Readings in

Social Development

Readings in

Social Development

Edited by

ROSS D. PARKE
University of Wisconsin

Holt, Rinehart and Winston, Inc.
New York—Chicago—San Francisco—Atlanta
Dallas—Montreal—Toronto—London—Sydney

Copyright © 1969 by Holt, Rinehart and Winston, Inc.

All rights reserved

Library of Congress Catalog Card Number: 69–13429

ISBN 0-03-074670-1

Printed in the United States of America

456 038 98765

to Richard H. Walters,
friend and mentor

Preface

Research in social development has expanded rapidly in the past few years, and it is the purpose of this book to make available, in a single volume, a set of readings that adequately reflects recent advances in theory and empirical research in this area. The outstanding characteristic of the recent research is its extensive and sophisticated employment of experimental methods for investigating social behavior in children. The studies selected, consequently, employ children as subjects, and they tend to be experimental rather than correlational in methodology. Although most of the readings are of recent vintage, older studies are included when they represent important methodological, empirical, or theoretical innovations.

I am not without biases. My social-learning-theory viewpoint is reflected in most of the papers selected, although I have tried to include articles representing other views that are clearly influential in guiding current research in an area. For example, the psychoanalytic concept of identification plays a central organizing role in research on sex-typing, and so I have included articles pertinent to identification theory. Similarly in the area of moral development, Piaget's stage theory approach is represented by Turiel's analysis of the development of moral judgments.

The current text that best reflects the viewpoint underlying my selection of articles is Bandura and Walters' *Social Learning and Personality Development*. To facilitate the use of these readings in conjunction with that book, I have tried to retain, in part, the organization of the earlier text. It should be noted that this organization departs from the more traditional approach, which traces the child's progress by age or stage. The emphasis here, as in Bandura and Walters, is on topics, such as dependency, achievement, aggression, sex-typing, and moral behavior. After the opening section on infant social behavior, which has received increased attention in recent years, are sections on social reinforcement and imitation. The readings relating to the five content areas noted above follow. The unity of the book lies in its emphasis of the social learning viewpoint and more specifically in its continual reference to the role played by reinforcement and imitation in the development, maintenance, and modification of each social behavior discussed. This organization permits examination of the specific theoretical and empirical issues that characterize the different topic areas. An introduction to each section highlights these issues and discusses the importance and implications of each of the articles.

Most of the articles are reprinted without abridgment, so that students, particularly advanced ones, can adequately evaluate the research design and the findings. To facilitate and encourage students to read in greater depth, the reference lists that originally appeared with the articles are reprinted. In addition, a list of books and review papers at the end of each section guides the student's further reading and library research.

The permission granted by authors and publishers to reprint the articles in this volume is greatly appreciated. Specific acknowledgments accompany each article. The comments of Professors Albert Bandura, Wesley C. Becker, Willard W. Hartup, and Richard H. Walters on a preliminary list of selections were very helpful. Professor E. Mavis Hetherington's suggestions and remarks on the introductory material were extremely valuable. I very much appreciate the assistance of Mrs. William Tishler in collecting and assembling the articles and Mrs. Willard Murray in proofreading and indexing the manuscript, and, finally, the efforts of the secretarial staff of the Psychology Department at the University of Wisconsin, especially Miss Linda Hutchinson.

Ross D. Parke

Madison, Wisconsin
December 1968

Contents

Dependency

Independence and Achievement

Aggression

Sex-role Development

Moral Development

Readings in
Social Development

chapter one

Infant Social Behavior

1.1 Introduction

For many years it has been assumed that social responsiveness in human infants developed out of oral activities. Historically emphasis on the feeding situation can be traced to two theoretical positions: psychoanalytic theory and learning theory. According to Freud, each stage of development is dominated by a particular bodily zone and the oral area is the focus in infancy. Sucking and related oral activities were viewed as innately pleasurable, and the infant's early attachment with the source of pleasure, usually the mother, was assumed to result from an innate desire to incorporate objects. Under the influence of psychoanalytic theory, learning approaches retained this emphasis on the feeding situation but argued that sucking, rather than being innately pleasurable, acquired positive value through association with the reduction of hunger, a primary drive. If we extend the learning interpretation to the development of social responsiveness, we see that the mother, as a result of being paired with drive-reducing feeding activity, acquires positive secondary reinforcement properties and consequently is valued in her own right.

A number of recent research findings have challenged the view that the feeding situation is the critical context for the development of social responsiveness. By using infant rhesus monkeys as subjects, Harlow (1958) has shown that feeding is of much less importance than "contact comfort" as an antecedent of attachment formation. The monkeys were raised on surrogate mothers—one of wire construction and one of terry cloth. Half the infants were fed on the wire mother and the remainder on the cloth mother. Infants fed on the lactating wire mother spent a decreasing amount of time in contact with her and an increasing amount of time with the non-lactating cloth mother. This is "a finding completely contrary to any interpretation of derived-drive in terms of which the mother-form becomes conditioned to hunger-thirst reduction" (Harlow, 1958, p. 676).

In subsequent reports, such as the Harlow-Zimmerman (1959) paper in this section, Harlow's initial findings were confirmed. In addition, infant monkeys favored the cloth mother as a safe base from which to explore the environment and tended to seek the proximity of the cloth rather than the wire mother in the presence of a fear stimulus. These findings support an earlier hypothesis suggested by Margaret Ribble (1944) that tactile stimulation is important for the development of the human infant.

Although Harlow's findings leave little doubt that physical contact is a variable of major importance in attachment formation, it is not the only mechanism involved. Later research has shown that the cloth surrogate cannot replace the real mother; in spite of Harlow's initial optimism that he had "engineered a very superior monkey mother . . . soft, warm, and tender, a mother with infinite patience, a mother available twenty-four hours a day, a mother that never scolded her infant and never struck or hit her baby in anger," it is now clear that surrogate-reared animals have real social deficits. Alexander and Harlow (1965) found that they were inferior to monkeys reared by real mothers in affiliative behavior, quality of play, dominance and competition, and sexual behavior.

Studies of attachment formation in human infants have similarly provided little support for the drive-reduction position. In the next paper, Schaffer and Emerson (1964) report the results of a recently completed longitudinal investigation of the development of social attachments during the first year and a half of life. Again the conclusion was that "satisfaction of physical needs does not appear to be a necessary precondition to the development of attachments, the latter taking place independently and without obvious regard to the experiences that the child encounters in physical care situations" (Schaffer & Emerson, 1964, p. 67). A variety of enticing findings have emerged from this project, many of them contrary to preconceived theoretical expectations. It was traditionally assumed that the mother is initially the sole object of attachment and that later attachments occur only after this relationship is firmly established. The finding that some infants do not initially develop a single specific attachment but instead display multiple attachments as soon as a specific attachment is apparent challenges this customary view. Moreover, even at the onset of the formation of specific attachments, the mother was not the single, or principal, object of attachment. Physical contact does not appear to be critical for attachment formation in human infants, for infants whose mothers used physical contact as the preferred mode of interaction were no more intensely attached to their mothers than infants whose mothers preferred nonphysical modes of social interaction. The extent to which the mothers interacted with their children and their responsiveness to the children's crying were the two main predictors of the strength of the children's attachment to their mothers.

This finding is consistent with the Rheingold (1956) study of the modification of social responsiveness in institutional infants. Both studies indicate that social stimulation is an important factor in promoting the development of social responsiveness.

Cairns (1966) has proposed a theory of attachment which is consistent with these data. According to his position, an animal will form an attachment to any perceptually salient object to which it is continuously exposed. Cairns provides data supporting his theoretical predictions in the experimental paper presented in this section. Working with sheep, Cairns raised ewes with dogs, other sheep, or an inanimate object (TV set) and found that sheep form attachments to any salient object with which they have been confined— other sheep, dogs, or even TV sets. However, the degree of attachment to the inanimate object (TV set) was considerably less than to the animate partners. This research provides a clearly positive answer to the question of whether an animal of one species can form an attachment to an animal of an alien species. Attachment to the same species is not an inevitable pattern, nor is it an irreversible pattern. Cairns found that the attachment of sheep who had been reared with members of their own species could be shifted merely by prolonged exposure to a canine cohabitant. Cairns' finding that physical contact is unnecessary for attachment is of particular theoretical importance. His results suggest that "contact comfort" may be a facilitating, but not a necessary, condition for attachment formation. However, differences in rearing and testing conditions and in the measures of attachment may account for the apparent inconsistency with the Harlow data, or species-specific differences may also be an important consideration. In fact, it is quite unlikely that the same sensory modalities and experiences will play an equally salient role in attachment formation in such a range of species as human infants, monkeys, and sheep. Nevertheless, both the Cairns and the Schaffer and Emerson studies clearly indicate that stimulation of the distance receptors may be important in attachment formation.

The evidence against the assumption that oral gratification is necessarily the principal antecedent of social responsiveness does not imply that the feeding situation itself is not of considerable importance for the development of attachment to the mother (Walters & Parke, 1965). Mothers often provide their infants with auditory and visual stimulation as well as with physical contact during feeding, and the stimulation provided in this context may contribute to the child's attachment to his caretaker. Moreover, Igel and Calvin (1960) have shown that need-reduction variables may play a role in attachment formation. In a study that paralleled Harlow's original experiment with mother surrogates in some respects, these investigators found that infant puppies preferred a lactating "comfortable" surrogate to an equally comfortable, but nonlactating surrogate. "Similarly one would expect a human infant to form a stronger attachment to a caretaker who feeds, provides contact comfort and visual and auditory stimulation than to one who supplies a similar amount of distance receptor stimulation, but little contact comfort or participates minimally in the feeding situation" (Walters & Parke, 1965, pp. 64–65). The implication of the research findings presented in this section, however, seems to be that these conditions may facilitate, but are not necessary for, the development of attachment.

In addition to developing attachments to familiar figures, infants often show a fear response to strangers during the second half of the first year. This "fear of strangers" or "8-months anxiety" reaction has often been observed (Preyer, 1888; Bridges, 1932; Spitz, 1950) but is still poorly understood. Two viewpoints have emerged. Some investigators favor the incongruity hypothesis, which treats this phenomenon as a special case of fear evoked by a discrepancy between familiar and slightly unfamiliar social objects (Hebb, 1946; Freedman, 1961; Schaffer, 1966). Others prefer a psychoanalytic interpretation, which stresses fear of separation or loss of a familiar figure as the primary factor in "fear of strangers" (Spitz, 1950). Both positions point to the importance of the relationship between this phenomenon and attachment. However, the order of appearance of the two phenomena is currently in dispute; according to Schaffer and Emerson (1964) stranger anxiety follows specific attachment, while other investigators suggest the reverse order (Tennes & Lampl, 1964). More clearly established are some of the factors that affect the age at which fear of strangers appears. Schaffer (1966), for example, found that the diversity of the child's social experiences was an important determinant: the greater the number of people the infant normally encountered in the course of his daily life, the later he tended to develop a fear of strangers. Moreover, once it emerges, specific mother-infant attachment may heighten the reaction to strangers. Schaffer and Emerson (1964) found that the more intensely the infant is attached, the more he will show stranger anxiety. Similarly, separating the infant from his mother increases the infant's stranger reaction, particularly in postattachment infants of 10 and 12 months of age (Morgan & Riccicuti, 1968). In tracing this fear reaction longitudinally, these latter investigators found an increased effect with age and no evidence of decline even in 12-month-old infants. No support was found for Spitz's (1950) claim that "stranger anxiety" is most intense at 8 months. More empirical research is required to settle these controversies.

What happens to the infant's social development if no mother figure is available? Orphanages and other institutions have provided a natural experimental situation in which to test the effects of "maternal deprivation." A host of studies (for example, Goldfarb, 1945; Spitz, 1945) demonstrated that institutionalization produced infants with emotional, social, and intellectual deficits. These effects were originally thought to be due to the lack of mother love (Spitz, 1945; Bowlby, 1952). However, more recent approaches (Casler, 1961; Yarrow, 1961, 1964) suggest that the traditional concept of "maternal deprivation" requires refinement if the effects of institutionalization are to be understood. Far from being a unitary construct, the maternal deprivation rubric has included, according to Yarrow (1961), four different kinds of deviation from a hypothetical mode of maternal care: institutionalization, separation from a mother or mother substitute, multiple mothers, and distortions in the quality of mothering (rejection, overprotection). In addition, pure conditions are rarely found; institutionalization is often combined with both separation from a maternal figure and a multiple mothering-caretaking arrangement. Hence the mother-love "explanation" is now viewed as simply too imprecise to be useful. An alternative and more clearly articulated hypothesis suggests that the cause of social and intellectual impairment may be the lack of sensory and perceptual stimulation that characterizes many institutional environments. In the case of postattachment infants, the impact of the separation from a mother figure may, in part, contribute to the detrimental effects of institutionalization. (See Yarrow, 1964;

for a review.) Therefore, the perceptual deprivation hypothesis is probably most applicable to infants who entered the institutional setting before 6 months of age.

Data supporting the hypothesis that sensory stimulation is important for normal social development come from a variety of animal studies (Harlow & Harlow, 1962; Thompson & Melzack, 1956), as well as from studies of extra stimulation of institutionalized infants (Casler, 1965; Rheingold, 1956; Skeels & Dye, 1939).

Casler (1965) has recently offered support for the role of tactile stimulation in overcoming the detrimental impact of the institutionalization experience. Institutionalized infants who were given extra tactile stimulation for a period of 10 weeks showed less of a drop in IQ over this period than nonstimulated subjects. Since the experimental as well as the control group showed some decline, other forms of stimulation, particularly visual and auditory, appear to be necessary for normal social and intellectual development. In a classic attempt to overcome the impact of institutionalization, Skeels and Dye (1939) transferred children reared in an institutional environment until approximately 19 months of age to a setting in which they received greater social and nonsocial stimulation. Children in the treatment group reached normal IQ levels and most of the group were eventually adopted. In contrast, the nontreated children had subnormal intelligence and the majority remained wards of the institution. According to a follow-up report (Skeels, 1966), the gains were maintained and in adulthood, educationally and occupationally, the adopted children were normal.

The Rheingold (1956) article in this section further supports the role of stimulation in social development. In a study of the effects of extra social stimulation on the social responsiveness of institutionalized babies, Rheingold substituted a single caretaker for the multiple caretakers usually found in institutional settings. After 8 weeks of intensive social stimulation from the experimental "mother," the infants were socially more responsive not only to the familiar caretaker, but also to an unfamiliar examiner than was a group of control infants who had stayed in the usual hospital regime. However, a follow-up study (Rheingold & Bayley, 1959) one year later, when the children were in adoptive homes, showed that the two groups did not differ in social responsiveness—a finding which suggests that the added mothering had only a short-term effect. Another noteworthy feature of the Rheingold study was her finding that most infants in the institution were not of subnormal intelligence. Combined with the follow-up data of Rheingold and Bayley, which showed both experimental and control children to be socially and intellectually normal, Rheingold's report clearly indicates that the often reported deleterious effects of institutionalization are not inevitable.

In the next papers in this section, three aspects of infant social behavior are examined: smiling, vocalizing, and play. Each of these behavior patterns has been used as an index of social responsiveness and is assumed to play an important role in adult-child interactions and in fostering the development of social attachments.

Smiling is one of the most frequently employed indices of infant social responsiveness and discriminability. The main bulk of the research in this area has been concerned with the types of stimulus conditions effective in eliciting the smiling response at various developmental stages. Even in the first week of life the infant smiles, but these early smiles appear to be dependent on the infant's internal state and are of little social significance. This period is relatively brief, however, and between the third and eighth weeks "social" smiling begins; the infant smiles in response to a wide variety of external, and often social, stimuli. Influenced by ethological conceptions of an innate releasing stimulus, it was originally proposed that the smiling face of an adult is the best elicitor of infant smiles. However, recent research has shown that a wide variety of stimuli are effective, including auditory and tactual, as well as visual, stimuli. Although the earliest elicitor of the smile appears to be a high-pitched human voice (Wolff, 1963), a combination of voice and face, particularly a moving face, is the most reliable elicitor of smiling in the first 6 months of life.

The developmental course of the smiling response in some ways parallels Schaffer and Emerson's outline of the development of attachments. In the fifth month of life, the infant smile comes under the control of select social stimuli; instead of smiling equally to both familiar and strange adult faces, for example, as he did in the previous phase, the infant smiles more readily at familiar social stimuli. The "fear of strangers" phenomenon is often indexed by this decline in smiling to a responsive, but strange, face.

A source of considerable controversy and disagreement has been the genesis of smiling responses. Some have regarded smiling as innately determined (Spitz, 1946), while others have laid emphasis on the role of instrumental or classical conditioning (Gewirtz, 1965).

Brackbill (1958), in her paper on smiling, clearly favors a learning approach to the development of smiling and provides some evidence for the modifiability of the smiling response. In her study she was able to successfully increase the frequency of smiling by operant conditioning procedures, and she further demonstrated that young infants' social behavior is modified by different reinforcement schedules. As expected, the intermittently reinforced infants smiled at a higher rate during extinction than the continuously reinforced infants. More recently, Etzel and Gewirtz (1967) have found that the smiling response can be instrumentally conditioned in infants as young as 8 weeks of age. However, as Wahler (1967) has shown, not all reinforcing agents are equally effective in shaping smiling; when mothers and strangers were compared, the familiar caretakers were more effective in obtaining reinforcement control of smiling behavior in 3½-month-old infants. The major significance of these studies is their demonstration that the smiling response may be strengthened or weakened according to well-established learning principles. Moreover, these findings suggest that cross-cultural variations in speed of development of smiling and other social responses may be due to different caretaking arrangements which provide differential opportunities for reinforcement of these social responses.

Infant vocalization, another index of social responsiveness, has received some attention recently. As the precursor of later language development and as a means of rudimentary communication, infant vocalization constitutes a significant class of responses. Studies of language development have indicated a relationship between the amount of environmental language stimulation and vocabulary and sentence length in preschool children (Day, 1932). Moreover, severe language retardation has been found in institutionalized children, whose early vocalizing attempts generally receive little or no reinforcement. Evidence that reinforcement may be important in modifying infant vocalizations has been reported by Rheingold, Gewirtz, and Ross (1959). In their study, an operant-conditioning technique was successfully employed to increase the frequency of vocalization among 3-month-old infants. A complex reinforcer—the experimenter smiled, talked, and touched the infant's abdomen—was presented whenever the infant vocalized. Although the procedure was effective in shaping the vocal behavior of the subjects, the claim that operant conditioning had been demonstrated was open to question. An alternative explanation suggested that some part of the reinforcing stimulus could have acted as a social "releaser." Or the stimulation may have been sufficient to elicit infant vocalizations, even if it had not been made contingent on the infants' responses (Rheingold et al., 1959). In a study controlling these possibilities, Weisberg (1963) unequivocally demonstrated that vocalizing could be instrumentally conditioned in young infants. Moreover, his findings suggest that social stimulation was a more effective reinforcer than nonsocial stimulation.

Studies of vocalization indicative of distress, such as crying, have yielded additional support for the conditionability of infant vocal behavior. Crying, while often elicited by painful stimulation, is frequently maintained by the caretakers' attention to a crying infant. In a recent study of crying in two infants, 6 to 20 weeks old, Etzel and Gewirtz (1967) demonstrated that crying is often continued because of the reinforcement it elicits from nurses in a hospital setting; moreover, by ignoring crying and reinforcing the infants for an incompatible prosocial response—smiling—they were able to extinguish the operantly maintained crying. Brackbill (1958) has noted a similar relationship between smiling and protest reactions.

These studies of operant conditioning clearly indicate that the infant's social behavior is modifiable and that mothers and other socializing agents play an important role in shaping the infant's social responses. However, it should be recognized that the infant is not a passive recipient of incoming stimulation, but an active and competent organism who modifies the behavior of other persons in his environment. The mother-infant relationship is clearly reciprocal. In fact, Bowlby (1958) has suggested that crying and smiling are congenital or innate releasers of maternal behavior and may play an important role in shaping maternal behavior patterns. Consistent with this view of affective responses as social signals is the Brackbill (1958) finding of an increase in protest following withdrawal of reinforcement. Crying, in this context, may represent the infant's attempt to regain the experimenter's attention.

Even more convincing evidence for the active role played by the infant comes from recent studies of infant exploratory behavior and play. Although there have been a variety of experimental demonstrations, using both humans and lower animals, that infants will actively seek stimulation from their environment, some of the best documentation of this phenomenon comes from Piaget's naturalistic observations of his own infants. In the excerpt from *Play, Dreams, and Imitation* included in this section, Piaget traces the development of play in infancy. According to Piaget, play is only one of a variety of behaviors resulting from the child's continuing attempt to understand his surroundings. It therefore can be understood only in relation to Piaget's general theory of behavior, which postulates two complementary processes—assimilation and accommodation. Assimilation is the process by which the child molds or bends incoming information to suit his existing forms of thought. Accommodation is the process whereby the child's thought structure is modified to conform to reality. Piaget regards play as "pure assimilation"; the child makes no attempt to adapt to reality, but merely bends incoming perceptions to fit his current inclinations and expectations. Since all behavior is a consequence of these complementary tendencies, all behavior has some playlike qualities. As

Gilmore (1966) noted, "One can't speak of play versus non-play in the Piagetian schema of things; behaviors are only less or more playful insofar as they do or do not make some attempt to cope with reality" (p. 348). Of particular interest is the picture that emerges from Piaget's descriptions—namely a curious organism actively exploring and manipulating new objects. It is in marked contrast to the traditional view of the infant as a passive, noninvolved recipient of environment inputs.

In conjunction with the laboratory findings (Berlyne, 1958: Fantz, 1961) that infants prefer complex, novel stimuli much more than simple, familiar stimuli, these kinds of observations have had a marked impact on motivational theory. In particular, the adequacy of the primary drive model, with its underlying assumption that such primary drives as hunger and thirst (and other tissue needs) are the main conditions motivating behavior, is questioned. In addition, the exploratory behavior studies present an organism not in search of stimulation reduction but often in pursuit of stimulation increases—a picture clearly inconsistent with the classical drive-reduction model. White (1959) and Hunt (1965) have argued for theoretical conceptualizations that give adequate recognition to classes of behavior like exploration, curiosity, and play. The findings of Harlow, Cairns, and Schaffer concerning the role of hunger reduction in the development of social responsiveness are consistent with the shift away from the centrality of drive reduction in motivational theories.

REFERENCES

Berlyne, D. E.   The influence of the albedo and complexity of stimuli on visual fixation in the human infant. *British Journal of Psychology,* 1958, **49**, 315–318.

Bowlby, J.   Maternal care and mental health. Monograph series, No. 2, Geneva: World Health Organization, 1951.

Bowlby, J.   The nature of the child's tie to his mother. *International Journal of Psycho-Analysis,* 1958, **39**, 350–373.

Bridges, K. M. B.   Emotional development in early infancy. *Child Development,* 1932, **3**, 324–341.

Cairns, R. B.   Attachment behavior of mammals. *Psychology Review,* 1966, **73**, 409–426.

Casler, L.   Maternal deprivation: A critical review of the literature. *Monographs of the Society for Research in Child Development,* 1961, **26**, No. 2 (Serial No. 80).

Casler, L.   The effects of extra tactile stimulation on a group of institutionalized infants. *Genetic Psychology Monographs,* 1965, **71**, 137–175.

Day, E. J.   The development of language in twins: I. A Comparison of twins and single children. *Child Development,* 1932, **3,** 179–199.

Etzel, B. C., & Gewirtz, J. L.   Experimental modification of caretaker-maintained high-rate operant crying in a 6- and a 20-week-old infant *(Infans tyrannotearus):* Extintion of crying with reinforcement of eye contact and smiling. *Journal of Experimental Child Psychology,* 1967, **3,** 303–317.

Fantz, R. L.   The origin of form perception. *Scientific American,* 1961, **204,** 66–72.

Freedman, D. G.   The infant's fear of strangers and the flight response. *Journal of Child Psychology and Psychiatry,* 1961, **2,** 242–248.

Gewirtz, J. L.   The course of infant smiling in four child-rearing environments in Israel. In B. M. Foss (Ed.), *Determinants of infant behavior,* III. London: Methuen, 1965. Pp. 205–248.

Gilmore, J. B.   Play: A special behavior. In R. N. Haber (Ed.), *Current Research in Motivation.* New York: Holt, Rinehart, and Winston, Inc., 1966. Pp. 343–355.

Goldfarb, W.   Psychological privation in infancy and subsequent adjustment. *American Journal of Orthopsychiatry,* 1945, **15,** 247–255.

Harlow, H. F.   The nature of love. *American Psychologist,* 1958, **13,** 673–685.

Harlow, H. F., & Harlow, M. K.   Social deprivation in monkeys. *Scientific American,* 1962, **207** (5), 136.

Harlow, H. F., & Zimmermann, R. R.   Affectional responses in the infant monkey. *Science,* 1959, **130,** 421–432.

Hebb, D. O.   On the nature of fear. *Psychological Review,* 1946, **53,** 259–276.

Hunt, J. M.   Intrinsic motivation and its role in psychological development. In D. Levine (Ed.), *Nebraska Symposium on Motivation.* Lincoln: University of Nebraska Press, 1965. Pp. 189–282.

Igel, G. J., & Calvin, A. D.   The development of affectional responses in infant dogs. *Journal of Comparative and Physiological Psychology,* 1960, **53,** 302–305.

Morgan, G. A., & Ricciuti, H. N.   Infants' responses to strangers during the first year. In B. M. Foss (Ed.), *Determinants of infant behavior,* IV. New York: Wiley, 1968.

Preyer, W. T.   *The mind of the child,* Vol. 1. New York: Appleton, 1888.

Rheingold, H. J.   The modification of social responsiveness in institutional babies. *Monograph of the Society for Research in Child Development,* 1956, Series 63, **21** (2).

Rheingold, H. L., Gewirtz, J. L., & Ross, H. W.   Social conditioning of vocalizations in the infant, *Journal of Comparative Physiological Psychology,* 1959, **52,** 68–73.

Ribble, M. A.   Infantile experiences in relation to personality development. In J. McV. Hunt (Ed.), *Personality and the behavior disorders,* II. New York: Ronald Press, 1944. Pp. 621–651.

Schaffer, H. R.   The onset of fear of strangers and the incongruity hypothesis. *Journal of Child Psychology and Psychiatry,* 1966, **7,** 95–106.

Schaffer, H. R., & Emerson, P. E.   The development of social attachments in infancy. *Monograph of the Society for Research in Child Development,* 1964, **29,** No. 3 (Serial No. 94).

Skeels, H. M.   Adult status of children with contrasting early life experiences. *Monographs of the Society for Research in Child Development,* 1966, **31,** No. 3 (Serial No. 105).

Skeels, H. M., & Dye, H.   A study of the effects of differential stimulation in mentally retarded children. *Proceedings and Addresses of the American Association on Mental Deficiency,* 1939, **44,** 114–136.

Spitz, R. A.   Hospitalism: An inquiry into the genesis of psychiatric conditions in early childhood. *Psychoanalytic Study of the Child,* 1945, **1,** 53–74.

Spitz, R. A.   The smiling response: A contribution to the ontogenesis of social relations. *Genetic Psychology Monographs,* 1946, **34,** 57–125.

Spitz, R. A.   Anxiety in infancy. *International Journal of Psycho-Analysis,* 1950, **31,** 139–143.

Tennes, K. H., & Lampl, E. E.   Stranger and separation anxiety in infancy. *Journal of Nervous and Mental Disease,* 1964, **139,** 247–254.

Thompson, W. R., & Melzack, R.   Early environment. *Scientific American,* 1956, 114(1), 38–42.

Walters, R. H., & Parke, R. D.   The role of distance receptors in the development of social responsiveness. In L. P. Lipsitt & C. C. Spiker (Eds.), *Advances in child development and behavior,* II. New York: Academic Press, 1965. Pp. 59–96.

Weisberg, P.   Social and nonsocial conditioning of infant vocalizations. *Child Development,* 1963, **34,** 377–388.

White, R. W.   Motivation reconsidered: the concept of competence. *Psychological Review,* 1959, **66,** 297–333.

Wolff, P. H.   Observations on the early development of smiling. In B. M. Foss (Ed.), *Determinants of infant behavior, II.* New York: John Wiley and Sons, Inc., 1963. Pp. 113–167.

Yarrow, L. J.   Maternal deprivation: Toward an empirical and conceptual re-evaluation. *Psychological Bulletin,* 1961, **58,** 459–490.

Yarrow, L. J.   Separation from parents during early childhood. In Lois W. Hoffman & M. L. Hoffman (Eds.), *Review of child development research,* I. New York: Russell Sage, 1964. Pp. 89–136.

SUPPLEMENTARY READING

Caldwell, B. M.   The effects of infant care. In L. W. Hoffman & M. L. Hoffman (Eds.), *Review of child development research, I.* New York: Russell Sage, 1964. Pp. 9–87.

Foss, B. M. (Ed.), *Determinants of infant behavior,* Vols. I–IV, New York: Wiley, 1961–1968.

Rheingold, H. L.   The development of social behavior in the human infant. *Monographs of the Society for Research in Child Development.* 1966, **31,** 1–17.

Walters, R. H., & Parke, R. D.   The role of the distance receptors in the development of social responsiveness. In L. P. Lipsitt & C. C. Spiker (Eds.), *Advances in child development and behavior, II.* New York: Academic Press, 1965. Pp. 59–96.

1.2 Affectional Responses in the Infant Monkey

Harry F. Harlow and Robert R. Zimmermann

Investigators from diverse behavioral fields have long recognized the strong attachment of the neonatal and infantile animal to its mother. Although this affectional behavior has been commonly observed, there is, outside the field of ethology, scant experimental evidence permitting identification of the factors critical to the formation of this bond. Lorenz *(16)* and others have stressed the importance of innate visual and auditory mechanisms which, through the process of imprinting, give rise to persisting following responses in the infant bird and fish. Imprinting behavior has been demonstrated successfully in a variety of avian species under controlled laboratory conditions, and this phenomenon has been investigated systematically in order to identify those variables which contribute to its development and maintenance (see, for example, Hinde, Thorpe, and Vince *(12)*, Fabricius *(7)*, Hess *(11)*, Jaynes *(13)*, and Moltz and Rosenblum *(17)*). These studies represent the largest body of existent experimental evidence measuring the tie between infant and mother. At the mammalian level there is little or no systematic experimental evidence of this nature.

Observations on monkeys by Carpenter *(5)*, Nolte *(18)*, and Zuckermann *(22)* and on chimpanzees by Kohler *(15)* and by Yerkes and Tomilin *(21)* show that monkey and chimpanzee infants develop strong ties to their mothers and that these affectional attachments may persist for years. It is, of course, common knowledge that human infants form strong and persistent ties to their mothers.

Although students from diverse scientific fields recognize this abiding attachment, there is considerable disagreement about the nature of its development and its fundamental underlying mechanisms. A common theory among psychologists, sociologists, and anthropologists is that of learning based on drive reduction. This theory proposes that the infant's attachment to the mother results from the association of the mother's face and form with the alleviation of certain primary drive states, particularly hunger and thirst. Thus, through learning, affection becomes a self-supporting, derived drive *(6)*. Psychoanalysts, on the other hand, have stressed the importance

Reprinted from *Science,* 1959, **130**, 421–432, by permission of the authors and the American Association for the Advancement of Science.

of various innate needs, such as a need to suck and orally possess the breast *(12)*, or needs relating to contact, movement, temperature *(19)*, and clinging to the mother *(2)*.

The paucity of experimental evidence concerning the development of affectional responses has led these theorists to derive their basic hypotheses from deductions and intuitions based on observation and analysis of adult verbal reports. As a result, the available observational evidence is often forced into a preconceived theoretical framework. An exception to the above generalization is seen in the recent attempt by Bowlby *(2)* to analyze and integrate the available observational and experimental evidence derived from both human and subhuman infants. Bowlby has concluded that a theory of component instinctual responses, species specific, can best account for the infant's tie to the mother. He suggests that the species-specific responses for human beings (some of these responses are not strictly limited to human beings) include contact, clinging, sucking, crying, smiling, and following. He further emphasizes that these responses are manifested independently of primary drive reduction in human and subhuman infants.

The absence of experimental data which would allow a critical evaluation of any theory of affectional development can be attributed to several causes. The use of human infants as subjects has serious limitations, since it is not feasible to employ all the experimental controls which would permit a completely adequate analysis of the proposed variables. In addition, the limited response repertoire of the human neonate severely restricts the number of discrete or precise response categories that can be measured until a considerable age has been attained. Thus, critical variables go unmeasured and become lost or confounded among the complex physiological, psychological, and cultural factors which influence the developing human infant.

Moreover, the use of common laboratory animals also has serious limitations, for most of these animals have behavioral repertoires very different from those of the human being, and in many species these systems mature so rapidly that it is difficult to measure and assess their orderly development. On the other hand, subhuman primates, including the macaque monkey, are born at a state of maturity which makes it possible to begin precise measurements within the first few days of life. Furthermore, their postnatal maturational rate is slow enough to permit precise assessment of affectional variables and development.

Over a 3-year period prior to the beginning of the research program reported here *(23)*, some 60 infant macaque monkeys were separated from their mothers 6 to 12 hours after birth and raised at the primate laboratory of the University of Wisconsin. The success of the procedures developed to care for these neonates was demonstrated by the low mortality and by a gain in weight which was approximately 25 percent greater than that of infants raised by their own mothers. All credit for the success of this program belongs to van Wagenen *(20)*, who had described the essential procedures in detail.

These first 3 years were spent in devising measures to assess the multiple capabilities of the neonatal and infantile monkey. The studies which resulted have revealed that the development of perception, learning, manipulation, exploration, frustration, and timidity in the macaque monkey follows a course and sequence which is very similar to that in the human infant. The basic differences between the two species appear to be the advanced postnatal maturational status and the subsequent more rapid growth of the infant macaque. Probably the most important similarities between the two, in relation to the problem of affectional development, are characteristic responses that have been associated with, and are considered basic to, affection; these include nursing, clinging, and visual and auditory exploration.

In the course of raising these infants we observed that they all showed a strong attachment to the cheesecloth blankets which were used to cover the wire floors of their cages. Removal of these cloth blankets resulted in violent emotional behavior. These responses were not short-lived; indeed, the emotional disturbance lasted several days, as was indicated by the infant's refusal to work on the standard learning tests that were being conducted at the time. Similar observations had already been made by Foley (8) and by van Wagenen (20), who stressed the importance of adequate contact responses to the very survival of the neonatal macaque. Such observations suggested to us that contact was a true affectional variable and that it should be possible to trace and measure the development and importance of these responses. Indeed there seemed to be every reason to believe that one could manipulate all variables which have been considered critical to the development of the infant's attachment to a mother, or mother surrogate.

To attain control over maternal variables, we took the calculated risk of constructing and using inanimate mother surrogates rather than real mothers. The cloth mother that we used was a cylinder of wood covered with a sheath of terry cloth (24), and the wire mother was a hardware-cloth cylinder. Initially, sponge rubber was placed underneath the terry cloth sheath of the cloth mother surrogate, and a light bulb behind each mother surrogate provided radiant heat. For reasons of sanitation and safety these two factors were eliminated in construction of the standard mothers, with no observable effect on the behavior of the infants. The two mothers were attached at a 45-degree angle to aluminum bases and were given different faces to assure uniqueness in the various test situations (Figure 1). Bottle holders were installed in the upper middle part of the bodies to permit nursing. The mother was designed on the basis of previous experience with infant monkeys, which suggested that nursing in an upright or inclined position with something for the infant to clasp facilitated successful nursing and resulted in healthier infants (see 20). Thus, both mothers provided the basic known requirements for adequate nursing, but the cloth mother provided an additional variable of contact comfort. That both of these surrogate mothers provided adequate nursing support is shown by the fact that the total ingestion of formula and the weight gain was normal for all in-

FIGURE 1. Wire and cloth mother surrogates.

fants fed on the surrogate mothers. The only consistent difference between the groups lay in the softer stools of the infants fed on the wire mother.

DEVELOPMENT OF AFFECTIONAL RESPONSES

The initial experiments on the development of affectional responses have already been reported (9) but will be briefly reviewed here, since subsequent experiments were derived from them. In the initial experiments, designed to evaluate the role of nursing on the development of affection, a cloth mother and a wire mother were placed in different cubicles attached to the infant's living cage. Eight newborn monkeys were placed in individual cages with the surrogates; for four infant monkeys the cloth mother lactated and the wire mother did not, and for the other four this condition was reversed.

The infants lived with their mother surrogates for a minimum of 165 days, and during this time they were tested in a variety of situations designed to measure the development of affectional responsiveness. Differential affectional responsiveness was initially measured in terms of mean hours per day spent on the cloth and on the wire mothers under two conditions of feeding, as shown in Figure 2. Infants fed on the cloth mother and on the wire mother have highly similar scores after a short adaptation period (Figure 3), and over a 165-day period both groups show a distinct preference

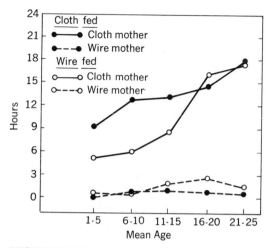

FIGURE 2. Time spent on cloth and wire
mother-surrogates. Short term.

for the cloth mother. The persistence of the differential responsiveness to
the mothers for both groups of infants is evident, and the overall differences
between the groups fall short of statistical significance.

These data make it obvious that contact comfort is a variable of critical
importance in the development of affectional responsiveness to the surrogate
mother, and that nursing appears to play a negligible role. With increasing
age and opportunity to learn, an infant fed from a lactating wire mother
does not become more responsive to her, as would be predicted from a derived-drive theory, but instead becomes increasingly more responsive to its

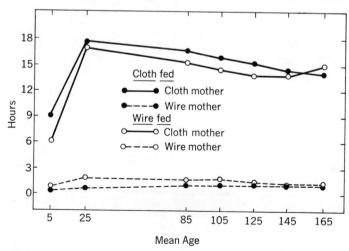

FIGURE 3. Time spent on cloth and wire mother-surrogates.
Long term.

nonlactating cloth mother. These findings are at complete variance with a drive-reduction theory of affectional development.

The amount of time spent on the mother does not necessarily indicate an affectional attachment. It could merely reflect the fact that the cloth mother is a more comfortable sleeping platform or a more adequate source of warmth for the infant. However, three of the four infants nursed by the cloth mother and one of the four nursed by the wire mother left a gauze-covered heating pad that was on the floor of their cages during the first 14 days of life to spend up to 18 hours a day on the cloth mother. This suggests that differential heating or warmth is not a critical variable within the controlled temperature range of the laboratory.

Other tests demonstrate that the cloth mother is more than a convenient nest; indeed, they show that a bond develops between infant and cloth-mother surrogate that is almost unbelievably similar to the bond established

FIGURE 4. Typical fear stimulus.

between human mother and child. One highly definitive test measured the selective maternal responsiveness of the monkey infants under conditions of distress or fear.

Various fear-producing stimuli, such as the moving toy bear illustrated in Figure 4, were presented to the infants in their home cages. The data on differential responses under both feeding conditions are given in Figure 5. It is apparent that the cloth mother was highly preferred to the wire mother, and it is a fact that these differences were unrelated to feeding conditions— that is, nursing on the cloth or on the wire mother. Above and beyond these objective data are observations on the form of the infants' responses in this situation. In spite of their abject terror, the infant monkeys, after reaching the cloth mother and rubbing their bodies about hers, rapidly come to lose their fear of the frightening stimuli. Indeed, within a minute or two most of the babies were visually exploring the very thing which so shortly before had seemed an object of evil. The bravest of the babies would actually leave the mother and approach the fearful monsters, under, of course, the protective gaze of their mothers.

These data are highly similar, in terms of differential responsiveness, to the time scores previously mentioned and indicate the overwhelming importance of contact comfort. The results are so striking as to suggest that the primary function of nursing may be that of insuring frequent and intimate contact between mother and infant, thus facilitating the localization of the source of contact comfort. This interpretation finds some support in the

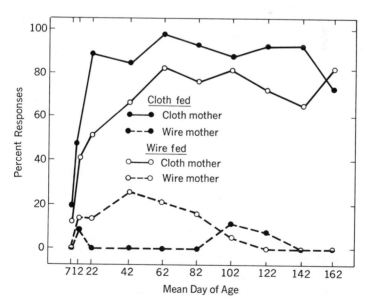

FIGURE 5. Home cage fear. First response dual-fed raised. Differential responsiveness in fear tests.

Infant Social Behavior

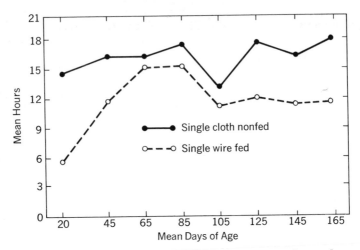

FIGURE 6. Time spent on cloth and wire, single mother-surrogates.

test discussed above. In both situations the infants nursed by the cloth mother developed consistent responsiveness to the soft mother earlier in testing than did the infants nursed by the wire mother, and during this transient period the latter group was slightly more responsive to the wire mother than the former group. However, these early differences shortly disappeared.

Additional data have been obtained from two groups of four monkeys each of which was raised with a single mother placed in a cubicle attached to the living-cage. Four of the infants were presented with a lactating wire mother and the other four were presented with a nonlactating cloth mother. The latter group was hand-fed from small nursing bottles for the first 30

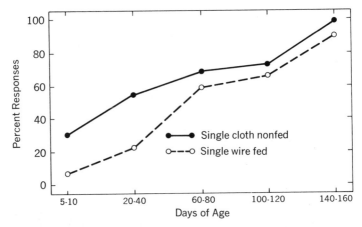

FIGURE 7. Home cage fear. Withdrawal to single surrogates mothers in fear tests.

days of life and then weaned to a cup. The development of responsiveness to the mothers was studied for 165 days; after this the individual mothers were removed from the cages and testing was continued to determine the strength and persistence of the affectional responses.

Figure 6 presents the mean time per day spent on the respective mothers over the 165-day test period, and Figure 7 shows the percentage of responses to the mothers when a fear-producing stimulus was introduced into the home cage. These tests indicate that both groups of infants developed responsiveness to their mother surrogates. However, these measures did not reveal the differences in behavior that were displayed in the reactions to the mothers when the fear stimuli were presented. The infants raised on the cloth mother would rush to the mother and cling tightly to her. Following this initial response these infants would relax and either begin to manipulate the mother or turn to gaze at the feared object without the slightest sign of apprehension. The infants raised on the wire mother, on the other hand, rushed away from the feared object toward their mother but did not cling to or embrace her. Instead, they would either clutch themselves and rock and vocalize for the remainder of the test or rub against the side of the cubicle. Contact with the cubicle or the mother did not reduce the emotionality produced by the introduction of the fear stimulus. These differences are revealed in emotionality scores, for behavior such as vocalization, crouching, rocking, and sucking, recorded during the test. Figure 8 shows the mean emotionality index for test sessions for the two experimental

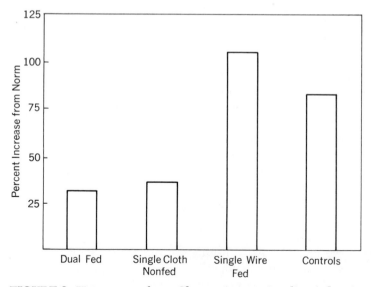

FIGURE 8. Home cage fear. Change in emotionality index in fear tests: total emotion score, increase from norm-mechanical stimuli.

groups, the dual-mother groups, and a comparable control group raised under standard laboratory conditions. As can be seen, the infants raised with the single wire mother have the highest emotionality scores of all the groups, and the infants raised with the single cloth mother or with a cloth and wire mother have the lowest scores. It appears that the responses made by infants raised only with a wire mother were more in the nature of simple flight responses to the fear stimulus and that the presence of the mother surrogate had little effect in alleviating the fear.

During our initial experiments with the dual-mother conditions, responsiveness to the lactating wire mother in the fear tests decreased with age and opportunity to learn, while responsiveness to the nonlactating cloth mother increased. However, there was some indication of a slight increase in frequency of response to the wire mother for the first 30 to 60 days (see Figure 5). These data suggest the possible hypothesis that nursing facilitated the contact of infant and mother during the early developmental periods.

The interpretation of all fear testing is complicated by the fact that all or most "fear" stimuli evoke many positive exploratory responses early in life and do not consistently evoke flight responses until the monkey is 40 to 50 days of age. Similar delayed maturation of visually induced fear responses has been reported for birds (7), chimpanzees (10), and human infants (14).

Because of apparent interactions between fearful and affectional developmental variables, a test was designed to trace the development of approach and avoidance responses in these infants. This test, described as the straight-alley test, was conducted in a wooden alley 8-feet long and 2-feet wide. One end of the alley contained a movable tray upon which appropriate stimuli were placed. The other end of the alley contained a box for hiding. Each test began with the monkey in a start box 1 foot in front of the hiding box; thus, the animal could maintain his original position, approach the stimulus tray as it moved toward him, or flee into the hiding box. The infants were presented with five stimuli in the course of five successive days. The stimuli included a standard cloth mother, a standard wire mother, a yellow cloth mother with the head removed, a blank tray, and a large black fear stimulus, shown in Figure 9. The infants were tested at 5, 10, and 20 days of age, respectively, and then at 20-day intervals up to 160 days. Figure 10 shows the mean number of 15-second time periods spent in contact with the appropriate mother during the 90-second tests for the two single-mother groups, and the responses to the cloth mother by four infants from the dual-mother group.

During the first 80 days of testing, all the groups showed an increase in response to the respective mother surrogates. The infants fed on the single wire mother, however, reached peak responsiveness at this age and then showed a consistent decline, followed by an actual avoidance of the wire mother. During test sessions 140 to 160, only one contact was made with the

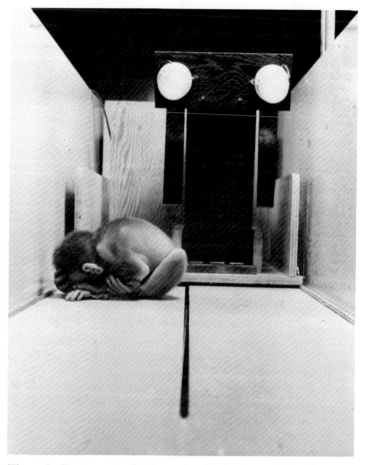

Figure 9. Response to the fear stimulus in the straight-alley test.

wire mother, and three of the four infants ran into the hiding box almost immediately and remained there for the entire test session. On the other hand, all of the infants raised with a cloth mother, whether or not they were nursed by her, showed a progressive increase in time spent in contact with their cloth mothers until approaches and contacts during the test sessions approached maximum scores.

The development of the response of flight from the wire mother by the group fed on the single wire mother is, of course, completely contrary to a derived-drive theory of affectional development.

A comparison of this group with the group raised with a cloth mother gives some support to the hypothesis that feeding or nursing facilitates the early development of responses to the mother but that without the factor of contact comfort, these positive responses are not maintained.

The differential responsiveness to the cloth mother of infants raised with

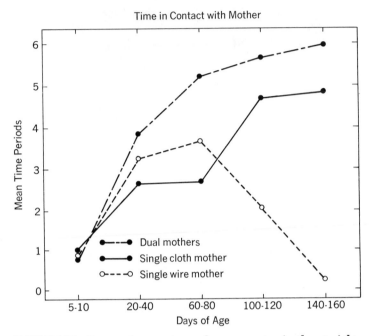

FIGURE 10. Responsiveness to mother-surrogates in the straight-alley tests.

both mothers, the reduced emotionality of both the groups raised with cloth mothers in the home-cage fear tests, and the development of approach responses in the straight-alley test indicate that the cloth mother provides a haven of safety and security for the frightened infant. The affectional response patterns found in the infant monkey are unlike tropistic or even complex reflex responses; they resemble instead the diverse and pervasive patterns of response to his mother exhibited by the human child in the complexity of situations involving child-mother relationships.

The role of the mother as a source of safety and security has been demonstrated experimentally for human infants by Arsenian (1). She placed children 11 to 30 months of age in a strange room containing toys and other play objects. Half of the children were accompanied into the room by a mother or a substitute mother (a familiar nursery attendant), while the other half entered the situation alone. The children in the first group (mother present) were much less emotional and participated much more fully in the play activity than those in the second group (mother absent). With repeated testing, the security score, a composite score of emotionality and play behavior, improved for the children who entered alone, but it still fell far below that for the children who were accompanied by their mothers. In subsequent tests, the children from the mother-present group were placed in the test room alone, and there was a drastic drop in the security scores. Contrariwise, the introduction of the mother raised the security scores of children in the other group.

We have performed a similar series of open-field experiments, comparing monkeys raised on mother surrogates with control monkeys raised in a wire cage containing a cheesecloth blanket from days 1 to 14 and no cloth blanket subsequently. The infants were introduced into the strange environment of the open field, which was a room measuring 6 by 6 by 6 feet, containing multiple stimuli known to elicit curiosity-manipulatory responses in baby monkeys. The infants raised with single mother surrogates were placed in this situation twice a week for 8 weeks, no mother surrogate being present during one of the weekly sessions and the appropriate mother surrogate (the kind which the experimental infant had always known) being present during the other sessions. Four infants raised with dual mother surrogates and four control infants were subjected to similar experimental sequences, the cloth mother being present on half of the occasions. The remaining four "dual-mother" infants were given repetitive tests to obtain information on the development of responsiveness to each of the dual mothers in this situation. A cloth blanket was always available as one of the stimuli throughout the sessions. It should be emphasized that the blanket could

FIGURE 11. Subsequent response to cloth mother and stimulus in the open-field test.

readily compete with the cloth mother as a contact stimulus, for it was standard laboratory procedure to wrap the infants in soft cloth whenever they were removed from their cages for testing, weighing and other required laboratory activities.

As soon as they were placed in the test room, the infants raised with cloth mothers rushed to their mother surrogate when she was present and clutched her tenaciously, a response so strong that it can only be adequately depicted by motion pictures. Then, as had been observed in the fear tests in the home cage, they rapidly relaxed, showed no sign of apprehension, and began to demonstrate unequivocal positive responses of manipulating and climbing on the mother. After several sessions, the infants began to use the mother surrogate as a base of operations, leaving her to explore and handle a stimulus and then returning to her before going to a new plaything. Some of the infants even brought the stimuli to the mother, as shown in Figure 11. The behavior of these infants changed radically in the absence of the mother. Emotional indices such as vocalization, crouching, rocking, and sucking increased sharply. Typical response patterns were either freezing in a crouched position, as illustrated in Figure 12, or running around the room on the hind feet, clutching themselves with their arms. Though no quanti-

FIGURE 12. Response in the open-field test in the absence of the mother-surrogate.

tative evidence is available, contact and manipulation of objects was frantic and of short duration, as opposed to the playful type of manipulation observed when the mother was present.

In the presence of the mother, the behavior of the infants raised with the single wire mothers was both quantitatively and qualitatively different from that of the infants raised with cloth mothers. Not only did these infants spend little or no time contacting their mother surrogates but the presence of the mother did not reduce their emotionality. These differences are evident in the mean number of time periods spent in contact with the respective mothers, as shown in Figure 13, and the composite emotional index for the two stimulus conditions depicted in Figure 14. Although the infants raised with dual mothers spent considerably more time in contact with the cloth mother than did the infants raised with single cloth mothers, their emotional reactions to the presence and absence of the mother were highly similar, the composite emotional index being reduced by almost half when the mother was in the test situation. The infants raised with wire mothers were highly emotional under both conditions and actually showed a slight, though nonsignificant, increase in emotionality when the mother was present. Although some of the infants reared by a wire mother did contact her, their behavior was similar to that observed in the home-cage fear tests. They did not clutch and cling to their mother as did the infants

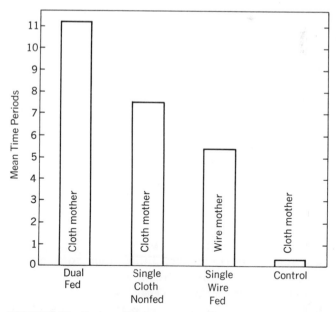

FIGURE 13. Responsiveness to mother-surrogates in the open-field test, with mean time periods in contact with mother.

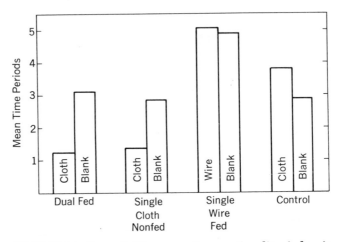

FIGURE 14. Open field, composite emotionality index in testing with and without the mother surrogates.

with cloth mothers; instead, they sat on her lap and clutched themselves, or held their heads and bodies in their arms and engaged in convulsive jerking and rocking movements similar to the autistic behavior of deprived and institutionalized human children. The lack of exploratory and manipulatory behavior on the part of the infants reared with wire mothers, both in the presence and absence of the wire mother, was similar to that observed in the mother-absent condition for the infants raised with the cloth mothers, and such contact with objects as was made was of short duration and of an erratic and frantic nature. None of the infants raised with single wire mothers displayed the persistent and aggressive play behavior that was typical of many of the infants that were raised with cloth mothers.

The four control infants, raised without a mother surrogate, had approximately the same emotionality scores when the mother was absent that the other infants had in the same condition, but the control subjects' emotionality scores were significantly higher in the presence of the mother surrogate than in her absence. This result is not surprising, since recent evidence indicates that the cloth mother with the highly ornamental face is an effective fear stimulus for monkeys that have not been raised with her.

Further illustration of differential responsiveness to the two mother surrogates is found in the results of a series of developmental tests in the open-field situation, given to the remaining four "dual-mother" infants. These infants were placed in the test room with the cloth mother, the wire mother, and no mother present on successive occasions at various age levels. Figure 15 shows the mean number of time periods spent in contact with the respective mothers for two trials at each age level, and Figure 16 reveals the composite emotion scores for the three stimulus conditions during these

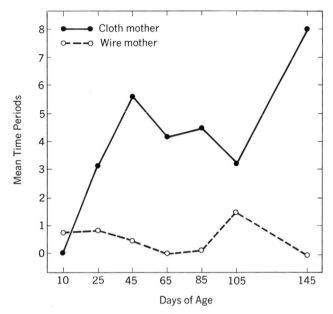

FIGURE 15. **Mean time periods in contact with mother of dual-fed raised. Differential responsiveness in the open-field test.**

same tests. The differential responsiveness to the cloth and wire mothers, as measured by contact time, is evident by 20 days of age, and this systematic difference continues throughout 140 days of age. Only small differences in emotionality under the various conditions are evident during the first 85 days of age, although the presence of the cloth mother does result in slightly lower scores from the 45th day onward. However, at 105 and 145 days of age there is a considerable difference for the three conditions, the emotionality scores for the wire-mother and blank conditions showing a sharp increase. The heightened emotionality found under the wire-mother condition was mainly contributed by the two infants fed on the wire mother. The behavior of these two infants in the presence of the wire mother was similar to the behavior of the animals raised with a single wire mother. On the few occasions when contact with the wire mother was made, the infants did not attempt to cling to her; instead they would sit on her lap, clasp their heads and bodies, and rock back and forth.

In 1953 Butler (3) demonstrated that mature monkeys enclosed in a dimly lighted box would open and reopen a door for hours on end with no other motivation than that of looking outside the box. He also demonstrated that rhesus monkeys showed selectivity in rate and frequency of door-opening in response to stimuli of different degrees of attractiveness (4). We have utilized this characteristic of response selectivity on the part of the monkey

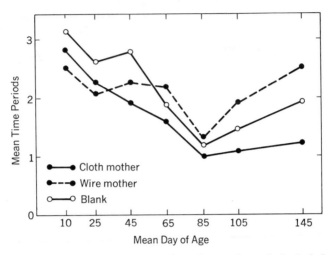

FIGURE 16. Composite emotionality index of dual fed
raised under three conditions in the open-
field test.

to measure the strength of affectional responsiveness of the babies raised
with mother surrogates in an infant version of the Butler box. The test
sequence involves four repetitions of a test battery in which the four stimuli
of cloth mother, wire mother, infant monkey, and empty box are presented
for a 30-minute period on successive days. The first four subjects raised with
the dual mother surrogates and the eight infants raised with single mother
surrogates were given a test sequence at 40 to 50 days of age, depending upon
the availability of the apparatus. The data obtained from the three experimental groups and a comparable control group are presented in Figure 17.
Both groups of infants raised with cloth mothers showed approximately
equal responsiveness to the cloth mother and to another infant monkey,
and no greater responsiveness to the wire mother than to an empty box.
Again, the results are independent of the kind of mother that lactated, cloth
or wire. The infants raised with only a wire mother and those in the control
group were more highly responsive to the monkey than to either of the
mother surrogates. Furthermore, the former group showed a higher frequency of response to the empty box than to the wire mother.

In summary, the experimental analysis of the development of the infant
monkey's attachment to an inanimate mother surrogate demonstrates the
overwhelming importance of the variable of soft body contact that characterized the cloth mother, and this held true for the appearance, development, and maintenance of the infant-surrogate-mother tie. The results also
indicate that, without the factor of contact comfort, only a weak attachment,
if any, is formed. Finally, probably the most surprising finding is that nursing or feeding played either no role or a subordinate role in the development

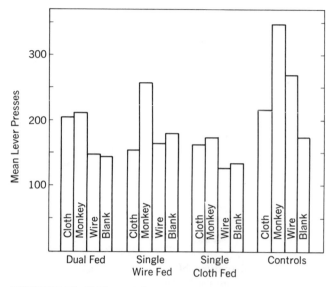

FIGURE 17. Differential responses to visual exploration.

of affection as measured by contact time, responsiveness to fear, responsiveness to strangeness, and motivation to seek and see. No evidence was found indicating that nursing mediated the development of any of these responses, although there is evidence indicating that feeding probably facilitated the early appearance and increased the early strength of affectional responsiveness. Certainly feeding, in contrast to contact comfort, is neither a necessary nor a sufficient condition for affectional development.

Retention of Affectional Responses

One of the outstanding characteristics of the infant's attachment to its mother is the persistence of the relationship over a period of years, even though the frequency of contact between infant and mother is reduced with increasing age. In order to test the persistence of the responsiveness of our "mother-surrogate" infants, the first four infant monkeys raised with dual mothers and all of the monkeys raised with single mothers were separated from their surrogates at 165 to 170 days of age. They were tested for affectional retention during the following 9 days, then at 30-day intervals during the following year. The results are of necessity incomplete, inasmuch as the entire mother-surrogate program was initiated less than 2 years ago, but enough evidence is available to indicate that the attachment formed to the cloth mother during the first 6 months of life is enduring and not easily forgotten.

Affectional retention as measured by the modified Butler box for the first 15 months of testing for four of the infants raised with two mothers is given in Figure 18. Although there is considerable variability in the total response

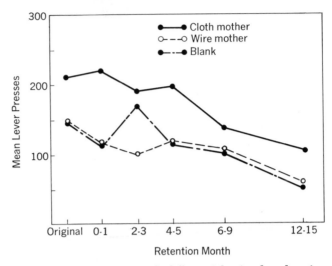

FIGURE 18. Retention of differential visual-exploration responses by the dual fed.

frequency from session to session, there is a consistent difference in the number of responses to the cloth mother as contrasted with responses to either the wire mother or the empy box, and there is no consistent difference between responses to the wire mother and to the empty box. The effects of contact comfort versus feeding are dramatically demonstrated in this test by the monkeys raised with either single cloth or wire mothers. Figure 19 shows the frequency of response to the appropriate mother surrogate and to the blank box during the preseparation period and the first 90 days of retention testing. Removal of the mother resulted in a doubling of the frequency of response to the cloth mother and more than tripled the difference between the responses to the cloth mother and those to the empty box for the infants that had lived with a single nonlactating cloth mother surrogate. The infants raised with a single lactating wire mother, on the other hand, not only failed to show any consistent preference for the wire mother but also showed a highly significant reduction in general level of responding. Although incomplete, the data from further retention testing indicate that the difference between these two groups persists for at least 5 months.

Affectional retention was also tested in the open field during the first 9 days after separation and then at 30-day intervals. Each test condition was run twice in each retention period. In the initial retention tests the behavior of the infants that had lived with cloth mothers differed slightly from that observed during the period preceding separation. These infants tended to spend more time in contact with the mother and less time exploring and manipulating the objects in the room. The behavior of the infants raised with single wire mothers, on the other hand, changed radically during the

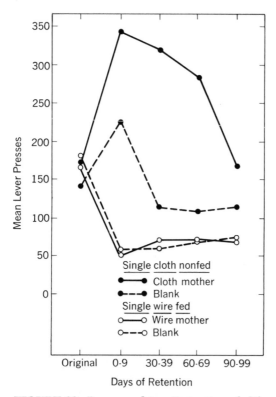

FIGURE 19. Love machine. Retention of differential visual-exploration responses by single-surrogate infants.

first retention sessions, and responses to the mother surrogate dropped almost to zero. Objective evidence for these differences is given in Figure 20, which reveals the mean number of time periods spent in contact with the respective mothers. During the first retention test session, the infants raised with a single wire mother showed almost no responses to the mother surrogate they had always known. Since the infants raised with both mothers were already approaching the maximum score in this measure, there was little room for improvement. The infants raised with a single nonlactating cloth mother, however, showed a consistent and significant increase in this measure during the first 90 days of retention. Evidence for the persistence of this responsiveness is given by the fact that after 15 months' separation from their mothers, the infants that had lived with cloth mothers spent an average of 8.75 out of 12 possible time periods in contact with the cloth mother during the test. The incomplete data for retention testing of the infants raised with only a lactating wire mother, or a nonlactating cloth mother indicates that there is little or no change in the initial differences

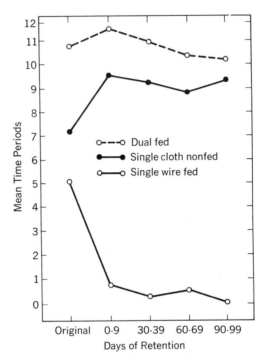

FIGURE 20. Mean time periods in contact with mother-surrogate compared with retention of responsiveness to mother in open-field tests.

found between these two groups in this test over a period of 5 months. In the absence of the mother, the behavior of the infants raised with cloth mothers was similar in the initial retention tests to that during the pre-separation tests, but with repeated testing they tended to show gradual adaptation to the open-field situation and, consequently, a reduction in their emotionality scores. Even with this overall reduction in emotionality, these infants had consistently lower emotionality scores when the mother was present.

At the time of initiating the retention tests, an additional condition was introduced into the open-field test: the surrogate mother was placed in the center of the room and covered with a clear plexiglas box. The animals raised with cloth mothers were initially disturbed and frustrated when their efforts to secure and contact the mother were blocked by the box. However, after several violent crashes into the plastic, the animals adapted to the situation and soon used the box as a place of orientation for exploratory and play behavior. In fact, several infants were much more active under these conditions than they were when the mother was available for direct contact.

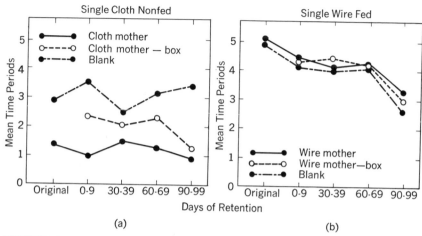

FIGURE 21. Composite emotionality index under three conditions in the open-field retention tests.

A comparison of the composite emotionality index of the babies raised with a single cloth or wire mother under the three conditions of no mother, surrogate mother, and surrogate-mother-box is presented in Figure 21. The infants raised with a single cloth mother were consistently less emotional when they could contact the mother but also showed the effects of her visual presence, as their emotionality scores in the plastic box condition were definitely lower than their scores when the mother was absent. It appears that the infants gained considerable emotional security from the presence of the mother even though contact was denied.

In contrast, the animals raised with only lactating wire mothers did not show any significant or consistent trends during these retention sessions other than a general overall reduction of emotionality, which may be attributed to a general adaptation, the result of repeated testing.

Affectional retention has also been measured in the straight-alley test mentioned earlier. During the preseparation tests it was found that the infants that had only wire mothers developed a general avoidance response to all of the stimuli in this test when they were about 100 days of age and made few, if any, responses to the wire mother during the final test sessions. In contrast, all the infants raised with a cloth mother responded positively to her. Maternal separation did not significantly change the behavior of any of the groups. The babies raised with just wire mothers continued to flee into the hiding booth in the presence of the wire mother, while all of the infants raised with cloth mothers continued to respond positively to the cloth mother at approximately the same level as in the preseparation tests. The mean number of time periods spent in contact with the appropriate mother surrogates for the first 3 months of retention testing are given in Figure 22. There is little, if any, waning of responsiveness to the cloth

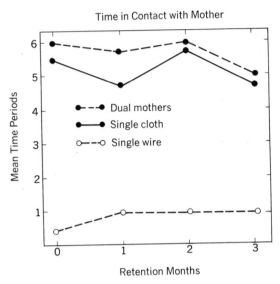

Time in Contact with Mother

FIGURE 22. Retention of responsiveness to mother-surrogates in the straight-alley test.

mother during these 3 months. There appeared to be some loss of reponsive-ness to the mother in this situation after 5 to 6 months of separation, but the test was discontinued at that time as the infants had outgrown the ap-paratus.

The retention data from these multiple tests demonstrate clearly the im-portance of body contact for the future maintenance of affectional responses. Whereas several of the measures in the preseparation period suggested that the infants raised with only a wire mother might have developed a weak attachment to her, all responsiveness disappeared in the first few days after the mother was withdrawn from the living-cage. Infants that had had the opportunity of living with a cloth mother showed the opposite effect and either became more responsive to the cloth mother or continued to respond to her at the same level.

These data indicate that once an affectional bond is formed it is main-tained for a very considerable length of time with little reinforcement of the contact-comfort variable. The limited data available for infants that have been separated from their mother surrogates for a year suggest that these affectional responses show resistance to extinction similar to the re-sistance previously demonstrated for learned fears and learned pain. Such data are in keeping with common observation of human behavior.

It is true, however, that the infants raised with cloth mothers exhibit some absolute decrease in responsiveness with time in all of our major test situations. Such results would be obtained even if there were no true decrease in the strength of the affectional bond, because of familiarization and adaptation resulting from repeated testing. Therefore, at the end of 1 year of retention testing, new tests were introduced into the experimental program.

Our first new test was a modification of the open-field situation, in which basic principles of the home-cage fear test were incorporated. This particular choice was made partly because the latter test had to be discontinued when the mother surrogates were removed from the home cages.

For the new experiment a Masonite floor marked off in 6- by 12-inch rectangles was placed in the open-field chamber. Both mother surrogates were placed in the test room opposite a plastic start-box. Three fear stimuli, selected to produce differing degrees of emotionality, were placed in the center of the room directly in front of the start-box in successive test sessions. Eight trials were run under each stimulus condition, and in half of the trials the most direct path to the cloth mother was blocked by a large plexiglas screen, illustrated in Figure 23. Thus, in these trials the infants were forced to approach and bypass the fear stimulus or the wire mother, or both, in order to reach the cloth mother. Following these 24 trials with the mothers present, one trial of each condition with both mothers absent was run, and this in turn was followed by two trials run under the most emotion-provoking condition: with a mechanical toy present and the direct path to the mother blocked.

We now have complete data for the first four infants raised with both a cloth and a wire mother. Even with this scanty information, the results are

FIGURE 23. Typical response to mother
in the modified open-field test.

obvious. As would be predicted from our other measures, the emotionality scores for the three stimuli were significantly different and these same scores were increased greatly when the direct path to the mother was blocked. A highly significant preference was shown for the cloth mother under both conditions (direct and blocked path), although the presence of the block did increase the number of first responses to the wire mother from 3 to 10 percent. In all cases this was a transient response and the infants subsequently ran on to the cloth mother and clung tightly to her. Objective evidence for this overwhelming preference is indicated in Figure 24, which shows the mean number of time periods spent in contact with the two

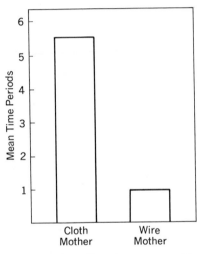

FIGURE 24. Time in contact with mothers of the dual fed. Differential responsiveness in the modified open-field test.

mothers. After a number of trials, the infants would go first to the cloth mother and then, and only then, would go out to explore, manipulate, and even attack and destroy the fear stimuli. It was as if they believed that their mother would protect them, even at the cost of her life—little enough to ask in view of her condition.

The removal of the mother surrogates from the situation produced the predictable effect of doubling the emotionality index. In the absence of the mothers, the infants would often run to the plexiglas partition which formerly had blocked their path to the mother, or they would crouch in the corner behind the block where the mother normally would have been. The return of the mothers in the final two trials of the test in which the most emotion-evoking situation was presented resulted in behavior near the normal level, as measured by the emotionality index and contacts with the cloth mother.

Our second test of this series was designed to replace the straight-alley test described above and provide more quantifiable data on responsiveness to fear stimuli. The test was conducted in an alley 8-feet long and 2-feet wide. At one end of the alley and directly behind the monkeys' restraining chamber was a small stimulus chamber, which contained a fear object. Each trial was initiated by raising an opaque sliding door which exposed the fear stimulus. Beginning at a point 18 inches from the restraining chamber, the alley was divided lengthwise by a partition; this provided the infant with the choice of entering one of two alleys.

The effects of all mother combinations were measured; these combinations included no mothers, two cloth mothers, two wire mothers, and a cloth and wire mother. All mother conditions were counterbalanced by two distance conditions—distances of 24 and 78 inches, respectively, from the restraining chamber. This made it possible, for example, to provide the infant with the alternative of running to the cloth mother which was in close proximity to the fear stimulus or to the wire mother (or no mother) at a greater distance from the fear stimulus. Thus, it was possible to distinguish between running to the mother surrogate as an object of security, and generalized flight in response to a fear stimulus.

Again, the data available at this time are from the first four infants raised with cloth and wire mothers. Nevertheless, the evidence is quite conclusive. A highly significant preference is shown for the cloth mother as compared to the wire mother or to no mother, and this preference appears to be independent of the proximity of the mother to the fear stimulus. In the condition in which two cloth mothers are present, one 24 inches from the fear stimulus and the other 78 inches from it, there was a preference for the nearest mother, but the differences were not statistically significant. In two conditions in which no cloth mother was present and the infant had to choose between a wire mother and no mother, or between two empty chambers, the emotionality scores were almost twice those under the cloth-mother-present condition.

No differences were found in either of these tests that were related to previous conditions of feeding—that is, to whether the monkey had nursed on the cloth or on the wire mother.

The results of these two new tests, introduced after a full year's separation of mother surrogate and infant, are comparable to the results obtained during the preseparation period and the early retention testing. Preferential responses still favored the cloth as compared to the wire mother by as much as 85 to 90 percent, and the emotionality scores showed the typical 2:1 differential ratio with respect to mother-absent and mother-present conditions.

The researches presented here on the analysis of two affectional variables through the use of objective and observational techniques suggest a broad new field for the study of emotional development of infant animals. The analogous situations and results found in observations and study of human infants and of subprimates demonstrate the apparent face validity of our tests. The reliability of our observational techniques is indicated, for example, by the correlation coefficients computed for the composite emotional index in the open-field test. Four product-moment correlation coefficients, computed from four samples of 100 observations by five different pairs of independent observers over a period of more than a year, ranged from .87 to .89.

Additional Variables

Although the overwhelming importance of the contact variable has been clearly demonstrated in these experiments, there is reason to believe that other factors may contribute to the development of the affectional response pattern. We are currently conducting a series of new experiments to test some of these postulated variables.

For example, Bowlby (2) has suggested that one of the basic affectional variables in the primate order is not just contact but *clinging* contact. To test this hypothesis, four infant monkeys are being raised with the standard cloth mother and a flat inclined plane, tightly covered with the same type of cloth. Thus, both objects contain the variable of contact with the soft cloth, but the shape of the mother tends to maximize the clinging variable, while the broad flat shape of the plane tends to minimize it. The preliminary results for differences in responsiveness to the cloth mother and responsiveness to the inclined plane under conditions that produce stress or fear or visual exploration suggest that clinging as well as contact is an affectional variable of considerable importance.

Experiments now in progress on the role of rocking motion in the development of attachment indicate that this may be a variable of measurable importance. One group of infants is being raised on rocking and stationary mothers and a second group, on rocking and stationary inclined planes. Both groups of infants show a small but consistent preference for the rocking object, as measured in average hours spent on the two objects.

Preliminary results for these three groups in the open-field test give additional evidence concerning the variable of clinging comfort. These data revealed that the infants raised with a standard cloth mother were more responsive to their mothers than the infants raised with inclined planes were to the planes.

The discovery of three variables of measurable importance to the formation and retention of affection is not surprising, and it is reasonable to assume that others will be demonstrated. The data so far obtained experimentally are in excellent concordance with the affectional variables named by Bowlby (2). We are now planning a series of studies to assess the effects of consistency and inconsistency with respect to the mother surrogates in relation to the clinical concept of rejection. The effects of early, intermediate, and late maternal deprivation and the generalization of the infant–surrogate attachment in social development are also being investigated. Indeed, the strength and stability of the monkeys' affectional responses to a mother surrogate are such that it should be practical to determine the neurological and biochemical variables that underlie love.

REFERENCES

1. Arsenian, J. M.   *J. abnorm. soc Psychol.*, 1943, **38**, 225.
2. Bowlby, J.   *Int. J. Psycho-anal.*, 1958, **39**, Part 5.
3. Butler, R. A.   *J. comp. & physiol. Psychol.*, 1953, **45**, 95.
4. Butler, R. A.   *J. exptl. Psychol.*, 1954, **48**, 19.
5. Carpenter, C. R.   *Comp. psychol. Monogr.*, 1934, No. 10, 1.
6. Dollard, J., & Miller, N. E.   *Personality and psychotherapy.* New York: McGraw-Hill, 1950, 133; Mussen, P. H. & Conger, J. J.   *Child development and personality.* New York: Harper & Row, 1956, 137–138.
7. Fabricius, E.   *Acta Zool, Fennica*, 1951, **68**, 1.
8. Foley, Jr., J. P.   *J. genet. Psychol.*, 1934, **45**, 39.
9. Harlow, H. F.   *Am. Psychologist*, 1958, **13**, 673; Harlow, H. F., & Zimmermann, R. R. *Proc. Am. phil. Soc.*, 1958, **102**, 501.
10. Hebb, D. O.   *The organization of behavior.* New York: Wiley, 1949, 241 ff.
11. Hess, E. H.   *J. comp. & physiol. Psychol.*, in press.
12. Hinde, R. A., Thorpe, W. H., & Vince, M. A.   *Behavior*, 1956, **9**, 214.
13. Jaynes, J.   *J. comp. physiol. & Psychol.*, in press.
14. Jersild, A. T., & Holmes, F. B.   *Child Develop. Monogr.*, 1935, No. 20, 356.
15. Kohler, W.   *The mentality of apes.* New York: Humanities Press, 1951.
16. Lorenz, K.   *Auk*, 1937, **54**, 245.
17. Moltz, H., & Rosenblum, L.   *J. comp. physiol. & Psychol.*, 1958, **51**, 658.
18. Nolte, A.   *Z. Tierpsychol.*, 1955, **12**, 77.
19. Ribble, M. A.   *The rights of infants.* New York: Columbia Univ. Press.
20. van Wagenen, G.   In E. J. Farris (Ed.), *The care and breeding of laboratory animals.* New York: Wiley, 1950, 1.
21. Yerkes, R. M., & Tomilin, M. I.   *J. comp. Psychol.*, 1935, **20**, 321.
22. Zuckerman, S.   *Functional affinities of man, monkeys, and apes.* London: Harcourt Brace, 1933.
23. Support for the research presented in this article was provided through funds received from the graduate school of the University of Wisconsin; from grant M-772, National Institute of Health; and from a Ford Foundation grant.
24. We no longer make the cloth mother out of a block of wood. The cloth mother's body is simply that of the wire mother, covered by a terry-cloth sheath.

1.3   The Development of Social Attachments in Infancy

H. Rudolph Schaffer and Peggy E. Emerson

The aims of the investigation are to supply descriptive data about the development of infant social attachment. They may be summarized as follows:

1. To explore some of the major parameters of social attachments in infancy, with special reference to:
   a. the age at onset,
   b. the intensity,
   c. the objects of attachments;
2. To search for variables that are related to individual differences in respect of the above parameters.

PROCEDURE

[The form was a short-term follow-up] from the early months of the first year until the age of 18 months. During this period identical data collection procedures were applied at regular intervals to each infant, the intervals being spaced four-weekly up to the child's first birthday, after which he was seen once more at 18 months. In this way the developmental trends of the phenomena under study could be traced and described.

Subjects

The subjects were 60 normal infants, of whom 31 were males and 29 females. Twenty-six of these infants were first-born children, while 24 had one sibling and a further 10 had two or more siblings. Developmental quotients, using the Cattell Infant Scale *(5)*, were obtained from all subjects around the age of 6 months and gave a mean figure of 110.1 and a range of 79 to 143.

Table 1 gives the ages of the infants at the beginning of the period of investigation. The oldest at that time was 23 weeks, the youngest 5 weeks.

TABLE 1. AGES OF INFANTS AT FIRST CONTACT

Age in Weeks	0–4	5–8	9–12	13–16	17–20	21–24	Total
N	0	10	16	10	17	7	60

Reprinted with abridgement from the *Monographs of the Society for Research in Child Development,* 1964, **29,** No. 3 (Serial #94), by permission of the authors and the Society for Research in Child Development.

[As] some contacts could not be made because of illness or absence of the family on holiday, and as three families moved elsewhere after the child's first birthday, the number of cases on which our data tends to vary somewhat from age to age.

The subjects were contacted and studied in two stages. First, a group of 23 infants was followed up until the age of 18 months, at which point it was decided to extend the project and add a further group of 37 infants. There are two differences between these groups: the initial contact was made rather earlier with the 37-group than with the 23-group (within the first 2 to 3 months rather than at 4 to 5 months of age), and some additional data (concerned with the elucidation of individual differences and to be described in due course) were gathered from the 37-group at 18 months which had not been obtained from the earlier group. In all other respects the two groups were similar, both in composition and with regard to the information sought from them.

Data Collection

The attachment measure. In our previous study *(12, 13)* the hospitalization situation was used to yield various indexes of separation upset as measures of attachment formation. While we wish to retain the separation criterion as a measure, other situations are clearly required for the purposes of a longitudinal study. Hospitalization, however, involves only a very much more intensified and prolonged form of an experience that occurs frequently in the everyday life of all infants, for every child is repeatedly exposed to separation from his mother, even though such a separation may last only a few minutes and involve a distance of not more than a few feet between mother and child. For the present investigation the index was based on a variety of such everyday separations.

After some preliminary enquiries the following seven situations were chosen . . . :

1. The infant is left alone in a room.
2. The infant is left with other people.
3. The infant is left in his pram outside the house.
4. The infant is left in his pram outside shops.
5. The infant is left in his cot at night.
6. The infant is put down after being held in the adult's arms or lap.
7. The infant is passed by while in his cot or chair.

These seven separation situations form the items in our attachment scale. For each, data about the infant's responses were obtained from interviews held with the mothers during our regular home visits, the data referring to the infant's behavior in the period since the last visit. The following information was required for each of the items:

a. Does the infant show any form of protest under the defined circumstances?

b. If protest occurs, does it invariably appear in this situation or only under certain conditions or at certain times?

c. If protest occurs, how intense is it (a "full-blooded" cry, for instance, or only a whimper, a moan, etc.)?

d. If protest occurs, at whom is it directed, i.e., whose departure elicits it?

The information asked for refers only to the infant's behavior immediately following the separation. . . .

From the end of the first year on, the development in the child's locomotor abilities frequently enabled him to react to a separation situation by following his object of attachment and thus avoiding loss of proximity from taking place at all. . . . We concentrated only on those instances where the infant was prevented from taking such action (either by his own lack of motor skills or by such physical obstacles as pram reins, playpens, or closed doors) and where separation therefore did actually take place.

The order and precise form of questions used to elicit the data were left to the interviewer, as it was found that the unstructured type of interview tended to be more productive and (though this was conjectural) more reliable. All information was recorded on the spot.

From the interview material . . . a number of measures could be obtained:

a. *The age at onset of attachments,* i.e., the point when protest behavior directed at particular individuals was first recorded. We arbitrarily defined this point as being midway between the interview which first yielded such information and the previous interview.

b. *The intensity of attachment.* Each of the seven separation situations was rated after every follow-up visit on the following four-point scale:

0—No protest reported.

1—Protests occur, but there are qualifications in respect of *both* the intensity with which they are expressed and their regularity—i.e., the protest is less than a "full-blooded" cry, consisting merely of whimpering, moaning, shouting, screwing up face, lip trembling, etc., and the infant is also reported as protesting on only some occasions that this particular situation arises.

2—Protests occur, but there are qualifications in respect of *either* intensity *or* regularity—e.g., loud protests on some occasions but not on others, or invariable protests but taking the form of just a brief whimper.

3—Protests occur, and there are no qualifications as to intensity or regularity, i.e., the infant cries loudly on each occasion.

The data obtained for the whole sample were rated for intensity independently by the two writers, and an agreement percentage of 93 was found. Disagreements were discussed and jointly decided.

By adding the ratings for the seven separating situations, a score with a maximum of 21 may be obtained for each interview, and this is taken to represent the intensity of the infant's attachment at that particular time. . . .

c. *The breadth of attachment.* This dimension refers to the number of objects of the attachment function, i.e., the number of individuals who at any one time evoke separation protest, irrespective of intensity or the number of situations in which this occurs.

By taking into account and identifying the various objects to whom attachments are formed by an infant, one can not only describe the growth of the attachment function as a whole, irrespective of the object(s) to which it is directed, but also isolate and trace the development of attachments as formed to particular individuals. . . .

In this report we shall be mainly concerned with two phenomena, namely the capacity to form attachments to specific individuals (taken as a whole, without considering the identity of these individuals), and, more narrowly, the attachment-to-mother.

The fear-of-strangers measure. An approach technique was used to investigate proximity avoidance, *i.e.,* fear of strangers, which involved the infant's reaction to the interviewer himself. Right at the beginning of every visit the interviewer related to the infant in a series of steps involving progressively greater proximity, in order to determine whether, and if so at what point, the infant began to show fear. Fear reactions were specified as whimpering, crying, lip trembling, screwed up face, looking or turning away, drawing back, running or crawling away, and hiding face. Not included are all instances where the child merely failed to respond positively, as when he stared solemnly without smiling or vocalizing back at the adult, or when he ceased all activity and remained quietly watchful.

The consecutive steps of the experiment, in order of progressively greater proximity, are as follows (the figures in parenthesis refers to the score allocated to an infant if he first showed fear at this particular point):

    a. The *Observer* (*O*) appears in the infant's visual range and remains standing still, looking at him but not in any other way stimulating him. (6)
    b. *O* smiles and talks to the infant without as yet moving any closer. (5)
    c. *O* approaches the infant, smiling and talking. (4)
    d. *O* makes physical contact with the infant by taking his hand or stroking his arm. (3)
    e. *O* offers to pick up the infant by holding out his hands. (2)
    f. *O* picks up the infant and sits him on his knee. (1)
    (If even the last type of contact elicited no fear response, a score of 0 was given.)

The score obtained by an infant depended on the step at which he first showed fear, and at this particular point the experiment was terminated.

Age at Onset of Attachments

The ages when the infants of the sample first showed attachments to specific individuals are given in Table 2. If we examine, first of all, specific

TABLE 2. AGE AT ONSET OF SPECIFIC ATTACHMENTS, OF ATTACHMENT-TO-MOTHER, AND OF FEAR-OF-STRANGERS

Age in Weeks	Specific Attachments (N)	Attachment-to-Mother (N)	Fear-of-Strangers (N)
21–24	4	3	0
25–28	15	13	10
29–32	17	18	15
33–36	7	8	19
37–40	7	8	7
41–44	4	4	4
45–48	3	3	2
49–52	1	1	0
53–78	2	2	3
Total	60	60	60

attachments irrespective of the identity of the individuals with whom they are formed, we see that the age at onset for the majority falls within the third quarter of the first year. The same applies if we take into account only that behavior which is specifically directed toward the mother, although there is a very slight shift in distribution which suggests that the mother was not the first attachment object in every case. [Our previous finding (12, 13)] is confirmed, namely that around 7 months of age the crucial period may be found when, in the majority of infants, this particular developmental milestone may be detected.

Attention must be drawn, however, to the existence of considerable individual differences. The youngest infant in the sample to reach this phase of development was only 22 weeks at the time, whereas two infants did not show separation protest toward specific individuals until they had passed their first birthday. Thus, despite the concentration in the third quarter of the first year, a very wide scatter is to be observed.

Table 2 also presents data about the age at onset of fear-of-strangers. Comparison with the attachment findings shows that the two phenomena do not coincide, but that the fear distribution follows in time that of the attachment distribution. In most of our cases there was an interval of approximately a month between the two crucial ages, though in 14 infants fear-of-strangers preceded, for some unknown reason, the emergence of specific attachments. It appears that the tendency to seek the proximity of certain familiar figures cannot simply be explained by the tendency to flee from (and therefore to seek protection from) strangers. The disparity in age at onset suggests that proximity seeking and proximity avoidance are not just the opposite sides of the same coin but that one can be found without the other. There is, however, a significant tendency for those who develop specific attachments early also to develop fear of strangers early: a rank order correlation (*rho*) of .412 was found ($p < .01$), indicating that the two functions may be part of a more general development trend.

When we examine more closely the manner in which the attachment milestone is reached, we find that the relevant phenomena are, in fact, new in only one respect, namely in the type of stimulus which evokes separation protest. Long before this age point, indeed from the very earliest months, proximity seeking is apparent. Thus the infant of 3 or 4 months may protest bitterly when social stimulation is withdrawn in the separation situations investigated by us and may not quieten until the other person returns. However, the crucial difference compared with the later behavior pattern is to be found in the *indiscriminate* nature of the early attachments: the infant in the first half year of life will cry for attention from anyone, familiar or stranger, and, though his responsiveness to the latter will become somewhat more delayed and less intense than to the former, both suffice to quieten him and the departure of both are likely to re-evoke his protests. It is only in the second six months that proximity seeking becomes focused on certain specific individuals only. This means that the 7-months milestone is not marked by the dramatic appearance of a new behavior pattern comparable to the first step or the first smile: it is distinguished rather by the child *ceasing* to cry after some people and confining his protests to certain selected figures in his environment. Thus the first sign of specific attachments usually emerged in the situation where the child is left with other people, for, while all our separation situations were able to furnish evidence of some form of protest, this particular situation appeared most sensitive in yielding evidence for the selective nature of protest.

Attachments . . . must be qualified according to the class of objects which elicit them. . . . Indiscriminate attachment, being a search for proximity in general instead of a concern for a particular individual, must be regarded as stimulus-oriented rather than object-oriented. It is thus a preliminary stage in the establishment of specific attachment and may be considered as a presocial phenomenon (analogous to the early smiling response). All infants in this sample showed evidence of indiscriminate attachments before reaching the specific phase, but we were unable to determine any point of onset for indiscriminate attachments, for no infants were studied in the first lunar month, and of the 10 infants with whom contact was established in their second lunar month eight were reported as already showing indiscriminate attachments at that time. . . .

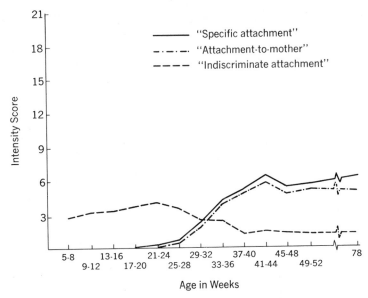

FIGURE 1. Developmental course of attachments.

Intensity of Attachments

In Figure 1 the developmental course of the attachment function is graphically indicated according to the mean intensity scores of the group obtained for the various age levels. . . . It is of interest to note that the indiscriminate attachment curve, though it descends after 6 months, does not completely disappear with the emergence of specific attachments but is still in evidence even at 18 months. While this is to some extent due to those infants who developed specific attachments rather late, it does [illustrate that] the onset of attachments to specific people does not necessarily completely displace evidence of indiscriminate attachment from the behavior repertoire of individual infants. The two may continue, at any rate within the age period covered by the present study, to exist side by side, in that the infant will show the one in some situations and the other in other situations. Sometimes an infant was also reported as crying for attention from anyone under normal circumstances but as insisting on the company of a particular person when tired or ill.[1] . . .

There are inevitably certain aspects of the developmental course of the attachment function which a curve based on group averages tends to ob-

---

[1] For scoring purposes, we allocated a specific score to an infant if, in the particular situation under consideration, he had given evidence during the period following the last visit that he was capable of forming attachments to specific individuals, even if he was reported as occasionally showing indiscriminate attachments as well in this situation.

scure. An examination of individual curves indicates two points worth commenting on. In the first place, most individual curves do not rise as gradually as the group curve, the shape of which is influenced by the differences in age at onset of specific attachments found in the sample as a whole. Twenty of the 60 infants obtained their highest score recorded within the period of the enquiry in the first lunar month following onset, thus suggesting that a stepwise development is by no means uncommon.

This point is further illustrated by . . . the increments in specific attachment intensity which occur for the group from one age period to the next. . . . By far the greatest increment occurs in the first lunar month following onset: not only are subsequent increments very much smaller but decrements occur too (in the second lunar month, for instance, decrements were found in 60 per cent of individual scores). The onset of specific attachments must therefore be seen, not as a gradual, tentative development slowly gaining in strength from month to month, but as a sudden emergence of a new developmental acquisition which, in many cases, manifests itself at full intensity from the very beginning. . . .

Turning now to the correlation between intensity and age at onset of specific attachments, no relation was found . . . in this sample. Two measures of intensity were used: that obtained for the first lunar month following onset and that obtained at 18 months. . . . The age at onset of specific attachments is therefore not related to the intensity with which they are manifested, either at the time that they first emerge or subsequently.

Both Spitz (17) and Freedman (6) have suggested that the intensity of a child's attachment is related to the age when fear of strangers is first evidenced, in that the strongly attached infant is likely to develop such fear early. We investigated this relation by taking as our intensity measure the score which the infant obtained on the same four-weekly visit on which fear was first detected. The correlation coefficient . . . did not . . . confirm . . . such a relation (rho = .149, ns).

The intensity of specific attachments did not, therefore, influence the age when fear of strangers appeared. But is it related to the *intensity* with which fear is manifested? Examining the association of these two phenomena separately for each age period (i.e., from the first lunar month following the emergence of *both* to 18 months), no statistically significant relation was found at any point. On the other hand, the relation was in every instance a positive one, and, when the mean of all the specific attachment scores that had been obtained from each infant was compared with the mean of all fear scores, a significant correlation (rho = .248, p < .05) was found. The relation appears thus to be a complex one: there is a tendency in general for the more intensely attached infant to show more fear to strangers, yet the fluctuation in the one phenomenon are not necessarily paralleled by fluctuations in the other, with the result that considerable discrepancies may be observed at any one point of time.

Objects of Attachments

Assessment of the attachment function at any given moment must involve . . . not only . . . its intensity dimension but also . . . its "breadth." We shall use this term to cover the number of objects with whom attachments are formed. . . . Here our attention will be given only to breadth as it is found in the specific phase.

The customary view of breadth is that the infant forms his first social relationship with one person (usually his mother) and that only when this has become firmly established is he able to make other subsidiary attachments. Table 3 confirms that the majority of infants in this sample did . . . form their initial attachment to one person only and that subsequently the number of attachment objects increased. However, the figures also show that the selection of a single object is apparently not a *necessary* first step, for 29 per cent of the sample first showed attachments directed at multiple objects, and 10 per cent even selected as many as five or more objects at the beginning of the specific phase.

TABLE 3. Number of Attachment Objects: Percentage of Subjects According to Number of Objects at Successive Age Periods

Number of Objects	Lunar Month Following Age at Onset in First Year						18-Months (CA)
	1st	2nd	3rd	4th	5th	6th	
1	71%	62%	41%	52%	47%	22%	13%
2	12	17	29	29	30	33	25
3	7	5	5	0	3	11	24
4	0	2	5	0	3	6	7
5 or more	10	14	20	19	17	28	31
Total	100	100	100	100	100	100	100
N	58	42	42	42	30	18	55

The other modification of the customary view refers to the speed with which, for the sample as a whole, breadth increases with age. This is not a slow and gradual process: by the third lunar month following onset over half the subjects were showing attachment towards more than one person, and by the sixth month this proportion had risen to three quarters of the group. By 18 months, finally, only 13 per cent were showing attachments to just one person, while almost a third of all cases now had five or more attachment objects.

A further question . . . refers to the identity of the individuals who are selected as attachment objects. From Table 4 we find, . . . that the mother is by far the most frequently chosen object. . . . However, she ceases to be the sole object of attachment for the majority of infants and, from about the third lunar month following the onset of specific attachments, more often than not shares this position with other people. What emerges strikingly from this analysis is the importance which fathers play in the child's world. . . . Twenty-seven per cent of the whole group . . . chose father as an attachment object jointly with other objects in this first month [following onset].

By 18 months 75 per cent of the sample showed attachments directed at the father, including 4 per cent for whom father was the only attachment object. Individuals other than the parents rarely formed an infant's sole object at any stage, but grandparents (and especially the maternal grandmother) were increasingly mentioned as joint objects. . . . In quite a number of instances, siblings or other children [were] selected as attachment objects. . . .

While an infant may show attachment towards a number of different individuals at any given time, . . . there will commonly be . . . a hierarchy of objects, and the individual at the top of this hierarchy to whom the most intense attachment is shown may be regarded as the infant's *principal object*. In order to establish the identity of these principal objects we calculated for every infant the intensity of attachment shown in relation to each of his specific objects at every age level, and in this way defined the individual located at the top of the hierarchy at each age period. . . .

At all stages the mother was most frequently chosen, either solely or,

TABLE 4. IDENTITY OF ATTACHMENT OBJECTS: PERCENTAGE OF SUBJECTS FORMING SPECIFIC ATTACHMENTS ACCORDING TO IDENTITY OF OBJECT AT SUCCESSIVE AGE PERIODS

Identity of Object	Lunar Month Following Age at Onset in First Year						18-Months (CA)
	1st	2nd	3rd	4th	5th	6th	
Mother (sole object)	65%	53%	32%	50%	47%	17%	5%
Mother (joint object)	30	35	54	43	50	77	76
Father (sole object)	3	9	7	2	0	5	4
Father (joint object)	27	23	42	29	44	59	71
Grandparent (sole object)	2	0	0	0	0	0	0
Grandparent (joint object)	9	12	14	12	10	29	45
Other relative (sole object)	0	0	0	0	0	0	2
Other relative (joint object)	5	5	5	14	10	18	16
Friend or neighbor (sole object)	0	0	2	0	0	0	0
Friend or neighbor (joint object)	3	7	7	9	3	12	26
Sibling (sole object)	0	0	0	0	0	0	2
Sibling (joint object)	2	5	7	7	7	12	22
Other child (sole object)	0	0	0	0	0	0	0
Other child (joint object)	3	5	14	7	3	12	14

occasionally, jointly with others, as the principal object. However, while in the first lunar month following onset the mother figures as a principal object in altogether 93 per cent of cases, at 18 months this percentage had decreased to 69. Thus, with increasing age, there was a tendency for other people to emerge as principal objects. Once again the important role played by fathers is emphasized: of all the instances in which individuals other than the mother were found to be principal objects (either solely or jointly with the mother), 62 per cent referred to fathers, 23 per cent to grandparents, and 15 per cent to other people. At 18 months father was chosen as sole principal object by 16 per cent of the subjects that showed specific attachments at that age and joint principal object by another 18 per cent.

Is breadth of attachment related to age at onset and intensity? Using two measures of breadth, that obtained for the first lunar month following onset and that obtained at 18 months, the median test reveals no association of either with age at onset.

Does the intensity of attachment to the infant's principal object have any bearing on the number of other figures to whom attachments are formed —whether, for instance, one can expect an intense attachment to the principal object to "drain" all such behavior away from other potential objects, or whether, quite the contrary, intensity and breadth are positively related. The results were again obtained from two age points—the first month following onset and the 18-month visit. For the former, a statistically significant relation between the two variables was found to exist: the infant with an intense attachment to his principal object was *more* likely to have selected other objects of attachment as well, whereas the weakly attached infant tended mainly to focus on only the one individual. At 18 months, however, this relation is no longer present.

Finally, the association of attachment breadth with intensity of fear-of-strangers may be examined. Our measures for these phenomena were taken at two points, namely at the first lunar month following the onset of *both* specific attachment and fear-of-strangers and at 18 months. Infants with many attachment objects tend to be more afraid when meeting a stranger than infants with few attachment objects.

FINDINGS: INDIVIDUAL DIFFERENCES

Individual Differences in Intensity

Although, as has been described, the intensity score obtained by any one infant may vary from age to age, the question still arises as to why, at any given point, certain infants show a far greater need for the presence of some particular individual than others. To investigate this problem, we arbitrarily selected the end point of the follow-up period, namely the age of 18 months, in order to locate the conditions which significantly vary with intensity at that time. As we were particularly interested in the effects of maternal behavior on the child, we further specified intensity of attachment-to-mother as the dependent variable to be studied here. . . .

Demographic and constitutional variables. . . . When the sample is divided at the median, neither sex nor birth order nor occupational level differentiates between infants who are respectively high and low on intensity of attachment-to-mother at 18 months. DQ also fails to reveal any significant association, *rho* being —.102.

Socializing variables. Writers such as Miller and Dollard (8) and Sears *et al.* (14) have suggested that the degree of the child's emotional dependence on the mother is a function of the severity of the socializing practices encountered in infancy. . . . At the 18-months interview with the group of 36 infants data were therefore systematically gathered about the following indexes:

a. Feeding rigidity during infancy. . . .
b. Age at weaning.
c. Length of weaning period.
d. Age when toilet training began.
e. Toileting severity. . . .

None of the socializing variables showed any relation to intensity of attachment-to-mother, and this applies not only to those socializing procedures that had taken place at some stage previous to 18 months (such as age at weaning of feeding rigidity) but also to those practices that were taking place concurrently (like severity of toilet training). . . .

Relationship variables. A group of variables which, on *a priori* grounds at least, may be regarded as having a more direct and immediate bearing on the extent to which an infant seeks the proximity of his mother are the mother's availability, the exclusiveness of maternal contact, the degree of maternal responsiveness to the infant, the amount of interaction initiated by the mother, and the customary mode of such interaction.

Maternal availability refers to the amount of time which a mother spends together with her child. Two measures were used to describe this variable. At the 18-months visit the 36 mothers were asked to make a note both of the number of times on which they left their infants for more than half an hour during the subsequent seven days and of the total time in hours which these absences involved.

. . . Although for both measures there is a tendency for infants above the median in attachment intensity to have mothers who are somewhat more available than infants below the median, this association is far from statistically significant. Mere "togetherness," it appears, is not sufficient to explain the difference in intensity. . . .

The remaining three variables (responsiveness, amount of interaction, and mode of interaction) all refer to the nature of the interaction process that takes place between mother and infant. . . . A particularly pertinent variable in this connection may be identified as the *degree of maternal responsiveness* in relation to the infant's crying. A six point scale ranging from—(1) mother generally leaves infant to cry indefinitely, mostly refuses to respond at all, to—(6) mother always responds quickly, goes almost at once, was used. . . .

This variably clearly differentiates between the high and the low attachment groups. Intensely attached infants are usually found in association with mothers who respond quickly to their demands for company, whereas weakly attached infants tend to have mothers who generally fail to reinforce such behavior.

Maternal responsiveness is only theoretically an "antecedent" variable. Its statistical association with attachment intensity does not demonstrate that it "comes first" and that it "causes" the infant's behavior. An interpretation in terms of *mutual adaptation* of mother and infant is likely to do most justice to the observed facts, so that attachment intensity may be viewed as the resultant of the strength of the infant's demands on the one hand and the degree to which the mother is prepared to respond on the other hand. . . .

In *amount of maternal interaction* we have another variable which describes the interchange between mother and infant, but, whereas responsiveness referred to infant-initiated episodes, this variable refers to those instances of interaction which are initiated by the mother. . . . At one extreme of the continuum is the mother who submits her infant to an almost continuous barrage of stimuli and relates to him unceasingly and intensely; at the other extreme we find the mother who follows a policy of "leave well alone," ignoring her baby as much as possible and spontaneously interacting with him on only rare occasions.

The following 6 point rating scale was used with items ranging from —(1) Interaction minimal—mother follows a policy of "leave well alone," does her best to avoid interaction outside routine care situations, tends to ignore infant to a considerable extent, to —(6) Considerable amount of interaction —fairly continuous stimulation of infant, often of a rather intense form, mother highly demonstrative in her relationship.

The results indicate that a significant relation exists with the intensity of attachment-to-mother. The highly stimulated infant does not like losing the proximity of his attachment object, whereas the infant who receives comparatively little stimulation rarely protests. Caution must be exercised in making cause-and-effect statements.

Observation of mothers suggests that two principal modes of interaction may be distinguished: the personal and the impersonal. In the *personal* approach stimulation is provided by the mother which stems in the main directly from herself. She responds to the infant's need for attention by offering herself, as it were: by picking up, handling, cuddling, talking, kissing, cooing, and providing other forms of stimulation which involve a direct and immediate contact between herself and the child. She thus puts herself at the center of the infant's attention, for, though she may also use toys and other objects in interacting with him, these are only used as subsidiary aids.

The personal approach can, however, be further subdivided, for it is possible to distinguish mothers whose primary mode of interaction involves a great deal of handling and other forms of physical contact and mothers where interaction, though still personal in nature, is expressed in other, non-contact ways. Thus a mother belonging to the latter category will generally provide visual and auditory stimulation rather than tactual and kinesthetic: when her baby cries she will not pick him up and cuddle him but will prefer to talk, coo, sing, smile, pull faces, etc. When playing with him, she will rarely have him on her knee but rely on more distant though still personal means of interaction.

In the *impersonal* approach the mother tends to use means of stimulation which draw the child's attention away from herself. She prefers to "divert" him and thus uses toys, food, and other objects in response to his demands for attention, supplying these in such a manner that the tendency to respond to her directly is minimized. Her manner of relating to the child is thus through various intermediate means and tends as far as possible to eliminate a more personal contact.

No mother ever employs just one of these three types to the exclusion of the other two, but most mothers do have a *preferred* mode of interaction which they customarily use. . . .

When compared with attachment intensity, no association is found with this maternal attribute. The impersonal group show no less attachment than the others; furthermore, those infants whose mothers were classified as predominantly "handlers" did not differ from the rest in attachment intensity.

We conclude that of the relationship variables only degree of maternal responsiveness and amount of maternal interaction have been shown to bear a significant relation to intensity of attachment-to-mother. Maternal availability, however, did not differentiate between the high and the low intensity groups: a mother's constant presence is apparently no sufficient guarantee that the infant will develop a very close attachment to her. What is required is a more active impinging of mother on child, so that somewhat limited availabilty may make a close tie feasible when combined with a high degree of responsiveness and a considerable amount of interaction. . . .

Finally, choice of attachment object does not depend on the alleviation of the child's physical needs. At the 18-months visit the mothers were asked to indicate who had chief responsibility for feeding and for changing, bathing, dressing, and putting to bed. They were also asked to list all those who participated to a minor degree in these activities. In 39 per cent of cases the individuals mainly responsible for feeding and other routines were not chosen as principal objects, and in that in 22 per cent the principal objects did not participate even to a minor degree in any aspect of the child's physical care. It appears that attachments may develop even when the individuals to whom they are formed have in no way been associated with physical satisfactions.

DISCUSSION

The ability to form an attachment to a specific individual arises, in the majority of cases, in the third quarter of the first year. Evidence indicates that the onset of specific attachments is but one expression of a more general development. Of particular significance here is the suggestion of Piaget (9, 10) that the beginnings of object conservation first manifest themselves in the third quarter of the first year. Similarly, studies of smiling (1, 16) have shown that within the same age period this aspect of social behavior ceases to be evoked by primitive configurational properties inherent in all human faces and becomes linked to specific individuals. All these developments may be regarded as based on a fundamental change in the infant's cognitive structure, i.e., in the manner in which perceptions are organized and related to each other and to their external sources. However, only further research can illuminate the details of the processes involved.

One point our data have definitely indicated, namely, that proximity seeking can be found long before the emergence of specific attachments. The need appears to be present even in the first six months and to give rise to behavior patterns that are identical to those found later on. In the second half-year, however, these responses become channeled into certain directions and are no longer indiscriminate in object choice. . . .

If proximity seeking is present from the early weeks on, must we regard the attachment need as primary, i.e., as an inborn motivational tendency to seek the presence of other people for its own sake and not, in the first place, for the satisfaction of the other needs? In this study we have not only failed to find any relation between attachment intensity and socializing severity, but we have also observed attachments to be formed to individuals who have never participated in routine care activities. Taken in conjunction with Bowlby's (3) theory, Harlow's (7) findings, and Ainsworth's (2) similar observations, the view that social behavior arises primarily in the context of the feeding situation must now be seriously questioned. Satisfaction of physical needs does not appear to be a necessary precondition to the development of attachments, the latter taking place independently and without any obvious regard to the experiences that the child encounters in physical care situations. . . .

There is, however, another interpretation which suggests itself, namely that the infant's need for the proximity of other people is not primary but arises, in the course of development, from his need for stimulation in general.

The notion that environmental stimulation is necessary for full development to take place is now widely accepted. In early infancy in particular, as studies of deprivation (15, 4) have shown, this requirement must be met. According to Rheingold (11), one of the most prominent characteristics of the young infant is his constant searching of the environment for stimulation—not only is his *responsiveness* well developed by 3 months of age, but by this time he is also already actively *seeking* for the arousing properties of his surroundings. But, as Rheingold further suggests, the most interesting object in his environment is the human object, with its high arousal potential and most varied stimulation propensity. In time, one may add, the infant learns that other human beings are particularly satisfying objects and that, moreover, the provision even of nonsocial stimulation is usually associated with their appearance. A need for their presence may thus be said to develop: the other person's proximity is initially sought as only one source of stimulation amongst many but will eventually be required in its own right once the infant has had the opportunity of learning about its special functional characteristics.

A three-stage development of early social behavior is thus envisaged. In the first stage, an asocial one, the individual seeks optimal arousal equally from all aspects of his environment. In time he learns to single out human beings as particularly satisfying objects and makes special efforts to seek their proximity. Thus we have the second stage, a presocial one, which is characterized by indiscriminate attachment behavior. Finally, a further narrowing down occurs, and in the last and only truly social stage attachments are formed to specific individuals. . . .

One of the more controversial findings of this investigation arises from the examination of the breadth dimension. This suggests that the choice of attachment object, even at the very beginning of the specific phase, is not necessarily confined to one person only, but that straightaway attachments may be formed to a number of different (though discriminated) individuals. . . . The substantial minority in whom attachments were focused on more than one person at this time indicates that this is neither a necessary nor an inherent feature in the development of this function. Moreover, although the mother was generally at the top of the hierarchy of the infant's objects, this choice was again not an inevitable one, for the importance of other people in the child's environment, particularly that of the father, was strongly emphasized throughout. To focus one's enquiry on the child's relationship with the mother alone would therefore give a misleading impression of the attachment function.

REFERENCES

1. Ahrens, R.   Beitrag zur Entwicklung des Physiognomie und Mimikerkennens. *Zeit. f. Experimentelle und Angewandte Psychol.*, 1954, **2**, 412–454.
2. Ainsworth, M. D.   The development of mother-infant interaction among the Ganda. In B. Foss (Ed.), *Determinants of infant behaviour, II*. London: Methuen, 1963.

3. Bowlby, J. The nature of the child's tie to his mother. *Int. J. Psycho-Anal.*, 1958, **39**, 350–373.
4. Casler, L. Maternal deprivation: a critical review of the literature. *Monogr. Soc. Res. Child Develpm.*, 1961, **26**, No. 2.
5. Cattell, P. *The measurement of intelligence of infants and young children.* Psychol. Corp., 1940.
6. Freedman, D. G. The infant's fear of strangers and the flight response. *J. Child Psychol. Psychiat.*, 1961, **2**, 242–248.
7. Harlow, H. F. The nature of love. *Amer. Psychologist*, 1958, **13**, 673–685.
8. Miller, N. E., & Dollard, J. *Social learning and imitation.* Yale Univer. Press, 1941.
9. Piaget, J. *The origin of intelligence in the child.* London: Routledge, 1953.
10. Piaget, J. *The child's construction of reality.* London: Routledge, 1955.
11. Rheingold, H. The effect of environmental stimulation upon social and exploratory behaviour in the human infant. In B. Foss (Ed.), *Determinants of infant behaviour, I.* London: Meuthuen, 1961.
12. Schaffer, H. R. Objective observations of personality development in early infancy. *Brit. J. med. Psychol.*, 1958, **31**, 174–184.
13. Schaffer, H. R., & Callendar, W. M. Psychologic effects of hospitalization in infancy. *Pediatrics*, 1959, **24**, 528–539.
14. Sears, R. R., Whiting, J. W. M., Nowlis, V., & Sears, P. S. Some childrearing antecedents of aggression and dependency in young children. *Genet. Psychol. Monogr.*, 1953, **47**, 135–236.
15. Spitz, R. A. Hospitalism: An inquiry into the genesis of psychiatric conditions in early childhood. *Psychoanal. Stud. Child*, 1945, **1**, 53–74.
16. Spitz, R. A. The smiling response: A contribution to the ontogenesis social relations. *Genet. Psychol. Monogr.*, 1946, **34**, 57–125.
17. Spitz, R. A. Anxiety in infancy: A study of its manifestations in the first year of life. *Int. J. Psycho-Anal.*, 1950, **31**, 138–143.

1.4   Development, Maintenance, and Extinction of Social Attachment Behavior in Sheep[1]

Robert B. Cairns

The experiments reported here had as their purpose the study of the mechanisms that control social attachment behavior in young sheep, a species

[1] The author expresses his thanks to D. L. Johnson and R. Webb for their help in the completion of these studies. This research was supported, in part, by grants from the Indiana University Foundation and the National Institute of Mental Health (07144-02 and 08757-01).

Reprinted from the *Journal of Comparative and Physiological Psychology* 1966, **62**, 298–306, by permission of the author and the American Psychological Association.

for which gregarious behavior is presumed to be prepotent (Miller, 1951; Scott, 1945).

EXPERIMENT 1

On the basis of assumptions discussed elsewhere (Cairns, 1966), it was expected that lambs would form an attachment with respect to any salient object with which they had been continuously confined. While tactile stimulation might facilitate attachment formation, such stimulation was not seen as essential to the process. Nor was it required that the object be alive and capable of developing patterns of dyadic interaction. The rearing conditions of the present study permitted a preliminary evaluation of these expectations.

This experiment was also concerned with the quantification of the reinforcement properties of the experimentally produced attachments. Previous work has shown that the ongoing behavior of lambs is usually disrupted when the cohabitant is removed from the confinement compartment (Cairns & Johnson, 1965; Hersher, Richmond, & Moore, 1963). It was expected, again on the basis of the association hypothesis (Cairns, 1966), that measures of the extent of the disruption would provide reliable indices of attachment strength. This proposition implied that the greater the amount of disturbance observed upon cohabitant separation, the greater the effectiveness of the cohabitant as a "social" reinforcement event.

Method

Subjects. From birth until the beginning of the experiment, when they were 4–8 wk. old, 20 purebred lambs (Hampshire Down) lived with the maternal ewes and other lambs in a small flock. One lamb died after 7 wk. in the control condition and was replaced with an S of the same age and sex.[2] In addition, 5 Rambouillet ewes and 10 mongrel dogs were used as cohabitants.

Apparatus. A U maze of plywood and wire construction was used for the assessment of social preferences. The 30-in.-wide runways were enclosed by 48-in. plywood walls and covered by translucent netting material. In length, the runway segments were: stem (start compartment to choice point) 12 ft.; arm (choice point to 90° turn) 6 ft.; entry (turn to goal area) 4 ft. The 8×8 ft. goal areas were enclosed by 48-in. plywood walls. Guillotine doors were located at the start compartment and at either side of the choice point. Five television sets, of various makes and external dimensions, provided the

---

[2] The relevant statistical analyses were performed with and without the inclusion of the substitute control S. The results of the two sets of analyses were strictly comparable. Unless otherwise noted, the product-moment correlations reported in Experiment 1 were based upon 20 Ss. The corresponding two-tailed significance levels ($df = 18$) are: $r \geq 45$, $p < .05$; $r \geq .57$, $p < .01$; $r \geq .68$, $p < .001$.

remaining items of equipment. All sets operated continuously, presenting both auditory and visual patterns.

Confinement compartments. Each of the 20 compartments was approximately 8 $\times$ 10 ft. in floor area, enclosed on all sides. Thus Ss were permitted no visual contact with animals other than the cohabitant. Ten of the compartments were partitioned into two equal parts by a wire fence, 5 ft. high, which extended the length of the midline of the compartment. The fence interstices were $1\frac{7}{8} \times 3\frac{7}{8}$ in.

Procedure. Five lambs were assigned at random to one of four confinement conditions. *(a)* Dog interaction: the lamb-dog pairs were housed in five different compartments. If the dog chewed, mauled, or otherwise abused the lamb, it was restricted by a neck harness to approximately one-half the compartment. It was necessary to so restrict two of the five dogs. All lambs were permitted free movement. *(b)* Dog separation: the two animals in each pair were housed together as above, except that the lamb was placed on one side of the wire partition, and the dog on the other. The interstices of the fence were small enough virtually to debar the animals from physical contact. *(c)* Inanimate: lambs were isolated from other animals, but were housed with a continuously operating television set. The sets emitted organized, but varied, patterns of visual and auditory stimulation. *(d)* Control: lambs were paired individually with nonmaternal Rambouillet ewes under conditions of restricted interaction, i.e., as in condition *b.* Once the experimental confinement had begun, the two animals were kept together 24 hr. per day, and separated only when required by the test sessions.

Two types of maze series were conducted: non-contrast, where the cohabitant was placed in one goal area, and the second goal compartment was empty; contrast, where a ewe was tethered in one goal area, and a dog was tethered or a television set was placed in the opposite compartment. One of the test objects was the lamb's cohabitant. The contrast stimulus for Ss in the three experimental groups was a ewe; the contrast stimulus for the control group was a dog.

Sets of 10 noncontrast trials were completed after 7, 14, 21, 28, and 63 days of confinement. The position of the cohabitant was alternated in each set of trials for each S: e.g., left, for Trials 1–10; right, Trials 11–20, etc. Prior to the first test trial in every set, S was forced twice to either goal area in an ABBA or BAAB sequence by closing off one arm of the U. During all trials the noncorrection method was followed: i.e., a guillotine door was closed immediately after S passed the choice point. The S remained in the goal area for 60 sec. and then was returned for the next test trial. On a given trial, S was permitted 5 min. to traverse the stem distance and enter either arm.

On Days 70–71, two blocks of 10 contrast trials were completed for each S. The placement of the cohabitant was the same on both test days. On Day

70, Ss were given four forced runs, two to either side, prior to the first test trial. On Day 71, prior to the beginning of the test series, Ss were given an additional forced run to either side. In other respects the procedure was the same as that followed in the noncontrast series.

To obtain an assessment of behavorial disruption contingent upon cohabitant removal, sets of short-term separation tests were conducted after Weeks 1, 2, 3, and 9 of confinement. In each series, S was observed for six successive 60-sec. periods. During half of these observations (Minutes 1, 3, 5) the cohabitant was present; during the remainder (Minutes 2, 4, 6) the cohabitant was removed.

Response measures. The behavior observed during the cohabitant removal tests was the amount of vocalization, i.e., bleating, which occurred during cohabitant separation relative to nonseparation. The confinement vocalization index, VI_c, was a difference score based upon the effects of cohabitant removal as observed in the confinement compartment: mean bleats per minute emitted during cohabitant absence minus mean bleats per minute emitted during cohabitant presence. A parallel measure, the maze vocalization index, VI_m, was the vocalization that occurred during two 60-sec. periods of confinement in the U-maze goal compartments with and without the cohabitant during the 4 preliminary trials of each noncontrast series.

The maze trials yielded two measures: *(a)* proportion of trials within each block of 10 trials that Ss selected the cohabitant; *(b)* running time, i.e., the time elapsed between the opening of the start compartment and S's passing the choice point into one of the two arms. The time scores, recorded to the nearest .1 sec., were transformed to common logarithms for analysis.

Results

Behavorial disruption. Vocalization was almost perfectly controlled by the experimental operations of cohabitant removal and replacement. Summing over observations and conditions, the difference in mean bleats per minute during cohabitant presence (.50) and cohabitant absence (8.05) was significant ($t = 5.72$, $df = 19$, $p < .001$). With the exception of 2 Ss assigned to the inanimate condition, every S tested demonstrated the essential disruption-quiescence pattern. As noted elsewhere (Cairns & Johnson, 1965; Hersher et al., 1963), recurrent bleating in this context was usually accompanied by agitated pacing, rapid breathing, and leaping against the walls of the enclosure.

To determine whether the magnitude of the disruption varied as a function of treatment conditions, a repeated-measure analysis of variance (4×4) was performed on the VI_c scores summarized in Table 1. The main treatment effect was statistically significant ($F = 4.27$, $df = 3/16$, $p < .05$). All between-group differences between the three experimental groups (interaction, separation, inanimate) surpassed the critical values of the Newman-Keuls

TABLE 1. Mean Confinement Vocalization Index of the
Four Treatment Groups for Cohabitant-Removal Tests
Conducted after 1, 2, 3, and 9 Wk. of Confinement
(Experiment 1)

Condition	Weeks				Total
	1	2	3	9	
Dog interaction	12.2	11.4	13.0	12.4	12.3
Dog separated	4.6	6.6	7.0	11.0	7.3
Inanimate	1.6	2.0	2.8	2.6	2.3
Control	11.0	11.4	11.8	15.0	12.3

procedure (Winer, 1962) at $p < .05$. Neither the repeated Tests effect nor the Test $\times$ Treatment interaction was significant.

An independent assessment of separation vocalization was obtained in the preliminary trials of each noncontrast U-maze series. During the initial weeks of testing, the correlations between the two independently derived vocalization indices, VI_c and VI_m, were of moderate magnitude ($r = .48$, .46, and .36 for Weeks 1, 2, and 3, respectively). By Week 9 of confinement, however, the vocalization scores obtained in the U maze were highly correlated with those obtained in the compartment cohabitant removal tests ($r = .90$). Both vocalization indices showed the expected differences in intensity of behavorial disruption as a function of treatment conditions.

Choice data. An analysis of variance of the noncontrast U-maze series data (Figure 1) indicated that the groups improved in performance over the successive five blocks of test trials ($F = 2.74$, $df = 4/64$, $p < .05$). In the final series (Week 9), Ss' preference for the cohabitant was clearly above the chance level ($F = 14.49$, $df = 1/19$, $p < .005$). A comparison of the "correct" responses produced by the four groups indicated that the experimental conditions did not have a significant differential effect on Ss' choice behavior in the noncontrast series. Neither the Treatment effect nor the Treatment $\times$ Trials interaction was statistically significant.

The contrast series permitted an assessment of the relative strength of the experimentally produced attachments. As shown in Figure 2, the experimental treatment effect was reliable ($F = 7.96$, $df = 3/16$, $p < .01$). Analysis by the Newman-Keuls procedure indicated that, with the exception of the two dog-paired groups, all group comparisons yielded significant differences: Ss in these two experimental conditions selected the ewe test object on fewer occasions than control Ss ($p < .001$) or Ss in the inanimate condition ($p < .01$) and the difference between the inanimate condition and the control condition was reliable ($p < .05$).

Running times. Over the five blocks of noncontrast trials, the lambs showed a systematic increase in the amount of time in mean log seconds (mls) that they remained in the stem of the maze prior to making a choice

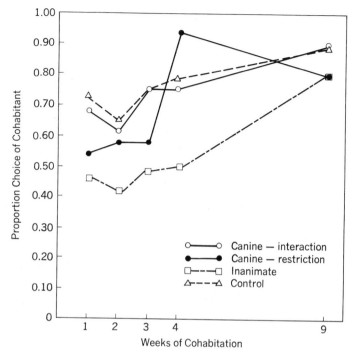

FIGURE 1. Choice behavior of lambs in noncontrast maze series, with 10 trials at each test week (Experiment 1).

$(F = 8.65, df = 4/64, p < .01)$. In all conditions, Ss tended to run faster in the first test series (Week 1 mls $= .94$) than they did in the final test series (Week 9 mls $= 1.40$). Unlike the choice scores, the running time index differentiated between the four treatment groups in the noncontrast series. The between-group effect was statistically significant, however, only in the final block of trials $(F = 4.20, df = 3/16, p < .05)$. A Newman-Keuls analysis of these data indicated that control Ss required significantly less time (mls $= .88$) than Ss assigned to the inanimate condition (mls $= 1.88$). The remaining between-group differences were nonsignificant.

The contrast series running times failed to yield significant differences between the various treatment groups. It is of some interest to note, however, that the lambs ran reliably faster in the contrast (mls $= 1.10$) series than in the final noncontrast (mls $= 1.40$) series $(F = 12.24, df = 1/16, p < .01)$. Analysis of the significant Test Type $\times$ Treatment interaction indicated that the main effect was due to the change in performance of one group: the inanimate condition. This group was the only one for which the contrast vs. final noncontrast latency difference was reliable $(t = 3.98, df = 4, p < .02)$.

Predictors of maze performance. A principal aim of the experiment was to determine whether attachment strength could be reliably quantified.

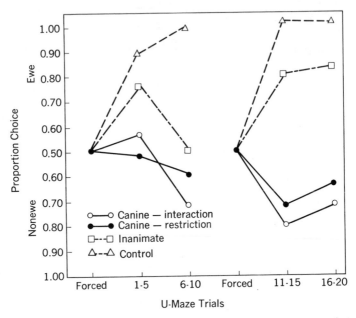

FIGURE 2. Choice behavior of lambs in contrast maze series over 4 blocks of 5 trials (Experiment 1).

Specifically, it was expected that the vocalization indices of behavioral disturbance, VI_c and VI_m, would be significantly related to the lamb's choice of its cohabitant.

The results indicated that neither vocalization index was significantly related to the choice performance of Ss in the noncontrast trial blocks. However, both indices were highly correlated with Ss' performance in the contrast series. For the final VI_c, the product-moment correlation was 8.1; for the final VI_m, the correlation was .75. If S showed considerable disruption during cohabitant separation, it would likely move in the direction of its cohabitant during the contrast trials. The within-group correlations were, with the exception of the control group, of the same order as those based upon the entire sample. The product-moment correlations between VI_m and choice of cohabitant in the contrast series within the various groups were: dog-paired conditions, $r = .75$ ($df = 8$, $p < .05$); inanimate condition, $r = .88$ ($df = 3$, $p < .05$); control, $r = -.06$ ($df = 3$, $p > .10$).

Similar correlational analyses were performed for the vocalization indices and running times. The data show that all of the correlations were in the expected direction: the greater the disturbance of S upon being separated from its cohabitant, the shorter its response latencies. But the relationships were reliable only for Ss' performance in the noncontrast series. For VI_c, the correlations between weekly vocalization scores and running times for Weeks 1, 2, 3, and 9 were $-.23$, $-.41$, $-.27$, and $-.50$. The corresponding correlations for VI_m and running times were $-.11$, $-.65$, $-.59$, and $-.56$.

Observations of following behavior. One of the more striking behavior patterns to emerge as a consequence of these experimental manipulations was the development of a strong following response: the lamb remained close to its dog cohabitant even when both animals were placed in an open field outside the maintenance compartment. If the cohabitant walked, the lamb would walk; if the cohabitant ran, the lamb would run; if the cohabitant jumped over a fence, the lamb would try to follow by going over, or through, the barrier.[3] This behavior, noted in earlier work (Cairns & Johnson, 1965), was specific to the cohabitant, and was obtained in all but two of the lambs assigned to the dog-paired conditions. Of the two Ss that did not follow their cohabitants, one was in the dog-interaction condition, and the other was in the dog-separation condition.

Discussion

Familar objects, animate or inanimate, can assume highly effective control over the behavior of young sheep. The attribution of reinforcement properties to a particular class of "social" objects, i.e., same-species animals, however, appears to be neither an inevitable nor an irreversible phenomenon. For lambs, at least, both the direction and the strength of social attachments are susceptible to experimental manipulation.

It should be noted that the experimentally produced attachments were often preceded by, or concurrent with, a same-species atttachment. All Ss in the present experiment had 4–8 wk. of constant exposure to various representatives of their own species prior to the experimental confinement. This experience presumably was sufficient for the lambs to develop a strong attachment response with respect to the same-species objects. Substantial evidence was later obtained (Experiment 3) which suggests that a same-species attachment not only had been established, but that it had not been entirely extinguished by the experimental procedures. This assumption—that the ewes possessed positive incentive properties for all lambs—was also consistent with the results of the choice and the time data of the present study. Indeed, the apparent conflicts between these two indices of incentive magnitude are resolved by this assumption.

Consider first the choice data. When obtained in single reward (noncontrast) series, the choice measure did not clearly differentiate between lambs that were strongly attached and those that were minimally attached to the cohabitant. All Ss learned to approach the "correct" goal area. But when a second reward event was introduced to the testing context—permitting Ss to select between the cohabitant and a presumably positive alternative—only the experimental Ss that were strongly attached to their cohabitant persisted in a cohabitant-appropriate turning response. With the resultant increase

---

[3] A short research film of these behaviors, shown at the 1964 American Psychological Association convention, is available from the Film Library, Audio-Visual Center, Indiana University (166 mm., silent, 10 min.).

in range of choice scores in the contrast series, the choice vs. vocalization correlation was enhanced.

The running time results also suggest that there was a residual, or rapidly learned, same-species attachment. Even though all lambs tended to move toward the location of the cohabitant in the noncontrast series, there were significant (and predictable) individual differences in how fast they got there. The most strongly attached animals, in terms of the VI measures, had shorter response latencies than Ss that were least strongly attached to their cohabitants. But those experimental Ss that had not formed strong alien-species social bonds, when tested in the contrast series, tended (a) to select the ewe test object instead of the cohabitant, and (b) to run faster to the ewe than they had to the cohabitant in the noncontrast trials. Under the particular conditions of this experiment, then, the time-dependent (latency) and time-independent (choice) measures of incentive magnitude yielded parallel and complementary results. In the light of the generally low or nonsignificant relationships that have been reported between incentive strength and discrimination learning (Pubols, 1960), the degree of the correlations obtained here between vocalization and maze performance was of particular interest.

Finally, preliminary support can be claimed for the hypothesized relationship between stimulus salience and attachment strength. As the cohabitant-removal tests demonstrated, the most salient objects in the lamb's compartment became the focus of an attachment response. Equally available, but less prominent, objects in the confinement context did not acquire effective control over the lamb's behavior. And the strongest attachments were formed within the conditions where the cohabitants were presumably most salient. Further evaluation of this hypothesis might include (a) the quantitative control of objective stimulus characteristics, such as intensity or mobility, and (b) assessments of the orienting behavior of the dependent animals.

EXPERIMENT 2

The principal aim of Experiment 2 was to determine the effects of various periods of short-term cohabitant separation on two indices of behavioral disruption (i.e., vocalization and gross movement). The study was also designed to yield information about the effects of water deprivation on these indices, and to permit thereby a direct comparison of the two different types of "deprivation."

Method

Subjects. Fourteen Hampshire lambs, all of which had participated as Ss in Experiment 1, were 17–21 wk. old at the time of the first deprivation series, and had been confined under conditions of experimental cohabitation for approximately 13 wk. (±1 wk.).

Water deprivation. Ten Ss were deprived of water for a 72-hr. period. The lamb's drinking dish was removed at 7:30 A.M. (± 1 hr.) on the first day of deprivation. Immediately following water removal, and at the end of 1, 2, 4, 8, 24, 48, and 72 hr., Ss were observed for two consecutive 15-min. periods. After the first 15-min. observation, Ss were given access to 200 cc of water in a nippled bottle for a 60-sec. period. At the end of the 60-sec. interval, the water was removed and a second 15-min. observation was conducted.

The Ss were maintained with their respective cohabitants under the conditions of confinement described in Experiment 1. The cohabitants were permitted to drink ad lib for brief periods approximately three times daily outside the confinement compartment. Dry food (grain, alafalfa, "Master Mix" dog pellets manufactured by McMillen Feed) was continuously available for both animals.

Social deprivation. Exactly parallel operations were followed with 10 lambs in assessing the effects of short-term social deprivation. Instead of water removal, the cohabitant (dog for 5 Ss and ewe for 5 Ss) was removed at 7:30 A.M. (± 1 hr.). The same observation schedule was followed. During the interval between each of the 15-min. observations, the cohabitant was reintroduced to the compartment for 60 sec., then removed. The Ss had ample food and water available at all times.

Six Ss were exposed to both types of deprivation separated by 1 wk., and the order of presentation counterbalanced (i.e., half of the group was exposed to the water deprivation treatment first, and the remainder to the social deprivation treatment first).

Measures. During the observation periods, two measures of behavorial disruption were recorded: (a) vocalization, and (b) gross movement. For each 15-min. period of continuous observation, the rate of vocalization was determined in mean bleats per minute. In addition to the vocalization measure, an index of general movement or locomotion, in mean number of occasions per minute that S entered a different quadrant of the compartment for each 15-min. observation period, was obtained.

Since each S was observed over 16 different 15-min. blocks in each deprivation series, it was possible to determine, for every S, the relationship between vocalization and movement. Ten independent correlations were computed from the social deprivation data and 10 from the water deprivation data. The median product-moment correlation between these two measures in the social deprivation series was $r = .89$ ($p < .001$), and in the water deprivation series, $r = .76$ ($p < .001$).

Results

The effects of water and social deprivation upon the vocalization and gross movement measures are shown in Figure 3. Both measures showed the

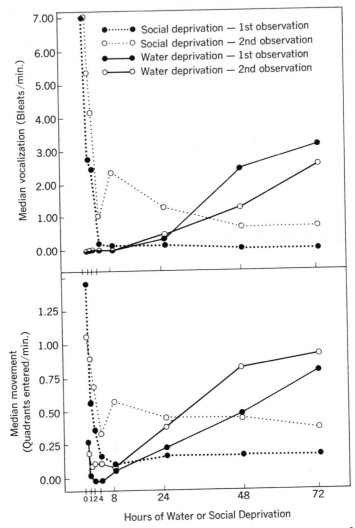

FIGURE 3. Lamb vocalization and movement as a function of hours since separation from cohabitant or water removal (Experiment 2).

expected increase with number of hours of water deprivation. Increments in rate of bleating and movement directly paralleled increments in rate of water consumption. The L test (Page, 1963) indicated that, in every instance, the trends were significant (Table 2).

Rather than showing that behavioral disturbance increased with hours of social deprivation, the data indicated exactly the opposite trend. The greatest disturbance was observed immediately upon removal of the cohabitant, followed by a sharp decrement in both indices in the early postsepara-

TABLE 2. Distribution-Free Trend Tests (L) Showing Effects of
Water and Cohabitant Removal (Experiment 2)

Index	Water removal		Cohabitant removal	
	1st Obs.	2nd Obs.	1st Obs.	2nd Obs.
Vocalization	1879 **	1924 **	1900 **	1909 **
Movement	1817 **	1865 **	1788 **	1765 *

* $p < .01$.
** $p < .001$.

tion observations. This effect was observed regardless of the species of the cohabitant. Note should be made that, except for the initial observation (i.e., 0 hr.), the amount of disruption occurring during the second set of observations (Minutes 16–30) was consistently greater than that observed in the first set (Minutes 1–15).

The Ls computed for the social deprivation curves surpassed the critical values for significance (Table 2).

Discussion

It appears that prolonged cohabitant separation provided the occasion for the initiation of an attachment-extinction process. It has been sometimes assumed that learned appetitive drives function in a fashion that is directly analogous to primary drives. In an extension of this model to social behavior, Gewirtz and Baer (1958) deduced that the longer the separation (presumably over a short-term period) from social objects, the higher the social drive level and the greater the reinforcement effectiveness of social events. Not only were the expectations of the primary drive analogue model not confirmed, but significant trends in the opposite direction were obtained. It must be noted, however, that concomitant changes in reinforcement effectiveness as a function of length of separation were not studied directly in this experiment.

EXPERIMENT 3

The final study in this series dealt with the reversal of a previously established social attachment.

Method

Subjects. Ten lambs from Experiment 1 were 23–25 wk. old at the beginning of the experimental procedures of this study.

Procedure. The original experimental conditions were reversed for Ss, i.e., 5 dog-paired lambs were reassigned to ewe cohabitants, and 5 control (ewe-paired) lambs were reassigned to the dog-paired conditions. The interaction-separation variable was ignored in the reassignment of all of the dog-paired Ss. The interchanges occurred after the lambs had been with the original cohabitant for 15–19 wk., excluding a 72-hr. period of social deprivation during the Confinement Weeks 12–14.

Under the same procedure followed in the original contrast series, U-maze trials were conducted after 7, 21–22, 35–36, and 49–50 days in the interchanged conditions. The original cohabitant was placed in one goal area, the contemporaneous cohabitant in the other goal area. Ten trials were involved in the first series, after Day 7 of confinement, and 20 trials in each of the succeeding series.

Results and Discussion

Performance in the final 10 trials of the original contrast series (Days 70–71 of Experiment 1) was taken as the prereversal index of social preference. These results, and those for tests following the interchange manipulation, are shown in Figure 4. The consequences of the interchange were seen after the first week in the new setting. An almost complete reversal of preference occurred in the case of the lambs moved from dog cohabitation

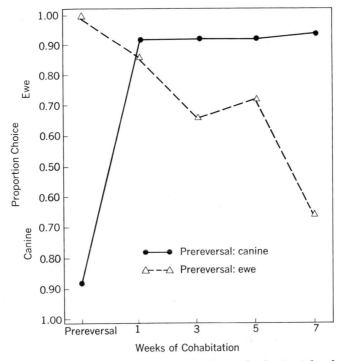

FIGURE 4. Choice behavior of lambs in final 10 trials of the preversal and postreversal contrast series (Experiment 3).

to ewe cohabitation; a minimal effect was observed in the opposite condition. By Day 50 of confinement, however, a significant reversal of preference was obtained in the latter group. Although the study was discontinued at this point, the trend in preferences seemed clear. Statistical analysis indicated that the Treatment $\times$ Time interaction was reliable ($F = 19.62$, $df = 4/32$, $p < .001$). Both experimental groups demonstrated a significant change in preference with respect to the dog cohabitants.

It has been suggested elsewhere (Cairns, 1966) that extended separation from an "attached" object would be associated with a progressive extinction of that relationship, coupled with the simultaneous development of an attachment to currently available stimuli. Certain factors might accelerate the relearning process: e.g., placement of the animal into an entirely unfamiliar setting, minimal or no contact with previously conditioned stimuli, or constant exposure to a highly salient stimulus in the "new" context. The very rapid reversal of attachments obtained in the dog to ewe interchanges may have been due to still another factor: the reestablishment of a previously acquired attachment response. It will be recalled that all lambs had been reared with sheep prior to the original (Experiment 1) confinement. The interchange manipulation was, for the animals assigned to the dog-paired condition in the original study, a reinstitution of the preexperimental context. For lambs assigned to the original control group, however, the reversal condition provided their first exposure to an alien animal in a non-test situation.

GENERAL DISCUSSION

Nonbiologic and derivative reinforcement events have been assigned a role of nuclear import in theories of personality and social behavior. It has been generally assumed that the reinforcement properties of such events will, under certain conditions, rival or exceed those which have been demonstrated for events more directly relevant to physiological need states. Only limited experimental evidence, however, can be cited in support of this proposition. Conditioned reinforcement events have rarely been shown to approach the stability or the intensity of primary reinforcers (Kelleher & Gollub, 1962; Myers, 1958). The present results provide a striking exception. Once acquired, the lamb's attachment to its cohabitant was strong and pervasive; its consequences were generalized across response systems and situations.

One of the more interesting findings of the present work was that the strength of the attachment response, and its corresponding reinforcement properties, could be experimentally manipulated. But the operation traditionally followed to enhance the effectiveness of primary reinforcement events diminished the effectiveness of social reinforcers. Though these deprivation effects appear to be contradictory, further analysis of the cue properties of drive stimuli involved suggest that the two functions represent one and the same process (Baumeister, Hawkins, & Cromwell, 1964; Cairns, 1966; Estes, 1958).

Finally, the limitations of the present studies due to species and organismic sample restrictions should be noted. The animals studied, young sheep, were ones in which gregarious behavior was readily elicited. Whether comparable effects might be obtained with older animals, or members of other species, requires further study. The results of other investigators indicate that the essential attachment-acquisition phenomena can be replicated, but at a diminished intensity, with a different species (Denenberg, Hudgens, & Zarrow, 1964), and with mature members of the same species (Hersher et al., 1963).

SUMMARY

Social attachment behavior of 20 purebred lambs was studied over a 6-mo. period. In the first of 3 experiments, the reinforcing properties of strong attachments formed by young lambs to the perceptually prominent objects, animate or inanimate, with which they had been continuously confined were demonstrated in a series of maze tests. The remaining 2 experiments dealt with the processes involved in the extinction of previously acquired social attachments by (a) analyzing some of the effects of short-term social and biological deprivation, and (b) examining the conditions under which the attachments might be reversed.

REFERENCES

Baumeister, A., Hawkins, W. F., & Cromwell, R. L.   Need states and activity level. *Psychol. Bull.,* 1964, **61,** 438–453.

Cairns, R. B.   Attachment behavior of mammals. *Psychol. Rev.,* 1966, **73,** 409–426.

Cairns, R. B., & Johnson, D. L.   The development of interspecies social attachments. *Psychon. Sci.,* 1965, **2,** 337–338.

Denenberg, V. H., Hudgens, G. A., & Zarrow, M. X.   Mice reared with rats: Modification of behavior by early experience with another species. *Science,* 1964, **143,** 380–381.

Estes, W. K.   Stimulus-response theory of drive. In M. R. Jones (Ed.), *Nebraska symposium on motivation: 1958.* Lincoln: University of Nebraska Press, 1958. Pp. 35–69.

Gewirtz, J. L., & Baer, D. M.   Deprivation and satiation of social reinforcers as drive conditions. *J. abnorm. soc. Psychol.,* 1958, **57,** 165–172.

Hersher, L., Richmond, J. B., & Moore, A. U.   Modifiability of the critical period for the development of maternal behavior in sheep and goats. *Behaviour,* 1963, **20,** 311–320.

Kelleher, R. T., & Gollub, L. R.   A review of positive conditioned reinforcement. *J. exp. Anal. Behav.,* 1962, **5,** 543–597.

Miller, N. E.   Learnable drives and rewards. In S. S. Stevens (Ed.), *Handbook of experimental psychology*. New York: Wiley, 1951. Pp. 435–472.

Myers, J. L.   Secondary reinforcement: A review of recent experimentation. *Psychol. Bull.*, 1958, **55,** 284–301.

Page, E. B.   Ordered hypotheses for multiple treatments: A significance test for linear ranks. *J. Amer. Statist. Assn.*, 1963, **58,** 216–230.

Pubols, B. H., Jr.   Incentive magnitude, learning, and performance in animals. *Psychol. Bull.*, 1960, **57,** 89–115.

Scott, J. P.   Social behavior, organization and leadership in a small flock of domestic sheep. *Comp. Psychol. Monogr.*, 1945, **18**(4, Whole No. 96).

Winer, B. J.   *Statistical principles in experimental design*. New York: Mc-Graw-Hill, 1962.

1.5   The Modification of Social Responsiveness in Institutional Babies

Harriet Lange Rheingold

This is an attempt to explore the effect upon infants of an experimental modification of the environment. For a group of institutional babies one "mother" was substituted for many "mothers" and the effect upon social responsiveness was assessed. This was the primary focus of the study, but the effects upon other kinds of behavior were also measured. The main question asked was, "What effect will an increase in social responsiveness to one person, the 'mother,' have upon responsiveness to other persons?"

From almost the beginning of life the infant is interested in people. His first active social response has been defined by Shirley (25) as the sober watching of an adult face early in the first month of life. At five weeks of age he is already smiling in response to an adult's overtures (6, 24). With time his social responsiveness becomes more elaborate; he laughs, vocalizes, stretches out his hands to be picked up, grasps another's clothes (5, 23).

Although at first he is interested in and responsive to all people, in the second month he discriminates his mother from the others about him and shows his recognition by change in expression, an intentness of regard, and by more ready and fuller smiling (18). In another month he sobers at the sight of a stranger (11, 15, 25). Facial expressions of distress and fear, crying, and physical withdrawal characterize later responses to strangers. Bayley (2) cites "discriminate strangers" as a normative item at 5.5 months which she defines as staring, frowning, withdrawal, or crying. Crying in response to

Reprinted with abridgement from the *Monographs of the Society for Research in Child Development* 1956, **21,** No. 2 (Serial #63), by permission of the author and the Society for Research in Child Development.

strangers in an examination situation increases up to 10 months of age (1). Gesell and Thompson (15) point to the period between 28 and 32 weeks for the change from "often discriminates strangers but usually adapts well to them" to "likely to withdraw from strangers." Hebb and Riesen (20) have described similar behavior in the young chimpanzee.

In social behavior, as in other kinds of behavior, the normative delineation of development obscures individual differences. For example, some babies appear never to be shy of strangers (25) and percentages reported by Gesell and Thompson (15) for withdrawing from strangers do not reach 50 at any age level. The causes of these differences have been attributed both to nature and to nurture. Social behavior, however, has been considered especially susceptible to environmental events (14, 25). It is the effect of environmental events which we will pursue here.

Institutions with their multiple "mothers," less frequent contact with adults, more impersonal care, provide an environment which differs markedly from family life and, as might be expected, the social behavior of institutionalized babies departs from normal development. These babies have been reported to be less interested in people, less responsive to them, less sensitive to changes in an adult's facial expression and tone of voice (13, 14, 26). That they also show interest in things and less competence in manipulating them has been attributed to this departure from the mother-child interplay of family life, rather than to the absence of material things in their environment.

For family babies, little is definitely known about environmental events which may affect their social responsiveness to known and strange persons or about the effect of social experience upon the manipulation of things. Normal social responsiveness did develop in the twins reared by the Denneses (10) under conditions of "minimum" social stimulation, although in a reprinting of the study (12) the experimental treatment was described as "controlled environmental conditions," conditions which Stone (28) believes qualify as "minimum *adequate* social stimulation." This experiment excepted, we have only opinion, such as Hebb's (19), based upon "common experience" that the fear of a stranger will be minimized or absent if a baby has already been exposed to the sight of a large number of persons; Jersild's suggestion (21) that awareness of a stranger will be affected by the experiences that babies have had with people; and Bayley's observation that, "When a child is old enough to make such differentiations, strange persons and places—if he is not taken about frequently—are a definite stimulus for crying" (1, p. 316).

For this experiment infants living in an institution were chosen as subjects because of their common background of experience and because of the relative care with which environmental conditions could be controlled and manipulated. We decided, also, to work with six-month-old infants because, by this age, family babies often give clear evidence of a difference in their responses to known and unknown persons.

Against this background the problem was set. The questions asked were:

1. Can six-month-old infants who have been cared for in an institution by many different persons learn to respond selectively to one person who assumes their care for a period?

2. If the infants learn this discrimination, how will it affect their responses to other persons? Specifically, will it produce an awareness of strangers? Will this awareness be characterized by signs of discomfort, fear, or physical withdrawal?

3. What will be the effect of care by one "mother" upon their achievements in certain other areas of behavior?

To answer these questions a series of propositions upon which experiment and observation might be expected to yield information was set forth, as follows:

1. Infants of six months of age who have been cared for by multiple "mothers," varying from day to day, should award special recognition to no one person.

2. These infants should show no awareness of a stranger.

3. If, now, one person, in contrast to many persons, assumes their care for a period of time, there should be an increase in social responsiveness to that person.

4. Following the appearance in the child of a differentiated response to the mother figure, there should appear an awareness of strangers, resembling in sequence and patterning of responses the course of development of normal babies, including responses of discomfort and withdrawal.

5. Finally, care by one person should result in improved performance in other areas of behavior. Postural achievements, success in manipulating cubes, and performance on a test of "intelligence" were chosen as tests of development in other areas of behavior.

The primary focus of this study was the infant's social behavior; other areas were considered as secondary to the purpose.

THE INSTITUTION

The institution was a large urban maternity hospital and orphan asylum which cared for children from birth through three years of age. The reasons for the children's residence in the institution included such causes as abandonment, financial inability of the parents to care for the child, and illness of the mother. Physical plant and care were excellent.

The institution observed the usual hospital practices to minimize the spread of infection. Wearing a gown (masks were not used) and scrubbing between handling babies were included in these practices. For the same reason, babies could not be put in a play pen or on the floor, or one baby brought into contact with another.

The babies were cared for by students in a one-year child-care course, by supervisors who were graduates of the course, and by volunteers. . . . A baby would ordinarily not be cared for by the same person from one time to the next. . . . The characteristic attitude of all caretakers, whether volunteers or hospital personnel, was benevolent. A majority of the caretakers were affectionate and playful in caring for the babies. . . . Thus most contacts between child and adult were pleasant. Departures from what is thought to be good mothering occurred more often because of insufficient personnel than because of emotional resistance of ignorance.

This sketch of the institution describes the environment of all the subjects before the experiment began. It describes also the environment for the control babies during the study.

THE SUBJECTS

The subjects were 16 infants, divided equally into experimental and control groups. Four pairs of experimental and control babies were studied in the first experiment; the other four pairs constituted a second and parallel experiment.

The design called for infants who were six months old, full-term, without marked physical or mental defect, who had lived in the institution for at least three months. An additional requirement was that there be a reasonably good likelihood that the subjects would remain in the hospital for the duration of the experiment. . . .

The eight subjects of each experiment were divided into four matched pairs on the basis of three variables, age, Cattell IQ, and social responsiveness. Because the sample was small, matching was perforce rough.

In the first experiment the assigning of subjects to experimental or control conditions was restricted by hospital arrangements over which we had little control. For the second experiment, however, the choice of the member in each pair to receive the experimental treatment was made at random. . . .

Four babies left the institution during the course of the experimental treatment. Two experimental babies, one in each experiment, left at the end of the third week. Two control babies of the second experiment left during the seventh week. After the end of the experimental treatment there were still other losses. No selective factor which might affect the results appeared to have been responsible for the removal of these babies from the institution.

Sex of subject was not used as a variable in matching or in the selecting of subjects. In the first experiment the experimental group was composed of two boys and two girls; the control group, of one boy and three girls. In the second experiment there were two boys and two girls in each group.

EXPERIMENTAL TREATMENT

The experimenter cared for, "mothered," the four subjects who were assigned to the experimental condition in each experiment. These babies lived in one room with their cribs side by side along one wall of the room. The experimenter fed, bathed, diapered, soothed, held, talked to, and played with these four babies for seven and one-half hours a day, from 7:30 A.M. to 3:00 P.M., five days a week, for eight weeks, a total of 300 hours. During these hours no one else cared for these babies. . . .

The experimenter deliberately and consistently tried to adapt her care to the individual needs of each baby as these were apparent to her, limited only by hospital routines and by the demands of caring for four babies at once. . . . The goal was to give the children maximal gratification.

During the experimental period of eight weeks, the experimenter had no contact of any kind with the control subjects, except for the weekly testing periods. These children had their cribs in another room and were cared for by hospital personnel and volunteers according to the routine described under *Institution*.

At the end of the eight weeks, the experimental subjects returned to the full-time care of the hospital, and the experimenter saw them only at the four subsequent weekly testing periods.

TIME-SAMPLING MEASURES OF TREATMENT

To obtain a measure of the difference between the experimental and the control conditions, a separate person, an observer, took time samples of the number of adults in each room and of their activities in relation to the babies. These variables were recorded on one half day (7:30 A.M. to noon or noon to 3:00 P.M.) of each week of the experimental treatment.

Studies of reliability were made during the course of each experiment, and the percentage of agreement on items checked was high. Table 1 shows that there was considerable resemblance between the two experiments in the variables measured by the time-sampling. The experimental children were less often alone, they were cared for more often, they were more often out of their cribs, they received more of their care from one person alone, and they were cared for by fewer persons. . . .

THE TESTS

. . . All tests throughout both experiments were administered by another person (not the observer), hereafter called the *examiner*. The examiner was a graduate student, trained by the experimenter, whom we tried to keep in ignorance of the experimental design. . . .

The battery of tests used was composed of the Cattell Infant Intelligence Scale, a test of social responsiveness, one of postural development, and one

TABLE 1. Time-Sampling Observations of Activities of Caretakers and Babies in the Experimental and Control Rooms

Item	Experiment 1				Experiment 2			
	E		C		E		C	
	N	%	N	%	N	%	N	%
Periods of observation	34		34		50		50	
Observations	945		1131		2233		2807	
Number of adults in room:								
0	212	22	728	64	574	28	2084	74
1	565	60	262	23	1371	61	381	14
2	145	15	88	8	233	10	214	8
3 or more	23	2	53	5	55	2	128	5
Caretakers	1		14		1		21	
Caretaking acts	215	23	83	7	435	19	185	7
Nature of act:								
talking	119	13	25	2	251	11	76	3
caring for	105	11	34	3	138	6	65	2
playing with	28	3	5	0	33	3	13	0
holding in arms	34	4	2	0	112	5	37	1
feeding	37	4	40	4	114	5	44	2
Child awake	829	88	791	70	1752	79	2146	76
awake and crying	17	2	11	1	43	2	101	4
asleep	116	12	340	30	481	21	661	24
Child in crib	567	60	1062	94	1401	63	2535	90
out of crib	120	13	58	5	339	15	108	4
seated in chair	258	27	11	1	493	22	152	5

Note.— Caretaking acts counted only once per observation; nature of acts not mutually exclusive.

of cube manipulation. The tests were given to all the subjects in the week preceding the beginning of the experiment, before assignment of subjects to the treatment condition. The Cattell test was given only once again, in the seventh week. All other tests were administered to both experimental and control subjects biweekly, on Saturdays, as follows: one part of the social test and the test of postural development were given at the end of the first week of treatment and on every other Saturday thereafter through the eleventh week (i.e., the third week after the end of treatment); the other part of the social test and the test of cube manipulation were given at the end of the second week of treatment and on alternating Saturdays thereafter through the twelfth week (the fourth week after the end of treatment).

Testing was carried out early in the morning, usually directly after the baby was fed.

The Social Tests

There were seven social tests, the first four composing Part A, the second three, Part B. These two parts were not equated; the second part was employed to yield additional information. Hereafter each separate test will be called a subtest. They do not correspond to the ordinary "personal-social" items of normative schedules, with the exception of Bühler's (5, 7), to which they owe a great deal.

The four situations for Part A were:

1. The adult stood approximately three feet from the child's crib, smiled at the child, but did not speak.

2. The adult went to the crib, leaned over the child, smiled, and said warmly, "Hello, baby, how are you?," which could be repeated a second time.

3. The adult tried by any means to get the child to smile, and as soon as the child smiled, frowned and scolded him in an angry tone of voice, saying, "You naughty baby, what did you do?" These words too could be repeated but only once.

4. After the lapse of at least 15 minutes (in order that the baby might forget the scolding), the adult, concealed behind a sheet thrown over the foot of the crib, called to the child, saying, "Hello, baby," or "Come on, baby."

The three situations for Part B were:

1. The adult stood at the side of the crib, smiled, and talked to the child as in A, 2.

2. The adult picked the child up, walked to the center of the room, held him in her arms so that the top of his head was level with her shoulder, smiled, and talked to him as in A, 2.

3. The adult returned the baby to his crib, placed him on his back, and stood at the crib, silent, and not looking at him.

The adults, or stimulus objects, to whom the babies' responses were obtained were (a) the experimenter, (b) the examiner, and (c) a volunteer. The experimenter was a known person to the experimental babies but unknown to the control subjects. The examiner was equally unknown to both groups of subjects. Because these tests were given so often, however, the possibility existed that both experimenter and examiner might in time become known to all subjects. This was especially true for the examiner who had more contact with the control subjects than did the experimenter. For this reason, a volunteer who had no prior contact with any of the subjects approached all the babies in both experiments in the eighth week only and then only for subtests 1 and 2 of Part A. . . .

The infants' responses to each subtest were recorded on a checklist on which the possible responses were set forth under the categories of:

1. Quickness of regard
2. Duration of regard
3. Kind and duration of facial expression
   a. positive: brightening, smiling, laughing; duration
   b. negative: sobering or frowning, whimpering, crying; duration
4. Nature of physical activity
5. Number of vocalizations.

The Other Tests

The test of postural development was composed of items from the developmental schedules of Gesell and Amatruda (14), whose procedure for testing was followed. All postural items were set down in chronological order as they appear in the 16-week through the 56-week schedules under the categories of supine, prone, pulled-to-sitting, and standing behavior. . . .

The test of cube manipulation was composed similarly of items from the same developmental schedules, for only the cube, not the massed cube, situation. The authors' directions were followed. Again, the items were enumerated in chronological order, this time from the 12-week through the 56-week schedule. . . .

The Catell Intelligence Scale for Infants was given and scored according to the author's directions (8). This scale, too, was given to the babies in the testing room.

The experimenter was not present at any of these tests.

THE RESULTS OF THE TESTS

Response to the Experimenter and the Examiner

Figure 1 shows that the curves for the experimental group in response to both stimulus persons, the experimenter and the examiner, exceed those of the control group. Further, the curve for the experimental group in response to the experimenter increases fairly rapidly in the first two weeks, maintains its height during the remaining six weeks of experimental treatment, then rises again after the end of the treatment. The curve for the experimental group in response to the examiner, on the other hand, rises gradually after an early decrease. One may speculate that at first an increase in responsiveness to one person is associated with, perhaps produces, a decrease in responsiveness to another person, but that, with time, increased responsiveness to one person is associated with increased responsiveness to another, though smaller in amount. The curves for the control group in response to both persons cross at points and until the last testing period are fairly stable.

It should be noted that number of cases decreased with time and that the

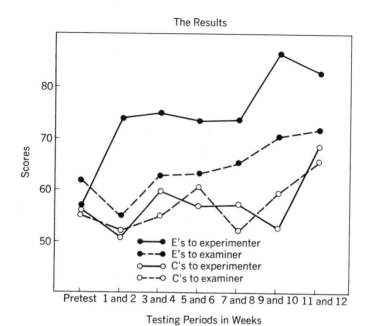

FIGURE 1. Means of social test for experimental and control groups in response to experimenter and examiner.

range of scores at each testing period was wide, with overlapping of scores between experimental and control groups.

An analysis of variance of scores for the smaller sample (six experimental and six control subjects at five testing periods, as described above) is presented in Table 2. The analysis suggests that it is very unlikely that the difference between the experimental and the control subjects in response to the experimenter could have arisen by chance, although the difference in response to the examiner may have. "Periods" had no statistically significant effect upon the scores, nor did the interaction of treatment with periods. It appears therefore that for these subjects it was treatment and not the passage of time which produced a statistically significant effect.

Although by this test there appears to be no statistically significant difference in the responses of experimental and control subjects to the *examiner,* the curves for these responses suggest the presence of some difference. A t test of paired comparisons based on the means for all experimental and control subjects at each testing period yields a value of 5.11, with p less than .005. (Differences between means were adjusted for N of cases by weighting.) We interpret these findings to mean that there is some tendency for the experimental babies to become more responsive to the examiner.

Finally, we can test for the effect of stimulus person by a t test of the

TABLE 2. ANALYSIS OF VARIANCE OF SOCIAL TEST SCORES FOR EXPERIMENTAL AND CONTROL GROUPS

Source of Variation	df	Experimenter as Stimulus			Examiner as Stimulus		
		MS	F	p	MS	F	p
Between subjects	11						
Treatment	1	4684.4	38.12	<.001	395.2	3.40	>.05
Error (b)	10	122.9			116.4		
Within subjects	48						
Periods	4	167.6	1.00	>.05	142.2	1.02	>.05
Treatment × periods	4	132.1	0.79	>.05	13.3	0.09	>.05
Error (w)	40	167.7			139.3		
Total	59						

differences between the means for experimental and control groups using for each subject the sum of the five measures. The experimental babies *were* more responsive to the experimenter than to the examiner (t equals 8.96, p is less than .001); the control subjects were no more responsive to the one than to the other (t equals 1.07, p is more than .1).

Response to the Stranger

At the eighth week, at the end of treatment, a person unknown to the babies served as stimulus objects in both experiments. Subtests 1 and 2 of Part A only were given, and these scores were compared with similar scores made in response to the experimenter and to the examiner. . . .

These data suggest that the experimental subjects were more responsive to the experimenter than to either of the other two stimulus persons; that the experimental subjects were more responsive to all three persons than the control subjects; and that the experimental subjects were as responsive to a "stranger" as to the examiner with whom they had experience.

Responses of all babies were predominantly positive, "negative" responses occurring in less than 12 per cent of all responses, about equally divided between experimenter and examiner. The number of vocalizations heard during the social tests increased over the course of the experiment for the experimental subjects, especially in their response to the experimenter. For the control subjects the number of the vocalizations appeared to decrease after the fifth week in response to both the experimenter and the examiner.

The experimental subjects made slightly higher scores on the postural, cube, and Cattell tests but the differences were not statistically significant.

DISCUSSION

In this experiment the chief element of the experimental treatment was the substitution of one "mother" for many "mothers." The primary goal of the treatment was to bring about an increase in social responsiveness to this one person and to measure the effects of this learning upon responsiveness to other persons. But in substituting one "mother" for many "mothers" other dimensions of the environment were changed as well. The one "mother" was with the children more of the time; she did more for them; and, coming to know the babies, she was more readily able to take into account their preferences, dislikes, irritabilities, and general reaction patterns. The results obtained in this study, therefore, cannot be related only to the substitution of one "mother" for many, or to any other single component of the treatment.

The design of this experiment. . . . does not cast any light on the mechanisms, that is, the reinforcers, responsible for the learning. . . . Our impression, based upon day-by-day observation of the infants during the experiment, is that the experimenter was an effective stimulus, not so much in terms of the services she was performing for the child, that is, whether feeding, bathing, or changing diapers, etc., but in relation to the attention she gave and received from the child. The attention seemed to be not just a general awareness as might well occur during a caretaking sequence, but a direct and clear act of attending. In any one day there were many such active interchanges of attending between child and experimenter, sometimes during, but often apart from, caretaking activities. Generally, these interchanges were playful or affectionate in nature. Could this sequence of responses be analyzed and made the subject of experiment apart from the caretaking activities, we expect it would yield some answers to the question of the mechanisms responsible for social learning.

We turn now to the chief question this experiment was designed to answer: the effect of increased responsiveness to a known person upon responses to other persons. It was predicted that as the infant's discrimination between known and unknown persons developed he would show signs of discomfort when approached by unknown persons. But in this study such signs did not accompany the discrimination. If "by nature some infants are more sensitive to strangers than others" (15, p. 262; 17), it seems unlikely that all eight experimental babies would belong to the less sensitive group. More likely, their past experience with many people, and their daily experience with some other people, are responsible for the absence of the behavior called awareness of the stranger.

Not only did the experimental babies not show signs of discomfort when approached by strange persons but instead they became more friendly, according to some of the evidence. One might say simply that a learned response has been transferred from the experimenter to other similar stimuli. An explanation which takes into account process as well as results can be considered: that the experimental treatment set up a continuously reinforcing environment. If it is true, as hospital personnel reported, that the experimental babies were more placid and better-natured, they themselves may have favorably altered the responses they received from the women who cared for them when the experimenter was not in the institution.

Finally, the results of this study must appear to confirm the hypothesis that social behavior in the infant is modifiable by environmental events. In contrast, postural, "adaptive," and "intellectual" behavior proved to be less modifiable by the experimental treatment. It is true that no special efforts were made to train the babies in these areas or even to give them special opportunity to practice. But neither did the experimental treatment offer systematic training in social responsiveness. Certainly the experimental babies were out of their beds more often, were given toys more frequently, etc. On the other hand, with more done for them, the experimental babies may have had less need to do for themselves. But if this were a significant variable, the control babies, who were more often left to themselves, should have surpassed the experimental babies. The experimental environment may have provided both more opportunity to practice and less need to practice, and the interaction of these variables may have been responsible for the lack of a statistically significant difference in their performances. It seems reasonable to conclude that the institution provided an environment as adequate for the development of these behaviors as did the experimental treatment.

REFERENCES

1. Bayley, Nancy. A study of the crying of infants during mental and physical tests. *J. genet. Psychol.*, 1932, **40**, 306–329.
2. Bayley, Nancy. The California First-Year Mental Scale. *Univer. of California Syllabus Series*, 1933, No. 243.
3. Bayley, Nancy. Consistency and variability in the growth of intelligence from birth to eighteen years. *J. genet. Psychol.*, 1949, **75**, 165–196.
4. Brodbeck, A. J., & Irwin, O. C. The speech behavior of infants without families. *Child Develpm.*, 1946, **17**, 145–156.
5. Bühler, Charlotte. *The first year of life* (trans. Greenberg, Pearl, & Ripin, Rowena) New York: Day, 1930.
6. Bühler, Charlotte. *From birth to maturity.* London: Kegan Paul, 1935.
7. Bühler, Charlotte, & Hetzer, Hildegarde. *Testing children's development from birth to school age* (trans. Beaumont, H.) New York: Farrar & Rinehart, 1935.
8. Cattell, Psyche. *The measurement of intelligence of infants and young children.* New York: Psychol. Corporation, 1940.
9. Dennis, W. An experimental test of two theories of social smiling in infants. *J. soc. Psychol.*, 1935, **6**, 214–223.

10. Dennis, W. Infant development under conditions of restricted practice and of minimum social stimulation. *Genet, Psychol. Monogr.*, 1941, **23**, 143–189.
11. Dennis, W., & Dennis, Marsena G. Behavioral development in the first year of life as shown by forty biographies. *Psychol. Rec.*, 1937, **1**, 349–361.
12. Dennis, W., & Dennis, Marsena G. Development under controlled environmental conditions. I. W. Dennis (Ed.), *Readings in child psychology*. New York: Prentice-Hall, 1951.
13. Freud, Anna, & Burlingham, Dorothy. *Infants without families*. New York: Int. Univer. Press, 1944.
14. Gesell, A., & Amatruda, Catherine S. *Developmental diagnosis*. New York: Hoeber, 1941.
15. Gesell, A., & Thompson, Helen. *Infant behavior, its genesis and growth*. New York: McGraw-Hill, 1934.
16. Goldfarb, W. Effects of psychological deprivation in infancy and subsequent stimulation. *Amer. J. Psychiat.*, 1945, **102**, 18–33.
17. Goodenough, Florence. *Developmental psychology*. New York: Appleton-Century, 1934.
18. Griffiths, Ruth. *The abilities of babies*. New York: McGraw-Hill, 1954.
19. Hebb, D. O. On the nature of fear. *Psychol. Rev.*, 1946, **53**, 259–276.
20. Hebb, D. O., & Riesen, A. H. The genesis of irrational fears. *Bull. Canad. Psychol. Ass.*, 1943, **3**, 49–50.
21. Jersild, A. T. *Child psychology*. (4th Ed.) New York: Prentice-Hall, 1954.
22. Lindquist, E. F. *Design and analysis of experiment in psychology and education*. Boston: Houghton-Mifflin, 1953.
23. Malrieu, P. La construction de l'objet et les attitudes sociales de l'enfant de la naissance à deux ans. *J. Psychol. norm. path.*, 1951, **44**, 425–437.
24. Piaget, J. *The construction of reality in the child*. (trans. Cook, Margaret) New York: Basic Books, 1954.
25. Shirley, Mary M. *The first two years, a study of twenty-five babies*. Vol. II. *Intellectual development*. Minneapolis: Univer. of Minnesota Press, 1933.
26. Spitz, R. A. Hospitalism. An inquiry into the genesis of psychiatric conditions in early childhood. *Psychoanal. Study of Child.*, 1945, **1**, 53–74.
27. Spitz, R. A. The smiling response: a contribution to the ontogenesis of social relations. *Genet. Psychol. Monogr.*, 1946, **34**, 57–125.
28. Stone, L. J. A critique of studies of infant isolation. *Child Develpm.*, 1954, **25**, 9–20.

1.6　Extinction of the Smiling Response in Infants as a Function of Reinforcement Schedule [1]

Yvonne Brackbill

Scheduling of reinforcement has been investigated extensively in relation to the conditioning of non-social responses. The results of these studies indicate in general that a schedule by which reinforcement follows every response is less effective in maintaining performance of that response during extinction than is a schedule by which reinforcement follows only some of those responses (4).

This investigation attempts to extend the study of frequency and patterning of reinforcement to the area of social learning and to cortically immature subjects. The purpose of the research is to evaluate the relative efficacy of intermittent as opposed to regular reinforcement upon frequency of smiling in infants.

The use of an instrumental conditioning paradigm in this study is in contrast to past studies of the conditioning of the smiling response (2, 7, 8), all of which, though differing in methodology, have utilized a classical conditioning paradigm in conceptualizing results. The inappropriateness of this framework in accounting for response change over time is most clearly illustrated in the study by Dennis (2).

METHOD

Subjects

Eight normal infants between the ages of three and one-half to four and one-half months served as Ss. Six were males and two, females. All came from intact middle class homes located within 10 miles of Stanford University.[2]

This particular age range was selected with the consideration in mind that the subject had to be old enough to remain awake for a short time

[1] This report is based upon a dissertation submitted to the Department of Psychology, Stanford University, in partial fulfillment of the requirements for the degree of Doctor of Philosophy. The writer wishes to thank Professors Albert Bandura, Quinn McNemar, Frances Orr Nitzberg, Robert Sears, William Verplanck, and C. L. Winder for their suggestions and help.

[2] The author is greatly indebted to Drs. John Anderson and Bruce Jessup for their cooperation in referring subjects.

Reprinted from *Child Development*, 1958, **29**, 1–12, by permission of the author and the Society for Research in Child Development.

period after feeding, yet not old enough to respond differentially to "mother" vs. "others." Other requirements for selection of Ss were: (a) that the infant not cry so often, with such intensity, and for so long a time that sessions very frequently had to be terminated, with consequent lack of experimental progress; (b) that the infant show an operant rate of at least two responses per five-minute interval; and (c) that the infant be able to maintain a supine position for intervals of five minutes without persistent struggling to regain the prone position.

Experimental Procedure

Ss were assigned to the regularly reinforced (RR) group or to the intermittently reinforced (IR) group in consecutive order of their acceptance as subjects. The first S was assigned to the IR group; the second, to the RR group; and so on.

For both groups, the experimental procedure was divided into three periods: In the first or *operant* period E stood motionless and expressionless at a distance of approximately 15 inches above S, and observed him for eight five-minute intervals to ascertain the operant level of smiling. In the second or *conditioning* period, reinforcement was meted out, contingent upon S's smile. Specifically, as soon as S smiled,[3] E smiled in return, began to speak softly to S, and picked it up. S was then held, jostled, patted and talked to for 30 seconds before being replaced in the crib.[4] In the third or *extinction* period, the procedure was again observation without reinforcement, as in the operant period. During extinction, Ss were observed for 13 five-minute intervals.

During all three periods, the basic interval for determining rate of responding was five minutes, and in the discussion to follow, *five-minute interval* (or simply, *interval*) refers to one five-minute period of continuous experimentation. The term *rate of response* refers to number of responses per interval. Also, the terms *response* and *trial* will be used interchangeably.

The two groups of Ss differed in respect to the reinforcement schedules used within the conditioning period. The RR group was maintained on a regular reinforcement schedule during the entire conditioning period. The IR group was maintained on a regular reinforcement schedule until each S had responded at maximum rate (see footnote 4) for 10 consecutive intervals. Immediately after the tenth interval at maximum rate, Ss were switched to a 2:1 randomized variable ratio reinforcement schedule for a total of 60

[3] Interjudge reliability concerning the decision as to whether a smile had or had not occurred was found to be .975, using a total N of 970 such decisions in the formula: twice number of agreements/total number of judgments. This reliability check was done prior to the experiment, with the assistance of Mr. Thomas Milburn.

[4] The reinforcement procedure was recorded on 12 feet of 8 mm. film.

responses (hence, 30 reinforcements), then to a 3:1 schedule for a total of 45 responses, and finally to a 4:1 schedule for 20 responses. Separate randomizations were used for each subject.

Maximum rate of response was determined as follows. Forty-five seconds were required for the administration of each reinforcement plus its accompanying events. (Five seconds were required for picking *S* up; 30 seconds for reinforcement; five seconds for putting *S* down; and five seconds for recording.) Therefore, no more than six responses could occur and be reinforced during any five-minute interval. *Maximum rate of response* was defined as no fewer than four responses per interval. That particular trial or response that marked the beginning of maximum response rate will be referred to as *criterion*.

Because of intersubject variation in total number of responses to criterion and because it was desired that the experimental results be a function only of reinforcement schedule and not a function of reinforcement schedule plus number of emitted responses, it was necessary to match the two groups for total number of trials during the conditioning period. The method of matching—like the method of group assignment mentioned earlier—was an individual one and was done in consecutive order of admission to the experiment. Specifically, *S* No. 2 (RR group) was matched for total number of trials with *S* No. 1 (IR group); *S* No. 4 was matched with *S* No. 3, and so on.

General Procedure

Each infant was placed on a schedule of social deprivation during the entire experimental period. Social deprivation was defined as minimized social and body contact between the infant and any other person in its environment, excluding *E*. In effect, this meant elimination of all social and body contacts that were not absolutely necessary for *S*'s well being.

Experimental conditions were kept as standard as possible for all sessions and for all Ss. *E* always wore a white laboratory coat. *S* was placed in a supine position near the open edge of his crib; placement of *S* and the crib was the same for all sessions. Source of light was standardized, and variance in intensity minimized. At the beginning of each session, *S* was freshly diapered, had just eaten to satiety, and had been awake for from 15 to 20 minutes. During the operant and extinction periods, at the end of every five-minute interval, *S* was placed in a prone position to rest for three minutes. While he was being turned over and during the rest period, *E* was not in his field of vision. During the experimental period, *S* was frequently required to work without rest for two successive intervals, but not for longer.

Typically, there were two to three sessions per day. Length of any one session ranged between 10 and 60 minutes, and was a function of the length of time *S* remained awake. The total number of days spent in experimentation with any one *S* ranged from eight to 16. Because of the very large

amount of time per day required for travel, experimentation, and maintenance of rapport with the mother, only one S was run at a time.

RESULTS AND DISCUSSION

Performance during the Operant Period

The two groups did not differ significantly in either mean operant re-
sponse rate ($t = .29$, 7 df) or total number of responses emitted ($t = .06$, 3
df). For this reason, scores have been combined for graphic presentation
(Fig. 1).

Figure 1 also includes a cumulative plot for a ninth, control S, who was
run, without reinforcement, for an extended operant period of 19 intervals
—or roughly three times the length of the operant period for experimental
Ss. These data provide some evidence against the possible explanation that
the mere presence of E—and not the reinforcement—is conducive to increased rate of response.

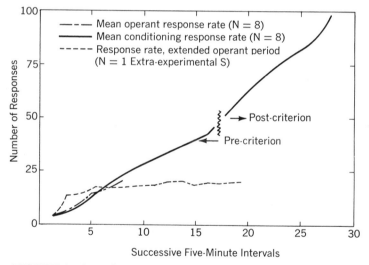

FIGURE 1. Cumulative curves showing rate of smiling response
during operant and conditioning periods.

Performance during the Conditioning Period

For the conditioning period, the total number of responses for each group
was 927, while the mean number of responses per subject was 231.7. Mean
group response rates are presented in Table 1; the most noticeable features
of these data are the abruptness of the change in mean response rate and in
variability following criterion.

Relative stability in response rate is also reflected in Table 2, which con-

TABLE 1. GROUP RESPONSE RATES DURING OPERANT AND CONDITIONING PERIODS

	Operant Response Rate		Conditioning Response Rate					
			Preceding Criterion		For First 10 Intervals following Criterion		For 11th–22nd Intervals following Criterion	
	Mean	σ	Mean	σ	Mean	σ	Mean	σ
Regular group	2.11	.63	2.70	.47	5.15	.06	5.15	.06
Intermittent group	2.88	.36	2.43	.44	5.10	.06	6.32 *	1.11 *
							8.12 †	.64 †
							13.00 ‡	1.51 ‡
Combined groups	2.49	.64	2.56	.50	5.12	.06		

* 2:1 schedule.
† 3:1 schedule.
‡ 4:1 schedule.

tains the individual post-criterion response rates emitted under the regular reinforcement schedule. For the IR Ss, percentages are based on the 10 intervals of regular reinforcement following criterion. For the RR Ss, percentages are based on the total number of intervals following criterion. From this table it can be seen that although most Ss habitually worked at one rate of response, there were interindividual differences in the habitual or "preferred" rate.[5]

Performance during the Extinction Period

Two statistical tests were applied to the extinction data in order to test the hypothesis that the IR group would be more resistant to extinction.

[5] One last datum concerning performance during conditioning was provided by S No. 8, who gave a clear demonstration of the type of response that Skinner has termed "superstitious behavior" (6). The behavioral sequence was as follows. During reinforcement, S kept his left fist doubled in his mouth. When placed in the crib, he withdrew the fist from the mouth and kept it suspended in air for the short time it took him to smile. Then, simultaneously with the beginning of the reinforcement procedure, the fist was promptly reinserted into the mouth, the head turned 90 degrees to the left, and the body musculature stiffened. The onset of this stereotyped response coincided with criterion (56th trial). It disappeared for three days during a period of . . . illness (90th through 118th trials), reappeared in full strength with recovery (119th trial), gradually diminished in intensity, and finally disappeared altogether by the 162nd trial.

TABLE 2. INDIVIDUAL RESPONSE RATES DURING CONDITIONING: PERCENTAGE OF INTERVALS FOLLOWING CRITERION DURING WHICH S EMITTED FOUR, FIVE, OR SIX RESPONSES PER INTERVAL

	Total Number of Intervals on Regular Reinforcement following Criterion	Percentage of These Intervals during Which Response Rate Was		
		4	5	6
Intermittent group				
S No. 1	10	10%	80%	10%
S No. 3	10	20	70	10
S No. 5	10	30	10	60
S No. 7	10	20	40	40
Regular group				
S No. 2	24	4.2	58.3	37.5
S No. 4	45	13.3	62.2	24.4
S No. 6	31	80.6	19.4	0
S No. 8	22	0	22.7	77.3

First, McNemar's pseudo three-way analysis of variance (5), with blocks representing the experimental variable of reinforcement schedule, was applied to the response frequencies over all 13 extinction intervals. (Summing across 13 intervals, the total number of responses for the IR group was 331; for the RR group, 130.) The resulting F of 17.14, with 1 and 6 df, is significant beyond the .01 level. Second, a mean difference was computed, using the four matched-pair differences in total number of responses during the last six extinction intervals. (In this case, total number of responses for the IR and RR groups were 113 and 3, respectively.) For 3 df the t of 6.77 is significant beyond the .005 level by a one-tailed test.

A noncumulative plot of mean response rates during extinction (Fig. 2), shows some interesting periods of sharp rise in response rate for both groups (interval No. 5 for the RR group; intervals No. 7 and No. 8 for the IR group). The point of occurrence of this "recovery" did not appear to be a function of the length of preceding rest period; e.g., in the IR group, two Ss recovered after a rest of several hours (i.e., at the beginning of a new session), while the other two Ss recovered after a rest of only three minutes (i.e., during a session).

Figure 2 also indicates that every member of the RR group extinguished not to his previous, operant rate of response, but to a zero rate. Coincident with the beginning of zero response rate was a conspicuous behavioral change: S would no longer fixate the discriminative stimulus (E's face). Instead, S's head turned to one side and remained there—an occurrence, it might be pointed out, that was in distinct contrast to S's persistent fixation

Infant Social Behavior

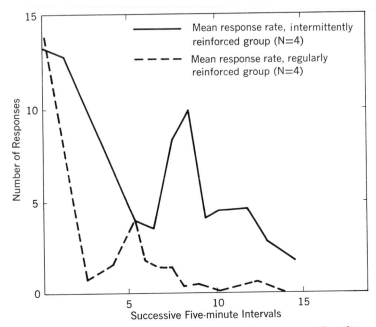

FIGURE 2. Noncumulative curves showing mean rates of smiling response during extinction period.

during conditioning. When this occurred, immediately preceding the last extinction interval, E propped S's head with rolled blankets or other material, making it impossible for the infant to turn his head to the left or right more than a few degrees. The "refusal" to fixate persisted even under these conditions; S's eyes then turned toward the ceiling. When withdrawal of reinforcement is conceptualized as frustration-producing (1), this persistent nonfixation may be regarded as an avoidance response that is elicited by continued frustration of the original (approach) response, is incompatible with the original response, and is reinforced by repeated escape from the frustrating situation.

The Relation of Protest to Smiling

As mentioned above, one of the criteria for subject selection was the frequency and intensity of crying. This criterion necessitated continued notations of such behavior during the operant period and first few conditioning intervals. Even after this point, however, E continued to record the incidence of crying, although at the time there seemed to be no particular reason for continuing to collect these data.

In recording crying, one of three types of notation was made, according to the intensity of response. In decreasing order of intensity, the notations were: (a) crying; (b) intense fussing: the same type of muscular and vocal involvement as in crying, but tears appeared only at the corners of eyes and did not course down the cheeks or temples; (c) fussing: considerable muscular and vocal involvement, but less than for the first two categories; no appearance of tears. In the presentation of data and discussions to follow, all three categories will be considered as one and referred to by the generic response term, *protest*.[6]

The data concerning protest show that during the conditioning period, as rate of smiling increased, rate of protest decreased—or more properly, protest extinguished with the counter-conditioning of smiling. Specifically, there is a perfect rank correlation between number of trials taken to extinguish the protest response and number of trials to conditioning criterion on the smile response. Similarly, during the extinction period, as rate of smiling decreased, rate of protest increased. In this case, the rank order correlation (tau) between rates of emission of the two responses from the beginning of extinction up to the first interval at zero rate of response, is —.69, significant at the .02 level by a two-tailed test. (First appearance of zero response rate was chosen as the referent point for the extinction period because it was the closest counterpart of the referent point for the conditioning period, i.e., criterion or beginning of maximum response rate.)

To express these results more generally, for all Ss combined, the ratio of protests to smiles during the conditioning period was 1:6.5 preceding criterion, and 1:276 following criterion. During the extinction period, the corresponding ratios were 1:40.5 (preceding first interval at zero rate of response) and 1:2.7 (during and following first interval at zero rate of response). Rates of protest response during operant, conditioning, and extinction periods are shown in Figure 3.

One might conceivably object to any interpretation of these correlations on the grounds that they merely reflect the fact that two such responses are mutually exclusive behaviors: an infant cannot protest and smile at the same time. Although this overlooks the important point that all Ss *changed* in the frequency of emission of both responses, there is a direct answer to such an objection in that the precriterion data show, for every S, both part and whole intervals during which neither protest nor smiling occurred at all.

There is a good deal of similarity between these findings and results obtained in a study by Estes (3), in which rats were reinforced for one instrumental response while a previously reinforced, competing response was being extinguished. Estes states that, "These results seem to lend some sup-

---

[6] It should be noted that interjudge reliability in discriminating protest from nonprotest was not determined. However, as indirect support for the objectivity or reproducibility of these data, the following points should be considered. First, this was a simple discrimination to make; even responses of lowest intensity represented a marked contrast to the infants' typical placid behavior. Second, the total numbers of protests for the two groups were approximately equal. Third, the orderliness of these data was not observed until the end of the experiment, when the results were actually tabulated.

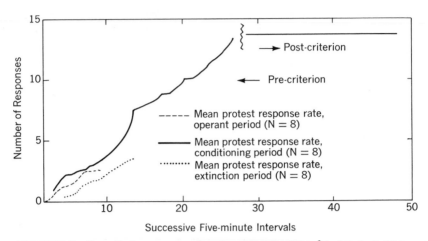

FIGURE 3. Cumulative curves showing mean rates of protest response during operant, conditioning, and extinction periods.

port to the view that the 'learning' of any one response involves the concurrent extinction of others and that the amount of initial acceleration in a learning curve is determined to an important extent by the relative initial strengths of all behaviors which may occur in the experimental situation" (3, p. 204).

In the present case, the most important determiner of rate of acquisition of the smiling response appears to be the initial strength of the functionally equivalent, competing protest response. The main difference between procedures is that in Estes' study, the conflicting response was both reinforced and extinguished as an integral part of the experiment, while in the present study only the extinction of the competing response took place during the experiment. Its establishment had already taken place prior to the beginning of the experiment—most probably via reinforcement by maternal care.

Perhaps the most appropriate way of conceptualizing these results is in terms of a habit family hierarchy of two responses for which the initially differing habit strengths were first reversed by selectively reinforcing only the weaker response, and then reversed again by extinguishing that response, allowing for recovery of the first. This leads to the general proposition that rate of acquisition and extinction is a function of the initial discrepancy in habit strength between competing responses.

SUMMARY

This investigation was concerned with the instrumental conditioning of a social response (smiling) in infants. Ss were two groups of four infants each; one group was maintained on a conditioning schedule of intermittent reinforcement and the other on a schedule of regular reinforcement. The reinforcement consisted of social and body contact between E and S. The dependent variable was relative resistance to extinction of smiling as a function of the differing reinforcement schedules.

Results confirmed the expectation that intermittent reinforcement is superior in maintaining continued performance of a response during extinction. Further, a negative correlation was found between rates of emission of protest and smiling responses during both conditioning and extinction periods. It was proposed that rate of acquisition and extinction is not only a function of reinforcement schedule but also of initial discrepancy in habit strength between competing responses.

REFERENCES

1. Adelman, H. M., & Maatsch, J. L.   Resistance to extinction as a function of the type of response elicited by frustration. *J. exp. Psychol.,* 1955, **50,** 61–65.
2. Dennis, W.   An experimental test of two theories of social smiling in infants. *J. soc. Psychol.,* 1935, **6,** 214–223.
3. Estes, W. K.   Effects of competing reactions on the conditioning curve for bar pressing. *J. exp. Psychol.,* 1950, **40,** 200–205.
4. Jenkins, W. O., & Stanley, J. C., Jr.   Partial reinforcement: A review and critique. *Psychol. Bull.,* 1950, **47,** 193–234.
5. McNemar, Q.   *Psychological statistics.* New York: John Wiley, 1955.
6. Skinner, B. F.   "Superstition" in the pigeon. *J. exp. Psychol.,* 1948, **38,** 168–172.
7. Thompson, J.   Development of facial expression of emotion in blind and seeing children. *Arch. Psychol.,* 1941, **37,** No. 264, 1–47.
8. Washburn, R.   A study of the smiling and laughing of infants in the first year of life. *Genet. Psychol. Monogr.,* 1929, **6,** 397–537.

1.7   Social and Nonsocial Conditioning of Infant Vocalizations [1]

Paul Weisberg

Basic to most views on the modification of an infant's early vocalizing are the stimuli afforded by the caretaker's behavior for the control of such social

[1] This paper is based upon a dissertation submitted to the Department of Psychology, University of Maryland, in partial fulfillment of the requirement for the

Reprinted from *Child Development* 1963, **34,** 377–388, by permission of the author and the Society for Research in Child Development.

behavior (3, 5, 6). Rheingold, Gewirtz, and Ross (7) found that an adult's responses contingent on the vocalizing of 3-month-old infants could bring about an increase in that behavior. Subsequently, when the reinforcing stimuli (tactual contact, "tsk" sounds, and smiles) were omitted during two days of extinction, the vocal rate declined to a level about 18 per cent above the operant rate. As Rheingold *et al.* point out, however, the question of whether vocalizing was operantly *conditioned* is equivocal since the reinforcing stimuli, per se, may have acted as social releasers. The possibility exists, then, that response-independent and dependent social events may have both stimulating and reinforcing properties for infant vocal behavior. Moreover, vocalizations may be affected by the presence in the infant's visual environment of a relatively unfamiliar and unresponding adult. That is, an immobile adult may serve as a discriminative stimulus for vocal behavior. Finally, if the infant's vocalizing effects any stimulus change in his external environment, then even such physical events (as well as social ones) might reliably strengthen the behavior.

The present investigation attempted to explore these possibilities by testing the effects of a series of short term experimental manipulations on the vocal behavior of infants.

METHOD

Institution and Environmental Setting

The institution in which the experiment was conducted was an urban Catholic orphan home equipped with fairly modern facilities for the care of children ranging from 2 weeks of age through preschool age. The infants were segregated in wards according to age group. The ward of concern here housed 16 infants of both sexes, with a median age of 3 months. The infants were multiply cared for by full time attendants, by resident "foster mothers," and occasionally by volunteers, but usually one attendant was left in charge of the 16 infants.

Subjects

Thirty-three 3-month-old full term infants, diagnosed as physically healthy, served as Ss. The groups to which the Ss were assigned (to be described below) did not differ significantly on such variables as age, birth weight, pre-experimental weight, and length of time in the institution. The ratio of males to females for each group varied from 5:1 to 3:3.

degree of Doctor of Philosophy. The writer is grateful to Drs. William S. Verplanck and Harriet L. Rheingold for their valuable suggestions and help throughout all phases of the study. Appreciation is extended to Sisters Mary Patricia and Thecla and to the personnel of St. Ann's Infant Asylum, Washington, D.C., where the experiment was carried out.

Procedure

The experiment took place in a small storage room relatively free from distraction by other infants or by the personnel of the orphanage. None of the infants had ever been in this room prior to the experiment. Once an S was ready for testing, that S was carried by E to the experimental room and seated in a canvas swing (Swyngomatic). E then concealed himself behind a partition in this room and waited 30 sec. before beginning an experimental session. If, within this time an S fell asleep, started to cry or to protest persistently, he was carried back to his crib and another session was attempted after half an hour had elapsed. Two 10-min. sessions were planned daily, but a session was terminated before the full 10 minutes had expired if any of these petulant behaviors appeared during the first 6 min. of a session. Thus every session reported lasted more than 6 min. without a prolonged disturbance by S. (76 per cent of all sessions ran the full 10 min.) If an S failed to complete two full daily sessions for one reason or another, that S was withdrawn from the experiment; five Ss were dropped following this criterion.

Each response consisted of a "discrete, voiced sound produced by S" (7, p. 69) appearing within each respiratory unit. Sounds classified as either "emotional" (protests, crying) or reflexive (coughs, sneezes, and certain digestive outbursts) were excluded. The phonetic topography of the response was not analyzed; the dependent variable was frequency of vocalizations made per min., i.e., rate of responding. Vocalizations and stimulus events were recorded on a kymograph. The recording speed was set at half an in. per sec., and each event could be marked by E's depression and release of a silent microswitch which was hidden from S. The median interobserver agreement on 20 sessions between E and another person trained to discriminate vocal behavior was 97 per cent (range 67 to 100 per cent). The rank-order correlation between the mean rates of both observers was .99.

Vocalizations of members of six groups were recorded through eight consecutive days. Either five or six Ss were randomly assigned to each group as they became available; if an S could not complete the experiment, he was replaced by the first available S. The experimental conditions of the fifth and sixth days were the basis for naming the groups. They were: No E present; E present; Noncontingent social stimulation; Noncontingent nonsocial stimulation; Contingent social stimulation; and Contingent nonsocial stimulation. These conditions include all that appeared in any part of the experiment. After describing them, the sequences appropriate to each group, each day, will be stated, providing the full experimental procedure.

1. *No E present.* The experimenter (E) remained behind a partition located about 5 ft. to the left of S. The upper part of the partition was transparent and allowed the E to observe all of S's behavior. E stationed himself at an angle which was about 135° from S's foveal line of vision so that, if S turned his head to the left, the chances of seeing E were minimized.

E, of course, minimized any auditory or movement cues that might indicate his presence. Under these conditions *S* oriented towards objects directly in front of himself (including parts of his body) and only occasionally turned to the left or right. *S*'s body size and the construction of the swing prevented him from making large torso movements.

2. *E present*. *E* seated himself facing *S* approximately 2 ft. away. *E* never smiled, frowned, or made rapid jerky movements of the head while in *S*'s presence; he did not open his mouth and maintained a "blank expression" fixating in the vicinity of *S*'s face. To keep his facial appearance invariant, *E* covertly counted numbers while fixating upon *S*.

3. *Noncontingent social stimulation*. *Ss* received stimulation on a pre-arranged schedule from *E* who was seated before them. The stimulation consisted of rubbing *S*'s chin with the thumb and forefinger followed and overlapped by an open-mouthed "toothy" smile and an aspirated "yeah" sound. Each such event lasted for about 2 sec. These events were given randomly four times a min. with the restriction that the interval between one event and the onset of the next be greater than 7 sec. On occasions when social stimulation was not given, *E* reverted to the facial expression described during the "*E* present" condition.

4. *Noncontingent nonsocial stimulation*. A door chime sounded on the same schedule as that followed with noncontingent social stimulation while *E* was seated faced toward *S*. Through successive sessions, the chime sounded 3 ft. to the left or right of *S* in an ABBA sequence.

5. *Contingent social stimulation*. The conditioning operations were performed by presenting the social stimulation described above immediately after each vocalization; that is, the smiles and the like were given contingent upon the infant's vocalizing. Responses made during the presentation of social stimulation were not further reinforced, and, during periods when *S* did not vocalize, *E* maintained the "blank expression."

6. *Contingent nonsocial stimulation*. The chime was sounded by *E* who was seated facing *S* immediately after each response. Vocalizations appearing during the chime's duration did not produce further auditory consequences. Spatial location of the chime also varied in an ABBA fashion from one session to the next.

The sequences through which the various *Ss* were run are presented in Table 1.

Group I controlled for changes in the operant rate of vocalizing with time in the experiment independent of an *E* being present. Group II served as a second control group, and any differences between the rates of groups I and II would indicate whether the presence of a human acted as an S^D for vocalizations. Groups III and IV were used to determine whether the reinforcing stimuli had eliciting properties and hence to clarify whether any changes in rates observed in groups V and VI could be attributed to rein-

TABLE 1. EXPERIMENTAL DESIGN

Group	1 and 2	3 and 4	5 and 6	7 and 8
			Days	
I (N=6)	No E	No E	No E	No E
II (N=5)	No E	E present	E present	E present
III (N=5)	No E	E present	Noncontingent social stimulation	Noncontingent social stimulation
IV (N=6)	No E	E present	Noncontingent nonsocial stimulation	Noncontingent nonsocial stimulation
V (N=5)	No E	E present	Contingent social stimulation	Extinction (E present)
VI (N=6)	No E	E present	Contingent nonsocial stimulation	Extinction (E present)

forcement (namely, social and nonsocial stimulation, respectively), *contingent* upon the occurrence of a response. Groups V and VI were used to show whether the rates of vocalizing shifted upward and downward by the imposition of reinforcement contingencies, and thus whether the behavior could be operantly conditioned.

RESULTS

Control Day Analysis (Days 1 to 4)

An analysis of variance of Ss' mean vocalization rates for days 1 to 4 (group variances as determined by the Bartlett test were homogeneous; uncorrected $X^2 = 10.65$; $p > .05$ with 5 df) revealed a significant day effect only ($F = 7.09$; $p < .001$ for 3 and 81 df). Further analysis of this day effect by t tests for correlated means based on all groups showed that the mean rates for each of the last three days were reliably greater than those of day 1 (all p's $< .02$). Days 2, 3, and 4 (means $= .91$, 1.13, and 1.21, respectively) were not significantly different from one another. The increase in rate after the low day 1 rates (mean $= .54$) probably indicate habituation of initial response to the relatively novel stimuli in the infant's environment. The day 2 rates provide good measures of the infant's vocal behavior when a human is absent from his environment, since the mean for all Ss on day 2 are close to the mean of the daily rates for just group I (*No E*) on subsequent days of the experiment (means $= .91$ and 1.00, respectively). Absence of an initial selection bias is suggested by the lack of any significant group differences on these control days and the fact that the days did not discriminate among the groups.

Effect of E

Upon the first introduction of E on day 3, 17 out of 27 Ss in groups II to VI (inclusive) increased in their rate over day 2 (binomial test = 1.15; p = .25, two-tailed test). The median gain for these 17 Ss was about the same for the 10 Ss who dropped in rate (medians = +.40 and —.37, respectively). By day 4, nine out of the 17 Ss whose rates were augmented on day 3 had declined in rate. The changes in mean rate of the six Ss in group I (*No E*) over this same time span were as follows: three Ss increased, one S decreased, and two Ss did not change in rate during days 2 to 3; four Ss increased and two Ss decreased in rate during days 3 to 4. Thus the presence relative to the absence of an unresponsive, immobile adult in the infant's visual environment is evidently not a releaser or discriminative stimulus for vocalizations.

Treatment Effects

The mean rates of days 3 and 4, 5 and 6, and 7 and 8 are plotted in Figure 1. (Pairs of treatment days were combined since each of these within-

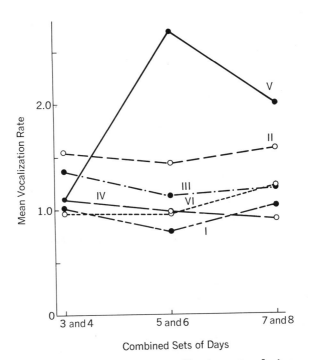

FIGURE 1. Group mean vocalization rates during the procedure of Days 3 and 4, 5 and 6, and 7 and 8. (See Table 1 for procedure).

group day effects were not significantly different from each other.) Treating the different groups as blocks and any particular set of days as columns with the Ss' mean response rate as row observations, the data lent themselves to a pseudo-three way analysis of variance design (4, p. 332). The analysis of the mean rates for each S on the control sessions (days 3 and 4) and experimental sessions (days 5 and 6) did not indicate any reliable differences either between these combined sets of days ($F = 1.63$; $p > .20$ for 1 and 27 df) or between groups ($F = 1.14$; $p > .20$ for 5 and 27 df). There was, however, a significant day $\times$ group interaction ($F = 4.94$; $p < .01$ for 5 and 27 df). The fact that all the Ss in group V showed considerable gains in their vocal rates between these two time spans indicates that social stimulation contingent on the infant's vocalizing acted to reinforce that behavior. However, when the chime was made contingent on vocalizations (i.e., group VI), the over-all rate for this group as well as groups I–IV remained fairly stable. When a similar analysis was performed for days 5 and 6 and days 7 and 8, there were no reliable differences between groups ($F = 1.65$; $p > .10$ for 5 and 24 df),[2] or between the combined pairs of days ($F < 1$; for 1 and 24 df) and the day $\times$ group interaction ($F = 2.38$; $p > .05$ for 5 and 24 df). However, note in Figure 1 that, although extinction operations on days 7 and 8 decreased the vocalization rates of the socially reinforced group, that group remained the most vocal.

Performance of Socially Reinforced Ss

The accumulated number of vocalizations per min. of the five Ss reinforced socially are plotted through each session in Figure 2. During social conditioning sessions (days 5 and 6), the median percentage increase based on all Ss over their operant level merely with E present exceeded 282 per cent. Note that there is no discontinuity associated with the almost 24 hour periods between sessions and that the rates under reinforcement are marked by periods of response bursts and of quiescence. Although the rates were lower on extinction than on conditioning days for four out of five Ss (the rates for S27 do not seem to fall off), the median percentage drop is only 47 per cent. There seems to be a direct relation between degree of conditioning success and resistance to extinction with the highly vocal-conditioned infants (especially S23 and S27) failing to extinguish. Only in the case of S24 did the rate toward the end of the experiment approximate the operant level.

DISCUSSION

The fact that the group receiving noncontingent social stimulation behaved like those responding under all other conditions except for the socially

---

[2] The reduction of the df for this analysis is due to the fact that three Ss (one from group IV and two from group VI) were not tested on days 7 and 8.

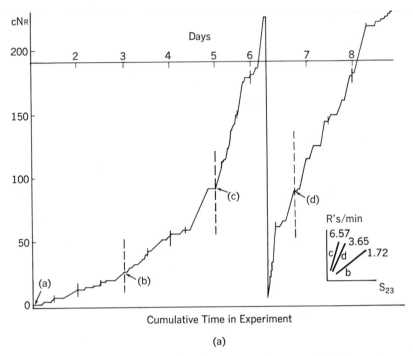

(a)

FIGURE 2. **Cumulative number of responses for group V Ss as a function of time in the experiment (in minutes). (a) No E;
(b) E present; (c) Contingent social stimulation; (d) Extinction. Short vertical lines separate sessions.**

reinforced group is consistent with the finding of Rheingold et al. (7) that
the vocalization of 3-month-old institutionalized infants can be conditioned
by actions of adults.

The present study and that of Rheingold et al. differ in a number of
ways. First, in the latter study, the infants' mean operant level (E present)
was more than four times higher than that found here. The discrepancy is
least likely due to subject differences, since both studies were done in the
same institution where the caretaking activities have remained invariant
over a span of years. More likely, at least three variables (or an interaction
among them) may have determined the difference in rates: (a) The infants
were observed in different experimental settings. In this study, response of
seated Ss to E were made in an unfamiliar room whereas in the Rheingold
et al. study, E leaned over S's crib. Since the infants were self-nursed in
their crib (by a propped bottle arrangement), a secondary or conditioned
reinforcement (or even a secondary drive stimulus reduction) explanation
cannot be ruled out. (b) The length and continuity of experimental sessions
differed. Rheingold et al. employed blocks of three three-min. testing sessions
spaced by two-min. "time out" or "rest" periods; this could have set up

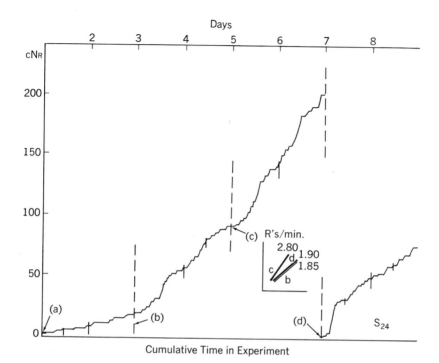

(b)

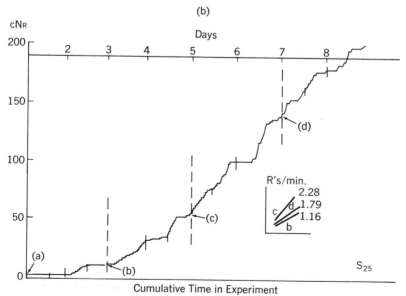

(c)

FIGURE 2. B & C

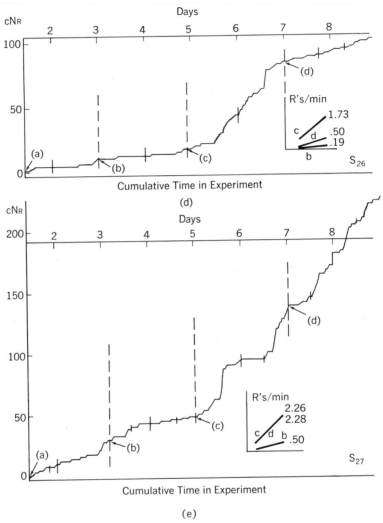

FIGURE 2. D & E

short term drive operations and allowed the response to recover between adjacent sessions. In this study in which "E present" sessions were run continuously for 6 to 10 min., the S's intrasessional response rate was frequently cyclical, suggesting that response recovery was an ongoing process. (c) The relation between the sex of E (male in this study and female in Rheingold's et al.) in an environment where all caretakers were female is a potentially important difference. While one can only speculate on the unknown dimensions of the human face to which infants respond, it should be pointed out that the greater opportunity for Ss to respond to "female"-like stimuli (faces, voices, etc.) would thus introduce greater "novelty" of E on S's operant level.

The results indicated that the initial presentation of an unresponding human did not serve as a discriminative stimulus (S^D) for vocal behavior. However, the relatively high resistance to extinction rates of the conditioned group suggest that the unresponding adult may have become a discriminative stimulus or, at least, a conditioned reinforcer. Admittedly, the high extinction rates could be due to the fact that not all vocalizing responses were reinforced on a continuous basis so that some of the S's responses could have been conditioned on a very low variable-ratio schedule (effectively, an interval one), thus developing high resistance to extinction. Brackbill (1) found that several values of intermittent social reinforcement provided by an adult for smiling in 4-month-old infants produced greater resistance to extinction than that resulting from a continuous schedule. In the Rheingold et al. study, however, vocalizations which were socially reinforced either on the average of 72 or 94 per cent of the time failed to produce any differential effect both during conditioning and extinction sessions. Since, in the present study the extinction process was not carried to completion, further work is necessary before it can be shown that the details of E's appearance can as stimuli become conditioned reinforcers for infant vocal behavior.

In the Brackbill and the Rheingold et al. studies, an inverse relation of protest (crying) to smiling and vocal behavior was found between conditioning and extinction sessions. Protest behavior was not directly measured in this study. However, the extinction sessions did not need to be terminated any earlier than any of the other conditions because of persistent protests. During extinction sessions there was, however, a change in the topography of the vocal response. After being emitted by S and then not reinforced by E, the full social response sequence on any one occasion might abruptly shift to pouts and whines only to return to smiles and the like. Both behaviors are mutually exclusive and compete with one another across time, so that, if extinction had been extended the "protest" might have gained in strength, eventually causing E to terminate the session and take the infant out of the situation. Substantiating evidence for this view is reported by Brackbill whose infants, after being extinguished to their operant level and below, refused to fixate to her face—"an occurrence, . . . that was in distinct contrast to S's persistent fixation during conditioning" (1, p. 120). The relation between "positive" and "negative" kinds of social behavior may be understood in terms of Estes' (2) finding that the conditioning of one behavior is a function of the initial strength of all behaviors and of the concurrent extinction of competing reactions.

There remains the question of the unsuccessful attempts to condition vocalizing using a nonsocial stumulus as a reinforcer. Since the noncontingent and contingent nonsocial Ss oriented towards the chime during its initial presentation, it is unlikely that the stimulus was not discriminated. The possibility exists that presenting the chime in the presence of an unresponding adult might facilitate habituation of responses to it. A test of this supposition would be to compare the effects of the chime as either an evoking or reinforcing stimulus when it is given either in the absence or presence of an adult.

The results of this study should not be taken to mean that nonsocial stimuli are necessarily inconsequential for the prediction and control of infant social behavior. These data show only that the particular chime used, under these conditions, in infants of this age, was ineffective. Rheingold et al., (8), Simmons (9), and Simmons and Lipsitt (10) have used nonsocial stimuli (lights and chimes) for the maintenance of behavior in older infants. The range of stimuli and subjects investigated must be extended.

SUMMARY

The vocal behavior of institutionalized 3-month-old infants in relation to manipulations in their physical and social environment through eight consecutive days was explored.

The results indicated that, after habituating to an unfamiliar setting devoid of humans, the S's rate of vocalizing did not reliably increase when an unresponding adult was introduced and made part of this environment, i.e., the immobile adult was evidently not a social releaser or S^D for vocal behavior. Taking the vocalizing rate in the presence of the unresponsive adult as the operant level, it was found that the behavior could be operantly conditioned by social consequences (the adult briefly touched S's chin and simultaneously smiled at and "talked" to him). Extinction operations subsequently reduced the rate but not to baseline performance. Conditions other than social reinforcement (e.g., presenting the reinforcing stimulus non-contingent upon vocalizing and giving an auditory stimulus in the presence of an unresponding adult both independently of and contingent upon vocalizing) did not seem to control infant vocal behavior.

REFERENCES

1. Brackbill, Y. Extinction of the smiling response in infants as a function of reinforcement schedule. *Child Develpm.*, 1958, **29**, 115–124.
2. Estes, W. K. Effects of competing reactions on the conditioning curve for bar pressing. *J. exp. Psychol.*, 1950, **40**, 200–205.
3. Lewis, M. M. *How children learn to speak*. Basic Books, 1959.
4. McNemar, Q. *Psychological statistics*. Wiley, 1955.
5. Miller, N. E., & Dollard, J. *Social learning and imitation*. Yale Univer. Press, 1941.
6. Mowrer, O. H. *Learning theory and personality dynamics*. Ronald, 1950.

7. Rheingold, H. L., Gewirtz, J. L., & Ross, H. W.   Social conditioning of vocalizations in the infant. *J. comp. physiol. Psychol.,* 1959, **52,** 68–73.
8. Rheingold, H. L., Stanley, W. C., & Cooley, J. A.   Method for studying exploratory behavior in infants. *Science,* 1962, **136,** 1054–1055.
9. Simmons, M. W.   Operant discrimination in infants. Unpublished doctoral dissertation, Brown Univer., 1962.
10. Simmons, M. W., & Lipsitt, L. P.   An operant-discrimination apparatus for infants. *J. exp. anal Behav.,* 1961, **4,** 233–235.

1.8   Play

J. Piaget

Play in its initial stages being merely the pole of the behaviours defined by assimilation,[1] almost all the behaviours we studied in relation to intelligence (*N.I.* and *C.R.*) [2] are susceptible of becoming play as soon as they are repeated for mere assimilation, *i.e.,* purely for functional pleasure.

Just as accommodation continually spreads beyond the framework of adaptation, so also does assimilation, and the reason for this is simple. Schemas [3] temporarily out of use cannot just disappear, threatened with atrophy for lack of use, but will become active for their own sake, for no other end than the functional pleasure of use. Such is play in its beginnings, the converse and complement of imitation. Imitation makes use of the schemas when these are adjustable to a model which corresponds with habitual activities, or when they can be differentiated by comparison with models which though new are related to these activities. Imitation is therefore, or at least becomes, a kind of hyperadaptation, through accommodation to models which are virtually though not actually usable. Play, on the

[1] Editor's note: Assimilation and accommodation are complementary processes by which the child deals with incoming environmental information. By assimilation Piaget means the infant's tendency to mold or bend reality to suit his existing forms of thought. Accommodation refers to the process whereby the infant's thought structure is modified to conform to reality.

[2] Editor's note: N.I. and C.R. refer to Piaget's earlier works, *The origins of intelligence in children,* New York: International Universities Press, 1952 (originally published 1936), and *The construction of reality in the child,* New York: Basic Books, 1954 (originally published 1937).

[3] Editor's note: Schema is Piaget's term to describe an organized and interrelated class of responses, e.g. sucking, prehension.

Reprinted from J. Piaget, *Play, Dreams, and Imitation.* New York: Norton, 1962 (originally published 1945), pp. 89–97, by permission of the author and publisher.

contrary, proceeds by relaxation of the effort at adaptation and by maintenance or exercise of activities for the mere pleasure of mastering them and
acquiring thereby a feeling of virtuosity or power. Imitation and play will
of course combine, but only at the level of representation, and will become
the set of what might be called "inactive" adaptations, in contrast to intelligence in action. During the sensory-motor stages, they are separate, even to
some extent antithetic, and therefore they must be studied separately.

When does play begin? The question arises at the *first stage*, that of purely
reflex adaptations. For an interpretation of play like that of K. Groos, for
whom play is pre-exercise of essential instincts, the origin of play must be
found in this initial stage since sucking gives rise to exercises in the void,
apart from meals (*N.I.*, Chap. I, § 2). But it seems very difficult to consider
reflex exercises as real games when they merely continue the pleasure of
feeding-time and consolidate the functioning of the hereditary set-up, thus
being evidence of real adaptation.

During the *second stage*, on the other hand, play already seems to assume
part of the adaptive behaviours, but the continuity between it and them is
such that it would be difficult to say where it begins, and this question of
boundary raises a problem which concerns the whole interpretation of later
play. "Games" with the voice at the time of the first lallations, movements
of the head and hands accompanied by smiles and pleasure, are these already
part of play, or do they belong to a different order? Are "primary circular
reactions" [4] generally speaking ludic, adaptive, or both? If we merely apply
the classical criteria, from the "pre-exercise" of Groos to the "disinterested"
(or as Baldwin calls it) the "autotelic" character of play, we should have to
say (and Claparède went almost so far) that everything during the first
months of life, except feeding and emotions like fear and anger, is play.
Indeed, when the child looks for the sake of looking, handles for the sake of
handling, moves his arms and hands (and in the next stage shakes hanging
objects and his toys) he is doing actions which are an end in themselves, as
are all practice games, and which do not form part of any series of actions
imposed by someone else or from outside. They no more have an external
aim than the later motor exercises such as throwing stones into a pond,
making water spirt from a tap, jumping, and so on, which are always
considered to be games. But all autotelic activities are certainly not games.
Science has this characteristic, and particularly pure mathematics, whose
object is immanent in thought itself, but if it is compared to a "superior"
game, it is clear that it differs from a mere game by its forced adaptation to

---

[4] Editor's note: Circular reactions refer to the infant's tendency to repeat a
sensory-motor response. Primary circular reactions generally center on and around
the infant's body (e.g. thumb-sucking), while secondary circular reactions are directed toward maintaining, through repetition, an interesting modification of the
external surroundings that was produced by the infant's own action.

an internal or external reality. In a general way, all adaptation is autotelic, but a distinction must be made between assimilation with actual accommodation and pure assimilation or assimilation which subordinates to itself earlier accommodations and assimilates the real to the activity itself without effort or limitation. Only the latter seems to be characterstic of play; otherwise the attempt to identify play with "pre-exercise" in general would involve the inclusion in it of practically all the child's activity.

But although the circular reactions have not in themselves this ludic character, it can be said that most of them are continued as games. We find, indeed, though naturally without being able to trace any definite boundary, that the child, after showing by his seriousness that he is making a real effort at accommodation, later reproduces these behaviours merely for pleasure, accompanied by smiles and even laughter, and without the expectation of results characteristic of the circular reactions through which the child learns. It can be maintained that at this stage the reaction ceases to be an act of complete adaptation and merely gives rise to the pleasure of pure assimilation, assimilation which is simply functional: the "Funktionslust" of K. Bühler. Of course, the schemas due to circular reaction do not only result in games. Once acquired, they may equally well become parts of more complete adaptations. In other words, a schema is never essentially ludic or non-ludic, and its character as play depends on its context and on its actual functioning. But all schemas are capable of giving rise to pure assimilation, whose extreme form is play. The phenomenon is clear in the case of schemas such as those of phonation, prehension (watching moving fingers, etc.) and certain visual schemas (looking at things upside down, etc.).

obs. 59. It will be remembered that T., at 0; 2 (21), adopted the habit of throwing his head back to look at familiar things from this new position (see *N.I.*, obs. 36). At 0; 2 (23 or 24) he seemed to repeat this movement with ever-increasing enjoyment and ever-decreasing interest in the external result: he brought his head back to the upright position and then threw it back again time after time, laughing loudly. In other words, the circular reaction ceased to be "serious" or instructive, if such expressions can be applied to a baby of less than three months, and became a game.

At 0; 3 T. played with his voice, not only through interest in the sound, but for "functional pleasure," laughing at his own power.

At 0; 2 (19 and 20) he smiled at his hands and at 0; 2 (25) at objects that he shook with his hand, while at other times he gazed at them with deep seriousness.

In short, during this second stage, play only appears as yet as a slight differentiation from adaptive assimilation. It is only in virtue of its later development that we can speak of two distinct facts. But the later evolution of play enables us to note the duality even at this stage, just as the evolution of imitation compels us to see the birth of imitation in the self-imitation of the circular reaction.

During the *third stage,* that of secondary circular reactions, the process remains the same, but the differentiation between play and intellectual assimilation is rather more advanced. Indeed, as soon as the circular reactions no longer involve only the child's own body or the perceptive canvas of elementary sensorial activity, but also objects manipulated with increasing deliberation, the "pleasure of being the cause" emphasised by K. Groos is added to the mere "functional pleasure" of K. Bühler. The action on things, which begins with each new secondary reaction, in a context of objective interest and intentional accommodation, often even of anxiety (as when the child sways new hanging objects or shakes new toys which produce sound) will thus unfailingly become a game as soon as the new phenomenon is grasped by the child and offers no further scope for investigation properly so called.

OBS. 60.   One need only re-read obs. 94–104 of the volume *N.I.* to find all the examples needed of the transition from assimilation proper to secondary reactions, to the pure assimilation which characterises play properly so called. For example, in obs. 94, L. discovered the possibility of making objects hanging from the top of her cot swing. At first, between 0; 3 (6) and 0; 3 (16), she studied the phenomenon without smiling, or smiling only a little, but with an appearance of intense interest, as though she was studying it. Subsequently, however, from about 0; 4, she never indulged in this activity, which lasted up to about 0; 8 and even beyond, without a show of great joy and power. In other words assimilation was no longer accompanied by accommodation and therefore was no longer an effort at comprehension: there was merely assimilation to the activity itself, *i.e.*, use of the phenomenon for the pleasure of the activity, and that is play.

These observations might be repeated in the case of each of the secondary reactions. But it is more curious to note that even the "procedures for prolonging an interesting spectacle," *i.e.*, the behaviours resulting from a generalisation of the secondary schemas (*N.I.*, obs. 110–118) give rise to an activity which is real play. Movements such as drawing oneself up so as not to lose a visual picture or a sound, carried out at first with great seriousness and almost with anxiety as to the result, are subsequently used on all occasions and almost "for fun." When the procedure is successful, the child uses it with the same "pleasure of being the cause" as in simple circular reactions, and moreover, even when the child himself sees it to be unsuccessful, he ends by repeating the movement without expecting anything from it, merely for amusement. This action must not be confused with the sensory-motor gestures of recognition, of which we spoke earlier (*N.I.*, obs. 107): the attitude of the child shows whether he is playing or striving to recognise the object.

During the *fourth stage*, that of co-ordination of the secondary schemas, two new elements related to play make their appearance. Firstly, the behaviours most characteristic of this period, or "the application of known schemas to new situations" (see *N.I.*, obs. 120–130) are capable, like the earlier ones, of being continued in ludic manifestations in so far as they are carried out for mere assimilation, *i.e.*, for the pleasure of the activity and without any effort at adaptation to achieve a definite end.

OBS. 61.   At 0; 7 (13), after learning to remove an obstacle to gain his objective, T. began to enjoy this kind of exercise. When several times in succession I put my hand or a piece of cardboard between him and the toy he desired, he reached the stage of momentarily forgetting the toy and pushed aside the obstacle, bursting into laughter. What had been intelligent adaptation had thus become play, through transfer of interest to the action itself, regardless of its aim.

Secondly, the mobility of the schemas (see *N.I.* 5, etc.) allows of the formation of real ludic combinations, the child going from one schema to another, no longer to try them out successively but merely to master them, without any effort at adaptation.

OBS. 62. At 0; 9 (3) J. was sitting in her cot and I hung her celluloid duck above her. She pulled a string hanging from the top of the cot and in this way shook the duck for a moment, laughing. Her involuntary movements left an impression on her eiderdown: she then forgot the duck, pulled the eiderdown towards her and moved the whole of it with her feet and arms. As the top of the cot was also being shaken, she looked at it, stretched up then fell back heavily, shaking the whole cot. After doing this some ten times, J. again noticed her duck: she then grasped a doll also hanging from the top of the cot and went on shaking it, which makes the duck swing. Then noticing the movement of her hands she let everything go, so as to clasp and shake them (continuing the preceding movement). Then she pulled her pillow from under her head, and having shaken it, struck it hard and struck the sides of the cot and the doll with it. As she was holding the pillow, she noticed the fringe, which she began to suck. This action, which reminded her of what she did every day before going to sleep caused her to lie down on her side, in the position for sleep, holding a corner of the fringe and sucking her thumb. This, however, did not last for half a minute and J. resumed her earlier activity.

A comparison between this sequence of behaviours and that of obs. 136 of *N.I.* at once makes plain the difference between play and strictly intelligent activity. In the case of the schemas successively tried out with new objects (obs. 136) J. merely sought to assimilate the objects, and, as it were, to "define them by use." Since there was adaptation of the schemas to an external reality which constituted a problem, there was intelligence properly so called. In the present case, on the contrary, although the process is the same, the schemas follow one after the other without any external aim. The objects to which they are applied are no longer a problem, but merely serve as an opportunity for activity. This activity is no longer an effort to learn, it is only a happy display of known actions.

But there is more in such behaviours than a mere sequence of aimless combinations with no attempt at accommodation. There is what might be called a "ritualisation" of the schemas, which, no longer in their adaptive context, are as it were imitated or "played" plastically. It is specially worth noting how J. goes through the ritual of all the actions she usually does when she is about to go to sleep (lies down, sucks her thumb, holds the fringe), merely because this schema is evoked by the circumstances. It is clear that this "ritualisation" is a preparation for symbolic games. All that is needed for the ludic ritual to become a symbol is that the child, instead of merely following the cycle of his habitual movements, should be aware of the make believe, *i.e.*, that he should "pretend" to sleep. In the sixth stage, we shall find just this.

During the *fifth stage* certain new elements will ensure the transition from the behaviours of stage IV to the ludic symbol of stage VI, and for that very reason will accentuate the ritualisation we have just noted. In relation to the "tertiary circular reactions" [5] or "experiments in order to see the result," it often happens that by chance, the child combines unrelated gestures without really trying to experiment, and subsequently repeats these gestures as a ritual and makes a motor game of them. But, in contrast to the combinations of stage IV, which are borrowed from the adapted schemas, these combinations are new and almost immediately have the character of play.

OBS. 63. At 0; 10 (3) J. put her nose close to her mother's cheek and then pressed it against it, which forced her to breathe much more loudly. This phenomenon at once interested her, but instead of merely repeating it or varying it so as to investigate it, she quickly complicated it for the fun of it: she drew back an inch or two, screwed up her nose, sniffed and breathed out alternately very hard (as if she were blowing her nose), then again thrust her nose against her mother's cheek, laughing heartily. These actions were repeated at least once a day for more than a month, as a ritual.

At 1; 0 (5) she was holding her hair with her right hand during her bath. The hand, which was wet, slipped and struck the water. J. immediately repeated the action, first carefully putting her hand on her hair then quickly bringing it down on to the water. She varied the height and position, and one might have thought it was a tertiary circular reaction but for the fact that the child's attitude showed that it was merely a question of ludic combinations. On the following days, every time she was bathed, the game was repeated with the regularity of a ritual. For instance, at 1; 0 (11) she struck the water as soon as she was in the bath, but stopped as if something was missing; she then put her hands up to her hair and found her game again.

At 1; 3 (19), with one hand, she put a pin as far away as possible and picked it up with the other. This behaviour, related to the working out of spatial groups, became a ritual game, started by the mere sight of the pin. Similarly, at 1; 4 (0), she had her leg through the handle of a basket. She pulled it out, put it back at once and examined the position. But once the gometrical interest was exhausted, the schema became one of play and gave rise to a series of combinations during which J. took the liveliest pleasure in using her new power.

At 1; 3 (11) J. asked for her pot and laughed a lot when it was given to her. She indulged in a certain number of ritual movements, playfully, and the game stopped there, to be taken up again the following days.

At 1; 1 (21) she amused herself by making an orange skin on a table sway from side to side. But as she had looked under the skin just before setting it in motion,

---

[5] Editor's note: Unlike secondary reactions, tertiary circular reactions involve not merely repetition, but also active experimentation, whereby the infant varies the activity in order to explore the consequences of variations on the external object.

she did it again as a ritual, at least twenty times; she took the peel, turned it over, put it down again, made it sway and then began all over again.

These behaviours are curious in that they are combinations not adapted to external circumstances. Obviously there is no necessity to screw up one's nose before wiping it on mother's cheek, to touch one's hair before hitting the water, or to look under a piece of orange peel (already well known) before making it move to and fro. But does the connection seem necessary to the child? We do not think so, although later on similar rituals may be accompanied by a certain feeling of efficacy, under the influence of emotion (as we are familiar with it in the game of avoiding walking on the lines between the stones in the pavement). In the present case, there is only adaptation at the starting point of such behaviours, secondary or tertiary circular reactions. But while in the normal circular reaction the child tends to repeat or vary the phenomenon, the better to adjust himself to it and master it, in this case the child complicates the situation and then repeats exactly all the actions, whether useful or useless, for the mere pleasure of using his activity as completely as possible. In short, during this stage, as before, play is seen to be the function of assimilation extended beyond the limits of adaptation.

The rituals of this stage are then a continuation of those of the previous one, with the difference that those of stage IV consist merely in repeating and combining schemas already established for a non-ludic end, while at this stage they become games almost immediately, and show a greater variety of combinations (a variety due no doubt to the habits following tertiary circular reaction). This progress in ludic ritualisation of schemas entails a corresponding development towards symbolism. Indeed, in so far as the ritual includes "serious" schemas or elements borrowed from such schemas (like the action of wiping one's nose, of asking for a pot, etc.), its effect is to abstract them from their context and consequently to evoke them symbolically. Of course, in such behaviours there is not necessarily as yet the consciousness of "make-believe," since the child confines himself to reproducing the schemas as they stand, without applying them symbolically to new objects. But although what occurs may not be symbolic representation, it is already almost the symbol in action.

With the *sixth stage*, owing to definite progress in the direction of representation, the ludic symbol is dissociated from ritual and takes the form of symbolic schemas. This progress is achieved when empirical intelligence becomes mental association, and external imitation becomes internal or "deferred" imitation, and this at once raises a whole set of problems. Here are some examples:

OBS. 64 (a). In the case of J., who has been our main example in the preceding observations, the true ludic symbol, with every appearance of awareness of "make-believe" first appeared at 1; 3 (12) in the following circumstances. She saw a cloth whose fringed edges vaguely recalled those of her pillow; she seized it, held a fold of it in her right hand, sucked the thumb of the same hand and lay down on her side, laughing hard. She kept her eyes open, but blinked from time to time as if she were alluding to closed eyes. Finally, laughing more and more, she cried "Néné" (Nono). The same cloth started the same game on the following days. At 1; 3 (13) she treated the collar of her mother's coat in the same way. At 1; 3 (30) it was the tail of her rubber donkey which represented the pillow! And from 1; 5 onwards she made her animals, a bear and a plush dog also do "nono."

Similarly, at 1; 6 (28) she said "avon" (savon = soap), rubbing her hands together and pretending to wash them (without any water).

At 1; 8 (15) and the following days she pretended she was eating various things, e.g., a piece of paper, saying "Very nice."

OBS. 64 (b). The development of these symbols which involve representation does not, of course, exclude that of purely sensory-motor rituals. Thus J., at 1; 6 (19), went the round of a balcony hitting the railings at each step with a rhythmical movement, stopping and starting again; a step, a pause; a blow, a step, a pause; a blow, etc.

Frequent relationships are formed between rituals and symbolism, the latter arising from the former as a result of progressive abstraction of the action. For instance, at about 1; 3 J. learnt to balance on a curved piece of wood which she rocked with her feet, in a standing position. But at 1; 4 she adopted the habit of walking on the ground with her legs apart, pretending to lose her balance, as if she were on the board. She laughed heartily and said "Bimbam."

At 1; 6 she herself swayed bits of wood or leaves and kept saying Bimbam and this term finally became a half generic, half symbolic schema referring to branches, hanging objects and even grasses.

OBS 65. In the case of L. "make believe" or the ludic symbol made its appearance at 1; 0 (0), arising, as in the case of J., from the motor ritual. She was sitting in her cot when she unintentionally fell backwards. Then seeing a pillow, she got into the position for sleeping on her side, seizing the pillow with one hand and pressing it against her face (her ritual was different from J.'s). But instead of miming the action half seriously, like J. in obs. 62, she smiled broadly (she did not know she was being watched); her behaviour was then that of J. in obs. 64. She remained in this position for a moment, then sat up delightedly. During the day she went through the process again a number of times, although she was no longer in her cot; first she smiled (this indication of the representational symbol is to be noted), then threw herself back, turned on her side, put her hands over her face as if she held a pillow (though there wasn't one) and remained motionless, with her eyes open, smiling quietly. The symbol was therefore established.

At 1; 3 (6) she pretended to put a napkin-ring in her mouth, laughed, shook her head as if saying "no" and removed it. This behaviour was an intermediate stage between ritual and symbol, but at 1; 6 (28) she pretended to eat and drink without having anything in her hand. At 1; 7 she pretended to drink out of a box and then held it to the mouths of all who were present. These last symbols had been prepared for during the preceding month or two by a progressive ritualisation, the principal stages of which consisted in playing at drinking out of empty glasses and then repeating the action making noises with lips and throat.

These examples show the nature of the behaviours in which we have seen for the first time pretence or the feeling of "make believe" characteristic of the ludic symbol as opposed to simple motor games. The child is using schemas which are familiar, and for the most part already ritualised in games of the previous types: but (1) instead of using them in the presence of the objects to which they are usually applied, he assimilates to them new objectives unrelated to them from the point of view of effective adaptation; (2) these new objects, instead of resulting merely in an extension of the schema (as is the case in the generalisation proper to intelligence), are used with no other purpose than that of allowing the subject to mime or evoke the schemas in question. It is the union of these two conditions—application of the schema to inadequate objects and evocation for pleasure—which in our opinion characterises the beginning of pretence. For instance, as early as the IVth stage, the schema of going to sleep is already giving rise to ludic ritualisations, since in obs. 62 J. reproduces it at the sight of her pillow. But there is then neither symbol nor consciousness of make-believe, since the child merely applies her usual movements to the pillow itself, *i.e.*, to the normal stimulus of the behaviour. There certainly is play, in so far as the schema is only used for pleasure, but there is no symbolism. On the contrary, in obs. 64 J. mimes sleep while she is holding a cloth, a coat collar, or even a donkey's tail, instead of a pillow, and in obs. 65 L. does the same thing, pretending to be holding a pillow when her hands are empty. It can therefore no longer be said that the schema has been evoked by its usual stimulus, and we are forced to recognise that these objects merely serve as substitutes for the pillow, substitutes which become symbolic through the actions simulating sleep (actions which in L.'s case go so far as pretence without any material aid). In a word, there is symbolism, and not only motor play, since there is pretence of assimilating object to a schema and use of a schema without accommodation.

REFERENCES

1. Baldwin, J. M. *Mental development in the child and in the race.* New York: Macmillan, 1895.
2. Buhler, K. *The mental development of the child.* New York: Harcourt, 1930.
3. Claparède, E. Sur la nature et la fonction du jue. *Arch. de Psychol,* 1934, **24,** 350–369.
4. Groos, K. *The play of men.* New York: Appleton, 1908.
5. Piaget, J. *The origins of intelligence in children.* New York: International Universities Press, 1952.
6. Piaget, J. *The construction of reality in the child.* New York: Basic Books, 1954.

chapter two

Social Reinforcement

2.1 Introduction

One of the most frequently employed methods of maintaining and modifying the behavior of children is adult approval or attention. Studies of infant behavior indicate that social reinforcement can, at a very early age, affect the developing child's behavior. In this section studies which aim at isolating the variables that affect the operation of social reinforcers for altering the behavior of children are presented. Systematic research in this area began only recently, but the picture that has emerged is exceedingly complex; the effects of social reinforcement are dependent upon sex of subject and examiner, type of task, and a variety of environmental variables.

Before reviewing the findings, the methodology employed by laboratory invesigators in this area will be examined. The principal task is a simple marble-dropping game in which the child places marbles into the holes of a wooden box or bin. The child's rate of responding, or his persistence at the game under different conditions of social reinforcement, is assessed. In another variation, a two-choice discrimination task is employed and the child is given social approval for choosing the hole that is designated by the experimenter as "correct." The increase in the frequency of the correct responses is the index of social reinforcer effectiveness. As Stevenson (1965) has noted in his recent review of social reinforcement, a variety of factors governed the choice of this laboratory task. The marble-dropping game possesses little intrinsic interest and thereby maximizes the effects of social reinforcement. It minimizes the effects of earlier learning and so reduces the impact of individual differences on task performance; individual differences often obscure the operation of experimental manipulations. Moreover, the game involves discrete responses which can be reliably measured in laboratory settings. However, even these relatively simple tasks and measures have encountered some serious methodological problems and criticisms (see Parton & Ross, 1965; Patterson, 1964). In spite of some shortcomings, these tasks have permitted the investigation of a wide range of social reinforcement parameters in highly controlled laboratory settings. Moreover, there is often a high degree of similarity between findings in these laboratory studies and results from studies in naturalistic settings involving more complex social responses.

Many socialization theories make the central assumption that children's behavior can be effectively controlled by social reinforcement from a variety of social agents, including parents, teachers, and peers. Well-controlled experimental studies executed in both laboratory and naturalistic settings have recently provided support for this basic assumption. For example, Patterson and his co-workers (Patterson, Littman, & Hinsey, 1964) have employed parents as reinforcing agents in laboratory studies of the effect of paternal and maternal approval upon a child's performance on a simple two-choice discrimination task. Their investigations have provided strong confirmation of the effectiveness of parents as reinforcing agents. In addition, they found a cross-sex effect that earlier investigators using strangers as reinforcing agents had found: mothers were more effective with their sons, while fathers were more effective with their daughters.

Support for the claim often made that the teacher, another important socializing agent, is important in maintaining and modifying children's social behavior, is provided in the lead article in this section. Using a wide variety of behaviors, Harris, Wolf, and Baer (1964) clearly demonstrate that teacher attention is a potent source of reinforcement for children. Their research indicates that problem or troublesome behavior is often inadvertently maintained by adult attention. The importance of this research lies in its demonstration that adult social reinforcement plays an important part in controlling children's social behavior in naturalistic settings.

Although often neglected in discussions of children's social devel-

opment, peers, as well as adults, often serve as agents of social
reinforcement. A number of investigators have very recently docu-
mented some of the effects of social reinforcement delivered by
peers. In a study that parallels the Wolf *et al.* research, Wahler
(1967) instructed peers to differentially attend to certain social behaviors of other preschoolers in a free-field setting. His results indicate that a variety of preschoolers' social behavior, including
cooperation, aggression, and speech, can be controlled by social
reinforcement contingencies established by peers.

Laboratory evidence of the effectiveness of peers is provided by a
pair of studies by Hartup (Hartup, 1964; Titkin & Hartup, 1965),
who has examined the effects of the sociometric status of the reinforcing peer on his capacity to influence another child. In the first
study, Hartup (1964) compared the effectiveness of verbal approval
administered by "liked" peers and by "disliked" peers. The results
indicated that for both 4- and 5-year-old subjects, the "disliked"
peer was more effective in maintaining the child's performance in a
simple marble-dropping game than was a "liked" peer. In a related
study, Titkin and Hartup (1965) reported a comparable set of results when the social status of the reinforcing agent was assessed in
terms of popularity in the peer group rather than in terms of friendship. Popular peers, unpopular peers, and isolated peers served as
reinforcing agents. Subjects reinforced by unpopular peers significantly increased in rate of response, those reinforced by popular
peers decreased, and children reinforced by isolates showed no
change in rate of response over the session. These peer studies, in
addition to confirming the effectiveness of peers as social reinforcers,
indicate that one of the important determinants of social reinforcer
effectiveness is the nature of the relationship between the agent and
the recipient of reinforcement.

The next study in this section (McCoy & Zigler, 1965) indicates
that the nature of the relationship is important in adult-child social
reinforcement situations as well as in peer interaction situations.
McCoy and Zigler, in a laboratory experimental investigation of
the effects of adult-child relationships on reinforcement effectiveness, exposed first and second grade boys to one of three interaction
conditions before administering a social reinforcement task. One
group had no contact with the reinforcing agent; a second group
had "neutral" contact—the agent was present but interacted with
the subject minimally; the third group experienced warm, positive
interaction with the experimenter. When the same experimenter
was the reinforcing agent in a marble-dropping game, children who
had previously experienced positive interaction elected to play
longer than the "neutral" interaction children, who, in turn, played

the game longer than the subjects encountering the experimenter for the first time. A number of other studies by Zigler and his colleagues (Berkowitz & Zigler, 1965; Berkowitz, Butterfield & Zigler, 1965) are consistent with this demonstration that the nature of the adult-child relationship is a crucial determinant of the effectiveness of the reinforcing agent for modifying children's social behavior. In addition, field studies (for example, Sears, Maccoby, & Levin, 1957) have consistently found that warm parents are most effective in shaping their children's behavior.

Just as the value of the reinforcing agent varies with the child's prior experience with the agent, the value of a reinforcing stimulus fluctuates with the events and experiences that precede it, or more generally with the context in which it occurs. Solomon (1964) makes a similar point in a recent discussion of punishment: "A punishment is not just a punishment. It is an event in the temporal and spatial flow of stimulation and behavior, and its effects will be produced by its temporal and spatial point of insertion in that flow" (Solomon, 1964, p. 242). The studies by Crandall (1963) and Crandall, Good, and Crandall (1964), based on a similar assumption, have investigated an important, but somewhat neglected aspect of social control: silence. This research clearly demonstrates that adult nonreactions have active reinforcing properties; silence after adult approval is analogous to negative reinforcement, and nonreaction after punishment is analogous to positive reinforcement. When the sequencing of reinforcement events is considered, silence emerges as a potentially potent means of shaping children's social responses.

Not all individuals are equally affected by social reinforcement manipulations, nor are all agents equally effective dispensers of social rewards. One of the most consistent findings in this area is the cross-sex effect: social reinforcement delivered by a male adult is more effective with girls, while a female reinforcing agent is more effective with boys. The Stevenson (1961) study in this section is one of a number of investigations to isolate this relationship (for example, Gewirtz, 1954; Gewirtz & Baer, 1958; Hartup, 1961). However, as Stevenson notes, this effect may not appear until the late preschool years; females are markedly effective social reinforcing agents with 3- and 4-year-old children, but males have little effect on children of this age. Once the cross-sex effect appears, however, it tends to persist, as evidenced by Stevenson and Allen's (1964) finding of a cross-sex effect in college age subjects. Therefore it is unlikely that the effect is limited to the late preschool or early elementary school age groups.

In addition to sex effects, personality variables, such as dependency, have been examined. Briefly, the literature on personality variables indicates that children who have well-developed dependency habits are influenced by social reinforcers to a greater degree than less dependent subjects (Ferguson, 1961; Hartup, 1958—see section on dependency).

The child's anxiety level may also be an important factor in determining his reaction to social reinforcers. Horowitz and Armentrout (1965), using fourth grade children, reported that highly anxious subjects (assessed by Children's Manifest Anxiety Scale) learn more effectively when given a social reinforcer than when reinforced by a buzzer. The type of reinforcement did not affect learning in children of low anxiety as indicated by the lack of difference between these subjects under buzzer and social reinforcement conditions. In addition, birth order, intellectual status, and social class have been found to affect a subject's response to social reinforcement. Together, these results suggest that the age and sex of the child, the sex and status of the reinforcing agents, and a host of personality characteristics of the subject are all determinants of social reinforcer effectiveness.

One of the intriguing problems in the social reinforcement literature concerns the effects of variations in the availability of social reinforcers on their subsequent effectiveness in modifying children's behavior. Gewirtz and Baer (1958a), in a now classic study, examined the effect of brief social isolation on children's responsiveness to social approval. Children were required to learn a simple two-choice discrimination task, during which the experimenter verbally reinforced subjects for "correct" responses. Children who had been isolated for 20 minutes modified their responses more readily than children tested immediately after being brought from the classroom. In a second study, children were either isolated (socially deprived), not isolated, or socially satiated by a 20-minute play period in the presence of a responsive adult. Children were most responsive to social reinforcers dispensed following isolation, intermediate under the nonisolation condition, and slowest following social interaction. Gewirtz and Baer employed a deprivation-satiation interpretation of their findings and argued that the effectiveness of social reinforcers is enhanced after deprivation of social stimuli and lowered after satiation in a manner paralleling the operation of appetitive drives, such as hunger or thirst. They argued that a "social drive" was operative in their situation. Landau and Gewirtz (1967) offer additional support for the satiation-deprivation analysis of social reinforcer effectiveness. Five-year-old Israeli boys were exposed to a social reinforcer either a few times (4 to 12) or many times (30 to 60) before being given a verbal conditioning task, in which reinforcement consisted of the same social stimulus used in the preceding satiation session. The results were consistent with the stimulus-satiation prediction that conditioning would be greatest for Ss given only limited preexposure to the reinforcing stimulus. Generally these findings suggest that the reinforcing efficacy of a stimulus is an inverse function of the degree of its availability to subjects in the preceding period (Landau & Gewirtz, 1967).

This explanation of social reinforcer effectiveness has led to considerable debate, and a number of alternative explanations have been offered. Walters and his colleagues (Walters & Karal, 1960; Walters & Ray, 1960; Walters, Marshall, & Shooter, 1960; Walters & Parke, 1964b) have suggested that the difference between the isolated and nonisolated subjects on the original Gewirtz and Baer studies could be due to the emotionally arousing nature of the isolation procedure, thereby rendering unnecessary the postulation of a "social drive." In a direct test of this interpretation, Walters and Ray (1960) examined the effects of both arousal and isolation on responsiveness to social reinforcement. The arousal manipulation consisted of employing a stranger as the experimenter's assistant and of failing to inform the child concerning the intentions of the experimenter. The isolation procedure and the learning task were similar to those used by Gewirtz and Baer. The results indicated that the arousal variable, not the isolation procedure per se, was the critical factor in facilitating learning. In the follow-up investigation, which is included in this section, Walters and Parke (1964) replicated these findings and strengthened the "arousal" argument by demonstrating a relationship between changes in finger temperature (an index of physiological arousal) and efficacy of learning. Moreover, learning was equally good when reinforcement consisted of either social approval or material rewards. The latter result argues against the social deprivation hypothesis, which suggests that it is the social nature of the reinforcer that accounts for the heightened susceptibility to social influence of previously isolated children. More generally, this study suggests that the subject's state of arousal may be an important determinant of his susceptibility to influence. Emotional arousal may alter perceptual thresholds and modify the range and nature of cues to which an observer will respond (see Walters & Parke, 1964a). This restriction of cues could result in the focusing of attention on the actions of a reinforcing agent, and the subject could thus learn more rapidly to identify the occasions on which reinforcements will be dispensed.

A variety of other interpretations of the original Gewirtz and Baer data are available. These include a frustration hypothesis (Hartup & Himeno, 1959), an anxiety hypothesis (Stevenson & Hill, 1963), and an information hypothesis (Cairns, 1963). Stevenson

(1965) has recently reviewed these different positions, and it is clear from his review that no one theoretical framework can adequately handle the diverse effects of social reinforcement.

REFERENCES

Berkowitz, H., Butterfield, E. C., & Zigler, E. The effectiveness of social reinforcers on persistence and learning tasks following positive and negative social interactions. *Journal of Personality and Social Psychology,* 1965, **2,** 706–714.

Berkowitz, H., & Zigler, E. Effects of preliminary positive and negative interactions and delay conditions on children's responsiveness to social reinforcement. *Journal of Personality and Social Psychology,* 1965, **2,** 500–505.

Cairns, R. B. Antecedents of social reinforcer effectiveness. Unpublished manuscript, University of Indiana, 1963.

Crandall, V. C. Reinforcement effects of adult reactions and nonreactions on children's achievement expectations. *Child Development,* 1963, **34,** 335–354.

Crandall, V. C., Good, S., & Crandall, V. J. Reinforcement effects of adult reactions and nonreactions on children's achievement expectations: A replication study. *Child Development,* 1964, **35,** 485–497.

Ferguson, P. E. The influence of isolation, anxiety, and dependency on reinforcer effectiveness. Unpublished M. A. thesis, University of Toronto, 1961.

Gewirtz, J. L. Three determinants of attention seeking in young children. *Monograph of the Society for Research in Child Development,* 1954, **19,** No. 2 (Serial No. 59).

Gewirtz, J. L., & Baer, D. M. The effects of brief social deprivation on behaviors for a social reinforcer. *Journal of Abnormal and Social Psychology,* 1958, **56,** 49–56.

Harris, F. R., Wolf, M. M., & Baer, D. M. Effects of adult social reinforcement on child behavior. *Young Children,* 1964, **20,** 8–17.

Hartup, W. W. Nurturance and nurturance withdrawal in relation to the dependency behavior of preschool children. *Child Development,* 1958, **29,** 191–201.

Hartup, W. W. Sex and social reinforcement effects with children. Paper read at the Annual Meeting of the American Psychological Association, New York, 1961.

Hartup, W. W. Friendship status and the effectiveness of peer as reinforcing agents. *Journal of Experimental Child Psychology,* 1964, **1,** 154–162.

Hartup, W. W., & Himeno, Y. Social isolation vs. interaction with adults in relation to aggression in preschool children. *Journal of Abnormal and Social Psychology,* 1959, **59,** 17–22.

Horowitz, F. D., & Armentrout, J. Discrimination-learning, manifest anxiety, and effects of reinforcement. *Child Development,* 1965, **36,** 731–748.

Landau, R., & Gewirtz, J. L. Differential satiation for a social reinforcing stimulus as a determinant of its efficacy in conditioning, *Journal of Experimental Child Psychology*, 1967, 5, 391–405.

McCoy, N., & Zigler, E. Social reinforcer effectiveness as a function of the relationship between child and adult. *Journal of Personality and Social Psychology*, 1965, *1*, 6, 604–612.

Parton, D. A., & Ross, A. O. Social reinforcement of children's motor behavior: A review. *Psychological Bulletin*, 1965, 64, 65–73.

Patterson, G. R., & Hinsey, W. C. Investigations of some assumptions and characteristics of a procedure for instrumental conditioning in children. *Journal of Experimental Child Psychology*, 1964, 1, 111–122.

Patterson, G. R., Littman, R., & Hinsey, C. Parental effectiveness as reinforcers in the laboratory and its relation to child rearing practices and child adjustment in the classroom. *Journal of Personality*, 1964, 32, 180–199.

Sears, R. R., Maccoby, E. E., & Levin, H. *Patterns of Child Rearing*, Evanston, Ill.: Row, Peterson, and Company, 1957.

Solomon, R. L. Punishment. *American Psychologist*, 1964, 19, 239–253.

Stevenson, H. W. Social reinforcement with children as a function of CA, sex of E, and sex of S. *Journal of Abnormal and Social Psychology*, 1961, 63, 147–154.

Stevenson, H. W. Social reinforcement of children's behavior. In L. P. Lipsitt and C. C. Spiker (Eds.), *Advances in Child Development and Behavior*, Vol. II. New York: Academic Press, 1965.

Stevenson, H. W., & Allen, S. Adult performance as a function of sex of subject. *Journal of Abnormal and Social Psychology*, 1964, 68, 214–216.

Stevenson, H. W., & Hill, K. The effect of social reinforcement following success and failure. Unpublished manuscript. University of Minnesota, 1963.

Stevenson, H. W., Keen, R., & Knights, R. M. Parents and strangers as reinforcing agents for children's performance. *Journal of Abnormal and Social Psychology*, 1963, 65, 429–431.

Titkin, S., & Hartup, W. W. Sociometric status and the reinforcing effectiveness of children's peers. *Journal of Experimental Child Psychology*, 1965, 2, 306–315.

Wahler, R. G. Child-child interactions in free field setting: Some experimental analyses. *Journal of Experimental Child Psychology*, 1967, 5, 278–293.

Walters, R. H., and Karal, P. Social deprivation and verbal behavior. *Journal of Personality*, 1960, 28, 89–107.

Walters, R. H., Marshall, W. E., & Shooter, J. R. Anxiety, isolation, and susceptibility to social influence. *Journal of Personality*, 1960, 28, 518–529.

Walters, R. H., & Parke, R. D. Social motivation, dependency, and susceptibility to social influence. *Advances in Experimental Social Psychology*, Vol. I. New York: Academic Press, 1964. Pp. 231–276. (a)

Walters, R. H. & Parke, R. D. Emotional arousal, isolation and discrimination learning in children. *Journal of Experimental Child Psychology*, 1964, *1*, 163–173. (b)

Walters, R. H., & Ray, E.   Anxiety, social isolation and reinforcer effectiveness. *Journal of Personality,* 1960, **28,** 358–367.

SUPPLEMENTARY READING

Stevenson, H. W.   Social reinforcement of children's behavior. In L. P.
Lipsitt & C. C. Spiker (Eds.), *Advances in child development and be-
havior,* II. New York: Academic Press, 1965. Pp. 97–126.
Ullman, L. P., & Krasner, L. (Eds.), *Case studies in behavior modification.*
New York: Holt, Rinehart and Winston, 1965.
Walters, R. H., & Parke, R. D.   Social motivation, dependency, and sus-
ceptibility to social influence. In L. Berkowitz (Ed.), *Advances in ex-
perimental social psychology,* Vol. I. New York: Academic Press, 1964.
Pp. 231–276.

2.2   Effects of Adult Social Reinforcement on Child Behavior [1]

Florence R. Harris, Montrose M. Wolf, and Donald M. Baer

There is general agreement among educators that one of the primary functions of a nursery school is to foster in each child social behaviors that
contribute toward more pleasant and productive living for all. However,
there is no similar consensus as to precisely how this objective is to be
attained. Many writers subscribe to practices based on a combination of
psychoanalytic theory and client-centered therapy principles, usually referred
to as a mental hygiene approach. Yet there are considerable variation and
vagueness in procedures recommended, particularly those dealing with such
problem behaviors as the child's hitting people, breaking valuable things,
or withdrawing from both people and things. Read (1955), for example,
recommends accepting the child's feelings, verbalizing them for him, and
draining them off through vigorous activities. Landreth (1942) advises keeping adult contacts with the child at a minimum based on his needs, backing
up verbal suggestions by an implicit assumption that the suggestion will be
carried out and, when in doubt, doing nothing unless the child's physical

[1] These studies were supported in part by research grants from the National Institute of Mental Health (MH-02208-07) and the University of Washington Graduate
School Research Fund (11-1873). The authors are also indebted to Sidney W. Bijou
for his general counsel and assistance.

Reprinted from *Young Children* 1964, **20,** 8–17, by permission of the authors and the
National Association for the Education of Young Children.

safety is involved. In addition to some of the above precepts, Taylor (1954) counsels parents and teachers to support both desirable and undesirable behaviors and to give nonemotional punishment. According to Standing (1959), Montessori advocates that teachers pursue a process of nonintervention, following careful preparation of a specified environment aimed at "canalizing the energy" and developing "inner command." Nonintervention does not preclude the "minimum dose" of instruction and correction.

Using some combination of such guidance precepts, teachers have reported success in helping some nursery school children who showed problem behaviors; but sometimes adherence to the same teaching principles has not been helpful in modifying the behavior of concern. Indeed, it is usually not at all clear what conditions and principles may or may not have been operative. All of these precepts have in common the adult behaviors of approaching and attending to a child. Therefore, it seemed to the staff of the Laboratory Preschool at the University of Washington that a first step in developing possible explicit criteria for judging when and when not to attend was to study the precise effects that adult attention can have on some problem behaviors.

This paper presents an account of the procedures and results of five such studies. Two groups of normal nursery school children provided the subjects studied. One group enrolled twelve three-year-olds and the other, sixteen four-year-olds. The two teachers of the younger group and the three teachers of the older group conducted the studies as they carried out their regular teaching duties. The general methodology of these studies was developed in the course of dealing with a particularly pressing problem behavior shown by one child at the beginning of the school year. It is worth considering this case before describing the procedures which evolved from it.

The study dealt with a three-year-old girl who had regressed to an excessive amount of crawling (Harris, Johnston, Kelley, and Wolf, 1964). By "excessive" is meant that after three weeks of school she was spending most of her morning crawling or in a crouched position with her face hidden. The parents reported that for some months the behavior had been occurring whenever they took her to visit or when friends came to their home. The teachers had used the conventional techniques, as outlined above, for building the child's "security."

Observations recorded in the third week at school showed, however, that more than 80% of the child's time was spent in off-feet positions. The records also showed that the crawling behavior frequently drew the attention of teachers. On-feet behaviors, such as standing and walking, which occurred infrequently, seldom drew such notice.

A program was instituted in which the teachers no longer attended to the child whenever she was crawling or crouching, but gave her continuous warm attention as long as she was engaging in behavior in which she was standing, running, or walking. Initially the only upright behaviors that the teachers were able to attend to occurred when the child pulled herself almost to her feet in order to hang up or take down her coat from her locker, and when she pulled herself up to wash her hands in the wash basin. Within a week of the initiation of the new attention-giving procedure, the child acquired a close-to-normal pattern of on-feet behavior.

In order to see whether the change from off- to on-feet behavior was related to the differential attention given by the teachers, they reversed their procedure, making attention once again contingent only upon crawling and other off-feet behavior. They waited for occasions of such off-feet behavior to "reinforce" with attention, while not attending to any on-feet behavior. By the second day the child had reverted to her old pattern of play and locomotion. The observational records showed the child was off her feet 80% of the class session.

To see whether on-feet behavior could be re-established, the teachers again reversed their procedure, giving attention to the child only when she was engaging in behaviors involving upright positions. On-feet behavior rose markedly during the first session. By the fourth day, the child again spent about 62% of the time on her feet.

Once the child was not spending the greater portion of her day crawling about, she quickly became a well-integrated member of the group. Evidently she already had well-developed social play skills.

As a result of this demonstration that either walking or crawling could be maintained and that the child's responses depended largely upon the teachers' attending behaviors, the teachers began a series of further experimental analyses of the relationship between teacher attention and nursery school child behavior.

Procedures

A specified set of procedures common to the next studies was followed. First, a child showing problem behavior was selected and records were secured. An observer recorded all of the child's behavior, the environmental conditions under which it occurred, and its immediate consequences under conventional teacher guidance. This was done throughout the 2½-hour school session, daily, and for several days. The records gave detailed pictures of the behavior under study. In each case, it became apparent that the problem behavior almost always succeeded in attracting adult attention.

As soon as these records, technically termed "baseline" records, of the typical behavior of the child and teachers were obtained, teachers instituted a program of systematically giving differential attention to the child. When the undesired behavior occurred, they did not in any way attend to him, but remained absorbed in one of the many necessary activities of teachers with other children or with equipment. If the behavior occurred while a teacher was attending to the child, she at once turned to another child or task in a matter-of-fact and nonrejecting manner. Concurrently, teachers gave immediate attention to other behaviors of the child which were considered to be more desirable than the problem behavior. The net effect of these procedures was that the child could gain a great deal of adult attention if he refrained from engaging in "problem behavior." If under this regime of differential attention the problem behavior diminished to a stable low level at which it was no longer considered a problem, a second procedure was inaugurated to check out the functional relationship between changes in the child's behavior and the guidance procedures followed.

The second procedure was simply to reverse the first procedure. That is, when the problem behavior occurred, the teacher went immediately to the child and gave him her full, solicitous attention. If the behavior stopped, she turned to other children and tasks, remaining thus occupied until the behavior recurred. In effect, one sure way for the child to secure adult attention was to exhibit the problem behavior. This procedure was used to secure reasonably reliable information on whether the teachers' special program had indeed brought about the changes noted in the child's behavior. If adult attention was the critical factor in maintaining the behavior, the problem behavior should recur in stable form under these conditions. If it did so, this was evidence that adult attention was, technically speaking, a positive social reinforcer for the child's behavior.

The final stage of the study was, of course, to return to procedures in which attention was given at once and continuously for behaviors considered desirable. Concurrently, adult attention was again withheld or withdrawn as an immediate consequence of the problem behavior. As the problem disappeared and appropriate behaviors increased, the intense program of differential adult attention was gradually diminished until the child was receiving attention at times and in amounts normal for the teachers in the group. However, attention was given only on occasions of desirable behavior, and never (or very seldom) for the undesirable behavior.

Crying and Whining

Following the above procedures, a study was conducted on a four-year-old boy who cried a great deal after mild frustrations (Hart, Allen, Buell, Harris, and Wolf, 1964). This child averaged about eight full-fledged crying episodes each school morning. The baseline observations showed that this crying behavior consistently brought attention from the teachers, in the form of going to him and showing solicitous concern. During the following days, this behavior was simply ignored. (The only exceptions to this were to have been incidents in which the child had hurt himself considerably and was judged to have genuine grounds for crying. Naturally, his hurts were to be attended to. Such incidents, however, did not occur.) Ten days of ignoring the outcries, but giving approving attention for verbal and self-help behaviors, produced a steady weakening of the crying response to a nearly zero level. In the final five days of the interval, only one crying response was recorded. The number of crying episodes on successive days is graphed in cumulative form in Fig. 1.

During the next ten days, crying was again reinforced whenever it oc-

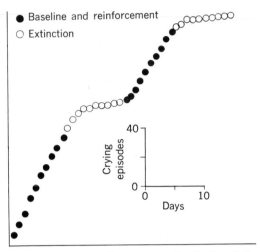

FIGURE 1. Cumulative record of the daily number of crying episodes.

curred, the teachers attending to the boy on these occasions without fail. At first, it was necessary to give attention for mere grimaces that might follow a bump. The daily crying episodes quickly rose to a rate almost as high as formerly. A second ten-day period of ignoring the outcries again produced a quick weakening of the response to a near-zero level, as is apparent in the figure. Crying remained at this low level thereafter, according to the informal judgment of the teachers.

The same procedures were used in another study of "operant crying" of a four-year-old boy, with the same general results.

Isolate Play

Two studies involved children who exhibited markedly solitary play behavior. Extremely little of their morning at nursery school was spent in any interaction with other children. Instead, these children typically played alone in a quiet area of the school room or the play yard, or interacted only with the teachers. For present purposes, both of these response patterns will be called "isolate play." Systematic observation showed that isolate play usually attracted or maintained the attention of a teacher, whereas social play with other children did so comparatively seldom.

A plan was initiated in which the teacher was to attend regularly if the child approached other children and interacted with them. On the other hand, the teacher was not to attend to the child so long as he engaged in solitary play. To begin with, attention was given when the child merely stood nearby, watching other children; then, when he played beside another child; and finally, only when he interacted with the other child. Teachers had to take special precautions that their attending behaviors did not result in drawing the child away from children and into interaction solely with the teacher. Two techniques were found particularly effective. The teacher directed her looks and comments to the other child or children, including the subject only as a participant in the play project. For example, "That's a big building you three boys are making; Bill and Tom and Jim (subject) are all working hard." Accessory materials were also kept at hand so that the teacher could bring a relevant item for the subject to add to the play: "Here's another plate for your tea party, Ann." In both isolate cases this new routine for giving adult attention produced the desired result: Isolate play declined markedly in strength while social play increased two- or threefold.

After about a week of the above procedure, the consequences of nonisolate and isolate play were reversed. The teachers no longer attended to the child's interactions with other children, but instead gave continuous attention to the child when he was alone. Within a week, or less, isolate play became the dominant form of activity in both cases.

The former contingencies were then reinstated: The teachers attended to social interactions by the child, and ignored isolate play as completely as they could. Again, isolate play declined sharply while social interaction increased as before. The results of one of these studies (Allen, Hart, Buell, Harris, and Wolf, 1964) are summarized in Fig. 2.

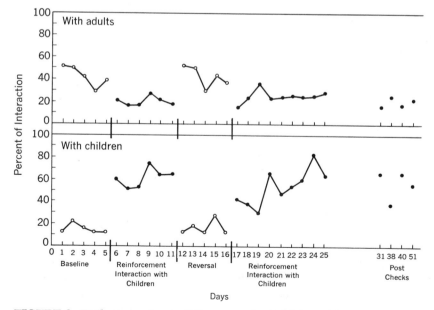

FIGURE 2. Daily percentages of time spent in social interaction with adults and with children during approximately two hours of each morning session.

Figure 2 shows the changes in behavior of a 4½-year-old girl under the different guidance conditions. The graph shows the percentage of play time that she spent in interaction with other children and the percentage of time spent with an adult. The remainder of her time was spent alone. It is apparent that only about 15% of this child's play time was spent in social play as long as the teachers attended primarily to her solitary play. But interacting behaviors rose to about 60% of total play time when the teachers attended only to her social play. At the same time, her interactions solely with teachers, not being reinforced, fell from their usual 40% of the child's playtime to about 20%. These were considered reasonable percentages for this nursery school child. During Days 17 through 25 the schedule of adult reinforcement of social play was gradually reduced to the usual amount of attention, given at the usual irregular intervals. Nevertheless, the social behavior maintained its strength, evidently becoming largely self-maintaining.

After Day 25, the teachers took care not to attend too often to the child when she was alone, but otherwise planned no special contingencies for attending. Four checks were made at later dates to see if the pattern of social behavior persisted. It is apparent (Fig. 2, Post Checks) that the change was durable, at least until Day 51. Further checks were not possible because of the termination of the school year.

A parallel study, of a three-year-old isolate boy (Johnston, Kelley, Harris, Wolf, and Baer, unpub.) yielded similar results showing the same pattern of rapid behavioral change in response to changing contingencies for adult attention. In the case of this boy, postchecks were made on three days during the early months of the school following the summer vacation period. The data showed that on those days his interaction with children averaged 55% of his play time. Apparently his social play was well established. Teachers reported that throughout the remainder of the year he continued to develop ease and skills in playing with his peers.

The immediate shifts in these children's play behavior may be partly due to the fact that they had already developed skills readily adapted to play with peers at school. Similar studies in progress are showing that, for some children, development of social play behaviors may require much longer periods of reinforcement.

Excessive Passivity

A fifth case (Johnston, Kelley, Harris, and Wolf, unpub.) involved a boy noted for his thoroughgoing lack of any sort of vigorous play activity. The teachers reported that this child consistently stood quietly about the play yard while other children ran, rode tricycles, and climbed on special climbing frames, trees, fences, and playhouses. Teachers also reported that they frequently attempted to encourage him, through suggestions or invitations, to engage in the more vigorous forms of play available. Teachers expressed concern over his apparent lack of strength and motor skills. It was decided to select a particular form of active play to attempt to strengthen. A wooden frame with ladders and platforms, called a climbing frame, was chosen as the vehicle for establishing this activity. The teachers attended at first to the child's mere proximity to the frame. As he came closer, they progressed to attending only to his touching it, climbing up a little, and finally to extensive climbing. Technically, this was reinforcement of successive approximations to climbing behavior. Fig. 3 shows the results of nine days of

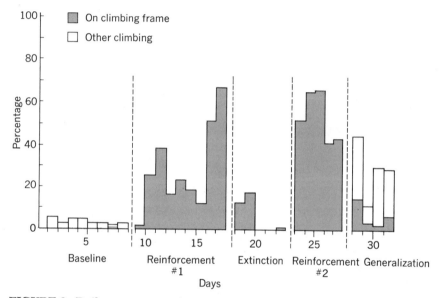

FIGURE 3. Daily percentage of time spent in using a climbing-frame apparatus. Open bars indicate time spent in climbing on other equipment.

this procedure, compared to a baseline of the preceding nine days. In this figure, black bars represent climbing on the climbing frame, and white bars represent climbing on any other equipment in the play yard. The height of the bars shows the percentage of the child's play time spent in such activities. It is clear that during the baseline period less than 10% of the child's time was spent in any sort of climbing activity, but that during the course of reinforcement with pleased adult attention for climbing on the frame, this behavior greatly increased, finally exceeding 50% of the child's morning. (Climbing on other objects was not scored during this period.) There then followed five days during which the teachers ignored any climbing on the frame, but attended to all other appropriate activities. The rate of climbing on the frame promptly fell virtually to zero, though the child climbed on other apparatus and was consistently given attention for this. Another five days of reinforcement of use of the climbing frame immediately restored the climbing-frame behavior to a high stable level, always in excess of 40% of the boy's play time. After this, the teachers began an intermittent program of reinforcement for climbing on any other suitable objects, as well as vigorous active play of all sorts, in an effort to generalize the increased vigorous activity. Frame-climbing weakened considerably, being largely replaced by other climbing activities, which were now scored again as data. Activities such as tricycle-riding and running were not systematically recorded due to difficulties in reliably scoring them. It is clear from the data obtained, however, that climbing activities were thoroughly generalized by this final procedure. Checks made the following school year in another play yard indicated that vigorous climbing had become a stable part of his behavior repertoire.

Summary and Discussion

The above studies systematically examined effects of adult attention on some problem behaviors of normal preschool children. The findings in each case clearly indicated that for these children adult attention was a strong positive reinforcer. That is, the behavior which was immediately followed by a teacher's giving the child attention rose rapidly to a high rate, and the rate fell markedly when adult attention was withheld from that behavior and concurrently given to an incompatible behavior. While it seems reasonable that for most young children adult attention may be a positive reinforcer, it is also conceivable that for some children adult attention may be a negative reinforcer. That is, the rate of a behavior may decrease when it is immediately followed by the attention of an adult, and rise again as soon as the adult withdraws. Actually, for a few children observed at the preschool, it has been thought that adult attention was a negative reinforcer. This seemed to be true, for instance, in the case of the climbing-frame child. Before the study was initiated, the teachers spent several weeks attempting to make themselves positively reinforcing to the child. This they did by staying at a little distance from him and avoiding attending directly to him until he came to them for something. At first, his approaches were only for routine help, such as buttoning his coat. On each of these occasions they took care to be smilingly friendly and helpful. In time, he began making approaches of other kinds, for instance, to show a toy. Finally, when a teacher approached him and commented with interest on what he was doing, he continued his play instead of stopping, hitting out, or running off. However, since his play remained lethargic and sedentary, it was decided that special measures were necessary to help him progress more rapidly. It was the use and effects of these special measures that constituted the study. Clearly, however, adult attention must be or become positively reinforcing to a child before it can be successfully used to help him achieve more desirably effective behaviors.

Studies such as those reported here seem to imply that teachers may help many children rapidly through systematic programming of their adult social reinforcements. However, further research in this area seems necessary. Some of our own studies now in progress suggest that guidance on the basis of reinforcement principles may perhaps bring rapidly into use only behaviors which are already available within the repertory of the child. If the desired behavior requires skills not yet in the child's repertory, then the process of developing those skills from such behaviors as the child has may require weeks or months. For example, a four-year-old child who could verbalize but who very rarely spoke was helped to speak freely within several days. On the other hand, a child of the same age who had never verbalized required a lengthy shaping process that involved reinforcing first any vocalization, and then gradually more appropriate sounds and combinations of sounds. The latter study was still incomplete at the close of a year of work. The time required to develop social behaviors in isolate children has likewise varied considerably, presumably for the same reasons.

Although the teachers conducted these studies in the course of carrying out their regular teaching duties, personnel in excess of the usual number were necessary. The laboratory school was staffed with one teacher to no more than six children, making it possible to assign to one teacher the role of principal "reinforcer teacher" in a study. This teacher was responsible for giving the child immediate attention whenever he behaved in specified ways. In addition, observers were hired and trained to record the behavior of each child studied. Each observer kept a record in ten-second intervals of his subject's behavior throughout each morning at school. Only with such staffing could reinforcement contingencies be precisely and consistently administered and their effects recorded.

Unless the effects are recorded, it is easy to make incorrect judgments about them. Two instances illustrate such fallibility. A boy in the laboratory preschool frequently pinched adults. Attempts by the teachers to ignore the behavior proved ineffective, since the pinches were hard enough to produce at least an involuntary startle. Teachers next decided to try to develop a substitute behavior. They selected patting as a logical substitute. Whenever the child reached toward a teacher, she attempted to forestall a pinch by saying, "Pat, Davey," sometimes adding, "Not pinch," and then strongly approving his patting, when it occurred. Patting behavior increased rapidly to a high level. The teachers agreed that they had indeed succeeded in reducing the pinching behavior through substituting patting. Then they were shown the recorded data. It showed clearly that although patting behavior was indeed high, pinching behavior continued at the previous level. Apparently, the teachers were so focused on the rise in patting behavior that, without the objective data, they would have erroneously concluded that development of a substitute behavior was in this case a successful technique. A second example illustrates a different, but equally undesirable, kind of erroneous assumption. A preschool child who had to wear glasses (Wolf, Risley, and Mees, 1964) developed a pattern of throwing them two or three times per day. Since this proved expensive, it was decided that the attendants should put him in his room for ten minutes following each glasses-throw. When the attendants were asked a few days later how the procedure was working, they said that the glasses-throwing had not diminished at all. A check of the records, however, showed that there was actually a marked decrease. The throwing dropped to zero within five days. Presumably, the additional effort involved in carrying out the procedure had given the attendants an exaggerated impression of the rate of the behavior. Recorded data, therefore, seem essential to accurate objective assessments of what has occurred.

The findings in the studies presented here accord generally with results of laboratory research on social development reviewed in this journal by Horowitz (1963). The importance of social reinforcement was also noted by Bandura (1963) in his investigations of imitation. Gallwey (1964) has replicated the study of an isolate child discussed here, with results "clearly confirmatory of the effectiveness of the technique." Further studies in school situations that can combine the function of research with that of service seem highly desirable.

REFERENCES

Allen, K., Eileen, Hart, Betty M., Buell, Joan S., Harris, Florence R., & Wolf, M. M. Effects of social reinforcement on isolate behavior of a nursery school child. *Child Develop.*, 1964, **35**, 511–518.

Bandura, Albert. The role of imitation in personality development. *J. Nursery Ed.*, 1963, **18**, 207–215.

Gallwey, Mary, Director of the Nursery School, Washington State University, Pullman, Wash., 1964. Personal communication.

Harris, Florence R., Johnston, Margaret K., Kelley, C. Susan, & Wolf, M. M. Effects of positive social reinforcement on regressed crawling of a nursery school child. *F. Ed. Psychol.*, 1964, **55**, 35–41.

Hart, Betty M., Allen, K. Eileen, Buell, John S., Harris, Florence R., & Wolf, M. M. Effects of social reinforcement on operant crying. *J. Exp. Child Psychol.* 1964, *I*, 145–153.

Horowitz, Frances Degen. Social reinforcement effects on child behavior. *J. Nursery Ed.*, 1963, **18**, 276–284.

Johnston, Margaret K., Kelley, C. Susan, Harris, Florence R., Wolf, M. M., & Baer, D. M. Effects of positive social reinforcement on isolate behavior of a nursery school child. Unpublished manuscript.

Johnston, Margaret K., Kelley, C. Susan, Harris, Florence R., & Wolf, M. M. An application of reinforcement principles to development of motor skills of a young child. *Child Development*, 1966, *37*, 379–387.

Landreth, Catherine. *Education of the Young Child.* New York: Wiley, 1942.

Read, Katherine H. *The Nursery School* (2nd ed.). Philadelphia: Saunders, 1955.

Standing, E. M. *Maria Montessori, Her Life and Work.* Fresno: American Library Guild, 1959.

Taylor, Katherine W. *Parents Cooperative Nursery Schools.* New York: Teachers College, Columbia University, 1954.

Wolf, Montrose M., Risley, T. R., & Mees, H. L. Application of operant conditioning procedures to the behavior problems of an autistic child. *Behav. Res. Ther.*, 1964, **1**, 305–312.

2.3 Friendship Status and the Effectiveness of Peers as Reinforcing Agents [1]

Willard W. Hartup

The purpose of this investigation was to study the performance of nursery school children on a simple, repetitive task under two conditions: with verbal approval administered by "liked" peers, and with approval administered by "disliked" peers. The study was motivated by the present paucity of empirical evidence concerning the effectiveness of peers as reinforcing agents.

Children have been used as Ss in numerous studies of social reinforcement (Horowitz, 1963; Stevenson, 1964). Almost exclusively, however, investigators have explored the effects of various contingencies of adult attentiveness and approval. Only one study has appeared in which peers were used as reinforcing agents (Patterson and Anderson, 1964). That study, plus one related investigation (concerning the incentive value of photographs of peers; Horowitz, 1962), constitutes the entire literature on the effectiveness of peers as reinforcing agents.

To be sure, many studies have focused on the relation between sociometric factors (social status, popularity, and the like) and strength of influence on peer behavior (e.g., Polansky, Lippitt, and Redl, 1950; Harvey and Rutherford, 1960; Harvey and Consalvi, 1960). In none of these studies, however, has the capacity of peers to reinforce the performance of other children been assessed. As Patterson and Anderson (1964) point out, information concerning the reinforcing effectiveness of peers is sorely needed in view of the widely held assumption that peers are second only to parents as socializing influences in most cultures.

Friendship status was selected as the independent variable in the present

[1] The author gratefully acknowledges the collaborative assistance of Barbara Boat, Robert G. Miller, Carolyn Thomson, and Frances Zavala in conducting this study. The data were collected at the Institute of Child Behavior and Development, State University of Iowa.

Reprinted from The *Journal of Experimental Child Psychology* 1964, **1**, 154–162, by permission of the author and Academic Press.

study for two reasons. First, frequencies and contingencies of reinforcement probably differ in the interactions of young children with liked as opposed to disliked peers. It has been found, for example, that preschool children who have high sociometric status engage more frequently in associative and friendly interaction with others than children who are not socially accepted (Marshall and McCandless, 1957). Such differences may well be antecedent to differences in the incentive value of attentiveness and approval by liked as opposed to disliked peers. Related to this conjecture is Horowitz's finding (1962) that photographs of "best friends" possess greater incentive value for younger nursery school children than photographs of "neutral" peers.

Second, when peers serve as reinforcing agents they may elicit a variety of responses by the S some of which may be relevant to task performance. For example, Patterson and Anderson (1964) report low negative correlations between performance increases and frequency of attention-getting behaviors shown by elementary school Ss during experimental sessions. It seems plausible that liked and disliked peers could differentially elicit responses such as bids for attention (which interfere with performance) and mild anxiety (which could facilitate performance).

The preceding paragraphs furnish the rationale for selecting friendship status as the independent variable in this study. No formal hypotheses guided this investigation, however, because so few data exist concerning the motivational and associative factors involved in peer influences on young children's behavior.

METHOD

Subjects

Ss consisted of 20 girls and 16 boys who attended two classes at a laboratory nursery school. Ages in this sample ranged between 4 years, 3 months and 5 years, 7 months. All Ss had attended nursery school for 6 months or more.

Male and female Ss in each preschool class were separately assigned, on a random basis, to Groups LP (reinforced by a liked peer) and DP (reinforced by a disliked peer). The 18 Ss in each of these groups were then divided at their respective median ages. These medians were between 5 years, 0 months and 5 years, 1 month for both Groups LP and DP. Thus four subgroups were constituted for the experiment: LP 4-year-olds, LP 5-year-olds, DP 4-year-olds, and DP 5-year-olds.

Assessment of Friendship Status

A female E administered a picture sociometric test (Moore and Updegraff, 1964) individually to each potential subject. The child was shown a board containing $2\frac{1}{2} \times 3$ inch photographs of the children in his nursery school class. The S was asked to name each child and was then asked to "look over all the pictures very carefully and find someone you especially like at school." Four such choices were elicited. Then *E* said "Now I want you to find someone you don't like very much at school." Four of these choices were also obtained.

In the experimental sessions which followed, each *S* in Group LP was reinforced by the child named first among the *S*'s positive choices on the sociometric. Each subject in Group DP was paired with his first negative choice.[2]

Apparatus

The apparatus was a modification of that described by Stevenson and Fahel (1961). It consisted of a 24 × 30 inch table top with two 6 × 8 × 5 inch bins on the side nearer the *S*. The left bin contained approximately 500 green, yellow, and white marbles. A plate, with six ⅝ inch randomly placed holes, covered the right bin. Beneath the right bin was a microswitch attached to an electronic counter which served to count each marble that was dropped into the bin. A panel, 3 inches high and running the length of the apparatus, was mounted behind the marble bins. Attached to this panel on the side opposite the *S* were two 6 V lights, one red and one blue. The lights were activated and the marble count recorded from a console in an observation booth.

Procedure

A testing sequence was established which permitted all the available children to serve as *Ss* (with one exception in each preschool class). Children who were designated as reinforcing agents participated first as *Ss*, then were trained in the reinforcement procedure during a second session, and served as reinforcing agents during a requisite number of subsequent sessions. One child, who did not first serve as a *S*, was needed as a reinforcing agent in each preschool class to begin the testing sequence. The two children picked for this purpose were randomly chosen from their respective classes before the other 36 *Ss* were assigned to subgroups as described above. Three women graduate students supervised the testing sessions.

[2] In view of recent findings concerning sex-of-experimenter effects on socially reinforced performance (Stevenson, 1961), it is pertinent to report that neither sex of reinforcing agent nor sex of agent relative to sex of *S* were seriously confounded by this selection procedure. Of 18 reinforcing agents in each experimental group, nine in Group LP and eleven in Group DP were boys. Eleven LP *Ss* had reinforcing agents of the same sex; nine DP *Ss* had same-sex reinforcers. Data analysis showed no performance differences associated with either sex of *S* or sex of agent.

It also should be noted that chronological age was, to some extent, confounded with preschool class attended, i.e., most of the 5-year-olds were in one class and most of the 4-year-olds in the other. Subsequent analyses, however, showed no significant performance differences between the two preschool classes.

Training the reinforcing agent. The reinforcing agent was brought to the laboratory and asked to be a "signalman" for the marble game. He was seated behind the apparatus and shown the panel lights. It was explained that these lights lit up when certain marbles hit a wire in the box and that the lights would enable him to tell S how he was doing. E then demonstrated the reinforcement procedure. After this, it was explained that the reinforcing agent should say "That's fine," when the red light came on and "That's good" to the blue. E coached the agent in this task, then dropped marbles, corrected mistakes, and approved correct responses. This continued until the reinforcing agent performed with consistent accuracy, usually a period of 5 or 6 minutes. Then E went out of the room and returned with an adult who dropped marbles for approximately 5 minutes while the agent practiced the reinforcement procedure. Corrections were given only if the reinforcing agent failed to respond or if accuracy declined noticeably. The session was terminated with the award of a small toy.

Criterion task. The S and the reinforcing agent were brought to the laboratory together, and S was asked to wait in an adjoining room while the game was being prepared. The reinforcing agent was then seated at the apparatus for a brief practice session. He was told to read the lights so that S would know how he was doing, to speak loudly, and to refrain from bothering S except to tell him "what the lights say." S was then brought in and the reinforcing agent was asked to wait in the other room. The instructions to S were: "The way to play this game is to pick up a marble from here and put it into one of these holes—like this. You can put them into any of these holes. Your job is to put as many marbles into these holes as there is time for. Only remember, you must pick the marbles up one at a time. I'll be sitting back of this screen [a one-way screen which completely concealed E] doing some work." E then moved behind the screen and asked S to go ahead. After 1 minute, E came from behind the screen and said, "OK, you stop now and we'll get_____ [the reinforcing agent] to come and watch you play the game."

E then said, when the reinforcing agent was seated across from S, "Now remember_____, you be a good signalman. And you,_____, put as many marbles in as you have time for. I will tell you when to stop." The session continued for 6 minutes, during which light signals were presented to the reinforcing agent once every 20 seconds. The light signals were presented in random order with the restriction that the two lights were flashed an equal number of times. If marbles were dropped on the floor E called over the screen and said they could be gotten later. If the reinforcing agent initiated conversation, was distracting in other ways, or ignored the lights, he was admonished gently and asked to remember that his job was to be the signalman. Interruptions were remarkably infrequent, but they did occur. After 6 minutes (excluding time consumed by interruptions) the session was terminated and both children were given toys.

Response Measure

The number of marbles dropped through the holes during each minute of the session was recorded by an observer. The number dropped during the first minute (while S was alone) was regarded as a base rate score. The base rate was then subtracted from the number of marbles inserted during each succeeding minute to furnish six difference scores for each S. These difference scores were used as indices of the effects of the reinforcing agent on S's response rate.

Mean base rate scores were 18.8, 19.4, 19.0, and 16.8 for LP 4-year-olds, LP 5-year-olds, DP 4-year-olds, and DP 5-year-olds, respectively. Analysis of these scores showed that the differences between Groups LP and DP and between 4- and 5-year-olds were not significant. These means closely approximate the midpoint between the mean base rates of 12.7 for 3- and 4-year-old children and 25.9 for 6- and 7-year-old children reported by Stevenson (1961). Thus, the base rates obtained under the conditions of the present study (peer reinforcing agent absent and adult E concealed) are comparable to base rate scores obtained under somewhat different circumstances (adult E present).

Correlations were computed between base rate and rate during each of the 6 reinforced minutes for Groups LP and DP separately. These correlations ranged between 0.37 and 0.86, with a mean of 0.66. Although relatively high, this average is somewhat below the intratask average correlation for older subjects of 0.86 reported by Stevenson (1964).

RESULTS

The data were analyzed by means of a Type III analysis of variance (Lindquist, 1953) in which the between-Ss factors were friendship status and chronological age and the within-Ss factor was minutes in the session. The results of this analysis, presented in Table 1, reveal that the effect of friendship status was significant ($p < 0.01$) as was the effect of chronological age ($p < 0.05$). Neither the effect of minutes in the session nor any of the interactions were significant. Figure 1 shows that performance was better maintained in Group DP than in Group LP and by 5-year-olds than by 4-year-olds. Figure 1 also shows that performance was enhanced among 5-year-old Ss in Group DP. In all other subgroups, performance deteriorated during the session, more so under some conditions than others.

DISCUSSION

Liked and disliked peers differentially affected performance in this study. A considerable decrement in response rate was precipitated in Group LP while in Group DP performance improved among 5-year-olds and deteriorated only slightly among 4-year-olds. The performance of the 5-year-olds in Group DP is comparable to the results of other social reinforcement studies with young children (e.g., Stevenson, 1961). Patterson and Anderson (1964)

TABLE 1. SUMMARY OF ANALYSIS OF VARIANCE OF DIFFERENCE
SCORES FOR 4- AND 5-YEAR-OLD SUBJECTS
REINFORCED BY LIKED AND DISLIKED PEERS

Source	df	MS	F
Liked vs. disliked reinforcer (A)	1	654.52	7.82 [b]
Age (B)	1	450.67	5.38 [a]
A × B	1	71.18	—
Error (b)	32	83.73	
Minutes (C)	5	24.74	1.90
C × A	5	26.64	2.04
C × B	5	9.94	—
C × A × B	5	9.31	—
Error (w)	160	13.03	

[a] $p < 0.05$
[b] $p < 0.01$

reported generally stronger positive effects of peer reinforcement than those obtained in this study, but their Ss and reinforcing agents were elementary rather than nursery school children.

Although it is clear from the results that liked and disliked peers differentially influenced performance, it is important to note that there are at least two possible determinants of this difference. Base-rate scores were obtained in a peer-absent situation while subsequent scores were obtained when S was in the presence of a peer who gave periodic verbal approval. It is possible that the performance differences obtained are attributable to differential effects of the *presence* of liked and disliked peers, differential effects of *approval* by liked and disliked peers, or some combination of both. Further study is required in order to determine which, if not both, of these factors is operative in producing the differential changes in rate associated with friendship status of the reinforcing agent.

The sharp decrement noted in the difference scores for Group LP suggests that the presence and comments of a liked peer interfered with marble-dropping. Quite probably friendly approach responses and bids for attention are more frequently reinforced in nursery school play by peers whom the child subsequently labels "someone I like" than by peers who are ultimately designated "someone I don't like." Anecdotal material gathered during the experimental session suggests that such social learning does take place and that it generalizes to the laboratory situation. Ten Ss in Group LP intensively attempted to converse with the reinforcing agent or to look at him during the 6-minute response period; the records of only five Ss in Group DP were similarly noted. Since bids for attention tend to interfere with

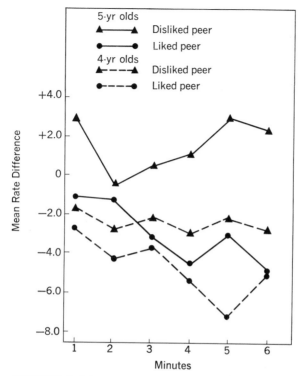

FIGURE 1. Mean rate difference scores for 6 one-minute intervals for 4- and 5-year-old Ss reinforced by liked and disliked peers.

performance on marble-dropping tasks (Patterson and Anderson, 1964), it is possible that differential performance by Groups LP and DP resulted from differential capacity of liked and disliked peers to elicit interfering dependency responses. The present data provide some further evidence on this point. Within Group LP, the mean difference scores for "talkers" and "nontalkers" were −5.77 and −1.58, respectively. A t-test indicated that the difference between these means is significant ($t = 2.54$, $df = 16$, $p < 0.05$). Ss in Group DP who "talked" also differed from those who did not attempt to interact with the reinforcing agent, but not significantly (−2.00 and +0.17, respectively).

An alternative explanation of the results is that the performance decrement in Group LP reflects conditions such as increasing boredom or fatigue, while other factors counteracted this trend in Group DP. It is very likely that preschoolers attach the sociometric designation "I don't like him" to peers who are threatening. With respect to this assumption, Moore (1964) found a negative correlation between popularity (based on both positive and negative sociometric choices) and aggressiveness as perceived by the peer group in nursery school. Aggressive, disliked peers could enhance performance on a socially reinforced task in several ways: (a) anxiety may be elicited, increasing the level of general motivation in the subject; (b) increased orientation to the task may be evoked by which the subject is able to avoid contact with the anxiety-producing stimulus; and (c) the nonaggressive attention and approval of a peer who is ordinarily frightening to the subject may be of particularly great incentive value. These are intriguing hypotheses for further investigation.

The results of the present study do not articulate straightforwardly with the previous findings of Patterson and Anderson (1964). These investigators found that friendship status affected changes in hole-preference on a marble-dropping task (a measure not employed in the present study) but did not affect response rate. Children in second and third grade showed greater changes in hole-preference when they were reinforced by friends, but fourth-graders showed greater changes when they were reinforced by nonfriends (not necessarily disliked). It would appear that the present findings parallel the findings of Patterson and Anderson with fourth-graders but not with second- and third-graders. However, methodological differences between the two studies are great and must be considered in interpreting results. Extensive developmental investigation of peer effectiveness as reinforcing agents, with a single methodology, is indicated in order to clarify the ambiguities noted here.

Although greater performance decrements were noted for 4-year-olds than 5-year-olds, this finding is not particularly relevant to the main purpose of the present study. It is possible that social reinforcement by peers of 4-year-old children has less incentive value than the attention and approval of 5-year-old peers. The age difference obtained, however, more probably stems from attention and fatigue differences between the two age groups.

SUMMARY

Performance on a marble-dropping task of 36 nursery school children was studied under two conditions. Half the Ss were given continuous attention and periodic verbal approval ("good," "fine") by liked peers; half were reinforced by disliked peers. Rate of marble-dropping was better maintained during the 6-minute testing period when the reinforcing agent was a disliked rather than a liked peer. Also, performance of 5-year-olds was better maintained than performance of 4-year-olds.

REFERENCES

Harvey, O. J., & Consalvi, C. Status and conformity to pressures in informal groups. J. abnorm. soc. Psychol., 1960, 60, 182–187.

Harvey, O. J., & Rutherford, Jeanne. Status in the informal group: Influence and influencibility at differing age levels. *Child Develpm.*, 1960, **31**, 377–386.

Horowitz, Frances D. Incentive value of social stimuli for preschool children. *Child. Develpm.*, 1962, **33**, 111–116.

Horowitz, Frances D. Social reinforcement effects on child behavior. *J. nur. Educ.*, 1963, **18**, 276–284.

Lindquist, E. F. *Design of experiments in psychology and education.* Boston: Houghton Mifflin, 1953.

Marshall, Helen R., & McCandless, B. R. A study in prediction of social behavior of preschool children. *Child Develpm.*, 1957, **28**, 149–150.

Moore, Shirley G. The relation between children's sociometric status and their social behaviors as perceived by peers. Unpublished manuscript, Univ. of Minnesota, 1964.

Moore, Shirley G., & Updegraff, Ruth. Sociometric status of preschool children related to age, sex, nurturance-giving, and dependency. *Child Develpm.*, 1964, **35**, 519–524.

Patterson, G. R., & Anderson, D. Peers as social stimuli. *Child Develpm.*, 1964, **35**, 951–960.

Polansky, N., Lippitt, R., & Redl, F. An investigation of behavioral contagion in groups. *Human Relat.*, 1950, **3**, 319–348.

Stevenson, H. W. Social reinforcement of children's behavior. Submitted for publication, 1964.

Stevenson, H. W. Social reinforcement wtih children as a function of CA, sex of E, and sex of S. *J. abnorm. soc. Psychol.*, 1961, **63**, 147–154.

Stevenson, H. W., and Fahel, Leila S. The effect of social reinforcement on the performance of institutionalized and non-institutionalized normal and feeble-minded children. *J. Pers.*, 1961, **29**, 136–147.

2.4   Social Reinforcer Effectiveness as a Function of the Relationship between Child and Adult [1]

Norma McCoy and Edward Zigler

Considerable evidence has now been presented indicating that a number of verbal responses, for example, "good," "right," emitted by adults are effective in influencing children's behavior. Attention has been given recently to

[1] This research was supported by Research Grant MH-06809 from the National Institute of Mental Health, United States Public Health Service. The authors wish to express their thanks to Dora Levy, Principal of Edgewood Elementary School for her cooperation and assistance during the course of this study. The authors are also indebted to Irvin Child and Jacob Gewirtz for their insightful criticisms of an earlier version of this paper.

Reprinted from the *Journal of Personality and Social Psychology*, 1965, **1**, 604–612, by permission of the authors and The American Psychological Association.

the degree to which a variety of situational, subject, and experimenter variables influence the effectiveness of these social reinforcers (Gewirtz, 1954; Gewirtz & Baer, 1958a, 1958b; Gewirtz, Baer, & Roth, 1958; Patterson, 1959; Patterson, Littman, & Hinsey, in press; Patterson & Ludwig, 1961; Stevenson, 1961; Stevenson, Hickman, & Knights, 1963; Walters & Ray, 1960; Zigler, 1961, 1963b, in press; Zigler & Kanzer, 1962; Zigler & Williams, 1963). Although the effects of a number of variables have been demonstrated, the process or processes by which these verbal responses of an adult acquire their reinforcing properties are far from clear. The simplest and most commonly advanced view is that parents or caretakers frequently pair positive verbal responses with primary reinforcers, and these responses thus acquire their reinforcing property. This view further holds that through generalization, these responses are also reinforcing when employed by other adults.

The difficulty in testing this position can be seen in recent studies which compare the effectiveness of social reinforcers dispensed by the mother or father of the child being reinforced or by a strange adult (Patterson, 1959; Patterson et al., in press; Patterson & Ludwig, 1961; Stevenson et al., 1963). The most logical prediction generated by the number-of-pairings position is that social reinforcers dispensed by parents would be more effective than social reinforcers dispensed by strange adults. However, Patterson (1959) found that although both fathers and strangers were positively reinforcing, fathers were not generally more reinforcing than were strange adults. Taking a somewhat different tack, Stevenson et al. (1963) predicted that parents would be less effective social reinforcers than would strange adults. Although subscribing to the number-of-pairings position, these investigators felt that the continuous supportive role played by parents results in the child being relatively satiated on his parents' supportive comments. Although Stevenson et al. did find that strangers were more effective reinforcing agents than were parents, their results remain surprising. These investigators, employing a measure involving the change in the rate of responding with the onset of reinforcement, found that the fathers' supportive comments were negative reinforcers for both boys and girls and that the mothers' supportive comments were negative reinforcers for boys and positive reinforcers for girls. These findings are hardly in keeping with the number-of-pairings hypothesis even when augmented by the satiation notion. In order to explain their findings, Stevenson et al. suggested that fathers in particular and men in general induced anxiety in children which inflated the rate of responding during the base period. The view that greater identification exists between girls and their mothers than between boys and either their mothers or fathers was employed to explain the finding that mothers and female adults were effective positive reinforcers with girls.

These explanations certainly suggest that it is inappropriate to view social reinforcers as operating in an automatic or mechanical manner or that the key variable is simply the number of pairings that these reinforcers have had with primary reinforcement. It would appear, rather, that the reinforcing agent and the responses he makes are complex stimuli which activate a variety of emotional, motivational, and cognitive responses. Depending upon the particular measure of reinforcer effectiveness employed, the responses of the child thus activated can result in either a facilitation or an attenuation in the effectiveness of the adults' supportive comments. Although reporting certain findings not in keeping with those of Stevenson et al. (1963), Patterson et al. (in press) have also taken the view that the reinforcing adult is best conceptualized as being both a general reinforcer and a complex cue eliciting a wide array of responses.

The problem in conceptualizing the reinforcing adult as the elicitor of responses is the difficulty in predicting just what responses he elicits and how such responses influence his effectiveness as a generalized reinforcer. The complexity of this problem has been noted by Patterson et al. (in press), and their effort to unravel it by investigating the relationship between parental practices in the home and the effectiveness of parents as reinforcers has been truly pioneering work.

Zigler and his colleagues (cf. Zigler, 1963b, in press) have also asserted that the typical experimental situation in which an adult verbally reinforces a child must be viewed as a complex interaction between adult and child. While also treating the adult as an elicitor, they have not been concerned with the entire spectrum of responses which are elicited in the child as a function of his total social conditioning history. Instead they have focused on those general tendencies elicited by the reinforcing adult which influence the adult's effectiveness as a reinforcer independent of the particular task being employed to assess this effectiveness. The view here is that while the adult is both an elicitor and a reinforcer, it should be possible to deduce certain general principles which determine the adult's reinforcer effectiveness. These investigators have argued that the history of every child is such that any adult elicits both a positive (approach) and negative (avoidance) reaction tendency. Thus, every interaction between an adult and child is viewed as a conflict situation for the child.

Stating that the reinforcing adult elicits a positive-reaction tendency in the child is simply another way of asserting that the history of all children is such that adults have been paired with primary or secondary reinforcers frequently enough to make adults general-positive reinforcers. What has received minimal attention in the literature is that parents and adults are not only general-positive reinforcers but through their history of pairings with punishing events, are general-negative reinforcers as well. Thus, how reinforcing the adult is for the child will depend on the interaction between both these positive and negative tendencies. Clearly, then, the relative magnitude of the tendencies will depend on the relative amount of positive and negative experiences the child has had with adults. Within such a framework the child minimally affected by social reinforcers would not necessarily be viewed as having low motivation for social reinforcers; he could be one whose negative-reaction tendency inhibits him from freely responding in order to secure positive reinforcement.

In the present study, the hypothesis was tested that the child's positive- and negative-reaction tendencies interact in determining an adult's effectiveness as a reinforcer. The assumption was made that the magnitude of these tendencies is affected by the general quality of the relationship existing between the reinforcing adult and the child. Three experimental conditions were employed. In the first, the reinforcing adult was a stranger; in the second, she was a familiar but neutral person; and in the third, she was a familiar and positive person. The general prediction tested was that the adult would be least reinforcing in the first condition, more reinforcing in the second condition, and most reinforcing in the third condition. This prediction was derived from the position that the strange adult would elicit the child's negative-reaction tendency which in turn would reduce the adult's effectiveness as a social reinforcer. In the familiar-neutral condition, the child would have learned that this particular adult was not a punishing agent; and this knowledge would reduce the child's negative-reaction tendency towards the adult prior to the reinforcing situation. The familiar-positive condition was viewed as one in which not only the negative-reaction tendency would be reduced but one in which the positive tendency would be enhanced as well.

A test of this position demands independent measures of both the child's positive and negative tendencies. As in previous studies (Zigler, 1961; Zigler, Hodgden, & Stevenson, 1958), the total time the child elected to play a two-part satiation task was employed as the measure of his positive-reaction tendency. A cosatiation index, that is, a score reflecting the relative amount of time spent playing each part of the game, was employed to assess the child's negative-reaction tendency. That this score is a valid measure of a child's negative-reaction tendency is suggested by a number of earlier studies in which relatively low cosatiation scores were found for subjects whose life histories were characterized by a high incidence of negative social encounters (Kounin, 1941; Zigler, 1961; Zigler et al., 1958). The rationale of this measure as advanced by Zigler (1961) is as follows: If the child has no negative-reaction tendency, he should play the first part of the game until he is satiated on the social reinforcers being dispensed. Such a child should play the second part for a shorter period of time than the first. The greater the negative-reaction tendency of the child, the shorter should be the time he spends on the first part. However, during the first part he is socially reinforced; he learns that the adult is not punishing and furthermore, he discovers upon the termination of the first part that he can indeed end the interaction whenever he likes. This should reduce the negative-reaction tendency with which he begins the second part. How long such a child plays the second part depends upon how large a negative-reaction tendency was present to be reduced during the first part. The greater the child's initial negative-reaction tendency, the greater the likelihood that he will play the second part longer than the first.

Further evidence that the cosatiation index is a valid measure of the child's negative-reaction tendency was provided by Shallenberger and Zigler (1961). These investigators found that both normal and retarded children who received the negative pretraining condition prior to the two-part game had lower cosatiation scores than children in a positive pretraining condition. For normal children, evidence to date suggests that the reduction in the negative-reaction tendency during Part I of the game is balanced by the satiation effects. Such children play Part II for about the same length of time as Part I. Thus, employing the two-part cosatiation procedure, the specific prediction made was that children in the stranger condition should play Part II about as long as Part I, while both familiar groups should show a marked decrease in playing time from Part I to Part II.

METHOD

Subjects

The sample consisted of 36 first- and second-grade boys attending the Edgewood Elementary School in New Haven, Connecticut. The school was located in a middle-class neighborhood having a predominantly Jewish population. Subjects were picked at random from all first- and second-grade boys with the restriction that no boy was included who was judged a behavior problem by the teacher or principal. The mean age of the group was 7.2 years. The sample was restricted to boys in order to avoid the complications of sex effects.

Experimenter

The experimenter was a 28-year-old female PhD in child psychology who had had considerable experience testing subjects in studies investigating social reinforcement effects on children. The experimenter was aware of the hypothesis under test, and any bias that this may have produced must be considered an uncontrolled variable in this experiment. In order to diminish the effect of any such bias, a highly structured procedure was employed during the administration of the experimental game. Considering the care exercised by the experimenter, it is the authors' belief that any examiner bias had minimal effect on the findings.

Experimental Manipulations

The sample was divided randomly into three groups of 12 boys each with the restriction that the mean CA of the groups be approximately equal. The three experimental conditions were:

Stranger (St).   The experimenter had no contact with any of the subjects in this condition prior to the administration of the experimental task.

Familiar-neutral (FN).   On three occasions the 12 subjects in this condition were taken from the classroom in two groups of 6 subjects each. The three sessions were separated by intervals of 1 week. Each group of 6 subjects was taken to an empty classroom and given drawing paper and attractive art materials consisting of pastels in 12 colors in Session 1, felt-top markers in 6 colors in Session 2, and presto paints in 6 colors in Session 3. The instructions were as follows:

> Hello. As you remember [Sessions 2 and 3 only] my name is Miss _____ and I've brought some things for you to have some fun with. I will give each of you some of these pastels [markers, paints] and some paper and you can make a picture of anything you like. You can begin as soon as you get some materials.

Following the instructions the experimenter distributed the art materials and told the subjects that she was going to be busy at her desk (located in the front of the room) and requested that they work quietly until it was time to return to their classroom. Any further comments by a child were reacted to minimally or not at all. Questions were answered briefly and the child was reminded to work quietly because the experimenter was very busy. If the children attempted to interact among themselves, the experimenter again requested that they work quietly. Very few children made more than one attempt to interact with the experimenter, and very little effort was required to keep the children quiet.

Familiar-positive (FP).   The initial procedure for this group was the same as for the FN group. Following the instructions, however, the experimenter responded at some length to all questions and comments as she passed out the materials. As the children began to work, the experimenter approached each boy individually and talked with him about what he was drawing. The experimenter then continued to interact with each subject attempting to establish a warm, positive relationship by being complimentary, helpful, and responsive. By the end of the three sessions the experimenter was employing the subjects' first names in her interactions with them. One boy in this group was absent for Session 3 but was retained in the study. Another boy was withdrawn from school during the course of the study; and this group, therefore, had 11 rather than 12 subjects.

Experimental Game (Marble-in-the-Hole)

The experimental game was a two-part satiation task consisting of a simple monotonous repetitive game called Marble-in-the-Hole which has been described previously (Zigler, 1961, 1963a). The game was made up of a wooden box having two holes on top. Inside the box was a chute connecting the holes with a single opening at the bottom of the box. The opening was filled with green and yellow marbles, thus insuring the subject a steady supply of marbles. The apparatus was automated so that it recorded the length of time the child played and the number of marbles he inserted. The subject's task was to insert a marble of one color into one hole and a marble of another color into the other hole.

Part I.   The game was placed in front of the subject with the experimenter directly behind it and facing the child. The experimenter said:

> Hello. As you remember [with FN and FP subjects only] my name is Miss _____, and we are going to play some games today. This is a game we call Marble-in-the-Hole. I'll tell you how to play it. You see these marbles. Some of them are green and some of them are yellow. They go in these holes. The green ones go in this hole [the experimenter's left] and the yellow ones go in this hole [the experimenter's right] [the experimenter pointed to the appropriate holes]. Now show me a green marble. Put it in the hole it goes in. Now show me a yellow marble. Put it in the hole it goes in. You can put as many marbles in the holes as you want to. You tell me when you want to stop. Remember, when you want to stop just tell me. OK, ready? Begin.

The subject then played the game until he indicated that he wished to stop, either by telling the experimenter he wanted to stop or by not inserting a marble for 30 seconds. A 15-minute time limit was used.

Part II.   After the subject indicated that he wished to stop, the experimenter said:

> Now I'll tell you how to play *this* game. This time we put the yellow marbles in this hole [the experimenter's left] and the green marbles in this hole [the experimenter's right]. Put a yellow marble where it goes. You can put as many marbles in the holes as you want to. You tell me when you want to stop. Remember, when you want to stop just tell me. OK, ready? Begin.

The subject again played the game until he indicated that he wished to stop, either by telling the experimenter he wanted to stop or by not inserting a marble for 30 seconds. A 15-minute time limit again was employed.

Procedure

The St subjects were administered the Marble-in-the-Hole game prior to any contact between the experimenter and FN and FP subjects. This was done so that none of the St subjects would become familiar with the experimenter by seeing her in the school or by hearing about her from subjects in the other groups. The FN and FP subjects were administered the Marble-in-the-Hole game 1 week following their third experimental session.

The subjects were tested individually in a small conference room. The subject was verbally reinforced twice a minute for as long as he played either part of the game. (The decision to verbally reinforce the child rather than to employ attention alone as a reinforcer was made in light of studies which have indicated that an attention-only condition has differential effects depending upon the reinforcement condition that has preceded it—Crandall, 1963; Stevenson & Snyder, 1960. While it might appear than an attention-only condition would provide the purest measure of the child's reaction tendencies, the particular contrast effects introduced by such a procedure mitigated against its use.) Reinforcements were administered approximately at the 15-second and 45-second points within each minute. Five statements were used: "You're doing very well," "That's very good," "You know how to play this game very well," "That's fine," and "You're really good at this game." These statements were made in a predetermined random order established separately for each subject. The experimenter was warm and friendly, smiling and nodding when administering the praise; but she did not respond to any attempts by the subject to engage her in conversation. If the subject dropped a marble on the floor, he was told not to pursue it but simply to continue playing the game.

RESULTS

The three groups' time scores are presented in Table 1 and Figure 1. Since the means and variances of these scores were correlated, a logarithmic

TABLE 1. PERFORMANCE OF THE THREE GROUPS ON THE EXPERIMENTAL GAME

Group N		Part 1		Part II		Total		Part I — Part II	Part I — Part II / Part I + Part II
		Min-utes	Log minutes	Min-utes	Log minutes	Min-utes	Log minutes		
Stranger	12	1.22	.3095	1.31	.3193	2.53	.6288	−.10	.0071
Familiar-neutral	12	6.72	.7327	2.85	.4702	9.57	1.2029	3.87	.3203
Familiar-positive	11	7.96	.8725	5.39	.6815	13.35	1.5540	2.56	.2455

transformation of the time scores ($\log X + 1$) was made. The log times spent by each group on each part of the game were subjected to a Lindquist Type I analysis of variance (Lindquist, 1956). The method of unweighted means was used to handle the unequal number of subjects in three groups. The results of this analysis are presented in Table 2.

A Pearson r of .977 was found between the subject's total time scores and the total number of marbles inserted. An analysis of the number-of-marbles-inserted data resulted in findings highly similar to those found with the time scores.

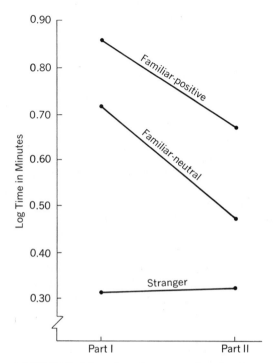

FIGURE 1. Mean log time spent by the three groups in part I and part II of Marble-in-the-Hole game.

As can be seen in Figure 1, the significant groups effect supported the prediction concerning how the groups would differ in the total time spent on the game. Further analyses of the total log-time scores using the between-subjects mean square as the estimate of error variance revealed that each group differed significantly from the other two. The FP group played significantly longer than both the FN ($t = 2.23$, $p < .05$) and St ($t = 5.88$, $p < .001$) groups. The St group also differed significantly from the FN group ($t = 3.73$, $p < .001$). The significant Parts effect reflected the overall tendency of the three groups to play Part I ($M \log = .6315$) longer than Part II ($M \log = .4849$). However, the St group did not contribute to this effect; and it was the failure of this group to decrease from Part I to Part II that resulted in the significant Conditions $\times$ Parts interaction. The performance pattern of the three groups on the two parts of the game supported the prediction that the two familiar groups would evidence a greater decrease from Part I to Part II than would the St group.

The prediction concerning the decrease from Part I to Part II was tested further through a direct examination of difference scores for each subject. A variation of Kounin's (1941) cosatiation index was employed to compute relative difference scores (Part I — Part II/Part I + Part II). Mean relative difference scores for each of the three groups are presented in Table 1. A simple one-way analysis of variance of these scores was significant ($F_{2/32} = 3.64$, $p < .05$). Further analyses revealed that the FN group had a significantly ($t = 2.59$, $p < .02$) greater decrease from Part I to Part II than did the St group. The difference between the FP and FN groups was not significant ($t < 1$), while the difference between the FP and St groups reached a borderline level of significance ($t = 1.93$, $p < .10$).

An examination was made of the number of subjects in each group who played Part II longer than Part I. As noted earlier, this pattern has been found in socially deprived children and in normal children who had negative experiences with an adult prior to being reinforced on the Marble-in-the-Hole game. The number of children playing Part II longer than Part I in the St, FN, and FP groups was seven, one, and two, respectively. The familiar groups were combined and a 2×2 contingency table was set up. Employing the Fisher exact test, this difference was found to be significant ($p < .01$). However, one subject in each of the familiar groups played both parts of the game for the total time allowed (15 minutes). Since it was possible that these two subjects might have played Part II longer than Part I had longer playing times been permitted, the analysis reported immediately above was recomputed with these two subjects excluded. The resulting differences remained significant ($p < .02$).

DISCUSSION

The findings of the present study clearly indicate that the nature of the relationship between a child and an adult influences how effective the adult will be in reinforcing the child's behavior. The experimenter was found to be significantly more reinforcing in the FP than in the FN condition. In turn, the experimenter was significantly more reinforcing in the FN than in the St condition. The significant differences between the groups in the decrease in playing time from Part I to Part II lent support to the view that

TABLE 2. ANALYSIS OF VARIANCE OF LOG-TIME SCORES

Source	df	MS	F
Conditions (A)	2	1.2622	8.87 **
Between subjects	32	.1422	
Parts (B)	1	.3761	13.51 **
A × B	2	.1190	4.28 *
Within subjects	32	.0278	

* $p < .025$.
**$p < .001$.

one factor resulting in an increase in an adult's effectiveness as a social reinforcer is a decrease in the child's negative-reaction tendency, that is, wariness of and/or reluctance to interact with an adult. However, the total pattern of performance of the three groups on the two parts of the game indicated that the enhanced effectiveness of the adult cannot be attributed solely to the reduction of the negative tendency.

If a reduction in the negative tendency were the only pertinent factor, then the FP group would show a greater decrease from Part I to Part II than would the FN group. However, the FP group not only played the total game longer than the FN group but also did not evidence any greater decrease from Part I to Part II. The overall findings thus suggest that the increased effectiveness of the adult in the FP condition was due to both a reduction in the negative-reaction tendency and to an increase in the positive-reaction tendency. It would appear that the reinforcers dispensed by the experimenter take on increased reinforcement value if the adult has been associated with warm, positive experiences in the child's recent past. This seems to be such a straightforward explanation that one is tempted to explain all the findings in terms of a differential increase in the positive tendency.

Thus, one could argue that the differences in total time found between the three groups reflect differences in the positive-reaction tendency and that the large decrease between Part I and Part II found for the familiar groups reflects nothing but fatigue and other satiation effects caused by playing Part I of the game so long. However, the finding that over half of the subjects in the St group play Part II longer than Part I constitutes strong evidence against this more simple view. The very nature of the game is such that one would expect every child to play the second part of the game for a shorter period than the first due to satiation and fatigue effects. No argument employing the positive tendency alone is capable of encompassing the finding that the majority of the children in the St group played Part II longer than Part I. As demonstrated by Shallenberger and Zigler (1961), playing the second part longer than the first is the clearest indication that a negative-reaction tendency is present. It would thus appear that the most appropriate conclusion derivable from the findings is that the treatment conditions differentially affected both the positive- and negative-reaction tendencies of the groups.

The results of the present study appear capable of shedding light on the effectiveness of parents versus strangers as social reinforcers. If it is assumed that parents have been more frequently associated with punishing events than have strange adults, then one would expect the negative-reaction tendency elicited by parents to be higher than that elicited by strange adults. It would be quite possible for this negative tendency to interfere with the parent's effectiveness as a reinforcer and given our usual experimental procedures, make him appear less effective as a social reinforcer than he really is. Given differences in the age of their children, their procedures, and the actual parents employed, it is not surprising that investigators have found that parents can be either negative or positive reinforcers (Patterson et al., in press; Stevenson et al., 1963). Certainly the context in which the parent serves as a reinforcer for his child and the particular child-rearing practices that have been employed by that parent would be factors influencing the magnitude of the child's negative-reaction tendency during the experimental task.

The findings of the present study also appear to be related to those of Sacks (1952) who investigated the effect of treatment conditions very similar to those employed in the present study on intelligence test performance. Three groups of children were tested. Following this, one group had positive interactions with the examiner, a second group had interactions similar to those employed in our neutral condition, and a third group had no interactions with the examiner. Upon retest, Sacks found that subjects in the first group showed the greatest increment; subjects in the second group the next largest increment; and those in the control group, the smallest increment in mean IQ. These findings suggest that negative-reaction tendencies evoked by a strange examiner interfere with children's test performance. Very high negative-reaction tendencies could explain the large discrepancies that have been reported (Sarason & Gladwin, 1958) between the test performance of institutionalized retardates, typically obtained while the child is interacting with a stranger, and the retardate's day-to-day capabilities, typically assessed through the child's interactions with familiar adults. Further investigations of the relative magnitudes of the positive- and negative-reaction tendencies referred to in this paper should also aid us in our understanding of the autistic child as well as illuminating the current controversy over whether extreme social deprivation leads to an increase in the interaction of the socially deprived individual or whether such deprivation leads to apathy and/or withdrawal (Cox, 1953; Goldfarb, 1953; Irvine, 1952; Wittenborn & Myers, 1957).

One final note is in order. Throughout this study longer playing time of the child has been interpreted as being due to the greater reinforcer effectiveness of the adult. The argument can be made that while longer playing time may reflect a heightened positive tendency towards the adult, it does not necessarily indicate that the adult has taken on greater social reinforcer effectiveness. The central issue here is whether the adult is effective only in maintaining the child's interaction with him or whether the adult has acquired a generally enhanced reinforcer effectiveness in respect to specific responses of the child. The investigation of the relationship between the child's positive or negative feelings towards an adult and that adult's effectiveness in shaping various behaviors of the child would appear to be an inviting area of future research.

SUMMARY

The hypothesis tested was that the child's positive- and negative-reaction tendencies interact to determine an adult's effectiveness as a reinforcer. Before administering a simple 2-part satiation task under conditions of positive reinforcement, 36 grade-school boys were divided randomly into 3 conditions. In the stranger (St) condition Ss had no prior contact with E. In the familiar-neutral (FN) condition Ss participated in 3 sessions at weekly intervals during which E provided attractive art materials but interacted minimally. The familiar-positive (FP) was identical to the FN condition except that E interacted freely and positively with Ss. Results showed that the FP group elected to play the experimental game significantly longer than the FN group ($p < .05$) which played significantly longer than the St group ($p < .001$). The pattern of results in time spent in Part I vs. Part II suggested that the experimental conditions influenced both the child's positive- and negative-reaction tendencies.

REFERENCES

Cox, F. The origins of the dependency drive. *Australian Journal of Psychology,* 1953, **5**, 64–73.

Crandall, Virginia C. Reinforcement effects of adult reactions and nonreactions on children's achievement expectations. *Child Development,* 1963, **34**, 335–354.

Gewirtz, J. L. Three determinants of attention-seeking in young children. *Monographs of the Society for Research in Child Development,* 1954, **19** (2).

Gewirtz, J. L., & Baer, D. M. Deprivation and satiation of social reinforcers as drive conditions. *Journal of Abnormal and Social Psychology,* 1958, **57**, 165–172. (a)

Gewirtz, J. L., & Baer, D. M. The effort of brief social deprivation on behaviors for a social reinforcer. *Journal of Abnormal and Social Psychology,* 1958, **56**, 49–56. (b)

Gewirtz, J. L., Baer, D. M., & Roth, C. H. A note on the similar effects of low social availability of an adult and brief social deprivation on young children's behavior. *Child Development,* 1958, **29**, 149–152.

Goldfarb, W. The effects of early institutional care on adolescent personality. *Journal of Experimental Education,* 1953, **12**, 106–129.

Irvine, E. Observations on the aims and methods of child rearing in communal settlements in Israel. *Human Relations,* 1952, **5**, 247–275.

Kounin, J. Experimental studies of rigidity: I. The measurement of rigidity in normal and feeble-minded persons. *Character and Personality,* 1941, **9**, 251–273.

Lindquist, E. F. *Design and analysis of experiments in psychology and education.* Boston: Houghton Mifflin, 1956.

Patterson, G. R. A preliminary report: Fathers as reinforcing agents. Paper read at Western Psychological Association, San Diego, April 1959.

Patterson, G. R., Littman, R. A., & Hinsey, C. Parents as social stimuli. *Child Development*, in press.

Patterson, G. R., & Ludwig, M. Parents as reinforcing agents. Paper read at Oregon Psychological Association, Eugene, April 1961.

Sacks, Elinor L. Intelligence scores as a function of experimentally established social relationships between child and examiner. *Journal of Abnormal and Social Psychology*, 1952, 47, 354–358.

Sarason, S. B., & Gladwin, T. Psychological and cultural problems in mental subnormality: A review of research. *Genetic Psychology Monograph*, 1958, 57, 7–269.

Shallenberger, Patricia, & Zigler, E. Rigidity, negative reaction tendencies, and cosatiation effects in normal and feebleminded children. *Journal of Abnormal and Social Psychology*, 1961, 63, 20–26.

Stevenson, H. W. Social reinforcement with children as a function of CA, sex of E, and sex of S. *Journal of Abnormal and Social Psychology*, 1961, 63, 147–154.

Stevenson, H. W., Hickman, R. K., & Knights, R. M. Parents and strangers as reinforcing agents for children's performance. *Journal of Abnormal and Social Psychology*, 1963, 67, 183–189.

Stevenson, H. W., & Snyder, Lelia C. Performance as a function of the interaction of incentive conditions. *Journal of Personality*, 1960, 28, 1–11.

Walters, R., & Ray, E. Anxiety, isolation, and reinforcer effectiveness. *Journal of Personality*, 1960, 28, 358–367.

Wittenborn, J., & Myers, B. *The placement of adoptive children*. Springfield, Ill.: Charles C Thomas, 1957.

Zigler, E. Social deprivation and rigidity in the performance of feebleminded children. *Journal of Abnormal and Social Psychology*, 1961, 62, 413–421.

Zigler, E. Rigidity and social reinforcement effects in the performance of institutionalized and noninstitutionalized normal and retarded children. *Journal of Personality*, 1963, 31, 258–269. (a)

Zigler, E. Social reinforcement, environmental conditions, and the child. *American Journal of Orthopsychiatry*, 1963, 33, 614–623. (b)

Zigler, E. The effect of social reinforcement on normal and socially deprived children. *Journal of Genetic Psychology*, in press.

Zigler, E., Hodgden, L., & Stevenson, H. W. The effect of support on the performance of normal and feebleminded children. *Journal of Personality*, 1958, 26, 106–122.

Zigler, E., & Kanzer, P. The effectiveness of two classes of verbal reinforcers on the performance of middle- and lower-class children. *Journal of Personality*, 1962, 30, 157–163.

Zigler, E., & Williams, Joanna. Institutionalization and the effectiveness of social reinforcement: A three-year follow-up study. *Journal of Abnormal and Social Psychology*, 1963, 66, 197–205.

2.5   Social Reinforcement with Children
As a Function of CA, Sex of *E*, and Sex of *S* [1]

Harold W. Stevenson [2]

The purpose of this study is to investigate the effectiveness of social reinforcement in modifying children's performance in a simple game. The
variables of primary concern are the sex of the adult providing the social
reinforcement, and the sex and age of the child being studied.

In two recent studies with preschool children (Gewirtz, 1954; Gewirtz &
Baer, 1958), women were found to have a significantly greater effect on the
performance of boys than of girls, and men were found to have a greater
effect on the performance of girls than of boys. Two types of tasks were
used: easel painting in the presence of a permissive adult and a simple game
in which one of two alternative responses was socially reinforced by the
adult. A significant interaction between sex of adult and sex of child
was found for amount of attention seeking while painting and for the
frequency with which the socially reinforced response was made. Although
as the authors indicate, other interpretations may account for the results,
the Oedipal theory of Freud provides perhaps the most meaningful focus
about which to view the data.

The results of these two studies lead one to speculate further about the
possible effects of social reinforcement by adults on the performance of
children of different ages. Again, even though other views may lead to
similar predictions, Freudian theory provides the most integrated series of
hypotheses for making such predictions.

During the early years of childhood the principal caretaker of both boys
and girls is usually the mother. Through her role in satisfying the child's
basic needs, the mother becomes the primary love-object of the young child
and her presence and comments acquire the capacity for reinforcing behaviors not associated with primary drives. Assuming the relationship with
the mother generalizes to other women, social reinforcement provided by
women should be more effective in modifying the performance of both
young boys and girls (2–4 years) than social reinforcement provided by men.

[1] This study was supported by Grant M-3519 from the National Institute of
Mental Health.
[2] The assistance of Richard Strate in the conduct of this study, and of Raymond
Collier in the analysis of the data is gratefully acknowledged.

Reprinted from *The Journal of Abnormal and Social Psychology*, 1961, **63**, 147–154,
by permission of the author and The American Psychological Association.

As the girl grows older and enters the Oedipal period a shift in object-choice from the mother to the father begins to occur. During this period the boy not only fails to change his love-object from the mother to the father, but comes to view the father negatively. Results such as those found in the Gewirtz studies are predicted for this stage (4–7 years); that is, women are predicted to have a significantly greater effect on the performance of boys than of girls, and men are predicted to have a significantly greater effect on the performance of girls than of boys. Later, the Oedipal relationships decrease in strength and the pattern of object-choice changes. The girl re-establishes a close affective relationship with the mother, and the boy shifts his object-choice from the mother to the father. During late childhood (7–11 years), women should be more effective reinforcing agents for girls' behavior than for boys', and men should now be more effective reinforcing agents for boys' behavior than for girls'.

The present study attempts to investigate the validity of such predictions by testing children at three age levels (3–4 years, 6–7 years, and 9–10 years) in a simple game in which either a male or female experimenter (*E*) makes supportive comments during the subject's (*S*'s) performance. In order to reduce the problems resulting from having only one male and one female *E*, six *E*s of each sex were employed. The use of more than one *E* also makes it possible to determine whether there are significantly different effects associated with different *E*s.

METHOD

Subjects

The *S*s were 252 boys and 252 girls selected on the basis of CA. One-third of the *S*s of each sex were within the CA range from 3–0 to 5–0 years, one-third from 6–0 to 8–0 years, and one-third from 9–0 to 11–0 years. The children were attending preschools or elementary schools in Minneapolis and St. Paul, and all of the children of the appropriate CAs in each group or class visited were used as *S*s.[3] The schools in general enrolled children of average socioeconomic and intellectual level and were selected on the basis of availability rather than any other criteria.

Experimenters

The *E*s were 12 persons who were willing to perform as *E*s and who were involved in some phase of the Institute of Child Development program.

[3] The writer wishes to thank Judith Rosen, Barbara Knight, Kristin Arnold, Stephanie Grossman, Evelyn Stern, Norma McCoy, Richard Strate, Norman Kass, Gerald Peterson, Peder Johnson, Mervyn Bergman, and Edward Dowd who served as *E*s, and the principals and teachers of the nursery schools and elementary schools visited for their cooperation in providing children for the study.

The female *E*s included two graduate students in psychology, three graduate students in child development, and a secretary. The male *E*s included a graduate student in psychology, a graduate student in child development, a postdoctoral research associate in child development, and undergraduate students in psychology, sociology, and industrial education. The age range for the *E*s was 19–25 years, with a mean CA of 22.8 years.

Apparatus

The apparatus has been described in detail elsewhere (Stevenson & Fahel, 1961). It consisted essentially of a table of adjustable height with two bins, 8 × 10 inches, and a short transverse upright panel to shield *E*'s recording from *S*. The left bin contained approximately 1,600 orange, blue, and green marbles. The right bin was covered by a plate with six 5/8 inch holes placed randomly about the surface. Below the right bin was a mechanism whereby each marble was counted as it fell to the bottom of the bin.

Procedure

The *S*s were tested individually. Each *S* was obtained from the classroom by *E* and taken to the experimental room, which in practically all of the schools visited was a quiet, isolated room. The *E* engaged *S* in friendly conversation and seated *S* at the table. The *E* affirmed *S*'s age and name, and said:

We're going to play a game. Let me tell you about it. This is called the Marble Game. See the marbles? We have blue ones and orange ones and this color green ones and this color green ones. Let me show you how to play it. The marbles go in these holes. [*E* indicated the marbles in the left bin and the holes of the plate covering the right bin.] You can put any color marble in any hole. These are the marbles and these are the holes. Pick the marbles up one at a time and put them in the holes. Let me show you how to do it. [*E* demonstrated how the marbles could be dropped in each hole.] O.K.? I'll tell you when to stop. Now you can play the game.

The first minute of the game was used to establish a baseline rate of response for each *S*. During this minute *E* played the role of an attentive, but nonreinforcing observer of *S*'s performance. Care was taken not to smile or to nod approval of *S*'s behavior during this period. After the first minute *E* continued to be attentive to *S*'s performance and did not avoid smiling and nodding when delivering one of the statements of verbal support. Twice a minute for the next 5 minutes *E* made a supportive statement about *S*'s performance. The statements were made after approximately 15″ and 45″ within each minute, and immediately following one of *S*'s responses. Five statements were used: "You're doing very well," "That's very good," "You know how to play this game very well," "That's fine," "You're really good at this game." These statements were made in a predetermined random order established separately for each *S*. Any attempts by *S* to engage *E* in conversation were not responded to by *E*.

Three departures from this procedure were allowed. First, if S stopped responding for 30 seconds during the course of the game, E said, "I'll tell you when to stop." If S failed to resume response or if S later stopped again for 30 seconds, the game was terminated. Second, if S picked up a handful of marbles, E said, "Put them in one at a time." If S did not heed this instruction, S was dropped from the experiment. Third, if S stopped responding during the first minute before a supportive comment was made, S was discarded. In addition to the last two criteria, Ss were also discarded if there were mechanical difficulties in the apparatus, or if any difficulties arose in the experimental procedure, such as someone's interrupting the game. A total of 35 Ss were eliminated from the experiment and replaced by other Ss on these bases.

Each E tested seven boys and seven girls at each of the three age levels. Most of the Es tested children from several schools within an age level. This was desirable from the standpoint of increasing the randomness of the sample of children tested by each E and was necessary because of the small number of children in some of the classes or groups visited. The children were obtained either alphabetically, according to seat order, or according to which children happened to be unoccupied or not engaged in group activities at the time E visited the class. There was no tendency for the first E visiting a group to obtain a different set of children from Es visiting the group later. When large groups were visited, several Es were available so that all children in a group were tested in a fairly uninterrupted sequence.

Before beginning to test children, each E practiced the procedure several times with an experienced E as the S.

Response Measures

The number of marbles inserted during each minute of the game was recorded by E. The number inserted during the first minute when E made no supportive comments was used as an index of S's base rate of response. The base rate was subtracted from the number of marbles inserted during each subsequent minute for each S and the mean of these difference scores was used as an index of the effectiveness of the social reinforcement in modifying S's rate of response. The two measures used in the major analyses of the results were, therefore, the base rate and the mean difference score.

RESULTS

The first prediction was that women would have a significantly greater effect than men on the performance of both boys and girls at the 3–4 year level. The mean difference score for boys and girls tested by men was —.04, and for boys and girls tested by women it was 1.38 (see Figure 1). This difference is significant at the .005 level ($t = 2.97$, $df = 166$).

In order to determine whether this difference might also be characteristic of the performance of Ss at the other age levels, the same comparison was

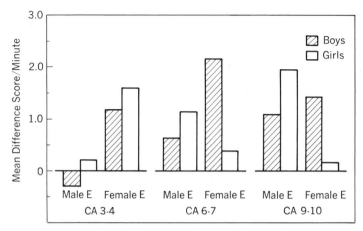

FIGURE 1. The average difference score obtained for each minute of the game for each CA and for each sex of SS and Es.

made for the other ages. The mean difference score for Ss tested by women at the 6–7 year level was 1.29 and for Ss tested by men, .90. The difference is not significant ($t = 1.08$). The mean difference score for Ss tested by women at the 9–10 year level was .80, and for Ss tested by men, 1.55. The difference is in the opposite direction from that found for younger Ss, but is not significant ($t = 1.68$, $df = 166$, $p > .10$).

The first prediction is therefore confirmed. Social reinforcement in the present setting is more effective in modifying the rate of response of boys and girls at the 3–4 year level when it is provided by women than when it is provided by men. The difference is significant at the 3–4 year level and at none of the other CA levels.

The second prediction was that for children of 6–7 years women would have a greater effect on the performance of boys than of girls, and men would have a greater effect on the performance of girls than of boys. The mean difference score for boys tested by women was 2.18 and for girls tested by women, .40. The difference is significant at less than the .025 level ($t = 2.37$, $df = 82$). The mean difference score for girls tested by men was 1.15, and for boys tested by men, .64. The difference is in the predicted direction, but is not statistically significant ($t = .66$).

Again, to determine whether this effect occurs only at the 6–7 year level, the same comparisons were made at the other age levels. The difference between the mean difference scores at the 3–4 year level for boys and girls tested by women was not significant ($t = .50$). The difference between the mean difference scores for boys and girls tested by men was also not significant ($t = .54$). At the 9–10 year level, the difference between the mean difference scores for boys and girls tested by women was not significant ($t =$

1.27), nor was the difference between the mean difference scores for boys and girls tested by men ($t = 1.13$).

The second prediction was thus only partly confirmed. At the 6–7 year level, and only at this CA level, women were more effective in modifying the behavior of boys than of girls. Social reinforcement provided by men did not have a significantly greater effect in modifying the behavior of girls than of boys at any of the CA levels.

The third prediction was that at the 9–10 year level boys tested by men would show a greater increment in response than would girls tested by men, and conversely, girls tested by women would show a greater increment in response than would boys tested by women. This prediction was not supported. The tendency was for the cross-sex effect suggested by the results at the 6–7 year level to be maintained at the 9–10 year level, but by the 9–10 year level the variability among Ss was so great that the differences were not statistically significant.

The average difference scores obtained for all Ss tested by men showed a consistent increase across the three age levels from —.04 to .90 to 1.55, while the average difference scores obtained for Ss tested by women showed a decrease across the three age levels from 1.38 to 1.29 to .80. The increase for the men from the 3–4 to the 9–10 year levels is highly significant ($t = 4.17$, $df = 166$, $p < .001$), but the corresponding decrease for the women is not significant ($t = 1.23$). Social reinforcement delivered by men therefore became increasingly effective as the Ss' CA increased, but no significant changes in the general effectiveness of social reinforcement delivered by women as a function of Ss' CA was found.

Base Rate

The question may be raised whether differences in performance among the various subgroups may not also have been manifest during the base rate period. The Es may have induced different levels of motivation during the initial stages of the task which would be reflected in different base rates of response. The data in Table 1, which presents the average base rates for each of the subgroups, indicate that this was not the case. Although, as might be expected, the rate of response increased with increasing CA, the

TABLE 1. Mean Base Rates for Each Subgroup

Sex of E and S	3–4	6–7	9–10
Male E			
Boys	12.4	26.0	36.0
Girls	14.4	27.1	34.0
Female E			
Boys	11.6	24.3	34.3
Girls	12.3	26.1	35.7

TABLE 2. Analysis of Variance of Base Rate Scores

Source	df	MS	Error	F
Sex E (A)	1	110.50	D	.64
Sex S (B)	1	97.78	B × D	2.01
Age S (C)	2	21137.50	C × D	1265.72 ***
Individual E (D)	10	173.66		5.25 ***
D$_M$	5	235.05		7.11 ***
D$_F$	5	112.27		3.40 **
A × B	1	24.90	B × D	.51
A × C	2	34.68	C × D	2.08
B × C	2	42.03	B × C × D	.50
B × D	10	48.69		1.47
C × D	20	16.70		.50
A × B × C	2	51.10	B × C × D	.61
B × C × D	20	83.20		2.52 ***
B × C × D$_M$	10	41.63		1.26
B × C × D$_F$	10	124.78		3.78 ***
Within	432	33.05		

** $p < .01$.
*** $p < .001$.

values for the subgroups within an age range are remarkably similar. None of the tendencies found in the analysis of the difference scores is seen.

An analysis of variance of the base rates was performed to determine whether the apparent similarities in performance were indeed nons;gnificant as well as to determine whether the mean rates of response of Ss tested by different Es differed significantly. This analysis is summarized in Table 2. There was no significant difference between the base rates of boys and girls, nor between the base rates of Ss tested by men and women. The difference associated with CA is highly significant, with each age level showing an increase in rate of response.

There is a highly significant difference in the average base rates of Ss tested by different Es. Significant differences occur among the base rates of Ss tested both by men and by women. Since the Ss tested by each E were determined at random, these differences in base rates cannot be attributed to characteristics of Ss. It must be concluded that the Es differed in ways which had significant effects on the rate with which Ss responded.

Finally, there is a highly significant interaction between Sex of S, Age of S, and Individual E. It is evident in the breakdown of this interaction according to sex of E that the major contribution to this interaction is derived from the women Es. The average base rates of Ss tested by men were rather evenly distributed within each age and sex grouping. For Ss tested by women, however, the dispersion of average base rates was similar for boys and girls at the 3–4 year level, but increased more for girls than for boys at the 6–7 and 9–10 year levels.

Difference Scores

An analysis of the changes in difference scores through the period in which social reinforcement of Ss' responses occurred indicates an increase in the average difference score from .35 for the second minute to 1.30 for the sixth minute. This increase is highly significant ($t = 4.62$, $df = 503$, $p <$ .001). The difference scores increased from the second through the sixth minute in 11 of the 12 subgroups. The only group in which a decrease through this period occurred was for girls at the 9–10 year level tested by women. Here the change was minimal; the average difference score for the second minute was .14, and for the sixth minute, .01.

Since the effect of social reinforcement was greatest during the sixth minute of the game, an analysis of variance was performed on the difference scores obtained for this period. Because of the lack of homogeneity of variance, a logarithmic transformation of the data was performed. The analysis is summarized in Table 3.

There was no significant difference in the sixth-minute difference scores

TABLE 3. Analysis of Variance of Difference Scores for Sixth Minute

Source	df	MS	Error	F
Sex E (A)	1	.002	D	.15
Sex S (B)	1	.006	B × D	2.14
Age S (C)	2	.014	C × D	.14
Individual E (D)	10	.013		6.84 ***
D_M	5	.010		5.26 ***
D_F	5	.015		7.89 ***
A × B	1	.012	B × D	4.28
A × C	2	.031	C × D	.31
B × C	2	.015	B × C × D	1.78
B × D	10	.003		1.47
C × D	20	.099		52.10 ***
C × D_M	10	.005		2.63 **
C × D_F	10	.015		7.89 ***
A × B × C	2	.010	B × C × D	1.19
B × C × D	20	.008		4.42 ***
B × C × D_M	10	.004		2.10 *
B × C × D_F	10	.013		6.84 ***
Within	432	.002		

   * $p < .05$.
  ** $p < .01$.
 *** $p < .001$.

for boys and girls or for Ss tested by men and women. There was a significant difference in the difference scores of Ss tested by individual Es, a significant double interaction between Individual E and Age of S, and a significant triple interaction between Individual E, Age of S, and Sex of S.

The tendency was for the dispersion of average difference scores to increase with increasing CA. The range tended to be more restricted, however, for boys than for girls at the youngest age level and the increase in range from one age level to the other tended to be greater for boys than for girls. In general, the findings are similar to those obtained in the analysis of the base rates in that the dispersion of average difference scores obtained for Ss tested by women tended to be greater than that obtained for Ss tested by men and in that the dispersion tended to be greater for girls than for boys at all ages.

An inspection of the sixth-minute difference scores indicates that there was some consistency in the ordering of the average difference scores of Ss tested by individual Es at the 3–4 and 9–10 year levels. Although the number of Es is small, rank order correlations were computed to give an indication of the degree of consistency found. The correlation for boys at the 3–4 and 9–10 year levels tested by men was .81 ($p < .05$), and for boys tested by women, .60. The correlation for girls tested by men was —.71, and for girls tested by women, —.76. In other words, the ordering of Es tended to be similar at the early and late ages for boys, while the ordering for girls indicated that women who produced high difference scores at the younger age levels tended to produce low difference scores at the highest age levels and vice versa.

The correlation between the number of marbles inserted during the first minute of the game and the difference score for the sixth minute was —.40. This r is highly significant ($p < .001$) and indicates a tendency for Ss with low base rates to have high increments in response and for Ss with high base rates to have lower increments in response.

DISCUSSION

The results at the 6–7 year level are similar to those reported by Gewirtz, Baer, and Roth (1958) for 4–6 year old children tested following a 20-minute period of social isolation. Since the index of the effectiveness of social reinforcement differs in the two studies, it is possible to compare the results only in terms of direction and not in terms of the absolute changes in behavior. In both studies social reinforcement provided by women had a significantly greater effect on the behavior of boys than of girls, and there is a tendency, not significant in either study, for social reinforcement provided by men to have a greater effect on the behavior of girls than of boys. The major discrepancy between the results from the two experiments is that the cross-sex effect was reliable in the Gewirtz, Baer, and Roth study only following social isolation and was not reliable when Ss were tested without such isolation.

The basis of this difference is not clear, and the present data indicate that deprivation immediately prior to testing is not a necessary condition for the effect to emerge.

The results provide some support for the predictions derived from psychoanalytic theory. There is clear support of the prediction that women are more effective than men in modifying the performance of boys and girls at the 3–4 year level in this type of task. As discussed above, the results are also in line with the prediction that adults should have a greater effect on children of the opposite sex at the 6–7 year level. The results for Ss tested by men are in the appropriate direction, but are not reliable. The strong effect of women on boys' performance at this age level, as contrasted with the more moderate effect of men on girls' performance, has some basis in the Freudian assumption that the Oedipal relationship is more intense with boys than with girls. The results do not support the prediction that the behavior of children at the 9–10 year level would be modified to a greater degree by social reinforcement provided by adults of the same sex as S compared to adults of the opposite sex. The view that the 9–10 year old children's close affective relationship with the like-sexed parent results in adults of this sex having a greater effect on the performance of the child is not supported.

The question arises as to whether other positions than the Freudian one may not provide a more satisfactory account for the results. Gewirtz and Baer (1958) have hypothesized that the effectiveness of social reinforcement is increased by social deprivation. A simple extension of this hypothesis may account for the cross-sex effect discussed above. It may be hypothesized that the effectiveness of social reinforcement provided by an adult in modifying children's performance is a function of the degree of social deprivation children have for contacts with members of the adult's sex.

It must be assumed that during the early years of the child's life the parent functions more frequently as a caretaker than as a source of social satisfaction for the child. As discussed earlier, the effectiveness of the mother as a reinforcing agent during the early years of the child's life may be posited as being a result of her gaining in secondary reinforcing value because of her presence in the satisfaction of the child's basic needs. The father has a relatively less important role at this time and only later does he begin to play a significant part in the child's daily activities. The increased effectiveness of the male Es with increasing CA of the child was found in this study. As the child grows older and becomes capable of satisfying his own basic needs or of delaying gratification of his needs, the importance of both parents as social agents increases.

Social forces begin to operate after the first years to direct boys' activities towards those of other boys and men and to direct girls' activities towards those of other girls and women. Masculine contacts and behavior are reinforced for boys and not for girls, and feminine contacts and behavior are reinforced for girls and not for boys. The boy is relatively more deprived of contact with females than with males and the girl is relatively more deprived of contact with males. This is assumed to be maximal during the early school years, for it is perhaps at this time that there is the greatest emphasis placed upon the child's adopting an appropriate sex role. Because of this deprivation, the effectiveness of women as reinforcing agents for boys and of men as reinforcing agents for girls is assumed to increase. The strength of the cross-sex deprivation is assumed to be greater for boys than for girls. Feminine activities and contacts are more likely to be discouraged for boys than masculine activities and contacts are for girls. Further, the boy has had a closer relationship and more frequent contact with the mother during the first years of life than the girl has had with the father, thus being forced to decrease or relinquish such relationships and contacts should have a greater effect on boys than on girls.

This general argument leads to an odd paradox, for it would be predicted that during these years the more effective reinforcement of masculine behavior for boys would be derived from the mother and the more effective reinforcement of feminine behavior for girls would be derived from the father. It may be important, therefore, to distinguish between the model for identification and the source of reinforcement for adopting behavior congruent with this model. Although the father may provide the model for masculine behavior for the young boy, the degree to which the boy identifies with this model may be a function of the degree to which the mother reinforces masculine behavior.

The results give several indications that there are differences between boys and girls in the degree to which the characteristics of individual adults influence their performance. The adults who were effective with younger girls tended to be less effective with older girls, while the adults who were effective with younger boys tended to remain effective with older boys. In view of the fact that the performance of 3–4 year old boys tested by different Es did not differ to so great a degree as did the performance of the young girls, it may be hypothesized that boys and girls differentiated the characteristics of the particular Es equally well, but that the performance of the young girls was influenced to a greater degree by the characteristics of particular Es than was the performance of young boys. The fact that the average difference scores obtained by the various groups of girls tended to differ to a greater degree at all age levels than did those obtained by the groups of boys indicates that the performance of girls in general was affected to a greater degree by particular characteristics of the individual Es than was the performance of boys. An examination of such factors as E's age, appearance, experience with children, scholastic status, or scores on the MMPI gave no indication of what characteristics of the Es produced these differences in base rates and difference scores. Further, there are no data which clarify why men in general tended to produce more homogeneous grouping of performance in children than did women.

SUMMARY

Six male and six female Es tested seven boys and seven girls at each of three age levels (3–4, 6–7, and 9–10 years) in a simple game. Following an initial minute during which a base line for performance was established, E made two of five standard supportive comments about S's performance each minute for the next 5 minutes. The increment in response occurring after the first minute of the game was used in the analysis of the results. The average difference score was greater for Ss tested by women than by men at the 3–4 year level, and was significantly greater for boys than for girls tested by women at the 6–7 year level. The increment was greater at the 6–7 year level for girls than for boys tested by men, but the difference was not significant. At the 9–10 year level the differences in performance associated with sex of E and sex of S were not statistically significant. An analysis of the increment of response during the sixth minute of the game indicated significant differences in the scores obtained by Ss tested by different Es, and significant interactions between individual Es and S's CA, and between individual Es, S's CA, and S's sex. The results were interpreted in terms of the hypothesis that the effectiveness of social reinforcement provided by an adult is a function of the degree to which children are deprived of contact with members of the adult's sex.

REFERENCES

Gewirtz, J. L. Three determinants of attention-seeking in young children. *Monogr. Soc. Res. Child Develpm.*, 1954, 19(2), No. 59.

Gewirtz, J. L., & Baer, D. M. The effect of brief social deprivation on behaviors for a social reinforcer. *J. abnorm. soc. Psychol.*, 1958, **56**, 49–56.

Gewirtz, J. L., Baer, D. M., & Roth, C. H. A note on the similar effects of low social availability of an adult and brief social deprivation on young children's behavior. *Child Develpm.*, 1958, **29**, 149–152.

Stevenson, H. W., & Fahel, Leila S. The effect of social reinforcement on the performance of institutionalized and noninstitutionalized normal and feebleminded children. *J. Pers.*, 1961, **29**, 136–147.

2.6 Deprivation and Satiation of Social Reinforcers as Drive Conditions

Jacob L. Gewirtz [1] *and Donald M. Baer* [2]

In an earlier study (6) we received what appeared to be an affirmative answer to the question: Are there social drives that respond to reinforcer deprivation as do the primary appetitive drives? In this investigation we extend the question, asking in addition if the behaviors maintained by social reinforcers are responsive also to a condition of relative satiation for such reinforcers. Children are again employed as subjects (*Ss*).

In the earlier study it was found that when an adult made words and phrases like "Good!" and "Hm-hmm" contingent upon an arbitrarily chosen response in nursery school children, that response was reinforced (i.e., conditioned). This effect was similar to that found in several other studies using verbal stimuli appealing to the concept of *approval* as reinforcers (e.g., 2, 9, 12, 16). It was found, in addition, that this reinforcing effect of approval could be increased when the children experienced a preceding 20-minute period of social isolation, relative to its effectiveness for the same children when they had not been isolated. While this result held primarily for boys tested by a female (rather than male) experimenter, other aspects of the data clearly supported the equating of isolation to the deprivation of social reinforcers: *social isolation increased reliably the reinforcing power of adult approval for children as a positive function of the degree to which they typically sought such approval in other settings.* Approval was taken to be representative of the reinforcers which control the purely social initiations made by children to adults.

Deprivation implies a period of unavailability of a given reinforcer, which results in an increase in behaviors for it; *satiation* implies a period of availability of a reinforcer, sufficient to effect a decrease in behaviors for it. Thus, deprivation and satiation represent two statements of a single concept, a dimension characterized by the relative supply of a reinforcer in the recent

[1] This study was carried out when the senior author was on the faculty of the University of Chicago, and was facilitated by a grant given to him by the Social Science Research Committee of that institution. The writers acknowledge with gratitude the discriminating assistance of Chaya H. Roth.

[2] At the time of this study, the junior author was a Public Health Service Predoctoral Research Fellow of the National Institute of Mental Health at the University of Chicago.

Reprinted from *The Journal of Abnormal and Social Psychology,* 1958, **57,** 165–172, by permission of the authors and The American Psychological Association.

history of an organism which determines the incidence of behaviors for that reinforcer. The concept of deprivation-satiation has considerable precedent as a drive operation in general behavior theory (e.g., 11, 14), where it has been employed to order contemporary conditions which account for variance in reinforcer effectiveness. As such, drive is generally defined as the functional relation between deprivation (or satiation) for a reinforcer and responding for that reinforcer. Further, concepts like deprivation have been somewhat loosely applied in a number of speculative formulations of the antecedents of certain social behaviors (e.g., 1, 8, 13, 15). Hence, laws relating social deprivation as an empirically defined dimension to certain basic characteristics of social behaviors would have considerable integrative value (5). But first, the experimental operations of deprivation and its inverse, satiation, must be implemented effectively in social terms.

In the earlier study cited (6), a beginning attempt was made to implement social deprivation: brief social isolation of a child was equated to a condition of deprivation of all social reinforcers (including approval), and the differential effects of that condition and of a comparison nonisolation (nondeprivation) condition were reflected in the reinforcing effectiveness of an adult's approval. The present study represents an attempt to simplify (and replicate) the social deprivation operation of the earlier study, as well as a beginning in the direction of establishing an operation of social satiation. Satiation will be equated to a condition in which an abundance of approval and social contact is supplied to a child by an adult. Experimental operations implementing the conditions of deprivation and of satiation for a class of social reinforcers are both reflected against an intermediate or nondeprivation (nonsatiated) condition. The hypothesis is that these conditions should enhance the effectiveness of the reinforcer in the order: Deprivation > Nondeprivation > Satiation.

METHOD

Sample

The Ss were 102 middle-class children selected from the classes of the first and second grades of a university laboratory school and randomly assigned to experimental conditions. Sixteen were Negro, the remainder white. Their mean age at the time of testing was seven years, six months, with a range from six and one-half to nine years. Their mean and median Stanford-Binet IQ score was 127 (the scores of only 3 Ss were below 100). One-half of the Ss under each condition were girls and one-half boys. The Ss were selected by their teachers according to the order in which their names appeared on alphabetical class lists. No S refused to participate.

Independent Variable

Deprivation. Seventeen boys and 17 girls were subjected to a condition of social isolation before playing the game. Each of these Ss was introduced to the experimenter (E) in the classroom by the teacher. The E was a young woman in her early twenties.[3] She walked with S a distance of several hundred feet through the school corridors to the experimental room. During this walk, E responded to S's questions and comments only when necessary, and maintained a somewhat distant but not unfriendly manner at all times. Upon reaching the experimental room, E showed S around the room, seated him and told him that someone else was using the game which he was to play and that she would have to fetch it but would be back in a little while. E then left the room and went (unobserved) to an adjacent observation booth from which S was observed during his isolation. She returned after 20 minutes with the toy. The game was then played in the usual fashion. The Ss, who occasionally accompanied adults in the school setting for tests, and who had experience in awaiting their turns, all accepted this condition without question.

Nondeprivation.   Seventeen boys and 17 girls were subjected to a condition of nonisolation, i.e., they played the game immediately upon their arrival at the experimental room. (Since this condition represents both relative nondeprivation and relative nonsatiation for approval, it served as an intermediate control condition for the other two conditions.) Until they entered the experimental room, Ss in this group were treated identically as were Ss in the Deprivation group.

Satiation.   Seventeen boys and 17 girls were subjected to a condition of relative satiation for approval from the adult before playing the game. Again, each of these Ss was introduced to E in the classroom by the teacher, but during the walk to the experimental room, E maintained a very pleasant and interested attitude toward S, responding to all details of his comments and questions, asking questions to draw out more of S's conversation, and generally approving of anything about S which might reasonably be praised or admired. Upon reaching the experimental room, E showed S around the room, seated him, told him that the game was in use elsewhere and that she would go fetch it in a little while when it would be free. She suggested that meanwhile S might like to draw pictures or cut out designs, and proffered the essential materials. Then, for 20 minutes S drew or cut out designs, while E maintained a stream of friendly conversation with him, inducing him to talk about himself if he did not do so naturally. The E alternated her praise and admiration of whatever S did with whatever he said about himself, all in an appropriate fashion, and attempted to dispense 30 such reinforcers during the 20-minute satiation period at an approximate rate of three every two minutes. In fact, E dispensed to the boys an average of 31.6 such reinforcers ($\sigma = 6.9$) and to the girls an average of 28.2 reinforcers ($\sigma = 8.1$).

[3] This E served as one of the two Es in a companion study (6).

The Game Setting

Following the experimental treatment, the central task for S (which was the same for all three groups) was to place marbles into either of the two holes of the toy (shown in Fig. 1) while E, who sat beside him, looked on.

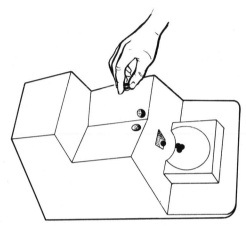

FIGURE 1. A schematic diagram of the experimental apparatus (The "Game").

(This procedure was identical to that employed in the earlier study (6) and is only summarized here.) The E observed S's play for a "baseline" period of four minutes, during which *no* reinforcers were dispensed. Meanwhile, E responded to any of S's comments and questions in a friendly but brief manner. Without pause, the baseline period was followed by a 10-minute test of reinforcer effectiveness. That is, E proceeded at this point to dispense the reinforcer, consisting of words like "Good," "Hm-hmm," and "Fine," according to a schedule incorporating several, successively higher, fixed ratios, whenever S dropped marbles into the *correct* hole, defined as that preferred *least* during the last (fourth) minute of the baseline period.

Dependent Variables

Reinforcer effectiveness score. The determination of the effectiveness of approval as a reinforcer was made from the "game" which followed immediately the treatment condition (i.e., the 20 minutes of Deprivation or of Satiation, or in the Nondeprivation condition, the arrival at the experimental room). The basic data were the numbers of marbles dropped in the correct and incorrect holes during each minute of play. These generated four pairs of frequency scores for the baseline period, and 10 such pairs of scores for the reinforcer effectiveness test period. For each minute of play, the *relative frequency* of a correct response was the ratio of correct responses to total responses, i.e., # correct/ (# correct + # incorrect). The score employed as dependent variable was taken as the difference, for each *S*, between the relative frequency of correct responses in the last (fourth) minute of the baseline period (when no reinforcers were dispensed) and the median relative frequency of correct responses of the 10 reinforcer test period minutes. This *reinforcer effectiveness score* represents the *gain* in relative frequency of the correct response attributable to the social reinforcer provided by the adult's approval.

Spontaneous social initiations. In addition, the verbal and purely social initiations of the child to the adult were tallied, but *only during the baseline period of the game,* before she began to dispense approval. The *E* treated the game as *S*'s central task and, while permissive, generally discouraged lengthy initiations on the part of *S*, suggesting, when necessary, that they could converse at length after the game. Where a reply to an initiation of *S* was required, *E*'s response was always friendly, yet brief, leaving responsibility for continuing that interaction sequence in *S*'s hands. All such responses by *S* were tallied by an observer in an observation booth. These responses took the form most frequently of Comments, less frequently of Questions, and least frequently of overt Attention-seeking.[4] They could be expected to represent behaviors by *S* for a variety of social reinforcers, in addition to approval. *Comments* were casual remarks which usually required no formal response from *E* (e.g., "We're going away for the holiday"). *Questions,* which were also casual, required only brief, token replies from *E* (e.g., "Do you think it will rain?"). When making a comment or asking a question, *S* typically continued responding in the game. *Attention-seeking* included responses characterized by urgency designed for active notice from *E*. Typically, *S* would pause to direct his complete attention to *E* while awaiting a response (e.g., "Watch me put the marble into this hole!"). Because of their generally infrequent occurrence in this study, these three behavior categories are scored in two different ways to produce two relatively independent response indices for the purpose of analysis:

a. The sum of the frequencies in the three social response categories, Comments, Questions, and Attention-seeking, which weights those categories in proportion to their frequency of occurrence (i.e., Comments contributes most and Attention-seeking least to that index).

b. The score of a *cumulative Guttman-like scale* (10), indexing what ap-

----

[4] These three observation categories are defined in detail in (3). High agreement between observers was found there on these behavior categories, and they entered into similar patterns of relationship with the independent variables. Moreover, they were found in (4) to have high loadings on a single factor and appeared to involve an active attempt to gain or to maintain the adult's attention, perhaps differing in the degree to which their initiations for attention were overt or direct.

pears to be the intensity of social contact, formed similarly as in (3) when the frequency scores for each verbal response category were dichotomized for each S into gross response alternatives, zero or nonzero frequency of occurrence.[5] A scale score of 3 indicated that an S had exhibited some of all three behaviors; a score of 2 indicated that some Comments and Questions were exhibited, but no Attention-seeking; a score of 1 indicated that only Comments were exhibited; and a score of zero indicated that no social response of any type was exhibited. Hence, the scale scores are weighted in favor of the less frequently occurring behavior categories, Questions and Attention-seeking.

RESULTS

The hypothesis advanced is that the mean reinforcer effectiveness scores for the treatment groups would rank in the order Deprivation > Nondeprivation > Satiation. To test this, two relatively independent statistical procedures are followed: the first is sensitive to the rank-order of the treatment means but does not take account of the degree of overlap between the distributions upon which the means are based; and the second, which takes such information into account and allows parametric statements about the means, is somewhat less sensitive to the rank-order hypothesis.

TABLE 1. TABLE OF MEANS

Sex	Deprivation (D)	Satiation (S)	½ (D + S)	Non-deprivation
Boys	.36 *	.18 *	.27 **	.21 *
Girls	.33 *	.07 *	.20 **	.23 *
Combined	.34 **	.13 **	.23 ***	.22 **

   * 17 cases; S.E. of a mean difference is .068.
   ** 34 cases; S.E. of a mean difference is .048.
   *** 68 cases.

[5] Of all 102 Ss in the four-minute baseline period, the proportion showing nonzero category frequencies was .71 for Comments, .53 for Questions, and .15 for Attention-seeking. When the response categories were arranged in the order of their decreasing popularities (the proportion of Ss exhibiting nonzero frequencies), it was concluded that, for present purposes, a satisfactory three-item Guttman-like scale was produced: only .03 of the 306 responses produced scale errors, the few scale errors found appeared random, and every observation category contained far less error than non-error. Of the 68 Ss in the Deprivation and Nondeprivation groups, five each produced one scale error in his response pattern. Such response patterns were assigned scale scores corresponding to the higher pattern which would have been attained had there been no scale error.

Reinforcer Effectiveness Score

Rank-order of the means. In Table 1, it is seen that the rank-order predicted for the three means is found separately for Boys and for Girls. The sex variable may be taken as an independent replication of the experiment. The theoretical probability of obtaining a predicted rank-order of three independent means is $\frac{1}{6}$, and with one independent replication the probability of obtaining two such orders is $\frac{1}{6} \times \frac{1}{6}$ or $\frac{1}{36}$. On this basis, we can conclude that the null hypothesis, that all six rank-orders of the three means are equally likely, is rejected at $p < .03$. Hence, the alternative hypothesis, that the predicted rank-order of the three means prevails, is accepted.

Regression analysis. For the purposes of the regression analysis (and for theoretical reasons as well), the three treatment conditions are considered as points along a single continuous dimension representing the degree of social deprivation. The analysis then proceeds from three working assumptions: (*a*) the units separating the treatments along this deprivation dimension are roughly equal in size, (*b*) their relationship to the reinforcer effectiveness means is linear, and (*c*) it is the *pattern* of the three means that is relevant to the rank-order hypothesis advanced, not the contrasts between mean pairs representing adjacent points on the postulated treatment dimension. On this basis, it appears most efficient to carry out the analysis of variance according to a regression model: in essence, to analyze the regression of the reinforcer effectiveness score means on the treatment dimension.

The reinforcer effectiveness scores of the Ss were classified in the six cells of a 3×2 factorial, there being three treatments and two sexes of Ss. After a Bartlett test indicated that the variances were homogeneous and an examination of the data suggested that the other assumptions underlying the analysis appeared to hold, the data were subjected to an analysis of variance. Table 2 indicates that there is no over-all sex difference, and that the treatment conditions do not affect the sex groups differentially. From Fig. 2, it is seen that the group means corresponding to the three levels of the experimental variable rank-order according to the hypothesis. It is seen in Table 2 that the Deprivation vs. Satiation comparison is reliable and in the order predicted. In the case of three means, this comparison represents the regression of those means on the treatment dimension. A Nondeprivation vs. $\frac{1}{2}$ (Deprivation $+$ Satiation) comparison, which represents the deviation of the Nondeprivation mean from the regression line, indicates that that mean falls remarkably close to the regression line. Hence, the regression predicted was found. (This result provides presumptive evidence only for the effectiveness of either of the extreme treatments, Deprivation or Satiation, relative to the intermediate Nondeprivation treatment.)

Approval as a reinforcer. A question of interest is whether the reinforcer dispensed was effective as such under Nondeprivation, which would be

TABLE 2. SUMMARY OF THE ANALYSIS OF VARIANCE OF THE
        REINFORCER EFFECTIVENESS SCORE

Source of Variation	df	Mean Square	F
Boys vs. girls (sex)	1	.0412	.524
Treatments			
Total	(2)	(.4032)	(5.123 *)
Deprivation (D) vs. satiation (S) [a]	1	.8031	10.200 **
Nondeprivation (N) vs. ½ (D + S) [b]	1	.0034	.043
Sex × treatment interaction			
Total	(2)	(.0356)	(.452)
Sex × D vs. S	1	.0268	.341
Sex × N vs. ½ (D + S)	1	.0444	.564
Error (within groups)	96	.0787	

[a] Due to regression.
[b] Due to the deviation of the N mean from the regression line.
* $p < .01$.
** $p < .005$.

comparable to the usual experimental case under which the effectiveness of
the reinforcer would be examined, as well as following Satiation, when the
reinforcer was relatively least effective in this experiment. The hypothesis is
tested that the mean reinforcer effectiveness score under Nondeprivation is
zero, employing an error term based only upon those 34 scores and a one-
tail t test. That mean score (.22) is found to be reliably greater than zero
at $p < .0005$. A similar test indicates that the Satiation condition of this
study did not reduce the reinforcing effectiveness of approval to a zero level;
the mean reinforcer effectiveness score following Satiation (.13) was reliably
greater than zero at $p < .01$. Hence, it may be concluded that approval
was effective as a reinforcer under all conditions, and that satiation was not
complete but only relative.

Spontaneous Social Initiations

An examination of Ss' spontaneous verbal initiations to E during *only*
the four-minute baseline period of the game can reinforce the conclusions
drawn from the reinforcer effectiveness score (which reflects only the susceptibility of Ss to approval as a reinforcer). These initiations could be
expected to represent behaviors by S for a variety of social reinforcers from
E and, hence, might be sensitive as well to the treatments. It should be
noted that E did not dispense approval during the baseline period, but
merely looked on as S put marbles into the toy. (Because the Satiation
treatment consisted of a period of intensive social contact between E and S,
which could encourage S to continue to make social initiations during the

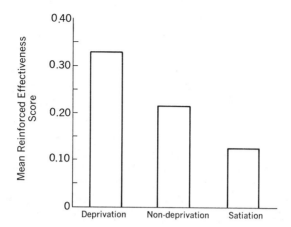

FIGURE 2. A pictorial representation of the means for the three levels of the experimental variable (34 Ss per condition).

game, only a comparison of the verbal social response scores between the Deprivation and Nondeprivation groups would be meaningful.)

The *total frequency of verbal initiation* scores was classified in a 2 × 2 factorial (Deprivation vs. Nondeprivation and Boys vs. Girls) and subjected to an analysis of variance. The mean number of verbal responses (Comments, Questions, and Attention-seeking) after Deprivation (4.4) was found to be reliably greater than that after Nondeprivation (2.3) at $p < .05$ ($F = 3.70$, 1 and 64 df, one-tail test). At the same time, the Treatment × Sex interaction effect was not reliable, indicating that the two treatments did not affect the sexes differentially.

The scale scores represent what appears to be the *intensity of social contact*, or the degree to which certain social reinforcers apart from approval (e.g., attention) are sought from the adult, and could take any one of the four values from zero to three. They were classified in a fourfold table, with *low* scores of zero and one taken to represent less intense social contact, and *high* scores of two and three taken to represent more intense social contact. It was found that 20 out of the 34 Ss exhibited high scale scores after Deprivation, while only 12 of the 34 Ss exhibited such high scale scores after Nondeprivation, indicating at $p < .05$ (chi square corrected for discontinuity = 2.89, 1 df, one-tail test) that a greater proportion of Ss exhibited more intense social contact scores after Deprivation than after Nondeprivation.

Hence, the two relatively independent indices derived from the three categories of spontaneous verbal initiations to E *both* reinforce the conclusions derived from the measure of the reinforcing effectiveness of E's approval.

DISCUSSION

In the earlier study cited (as in this study), the experimental operation of brief social isolation of the child was equated to a condition of deprivation [6] of all social reinforcers (including approval). Hence, it became important to demonstrate that this condition increases the incidence of behaviors for approval relative to an empirically defined level of satiation for that reinforcer. The results suggest that this has been accomplished. And since under the Nondeprivation condition Ss had just come from class, with no further experimental treatment, it seemed reasonable that it would represent some point intermediate between the other conditions. The rank-order of the mean reinforcer effectiveness scores for these three conditions followed this logic precisely and was uncomplicated by an interaction involving sex of Ss. Hence, the results replicate the finding of the earlier study concerning the greater effectiveness of approval after Deprivation, relative to Nondeprivation. While the mean difference between reinforcer effectiveness scores for Deprivation and Nondeprivation for the Ss in this study (ranging in age from 6–6 to 9–0) appears to be of the same order as that for the Ss in the earlier study (who ranged in age from 3–10 to 5–3), the absolute level of the means appears to be higher.

The two indices drawn from the three spontaneous verbal social initiation categories reinforced the conclusions based on the index of the reinforcing effectiveness of E's approval for the Deprivation and Nondeprivation conditions (where a difference test was meaningful). It seems likely then, if the game-set were dispensed with and the natural or spontaneous social initiations to E were employed as the sole dependent variable, that similar conclusions would be drawn from the results. However, if the present establishing operation for satiation were to be employed in such a study, it would still be almost impossible to separate the social effects of satiation from the artifactual effects of Ss' greater familiarity with E.

The essence of the parallel between our use of the term drive for social reinforcers and the traditional use of the term for the deprivation of food and water reinforcers, as in hunger and thirst, lies in the definition of a drive as the functional relation between deprivation for a reinforcer and responding for that reinforcer. In that special sense, then, it would appear that there exist for children social drives that respond to social reinforcer deprivation similarly as do many primary appetitive drives. Yet it should not be supposed that the results of this study validate decisively the conclusion that a social reinforcer follows a deprivation-satiation logic. The responsiveness of a reinforcer to relative values of both deprivation and satiation represents only one requirement under this logic. Social reinforcers may be supplied and deprived in a variety of ways, and it is important to discover

[6] An analysis of some possible Deprivation condition artifacts is made in (6).

their responsiveness to many of these ways. It would be especially important, for example, to implement the deprivation of a *single* social reinforcer, rather than of all social reinforcers. Further, it is essential to have some assurance that the social reinforcers are more or less homogeneous in this regard, for verbal approval may not be representative of the reinforcers controlling the purely social initiations made by children to adults. Replications of these effects with other social reinforcers (e.g., attention) would strengthen the conclusions, as would parametric studies of the deprivation-satiation dimension. Another assumption is that approval had acquired reinforcing value for children through a history of conditioning. A stronger case would result if approval were demonstrated to be a more effective reinforcer than, say, a comparable nonsocial noise produced by a machine; or if that noise were shown to be less affected than approval by deprivation-satiation conditions like those employed here. Even so, the earlier finding (6) that isolation enhanced the reinforcing power of adult approval for *S*s as a positive function of the degree to which they sought adult approval in other settings would indicate against both these possibilities. And the difference in spontaneous social initiations following Deprivation and Nondeprivation supports the more general conclusions drawn here; those behaviors were very likely employed for social reinforcers other than approval.

While the results of this study can stand in their own right, several additional experimental conditions could help elucidate the processes at issue. Thus, it would be useful to separate the effects of some of the three components of the satiation condition employed, namely, (a) *E*'s physical presence, (b) the social interaction between *E* and *S*, and (c) the approval reinforcers dispensed by *E* to *S*. To do this, it would be necessary to employ such conditions as, for example, one in which *E* sits with *S* for 20 minutes but says nothing, or one in which approval is dispensed without *E*, possibly out of "thin air." While some such conditions might be difficult to implement, the attempt to establish conditions like these would be worth while in the context of this experiment. Even so, the results of an experiment (3) on related behavior (for attention) suggest that a condition in which *E* sits near *S* but interacts minimally with him (only upon request) functions more as a condition of social deprivation than as one of satiation (7).

Apart from these considerations, the standard primary-conditioned reinforcer issue in the study of animal drives cannot be involved as such in this case. We have assumed that some sort of conditioned reinforcer is at issue, but haven't separated out conclusively the effects of the several stimulus components of that conditioned reinforcer. At the very worst, then, it isn't clear that the social reinforcer dispensed is independent of *E*. We have already noted the possibility that noise, rather than social noise, might constitute the reinforcing stimulus. Apart from this, however, it does not seem significant to consider social reinforcers as separate from the person dispensing them: they are eminently social noises in our logic; and their social character refers not only to their presumed history but also to the method of their delivery.

Additional considerations. In the earlier study, two *E*s were employed to dispense the social reinforcer, one male and one female. An interaction effect was found which indicated, among other things, that the increase in the effectiveness of approval as a reinforcer, brought on by Deprivation relative to Nondeprivation, was greatest for boys with the female *E*. This change was not reliable for the other three Sex of *S* × Sex of *E* groups. In this experiment, in which both boys and girls were tested by a female *E*, no Treatment × Sex interaction was found (although the Satiation mean of girls may not have differed from zero). Hence, to that extent, the previous results are not replicated, but the conclusions can be drawn more generally. (This finding could be referred to the postulate that *S*s of this study are "latent" [in the Freudian sense], while those in the earlier study were "Oedipal." However, there exist other possibilities, including slight changes in method, to explain the discordant results of the two studies on this issue.)

Only one reinforcer-dispensing *E* was employed, and she was not unaware of the expected direction of the results. Her behavior was scored by objective and easily discriminated criteria and judged satisfactory. Still, there remains some reason for caution; for the findings of this experiment cannot be conclusive until they are widely replicated with similar and improved procedures. Nevertheless, the reliability of the results is supported by the difference between the Deprivation and Nondeprivation groups on the spontaneous social initiations made to *E* before she began to dispense the reinforcer: there, where it was even less likely that *E* could influence the outcome, the finding paralleled precisely that derived from the reinforcer effectiveness index.

SUMMARY

On the assumption that approval is representative of the reinforcers controlling the purely social initiations of children to adults, the verbal approval of a female *E* was made contingent upon one response in a two-response game for 102 first- and second-grade children (*S*s) of a university laboratory school. The change in relative response frequency from a baseline level following introduction of the reinforcer indicated the degree to which approval was reinforcing for an *S*.

Before playing the game, *S*s were subjected to one of three experimental conditions: 34 *S*s were subjected to a 20-minute period of isolation (conceived to be social *Deprivation*); 34 *S*s played the game immediately upon coming from class (conceived to be an intermediate condition between deprivation and satiation, and called *Nondeprivation*); and 34 *S*s devoted 20 minutes to drawing and cutting out designs, while *E* maintained a stream of friendly conversation with each of them and approved and admired their art efforts and statements in an appropriate fashion (conceived to be *Satiation* for approval and social contact). There were 17 boys and 17 girls in each experimental group.

Employing two independent tests (one on the order of the means, the other on the regression of the means on the treatment dimension), it was found that the rank-order hypothesis advanced was reliably supported (at $p < .03$ and $p < .005$ respectively). The reinforcing effectiveness of approval was relatively greatest after Deprivation, intermediate after Nondeprivation, and least after Satiation. Approval functioned as a reinforcer after all conditions, even Satiation ($p < .01$). Boys and girls were affected similarly on this measure by the experimental conditions.

The spontaneous social initiations made by Ss to E, before she had begun to dispense approval in the game, supported the results based on the index of the effectiveness of approval as a reinforcer. Following the Deprivation condition, there resulted a greater mean frequency of social initiations ($p < .05$), and a larger proportion of Ss exhibiting apparently intense social interaction ($p < .05$), than there did following the Nondeprivation condition. (The nature of the establishing operation for the Satiation condition precluded a meaningful comparison of the other conditions with it on these social behaviors.)

Thus, a reinforcer appearing to be typical of those involved in children's social drives appears responsive to deprivation and satiation operations of a similar order as those controlling the effectiveness of reinforcers of a number of the primary appetitive drives.

REFERENCES

1. Bowlby, J. Maternal care and mental health. *Bull. World Hlth. Org. Monogr.*, 1951, 3, 355–533.
2. Chase, Lucille. Motivation of young children: An experimental study of the influences of certain types of external incentives upon the performance of a task. *Univer. Iowa Stud. Child Welf.*, 1932, 5, No. 3. Pp. 119.
3. Gewirtz, J. L. Three determinants of attention-seeking in young children. *Monogr. Soc. Res. Child Develpm.*, 1954, 19, No. 2 (Serial No. 59).
4. Gewirtz, J. L. A factor analysis of some attention-seeking behaviors of young children. *Child Develpm.*, 1956, 27, 17–36.
5. Gewirtz, J. L. A program of research on the dimensions and antecedents of emotional dependence. *Child Develpm.*, 1956, 27, 205–221.
6. Gewirtz, J. L., & Baer, D. M. The effect of brief social deprivation on behaviors for a social reinforcer. *J. abnorm. soc. Psychol.*, 1958, 56, 49–56.
7. Gewirtz, J. L., Baer, D. M., & Roth, Chaya H. A note on the similar effects of low social availability of an adult and brief social deprivation on young children's behavior. *Child Develpm.*, 1958, 29, 149–152.

8. Goldfarb, W. Psychological privation in infancy and subsequent adjustment. *Amer. J. Orthopsychiat.*, 1945, **15**, 247–255.

9. Greenspoon, J. The reinforcing effects of two spoken words on the frequency of two responses. *Amer. J. Psychol.*, 1955, **68**, 409–416.

10. Guttman, L. The basis of scalogram analysis. In S. A. Stouffer *et al. Measurement and prediction.* Princeton, N.J.: Princeton Univer. Press, 1950. Pp. 60–90.

11. Hull, C. L. *A behavior system.* New Haven: Yale Univer. Press, 1952.

12. Hurlock, Elizabeth B. The value of praise and reproof as incentives for children. *Arch. Psychol., N.Y.,* 1924, **11**, No. 71, 5–78.

13. Ribble, Margaret. Infantile experience in relation to personality development. In J. McV. Hunt (Ed.), *Personality and the behavior disorders.* New York: Ronald, 1944. Pp. 621–651.

14. Skinner, B. F. *Science and human behavior.* New York: Macmillan, 1953.

15. Spitz, R. A. Hospitalism: An inquiry into the genesis of psychiatric conditions in early childhood. In Anna Freud *et al.* (Eds.), *The psychoanalytic study of the child.* Vol. 1. New York: Int. Universities Press, 1945. Pp. 53–74.

16. Wolf, Theta H. The effect of praise and competition on the persistent behavior of kindergarten children. *Univer. Minn. Child Welf. Monogr. Series,* 1938, No. 15. P. 138.

2.7   Emotional Arousal, Isolation, and Discrimination Learning in Children [1]

Richard H. Walters and Ross D. Parke

Gewirtz and Baer (1958a,b) reported that children who had experienced a 20-minute period of social isolation conditioned more readily in a simple discrimination-learning task, when verbal approval was used as a reinforcer, than did children who had not been isolated. They attributed their findings to the arousal by isolation of a social drive which motivated behavior "for" a social reinforcer. Walters and Karal (1960) criticized this interpretation on the grounds that the isolation procedure may have aroused "anxiety" in young children and that the findings could therefore be interpreted without

[1] This study was supported by a Public Health grant (605/5/293) of the (Canadian) National Health Grants Programme. It was made possible through the cooperation of the York Township Board of Education and the principals and staff of Keelesdale and Humbercrest Schools. The assistance in this project of Valerie A. Cane, Jeanette Cochrane, Betty Lou Joynt, and Susan J. Parke is gratefully acknowledged.

Reprinted from *Journal of Experimental Child Psychology* 1964, **1**, 163–173, by permission of the authors and Academic Press.

the postulation of a social drive.[2] This latter interpretation is consonant with evidence from a variety of studies showing that moderate arousal or moderately heightened drive improves performance in some kinds of learning task (Bindra, 1959; Malmo, 1959).

Walters and Ray (1960) repeated the conditioning procedures of Gewirtz and Baer by using a 2×2 design in which both degree of social contact and "anxiety" level were experimentally manipulated. In this study it was assumed that the placing of Grade 1 and Grade 2 children in a strange environment by a strange adult would be a stimulus for anxiety and that this anxiety would be reduced by the use of a familiar adult as E's assistant. It was assumed also that a 20-minute period of isolation would, in itself, have little influence on responsiveness to social reinforcers. The results indicated that the "anxiety" variable was far more effective than the variable of isolation-interaction in facilitating conditioning.

However, Walters and Ray failed to provide any validating measure of the effectiveness of their manipulation for inducing arousal in young children. Moreover, during the conditioning procedure they employed only social reinforcement of precisely the same kind as that used by Gewirtz and Baer. Since it is crucial to the social-drive hypothesis that this drive increases motivation for *social* reinforcers, the effects of varying the degree of social responsiveness of the experimenter during testing should perhaps also have been investigated.

This paper reports a partial replication of the Walters and Ray study in which a physiological index of emotional arousal was secured and both verbal approval and impersonally dispensed material rewards were used as reinforcers. Children older than those used by Walters and Ray were selected as subjects partly to facilitate the use of a physiological index, and partly to increase the range of subjects with whom the phenomenon under investigation might be demonstrated. The simple discrimination task utilized by Walters and Ray is unsuitable for older children; consequently, a task devised by Miller and Estes (1961) was substituted.

The choice of a physiological index was limited by the necessity of carrying out the study within a school setting. Since there is some evidence that a fall in finger temperature is a concomitant of emotional arousal (Mittelman and Wolff, 1953, Mandler, Mandler, Kremen, and Sholiton, 1961) and equipment for recording this index is battery-operated and easily portable, the finger temperatures of S's were recorded at the same time as the children carried out a discrimination-learning task.

---

[2] In earlier studies by the senior author and his collaborators (e.g., Walters and Karal, 1960), the term "anxiety" was utilized to denote an emotional response to a specific threat situation. Theoretical considerations, outlined by Walters and Parke (1964), led to the substitution of the term "arousal" in this and other more recent publications (e.g., McNulty and Walters, 1962).

METHOD

Subjects

Subjects were 40 Grade 4 boys and 40 Grade 4 girls from two schools in a single area of metropolitan Toronto. Five girls and five boys were randomly assigned to each of eight conditions in a $2 \times 2 \times 2 \times 2$ factorial design involving high versus low arousal, isolation versus no isolation, material versus verbal rewards, and sex of Ss.

Apparatus

A 35 mm slide viewer was attached to a box containing a transformer, which operated the viewer light. When E pushed a button at the rear of the box, a slide was illuminated. When S pressed either of two buttons on the front of the box, the viewer light was extinguished; at the same time, one of two red lights on E's side of the panel was illuminated, thus indicating to E which button S had pushed.

The stimuli presented to S consisted of line drawings of a pair of faces which were identical except that the eyebrows on one face were drawn close to the eyes, whereas they were high up over the eyes on the other face. Four slides were used, two with the high-eyebrow face on the right and two with the high-eyebrow face on the left. Two pairs of slides were used in order to facilitate presentation.

A Yellow Springs battery-operated telethermometer with thermistor probe was used to record S's finger temperatures during testing. The thermistor probe was tightly secured with adhesive tape to the second finger of S's left hand, which was placed on a table with the probe upwards. Ss were instructed to keep the hand as still as possible through the testing period. The dial of the telethermometer permitted readings accurate to the nearest half degree; these were read by inspection and recorded on a data sheet.

Procedure

High-arousal, isolation condition. A female psychology student (E_1) appeared at the door of the classroom and asked for S. The E instructed S to come with her without offering any explanation of her intentions. No conversation was initiated and any questions were answered in a brief and formal manner. The S was then taken to an unfamiliar room, seated in a chair facing the wall, and told: "I have something for you to do, but the machine is broken. Sit in this chair and do not move until I come back." The E then left the room. Ten minutes later she returned with the second E (E_2), and seated S in front of the slide-viewer cabinet which until then had been concealed from S. The E taped a thermistor probe to S's middle finger, again without explanation of what she was doing, and instructed S to keep his finger in one position on the table. Both Es then left the room. The S was left alone for 3 minutes to allow the finger temperature to stabilize. The Es then returned and commenced the conditioning procedure. E_1

recorded S's finger temperature while E_2, with whom S had had least contact, supervised the learning task and dispensed the reinforcers.

High-arousal, no-isolation condition. The procedure was identical with that used for high-arousal, isolation Ss, except that the 10-minute isolation period was omitted. While the finger temperature stabilized, both Es remained in the room. In order to maintain the presumably stressful atmosphere, their responses to S's questions consisted only of the statement, "Just keep still and wait for a while," and brief sentences and phrases of equivalent meaning. The Ss in the no-isolation groups were tested after mid-morning or noon-hour breaks, during which they had been interacting in play sittings with classmates for a period of at least 10 minutes.

Low-arousal, isolation condition. While E fetched S from the classroom, she maintained a very pleasant and friendly manner. She explained to S that he was going to play a game and kept up a running conversation with him in an effort to make S feel at ease. The S was taken to the experimental room, where E said, "We want to play a game with you, but it is broken right now. I do not want you to miss your turn, so just wait in this room while we fix it. We'll come for you when the game is ready."

After 10 minutes, Es returned, and the thermistor probe was attached to S's finger. It was explained to S that this would not hurt and that it was just the same as having a thermometer placed in his mouth, except that it would be placed on his finger. The Es then left the room for 3 minutes while the temperature stabilized.

Low-arousal, no isolation condition. Ss were treated in the same manner as in the previous condition, except that the isolation period was omitted and consequently no explanation of a delay was needed.

Conditioning procedure. All Ss were given the following instructions: "We are going to show you pictures of two twins, Bob and Bill, in this viewer in front of you, and we want you to try to tell them apart. When the light comes on and you see the two twins, push the button underneath the twin you want to call Bill. You may choose either one the first time. After that, each time you see the twins try to pick that same one which you first called Bill."

Following these instructions, the slides were shown one at a time with the position of the twins varied according to a predetermined, randomly arranged schedule. Stimuli were presented and Ss' responses recorded by E_2 while finger temperature readings were taken every 15 seconds by E_1. The slides were presented for 80 trials or until S had made eight consecutive correct responses.

Rewards

Half the children in each arousal condition were reinforced with verbal approval, while half were given material rewards. Verbal reinforcement consisted in E's saying, "That's good," "That's right," or "That's fine," following every correct response which S gave.

The Ss in the material-reward condition had every correct response rein- forced with tokens, which were exchangeable for toys. After the learning instructions, these Ss were told: "Each time you push the right button, that is, the one that is under Bill, you will receive one of these little green disks. If you make enough right choices and collect enough green tokens, we shall give you a prize." The Ss were then shown a tray of the toys that

TABLE 1. Means and SDs of Trials to Criterion and Errors for All Subgroups [a] of Ss

	Boys							
	High Arousal, Isolation				Low Arousal, Isolation			
	Trials		Errors		Trials		Errors	
Reward	Mean	SD	Mean	SD	Mean	SD	Mean	SD
Verbal	20.8	17.82	5.8	9.22	50.4	28.76	22.2	17.44
Material	17.0	13.02	3.2	4.93	47.2	27.11	20.2	17.43
	High Arousal, No Isolation				Low Arousal, No Isolation			
	Trials		Errors		Trials		Errors	
	Mean	SD	Mean	SD	Mean	SD	Mean	SD
Verbal	36.4	24.22	15.4	11.88	34.8	31.51	15.4	19.72
Material	24.2	12.07	8.6	6.83	25.4	27.43	7.0	11.56
	Girls							
	High Arousal, Isolation				Low Arousal, Isolation			
	Trials		Errors		Trials		Errors	
	Mean	SD	Mean	SD	Mean	SD	Mean	SD
Verbal	20.2	10.81	4.2	3.82	19.6	16.31	5.4	7.86
Material	30.2	26.73	8.8	12.42	47.4	27.16	20.4	16.13
	High Arousal, No Isolation				Low Arousal, No Isolation			
	Trials		Errors		Trials		Errors	
	Mean	SD	Mean	SD	Mean	SD	Mean	SD
Verbal	28.2	24.83	9.6	11.76	53.6	25.29	26.0	11.06
Material	20.8	12.62	6.8	6.79	43.0	27.25	18.0	13.74

[a] $N = 5$ in each subgroup.

they could win, and the learning task was begun. Whenever S made a correct response, E, who was concealed from S's view by a screen, pushed a token through an aperture, from which it fell into a tray that had been set in front of S. The E made no comment of any kind during the dispersing of these reinforcers. At the end of the game, S was given a disk and told that in about a week's time he could exchange it for a toy. The S was then taken back to his classroom.

RESULTS

Table 1 presents means and SDs of trials to criterion of boys and girls under each of the eight experimental conditions. The table also includes parallel results in terms of number of errors. The two measures are, of course, not entirely independent.

A $2 \times 2 \times 2 \times 2$ analysis of variance of trials to criterion yielded a significant main effect for arousal level ($F = 7.20$; $p < 0.01$ for 1 and 64 df). The effects of isolation, sex of subject, and type of reward, and all interactions were nonsignificant. An analysis of variance of number of errors produced a similar result ($F = 7.80$ for arousal, no other significant effect).

Because of the variability of room temperature and humidity, finger-temperature recordings were not entirely satisfactory. Moreover, readings from the dial of the telethermometer can only be gross when made by inspection. However, the selected criterion of arousal was the direction of change in temperature during the testing period, which could be adequately assessed from the data secured by E_1. Table 2 gives the number of Ss who

TABLE 2. FINGER TEMPERATURE CHANGES

Change	High Arousal		Low Arousal	
	Isolation	No Isolation	Isolation	No Isolation [a]
Fall	17	13	7	7
No change or slight rise	3	7	13	12
	Chi-square = 13.87; p < 0.001			

[a] The data for one S were lost on account of a loose thermistor probe.

showed drops in finger temperature during the learning task. Data are based only on the first 2 minutes of learning, since some Ss had reached the criterion of learning by the end of this period and consequently the recording of their finger temperatures was discontinued. Moreover, the effects of the experimental manipulation might be expected to be most marked, and most important as a determinant of performance, near the commencement of the learning task. The data for boys and girls were combined in order to increase the number of cases in each cell and thus permit a chi-square test.

This test indicated that the distribution of Ss under the four experimental conditions significantly differed.

As a further check on the relationship between temperature fall and speed of learning, the mean number of trials to criterion was calculated for all Ss who showed a drop in finger temperature and also for all Ss whose temperature did not drop. These means were 26.45 and 38.63, respectively, a difference large enough to reach significance ($t = 2.13$; $p < 0.05$, for 77 df).

DISCUSSION

The results of this study and those of previous related investigations (Walters and Ray, 1960; Walters, Marshall, and Shooter, 1960) indicate that children learn a relatively simple task more readily when their arousal level is moderately high than when their arousal level is low.

Walters and Ray interpreted similar findings as indicating that *reinforcers are more effective* if the recipient of reinforcers is anxious or aroused. However, there is also evidence that observational learning that occurs *in the absence of reinforcement* is facilitated if the observer is aroused (Bandura and Walters, 1963). Consequently, a more general explanatory principle is required to account for the effects of arousal.

One possible explanation is that under moderate emotional arousal the learner is more attentive to relevant cues (Easterbrook, 1959; Kausler and Trapp, 1960). If this is so, it is reasonable to suppose that children under our high-arousal conditions confined their attention more closely to the visually presented stimuli, so facilitating the recognition of differences, and were also more alert to the associations between their choices and the responses of the experimenter.

Erickson (1962) reported more effective verbal conditioning in children who had been deprived of adult contact than in children with whom an adult had been continually communicating during a 15-minute "digit game." Moreover, improved learning following deprivation was apparent only when verbal approval was used as the reinforcer; when reinforcement consisted of marbles delivered by a dispenser, deprived and satiated groups of children did not greatly differ. In fact, Erickson's graphs suggest that conditioning was successful *only* with subjects who had been first deprived of social interaction and then rewarded with verbal approval.

Erickson's marble-dispensing procedure was not, however, comparable to the manner in which material rewards were dispensed in the present study. Under our material-reward condition, Ss were explicitly set a discrimination task and were told that the tokens they received for correct responses could be later exchanged for a prize. In Erickson's experiment, the children who received marbles were not told that these signified the occurrence of a correct response or could be interpreted as rewards. Under these circumstances, it seems unlikely that the dropping of a marble was an adequate stimulus for the production of discrimination learning. Moreover, the *intrinsic* re-

ward value of a marble is probably highly dependent on the sex and age of
a child and whether the marble season is "on." Erickson included girls as
well as boys and used Grade 6 children, who are beyond the age at which
marbles arouse maximum interest; no information is given concerning the
time of year when her children were tested. Finally, she did not tell the
children that they might keep any marbles that were delivered. Consequently, the marbles probably lacked incentive value, in addition to being
inadequate as discriminative stimuli.

The above objections do not, of course, apply to Erickson's findings for
verbally reinforced children, who learned more readily after social deprivation. Her deprivation procedure, however, was more of a withdrawal-of-
attention operation than a simple isolation condition; her E first gave the
children instructions and practice for the verbal conditioning task and then
withdrew her attention while remaining in the room with the child. Somewhat similar procedures have been shown to lead to faster learning in nursery-school children (Hartup, 1958). In fact, Erickson's findings for the
verbally reinforced group are consistent with the view that a variety of conditions, including both withdrawal of reinforcers and the creation of threat,
may produce emotional arousal and consequently more effective learning
in social situations (Bandura and Walters, 1963).

The design of the study did not permit a full examination of the cross-sex
effect reported by Gewirtz and Baer (1958a,b), who noted that social isolation was more likely to enhance the reinforcer effectiveness of verbal approval when the E was of the opposite sex from the Ss. Some data relevant
to this cross-sex effect were, nevertheless, secured. When the arousal manipulation was omitted and verbal approval served as the reinforcer, isolated
girls took considerably fewer trials to learn the discrimination task than did
isolated boys. In fact a selective post hoc two-tailed Mann-Whitney test
indicated that the difference, which is in the opposite direction to that
noted by Gewirtz and Baer, had reached significance ($U = 2$ for $n_1 = 5$,
$n_2 = 5$; $p = 0.032$). However, not too much weight should be placed on this
finding, since the five girls in question performed, on the average, as well
as, or better than, most other subgroups of Ss, including those under the
high-arousal isolation condition. Moreover, the Ss in our study were considerably older than the nursery-school children used by Gewirtz and Baer;
cross-sex effects, which are by no means confined to adult interactions with
previously isolated children, seem to vary according to the age of the Ss
(Stevenson, 1961).

Although the analyses of variance of trials to criterion and errors yielded
no clearly significant interaction effects, the anxiety $\times$ isolation $\times$ sex interactions approached significance ($p < 0.10$). This trend was largely due
to the relatively poor performance of boys under the low-arousal-isolation
condition, a finding that is again at variance with the Gewirtz-and-Baer
hypothesis concerning cross-sex effects in relation to isolation.

According to the social-deprivation theory, it is the nature of approval or

attentiveness as a specifically *social* reinforcer that accounts for the heightened susceptibility to social influence of children who are rewarded for
conformity following social deprivation. Our failure to find any interaction
effects involving isolation and type of reward suggests that this aspect of
the theory is mistaken and consequently lends some support to the arousal
hypothesis, which demands only that the rewards be appropriate to the age,
sex, and socioeconomic status of the recipients. Perhaps the weight of evidence would have been greater if an automatic dispenser had been used to
deliver the material rewards. However, the manner in which material rewards were dispensed closely approximates automatic dispensing, except
for the fact that the *E* was quite evidently the controller of resources. It
may even be claimed that our procedure is the better parallel to the dispensing of "nonsocial" rewards in real-life situations, in which material
rewards are ordinarily perceived as being mediated by socialization agents.
In any case, the manner in which the material rewards were dispensed involved a minimum of social interaction and departed radically from the
conditions under which, according to Gewirtz and Baer, reinforcer effectiveness should be enhanced.

Since *S* was permitted initially to *select* the twin he would call Bill, it is
possible that arousal facilitated learning only because, in the two-choice
discrimination task, the "correct" discrimination was prepotent in *S*s' response hierarchy to the pairs of perceptual stimuli. In this case, of course,
the results would be consistent with Spence's (1958) theorizing concerning
the influence of strength of drive on learning. In the study by Walters and
Ray (1960), however, the "correct" response was *S*'s nonpreferred choice
during the first 4 (baseline) minutes of responding in a two-choice situation.
Nevertheless, these findings are only paradoxical if one fails to distinguish
situationally induced arousal or "anxiety" from "anxiety" or "emotionality"
as a personality characteristic that may be assessed from paper-and-pencil
tests. Whereas inventory and questionnaire measures of anxiety such as the
MAS may reflect primarily the *range* of cues to which a person will respond
in an emotional manner, physiological measures of arousal and self-reports
of reactions to specific threatening situations may reflect primarily the *intensity* with which the subject reacts. If this speculation is correct, one
would not expect "manifest anxiety" and "emotional arousal" to influence
learning in precisely equivalent ways (Walters and Parke, 1964).

A fairly lengthy series of isolation studies has thus led to several conclusions. In the first place, there is some evidence to support the hypothesis
that isolation may, under some circumstances, be a conditioned stimulus for
"anxiety." This conclusion can draw further support from Schachter's
(1959) studies of affiliation. Second, isolation may be a condition under
which "anxiety" induced by preceding events may mount, again a conclusion that is consonant with Schachter's data. Third, moderate emotional
arousal (accompanying or not accompanying isolation) may lead to faster

learning, at least of some kinds of discrimination tasks. Finally, it is now proposed that this faster learning is in no way related to changes in reinforcer effectiveness, but rather reflects the improved perceptual organization and cue utilization that appears to accompany moderate emotional arousal.

SUMMARY

The social-drive hypothesis states that social deprivation arouses a social drive that motivates behavior "for" social reinforcers. An alternative explanation is that social deprivation can be an emotionally arousing stimulus and that faster learning by children following isolation reflects the arousal of a nonspecific drive condition. Eighty Grade IV children, 40 boys and 40 girls, learned a simple discrimination task following one of four manipulations: high arousal with isolation; high arousal without isolation; low arousal with isolation; and low arousal without isolation. Half the Ss under each manipulation were rewarded with verbal approval; the remainder received material rewards. Results indicated that the only important influence on learning was Ss' level of arousal.

REFERENCES

Bandura, A., & Walters, R. H. *Social learning and personality development.* New York: Holt, 1963.

Bindra, D. *Motivation: a systematic reinterpretation.* New York: Ronald Press, 1959.

Easterbrook, J. A. The effect of emotion on cue utilization and the organization of behavior. *Psychol. Rev.,* 1959, **66,** 183–201.

Erikson, Marilyn T. Effects of social deprivation and satiation on verbal conditioning in children. *J. comp. physiol. Psychol.,* 1962, **55,** 953–957.

Gewirtz, J. L., & Baer, D. M. The effects of brief social deprivation on behaviors for a social reinforcer. *J. abnorm. soc. Psychol.,* 1958, **56,** 49–56. (a).

Gewirtz, J. L., & Baer, D. M. Deprivation and satiation of social reinforcers as drive conditions. *J. abnorm. soc. Psychol.,* 1958, **57,** 165–172. (b)

Hartup, W. W. Nurturance and nurturance-withdrawal in relationship to the dependency behavior of preschool children. *Child Develpm.,* 1958, **29,** 191–201.

Kausler, D. H., & Trapp, E. P. Motivation and incidental learning. *Psychol. Rev.,* 1960, **67,** 373–379.

McNulty, J. A., & Walters, R. H. Emotional arousal, conflict, and susceptibility to social influence. *Canad. J. Psychol.,* 1962, **16,** 211–220.

Malmo, R. B. Activation: a neurophysiological dimension. *Psychol. Rev.,* 1959, **66,** 367–386.

Mandler, G., Mandler, Jean M., Kremen, I., & Sholiton, R. D. The response to threat: Relations among verbal and physiological indices. *Psychol. Monogr.,* 1961, **75,** No. 9 (Whole No. 513).

Miller, Louise B., & Estes, Betsy W.   Monetary reward and motivation in discrimination learning. *J. exp. Psychol.,* 1961, **61,** 501–504.

Mittelman, B., & Wolff, H. G.   Emotions and skin temperature: Observations on patients during psychotherapeutic (psychoanalytic) interviews. *Psychosom. Med.,* 1943, **5,** 211–231.

Schachter, S.   *The psychology of affiliation.* Stanford: Stanfodr Univer. Press, 1959.

Spence, K. W.   A theory of emotionally based drive (D) and its relation to performance in simple learning situations. *Amer. Psychol.,* 1958, **13,** 131–141.

Stevenson, H. W.   Social reinforcement with children as a function of CA, sex of E, and sex of S. *J. abnorm. soc. Psychol.,* 1961, **63,** 147–154.

Walters, R. H., & Karal, Pearl.   Social deprivation and verbal behavior. *J. Pers.,* 1960, **28,** 89–107.

Walters, R. H., Marshall, W. E., & Shooter, J. R.   Anxiety, isolation, and susceptibility to social influence. *J. Pers.,* 1960, **28,** 518–529.

Walters, R. H., & Parke, R. D.   Social motivation, dependency, and susceptibility to social influence. In L. Berkowitz (Ed.), *Advances in experimental social psychology.* New York: Academic Press, 1964, in press.

Walters, R. H., & Ray, E.   Anxiety, social isolation, and reinforcer effectiveness. *J. Pers.,* 1960, **28,** 358–367.

chapter three

Imitation

3.1 Introduction

Although social reinforcement is an important means of shaping social behavior, many social responses are learned merely through observing the behavior of other persons. Since imitation often short-circuits the shaping procedures involved in the use of social reinforcement, it is one of the most important means through which social responses are acquired and maintained.

A number of attempts have been made to account for the way in which imitative responses are acquired and these have recently been reviewed by Bandura (1965). Around the turn of the century, social psychologists like Morgan (1896) and McDougall (1908) offered explanations of imitation; however, like most instinct-based theories, their explanations have not had much influence.

More influential was a classical conditioning of imitation advocated by Humphrey (1921), Allport (1924), and Holt (1931). According to this approach, person A makes a response that is copied by person B. Then A may repeat the response, and a circular associative sequence is set up whereby B's matching behavior becomes a stimulus for A's behavior. Critics of the theory (e.g., Bandura, 1965; Bandura and Walters, 1963) note that it fails to adequately account for the emergence of novel responses during the model-observer interaction sequence.

The instrumental learning paradigm has been used most frequently to explain the development of imitation. Miller and Dollard provided the classic statement of this position over a quarter of a century ago in *Social Learning and Imitation* (1941). The authors describe a form of imitation called matched-dependent behavior. In a two-choice discrimination situation, children always saw the choice made by another subject rewarded. Whenever the observer matched the choice of the model, he was reinforced; nonmatching resulted in nonreinforcement. After a few trials children learned to use the behavior of the model as a discriminative cue and thereby gained reinforcement. In this way, Miller and Dollard argued, children as well as rats could be taught to imitate the behavior of another person. In a variety of studies they showed that imitative responses acquired in this manner would generalize across situations, models, and motivational states.

In addition to requiring that the responses imitated already exist in the observer's repertoire, the theory "does not account for the occurrence of imitative behavior in which the observer does not perform the models' responses during the acquisition process and for which reinforcers are not delivered to the models or the observers. Moreover, it presents imitative learning as contingent on the observer's performing a close approximation to the matching response before he can acquire it imitatively and thus places a severe restriction on the behavioral changes that can be attributed to the influence of a model" (Bandura & Walters, 1963, p. 55).

Recent evidence favoring an operant-reinforcement analysis of imitation is presented in the Baer and Sherman paper. According to this position (Skinner, 1953, 1957), imitative responses develop from a learning history in which reinforcement is contingent on a response similar to the model's. As a result of being reinforced, the matching response itself may acquire secondary reinforcement. Through generalization a child may eventually imitate responses of the model which have not previously been reinforced. In the research, Baer and Sherman (1964) have employed an automated puppet who served as both the model and the reinforcing agent for shaping imitative behavior in children. They established a diverse repertoire of imitative responses (mouthing, head nodding, and novel verbalizations) by socially reinforcing their subjects for matching the responses of the puppet. Secondly, these authors demonstrated that this imitative behavior will generalize to new behaviors (bar pressing in this case) without specific training in the new response. Finally, their research indicated that the generalized imitative response can persist in a context of reinforcement of other imitative responses without being specifically reinforced. The study provides a very clear demonstration of the role of reinforcement in controlling and maintaining generalized imitation in children.

In a later study, Baer, Peterson, and Sherman (1965) taught several imitative responses to retarded children whose behavior repertoires did not originally include imitation by physically assisting the child to make the desired responses initially and by providing immediate reinforcement for successful responses. The subjects were eventually capable of imitating new responses without assistance and showed evidence of generalized imtiation as well. Lovaas, Berberich, Perloff, and Schaeffer (1966) successfully used a similar paradigm for conditioning imitation of verbal responses by mute schizophrenic children, and Metz (1964) showed that generalized imitative responding can be established by operant procedures in autistic children.

In the next contribution to this topic, Hartup and Coates (1967) report the results of a recent test of Mowrer's secondary reinforcement theory of imitation. According to Mowrer, when a model performs an action and at the same time rewards the observer through the process of secondary reinforcement, the model's behavior acquires value for the observer. Owing to stimulus generalization, whenever the observer reproduces the model's behavior, the proprioceptive feedback accompanying the execution of the imitative act is experienced as rewarding. The observer, therefore, is motivated to reproduce the model's behavior, even in the model's absence, in order to secure the secondary reinforcing feedback. Mowrer's theoretical position emphasizes the importance of the model-observer relationship and explicitly predicts that the amount of reward given by the model is a critical determinant of whether the model will be imitated. As in the case of social reinforcement, research has shown that the relationship variable is important. Specifically, a model who has been warm and affectionate will be imitated more than a neutral model (Bandura & Huston, 1961; Mussen & Parker, 1965).

However, as Hartup and Coates (1967) note, there are important situational and individual differences which may alter the extent to which a rewarding model is imitated. In their experiment, when the effect of the child's history of prior peer reinforcement was examined, it was found that nursery school children who had frequently been rewarded by peers imitated a rewarding peer more than a nonrewarding peer. While this result clearly supports Mowrer's theory, their finding that subjects with a socialization history of relatively infrequent peer reinforcement imitated a nonrewarding model to a greater degree clearly limits it. This study indicates not only that prior socialization experiences are important determinants of model choice, but that both peer models and adult models play an important role in modifying children's social behavior.

The next paper (Bandura, 1965) further highlights the role of reinforcement in the imitative process. Specifically, Bandura's results indicate that the consequences of the model's participation in an activity will be an important determinant of whether the observer will engage in a similar activity. Children imitated the actions of the model more frequently when the model was rewarded than when the model was punished. However, the consequences of the model's response affect primarily whether or not the response is performed and have relatively little effect on the learning of the behavior patterns. In a posttest, all subjects, regardless of whether they had been exposed to a rewarded model or a punished model, could accurately demonstrate the sequence of aggressive responses that the model had displayed. Moreover, in the Bandura study, the subject was never reinforced for imitating, which suggests that imitative learning can occur independently of reinforcement delivered either to the model or the observer.

In order to account for the occurrence of imitative learning in the absence of reinforcement, Bandura (Bandura, 1965; Bandura & Walters, 1963) has offered a stimulus contiguity theory of observational learning. He has summarized this contiguity-mediational theory as follows: "During the period of exposure, modeling stimuli elicit in observing subjects configurations and sequences of sensory experiences which, on the basis of past associations, become centrally integrated and structured into perceptual responses" (Bandura, 1965b, p. 10). According to this theory the observer's symbolic or representational responses in the form of images and verbal associates of the model's behavior are clearly central in accounting for observational learning. In this section, Bandura, Grusec, and Menlove (1966) report the results of a recent test of this theory. On the assumption that the observer's verbalizations would affect the representational process, subjects were instructed to verbalize the model's actions in order to facilitate the development of symbolic representations of the model's responses. While other children passively observed, a third group verbalized competing or irrelevant responses in order to retard the acquisition of imaginal correlates of the model's behavior. In support of the theory, subjects in the facilitating symbolization condition were clearly superior in reproducing the model's responses. The study indicates that the nature of the activity during the viewing period can markedly influence observational learning. More specifically, this research suggests that symbolization clearly enhances the acquisition of imitative responses. Finally, the study questions the adequacy of theories which stress the necessity of reinforcement for the occurrence of imitative learning.

In the final paper in this section, Hicks (1965) has explored the long-term effects of exposure to models. Children of nursery school age saw aggressive peer or adult models and were tested for retention of the model's responses immediately after exposure and again after a 6-month interval. Although the subjects saw the model only once, they were able to perform some of the model's responses even after the lengthy interval. Hicks found that, when questioned, subjects remembered even more than they spontaneously performed. This demonstration that the effects of exposure to models is more than transitory and may endure over a lengthy time span is an important contribution to the imitation literature. A further significant feature of both Hicks' contribution and the Hartup and Coates' article is the explicit recognition of the potentially important role played by peer models in social development. In fact, Hicks' study represents one of the few experimental comparisons of the effectiveness of peer and adult models. The complexity of his results clearly indicates the need for additional systematic comparisons of these two groups. Since the influence of peers as shapers of social behavior patterns seems to increase with age, investigations of the influence of adult and peer models with children at various age levels may clarify the complex relationships in this area.

REFERENCES

Allport, F. H. *Social psychology,* Cambridge, Mass.: Riverside Press, 1924.

Baer, D. M., Peterson, R. F., & Sherman, J. A. Building an imitative repertoire by programming similarity between child and model as discriminative for reinforcement. Paper read at biennial meeting of the Society for Research in Child Development, Minneapolis, Minnesota, March, 1965.

Baer, D. M., & Sherman, J. A. Reinforcement control of generalized imitation in young children. *Journal of Experimental Child Psychology,* 1964, 1, 37–49.

Bandura, A. Influence of models' reinforcement contingencies on the acquisition of imitative responses. *Journal of Personality and Social Psychology,* 1965b, 1, 589–595.

Bandura, A., Grusec, J. E., & Menlove, Frances L. The influence of symbolization and incentive set on observational learning. *Child Development,* 1966, 37, 499–506.

Bandura, A., & Huston, A. C. Identification as a process of incidental learning, *Journal of Abnormal and Social Psychology,* 1961, 63, 311–318.

Bandura, A., & Walters, R. H. *Social Learning and Personality Develop-*
ment, New York: Holt, Rinehart and Winston, Inc., 1963.

Hartup, W. W., & Coates, B. Imitation of peers as a function of reinforcement from the peer group and rewardingness of the model. *Child*
Development, 1967, *38,* 1003–1016.

Hicks, D. J. Imitation and retention of film-mediated aggressive peer and
adult models. *Journal of Personality and Social Psychology,* 1965, **2,**
97–100.

Holt, C. B. *Animal drive and the learning process,* Vol. I. New York:
Holt, 1931.

Humphrey, C. Imitation and the conditioned reflex. *Pedagogical Semi-*
nary, 1921, **28,** 1–21.

Lovaäs, O. I., Berberich, J. P., Perloff, B. F., & Schaeffer, B. Acquisition
of imitative speech by schizophrenic children. *Science,* 1966, **151,** 705–
707.

McDougall, W. *An introduction to social psychology.* London: Methuen,
1908.

Metz, J. R. Teaching autistic children generalized imitation. Paper read
at the American Psychological Association, Los Angeles, 1964.

Miller, N. E., & Dollard, J. *Social learning and imitation.* New Haven:
Yale University Press, 1941.

Morgan, C. L. *Habit and Instinct.* London: Arnold, 1896.

Mussen, P. H., & Parker, A. L. Mother nurturance and girls' incidental
imitative learning. *Journal of Personality and Social Psychology,* 1965,
2, 94–97.

Piaget, J. *Play, dreams, and imitation in childhood.* New York: Norton,
1951.

Skinner, B. F. *Science and human behavior.* New York: Macmillan, 1953.

Skinner, B. F. *Verbal behavior.* New York: Appleton, 1957.

SUPPLEMENTARY READING

Bandura, A. Vicarious processes: A case of no-trial learning. In L. Berkowitz (Ed.), *Advances in experimental social psychology,* Vol. II. New
York: Academic Press, 1966. Pp. 1–55.

Bandura, A., & Walters, R. H. *Social learning and personality develop-*
ment. New York: Holt, 1963. Pp. 47–108.

Maccoby, E. E. Effects of mass media. In L. W. Hoffman & M. L. Hoffman
(Eds.), *Review of child development research,* Vol. I. New York:
Russell Sage, 1964. Pp. 323–348.

3.2 Reinforcement Control of Generalized Imitation in Young Children [1]

Donald M. Baer and James A. Sherman [2]

The term "imitation" has seen much use in the literature of child psychology. However, experimental work in this area has often failed to invoke its most powerful meaning. In experimental situations, behavior frequently has been called imitative because it resembled that of a model previously observed by the subject. But there rarely has been any guarantee that the *similarity* of the two behaviors was functional in producing the behavior in the observer. Instead, it has been common to require the observer to learn a reinforced response after having watched a model perform the same response and receive reinforcement for it. The observer often does profit from this observation of a correct performance. However, it is quite possible that he does so because certain stimuli of the situation have been paired with the sight of the reinforcement secured by the model. Since the sight of reinforcement should be a powerful secondary reinforcer, observational learning, not of a similar response, but of the cues which will facilitate that response may very well take place. When the observer is placed in the situation, his learning (of what typically is the only reinforced response in the situation) is speeded by his previously acquired sensitivity to the cues in the situation.

For example, a child may watch a model turn a crank on a green box and receive nothing, then turn a crank on a red box and receive reinforcement consistently and repeatedly. As a result of this observation, the observer subsequently may learn the same discrimination more quickly than a control subject. This may be due simply to the establishment of red as a discriminative cue for reinforcement. The observer is better reinforced for approaching red than green as a consequence of his observation, and thereby is more likely to turn the crank on the red box and be reinforced for it. There is no need in this example to assume that the *similarity* of his crank-turning response and the model's is involved. The similarity may lie in the eye of the

[1] This research was supported in part by grant M-2208 from the National Institutes of Health, United States Public Health Service.

[2] The authors are grateful to Miss Judith Higgins and Miss Sharon Feeney for their reliable and intelligent assistance as *A*s. Appreciation is also due to Mrs. Mildred Reed, Director, and Mrs. Mildred Hall, Seattle Day Nursery Association, for their cooperation and assistance.

Reprinted from *Journal of Experimental Child Psychology,* 1964, **1,** 37–49, by permission of the authors and Academic Press.

experimenter rather than in the eye of the observer, and, in this situation, only a similar response will be reinforced. Hence the similarity is both forced and (perhaps) irrelevant.

However, there can be a more powerful use of imitation in the experimental analysis of children's learning if it can be shown that similarity per se functions as an important stimulus dimension in the child's behavior. The purpose of the present study is to add another demonstration of this role of similarity to the small body of literature already produced (e.g., Bandura and Huston, 1961) and to show the function of certain social reinforcement operations in promoting responding along the dimension of similarity in behavior. Specifically, a response is considered which is imitative of a model but never directly reinforced. Instead, other responses, also imitative of a model, are controlled by reinforcement operations. The strength of the unreinforced imitative response is then observed as a function of these reinforcement operations. An animated talking puppet, used previously in studies of social interaction with children (Baer, 1962), serves both as a model to imitate and as a source of social reinforcement.

METHOD

Apparatus

The apparatus was an animated talking puppet dressed as a cowboy and seated in a chair inside a puppet stage. The puppet was capable of making four kinds of responses: (1) raising and lowering his head, or *nodding;* (2) opening and closing his mouth, or *mouthing;* (3) *bar-pressing* on a puppet-scaled bar-pressing apparatus located beside his chair, almost identical in appearance to a regular-sized bar-pressing apparatus located beside the child; and (4) *talking,* accomplished by playing *E*'s voice through a loud-speaker mounted behind the puppet's chair, while the puppet's jaw was worked in coordination with the words being spoken. (For a more complete description and a photograph, cf. Baer, 1962.)

First Sequence of Procedures

Introduction. The experiment was conducted in a two-room mobile trailer-laboratory (Bijou, 1958) parked in the lot of a day-care nursery. *E* observed the child and puppet through a one-way mirror from the other room. The child sat in a chair immediately in front of the puppet stage. An adult assistant, *A,* brought the child to the laboratory, introduced him to the puppet, seated him in his chair, and then sat in a screened corner of the room, out of the child's sight. The introduction for the first session was, "This is Jimmy the puppet. He wants to talk to you. And this (pointing) is your bar. See, it's just like Jimmy's bar, only bigger (pointing). Do you know how it works?" The usual answer was "No," in which case *A* demonstrated a bar-press, saying "Now you try it." (Some children pressed the bar without demonstration.) *A* then said, "You can talk to Jimmy now." On all later sessions, *A* said simply, "Hello Jimmy, here's (child's name) to talk to you again," and, to the child, "Now you can talk to Jimmy again."

After *A*'s introduction, the puppet raised his head and began speaking to the child. He followed a fairly standard line of conversation, starting with greetings, and progressing through expressions of pleasure over the chance to talk with the child to alternating questions about what the child had been doing and colorful stories about what the puppet had been doing. This type of conversation was maintained throughout all the sessions; the social reinforcement procedures used as the independent variables in this study were interjected within the conversation according to the experimental design.

Operant level. The first session was to acquaint child and puppet and to collect an operant level of the child's bar-pressing, imitative or otherwise. Shortly after the puppet began talking to the child, he began to press his bar, alternating between a slow rate of 1 response per 15 seconds and a fast rate of about 3 responses per second. The puppet's bar-pressing was recorded on a cumulative recorder.

The operant level period was interrupted after 5–10 minutes of the puppet's bar-pressing for a special procedure. The special procedure was designed to establish whether the child could generalize from the puppet's bar to his own. After the puppet had stopped bar-pressing, he would nod twice and say, "This is my head. Show me your head." Invariably, the child would move his head or point to it. The puppet then said, "Good," and began mouthing, saying, "This is my mouth. Show me your mouth." The child would move his mouth or point to it. Then the puppet said, "Good," and bar-pressing twice, said, "This is my bar. Show me your bar." Some children imitated the response; some pointed to their bar. A few did neither; of these, some appeared puzzled, and others tentatively reached for the puppet's bar. These were the children the procedure was designed to detect. In their cases, the puppet explained that they had a bar of their own and helped them find it, which usually sufficed to produce either a bar-press or a pointing toward the bar. The puppet gave no reinforcement for the bar-pressing response, and instead resumed the conversation about his adventures or the child's. With some subjects there then followed another 5–10 minutes of bar-pressing by the puppet to determine whether this procedure in itself had promoted imitative bar-pressing by the child. No imitative bar-pressing ever did develop as a result of this procedure alone in the children subjected to it. For the rest of the subjects, this extra portion of the operant level period was dropped.

Still another 5–10 minutes of bar-pressing by the puppet was sometimes displayed. On these occasions, the puppet took up a very approving line of conversation, dispensing a great deal of "Good," "Very good," and "You're really smart" to the child. This was to determine the effect of noncontingent social reinforcement on the child's imitative bar-pressing. However, no child subjected to this procedure ever developed imitative bar-pressing as a result. The other subjects had a similar kind of noncontingent approval incorporated into the earlier portions of their operant level periods.

The typical rate of imitative bar-pressing during operant level periods was zero. In fact, of 11 children seen in this study, only one showed a slight tendency to imitate the puppet's bar-pressing, but this disappeared early in her operant level period. Two others showed a non-imitative bar-pressing rate during the initial session.

Reinforcement of some imitative responses. After collecting the child's operant level of bar-pressing, the puppet stopped bar-pressing and began to present a series of other responses, one after another at first, and then at scattered points in his conversation. Each time he would first ask the child, "Can you do this?" These responses consisted of nodding, mouthing, and a variety of nonsense statements (such as "Glub-flub-bug," "One-two-three-four," or "Red robins run rapidly"). In each case, if the child imitated the responses, the puppet reinforced the child's response with approval, consisting mainly of the words "Good," "Very good," and "Fine." Almost without exception, the children did imitate virtually every response the puppet presented in this way, and after a few reinforcements, the puppet stopped asking "Can you do this?" in preface to the response.

After the child was consistently imitating each of these other responses without the prefatory "Can you do this?", the puppet resumed bar-pressing, alternating fast and slow rates. He continued to display nodding, mouthing, and verbal nonsense statements at scattered points in his conversation, and maintained a continuous schedule of reinforcement for every imitation of these by the child. The child's bar-pressing from this point on was the basic dependent variable of the study. An increase over operant level in this never-reinforced [3] bar-pressing by the child, especially insofar as it matched the puppet's bar-pressing, would be significant: It would be attributable to the direct reinforcement of the other responses (nodding, mouthing, and verbal). These responses have very slight topographical resemblance to bar-pressing; they are like it essentially in that they all are imitative of a model's behavior. Thus an increase in imitative bar-pressing by the child would indicate that similarity of responding per se was a functional dimension of the child's behavior, that is, similarity of responding could be strengthened as could responding itself.

This program of reinforcement for all imitative responding (other than bar-pressing) was usually begun during the first session. With some children, it was started early in their second session. Children were seen as many as 7

[3] On one occasion with one child, a bar-press was accidentally reinforced. This will be noted in the results.

sessions in the course of the study. These sessions were separated by 3–7 days.

RESULTS

In the design of this study, both individual and group performances are relevant to the central question. If any child showed a significant increase in imitative bar-pressing over his operant level, as a result of direct reinforcement of other imitative responses, this would demonstrate the functional role of similarity in behavior for that child. Hence each child represented an experiment in himself. As a group, the sample allows some estimation of the probability of the effect occurring in children from this population.

Of 11 children studied, 4 failed to show any development of an imitative bar-pressing response during the course of reinforcement of nodding, mouthing, and verbal imitations. Two of these were the only two children showing a high level of non-imitative bar-pressing during their operant level periods. The remaining 7 children showed varying degrees of increase in bar-pressing, as illustrated in Fig. 1. This figure shows 4 records, selected to indicate the range of increase in bar-pressing obtained. A fact not always apparent in these records (necessarily compressed for publication) is that virtually

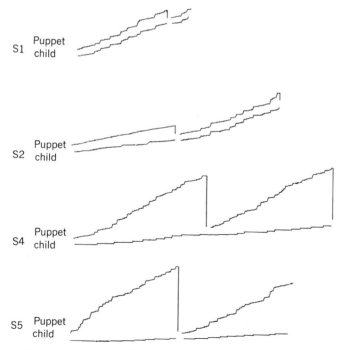

FIGURE 1. The development of generalized imitative bar-pressing in four representative Ss.

every bar-pressing response by the child occurs closely following a response (or response burst) by the puppet, and hence is clearly imitative.

FURTHER PROCEDURE AND RESULTS

The increased imitative bar-pressing by some of the children was brought about by reinforcement of other imitative responding by the child (nodding, mouthing, and verbal performances). Further procedures were developed to show the dependence of the generalized imitative bar-pressing on this reinforcement. These procedures were of two kinds: extinction of the other imitative responding, and time-out from the other imitative responding.

Extinction of imitation. Extinction was instituted with two children, one of whom had developed a near-perfect rate of imitative bar-pressing, the other showing a low rate. After a stable rate of imitative bar-pressing had been established by each child, the puppet stopped giving any reinforcement for imitation of his nodding, mouthing, or verbal nonsense performances (imitation of which in the immediate past he had reinforced continuously). However, he continued performing these actions at the same rate. He also continued to reinforce the child at the same rate, but at appropriate points in the child's conversation rather than for imitation. This continued for several sessions, until the child had shown a stable or marked decrease in imitative bar-pressing. Then reinforcement was shifted back to imitations of nodding, mouthing, or verbal nonsense performances and maintained as before, until the child showed a stable or marked increase in imitative bar-pressing. As usual, bar-pressing was never reinforced.

The subjects chosen for this procedure were $S1$ and $S4$ of Fig. 1; both were girls. Their records (Fig. 2) include the early sessions that show operant level and the development of generalized imitation, already seen in Fig. 1, as a baseline against which the effect of extinction of other imitative responding is seen. (Sessions 4 and 5 are omitted from the record of $S4$ because they are virtually identical in procedure and performance to Session 3 and would needlessly enlarge Fig. 2 if included.) It is clear that $S1$ was very responsive to the extinction and reinforcement operations: Her near-perfect rate of imitative bar-pressing weakened considerably after nearly one complete session of extinction for other imitative responding, but promptly recovered its near-perfect aspect when reinforcement was resumed.[4] The record of $S4$ shows the same pattern, but the differences are not so apparent. This may be due to the low rate of imitative bar-pressing induced in $S4$

[4] In the case of $S1$, it can be seen that the effects of extinction are markedly stronger with the beginning of Session 4, and that the effects of resumed reinforcement, clear in the last half of Session 5, are even more pronounced with the beginning of Session 6. This interaction between session changes and experimental conditions remains an unexplained complication of the data; however, it need not greatly alter the conclusions drawn.

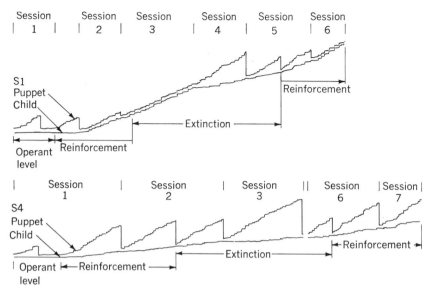

FIGURE 2. The effects of extinction of previously reinforced imitation on generalized imitative bar-pressing in two Ss.

under the previous reinforcement conditions. Sighting along the curve, however, will make clear the same pattern of rate changes apparent in the record of S1.

Time-out from imitation. Time-out procedures were instituted with two other children, one of whom had a high rate of imitative bar-pressing, and the other only a modest rate. After a stable rate of imitative bar-pressing had been established by each child, the puppet ceased providing any nodding, mouthing, or verbal nonsense performances for the child to imitate, hence eliminating any reinforcement of imitation by eliminating the previously established cues for the occurrence of imitation. Social reinforcement was continued at the same rate, but was delivered for appropriate comments in the child's conversation rather than for imitation.

This time-out was continued until the child showed a stable or marked decrease in imitative bar-pressing. Then the puppet resumed performances of nodding, mouthing, and verbal nonsense statements, and shifted his reinforcement back to the child's imitations of these performances until the child showed a stable or marked increase in imitative bar-pressing. Then the whole cycle of time-out and reinforcement was repeated in exactly the same way. Bar-pressing, of course, was never reinforced.

The subjects chosen for this procedure were S2 of Fig. 1 and S3, both girls. Their records are shown in Fig. 3. (The early portion of the record of S2 has already been seen in Fig. 1.) It is apparent that the time-out condition produced a quick and drastic weakening of imitative bar-pressing in

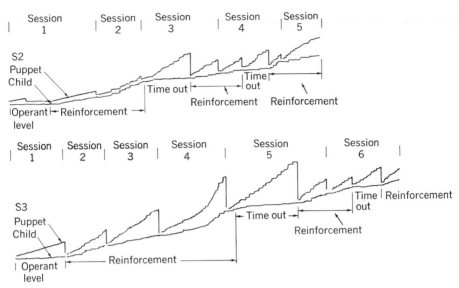

FIGURE 3. The effects of time-out from reinforced imitation on generalized imitative bar-pressing in two Ss.

these children, and that a resumption of reinforcement of other imitative responses, when these were again displayed by the puppet for the child to imitate, quickly generalized to the nonreinforced imitative bar-pressing. (By accident, S3 received one reinforcement for bar-pressing during Session 1. It is assumed that the effect of this single reinforcement was negligible.)

DISCUSSION

In this study, social reinforcement has been used to strengthen a set of behaviors directly. The responses of nodding, mouthing, and saying nonsense syllable chains have been established through instructions ("Can you do this?") and reinforcement, and maintained with reinforcement. These responses have in common the fact that they are all imitative of a model's behaviors and that the child does them only when the model does. It is in this context that the strengthening of imitative bar-pressing becomes significant. Bar-pressing was never reinforced directly; nor was the child ever instructed to bar-press imitatively. (The simple instructions dealing with the child's bar—"Show me your bar"—never promoted imitative bar-pressing in the children observed specifically for this possibility.) Bar-pressing has little physical or topographical resemblance to nodding, mouthing, and verbal nonsense chains. What it does have in common with these responses is the fact that it too is imitative of one of the model's performances. Hence its strengthening, following the direct strengthening of nodding, mouthing, and verbal responses, may be attributed to generalization along a dimension of similarity between the child's response and the model's response. In other words, the child is responsive to the stimulus of similarity between responses per se, apparently independently of the particular physical stimuli involved in specific responses.

It can be important to demonstrate that similarity between behaviors of model and child can be a functional stimulus dimension. Such a demonstration would be essential in at least some reinforcement analyses of imitation, especially in any analysis trying to show that imitation should be a strong response in a child, even when it does not produce extrinsic reinforcement. One such analysis might proceed as follows:

In the ordinary course of his early life, a child will form many hundreds of discriminations that involve the sight or sound of a model's behavior as a cue for a response by the child which achieves the same (or a similar) reinforcing outcome. In effect, in all such situations, the child is in a position to learn what response on his part reproduces the effect produced by the model's behavior. Many times, the world will be such that only a response similar in physical make-up or topography will reproduce the same effect. For example, many times a child will need to get through a latched door. He will often observe an older or more skillful model turn the knob and pass through. The child will eventually differentiate his own behavior to the point where it succeeds in opening the door. But doors are such that very few responses will succeed, and consequently the child's behavior will be very similar to the model's. In this situation, and in many others like it, the stimulus of similarity between the child's behavior and the model's is consistently programmed and sets the occasion for reinforcement of the child. Given enough of these situations, of adequate consistency and variety, the stimulus of similarity between behaviors in general may become discriminative for reinforcement. Since a stimulus which is discriminative for reinforcement becomes (secondarily) reinforcing in its own right, then responses which produce similarity between behaviors will thereby be strengthened. Responses of the child which "produce similarity" are those responses which have a topography that the child can compare to the topography of the model's responses, e.g., he can see both his response and the model's or can hear both. Hence the child will become generally "imitative," and, if similarity has great strength as a discriminative and therefore reinforcing stimulus, imitative behavior will be correspondingly more prevalent and apparently autonomous.

Certain details of procedure in this study may be worthy of note. One involves the fact that noncontingent social reinforcement given by the puppet to the child was not sufficient to induce imitation of the puppet. Furthermore, once a generalized imitation had been set up, noncontingent reinforcement was not sufficient to maintain it. Only when other imitative responses were being reinforced would imitative bar-pressing (never directly reinforced) remain at any strength. The puppet would, as the design required, shift his reinforcement from imitative responses to other appropriate moments in the interactions, but the general amount and spacing of this reinforcement remained the same. Hence the effects on imitative bar-pressing noted here cannot be attributed to the simple presence or absence of reinforcement, but rather are related to its contingent or noncontingent use. This is at some variance with the results of other studies (cf. Bandura and Huston, 1961), in which a prior condition of noncontingent social reinforcement from a model evoked more imitation of the model from the child than otherwise. This may be due to the particular response used in this study to observe generalized imitation, which was bar-pressing. Bar-pressing may be an unusual response for a young child and may have relatively little resemblance to the strong responses already in his repertoire. For this reason, it may be a relatively inefficient response with which to demonstrate a generalized imitation of the puppet. On the other hand, it may be that while similarity between behaviors is reinforcing for children, this reinforcing value is closely dependent on similarity remaining discriminative for at least some reinforcement in the situation. Possibly, when similarity clearly is no longer discriminative for reinforcement, it loses its own reinforcing function rather quickly. It will take an extensive program of research to provide useful data on this question, but the question may well be worth it, since such arguments about imitation can figure heavily in a conceptual account of socialization or "identification."

Another point, possibly important, is that all of the subjects showing imitation were girls. Since the group sampled was composed largely of girls, this may not be unusual. However, the puppet was clearly a male cowboy, and since cross-sex interactions are prevalent where social reinforcement is involved (especially with young children), it may be that later data will demonstrate that the sex of the subject and the model is an important variable. No conclusion is possible from the present data.

Finally, the increased imitative bar-pressing demonstrated here is not simply part of a generalized increase in activity; its clearly imitative nature denies that. Furthermore, it was apparent to the observers that there was no general increase of other observable activities as imitative bar-pressing developed in the child.

SUMMARY

Three imitative responses (head nodding, mouthing, and strange verbalizations) were established in young children by social reinforcement from a puppet. A fourth imitative response (bar-pressing), which was never reinforced, was found to increase in strength when reinforcement followed the other three imitative responses. This increase in imitative bar-pressing was taken to indicate that a generalized similarity of responding between puppet and child could be a reinforcing stimulus dimension in the child's behavior.

Two additional procedures were applied to demonstrate further the dependence of imitative bar-pressing upon the reinforcement following the other imitative responses. These additional procedures were extinction of the other imitative responding, and time-out from the other imitative responding. In extinction, reinforcement was no longer presented following imitative head nodding, mouthing, and strange verbalizations, but was instead presented in a noncontingent manner during the normal conversation between puppet and child. As a consequence, imitative bar-pressing decreased in strength. When reinforcement was reinstated for the other imitative responses, imitative bar-pressing again rose in strength. During time-out periods, the puppet ceased to provide the child with head nodding, mouthing, and strange verbalization performances for the child to imitate. Again, social reinforcement was continued at the same rate but was delivered during the normal puppet-child conversation. The effect of the time-out was to decrease the strength of imitative bar-pressing. Reinstatement of the cues and reinforcement for imitative head nodding, mouthing, and strange verbalizations produced increased imitative bar-pressing.

REFERENCES

Baer, D. M. A technique of social reinforcement for the study of child behavior: Behavior avoiding reinforcement withdrawal. *Child Develpm.*, 1962, **33**, 847–858.

Bandura, A., & Huston, Aletha C. Identification as a process of incidental learning. *J. abnorm. soc. Psychol.*, 1961, **63**, 311–318.

Bijou, S. W. A child study laboratory on wheels. *Child Develpm.*, 1958, **29**, 425–427.

3.3 Imitaion of a Peer as a Function of Reinforcement from the Peer Group and Rewardingness of the Model [1]

Willard W. Hartup and Brian Coates

Considerable research has been generated by the hypothesis that rewarding models are imitated to a greater extent than nonrewarding models. This

[1] This study was completed with the assistance of a stipend awarded to Brian Coates from grant 5-T01-MHO-6668, National Institute of Mental Health. The authors are particularly grateful to Rosalind Charlesworth for her help and to the collaborating nursery school teachers.

hypothesis figures prominently in several general theories of identification, including the theory of anaclitic identification developed by Freud (1914), the secondary reinforcement interpretation of imitation by Mowrer (1950; 1960), and the extension of these theories formulated by Sears (1957) and Sears, Rau, and Alpert (1965).

The formulation developed by Mowrer is particularly specific concerning the mechanisms underlying imitation. Mowrer suggested that rewards given to S by a model increase the secondary reinforcing value (for S) of behaviors manifested by the model. When S reproduces these behaviors, the proprioceptive feedback from the imitative acts is presumed, as a consequence of stimulus generalization, to be secondarily reinforcing. This secondary reinforcement predisposes S to reproduce the behavior of the model. Although Mowrer originally provided this theory as an explanation for the imitation of verbal behavior, the theory has since been extended to account for all imitative acts (Mowrer, 1960; Sears, 1957).

Both differential and experimental strategies have been used to test the prediction that rewarding models produce more imitation in children than nonrewarding models. One kind of evidence is provided by studies of the relation between parental affection and nurturance, on the one hand, and identification-related behaviors in children, on the other. Sears (1953) reported that boys with warm, affectionate fathers employed the father doll more frequently in doll play than boys of colder, less affectionate fathers. Mussen and Distler (1960) reported that fathers of highly masculine kindergarten boys were more affectionate than fathers of less masculine subjects, and, in a series of other studies by Mussen and his associates (Mussen & Distler, 1959; Mussen, 1961; Mussen & Rutherford, 1963), highly masculine boys were found to perceive their fathers as more rewarding and nurturant (as well as strong and powerful) than less masculine boys. The results of a recent study by Sears et al. (1965), however, failed to support the hypothesis that warmth and nurturance are related to identification in either girls or boys.

Experimental evidence concerning this hypothesis has been provided by Bandura and Huston (1961), who found that preschool Ss who had received social rewards from the model during two 15-minute play periods reproduced "incidental" verbal and motor responses displayed by the model to a greater extent than Ss experiencing nonrewarding interaction. These two groups, however, did not differ significantly in duplicating the model's choices in a discrimination task. Next, Bandura, Ross, and Ross (1963) reported that nursery school children more frequently imitated models from whom they received social and material rewards than models with whom they competed for such rewards. Mischel and Grusec (1966) found that the rewardingness of the model facilitated imitation, but this effect depended on the type of behavior being modeled ("aversive" or "neutral") and whether imitation was measured in terms of "rehearsal" or "transmission."

More recently, Grusec (1966) reported that the model's rewardingness influenced children's imitation of self-criticism, depending on whether the model had previously used withdrawal of love, as opposed to withdrawal of material rewards.

Other evidence pertinent to the secondary reinforcement theory of imitation is provided by Rosenblith (1959), who reported that the attentiveness of the experimenter-model, as compared to attention withdrawal, enhanced imitation, but only in girls. Rosenhan and White (1967) reported no effect of the prior relation existing between S and model on the imitation of altruistic behavior, except that boys whose relations with the model were "negative" showed greater continuity in amount of imitation from model-present to model-absent conditions than boys whose relations with the model were positive or boys who had no prior relations with the model.

Stein and Wright (1964) reported that nurturance by an adult model affected imitation in preschool children, depending on the extent of change in the manifestation of dependency by the child during the experimental session. The Ss who responded to withdrawal of nurturance or to isolation with *increased* dependency and Ss who responded to continuous nurturance from E with *decreased* dependency imitated the model to a greater extent than Ss whose changes in dependency were in directions opposite to those mentioned. Lastly, Kobasigawa (1965) reported that adult models who had previously dispensed social rewards and were then observed to undergo a frustration experience elicited no greater emotionality in first-grade boys than models not dispensing social reinforcement.

Many of the findings reviewed above support the secondary reinforcement theory of imitation. Simultaneously, they suggest that situational and individual differences modify the effect of reward from the model on imitation. Sex of S, personality characteristics, and type of response being imitated are examples of such modifiers. But what antecedents are responsible for these interaction effects? What, for example, are the antecedents of sex differences in the impact of rewarding models on imitation? Differences in the socialization history of boys and girls are probably responsible, but which?

The main purpose of this experiment was to study one likely source of variation in the effect of the model's rewardingness on imitation—S's general history of reinforcement from persons resembling the model. The study was based on the hypothesis that the effects of exposure to a rewarding model, as compared to a nonrewarding model, depend on the nature of S's previous experience with people who are like the model. Peers were selected as the class of models to be used. Nursery school children were believed to be appropriate Ss because, even in nursery school groups, the range of reward frequencies exchanged among them is large.

The study was guided by the dimensional prediction stated above. Directional predictions were partially formulated prior to the experiment. For example, it was expected that rewarding peer models would produce more imitation than nonrewarding models for children with a history of frequent reinforcement from their peers. The results for children with histories of infrequent peer reinforcement were more difficult to predict because low frequencies of reinforcement from peers are often characteristic of children who are actively rejected or who are fearful in social situations. Solely on the basis of Mowrer's hypothesis, it would be expected that the rewarding-model effect would be diminished for such Ss. To the extent that such Ss are socially anxious, however, it is possible that nonrewarding peers may exert greater imitative influence than peers who, in the past, have been sources of reassurance and support.

The behaviors modeled in the experiment consisted of an altruistic response plus a group of verbal and motoric actions "incidental" to the altruistic act. Since the study involved peers as models and altruistic behavior as the major dependent variable, it accomplishes two secondary purposes: (a) it contributes to the slowly growing literature concerning the influence of peer models on the socialization of the child (e.g., Bandura & Kupers, 1964; Clark, 1965; Grosser, Polansky, & Lippitt, 1951; Hicks, 1965), and (b) it adds to the sparse evidence concerning imitation as a determinant of altruism (Rosenhan & White, 1967).

METHOD

Subjects

The pool from which Ss were drawn consisted of 64 children enrolled in four groups at the Laboratory Nursery School of the University of Minnesota. This pool included all children enrolled both at the time observations were conducted in the peer group and during a later experimental period. The Ss were 56 children from this pool. Excluded were two children who were receiving psychotherapy, two children who refused to participate, two children whose models failed to carry out the prescribed procedure, and two who were dropped to yield equal cell frequencies. These Ss ranged in age from 3–9 through 5–4, with a mean age of 4–6.

Experimental Design

The experimental design consisted of the following groups:

Frequent reinforcement from peers (FR):
    Rewarding peer model (RM) ($N = 12$)
    Nonrewarding peer model (NRM) ($N = 12$)
Infrequent reinforcement from peers (IR):
    Rewarding peer model (RM) ($N = 12$)
    Nonrewarding peer model (NRM) ($N = 12$)
No model (control) ($N = 8$)

Assignment of Subjects

The initial step in the assignment of Ss was the measurement of rein-forcement frequencies occurring in the nursery school peer group. For this purpose, observations were conducted extending over a 5-week period.[2] Briefly, the observations produced 12 3-minute samples of each child's be-havior, recorded in running account form by observers stationed in the nursery school. These records contained information concerning the child's activity, persons in his vicinity, and accounts of the interaction occurring between the child and other persons.

The 3-minute protocols were then rated by two judges. The records were screened for instances in which the child dispensed or received "generalized social reinforcers" (Skinner, 1953). Four types of positive social reinforcers were tabulated: (*a*) attention and approval (e.g., attending, offering praise, smiling and laughing, offering guidance or suggestions); (*b*) affection and personal acceptance (both physical and verbal); (*c*) submission (e.g., passive acceptance of another child's demands, sharing, compromise); (*d*) tokens (tangible objects).

A total of 161 protocols were rated by both raters. The ratio of agree-ments concerning the occurrence of social reinforcement divided by agree-ments plus disagreements was .77.

It was possible to compute the total number of reinforcements dispensed by each child to his peers and the number received. The latter score was assumed to be an index of the total frequency of positive reinforcement the child received from the peer group.[3] It was on the basis of these scores, which ranged from 0 to 55, that the children were divided into two groups: those above the median, for their own nursery school class, in number of reinforcements received (frequent reinforcement group) and those below (infrequent reinforcement group). The mean number of reinforcers re-ceived from peers in the FR group was 24.9, while the mean for the IR group was 9.0.

The children in each of the two reinforcement groups were then randomly assigned to model conditions: rewarding peer model (RM) or nonrewarding peer model (NRM). The observational records for each S assigned to group RM were searched for the name of the like-sex peer who had given S the most frequent reinforcement during the observations. This peer was desig-

[2] A detailed description of the observational procedure can be found in Charles-worth and Hartup (1967).

[3] The extent to which the total number of positive reinforcements received serves as an index of total social interaction is not known. It was possible to compute cor-relations between receipt of positive and receipt of negative reinforcements for Ss in two of the preschool groups. These correlations were .43 ($p < .10$) and .51 ($p < .05$). Incidents of nonreinforcing contacts among peers were numerous but were not tabulated.

nated as S's model. The RM Ss had received a mean of 5.4 reinforcements from their models during the 36 minutes of observation. Next, a list was prepared for each S in group NRM consisting of all like-sex children in the class who had never been observed to furnish S with reinforcement. One child, randomly selected from this list, was designated as S's model. The mean reinforcements given to the NRM Ss by their models had, of course, been zero.

The final preliminary step consisted of establishing a testing sequence permitting all the available children to serve as Ss. Some children participated only as Ss; others, who were designated as models, participated first as Ss, then were trained and served as models during subsequent sessions (not more than two for any child).

One boy and one girl from each preschool class were required to start the testing by serving as "first" models. These children were randomly selected. If this selection did not make it possible to test all of the children in that preschool class in sequence, substitute first models were picked. Those children designated as first models completed the experimental task prior to being trained as models. This group of eight children (two from each preschool class) thus comprised a no-model control group (C).

PROCEDURE

No-Model Condition

The S was brought to a laboratory room which contained three hats (maroon, green, and yellow) hung on pegs, three feathers (white, yellow, and orange) placed on a chair, three pencils (black, brown, and green) also hung on pegs, and a table containing a stack of dittoed mazes (simple one-turn puzzles) and three bowls. One bowl, placed in front of the child, was a receptacle for trinkets released by a dispensing device. The other bowls were placed to S's left and right (counterbalanced across Ss); one was designated as belonging to a preschool child (not known to S) whose picture was attached, the other was designated as S's bowl. The following instructions were given:

We have a game for you today. It is a puzzle game and these are the puzzles. (E displays puzzles.) The way you play this game is to draw a line from one flower to another flower, like this. (E demonstrates.) Now you can do some. (S was helped to complete two or three of the puzzles.) There is one other thing that I want to tell you about the game. Whenever you are doing a good job on the puzzle, some little cats will come out of the machine back there. They will come down this chute and fall in this bowl. Whenever some cats come down the chute I want you to put them in one of these other bowls. Either put them over here in Alec's bowl (Kathy's for female Ss) or over here in your bowl. Alec is another boy in the nursery school. Now remember, whenever you are doing a good job on the puzzle, some little cats will come out of the machine into this bowl here and you are to put them in one of these two bowls, either Alec's bowl or your bowl, your bowl or Alec's bowl. Do you understand? I have to do some work so I will sit in here.

Nothing further was said concerning whether S could keep the trinkets in his bowl at the conclusion of the session. The E then went into an adjoining room, left the door ajar, and seated himself out of sight. S was told to proceed, and after each maze was completed six trinkets were ejected through the chute. The session consisted of ten mazes, each followed by the dispensing and allocation of six trinkets. If S failed to pick up the trinkets, E urged him to do so by saying, "Put the cats in the bowls; in Alec's bowl or your bowl, your bowl or Alec's bowl."

Model Conditions

Training the model. Each child designated as a model was brought to the laboratory several days after he had participated as S. He was reminded of the earlier session, given an opportunity to complete two mazes, and asked to help E by demonstrating the game for another child from his class. The E stressed that it was necessary to play the game in a particular way. First, M was told that he should go to the hats, pick out the green one (color alternated across Ss), attach the white feather (also alternated) to the hole in the hat, and put the hat on his head. Next, he was told to select the black pencil (color also alternated), to seat himself at the table, and begin work on the puzzles. Then M was instructed to pick up the six trinkets ejected after each maze, place them in a row on the table, and to pick them up one at a time, placing all but the last one in Alec's (or Kathy's) bowl. The M was also instructed to repeat the words "One for Alec" each time a trinket was placed in "Alec's bowl." The E stressed that only the last trinket should be placed in M's own bowl. This procedure was practiced, with E coaching and sometimes demonstrating, until M was able to perform the task with consistent accuracy. The M accompanied E to the nursery school for the purpose of inviting S to play the game.

Experimental session. When the children arrived in the laboratory, E described the game using the instructions given above. He also explained that the children would take turns and that M would be first. The S was seated so as to face M at a 90° angle and was told that he should try not to bother M. The E entered the adjoining room, leaving the door partly open. Then M was told to proceed. If M failed to respond or engaged in distracting behavior, E prompted him from the other room. In no case, however, were mistakes in allocating trinkets corrected. Such mistakes were made by only two Ms whose Ss were subsequently excluded from the experiment.

After ten mazes, the children were told it was time for S to play the game. The M was invited to wait in the adjoining room with E, and the instructions were repeated briefly to S. When everyone had reached his appropriate spot, S was told to begin.

Response Measures

The following information was recorded by E (observing through a small one-way window): (a) whether or not S chose a hat, a feather, and/or a pencil and the colors of these objects; (b) whether or not S lined up the trinkets and whether the trinkets were placed in the bowls one at a time or in groups; (c) frequency with which S reproduced the verbalization of M; and (d) the particular bowl chosen for allocation of each trinket.

The response measures derived from these records included: (a) presence-absence of imitative hat, feather, and pencil choices; (b) presence-absence of "line up" behavior on each trial (ranging from 0 to 10 over entire session); (c) presence-absence of imitative verbalization (ranging from 0 to 6 on each trial); (d) number of trinkets placed in the "other's" bowl (ranging from 0 to 6 on each trial); (e) latency of the first nonaltruistic choice—the number of trinkets placed in "other's" bowl before placement of the first trinket in S's own bowl (ranging from 0 to 7 on each trial).

RESULTS

Intercorrelations among four of the dependent measures are shown in Table 1. All of these measures represent components of the response se-

TABLE 1. INTERCORRELATIONS AMONG FOUR IMITATION SCORES ($N = 48$)

Score	Giving to Other (Total)	Latency of Giving to Self (Total)	Verbalization (Total)	Line Up (Total)
Giving to other				
Latency of giving to self	.92 **			
Verbalization	.28 *	.32 *		
Line up	.32 *	.36 *	.54 **	

* $p < .05$.
** $p < .01$.

quence used in allocating the trinkets. The correlations, which were computed only for S's who observed a model, are all significantly positive, but five are relatively small. It should be noted that the two altruism scores (frequency of "giving to other" and latency of "giving to self") are highly correlated. This relation is artifactual. Consequently, "giving to other" was used alone as the altruism index in the data analysis.

Wherever possible, subsequent analyses were completed with scores divided into five-trial blocks. Inspection revealed that the treatment effects varied over time.

Effect of Model

To assess the effects of observing a model on altruistic behavior, a one-way analysis of variance was conducted on the data for all five of the groups in the experiment. "Giving to other" scores were analyzed separately for the first and second blocks of five trials. The treatments effect was significant in all instances. For the first trial block, $F = 7.49$, $df = 4/51$, $p < .005$; second trial block, $F = 3.39$, $df = 4/51$, $p < .02$.

Contrasts between the amount of "giving to other" in group C and in each of the model groups (t tests) revealed significant differences for each contrast in both trial blocks. Thus, observation of the model produced significantly more altruism than occurred when no opportunity to observe a model was provided (see Table 2).

TABLE 2. MEAN "GIVING TO OTHER" SCORES IN
BLOCKS OF FIVE TRIALS BY REINFORCEMENT
CONDITION AND TYPE OF PEER MODEL

	Trial Block	
Group	1	2
Frequent reinforcement		
Rewarding model	21.00	19.25
Nonrewarding model	13.42	13.83
Infrequent reinforcement		
Rewarding model	17.50	17.08
Nonrewarding model	22.83	18.58
No model	5.63	3.75

Observing the model also affected the frequency of "incidental" behaviors. Statistical analysis was not performed, but it can be seen in Table 3 that no verbalization or "line up" behavior occurred in group C, although appreciable amounts were displayed by Ss who had observed a model.

Effects of Peer Reinforcement
and Rewardingness of Model

The "giving to other" scores for Ss who observed models were subjected to mixed-design analysis of variance. The between-Ss factors were reinforcement from peers (FR vs. IR) and type of peer model (RM vs. NRM). The within-Ss factor consisted of trial blocks (first vs. second five trials). Mean scores for each subgroup may be seen in Table 2.

The analysis revealed a significant effect of trial blocks ($F = 7.80$, $df = 1/44$, $p < .01$), indicating that fewer altruistic responses were made during the second block of five trials than during the first. In addition, the interaction between reinforcement from peers and type of model was significant

TABLE 3. Mean Number of "Incidental" Behaviors
According to Reinforcement Condition
and Type of Peer Model

Group	Verbalization (Total)	Line-Up Responses (Total)
Frequent reinforcement		
Rewarding model	36.83	4.50
Nonrewarding model	7.58	1.67
Infrequent reinforcement		
Rewarding model	21.08	3.92
Nonrewarding model	18.00	3.92
No model	0.00	0.00

($F = 4.59$, $df = 1/44$, $p < .05$), as was the interaction between reinforcement from peers, type of model, and trial blocks ($F = 7.80$, $df = 1/44$, $p < .01$). Further analyses revealed that the treatments effects were confined principally to the first five trials. There was a significant interaction between reinforcement from peers and type of model in the data for the first five trials ($F = 8.44$, $df = 1/44$, $p < .01$), but not for the second. During the first trials, Ss who had received frequent reinforcement from their peers imitated a rewarding peer model more frequently than a nonrewarding model ($t = 3.17$, $p < .01$). On the other hand, Ss who were observed to receive infrequent peer reinforcement imitated a nonrewarding model more frequently than a rewarding model ($t = 2.61$, $p < .02$). Additional contrasts made on the data for the first five trials revealed: (a) among Ss who observed a rewarding model, those with a history of frequent peer reinforcement did not differ significantly from those with a history of infrequent reinforcement ($t = 1.41$, $p < .20$); (b) among those who observed a nonrewarding model, Ss who had received infrequent reinforcement from the peer group imitated significantly more than those who had received frequent peer reinforcement ($t = 4.88$, $p < .01$).

Analysis of imitative verbalization scores was conducted as described for the preceding measure. None of the interactions was significant. Rather, a significant main effect of type of model was obtained ($F = 5.39$, $df = 1/44$, $p < .02$). As can be seen from Table 3, Ss who observed a rewarding model reproduced the model's verbal behaviors more frequently than Ss who observed nonrewarding models. This trend is less clear for IR Ss than for FR Ss, and the interaction between reinforcement from peers and type of model approached significance ($F = 3.53$, $df = 1/44$, $p < .10$).

"Line up" scores were collapsed over all ten trials prior to analysis because this score consisted of presence-absence on single trials. None of the main or interaction effects was significant.

The data concerning the child's behavior with the hats, feathers, and pencils were analyzed by means of χ^2. All possible contrasts between pairs of experimental groups were completed. The only significant difference to emerge from these analyses showed that FR-RM Ss reproduced the pencil choices of the model more frequently than IR-NRM Ss ($\chi^2 = 4.45$, $p < .05$). This single finding may be attributed to chance. With respect to these particular incidental behaviors, then, the experimental conditions failed to influence differentially the child's imitative behavior.

DISCUSSION

Effects of Model

Observation of altruistic models increased the frequency of altruistic behavior of the Ss, a finding which confirms the results of Rosenhan and White (1967). Since frequency of altruism was highly correlated with the latency of nonaltruistic behavior, the evidence suggests that two parameters of altruism were imitated. As pointed out earlier, however, the most conservative description of the results is in terms of one altruism index, not both.

Can it be assumed that the behavior displayed by the model was construed by S as "altruism"? It is true that S was not told explicitly that he would be able to keep the trinkets in his own bowl and that those in the other child's bowl were to be given away. Nevertheless, in postsession interviews with ten Ss, all ten thought they could keep the trinkets in their own bowl, and seven thought the trinkets in the second bowl would be given to the child whose picture was attached to the bowl. Consequently, the assumption that the experiment involved imitative effects on altruism is tenable.

Among Ss who observed a model, those showing imitative altruism tended to imitate other components of the altruistic response sequence. Most of the intercorrelations among response measures were low, however, indicating that the effects of observing a model were not highly pervasive. The experimental findings are consistent with the intercorrelations. The peer reinforcement history tended to have significant effects on behavior which was central in the altruistic response sequence (frequency of "giving to other"). Borderline effects of peer reinforcement were found with respect to imitative verbalization, and no effects were obtained with respect to less central actions ("lining up" behavior or choices of hat, feather, and pencil). This failure of the treatment effects to generalize to all measures could simply have been a function of "response centrality." It is also possible that the treatment effects did not generalize to "lining up" scores and hat, feather, and pencil choices because these behaviors occurred much less frequently than trinket sorting or verbalization.

Effects of Peer Reinforcement

The relation between rewardingness of the peer model and imitative altruism was positive when S was reinforced frequently by the peer group but negative when reinforcement was infrequent. It is known that peer reinforcement is correlated with social acceptance (e.g., Hartup, Glazer, & Charlesworth, 1967; Marshall & McCandless, 1957). Therefore, the four experimental groups were contrasted with respect to the social acceptance of the models, the acceptance of the Ss, and the friendliness existing between the models and their respective Ss. Data from a picture sociometric test were used for this purpose. First, no significant differences were found in the frequency with which the models in the four groups were chosen by their peers as "liked," as "disliked," or in total times mentioned. Similarly, the social acceptance of the Ss themselves did not differ significantly among the four groups. Finally, children in group FR-RM were significantly more friendly toward their models, as revealed by the frequency with which the model was included among S's sociometric choices, than were the children in the other three groups. However, Ss in group IR-NRM, which imitated as much as group FR-RM, were less friendly toward their models than Ss in the latter group. Thus, overall, status differences among the groups do not account for the observed differences in imitation.

It is concluded that the results support Mowrer's secondary reinforcement theory of imitation when S's history includes relatively frequent reinforcement from persons resembling the model. For infrequently reinforced Ss, the influence of model rewardingness did not diminish; rather, nonrewarding models proved to be more efficacious than rewarding ones.

One explanation for these results is based on the assumption that children who receive little reinforcement are also anxious when placed in contact with other children. For them, exposure to a nonrewarding model may arouse discomfort or anxiety, adding motivation to perform the actions which the situation elicits (including, in the present instance, imitation). Exposure of such children to a rewarding model, however, could result in anxiety reduction, thereby lowering S's motivation for imitative behavior.

This argument implies a dual theory of peer imitation: (a) when reinforcement from peers is frequent, matching the behavior of a rewarding model has greater incentive value than matching a nonrewarding model (the Mowrer hypothesis); (b) when peer reinforcement is not frequent, a nonrewarding model sustains or increases anxiety, whereas the presence of a rewarding model reduces such motivation for imitation. This theory is similar to the hypothesis advanced by Hill (1967) concerning the role of anxiety in task performance under social reinforcement and, in some respects, parallels the dualism in psychoanalytic theories of identification. For example, it could be hypothesized that (*a*) nurturant models are emulated (anaclitic identification) when reinforcement from persons like the model has been frequent, and (*b*) when reinforcement has been infrequent, the model who elicits anxiety (or who does not behave in such a way as to reduce it) is defensively emulated. Thus, the present speculations contain interesting implications for predicting the conditions under which anaclitic and defensive identification operate.

It is also possible to consider the present results in terms of perceived similarity. It is known that, in the peer group, the correlation between "giving reinforcement to others" and "getting reinforcement from others" is positive and high (Charlesworth & Hartup, 1967). Thus, it is possible that FR-RM Ss perceive themselves to be similar to the model (both give as well as receive frequent reinforcements) as do IR-NRM Ss (both receive and give few reinforcements). On the other hand, perceived similarity would not be great in the other two experimental groups, FR-NRM and IR-RM. Earlier studies have shown that if S perceives himself as similar to M, conformity is enhanced (e.g., Stotland & Patchen, 1961) as well as imitation (Maccoby, 1959; Rosekrans, 1967). The perceived similarity (or reduced dissimilarity) existing for frequently reinforced Ss with rewarding models and for infrequently reinforced Ss with nonrewarding models would thus account for the greater amounts of imitation shown by these two groups than by the other groups in the experiment.

The present study helps to clarify the influence of the model's rewardingness on imitation. The generality of the results needs to be assessed in further research and theoretical implications explored. It appears, however, that the child's socialization history contributes importantly to the effects on imitation of rewards from the model.

SUMMARY

This study is based on the hypothesis that the effect of exposure to rewarding peer models, as compared to nonrewarding models, depends on the subject's general history of reinforcement from the peer group. 56 nursery school children were selected as Ss, and the behavior modeled consisted of a series of altruistic and "incidental" responses. It was found that Ss exposed to an altruistic peer model displayed significantly more altruism than Ss not exposed to a model. It was also discovered that Ss who had a history of frequent reinforcement from their peers imitated a rewarding model significantly more than a nonrewarding model; on the other hand, children who received infrequent reinforcement from peers imitated nonrewarding peers significantly more than rewarding peers. The results are discussed in relation to Mowrer's secondary reinforcement theory of imitative behavior.

REFERENCES

Bandura, A., & Huston, Aletha C.   Identification as a process of incidental learning. *Journal of abnormal and social Psychology*, 1961, **63**, 311–318.

Bandura, A., & Kupers, Carol J.   Transmission of patterns of self-reinforcement through modelling. *Journal of abnormal and social Psychology*, 1964, **69**, 1–9.

Bandura, A., Ross, Dorothea, & Ross, Sheila A.   A comparative test of the status envy, social power, and secondary reinforcement theories of identificatory learning. *Journal of abnormal and social Psychology*, 1963, **67**, 527–534.

Charlesworth, Rosalind, & Hartup, W. W.   Positive social reinforcement in the nursery school peer group. *Child Development*, 1967, **38**, 993–1002.

Clark, Barbara S.   The acquisition and extinction of peer imitation in children. *Psychonomic Science*, 1965, **2**, 147–148.

Freud, S.   On narcissim: an introduction (1914). In J. D. Sutherland (Ed.), *Collected papers of Sigmund Freud*. Vol. 4. London: Hogarth, 1957. Pp. 30–60.

Grosser, D., Polansky, N., & Lippitt, R.   A laboratory study of behavioral contagion. *Human Relations*, 1951, **4**, 115–142.

Grusec, Joan.   Some antecedents of self-criticism. *Journal of Personality and social Psychology*, 1966, **4**, 244–253.

Hartup, W. W., Glazer, Jane, & Charlesworth, Rosalind.   Peer reinforcement and sociometric status. *Child Development*, 1967, **38**, 1017–1024.

Hicks, D. J.   Imitation and retention of film-mediated aggressive peer and adult models. *Journal of Personality and social Psychology*, 1965, **2**, 97–100.

Hill, K. T.   Social reinforcement as a function of test anxiety and success-failure experiences. *Child Development*, 1967, **38**, 723–737.

Kobasigawa, A.   Observation of failure in another person as a determinant of amplitude and speed of a simple motor response. *Journal of Personality and social Psychology*, 1965, **1**, 626–631.

Maccoby, Eleanor E.   Role-taking in childhood and its consequences for social learning. *Child Development*, 1959, **30**, 239–252.

Marshall, Helen R., & McCandless, B. R.   A study in prediction of social behavior of preschool children. *Child Development*, 1957, **28**, 149–159.

Mischel, W., & Grusec, Joan.   Determinants of the rehearsal and transmission of neutral and aversive behaviors. *Journal of Personality and social Psychology*, 1966, **3**, 197–206.

Mowrer, O. H.   Identification: a link between learning theory and psychotherapy. In *Learning theory and personality dynamics*. New York: Ronald Press, 1950. Pp. 69–94.

Mowrer, O. H.   *Learning theory and the symbolic processes*. New York: Wiley, 1960.

Mussen, P. H.   Some antecedents and consequents of masculine sex-typing in adolescent boys. *Psychological Monographs*, 1961, **75** (Whole No. 506).

Mussen, P. H., & Distler, L.   Masculinity, identification, and father-son relationships. *Journal of abnormal and social Psychology*, 1959, **59**, 350–356.

Mussen, P. H., & Distler, L.   Child-rearing antecedents of masculine identification in kindergarten boys. *Child Development*, 1960, **31**, 89–100.

Mussen, P. H., & Rutherford, E.   Parent-child relations and parental personality in relation to young children's sex-role preferences. *Child Development,* 1963, **34,** 589–607.

Rosekrans, Mary A. Imitation in children as a function of perceived similarity to a social model and vicarious reinforcement. *Journal of Personality and social Psychology,* 1967, in press.

Rosenblith, Judy F. Learning by imitation in kindergarten children. *Child Development,* 1959, **30,** 69–80.

Rosenhan, D., & White, G. M. Observation and rehearsal as determinants of prosocial behavior. *Journal of Personality and social Psychology,* **5,** 424–431.

Sears, Pauline S. Child rearing factors related to the playing of sex-typed roles. *American Psychologist,* 1953, **8,** 431. (Abstract)

Sears, R. R. Identification as a form of behavior development. In D. B. Harris (Ed.), *The concept of development.* Minneapolis: University of Minnesota Press, 1957. Pp. 149–161.

Sears, R. R., Rau, Lucy, & Alpert, R. *Identification and child rearing.* Stanford, Calif.: Stanford University Press, 1965.

Skinner, B. F. *Science and human behavior.* New York: Macmillan, 1953.

Stein, Aletha H., & Wright, J. C. Imitative learning under conditions of nurturance and nurturance withdrawal. *Child Development,* 1964, **35,** 927–937.

Stotland, E., and Patchen, M. Identification and change in prejudice and in authoritarianism. *Journal of abnormal and social Psychology,* 1961, **62,** 254–274.

3.4 Influence of Models' Reinforcement Contingencies on the Acquisition of Imitative Responses [1]

Albert Bandura [2]

It is widely asumed that the occurrence of imitative or observational learning is contingent on the administration of reinforcing stimuli either to the model or to the observer. According to the theory propounded by Miller and Dollard (1941), for example, the necessary conditions for learning through imitation include a motivated subject who is positively reinforced for matching the rewarded behavior of a model during a series of initially random, trial-and-error responses. Since this conceptualization of observational learning requires the subject to perform the imitative response before he can learn it, this theory evidently accounts more adequately for the emission of previously learned matching responses, than for their acquisition.

[1] This investigation was supported by Research Grant M-5162 from the National Institutes of Health, United States Public Health Service.

[2] The author is indebted to Carole Revelle who assisted in collecting the data.

Reprinted from the *Journal of Personality and Social Psychology* 1965, **1,** 589–595, by permission of the author and the American Psychological Association.

Mowrer's (1960) proprioceptive feedback theory similarly highlights the role of reinforcement but, unlike Miller and Dollard who reduce imitation to a special case of instrumental learning, Mowrer focuses on the classical conditioning of positive and negative emotions to matching response-correlated stimuli. Mowrer distinguishes two forms of imitative learning in terms of whether the observer is reinforced directly or vicariously. In the former case, the model performs a response and simultaneously rewards the observer. If the modeled responses are thus paired repeatedly with positive reinforcement they gradually acquire secondary reward value. The observer can then administer positively conditioned reinforcers to himself simply by reproducing as closely as possible the model's positively valenced behavior. In the second, or empathetic form of imitative learning, the model not only exhibits the responses but also experiences the reinforcing consequences. It is assumed that the observer, in turn, experiences empathetically both the response-correlated stimuli and the response consequences of the model's behavior. As a result of this higher-order vicarious conditioning, the observer will be inclined to reproduce the matching responses.

There is some recent evidence that imitative behavior can be enhanced by noncontingent social reinforcement from a model (Bandura & Huston, 1961), by response-contingent reinforcers administered to the model (Bandura, Ross, & Ross, 1963b; Walters, Leat, & Mezei, 1963), and by increasing the reinforcing value of matching responses per se through direct reinforcement of the participant observer (Baer & Sherman, 1964). Nevertheless, reinforcement theories of imitation fail to explain the learning of matching responses when the observer does not perform the model's responses during the process of acquisition, and for which reinforcers are not delivered either to the model or to the observers (Bandura et al., 1961, 1963a).

The acquisition of imitative responses under the latter conditions appears to be accounted for more adequately by a contiguity theory of observational learning. According to the latter conceptualization (Bandura, in press; Sheffield, 1961), when an observer witnesses a model exhibit a sequence of responses the observer acquires, through contiguous association of sensory events, perceptual and symbolic responses possessing cue properties that are capable of eliciting, at some time after a demonstration, overt responses corresponding to those that had been modeled.

Some suggestive evidence that the *acquisition* of matching responses may take place through contiguity, whereas reinforcements administered to a model exert their major influence on the *performance* of imitatively learned responses, is provided in a study in which models were rewarded or punished for exhibiting aggressive behavior (Bandura et al., 1963b). Although children who had observed aggressive responses rewarded subsequently reproduced the model's behavior while children in the model-punished condition failed to do so, a number of the subjects in the latter group described in postexperimental interviews the model's repertoire of aggressive responses with considerable accuracy. Evidently, they had learned the cognitive equivalents of the model's responses but they were not translated into their motoric forms. These findings highlighted both the importance of distinguishing between learning and performance and the need for a systematic study of whether reinforcement is primarily a learning-related or a performance-related variable.

In the present experiment children observed a film-mediated model who exhibited novel physical and verbal aggressive responses. In one treatment condition the model was severely punished; in a second, the model was generously rewarded; while the third condition presented no response consequences to the model. Following a postexposure test of imitative behavior, children in all three groups were offered attractive incentives contingent on their reproducing the models' responses so as to provide a more accurate index of learning. It was predicted that reinforcing consequences to the model would result in significant differences in the performance of imitative behavior with the model-rewarded group displaying the highest number of different classes of matching responses, followed by the no-consequences and the model-punished groups, respectively. In accordance with previous findings (Bandura et al., 1961, 1963a) it was also expected that boys would perform significantly more imitative aggression than girls. It was predicted, however, that the introduction of positive incentives would wipe out both reinforcement-produced and sex-linked performance differences, revealing an equivalent amount of learning among children in the three treatment conditions.

METHOD

Subjects

The subjects were 33 boys and 33 girls enrolled in the Stanford University Nursery School. They ranged in age from 42 to 71 months, with a mean age of 51 months. The children were assigned randomly to one of three treatment conditions of 11 boys and 11 girls each.

Two adult males served in the role of models, and one female experimenter conducted the study for all 66 children.

Exposure Procedure

The children were brought individually to a semi-darkened room. The experimenter informed the child that she had some business to attend to before they could proceed to the "surprise playroom," but that during the waiting period the child might watch a televised program. After the child was seated, the experimenter walked over to the television console, ostensibly tuned in a program and then departed. A film of approximately 5 minutes duration depicting the modeled responses was shown on a glass lenscreen in the television console by means of a rear projection arrangement, screened from the child's view by large panels. The televised form of presentation was utilized primarily because attending responses to televised stimuli are strongly conditioned in children and this procedure would therefore serve to enhance observation which is a necessary condition for the occurrence of imitative learning.

The film began with a scene in which the model walked up to an adult-size plastic Bobo doll and ordered him to clear the way. After glaring for a moment at the noncompliant antagonist the model exhibited four novel aggressive responses each accompanied by a distinctive verbalization.

First, the model laid the Bobo doll on its side, sat on it, and punched it in the nose while remarking, "Pow, right in the nose, boom, boom." The model then raised the doll and pommeled it on the head with a mallet. Each response was accompanied by the verbalization, "Sockeroo . . . stay down." Following the mallet aggression, the model kicked the doll about the room, and these responses were interspersed with the comment, "Fly away." Finally, the model threw rubber balls at the Bobo doll, each strike punctuated with "Bang." This sequence of physically and verbally aggressive behavior was repeated twice.

The component responses that enter into the development of more complex novel patterns of behavior are usually present in children's behavioral repertoires as products either of maturation or of prior social learning. Thus, while most of the elements in the modeled acts had undoubtedly been previously learned, the particular pattern of components in each response, and their evocation by specific stimulus objects, were relatively unique. For example, children can manipulate objects, sit on them, punch them, and they can make vocal responses, but the likelihood that a given child would spontaneously place a Bobo doll on its side, sit on it, punch it in the nose and remark, "Pow . . . boom, boom," is exceedingly remote. Indeed, a previous study utilizing the same stimulus objects has shown that the imitative responses selected for the present experiment have virtually a zero probability of occurring spontaneously among preschool children (Bandura et al., 1961) and, therefore, meet the criterion of novel responses.

The rewarding and punishing contingencies associated with the model's aggressive responses were introduced in the closing scene of the film.

For children in the model-rewarded condition, a second adult appeared with an abundant supply of candies and soft drinks. He informed the model that he was a "strong champion" and that his superb aggressive performance clearly deserved a generous treat. He then poured him a large glass of 7-Up, and readily supplied additional energy-building nourishment including chocolate bars, Cracker Jack popcorn, and an assortment of candies. While the model was rapidly consuming the delectable treats, his admirer symbolically reinstated the modeled aggressive responses and engaged in considerable positive social reinforcement.

For children in the model-punished condition, the reinforcing agent appeared on the scene shaking his finger menacingly and commenting reprovingly, "Hey there, you big bully. You quit picking on that clown. I won't tolerate it." As the model drew back he tripped and fell, the other adult sat on the model and spanked him with a rolled-up magazine while reminding him of his aggressive behavior. As the model ran off cowering, the agent forewarned him, "If I catch you doing that again, you big bully, I'll give you a hard spanking. You quit acting that way."

Children in the no-consequences condition viewed the same film as shown to the other two groups except that no reinforcement ending was included.

Performance Measure

Immediately following the exposure session the children were escorted to an experimental room that contained a Bobo doll, three balls, a mallet and pegboard, dart guns, cars, plastic farm animals, and a doll house equipped with furniture and a doll family. By providing a variety of stimulus objects the children were at liberty to exhibit imitative responses or to engage in nonimitative forms of behavior.

After the experimenter instructed the child that he was free to play with the toys in the room, she excused herself supposedly to fetch additional play materials. Since many preschool children are reluctant to remain alone and tend to leave after a short period of time, the experimenter reentered the room midway through the session and reassured the child that she would return shortly with the goods.

Each child spent 10 minutes in the test room during which time his behavior was recorded every 5 seconds in terms of predetermined imitative response categories by judges who observed the session through a one-way mirror in an adjoining observation room.

Two observers shared the task of recording the occurrence of matching responses for all 66 children. Neither of the raters had knowledge of the treatment conditions to which the children were assigned. In order to provide an estimate of interscorer reliability, the responses of 10 children were scored independently by both observers. Since the imitative responses were highly distinctive and required no subjective interpretation, the raters were virtually in perfect agreement (99%) in scoring the matching responses.

The number of different physical and verbal imitative responses emitted spontaneously by the children constituted the performance measure.

Acquisition Index

At the end of the performance session the experimenter entered the room with an assortment of fruit juices in a colorful juice-dispensing fountain, and booklets of sticker-pictures that were employed as the positive incentives to activate into performance what the children had learned through observation.

After a brief juice treat the children were informed, that for each physical, or verbal imitative response that they reproduced, they would receive a pretty sticker-picture and additional juice treats. An achievement incentive was also introduced in order to produce further disinhibition and to increase the children's motivation to exhibit matching responses. The experimenter attached a pastoral scene to the wall and expressed an interest in seeing how many sticker-pictures the child would be able to obtain to adorn his picture.

The experimenter then asked the child, "Show me what Rocky did in the TV program," "Tell me what he said," and rewarded him immediately following each matching response. If a child simply described an imitative response he was asked to give a performance demonstration.

Although learning must be inferred from performance, it was assumed that the number of different physical and verbal imitative responses reproduced by the children under the positive-incentive conditions would serve as a relatively accurate index of learning.

RESULTS

Figure 1 shows the mean number of different matching responses reproduced by children in each of the three treatment conditions during the no-incentive and the positive-incentive phases of the experiment. A square-root transformation $(y = \sqrt{f} + \frac{1}{2})$ was applied to these data to make them amenable to parametric statistical analyses.

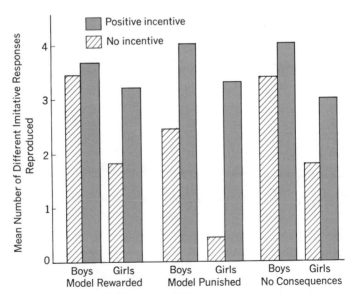

FIGURE 1. Mean number of different matching responses reproduced by children as a function of positive incentives and the model's reinforcement contingencies.

Performance Differences

A summary of the analysis of variance based on the performance scores is presented in Table 1. The findings reveal that reinforcing consequences to the model had a significant effect on the number of matching responses that the children spontaneously reproduced. The main effect of sex is also highly significant, confirming the prediction that boys would perform more imitative responses than girls.

TABLE 1. ANALYSIS OF VARIANCE OF
IMITATIVE PERFORMANCE SCORES

Source	df	MS	F
Treatments (T)	2	1.21	3.27 *
Sex (S)	1	4.87	13.16 **
T × S	2	.12	<1
Within groups	60	.37	

* $p < .05$.
** $p < .001$.

Further comparisons of pairs of means by t tests (Table 2) show that while the model-rewarded and the no-consequences groups did not differ from each other, subjects in both of these conditions performed significantly more matching responses than children who had observed the model experience punishing consequences following the display of aggression. It is evident, however, from the differences reported separately for boys and girls in

TABLE 2. COMPARISON OF PAIRS OF MEANS BETWEEN TREATMENT CONDITIONS

Performance measure	Treatment conditions		
	Reward versus punishment (t)	Reward versus no consequences (t)	Punishment versus no consequences (t)
Total sample	2.20 **	0.55	2.25 **
Boys	1.05	0.19	1.24
Girls	2.13 **	0.12	2.02 *

* $p < .05$.
** $p < .025$.

Table 2, that the significant effect of the model's reinforcement contingencies is based predominantly on differences among the girls' subgroups.[3]

Differences in Acquisition

An analysis of variance of the imitative learning scores is summarized in Table 3. The introduction of positive incentives completely wiped out the previously observed performance differences, revealing an equivalent amount

TABLE 3. ANALYSIS OF VARIANCE OF
IMITATIVE LEARNING SCORES

Source	df	MS	F
Treatments (T)	2	0.02	<1
Sex (S)	1	0.56	6.22 *
T × S	2	0.02	<1
Within groups	60	0.09	

* $p < .05$.

of imitative learning among the children in the model-rewarded, model-punished, and the no-consequences treatment groups. Although the initially large sex difference was substantially reduced in the positive-incentive condition, the girls nevertheless still displayed fewer matching responses than the boys.

Acquisition-Performance Differences

In order to elucidate further the influence of direct and vicariously experienced reinforcement on imitation, the differences in matching responses displayed under nonreward and postive-incentive conditions for each of the three experimental treatments were evaluated by the t-test procedure for correlated means. Table 4 shows that boys who witnessed the model either rewarded or left without consequences performed all of the imitative responses that they had learned through observation and no new matching responses emerged when positive reinforcers were made available. On the other hand, boys who had observed the model punished and girls in all three treatment conditions showed significant increments in imitative behavior when response-contingent reinforcement was later introduced.

[3] Because of the skewness of the distribution of scores for the subgroup of girls in the model-punished condition, differences involving this group were also evaluted by means of the Mann-Whitney U test. The nonparametric analyses yield probability values that are identical to those reported in Table 2.

TABLE 4. Significance of the Acquisition-Performance Differences in Imitative Responses

Group	Treatment conditions		
	Reward (t)	Punishment (t)	No consequences (t)
Total sample	2.38 *	5.00 ***	2.67 **
Boys	0.74	2.26 *	1.54
Girls	3.33 **	5.65 ***	2.18 *

* $p < .025$.
** $p < .01$.
*** $p < .001$.

DISCUSSION

The results of the present experiment lend support to a contiguity theory of imitative learning; reinforcements administered to the model influenced the observers' performance but not the acquisition of matching responses.

It is evident from the findings, however, that mere exposure to modeling stimuli does not provide the sufficient conditions for imitative or observational learning. The fact that most of the children in the experiment failed to reproduce the entire repertoire of behavior exhibited by the model, even under positive-incentive conditions designed to disinhibit and to elicit matching responses, indicates that factors other than mere contiguity of sensory stimulation undoubtedly influence imitative response acquisition.

Exposing a person to a complex sequence of stimulation is no guarantee that he will attend to the entire range of cues, that he will necessarily select from a total stimulus complex only the most relevant stimuli, or that he will even perceive accurately the cues to which his attention is directed. Motivational variables, prior training in discriminative observation, and the anticipation of positive or negative reinforcements contingent on the emission of matching responses may be highly influential in channeling, augmenting, or reducing observing responses, which is a necessary precondition for imitative learning (Bandura, 1962; Bandura & Walters, 1963). Procedures that increase the distinctiveness of the relevant modeling stimuli also greatly facilitate observational learning (Sheffield & Maccoby, 1961).

In addition to attention-directing variables, the rate, amount, and complexity of stimuli presented to the observer may partly determine the degree of imitative learning. The acquisition of matching responses through observation of a lengthy uninterrupted sequence of behavior is also likely to be governed by principles of associate learning such as frequency and re-

cency, serial order effects, and other multiple sources of associative interference (McGuire, 1961).

Social responses are generally composed of a large number of different
behavioral units combined in a particular manner. Responses of higher-
order complexity are produced by combinations of previously learned
components which may, in themselves, represent relatively complicated
behavorial patterns. Consequently, the rate of acquisition of intricate matching responses through observation will be largely determined by the extent
to which the necessary components are contained in the observer's repertoire.
A person who possesses a very narrow repertoire of behavior, for example,
will, in all probability, display only fragmentary imitation of a model's
behavior; on the other hand, a person who has acquired most of the relevant components is likely to perform precisely matching responses following several demonstrations. In the case of young preschool children their
motor repertoires are more highly developed than their repertoires of verbal
responses. It is, perhaps, for this reason that even in the positive-incentive
condition, children reproduced a substantially higher percentage (67%) of
imitative motor responses than matching verbalizations (20%). A similar
pattern of differential imitation was obtained in a previous experiment
(Bandura & Huston, 1961) in which preschool children served as subjects.

It is apparent from the foregoing discussion that considerably more research is needed in identifying variables that combine with contiguous
stimulation in governing the process of imitative response acquisition.

It is possible, of course, to interpret the present acquisition data as reflecting the operation of generalization from a prior history of reinforcement of imitative behavior. Within any social group, models typically
exhibit the accumulated cultural repertoires that have proved most successful for given stimulus situations; consequently, matching the behavior
of other persons, particularly the superiors in an age-grade or prestige
hierarchy, will maximize positive reinforcement and minimize the frequency
of aversive response consequences. Since both the occurrence and the positive reinforcement of matching responses, whether by accident or by intent,
are inevitable during the course of social development, no definitive resolution of the reinforcement issue is possible, except through an experiment
utilizing organisms that have experienced complete social isolation from
birth. It is evident, however, that contemporaneous reinforcements are unnecessary for the acquistion of new matching responses.

The finding that boys perform more imitative aggression than girls as a
result of exposure to an aggressive male model, is in accord with results from
related experiments (Bandura et al., 1961, 1963a). The additional finding,
however, that the introduction of positive incentives practically wiped out
the prior performance disparity strongly suggests that the frequently observed sex differences in aggression (Goodenough, 1931; Johnson, 1951;
Sears, 1951) may reflect primarily differences in willingness to exhibit ag-

gressive responses, rather than deficits in learning or "masculine-role identification."

The subgroups of children who displayed significant increments in imitative behavior as a function of positive reinforcement were boys who had observed the aggressive model punished, and girls for whom physically aggressive behavior is typically labeled sex inappropriate and nonrewarded or even negatively reinforced. The inhibitory effects of differing reinforcement histories for aggression were clearly reflected in the observation that boys were more easily disinhibited than girls in the reward phase of the experiment. This factor may account for the small sex difference that was obtained even in the positive-incentive condition.

The present study provides further evidence that response inhibition and response disinhibition can be vicariously transmitted through observation of reinforcing consequences to a model's behavior. It is interesting to note, however, that the performance by a model of socially disapproved or prohibited responses (for example, kicking, striking with objects) without the occurrence of any aversive consequences may produce disinhibitory effects analogous to a positive reinforcement operation. These findings are similar to results from studies of direct reinforcement (Crandall, Good, & Crandall, 1964) in which nonreward functioned as a positive reinforcer to increase the probability of the occurrence of formerly punished responses.

Punishment administered to the model apparently further reinforced the girls' existing inhibitions over aggression and produced remarkably little imitative behavior; the boys displayed a similar, though not significant, decrease in imitation. This difference may be partly a function of the relative dominance of aggressive responses in the repertoires of boys and girls. It is also possible that vicarious reinforcement for boys, deriving from the model's successful execution of aggressive behavior (that is, overpowering the noncompliant adversary), may have reduced the effects of externally administered terminal punishment. These factors, as well as the model's self-rewarding and self-punishing reactions following the display of aggression, will be investigated in a subsequent experiment.

SUMMARY

In order to test the hypothesis that reinforcements administered to a model influence the performance but not the acquisition of matching responses, groups of children observed an aggressive film-mediated model either rewarded, punished, or left without consequences. A postexposure test revealed that response consequences to the model had produced differential amounts of imitative behavior. Children in the model-punished condition performed significantly fewer matching responses than children in both the model-rewarded and the no-consequences groups. Children in all 3 treatment conditions were then offered attractive reinforcers contingent on their reproducing the model's aggressive responses. The introduction of positive incentives completely wiped out the previously observed performance differences, revealing an equivalent amount of learning among children in the model-rewarded, model-punished, and the no-consequences conditions.

REFERENCES

Baer, D. M., & Sherman, J. A.   Reinforcement control of generalized imitation in young children. *Journal of Experimental Child Psychology*, 1964, **1**, 37–49.

Bandura, A.   Social learning through imitation. In M. R. Jones (Ed.), *Nebraska symposium on motivation: 1962*. Lincoln: Univer. Nebraska Press, 1962. Pp. 211–269.

Bandura, A.   Vicarious processes: A case of no-trial learning. In L. Berkowitz (Ed.), *Advances in experimental social psychology*. Vol. 2. New York: Academic Press, 1965, in press.

Bandura, A., & Huston, Aletha C.   Identification as a process of incidental learning. *Journal of Abnormal and Social Psychology*, 1961, **63**, 311–318.

Bandura, A., Ross, Dorothea, & Ross, Sheila, A.   Transmission of aggression through imitation of aggressive models. *Journal of Abnormal and Social Psychology*, 1961, **63**, 575–582.

Bandura, A., Ross, Dorothea, & Ross, Sheila A.   Imitation of film-mediated aggressive models. *Journal of Abnormal and Social Psychology*, 1963, **66**, 3–11. (a)

Bandura, A., Ross, Dorothea, & Ross, Sheila A.   Vicarious reinforcement and imitative learning. *Journal of Abnormal and Social Psychology*, 1963, **67**, 601–607. (b)

Bandura, A., & Walters, R. H.   *Social learning and personality development*. New York: Holt, Rinehart, & Winston, 1963.

Crandall, Virginia C., Good, Suzanne, & Crandall, V. J.   The reinforcement effects of adult reactions and non-reactions on children's achievement expectations: A replication study. *Child Development*, 1964, **35**, 385–397.

Goodenough, Florence L.   *Anger in young children*. Minneapolis: Univer. Minnesota Press, 1931.

Johnson, Elizabeth Z.   Attitudes of children toward authority as projected in their doll play at two age levels. Unpublished doctoral dissertation, Harvard University, 1951.

McGuire, W. J.   Interpolated motivational statements within a programmed series of instruction as a distribution of practice factor. In A. A. Lumsdaine (Ed.), *Student response in programmed instruction: A symposium*. Washington, D. C.: National Academy of Sciences, National Research Council, 1961. Pp. 411–415.

Miller, N. E., & Dollard, J. *Social learning and imitation*. New Haven: Yale Univer. Press, 1941.

Mowrer, O. H.   *Learning theory and the symbolic processes*. New York: Wiley, 1960.

Sears, Pauline S.   Doll play aggression in normal young children: Influence of sex, age, sibling status, father's absence. *Psychological Monographs*, 1951, **65** (6, Whole No. 323).

Sheffield, F. D. Theoretical considerations in the learning of complex sequential tasks from demonstration and practice. In A. A. Lumsdaine (Ed.), *Student response in programmed instructions: A symposium.* Washington, D. C.: National Academy of Sciences, National Research Council, 1961. Pp. 13–32.

Sheffield F. D., & Maccoby, N. Summary and interpretation on research on organizational principles in constructing filmed demonstrations. In A. A. Lumsdaine (Ed.), *Student response in programmed instruction: A symposium.* Washington, D. C.: National Academy of Sciences, National Research Council, 1961. Pp. 117–131.

Walters, R. H., Leat, Marion, & Mezei, L. Inhibition and disinhibition of responses through emphatic learning. *Canadian Journal of Psychology,* 1963, **17,** 235–243.

3.5 Observational Learning as a Function of Symbolization and Incentive Set [1]

Albert Bandura, Joan E. Grusec, and Frances L. Menlove

Most conceptualizations of imitative or observational learning have been developed and tested largely on the basis of a limited paradigm requiring observing Ss to perform matching responses and to secure positive reinforcers as a precondition for their acquisition (Baer & Sherman, 1964; Miller & Dollard, 1941; Skinner, 1953). These theories, however, fail to account for the occurrence of delayed reproduction of modeling behavior originally learned by observers under exposure conditions permitting no overt performance of matching responses (Bandura, 1962; 1965a; Bandura & Walters, 1963). Since observers can acquire only perceptual and other implicit responses resembling the sequences of modeling stimuli while they are occurring, symbolic processes which mediate subsequent behavioral reproduction must play a prominent role in observational learning.

Recent theoretical analyses of observational learning (Bandura, 1965c; Sheffield, 1961) emphasize the role of stimulus contiguity and associated cognitive or representational responses in the acquisition process. According to contiguity-mediational theory, during the period of exposure modeling stimuli elicit in observing Ss configurations and sequences of sensory experiences which, on the basis of past associations, become centrally integrated and structured into perceptual responses.

There is some evidence from research in sensory conditioning (Conant,

[1] This work was supported by Public Health Service research grant M-5162 from the National Institute of Mental Health.

Reprinted from *Child Development* 1966, **37,** 499–506, by permission of the authors and the Society for Research in Child Development.

1964; Leuba, 1940; Naruse & Abonai, 1953) to suggest that, in the course of observation, transitory sensory and perceptual phenomena can be converted to retrievable images of the corresponding stimulus events. In addition to imaginal responses, the observer acquires, once verbal labels have become attached to objective stimuli, verbal equivalents of the model's behavior during the period of exposure (Bandura, 1965b; Bandura, Ross, & Ross, 1963). The latter findings thus provide some basis for assuming that symbolic or representational responses in the form of images and verbal associates of the model's behavior constitute the enduring learning products of observational experiences. It is likewise assumed in the contiguity-mediational theory that symbolic matching responses possess cue-producing properties that are capable of eliciting, some time after observation, overt responses corresponding to those that were modeled, provided the requisite components exist in the observer's behavioral repertoire.

In order to test the proposition advanced in the above theory that symbolization enhances observational learning, a modeling study was conducted in which an attempt was made to manipulate the relevant symbolic responses. Viewers' verbalizations of modeling stimuli would be expected to influence mediating or representational response processes. Therefore, during the response-acquisition phase of the experiment, one group of children engaged in facilitative verbalization designed to enhance the development of imaginal and verbal associates of the model's behavior. A second group of children simply observed passively, while the third group of children assigned to a competing symbolization condition produced interfering verbal responses intended to counteract the establishment of representational responses.

The degree of observational learning may also be partly governed by incentive-related sets which exert selective control over the direction, intensity, and frequency of observing responses. It is also entirely possible that different symbolization instructions could create in observers differential anticipations as to the possibility of their later being called upon to demonstrate what they had learned from the modeled stimulus presentation. Such self-induced sets, if operative, might affect attending behavior and thus confound the effects of symbolization processes. Hence, in the present study half of the Ss in each of the three observational treatments were offered positive incentives to learn the model's response patterns, while the remaining children were provided no incentives.

It was predicted that the number of matching responses acquired observationally by children in the facilitative symbolization condition would exceed the corresponding scores for the passive observers, who, in turn, would show a higher level of acquisition than Ss in the competing symbolization treatment. It was also hypothesized, for reasons given above, that incentive set would enhance observational learning.

Subjects

The Ss were 36 boys and 36 girls ranging in age from 6 to 8 years. They were drawn from two elementary schools in a lower-middle-class community.

Design and Procedure

The investigation utilized a $2 \times 2 \times 3$ factorial design. Children of each sex were randomly assigned to either the facilitative symbolization, the passive observation, or the competing symbolization conditions. Half of the Ss in each of the latter experimental treatments participated in the incentive-set condition, while the remaining children were assigned to the no-incentive-set group. Thus, there were six groups of six Ss each.

The Ss in the facilitative symbolization group were instructed to verbalize every action of the model as it was being performed in the movie. With children in the competing symbolization group, E explained that she was interested in determining whether children could pay close attention to a movie while engaging in another activity simultaneously. They were therefore to count "1 and a 2, and a 3, and a 4, and a 5" repeatedly, at the same time that they watched closely the filmed presentation. The Ss in the passive observation group were instructed simply to pay close attention to the movie.

Children who were assigned to the incentive-set condition were also informed that following the movie they would be asked to demonstrate what they had learned and that they would receive candy treats for each item that they reproduced correctly. On the other hand, Ss in the no-incentive-set group were told that they would return to their classroom immediately following the movie.

Following the instructional procedures, E turned on the movie projector, which displayed the modeling stimuli on a glass lens screen in the television console.

The movie consisted of a 4-minute color film in which an adult male model exhibited a series of relatively novel patterns of behavior and often utilized play materials in unusual ways. Since this study was concerned with issues of response acquisition, it was necessary to devise unusual response sequences that have virtually a zero probability of occurring spontaneously in preschool children and hence meet the criterion of novel responses. In the opening scene the model entered the room with his right hand cupped over his eyes. He then clasped his hands behind his back as he surveyed the various play materials.

In the first action sequence the model built a tower with blocks arranged in a unique manner and set a plastic juice dispenser, which was to serve as a target, on top of the tower. After picking up a dart gun and a baton, the model paced off a specified number of steps from the target, placed the baton on the floor to mark the range, got down on one knee, and fired the dart gun at the plastic container. The block tower was then disassembled in a distinctive way. In the next action sequence, which was directed toward a large Bobo doll, the model sat on the doll, punched it in the nose, pummeled it with a mallet, tossed rubber balls at it, lassoed it with a hoola hoop, and dragged it with the improvised lariat to a far corner of the room. The model then picked up two bean bags and paced off backward a designated number of steps from the target, which consisted of an upright board with three large holes. After reaching the starting point, the model tossed the bean bags between his legs with his back to the target. He then retrieved the bags, paced backward, squatted with his back to the target, and tossed a bean bag over each shoulder. The closing scene showed the model walking across the room whirling the hoola hoop over his right arm.

Delayed imitative performance is determined not only by observational variables but also by rehearsal processes which typically improve retention. An incentive set may, therefore, influence the amount of behavioral reproduction by both augmenting and channeling observing responses during acquisition, and actuating deliberate implicit rehearsal of matching responses immediately after exposure. Since the present experiment was primarily concerned with issues of response acquisition, and the occurrence of differential anticipatory rehearsal would obscure results, children in all groups were assigned the task of counting out loud during the brief period between the end of the movie and reproduction. By this procedure, an attempt was made to hold interpolated activities constant for all groups and to prevent facilitative rehearsal of responses. Immediately after the completion of the movie, E announced that they would now proceed to another room in the mobile laboratory, and that she was interesting in seeing how high they could count while they walked to the other end of the trailer. Since the interpolated task was highly dissimilar to the modeled activities, it was not expected to reduce retention to any great extent.

Test for Acquisition

The test for acquisition was administered by a second female experimenter in a room containing the stimulus items that were utilized by the model in the filmed performance. In order to control for any possible E influences, the person who conducted this phase of the study did not know to which treatment conditions Ss had been assigned.

The children were asked by E to demonstrate all of the model's responses they could recall, and were praised and rewarded with candy for each matching response correctly reproduced. A standardized cuing procedure was employed to insure the same order of reproduction for all Ss. They were asked to show the way in which the model behaved in the opening scene of the movie; to demonstrate what he did with the dart gun, the Bobo doll, and the bean bags; and to portray the model's behavior in the closing scene of the film. The children were thus given a fragmentary cue and asked to reproduce the entire response sequence in which the particular stimulus object was employed.

The E recorded the children's matching responses on a checklist containing the 38 responses that had been exhibited by the model. In order to provide an estimate of interscorer reliability, the performances of ten children were recorded simultaneously but independently by another rater who observed the test sessions through a one-way mirror from an adjoining observation room. The two raters were in perfect agreement on 96 per cent of the specific matching responses that were scored.

RESULTS

Table 1 presents the mean number of matching responses achieved by children in the various treatment conditions. In each incentive condition,

TABLE 1. MEAN NUMBER OF MATCHING RESPONSES REPRODUCED AS A FUNCTION OF SYMBOLIZATION AND INCENTIVE-SET CONDITIONS

	Observational Conditions		
Incentive	Facilitative Symbolization	Passive Observation	Competing Symbolization
No incentive set			
Boys	16.8	14.5	11.5
Girls	17.5	13.2	6.0
Total	17.2	13.8	8.7
Incentive set			
Boys	16.2	15.3	13.0
Girls	14.8	11.7	9.8
Total	15.5	13.5	11.4

for both boys and girls, the mean reproduction scores attained by the active symbolizers exceeds the corresponding means for the passive observers who, in turn, show a higher level of acquisition than Ss in the competing symbolization treatment. Analysis of variance of these data reveals that symbolization is a highly significant source of variance ($F = 13.01$; $p < .001$).

Further comparisons of pairs of means by the t test indicate that Ss who generated verbal equivalents of the modeling stimuli during presentation subsequently reproduced significantly more matching responses than children who either observed passively ($t = 2.18$; $p < .025$) or engaged in competing symbolizations ($t = 5.12$; $p < .001$). Moreover, the passive viewers acquired more of the model's repertoire of behavior than children who engaged in verbalizations designed to interfere with the development of representational responses ($t = 2.94$; $p < .01$).

It is of interest that boys reproduced a significantly higher number of matching responses than girls ($F = 5.70$; $p < .05$). Contrary to prediction, however, observational learning was not influenced by incentive set nor were there any significant interaction effects.

DISCUSSION

Although the results of the present study provide confirmatory evidence for the facilitative role of symbolization in observational learning, alternative interpretations of these findings might be examined. It is conceivable that the method utilized for preventing the acquisition of representational responses may have interfered with observation of the modeling stimuli. Considering, however, that the modeling stimuli were projected on a large television screen directly in front of the S seated in a dark room, it is improbable that, under such conditions of highly focused attention, concurrent competing verbalization could reduce appreciably the occurrence of observing responses. Indeed, the replies of children in the incentive-set condition to questions in the postexperiment interview indicate that they exerted strong efforts to observe and to retain the responses exhibited by the model ("While I was counting, I was paying attention to the thing. I thought back about it in my head . . . I look at it all the time so I remember it all the time").

The marked external control of observing responses through the televised mode of stimulus presentation in all likelihood accounts to some extent for the absence of a significant incentive effect on the acquisition of matching behavior. As several of the children put it, "I didn't look all over the place. I just watched the movie and kept my eyes on it. . . . I kept watching. I couldn't take my eyes off it."

In situations where a person is exposed to multiple models exhibiting diverse patterns of behavior, knowledge of the reinforcement contingencies associated with the corresponding response patterns and anticipation of positive or negative reinforcement for subsequent reproduction may exert selective control over the nature and frequency of attending responses. The effects of incentive set on observational learning would, therefore, be most clearly elucidated by a comparative study utilizing stimulus situations ranging from (a) highly focused observation of a single sequence of modeling stimuli or (b) controlled exposure to multiple models requiring selective attentiveness to competing social cues presented simultaneously to (c) self-selection of frequency and duration of exposure to specific types of models. The latter condition, which corresponds most closely to observational learning in naturalistic situations, would probably maximize the influence of reinforcement-oriented set.

The hypothesis concerning the influence of anticipated positive reinforcement for matching responses on observational learning was based on presumed perceptual sensitizing effects of an incentive set induced prior to exposure. The fact, however, that Ss who expected to be subsequently tested and rewarded for their imitative behavior generally achieved slightly lower acquisition scores than their uninformed counterparts suggests that the benefits of incentive set may have been offset by detrimental effects. There were indications in the interview data, elicited by questions about the children's thoughts during the film-viewing, that the incentive-set instructions generated achievement anxieties in some of the children. ("I was thinking what should I tell you and what should I do. . . . I was just thinking, I hope I remember everything.") Observational learning could be adversely affected by implicit rehearsal of preceding events and disruptive thoughts concerning an impending test if these competing cognitive activities occur while the modeling stimuli are being presented at a relatively rapid rate. Any deleterious consequences should be greatest, as was the case, among the active symbolizers who were in the optimal film-viewing condition and, therefore, would most likely be hindered by the additional motivational effects of expectation of a performance test following the exposure session.

The small but nevertheless significant sex differences in acquisition scores is probably due, in part, to the fact that the modeled responses involved physical masculine-typed activities. The girls' more adverse reaction to the incentive set may also have been a contributing factor.

A single brief exposure to a continuous series of modeling stimuli is likely to produce some interference in the acquisition and correct sequencing of novel matching responses. Dramatic intrusions from the various sequential patterns were occasionally evident in Ss' behavioral reproductions, as in the case of the child who fired the dart gun at the Bobo doll, when, in fact, the plastic container served as the modeled target. Massed exposure conditions may thus result in the development of some erroneous modeling responses and the loss, through interference, of previously acquired ones.

Simultaneous competing verbalizations during observation of modeling displays would not be expected to interfere too extensively with the development of visual imagery, particularly when the modeling stimuli are highly salient, as in the present experiment. It would, therefore, be of considerable theoretical significance to determine whether any matching responses could be reproduced if, in addition to preventing the development of verbal associates, visual imaginal responses were likewise precluded, masked, or obliterated. Such imagery-interference procedures would provide the most decisive evidence as to whether representational mediators are necessary for long-term retention and delayed behavioral reproduction of modeling stimuli.

SUMMARY

This study investigated the effects of symbolization on delayed reproduction of modeling stimuli in a test of the contiguity-mediational theory of observational learning. During exposure to the behavior of a film-mediated model, one group of children engaged in concurrent verbalization, a second group observed passively, while a third group engaged in competing symbolization. Half of the children in each of the treatment conditions observed the model's behavior under a positive incentive set; the remaining Ss were provided no incentive to learn the model's responses. Ss who generated verbal equivalents of the modeling stimuli during exposure subsequently reproduced more matching responses than the passive viewers, who, in turn, showed a higher level of acquisition than children in the competing symbolization treatment. Observational learning, however, was not influenced by incentive set.

REFERENCES

Baer, D. M., & Sherman, J. A.   Reinforcement control of generalized imitation in young children. *J. exp. child Psychol.,* 1964, **1,** 37–49.

Bandura, A.   Social learning through imitation. In M. R. Jones (Ed.), *Nebraska symposium on motivation: 1962.* Lincoln: Univer. of Nebraska Pr., 1962. Pp. 211–269.

Bandura, A.   Behavioral modifications through modeling procedures. In L. Krasner & L. P. Ullmann (Eds.), *Research in behavior modification.* New York: Holt, Rinehart & Winston, 1965. Pp. 310–340. (a)

Bandura, A.   Influence of models' reinforcement contingencies on the acquisition of imitative responses. *J. Pers. soc. Psychol.,* 1965, **1,** 589–595. (b)

Bandura, A.   Vicarious processes: a case of no-trial learning. In L. Berkowitz (Ed.), *Advances in experimental social psychology.* Vol. 2. New York: Academic Press, 1965. Pp. 1–55. (c)

Bandura, A., Ross, Dorothea, & Ross, Sheila A.   Vicarious reinforcement and imitative learning. *J. abnorm. soc. Psychol.,* 1963, **67,** 601–607.

Bandura, A., & Walters, R. H.   *Social learning and personality development.* New York: Holt, Rinehart & Winston, 1963.

Conant, M. B.   Conditioned visual hallucinations. Unpublished manuscript, Stanford Univer., 1964.

Leuba, C.   Images as conditioned sensations. *J. exp. Psychol.,* 1940, **26,** 345–351.

Miller, N. E., & Dollard, J.   *Social learning and imitation.* New Haven, Conn.: Yale Univer. Pr., 1941.

Naruse, G., & Abonai, T.   Decomposition and fusion of mental images in the drowsy and posthypnotic hallucinatory state. *J. clin. exp. Hypnosis,* 1953, **1,** 23–41.

Sheffield, F. D.   Theoretical considerations in the learning of complex sequential tasks from demonstration and practice. In A. A. Lumsdaine (Ed.), *Student responses in programmed instructions: a symposium.* Washington, D.C.: National Academy of Sciences, National Research Council, 1961. Pp. 13–52.

Skinner, B. F.   *Science and human behavior.* New York: Macmillan, 1953.

3.6   Imitation and Retention of Film-mediated Aggressive Peer and Adult Models [1]

David J. Hicks

Research on the influence of film-mediated aggressive models in shaping children's aggressive behavior has utilized adults or cartoons as the stimuli to be observed with the measurement of subsequent aggression closely following exposure to a model (Bandura, Ross, & Ross, 1963a, 1963b; Lovaas, 1961; Mussen & Rutherford, 1961). Minor attention has been devoted to the effects of peer models on children's performance of aggressive responses while the long-term effects of aggressive models on children's behavior has not been studied. The present study was aimed at investigating the immediate and post-interval effectiveness of film-mediated peers and adults as transmitters of aggressive patterns of behavior.

METHOD

Subjects

The subjects were 30 boys and 30 girls enrolled in the Chico State College Laboratory School and Child Development Laboratory. They ranged in age from 41 to 76 months, with a mean age of 61 months. A female experimenter conducted the study for all 60 children.

Procedure

Subjects were assigned to four experimental groups and one control group of 12 subjects each. One group of experimental subjects observed an adult male model while a second, a third, and a fourth group of experimental subjects were exposed to a female adult model, a peer male model, and a peer female model, respectively. The models were presented to the subjects by means of 8-minute films projected on a plastic lenscreen in a television console. Children in the experimental conditions were equally divided into male and female subgroups so that half of the subjects in each condition were exposed to same-sex models, while the remainder viewed models of the opposite sex.

Subjects in the experimental and control groups were matched on ratings

[1] This investigation was supported in part by Research Grant MH-7401 from the National Institutes of Health, United States Public Health Service.

Reprinted from the *Journal of Personality and Social Psychology* 1965, **2**, 97–100, by permission of the author and the American Psychological Association.

of the amount of physical aggression, verbal aggression, and aggression toward inanimate objects as observed prior to experimentation by two raters on the staff of the laboratory school and child development laboratory who were familiar with the behavior of the subjects. In addition to sex and preexperimental aggressiveness, subjects were also matched on the basis of age.

The children were brought individually by the experimenter to the exposure room. The experimenter seated the child at a table placed in front of a television console. The experimenter suggested that they watch a television program and walked over to the set and turned it on. A film containing the appropriate model condition appeared and the experimenter moved to a chair placed to the side and behind the child. From this position the experimenter measured the amount of time the children observed the films. The experimenter remained with the child during the exposure period.

The films to which children in the experimental conditions were exposed began with a commentator introducing the model who was walking about a room looking at some toys which were on the floor. The toys consisted of a plastic bat, four plastic balls, and a pounding board with a mallet. During this time an inflated plastic doll was shown and introduced by the commentator. The model moved to the doll and then looked about the room to the toys placed on the floor. The model then picked up the plastic bat and started to hit the doll. Following the bat aggression the model picked up the plastic balls and threw them at the doll. The model started striking the doll with the mallet from the pounding-board set following the ball-throwing sequence. The final aggressive behavior performed by the model was to sit on the doll and punch it repeatedly in the nose. Each of the distinctive aggressive acts was shown for a period of 30 seconds before the next behavior in the sequence was presented. Each sequence of four behaviors was repeated three times. The model made four verbally aggressive responses which were interspersed throughout the sequences of physically aggressive acts. The verbal stimuli used were "Batter up," "Smacko," "Take that," and "Bingo." The films were edited so the duration of the physical acts and the number of verbal responses were the same in all the experimental conditions.

Following exposure to a film subjects were mildly frustrated. This was accomplished by taking them to another room containing a variety of attractive toys which the children were told that they could play with. As soon as a subject demonstrated involvement with the toys the experimenter said that the child could no longer play with the materials for it had been decided to save them for other children. The children were told that there were toys in another room and that they could play with any of those. The experimenter and subject then entered the experimental room.

The experimenter remained in the experimental room with the child. In order to minimize her influence on the children's behavior the experimenter remained at a desk in the corner with her back to the subject and avoided any contact.

Children assigned to the control condition were not shown films, but were mildly frustrated prior to entering the experimental room.

Test for Imitation

The experimental room contained a variety of play materials, some of which could presumably be used for imitative or nonimitative aggression and others which would tend to elicit nonaggressive behaviors. The aggressive toys consisted of a large inflated plastic doll, a mallet and pounding board, a plastic bat, four plastic balls, two dart guns, and a plastic rifle. The nonaggressive toys included a farm set with animals, two small dolls with clothing, a tea set, two cars, and a truck. These materials were arranged in a fixed order prior to the entrance of each of the subjects.

The subject was in the experimental room for a period of 20 minutes during which time his behavior was scored by two judges on predetermined response categories. The judges viewed the subject through one-way vision glass in an adjoining observation room. The 20-minute period was divided in 5-second intervals by use of a prerecorded tape which sounded the interval numbers. This procedure yielded a total number of 240 responses for each subject.

A subject's behavior was scored as an imitative aggressive response when the child struck the doll with the bat, threw balls at the doll, hit the doll with the mallet, or sat on the doll and punched it in the nose. The number of nonimitative aggressive responses and nonaggressive responses was also scored. The degree of interjudge agreement on the type of behavior performed was calculated with the resulting product-moment coefficient being .93.

Retest Procedure

Approximately 6 months after their exposure to a film and the initial observation of behaviors all subjects were reobserved. The mean number of days in this interval was 178 with a range of 166–187 days.

The subjects were brought individually by the same experimenter to the instigation room. The children were not reexposed to the films. The frustration procedure was identical with that used during the initial phase of the experiment with the exception that a different set of attractive toys was presented. Following the frustration the experimenter reintroduced the children to the same experimental room which was arranged as it had been previously. Again the children remained in the room for 20 minutes during which time the subjects' behaviors were scored by judges watching through one-way vision glass in an adjoining room. During this second 20-minute period the experimenter remained with the children and avoided contact.

Test for Retention

At the end of the second performance period the experimenter turned to the children and asked if they recalled the television show that they had seen together. When the children indicated memory of the exposure the experimenter produced a large candy sucker and informed the children that she would give them the sucker if they could tell her all the things they had seen on the film. The sucker was withheld until a child was consistently incorrect or obviously had terminated effort to recall. When a child had difficulty with verbalization or ceased to verbalize the experimenter asked the child, "Show me what you saw on the television program." The number of descriptions of an imitative response and/or performance demonstrations made by the children were scored by the judges in the adjoining room.

RESULTS

Table 1 presents the mean imitation scores for children in the four experimental conditions and the control group obtained shortly after exposure

TABLE 1. INITIAL MEAN IMITATIVE AGGRESSION SCORES FOR EXPERIMENTAL
AND CONTROL GROUPS

Response category	Experimental conditions				Control
	Adult male	Adult female	Peer male	Peer female	
Imitative aggression	9.58	16.33	22.75	13.42	.00
Boys	14.00	27.50	29.83	20.33	.00
Girls	5.17	5.17	15.67	6.50	.00

to the models. The original scores were transformed to the logarithm of the scores plus one to make the data amenable to parametric statistical analysis. The transformation was necessitated by the presence of many zero imitation scores found in the control group and used because the increases in group means and variances were essentially proportional.

TABLE 2. ANALYSIS OF VARIANCE OF TRANSFORMED INITIAL
IMITATIVE RESPONSES

Source	df	MS	F
Between subjects	11		
Sex (S)	1	2.41	12.78 *
Error (b)	10	1.88	
Within subjects	48		
Treatments (T)	4	9.56	10.54 **
S × T	4	2.02	2.23
Error (w)	40	.23	

* $p < .01$.
** $p < .001$.

The results of the analysis of variance based on the initial imitation scores are presented in Table 2. The findings reveal that exposure of children to aggressive models is a relevant antecedent in determining the subsequent form of a child's aggressive behavior. The sex of the child was shown to be a significant main effect indicating that the performance of imitative aggressive behavior is greater for boys than for girls.

When compared with the control condition the adult-male ($t = 3.79$, $p < .001$), adult-female ($t = 4.61$, $p < .001$), peer-male ($t = 6.24$, $p < .001$), and peer-female ($t = 4.13$, $p < .001$) model conditions were all found to be highly effective in shaping the children's aggressive responses. The performance level of subjects who viewed peer-male models was shown to be significantly higher than those of either the adult-male ($t = 2.45$, $p < .05$) or peer-female ($t = 2.10$, $p < .05$) model conditions.

The mean imitation scores for the same children in the four experimental conditions and the control group 6 months after exposure to the models are presented in Table 3.

TABLE 3. SUBSEQUENT MEAN IMITATIVE AGGRESSION SCORES FOR EXPERIMENTAL AND CONTROL GROUPS

Response category	Experimental conditions				Control
	Adult male	Adult female	Peer male	Peer female	
Imitative aggression	8.92	3.92	6.42	4.33	.33
Boys	7.33	7.17	5.17	6.50	.67
Girls	10.50	.67	7.67	2.17	.00

Though the results of the analysis of variance based on the transformed imitation scores obtained from the reobservation of subjects failed to reveal any significant treatments, sex, or interaction effects, a comparison of pairs of means from the performance of subjects during this subsequent test was performed. The results showed that only exposure to an adult-male model remains a relevant antecedent experience in shaping the form of children's aggressive behavior ($t = 2.49$, $p < .05$).

In each of the films utilized in the experimental conditions the model performed four distinctive physical aggressive behaviors. In order to evaluate further the variety of the models' behaviors which were transmitted to the subjects an analysis of the number of *different* model-provided behaviors found in the initial performances, subsequent performances, and the post-experimental retention tests of the experimental subjects was evaluated by the *t*-test procedure for correlated means. The differences between the initial and subsequent performance phases of the experiment were significant for boys ($t = 6.39$, $p < .01$) and for girls ($t = 3.24$, $p < .01$) indicating that the number of modeled behaviors found in a subject's performance is greatly reduced 6 months after exposure to an aggressive model.

The evaluation of the differences of the number of different model-provided behaviors found in the performance and retention of subjects 6 months after exposure to the films showed that the children retained more elements of the model's behavior than they performed. The differences found were significant for boys ($t = 4.30$, $p < .01$) and for girls ($t = 4.02$, $p < .01$).

DISCUSSION

The results of the present study confirm the finding reported by Bandura et al. (1963a) that exposure to filmed aggression effectively shapes the form of children's aggressive responses.

In studies by Jakubczak and Walters (1959) and Bandura and Kupers (1964) it was found that an increased probability of receiving positive consequences or preventing negative ones when adults rather than peers were modeled apparently determined the model choice and imitative performance levels of children. When aggression is the type of behavior under investigation the age-status of the model does not appear to operate as a discriminative cue which alters the amount of imitation.

The relatively low imitation scores obtained by girls could be attributed to either response inhibition or inhibition of observational tendencies. Bandura and Walters (1963) have proposed that the probability of occurrence of observing responses may increase or decrease depending on the observer's anticipation of positive or negative reinforcement. The difference in imitative responses between boys and girls could, then, be due to the increased tendency by male subjects to observe what would be a sex-appropriate behavior and a decreased predisposition to observe a sex-inappropriate behavior on the part of female subjects. A comparison of the observational responses of boys and girls does not support this differential observation hypothesis. Boys did not differ significantly from girls in the amount of time spent in observing the model's behavior ($t = .05$). An observer's willingness to perform a model's behavior rather than a willingness to observe would appear to account for the significant difference in imitative responses between sexes.

The exposure of children to aggressive films appears to remain a relevant antecedent in shaping the form of their aggressive responses for a considerable length of time. The continued performance of aggressive matching responses is most significant when the model is an adult male. This finding would be of particular importance in light of the frequency with which aggressive adult males are presented in movies and television.

SUMMARY

The relative effect of peer and adult models as transmitters of novel aggressive responses was investigated. Children viewed either male or female adult or male or female peer models presented on film and a test for imitative aggression was made. 6 mo. after seeing the films the same children were reobserved in order to assess the long-term influence of the models. In addition, a test of retention was made after the 6-mo. interval. It was found that the male peer had the most immediate influence in shaping children's aggressive behaviors while the adult male had the most lasting effect. A significantly greater number of the models' behaviors were retained after 6 mo. than were performed.

REFERENCES

Bandura, A., & Kupers, Carol J. Transmission of patterns of self-reinforcement through modeling. *Journal of Abnormal and Social Psychology,* 1964, **69,** 1–9.

Bandura, A., Ross, Dorothea, & Ross, Shiela A. Imitation of film-mediated aggressive models. *Journal of Abnormal and Social Psychology,* 1963, **66,** 3–11. (a)

Bandura, A., Ross, Dorothea, & Ross, Shiela A. Vicarious reinforcement and imitation. *Journal of Abnormal and Social Psychology,* 1963, **67,** 601–607. (b)

Bandura, A., & Walters, R. H. *Social learning and personality development.* New York: Holt, Rinehart, & Winston, 1963.

Jakubczak, L. F., & Walters, R. H. Suggestibility as dependency behavior. *Journal of Abnormal and Social Psychology,* 1959, **59,** 102–107.

Lovaas, O. I. Effect of exposure to symbolic aggression on aggressive behavior. *Child Development,* 1961, **32,** 37–44.

Mussen, P. H., & Rutherford, E. Effects of aggressive cartoons on children's aggressive play. *Journal of Abnormal and Social Psychology,* 1961, **62,** 461–464.

chapter four

Dependency

4.1 Introduction

One of the most pervasive social behaviors involves our reliance from infancy through adulthood on other people for approval, reassurance, help, attention, and physical contact. Although the form in which this behavior is expressed changes over the developmental sequence and the objects may differ, culturally sanctioned opportunities to seek nurturant responses from others are always available. This class of responses is generally referred to as dependency, and a person who exhibits them is viewed as behaving in a dependent manner.

Two varieties of dependency have been distinguished: task-oriented and person-oriented (Bandura & Walters, 1963) or instrumental and emotional (Heathers, 1955). In the case of task or instrumental dependency, a person seeks help from someone else in order to reach a goal. The infant, for example, is dependent on the mother for food. Of greater interest is person-oriented or emotional dependence, in which the social responses of others are the goals of the behavior and not merely the means of reaching some other goal. The early instrumental dependence in the mother-child relationship is often regarded as the precursor of emotional dependency. The development of emotional dependence on other persons is viewed as a precondition for adequate social adjustment, and much attention has been paid to people with deficits, such as autistic children and institutionalized infants.

However, most behavioral categories that are generally employed in discussions of social development, such as dependency, independence, achievement, and aggression, have not been defined unambiguously.[1] For example, in defining dependency as a set of response tendencies which are instrumental in obtaining social reinforcement or nurturance (Hartup, 1963), difficulties immediately arise, because many of the approval-eliciting responses could be easily viewed as achievement-oriented behaviors. However, achievement has often been employed as an index of independence, a construct that has traditionally been seen as the opposite of dependency. To what category does one assign behaviors which seem achievement-oriented but are contingent on social reinforcers for their maintenance—achievement or dependency?

The confusion found in trying to define or classify social-psychological behaviors stems from the fact that the basis for categorizing a response as dependent, achievement oriented, or aggressive involves a judgmental process (Walters & Parke, 1964). Behavior that is judged dependent in one context may not be judged dependent in another context. The implication of this position is that the child does not, strictly speaking, acquire dependency habits or develop a dependency drive; "he develops a variety of possibly interrelated responses, such as asking for help and soliciting approval, that may or may not be regarded as dependent according to the circumstances in which they occur and the value system within which his behavior is judged" (Walters & Parke, 1964, p. 240). "Dependency," then, is a quasi-evaluative label reflecting social judgments that are made within particular cultural contexts. For example, behavior that is regarded as dependent within one cultural or subcultural framework (or for males but not for females) is not so classified in another. In the case of dependency, the value judgments often take into account the appropriateness of a response for an agent having a known or assumed level of capacity for coping with a situation. In a situation where the individual is incapable of achieving his goal alone, help-seeking, for example, will be judged differently than equivalent behavior under circumstances in which the individual's goals can be economically and readily attained without the mediation of others. Persons who tend to rely on others

---

[1] For a fuller discussion of these issues, see Walters and Parke, 1964.

even when capable of carrying out activities efficiently and unaided are likely to be called "dependent."

An adequate understanding of social development requires a thorough investigation of the process whereby children learn to make social judgments that enable them to discriminate acceptable from nonacceptable responses, which are classified as dependent or nondependent on the basis of their acceptability within the cultural system (Walters & Parke, 1964, p. 241). Labels, such as dependency, have some objective reference to certain classes of behavior, although it is not often well defined. The investigation of the conditions under which such behavioral referents as help-seeking or approval-seeking are acquired and maintained has been the research focus of the studies reported in this section.

In studying the development of any social behavior, the investigator is concerned with the changes in the form of the response that occur as the child develops, and in isolating the child-rearing antecedents of the behavior. Heathers, in his research on the development of dependency, has been concerned with both of these questions. In a study that preceded the experimental study in this section, he observed 2-year-olds and 4- and 5-year-olds in a nursery school situation and noted that changes occurred with age, both in the form of the dependent response and in the objects to whom the dependent response was directed. Clinging and affection-seeking decline with age, relative to attention or approval-seeking. Similarly, the object of dependency shifts with age; as the child matures, emotional dependence on adults declines while dependence on one's peers tends to increase. This shift to peers is probably due to the fact that older nursery schoolers provide social reinforcers to their classmates more frequently than younger pre-school-age children (Charlesworth & Hartup, 1967).

The relative stability of dependency behavior from childhood to adulthood has been assessed in a longitudinal study by Kagan and Moss (1960), who found a relatively stable degree of dependency for girls but no relationships between childhood and adult dependency for boys. As Kagan and Moss note, in our culture dependency is clearly a feminine sex-typed behavior pattern, and the differential stability is probably due to the greater encouragement of dependency in females and the discouragement of these behaviors in males. (See the Kagan and Moss article in the section on sex typing.)

Another means of studying dependency is to place children in an experimental situation which will be likely to elicit dependent responses, then assess the differences in the amount of dependency shown by children who differ in background, age, or sex. Heathers, in his article in this section, used a novel fear-inducing situation and assessed the extent to which different children would exhibit dependent responses. As in the earlier observational study, age was an important variable; younger children were more dependent than older children. In addition, Heathers found that certain child-rearing experiences can differentiate between children exhibiting different amounts of dependency. The high-dependent children were products of child-centered homes in which parents encouraged their children to rely on others rather than take care of themselves. Similarly, Finney (1961) has reported a positive correlation between the mother's tendency to selectively reward dependent behavior and the child's dependency level. Further evidence that parental reinforcement and encouragement of dependent responses are important antecedents of childhood dependency comes from a variety of other field studies. For example, Sears, Maccoby, and Levin (1957), in a large-scale study of the child-rearing practices of over three hundred Boston mothers, found a positive relationship between maternal demonstrativeness and child dependency. However, as Levy (1943) has noted, excessive encouragement of infantile dependent behavior combined with attempts at preventing the emergence of independent forms of behavior may result in the development of extremely maladaptive degrees of submissive dependency.

In addition to positive reinforcement, parental rejection in the form of either inconsistent reinforcement or intermittent reward and punishment may be an important antecedent of dependency. Sears, Maccoby, and Levin (1957) found a positive correlation between maternal punitiveness for dependency behavior and the strength of the child's dependency habits, but only when these responses were also frequently rewarded. When dependency received little reinforcement, rejection was not predictive of the child's dependency level. A study by Fisher (1955), using dogs, yielded similar results, namely, greater dependency for the puppies who had been trained to make social approach responses under a schedule involving both reward and punishment than for those animals trained to approach a human under a schedule involving only positive reinforcement.

The experimental study by Hartup (1958) presented in this section can be viewed within this same framework. Hartup found that withdrawal of attention led to a greater increase in dependency than did consistent attention. The effects were more noticeable with girls who presumably have highly developed dependency habits, and with high-dependent boys. An earlier experimental study by Gewirtz (1954), in which children engaged in more attention-seeking from a nonresponsive rather than a responsive adult, and the Gewirtz and Baer (1958) study (see section on social reinforcement) of social isolation are consistent with Hartup's findings.

The last two papers in this section deal with the behavioral consequences of high or low dependency. One study sought to determine whether children of differing dependency levels vary in their susceptibility to social influence. Jakubezak and Walters (1959), working on the assumption that suggestibility is another form of dependent behavior, hypothesized that high-dependent subjects would conform more than low-dependent subjects to the suggestions of others. Their data strongly supported the hypothesis. Moreover, adults were more effective than peers in modifying the judgments of their adolescent subjects. Studies with adults have found a similar relationship between dependency and conformity. Mussen and Kagan (1956), for example, using a projective measure of dependency found that high-dependent subjects were more influenced in a group conformity situation. As indicated in the discussion of social reinforcement, high-dependent subjects are also more responsive and more readily influenced by social reinforcers than low-dependent children (Endsley, 1960; Ferguson, 1961; Cairns & Lewis, 1962).

In addition, the dependency level of a child has clear implications for his sociometric status among peers. A number of studies by McCandless and his colleagues (Marshall & McCandless, 1957; McCandless, Bilous, & Bennett, 1961) have reported that high dependency is often linked with low popularity with peers.

In the final paper in this section, the tendency of dependent and nondependent subjects to imitate is explored. Ross's findings are generally in agreement with earlier studies (Bandura & Huston, 1961; Bandura, Ross, & Ross, 1961, 1963) which indicated that high-dependent children show more imitative behavior than low-dependent children. Moreover, Ross has extended our understanding of this relationship by showing that high- and low-dependent children imitate different aspects of the model's behavior. In a learning situation, low-dependent subjects tend to select for imitation those aspects of the model's behavior which are task relevant and tend to ignore irrelevant or incidental actions of the model. High-dependent subjects, however, tend to pay approximately equal attention to all aspects of the model's behavior, regardless of their relevance for task solution. These results suggest that high- and low-dependent children differ not only in their tendency to imitate, but also in their strategies in the imitation situation.

REFERENCES

Bandura, A., & Huston, A. C. Identification as a process of incidental learning. *Journal of Abnormal and Social Psychology*, 1961, **63**, 311–318.

Bandura, A., Ross, D., & Ross, S. A.   Imitation of film-mediated aggressive models. *Journal of Abnormal and Social Psychology,* 1963, **66,** 3–11 (a).

Bandura, A., Ross, D., & Ross, S. A.   Transmission of aggression through imitation of aggressive models. *Journal of Abnormal and Social Psychology,* 1961, **63,** 575–582.

Bandura, A., & Walters, R. H.   *Social learning and personality development.* New York: Holt, Rinehart and Winston, Inc., 1963b.

Cairns, R. B., & Lewis, M.   Dependency and the reinforcement value of a verbal stimulus. *Journal of Consulting Psychology,* 1962, **26,** 1–8.

Charlesworth, R., & Hartup, W. W.   Positive social reinforcement in the nursery school peer group. *Child Development,* 1967, *38,* 993–1002.

Endsley, R. C.   Dependency and performance by preschool children on a socially-reinforced task. Unpublished M.A. Thesis, State University of Iowa, 1960.

Ferguson.   The influence of isolation, anxiety, and dependency on reinforcer effectiveness. Unpublished M.A. Thesis, University of Toronto, 1961.

Fisher, A. E.   The effects of differential early treatment on the social and exploratory behavior of puppies. Unpublished doctoral dissertation, Pennsylvania State University, 1955.

Gewirtz, J. L.   Three determinants of attention seeking in young children. *Monograph of the Society for Research in Child Development,* 1954, **19,** No. 2 (Serial No. 59).

Gewirtz, J. L., & Baer, D. M.   The effects of brief social deprivation on behaviors for a social reinforcer. *Journal of Abnormal and Social Psychology,* 1958, **66,** 49–56.

Hartup, W. W.   Nurturance and nurturance-withdrawal in relation to the dependency behavior of preschool children. *Child Development,* 1958, **29,** 191–201.

Hartup, W. W.   Dependency and independence. In *Child Psychology, the Sixty-second Yearbook of the National Society for the Study of Education,* Part I. Chicago: The National Society for the Study of Education, 1963. Pp. 333–363.

Heathers, G.   Emotional dependence and independence in nursery school play. *Journal of Genetic Psychology,* 1955, **87,** 37–57.

Jakubezak, L. F., & Walters, R. H.   Suggestibility as dependency behavior. *Journal of Abnormal and Social Psychology,* 1959, **59,** 102–107.

Kagan, J., & Moss, H. A.   The stability of passive and dependent behavior from childhood to adulthood. *Child Development,* 1960, **31,** 577–591.

Levy, D. M.   *Maternal overprotection.* New York: Columbia University Press, 1943.

McCandless, B. R., Bilous, C. B., & Bennett, H. L.   Peer popularity and dependence on adults in preschool-age socialization. *Child Development,* 1961, **32,** 511–518.

Marshall, H. R., & McCandless, B. B.   Relationship between dependence on adults and social acceptance by peers. *Child Development,* 1957, **28,** 413–419.

Sears, R. R., Maccoby, E. E., & Levin, H. *Patterns of child rearing*. New York: Harper, 1957.

Walters, R. H., & Parke, R. D. Social motivation, dependency, and susceptibility to social influence. In L. Berkowitz (Ed.), *Advances in Experimental Social Psychology*, Vol. 1. New York: Academic Press, 1964. Pp. 231–276.

SUPPLEMENTARY READING

Bandura, A., & Walters, R. H. *Social learning and personality development*. New York: Holt, Rinehart and Winston, Inc., 1963. Pp. 137–148.

Hartup, W. W. Dependence and independence. In H. W. Stevenson (Ed.), *Child psychology: The sixty-second yearbook of the National Society for the Study of Education*, Part 1. Chicago: University of Chicago Press, 1963. Pp. 333–363.

Walters, R. H., & Parke, R. D. Social motivation, dependency and susceptibility to social influence. In L. Berkowitz (Ed.), *Advances in experimental social psychology*, Vol. I. New York: Academic Press, 1964. Pp. 231–276.

4.2   Emotional Dependence and Independence in a Physical Threat Situation

Glen Heathers [1]

This paper reports an approach to measuring emotional dependence and independence in grade school children responding to a novel situation involving the threat of physical injury. One way in which people depend on others is by seeking reassurance in situations they perceive as threatening to themselves. We assume that a child develops the tendency to look to others for reassurance in threatening situations because others protect him from injury. Thus he learns to associate their presence, their encouraging remarks, or their help with being safe from harm. Thereafter, when he becomes anxious in anticipation of injury, the child may seek reassurance as a means of relieving his anxiety. In a study of children's fears of the dark and of high places, Holmes (2) demonstrated how children may utilize the reassuring presence of an adult as an emotional support in facing feared situations.

[1] The writer is grateful to Mrs. Ruth Bean, Edna Small and Suzanne Hamberger for assistance in conducting this study.

Reprinted from *Child Development* 1953, **24**, 169–179, by permission of the author and the Society for Research in Child Development.

A child exhibits independence when physically threatened if he copes with the situation without requiring reassurance or help. It is assumed that he will tend to rely on himself if he expects that he can avoid injury or that he can tolerate whatever injury he may suffer. Also, the child may show independence as a way of winning approval from others, or as a way of avoiding their disapproval. Finally, he may express independence in order to experience the self-approval which comes from knowing that he has mastered a difficult or threatening situation.

METHOD AND SUBJECTS

In selecting a task for measuring dependence and independence under physical threat, six criteria were employed: (a) the task should involve the possibility of physical injury which all subjects will perceive; (b) it should not be so threatening that any grade school children will refuse to perform it; (c) it should be a task which children in the 6–12 age range are capable of performing independently; (d) it should be novel in order to minimize differences in the children's experience with similar tasks; (e) it should allow a clear choice between dependent and independent modes of coping with it; and (f) it should provide a series of trials to permit adjustive changes to be measured.

The physical threat situation devised for this exploratory study was the Walk-the-Plank Test, a task which meets the six requirements relatively well. In this test, the subject was blindfolded and instructed to walk the length of a plank balanced on springs and raised eight inches off the floor. The plank was six feet long and 12 inches wide, with sideboards rising two inches above the level of the plank to prevent stepping off the side. It was pivoted at the center like a teeter-totter, and was attached at either end to a baseboard by two springs. It required a weight of about sixty pounds applied to the end of the plank to tip it downward until it touched the floor. To add to the instability of the plank, the cross-board on which it was pivoted was an inch higher at the center of the plank than at either side so that the plank tipped sidewise as well as endwise. One foot from the exit end of the plank, a small strip of wood was nailed across it so that the subject, when his foot bumped against the strip, would know he was near the end.

The subject was led into the testing room past the apparatus and seated at a desk facing away from the apparatus. When he went by the apparatus, he was not permitted to inspect it or test it in any way. After he was interviewed for about fifteen minutes in connection with another study, the subject was administered the Walk-the-Plank Test. For this, he was blindfolded with rubber goggles adapted for the purpose, then given the instructions which follow.

"This is a game where you walk along a wiggly board and step down to the floor when you get to the end. (E leads S to starting end of plank.) Step up. (E holds S's arm while S gets into position.) Turn this way. (E exerts pressure to turn S facing toward exit end of plank.) Feel the sides. (If necessary, E helps S bring his feet against both edge boards.) You will know when you get to the end because your toe will bump against a board stretched across the end. Walk between the sides till your toe bumps against the board, then step down to the floor."

"O.K. Do you want me to walk along with you this time?" (E touches back of S's hand and waits for him to accept or reject the help offered. If S takes the hand, E walks beside him to the end of the plank. If he ignores or rejects the hand, E walks silently behind him to catch him if he loses his balance.)

Five trials were given in immediate succession, with the subject led back to the starting end and helped into the starting position after each trial. At the beginning of each trial, the helping hand was offered in the same way and with the same statement as on the first trial. A record was kept of acceptance or rejection of the offer and of the subject's remarks. The reason for limiting the test to five trials was that previous exploratory work with the test indicated that a fair proportion of children become resistant if the number of trials exceeded five or so.

The subjects were 56 children, 31 boys and 25 girls, between six and 12 years of age. All were members of the Fels Research Institute's longitudinal research population which draws almost exclusively from the middle socio-economic class. The writer served as experimenter.

RESULTS

General Reactions to the Test

We may infer that a high proportion of the subjects perceived the task as physically threatening from the fact that two-thirds of them accepted the helping hand on the first trial while, of the remaining one-third, most were obviously tense and cautious while walking the plank. Subjects' spontaneous remarks, such as "It's scary," "I'm afraid I'll fall," and "It feels funny," verbalized the anxiety which they felt while performing the task. A small proportion of the subjects (about one in ten) behaved from the start with calm assurance, walking quickly and confidently along the plank and offering remarks such as "I like it" and "It's fun." Although nearly all of the subjects perceived the task as threatening, none of them refused to perform any of the five trials.

Concerning the novelty of the task, all 56 children reported, when interviewed at the end of the task, that they had rarely been blindfolded before and never before had walked a springy board when blindfolded. Their experiences with blindfolds had been limited to occasional games of pin-the-tail-on-the-donkey, blind-man's buff, or the like.

The need for reassurance in coping with the situation was shown not only by taking the helping hand but, with several subjects, by leaning toward the experimenter while walking the plank. Some subjects rejected the hand but asked the experimenter to walk along beside them.

In interpreting the independence most subjects showed on the first or later trials, it is important to note that they were never instructed to walk the plank alone. The fact that most did so indicates their own tendencies toward independence, either because they assumed this was expected of them or because they desired to master the task. Typical remarks indicating their desire to perform the task alone were, "I'll try it by myself," "I believe I can," and "I'll do it alone."

Sex Differences

A popular notion is that girls are more fearful than boys in physical threat situations, and more inclined to be dependent on others for protection against injury. The present test offers the opportunity to check this notion in a situation which was highly novel for both the boys and girls who served as subjects.

For the sex comparison, twenty boys and twenty girls were selected from the 56 children on the basis of closest possible age matching. The means of both groups were 121.4 months. The median age of the boys' group was 129 months; of the girls' group, 130 months. Both groups had a semi-interquartile range of 17 months. On the first trial of the test, 12 of the boys and 14 of the girls accepted the helping hand. On all five trials taken together, the twenty boys accepted the helping hand a total of 32 times, the twenty girls also 32 times. The evidence of this study thus failed to support the view that girls are more fearful or less self-reliant than boys in physical threat situations when the factor of experience with the situation is controlled. If the boys did have more experience than the girls in facing physical threats, or if they were generally under more social pressure to exhibit courage, these differences did not generalize to this task.

Trial-to-Trial Differences

The Walk-the-Plank Test confronted the subjects with a situation which was novel in that it required them to walk an unstable platform without visual cues to direct them and to help them keep their balance. While almost all of the subjects were capable of doing the task without help, on Trial 1 they could not be sure of the hazards ahead or of their ability to cope with them. This meant that on Trial 1, anxiety and the associated need for reassurance should have been at a relatively high level, and a higher proportion of subjects would be expected to accept the helping hand on this trial than on later trials. After Trial 1, all the subjects had a more realistic basis for knowing the requirements of the task and for estimating their ability to perform it without aid. From this, it was reasonable to predict a greater decline in the number of subjects accepting the hand on Trial 2 (as compared with Trial 1) than would occur on Trials 3, 4, or 5 as compared to Trials 2, 3 or 4, respectively.

The results strongly supported this prediction. Thirty-six of the 56 subjects accepted the helping hand on Trial 1, 18 on Trial 2, 16 on Trial 3, 16 on Trial 4, and 15 on Trial 5. Figure 1 presents graphically the per-

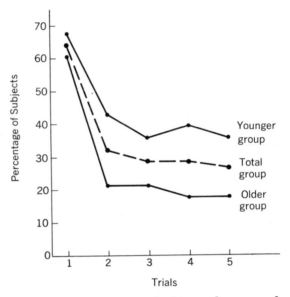

FIGURE 1. Percentages of subjects who accepted the helping hand on each of five trials in the Walk-the-Plank Test. The curves give results for 28 younger and 28 older children and for the total group of 56 children.

centages of the 56 subjects who accepted the hand on each trial (note curve marked "Total Group"). The decline in the proportion of subjects who accepted the hand on Trial 2 as compared with Trial 1 was significant beyond the .01 level.[2] The further declines which occurred on Trials 3 and 5 were not significant.

Ten of the 56 children (six boys and four girls) accepted the hand on all five trials. Their failure to learn to walk without help raises significant questions for independence training in threatening situations. Five of the

---

[2] The proportion of subjects accepting the hand in Trial 1 was .643. Using the formula $\sigma_p = \sqrt{pq/N}$, the fiducial limits of $\pm 3\sigma_p$ for the population sampled in Trial 1 are .829 and .457. The proportion of subjects accepting the hand in Trial 2 was .321 which is outside these limits.

ten not only held the experimenter's hand but leaned on him as they walked the plank. This meant they were giving themselves no chance to learn to balance themselves and it is not surprising they remained dependent throughout the task. The conditions under which a person "throws away his crutches" in a threat situation is an important research problem.

The fact that nine subjects "regressed" by accepting the helping hand after walking without help on one or more trials indicates a conflict between dependent and independent tendencies. The most likely explanation is that, with these subjects, the experience of walking the plank by themselves increased their anxiety in anticipation of injury to the point where they resorted to help as a way of lessening their anxiety. The Walk-the-Plank Test evidently provides a good situation for further research on dependence-independence conflict directed to the question, "What situational variables determine the choice of dependent or independent responses in a physical threat situation?"

Age Differences

In this study it was assumed that dependent responses (taking the helping hand) indicated relatively high anxiety in anticipation of injury and/or relatively low tendencies to assert independence. By and large, older children were expected to have less anxiety than younger children in a given physical threat situation as a result of their greater capacities. Also, it was assumed that, in this culture, older children would have stronger needs to behave independently than younger children as a reflection of stronger social expectations that they handle situations on their own. These assumptions led to the prediction that older children would be less dependent (or more independent) than younger children in the Walk-the-Plank Test.

Considering that the test was a highly novel situation for the subjects and that none of them could know what to expect until after the first trial, it was predicted that on this trial the older children would express more nearly the same amount of dependence as younger children than would be true on later trials. In other words, it was assumed that the older subjects would be unable to utilize fully the advantages their greater capacities and experience gave them until they knew what the task required of them.

The age differences obtained support the analysis given above. The 56 children were divided into younger and older groups of 28 each. The younger group ranged from 80 to 114 months of age with a median age of 98 months, the older group from 114 to 150 months with a median age of 134 months. On trial 1, 19 of the younger and 17 of the older children accepted the helping hand. Thus, on the initial trial, age differences were at a minimum. On later trials, age differences were larger. On Trials 2, 3, 4 and 5, respectively, the numbers of younger children accepting the helping hand were 12, 10, 11 and 10. Corresponding numbers of older children were 6, 6, 5 and 5. These results are presented graphically in Figure 1. Another indication of age differences in the task was the fact that, of the ten children who accepted help on all five trials, eight were in the younger group.

While the age-differences found in this study were consistent with theoretical expectations, the data were insufficient to yield statistically significant differences.

Mothers' Behavior in Relation to Dependence-Independence

It is generally assumed that a child's parents play critical roles in determining his ways of dealing with problem situations. At the Fels Research Institute, data on the mothers' ways of relating to their children are available in the form of periodic ratings using the Fels Parent Behavior Rating Scales. These thirty scales deal with various aspects of mothers' behavior toward their children. The ratings are made following a visit to the home by the Fels Home Visitor who observes the mothers' interaction with her children. These ratings offer the basis for an exploratory test of the relationships between certain aspects of mothers' behavior and the dependence-independence behavior of their children in the Walk-the-Plank Test.

Five of the 30 aspects of mothers' behavior rated in the Scales were selected on theoretical grounds as having particular relevance for learning to express dependent or independent tendencies in physical threat situations. These are Child-centeredness of Home, General Babying, Protectiveness, Accelerational Attempt, and Democracy of Policy. These scales have been described in detail by Baldwin, Kalhorn and Breese (1). They are characterized in briefest terms in this report.

High child-centeredness of the home means that the household revolves around the children, with major sacrifices made for the children's trivial comforts. Low child-centeredness means that the children's welfare is subordinated to that of other family members, with the children being left largely to fend for themselves. It was predicted that high child-centeredness would be associated with high dependence in the Walk-the-Plank Test on the assumption that it encourages the child to lean on others rather than taking care of himself in problem situations.

High babying means that the child is continually helped, even when he is fully capable of doing things by himself. Low babying means the child is left alone to solve his problems, and is often refused aid when he asks for it. It was predicted that high babying would be associated with high dependence in the Walk-the-Plank Test.

High protectiveness means that the child is sheltered from discomforts and difficulties, while low protectiveness means he is deliberately exposed to hazards or dangers. It was predicted that high protectiveness would be associated with high dependence on the Walk-the-Plank Test.

High acceleration means that the child is deliberately trained to develop skills, while low acceleration means he is held back from "growing up." It was predicted that high acceleration would be associated with high independence on the Walk-the-Plank Test on the assumption that acceleration involves training for mastery of situations.

High democracy of policy means that a child is given a definite share in deciding policies which concern him, while low democracy means that he is dictated to without regard to his own wishes. It was predicted that high democracy would be associated with high independence, assuming that it fosters self-reliance and discourages passive dependence.

To test the predictions, only the results for Trial 1 of the Walk-the-Plank Test were used. On later trials, too few subjects accepted the helping hand to permit adequate statistical analysis of differences between those subjects who accepted and those who rejected the helping hand. On Trial 1, thirty-six subjects accepted help and twenty rejected it. From the thirty-six who accepted help, twenty were selected strictly on the basis of choosing the group which most closely matched, in terms of sex and age, the group of twenty subjects who rejected help. Both groups contained 11 boys and nine girls. The Dependent Group (composed of subjects who accepted help) had a mean age of 119.9 months, the Independent Group (composed of subjects who rejected help) a mean age of 119.6 months. As further evidence that the groups were satisfactorily matched in terms of age, the Dependent Group had a median age of 124.5 months and a semi-interquartile range of 17.2 months, while the Independent Group had a median age of 127.0 months and a semi-interquartile range of 19.3 months.

In selecting ratings for use in this study, those made following the last home visit prior to the time the child was given the Walk-the-Plank Test were used. Since home visits are not conducted with children past the age of (approximately) ten years, the interval between the time the ratings were made and the time the data of this study were obtained was almost three years for some of the older subjects. The mean interval for the forty subjects involved in this part of the study was 18.3 months. With 63 per cent of the subjects, the interval was between 11 and 15 months; with eight per cent, between 16 and 24 months; and with 29 per cent, between 25 and 34 months. If one makes the plausible assumption that there is marked consistency from year to year in a mother's way of relating to her children, the time discrepancy should not render the home visit ratings selected inapplicable to the purpose of exploring relationships between mothers' behavior and the subjects' performance of the Walk-the-Plank Test.

The home visit ratings used were in the form of T-Scores, which place the individual in relation to other children in the Fels research population. A rating of 50 thus places the child at the mean of the norming group, a rating of 40 places him one sigma below the mean, while a rating of 60 places him one sigma above the mean. In comparing the parent-behavior ratings given children in the Dependent and Independent Groups, the mean T-Scores were computed for each group for each of the five mother-behavior variables. The reliabilities of differences in means of the Dependent and the

Independent Groups were determined using Wilcoxon's non-parametric test for unpaired replicates (3).

Table 1 summarizes the results obtained with each of the five variables. It was predicted that high child-centeredness, high babying and high protectiveness would be associated with dependence rather than independence in the Walk-the-Plank Test. The results for child-centeredness and babying were in the predicted direction, though babying did not yield a significant difference. With protectiveness, a slight and insignificant difference was found in the opposite direction from that predicted. This finding may reflect unreliability of the measures employed, or it may indicate that the prediction made with respect to the protectiveness variable was incorrect.

It was predicted that high acceleration and high democracy would be associated with independence in the Walk-the-Plank Test. The results with both variables were in the predicted direction, though the difference in means was not significant with respect to democracy.

The results of this analysis support the view that a child's behavior in a physical threat situation is related to certain aspects of his mother's behavior toward him. Further research is needed to establish the nature and degree

TABLE 1. Mean Ratings on Five Mother-Behavior Variables for 20 Subjects Who Accepted the Helping Hand (Dependent Group) and 20 Subjects Who Rejected the Helping Hand (Independent Group) on Trial 1 of the Walk-the-Plank Test

Mother-Behavior Variable	Mean of Dependent Group	Mean of Independent Group	Difference	Predicted Direction?	Reliability
Child-centeredness	51.8	44.6	+7.2	Yes	$<.02$
Babying	47.6	44.0	+3.6	Yes	Non-signif.
Protectiveness	48.7	49.8	−1.1	No	Non-signif.
Acceleration	48.4	54.0	−5.6	Yes	$<.05$
Democracy	47.6	51.3	−3.4	Yes	Non-signif.

of such relationships because of several limitations of this exploratory analysis. The results presented here involved too few subjects to be conclusive with some of the variables employed. The ratings of mothers' behavior used may be unrepresentative because they were based on a single home visit and because they were made from one to three years prior to the subjects' performance of the Walk-the-Plank Test. Also, no measure of the reliability of the Walk-the-Plank Test was available.

It should be noted that differences in mothers' behavior toward the children in the Dependent and the Independent Groups may reasonably be interpreted in two ways. It may be that a mother influences her child's performance in threat situations by indulging him or coaching him, or it may be that the child's behavior in problem situations influences the way his mother treats him. For example, a child may be fearful and dependent because his mother babies him, or his mother may baby him because he is fearful and dependent. Thus the data of this study do not permit determining whether the mother's behavior or the child's behavior was the independent variable.

DISCUSSION

The Walk-the-Plank Test is a promising technique for investigating dependent and independent responses to physical threat in grade school children. The task is threatening enough to arouse marked anxiety and to induce a high percentage of children to seek reassurance, particularly on the initial trial. At the same time it is not so threatening or so difficult that children as young as six years of age cannot perform it independently. The blindfold, in combination with the raised and unstable platform, offers a highly novel situation for children in the age range studied. Acceptance or rejection of the helping hand offers a clear differentiation of dependent and independent modes of coping with the task. The task as designed for this study is not well suited for studying individual adjustment to threats because, with most subjects, adjustment occurs within a trial or two. Also, the all-or-none measurement of dependent and independent responses does not permit ranking individuals in terms of fine differences in their adjustive responses to the situation. For these reasons, the task is primarily of value in differentiating groups of subjects in terms of dependent and independent behavior.

A major limitation of the task as employed in this study is that no measure was obtained of the amount of threat the subject perceived in the situation, or the amount of tension or anxiety it aroused. If measures of autonomic arousal or verbal reports of anxiety were obtained on each trial, dependent and independent modes of response could be interpreted more meaningfully. The task would probably be improved by blindfolding the subjects before they saw the apparatus. Also, it would probably be an improvement to reduce the instability of the plank since this would place less emphasis on differences in the subjects' skills in maintaining balance.

In considering further studies for which the Walk-the-Plank Test is suited, the investigation of factors which affect the shift from dependent to independent modes of coping with the situation seems particularly promising. Thus different techniques of offering reassurance might be employed with comparable groups of subjects. A comparison of the groups on, say, the fifth trial of the test would indicate the relative effects of the different techniques employed. Similarly, one group of subjects might be offered reassurance and help on each trial and another group required to perform the task on a "sink-or-swim" basis without any form of support. Also, the test lends itself to study of the effects of social factors such as the presence of one's parents or one's peers on performance of the task.

SUMMARY

1. This paper reports an exploratory study of emotional dependence and independence in the Walk-the-Plank Test which required the subject while blindfolded to walk the length of a six-foot plank balanced by springs and raised eight inches off the floor. Fifty-six children, 31 boys and 25 girls, between six and 12 years of age individually performed five trials on the apparatus. On each trial, the subject might exhibit dependence by holding the experimenter's hand while he walked the plank, or he might exhibit independence by walking the plank without help.

2. Evidence was presented to indicate that almost all of the subjects perceived the task as threatening. However, the task was not so threatening that any of the subjects refused to perform any of the five trials.

3. No sex differences were found in the subjects' performance of the Walk-the-Plank Test.

4. Two-thirds of the subjects accepted the helping hand on the first trial of the test and approximately one-third on each of the succeeding four trials. The difference in the proportion of subjects accepting the helping hand on Trials 1 and 2 was significant. The fact that a very high proportion of the shifts from dependence to independence occurred on the second trial was interpreted as related to the novelty of the task on the first trial.

5. Almost the same proportion of younger and older children accepted the helping hand on the first trial of the test. However, on later trials, the younger children accepted the helping hand twice as often as the older children. The lack of evidence for age differences on Trial 1 was interpreted as related to the novelty of the task on that trial.

6. There was evidence that the amount of dependence or independence children showed in the Walk-the-Plank Test was related to certain aspects of their mothers' behavior toward them at home as rated with the Fels Parent Behavior Rating Scales.

7. The Walk-the-Plank Test was discussed in relation to its suitability for use with further studies of dependence and independence.

REFERENCES

1. Baldwin, A. L., Kalhorn, J. and Breese, F. H.   The appraisal of parent behavior. *Psychol. Monogr.*, 1949, **63**, No. 4.
2. Holmes, F. B.   An experimental investigation of a method of overcoming children's fears. *Child Develpm.*, 1936, **7**, 6–30.
3. Wilcoxon, Frank. *Some rapid approximate statistical procedures.* (Rev. July 1949.) American Cyanamid Co., 30 Rockefeller Plaza, New York City.

4.3 Nurturance and Nuturance-Withdrawal in Relation to the Dependency Behavior of Preschool Children [1]

Willard W. Hartup

This investigation is based on the hypothesis that non-nurturance by an adult is more strongly associated with the occurrence of dependency behavior in young children than is nurturance alone. The naturalistic studies of Sears *et al.* (11), Beller (1), and Smith (12) all contain data which show a positive relationship between amount of parental frustrations (non-nurturance) and the frequency of dependency behavior observed in young children. Similar results were obtained in the laboratory studies of Gewirtz (5, 6, 7), although Carl's laboratory findings with respect to this hypothesis were inconclusive (2).

The present study was designed to explore the relationship between one specific form of non-nurturance—the withdrawal of nurturance—and young children's acquisition of responses which elicit adult approval. This relationship was studied in the laboratory where some manipulation of the relevant antecedent conditions was possible.

The method of this study has been to provide a comparison in the learning of simple responses which elicit adult approval between a group of children consistently nurtured by an experimenter and another group who were nurtured and then rebuffed (nurturance-withdrawal). It was predicted that children in the presence of an adult female experimenter who withdraws her nurturance in this fashion will learn simple tasks eliciting adult approval in fewer trials and with fewer errors than children in the presence of an experimenter who has been consistently nurturant. This prediction is based, in part, on those aspects of psychoanalytic theory which suggest that attempts by the child to institute closeness and seek affection are most strongly related to the anxiety generated at times of separation from the mother or when the child has experienced loss of the mother's love (4). It is believed that the withdrawal of nurturance by a female experimenter is

[1] This study is based on a doctoral dissertation submitted by the author to the Graduate School of Education of Harvard University. Parts of this investigation were reported at the 1956 meetings of the American Psychological Association in Chicago, Illinois. The author wishes to acknowledge the helpful criticisms of Dr. Harry Levin in the preparation of this study.

Reprinted from *Child Development* 1958, **29**, 191–201, by permission of the author and the Society for Research in Child Development.

similar to certain aspects of the caretaker-child relationship. If so, such behavior by the experimenter should generate certain amounts of anxiety in young children which, in turn, should motivate dependency behavior.

Certain aspects of behavior theory are also relevant to the present prediction. Miller (9) and Mowrer (10) suggest that the capacity of a neutral stimulus to evoke anxiety is strengthened through association with increases in drive or delay in primary reinforcement; presumably it is association such as this which results in children becoming anxious when the mother is absent or non-nurturant. If children in our culture commonly do learn to respond in this way to the non-nurturance of adults, if anxiety does motivate behavior, and if adult nurturance has acquired the capacity to reduce anxiety and thereby reinforce behavior for the young child, the experimental prediction formulated for this investigation can be made.

METHOD

Subjects

Subjects used in this investigation were 34 preschool children—15 boys and 19 girls—in attendance at the Harvard University Preschool during the spring of 1954. The subjects ranged in age from three years, ten months, to five years, six months. The mean age of the children in the sample was four years, seven months; the standard deviation was 4.7 months. The preschool population at the time of the experiment was typical of many laboratory nursery schools in that the children were all from academic, professional, or business homes, and were free from severe emotional disturbances and physical handicaps. Two subgroups were drawn from this sample. These subgroups were counterbalanced with respect to sex of child and dependency ratings made by the preschool teachers on scales of the type used by Beller (1). Two young women served as experimenters.[2] Each experimenter worked with a randomly-assigned half of the subjects in each group.

Procedure

Each child was brought individually to the laboratory room for the experimental session. This room was equipped with one-way mirrors for observation and was furnished with a child's table and chairs, an adult-sized table with comfortable chair, and a large bench. The experimental session proceeded as follows:

1. For a period of five minutes, the experimenter interacted nurturantly with the child while the child played with toys. For purposes of this experiment nurturance consisted of adult behavior which rewarded, encouraged,

[2] The author wishes to thank Mrs. Carla F. Berry and Miss Willa Dinwoodie for their assistance in this regard.

supported, or showed affection to the child; during this five-minute period the experimenter attempted to maximize these qualities in her behavior toward the child. Children in both experimental groups experienced this period of nurturant interaction with the experimenter.

2. Children in the consistent-nurturance group (hereafter called group C) then immediately experienced a second five-minute period like the first.

3. The second five minutes for the nurturance-withdrawal group (group NW) were marked by the experimenter's behaving non-nurturantly toward the child. She ceased to interact with the child, withdrew from his proximity, and did not reward any of the child's supplications beyond telling him that she was "busy." The experience of children in group NW, having first a period of nurturant interaction, then a period of non-nurturance from the experimenter, has been called "nurturance-withdrawal."

4. Children in both experimental groups were then asked by the experimenter to learn two tasks, the reward for which was the verbal approval of the experimenter. Task I consisted of learning a simple *position* concept in an arrangement of two blue and two red one-inch blocks. The task was presented to the child as a guessing game. The experimenter placed the blocks on the floor first in this order (reading from the child's left): red, red, blue, blue. She then said: "I'm thinking of one of the blocks and I want to see if you can guess which one it is. Point with your finger to the one you think is right and I'll tell you if it's the right one." The child's first guess was always unsuccessful, as was his second. The third guess was always successful. This introductory procedure was followed to eliminate chance successes on the first guess. On each succeeding trial the arrangement of the blocks was changed through all the possible order-permutations. The correct block was always the block in the same position in the row as the one which the child chose on his third guess. The performance criterion was three consecutive correct trials. Task II consisted of copying from memory a row of adjacent blue, red, and yellow one-inch cubes which were shown to the child for five seconds per trial. Six blocks were arranged in the following order: red, yellow, blue, blue, yellow, red. The performance criterion was one perfect reproduction of the arrangement completed by the child from his own supply of blocks. Measures used in the subsequent analysis of the data were: (a) number of errors to criterion on task I; (b) number of trials to criterion on task I; (c) number of errors to criterion on task II; (d) number of trials to criterion on task II. Error- and trial-scores were correlated .93 on task I, .96 on task II.

Measures of the child's tendency to be dependent on adults were from three sources: (a) observation during the period of nurturant interaction in the laboratory; (b) ratings of the child's dependency on adults made by the preschool teachers; and (c) observations of the child's dependency on adults in preschool made by observers.

Behavior categories used for the laboratory observations were as follows:

1. Asks for verbal help and information
2. Asks for material help
3. Seeks reassurance and rewards
4. Seeks positive attention
5. Seeks to be near
6. Seeks physical contact
7. Seeks negative attention
8. Initiates verbal interaction with experimenter

Frequencies in categories 1 through 7 were summed to yield a measure of dependence on the experimenter. Category 8, "verbal interaction," was used independently in the analysis of data.

The following seven-point scales were used for the teacher ratings of the child's dependence on adults in the preschool situation:

1. Seeks recognition
2. Seeks unnecessary help
3. Seeks necessary help
4. Seeks physical contact and proximity
5. Seeks attention

Each child was rated by two of his teachers (reliability coefficients ranged between .73 and .99). The ratings of the two teachers on each scale were pooled; a summary rating score was then obtained by summing the pooled ratings on all five scales. This summary rating score was used to counterbalance the two subgroups as described above and was also used in analyzing the learning scores.

Behavior categories used for the preschool observations of dependency on the teacher were:

1. Seeks recognition and approval
2. Seeks unnecessary help
3. Seeks necessary help
4. Seeks physical contact
5. Seeks to be near
6. Seeks positive attention
7. Seeks negative attention

Frequencies in the seven categories were summed to yield the preschool observation measure of dependence on the teacher which was used in the statistical analysis.

The intercorrelations among the two laboratory scores, the summary teacher rating, and the preschool observation total score are reported in Table 1.

TABLE 1. Intercorrelations among Four Measures of Dependency ($N = 34$)

	1	2	3	4
1. Verbal interaction with experimenter: laboratory				
2. Dependence on experimenter: laboratory	.13			
3. Dependence on preschool teacher: teacher rating	.03	.40 *		
4. Dependence on preschool teacher: observer score	.00	.11	.31	

* Significant beyond .05 level.

The data from the learning tasks were studied by a triple-classification analysis of variance technique for unequal cell-entries (13). The three independent variables in this analysis were (a) sex of child; (b) dependency scores as described above and by which the group was separated into two subgroups—high dependency (all cases above the median on the score being used) and low dependency (all cases below the median); (c) experimental treatment, consistent nurturance versus nurturance-withdrawal. Four analyses of variance were completed for each trial- or error-score from the learning tasks: one for each summary dependency score described above. The results of these analyses are summarized in the tables which follow.

TABLE 2. F Ratios from Four Analyses of Variance Based on Number of Trials on Task I according to Sex of Child, Dependence, and Experimental Condition

Source	Analysis 1 * ($N = 27$)	Analysis 2 * ($N = 33$)	Analysis 3 * ($N = 32$)	Analysis 4 * ($N = 31$)
Sex of child	16.153 §	2.618	3.988	2.953
Dependence	7.163 †	.002	.527	6.571 †
Experimental condition	13.859 ‡	4.574 †	1.759	1.438
Sex × dependence	3.053	3.630	.028	.015
Sex × condition	6.744 †	2.098	3.549	6.437
Dependence × condition	2.224	.792	2.249	1.488
Sex × dependence × condition	.215	.570	.005	1.186

* The measures of dependence used were: analysis 1, frequency of verbal interaction initiated by child in the laboratory session; analysis 2, frequency of dependence on adults observed on the laboratory session; analysis 3, teachers' ratings of dependence; analysis 4, dependence on preschool teachers as recorded by observers.
† Significant between .05 and .01.
‡ Significant between .01 and .001.
§ Significant beyond .001.

RESULTS

Task I—Number of Trials

Table 2 shows that the *F* ratio for the experimental variable was significant beyond the .01 level in analysis 1 and beyond the .05 level in analysis 2. The means for groups C and NW are reported in Table 3 along with the *t* ratio for the difference between means. These data show that NW children (who had experienced nurturance-withdrawal) took fewer trials to complete the task than C children (who had experienced consistent nurturance). Table 2 also shows that in two analyses there was a significant interaction between experimental condition and the sex of child. This interaction may be interpreted to indicate that the effects of nurturance-withdrawal by a female adult are dependent on the sex of the child. The data reported in Table 3 show more clearly the effects of this interaction: nurturance-withdrawal was clearly associated with faster learning of the task for girls, but there was no difference between the means for boys in group C and in group NW.

TABLE 3. Mean Number of Trials on Task I for Boys and Girls in Two Experimental Groups

	Group C	N	Group NW	N	t	p
Boys	15.86	7	16.14	7	. .	n.s.
Girls	35.22	9	16.10	10	2.570	.02>*p*>.01
Boys and Girls	26.77	16	16.11	17	2.041	.05>*p*>.01

The *F* ratio for sex of child was significant in one of the analyses reported in Table 2, and the direction of mean differences showed that boys as a group learned the task in fewer trials than girls. This difference is believed to relate to some feature of the task itself rather than the social conditions of the experiment since the same difference was not found in the data for task II; however, the aspect of task I producing the sex difference was not clear from observation of the children in the experiment. The dependency variable was also significant in two analyses; subgroup means showed that the more dependent children (as measured by verbal interaction) learned task I more quickly than the less dependent children, but that more dependent children (as measured by preschool observation) learned task I less quickly than the less dependent children.

Task I—Number of Errors

Since the error-measure was highly correlated with the trials-measure on task I similar results would be expected and were obtained from the analyses of variance. *F* ratios for the experimental variable were significant in analyses 1 and 2 (Table 4). Again, significant interaction between sex of child and experimental condition was found (in analysis 4, Table 4). Table 5 reports the means for the experimental groups according to sex of child, and once more the results show significant differences between the experimental groups for girls but not for boys.

TABLE 4. F Ratios from Four Analyses of Variance Based on Number of Errors on Task I according to Sex of Child, Dependence, and Experimental Condition

Source	Analysis 1 * (N = 27)	Analysis 2 * (N = 33)	Analysis 3 * (N = 32)	Analysis 4 * (N = 31)
Sex of child	9.421 ‡	1.360	2.581	1.385
Dependence	5.060 †	.190	1.050	6.577 †
Experimental condition	10.519 ‡	4.640 †	1.232	.924
Sex × dependence	1.943	4.063	.003	.532
Sex × condition	4.267	1.560	3.262	6.118 †
Dependence × condition	2.458	1.364	1.610	.772
Sex × dependence × condition	.074	1.219	.003	1.414

* The measures of dependence used were: analysis 1, frequency of verbal interaction initiated by child in the laboratory session; analysis 2, frequency of dependence on adults observed in the laboratory session; analysis 3, teachers' ratings of dependence; analysis 4, dependence on preschool teachers as recorded by observers.
† Significant between .05 and .01.
‡ Significant between .01 and .001.

The F ratio for sex of child was significant in one analysis indicating that boys learned the task faster than girls. The dependency variable was significant in two analyses, but mean differences were in the same inconsistent directions as in the analysis of trial scores on task I.

TABLE 5. Mean Number of Errors on Task I for Boys and Girls in Two Experimental Groups

	Group C	N	Group NW	N	t	p
Boys	18.14	7	18.71	7	. .	n.s.
Girls	39.33	9	17.30	10	2.71	.02 > p > .01
Boys and Girls	30.06	16	17.88	17	1.90	.10 > p > .05

Task II—Number of Trials

The distribution of scores on this measure significantly departed from normality; hence the results are not reported here.

Task II—Number of Errors

The results for errors on task II were consistent with respect to experimental condition with those found on task I, although at a lesser level of significance. Table 6 shows that one F ratio for the conditions variable was significant beyond the .05 level.

TABLE 6. F RATIOS FROM FOUR ANALYSES OF VARIANCE BASED ON
NUMBER OF ERRORS ON TASK II ACCORDING TO SEX OF CHILD,
DEPENDENCE, AND EXPERIMENTAL CONDITION

Source	Analysis 1 * (N = 24)	Analysis 2 * (N = 29)	Analysis 3 * (N = 28)	Analysis 4 * (N = 28)
Sex of child	.169	1.567	.170	.056
Dependence	2.146	.493	5.318 †	1.359
Experimental condition	.501	2.788	4.755 †	.521
Sex × dependence	2.332	1.691	2.667	.314
Sex × condition	.003	.014	.373	1.682
Dependence × condition	1.155	.037	.311	.167
Sex × dependence × condition	.263	.048	.376	1.983

* The measures of dependence used were: analysis 1, frequency of verbal interaction initiated by child in the laboratory session; analysis 2, frequency of dependence on adults observed in the laboratory session; analysis 3, teachers' ratings of dependence; analysis 4, dependence on preschool teachers as recorded by observers.
† Significant between .05 and .01.

The mean number of errors on task II made by the two experimental groups are reported in Table 7. These data are consistent with those for task I and suggest that faster learning was produced under the nurturance-withdrawal condition than under a condition of uninterrupted nurturance. No significant interaction effects were discovered in the analyses of variance.

The F ratios for sex of child were not significant in these analyses; the dependency variable (when measured by teacher ratings) yielded a significant F, and the means suggest that more dependent children learned task II faster than less dependent children.

TABLE 7. MEAN NUMBER OF ERRORS ON TASK II FOR BOYS AND GIRLS IN
TWO EXPERIMENTAL GROUPS

	Group C	N	Group NW	N	t	p
Boys	12.40	5	6.17	6	1.121	$.30 > p > .20$
Girls	8.33	9	4.44	9	1.420	$.20 > p > .10$
Boys and Girls	9.79	14	5.07	15	1.750	$.10 > p > .05$

DISCUSSION

The findings for girls uniformly support the hypothesis that nurturance-withdrawal is associated with more efficient performance on the learning tasks than consistent nurturance. The results for boys, however, showed that there were no differences between the nurturance-withdrawal and the consistent nurturance groups. Actually, the results for boys were not so clearly negative. When the boys' groups were divided according to the measures of dependence, *highly* dependent boys were found to respond much as the girls while *low* dependent boys responded in the reverse fashion. Thus, highly dependent boys (who may be assumed to be generally anxious concerning their relationships with adults) did learn more efficiently when the experimenter withdrew her nurturance. The boys in the low dependency group who were consistently nurtured learned more efficiently than boys in this group who experienced nurturance-withdrawal. Although the number of cases in these subgroups was small, this trend in the data suggests support for the hypothesis concerning the influence of nurturance-withdrawal for highly dependent boys as well as for the girls.

The fact that the findings for boys were so equivocal is an interesting one for further exploration. It may be that boys respond differently from girls to the nurturance-withdrawal of a *female* experimenter. Psychoanalytic theory regarding Oedipal relationships suggests that the punitiveness of a like-sexed adult should be more threatening to a child than the punitiveness of an opposite-sexed adult. It would be comparatively easy to incorporate sex of experimenter as a variable in a study such as this. However, since the results of this study suggest that nurturance-withdrawal fails to motivate only *low* dependent boys, there may be some sort of complex interaction among experimental conditions which this study failed to bring to light. For example, boys of this age who are not overtly dependent on adults may have moved further than highly dependent boys toward identifying with the male sex role, which in our culture contains certain elements of independence and self-reliance. Boys who *are* highly identified with the male role might well respond with greater anxiety to the mothering nurturance of the experimenter than to the condition in which the experimenter ceases to be attentive and leaves the child alone. If this were the case, most efficient learning would then have taken place in the low dependency boys under conditions of consistent nurturance. The experiment contains no measure of identification by which this interpretation can be checked.

The relationships of sex of child and dependence to speed of learning on the experimental tasks are far from being clear-cut in these data. Boys tended to learn task I faster than girls, but not task II. Dependence, as measured either by verbal interaction in the laboratory session or by teacher ratings, was positively associated with speed of learning; however, dependence as rated by observers in the preschool proved to be negatively associated with speed of learning. The sources of these inconsistencies probably lie in the situational and procedural differences involved in the various measures of dependence; the intercorrelations among the dependency measures suggest that the various measures did *not* measure similar behavioral traits. It does not appear possible, therefore, without further study, to suggest the manner in which motivation to be dependent modifies the effects of nurturance-withdrawal on speed of learning in young children.

The general significance of these findings is felt to be clear and in the direction suggested by the hypothesis tested: nurturance-withdrawal stimulates faster learning than nurturance alone on simple cognitive tasks for girls, and probably also for boys. There may be, however, some second- or third-order interaction between nurturance-withdrawal, sex of child, sex of experimenter, and dependence which influences the behavior of boys under conditions like those of this experiment.

SUMMARY

Thirty-four four-year-old preschool children were divided into two experimental groups equated on the basis of sex and teachers' ratings of dependence on adults in preschool. Individual subjects in one group (C) were consistently nurtured by a female experimenter during a 10-minute period of interaction, after which two simple tasks were learned by the child. The subjects in the second group (NW) experienced nurturant interaction with the experimenter during only five minutes, then experienced five minutes of non-nurturant response from the experimenter, and finally were asked to learn the tasks. The data were treated by an analysis of variance technique in which learning scores were divided according to sex of child, dependency ratings, and experimental condition.

Children in group NW took fewer trials to learn task I than children in group C. Although the group findings were significant, analysis according to sex of child showed that nurturance-withdrawal was most clearly associated with faster learning in girls. Children in group NW made fewer errors in learning both task I and task II, although these findings were most significant for girls.

It is felt that these results support the hypothesis that nurturance-withdrawal supplies greater motivation than consistent nurturance for children's behavior which is designed to gain the reassurance of adults.

REFERENCES

1. Beller, E. K. Dependency and independence in young children. *J. genet. Psychol.*, 1955, **87**, 25–35.

2. Carl, J. An experimental study of the effect of nurturance on preschool children. Unpublished doctoral dissertation, State Univer. of Iowa, 1949.
3. Dollard, J., & Miller, N. E. *Personality and psychotherapy.* New York: McGraw-Hill, 1950.
4. Freud, S. Three contributions to the theory of sex. In *The Basic Writings of Sigmund Freud.* New York: Random House, 1938.
5. Gewirtz, J. L. Succorance in young children. Unpublished doctoral dissertation, State Univer. of Iowa, 1948.
6. Gewirtz, J. L. Three determinants of attention-seeking in young children. *Monogr. Soc. Res. Child Develpm.,* 1954, **19,** No. 2. (Serial No. 59)
7. Gewirtz, J. L. Does brief social deprivation enhance the effectiveness of a social reinforcer ("approval")? *Amer. Psychologist,* 1956, **11,** 428. (Abstract)
8. Hartup, W. W. Nurturance and nurturance-withdrawal in relation to the dependency behavior of preschool children. Unpublished doctoral dissertation, Harvard Univer., 1955.
9. Miller, N. E. Studies of fear as an acquirable drive. I. Fear as motivation and fear-reduction as reinforcement in the learning of new responses. *J. exp. Psychol.,* 1948, **38,** 89–101.
10. Mowrer, O. H. *Learning theory and personality dynamics.* New York: Ronald, 1950.
11. Sears, R. R., *et al.* Some child-rearing antecedents of dependency and aggression in young children. *Genet. Psychol. Monogr.,* 1953, **47,** 135–234.
12. Smith, H. T. A comparison of interview and observation measures of mother behavior. Unpublished doctoral dissertation, Harvard Univer., 1953.
13. Walker, H. M., & Lev, J. *Statistical inference.* New York: Holt, 1953.

4.4 Suggestibility as Dependency Behavior [1]

Leonard F. Jakubczak and Richard H. Walters

An analysis of experimental procedures used in studies of suggestibility supports an interpretation of suggestibility as a form of dependency behavior.

[1] This paper is based in part on a thesis submitted by the first-named author in partial fulfilment of the requirements for the degree of M.A. at the University of Toronto. The authors wish to express appreciation to G. B. Thornton and E. Tulving for constructive advice and assistance and, also, to the Institute of Child Study of the University of Toronto and the Forest Hill Village Board of Education for their cooperation in this study. They wish in particular to express gratitude to Dorothee Keschner for permission to adapt and revise her test of dependency and independence and for her ready assistance in the development of a parallel test for older children.

In the experiments of Sherif (1935) and Asch (1940), designed to demonstrate the influence of group norms, suggestions were given to subjects(Ss) which resulted in increased conformity of their judgments to those of other members of the group. The changes in judgments were said by Asch to result from S's need for social support, in other words, they were evidence of S's dependency on the group. When the autokinetic effect is employed as a means of demonstrating the influence of suggestion, S is confronted with a highly ambiguous stimulus and is asked to make judgments in the absence of customary cues. A second person also makes judgments that S may accept as criteria against which to validate his own. Under these circumstances the judgments of another person become cues which S may accept or reject. If S accepts them, he is accepting help; if he accepts help, he is responding in a dependent manner.

Both experimental and clinical evidence support an interpretation of suggestibility in terms of dependency behavior. Inverse relationships between suggestibility and ascendancy (Kelman, 1950) and between suggestibility and self-sufficiency (Young & Gaier, 1953) have been found. Moreover, suggestibility and dependency have been traditionally associated in clinical descriptions of hysterical reactions. However, in spite of implicit and explicit treatment of suggestibility in terms of dependency behavior, there has been little attempt to relate suggestibility to the development of dependency and independence in young children.

Sears, Whiting, and their collaborators (Sears, Maccoby, & Levin, 1957; Sears, Whiting, Nowlis, & Sears, 1953; Whiting & Child, 1953; Beller, 1955) have regarded dependency as a learned motivational system of which help-seeking and approval-seeking are manifestations. From this point of view, dependency behavior is acquired in the earliest relationship of the child to its parents, and is generalized to other adults and also, to a lesser extent, to peers. Dependent responses are necessarily to some degree reinforced in the first year or two of life, if only because the young child is too helpless and immature to care for its own needs. On the other hand, independence training also commences early and results in the partial inhibition of dependency behavior. Thus the conditions for a conflict in the area of dependency are present very early in the life of every child.

Miller (1948) has provided a theoretical model for the displacement of responses under conditions of conflict. This model assumes that the gradient of generalization of an inhibitory response is steeper than that of the response which it inhibits. The assumption permits predictions about the strength of overt responses, under conditions of strong and of weak inhibition, both to the persons in whose presence the conflict is originally learned and to persons of increasing dissimilarity from the original instigators of conflict. The relative strength of displaced overt responses may be depicted by subtracting the height of the curve representing the inhibitory response from the height of the curve representing the response that is inhibited, and plotting this set of differences as a new curve (Whiting & Child, 1953, p. 293). Since dependency on the parents is rarely, if ever, completely inhibited in children, only the right-hand portion of Miller's model was taken into account in constructing curves for predictions concerning dependency behavior (Fig. 1).

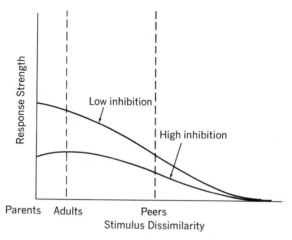

FIGURE 1. **Hypothetical strength of displaced dependency responses at varying points on a stimulus dissimilarity continuum for conditions of strong and weak inhibition.**

Dependency behavior was regarded, for the purposes of this study, as a class of responses that included both help-seeking behavior and the acceptance of suggestions. High-dependent children were defined as those who readily accepted help even in tasks that they could perform by themselves; low-dependent children as those who showed reluctance to accept help even when a task was beyond their level of skill. In view of the description of the development of dependency and independence provided by Sears, Maccoby, and Levin (1957), it was assumed that the low-dependent group showed considerable inhibition of dependency responses, whereas the high-dependent group showed little such inhibition. On the basis of these assumptions, and those reflected in the hypothetical curves shown in Fig. 1, the following hypotheses were developed:

1. High-dependent children are more suggestible than low-dependent children.
2. Children respond more strongly when adults give suggestions than when peers give suggestions.
3. The difference in suggestibility between high-dependent and low-

dependent children is greater when suggestions are given by adults than when suggestions are given by peers.

Subjects

Subjects (Ss) were chosen on the basis of a modified form of a test of dependency and independence first developed by Keschner (1957) for use with five- to eight-year-old children.[2] For the purposes of this study, the test was extended for use with eight- to ten-year-old boys. The modified test consisted of 24 cartoon-like drawings, each depicting an adult offering help to a child. The child was asked to indicate, by circling Yes or No beneath each drawing, whether he would, or would not, accept help. The test was administered to 60 nine-year-old boys in an elementary public school. At the same time, a list of the situations depicted in the test was sent to the boys' parents who were asked to indicate whether or not the child could carry out the tasks unaided.

If a child indicated that he would accept help when his parent indicated that he could carry out the task in question, he was given a score of 1; if he indicated that he would not accept help when his parent indicated that he could not carry out the task in question, he was given a score of -1. The 12 boys with the highest total score for the 24 situations were selected as high-dependent Ss; the 12 boys who scored lowest were selected as low-dependent Ss.

Each S was twice exposed to suggestions, once by a peer and once by an adult. Half the high-dependent Ss and half the low-dependent Ss were exposed on the first experimental session to the peer and on the second session to the adult; the remaining Ss were exposed to the adult on the first session and to the peer on the second session. Ss were randomly assigned to the two orders.

Confederates

Four eleven-year-old boys and four adults were trained to give suggestions. Three boys and three adults bore the major load of suggesting; the remaining two confederates were substitutes in case the scheduled suggester was not available at the time he was required. Each regular confederate had four high-dependent and four low-dependent Ss assigned to him. Care was

[2] A copy of the revision of Keschner's test for dependency and independence used in this study has been deposited with the American Documentation Institute. Order Document No. 5903 from ADI Auxiliary Publications Project, Photoduplication Service, Library of Congress, Washington 25, D. C., remitting $1.75 for microfilm or $2.50 for photocopies. Keschner's original test is included in her doctoral thesis (University of Toronto, 1957).

taken to insure that the average time interval between the first and second exposure to suggestion was approximately the same for the high-dependent and the low-dependent Ss, and for the two orders of suggestion. The substitute adult and peer suggesters had each to be used on two occasions to keep time intervals controlled. First sessions were completed for all Ss before second sessions were begun; as far as other conditions allowed, high-dependent and low-dependent Ss were run in random order.

Apparatus

The apparatus used for the autokinetic sessions was an approximate duplicate of that described by Sherif (1935) and used by more recent investigators (Kelman, 1950; Linton, 1954). It was located at one end of a photographic darkroom, 7 ft. from S, and was screened from S's view when the autokinetic effect was not actually being induced.

Both S and the confederate were given toy "crickets" which they used to indicate that the light was beginning to move. The "cricket" used by the confederate was slightly muted to allow E to identify the producer of the signal. S was supplied with a pencil and pad on which to record his judgments concerning the apparent movement of light. In order to prevent S from suspecting that the confederate was not just another S, the latter also wrote on a pad at appropriate times during the experiment.

Crutchfield and Edwards (1945) found that the hum of a motor enhances the autokinetic effect. Consequently, to simulate the sound of a motor, a portable electric fan was located immediately behind the autokinetic apparatus and was kept in operation throughout the experiment.

Procedure

S was given the following preliminary instruction immediately before entering the experimental room:

I'm doing an experiment. I'm trying to find out how well people see a light move in a completely dark room. I want you to look at this light, and tell me how many inches it moves. O.K?

S was also told that another person was already in the room, and that he, too, was taking part in the experiment. When S was seated in a chair, adjacent to the suggester, E gave the following instructions:

In a little while, I shall close the door and turn off the light, so that it will be completely dark in here. Then I shall turn on a little point of light. It will be located directly in front of you. I want you to look for this light, and as soon as you see it, let me know. Then we'll start the experiment. I'll turn on the motor, and then the light. I want you to look at it very carefully, and signal me as soon as you see it starting to move. Signal me by pressing your "cricket," like this [E demonstrates]. A few seconds after you have signaled, the light will be turned off. Then I want you to take your pad and pencil, and write down how many inches you think the light has moved. After you write down the number, turn the page over, so that there is only one number on each page. O.K.? Any questions?

Pretraining trials. On each trial, the autokinetic light was turned on for a period of approximately 5 sec. beyond the time at which S signaled, or for a period of 20 sec. if no signal was made. The confederate signaled immediately after S signaled. This procedure was followed for eight trials.

Training trials. S was now instructed as follows:

Now in this part of the experiment, I want both of you to call out your judgments after writing them down. So for the next few trials, you do the same thing that you did before, except that you also call out how far you think that the light has moved. Since I have to keep track of who gives the judgment, why don't you answer in a definite order? Let's say you (S's first name), and then you, Mr. _____ (if adult), or you _____ (confederate's first name, if peer).

After S gave his estimate, the confederate gave an estimate 5 in. greater than S's. Eight training trials were carried out in this manner.

Posttraining trials. A final series of four trials was given. S was instructed as follows:

In the remaining part of this experiment, keep quiet and don't say anything out loud. Just mark down your judgments on your pads.

At this point, the experimental session was terminated, and the child was allowed to return to class.

The second session was carried out in the same manner as the first, except for two adjustments in procedure necessitated by some Ss' reactions to the first session. Since, in the pretraining trials of the first session, some Ss appeared to delay signaling until the confederate had indicated that he had seen the light move, during the second session the confederate signaled before S on every other pretraining trial. Two or three Ss had noted that the confederate's judgment had always been 5 in. greater than theirs. Consequently, during the second session, instead of adding five to each of S's estimates, the confederate added a variable amount, averaging five over eight trials. The implications of these changes are considered later in the discussion.

One S was lost from the low-dependent group on the second session. This S claimed that he could no longer see the light and, consequently, further training was impossible.

Measures

A suggestion that the light would move was given at the outset of the experiment. This suggestion was reinforced during the pretraining trials by the confederate's signal indicating that he had seen the light move. Consequently, one measure of suggestibility could be obtained from S's responses in the pretraining trials. The median of S's responses on the pretraining trials was taken as his pretraining response. The effect of training was measured by subtracting S's median response on the pretraining trials from his median response on the posttraining trials.

Not every S wrote down a response each time he signaled with his "cricket." In addition, some Ss gave an occasional extreme and unrealistic response. A nonparametric analysis of data was clearly indicated.

RESULTS

Table 1 shows the median pretraining judgment of each S and, also, the difference between his median pretraining and his median posttraining judgment for both sessions.

On the pretraining trials of the first session, high-dependent Ss were significantly more suggestible than were low-dependent Ss ($U = 41$; $p < .05$). A finer analysis of results on these trials, which took into account the status of the suggester, revealed a marked difference between high dependent and low-dependent Ss in their suggestibility to adults ($U = 3$; $p = .008$); on the other hand, the difference between high-dependent and low-dependent Ss in their suggestibility to peers was much smaller and failed to reach significance. No significant difference between high-dependent and low-dependent Ss was found after the first pretraining session.

Data for high-dependent and low-dependent Ss were now combined for assessing differences attributable to the status of the suggester. On the pretraining trials of the first session adults were significantly more effective in their suggestions than were peers ($U = 21$; $p < .01$). In addition, adults were more effective than peers in training during the second session ($U = 32.5$; $p < .01$). There was no difference in the effectiveness of adults and peers in training during the first session or in pretraining trials of the second session.

The order of exposure to adult and peer suggesters had an important influence on results. Both the adult and the peer were significantly more effective in the second, than in the first, pretraining session ($U = 22$; $p < .01$ for adults; $U = 5.5$; $p < .001$ for peers). The adult was no more effective in changing responses from the pretraining to the posttraining sessions when he preceded the peer than when he followed the peer. On the other hand, the peer was much more effective in changing responses if he preceded the adult than if he followed him ($U = 20$; $p < .01$).

The greater effectiveness of both the adult and of the peer in the second pretraining session strongly suggested that transfer of learning from the first to the second session had occurred. Accordingly, transfer effect from the first to the second session, both for pretraining responses and for effects of training, was assessed by the Wilcoxon test (Siegel, 1956). While there was a highly significant increase in pretraining responses on the second session ($T = 1$; $p < .001$), the effect of training was, if anything, somewhat reduced.

TABLE 1. MEDIAN RESPONSES OF HIGH-DEPENDENT AND LOW-DEPENDENT SUBJECTS
TO ADULTS AND PEERS ON FIRST AND SECOND SESSIONS [a]

Order	Subject	First Session		Second Session	
		Pretraining Trials	Effect of Training [b]	Pretraining Trials	Effect of Training
High-dependent Ss					
Peer first	9	1.50	38.50	7.00	36.50
	11	1.00	5.00	2.00	4.00
	8	2.50	11.00	4.00	6.50
	10	1.00	3.00	6.50	2.50
	7	3.00	49.50	22.00	68.00
	12	2.00	4.00	2.00	2.00
Adult first	5	3.50	−1.00	3.00	−0.50
	3	3.00	11.00	9.00	2.00
	2	2.50	18.00	18.00	−3.00
	1	3.00	3.00	3.00	9.50
	25	4.00	2.50	9.00	0.00
	26	3.50	24.00	15.00	37.00
Low-dependent Ss					
Peer first	20	1.00	19.50	13.00	27.00
	21	0.00	12.50	13.00	3.50
	23	0.00	4.50	6.00	7.50
	22	2.00	9.50	5.00	0.50
	24	2.50	6.00	4.00	6.50
	19	2.00	55.50	12.00	638.00
Adult first	17	2.50	9.00	5.00	2.00
	18	2.00	3.50	2.00	1.50
	16	2.00	5.50	4.50	2.50
	13	2.50	7.00	4.00	3.00
	14	3.00	14.50	14.00	6.00
	15	2.00	6.00 [c]		

[a] Responses reported in terms of inches.
[b] Calculated by subtracting S's median pretraining response from his median posttraining response.
[c] This S failed to make any response on the second session.

In order to estimate both the effects of learning and of procedural changes during the experiment, trial-by-trial graphs of Ss' responses were constructed for each of the experimental sessions (Figs. 2 and 3). In order to give each S's series of responses equal weight in determining the form of the curves, a nonparametric procedure was used in their construction. Each S should have made 20 responses on each experimental session, eight in the pretraining period, eight in the training period, and four in the posttraining period.

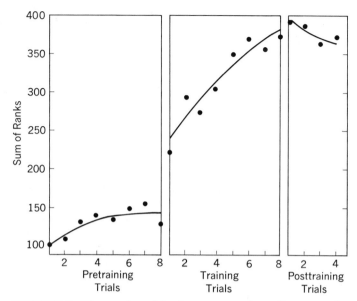

FIGURE 2. Change in subject's responses from first pretraining to last posttraining trial: First session (N = 24).

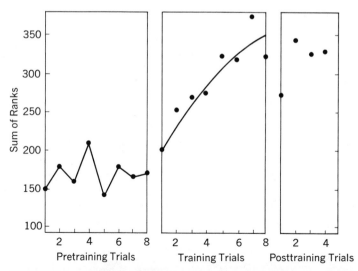

FIGURE 3. Change in subject's responses from first pretraining to last posttraining trial: Second session (N = 23).

If S had not recorded a response, his median response for the series of four or eight trials, as the case might be, was substituted. Since E could not know on which trial S had failed to respond, substitute scores were randomly assigned to trials. A complete set of 20 scores was thus obtained for each S. These series of 20 responses were then ranked for each S. S's smallest response during the series was given a rank of 1, his largest response a rank of 20. Twenty-four sets of ranked responses were thus obtained for the first session, 23 for the second session. The sum of the ranks for each trial was calculated and used to construct the graphs shown in Figs. 2 and 3.

DISCUSSION

While predictions were not consistently confirmed, the results of the experiment provide considerable support for the interpretation of suggestibility in terms of dependency behavior. On the pretraining trials of the first session, all three experimental hypotheses were confirmed. It should be noted that in these pretraining trials the only suggestion given was the confederate's signal that he had seen the light move; no verbalized judgment was given.

Failure to obtain consistent differences beyond the first pretraining trials may be due in part to undetermined effects of the experimental procedure itself. Predictions were, in fact, based on hypothesized differences in child-training procedures prior to the experiment. These differences were expected to produce different responses from high-dependent and low-dependent Ss in the experimental situation. While such differences were found at the very outset of the experiment, the experimental procedure may, by training all Ss to respond in a dependent manner, have served largely to reduce differences which previously existed.

Ss' responses were greatly influenced by the order of exposure to adult and peer suggesters. The increased responsiveness to both adult and peer during the pretraining trials of the second session can be simply explained as a positive transfer effect. Such an effect cannot, however, explain the finding that peers are less effective in producing change from pretraining to posttraining trials when they follow adults than when they precede them. If considerable learning occurs during the first session, possibly only an adult (presumably a stronger reinforcer than a peer) can produce a further increase in suggestibility.

The graphical presentation of data (Figs. 2 and 3) suggests that learning may occur even during the pretraining trials of the first session, though it is, of course, possible that the changes during these trials reflect a "warm-up" effect. These changes have, in any case, marked implications for prior studies of the autokinetic effect in which practice sessions have been given Ss before the experiment proper begins. With child Ss it is apparently unnecessary to make a judgment contrary to Ss' in order to enhance the autokinetic effect; one has only to imply that the light has moved. It is possible that a similar effect could be produced with adults.

During the first session's training trials Ss' responses form a negatively accelerated curve (Fig. 2) analogous to many learning curves. On the other hand, the curve for posttraining trials indicates that extinction begins when verbal suggestions are no longer given. Suggestion can thus be interpreted as reinforcement of dependency behavior.

The results for the second session are of considerable interest. During the pretraining trials of this session the confederate signaled before Ss on half the trials and after Ss on the other half. The effect of this alternation is clearly reflected in Fig. 3. Ss' judgments are greater if they occur on a trial on which the confederate signals first and follow a trial on which their own signal is reinforced by a subsequent signal from the confederate, i.e., on occasions when their responses are doubly reinforced.

The addition of a variable increment, averaging 5 in., to Ss' judgments in the training trials has approximately the same effect as the addition of a constant 5 in. on each trial. A rather steep, negatively accelerated curve is obtained both from Ss' responses in the first training period and from their responses in the second training period. On the second set of posttraining trials Ss' responses again decrease, but not in as steady a manner as on the first posttraining trials. The last three of these trials, however, again suggest that over a longer series of trials, gradual extinction might take place.

SUMMARY

Two groups, each consisting of 12 nine-year-old boys, were exposed to the autokinetic effect. The low-dependency groups consisted of boys who indicated unwillingness to accept help in tasks which they were unable to accomplish themselves; the high-dependency group consisted of boys who indicated willingness to accept help even when they required none. Each child was twice exposed to the autokinetic effect; on one occasion, judgments contrary to the child's were given by an adult; on the other occasion, contrary judgments were given by a peer. Half the Ss in each group received suggestions first from an adult, then from the peer; for the other half, the suggesters were employed in the reverse order.

Predictions were made (a) on the assumption that suggestibility was a form of dependency behavior and (b) were partly based on Miller's (1948) theoretical model for the displacement of responses under conditions of strong and weak inhibition. These predictions were confirmed by the results for the pretraining trials of Ss' first experimental session. High-dependent Ss were significantly more suggestible than low-dependent Ss, and adults were more effective as confederates than were peers. In addition, the difference in suggestibility between high-dependent and low-dependent Ss was much greater when adults were used as confederates than when suggestions were given by peers.

Though findings were not consistent for the remaining stages of the experiment, confirmatory evidence of the greater effectiveness of adult suggesters was provided on the second session; on this session, adults produced a greater change in Ss' responses from pretraining to posttraining trials than did peers. The effect of order of exposure to adult and peer suggesters proved to be important, and complex transfer effects apparently occurred.

A graphical analysis of changes over the series of trials suggested that learning may occur even before contrary judgments are given by confederates in the training trials. Learning is considerably increased, however, when contrary judgments are given; steeply rising, negatively accelerated curves were obtained for the training sessions. When suggestion is no longer given in the posttraining trials, Ss' responses apparently begin to extinguish.

The findings as a whole support the interpretation of suggestibility in terms of dependency behavior, especially if dependency is itself regarded as a class of learned responses which may be reinforced or extinguished by the responses of other persons.

REFERENCES

Asch, S. E.   Studies in the principles of judgments and attitudes: II. Determination of judgments by group and by ego standards. *J. soc. Psychol.*, 1940, **12**, 433–465.

Beller, E. K.   Dependency and independency in young children. *J. genet. Psychol.*, 1955, **87**, 25–35.

Crutchfield, R. S., & Edwards, W.   The effect of a fixated figure on autokinetic movement. *J. exp. Psychol.*, 1949, **39**, 561–568.

Kelman, H. C.   Effects of success and failure on suggestibility in the autokinetic situation. *J. abnorm. soc. Psychol.*, 1950, **45**, 267–285.

Keschner, Dorothee A.   Dependence and independence in primary-school children. Unpublished doctoral thesis, Univer. of Toronto, 1957.

Linton, Harriet B.   Rorschach correlates of response to suggestion. *J. abnorm. soc. Psychol.*, 1954, **49**, 75–83.

Miller, N. E.   Theory and experiment relating psychoanalytic displacement to stimulus-response generalization. *J. abnorm. soc. Psychol.*, 1948, **43**, 155–178.

Sears, R. R., Maccoby, Eleanor E., & Levin, H. *Patterns of child training.* Evanston: Row Peterson, 1957.

Sears, R. R., Whiting, J. W. M., Nowlis, V., & Sears, P. S.   Some child-rearing antecedents of aggression and dependency in young children. *Genet. Psychol. Monogr.*, 1953, **47**, 135–235.

Sherif, M.   A study of some social factors in perception. *Arch. Psychol., N. Y.*, 1935, No. 187.

Siegel, S.   *Nonparametric statistics for the behavioral sciences.* New York: McGraw-Hill, 1956.

Young, M., & Gaier, E. L.   A preliminary investigation into the prediction of suggestibility from selected personality variables. *J. soc. Psychol.*, 1953, **37**, 53–60.

Whiting, J. W. M., & Child, I.   *Child training and personality.* New Haven: Yale Univer. Press, 1953.

4.5   Relationship between Dependency, Intentional Learning, and Incidental Learning in Preschool Children [1]

Dorothea Ross

Dependency means learning to value other people; dependent behavior refers to a class of responses that includes seeking approval, attention, help, physical contact, and proximity (Sears, Maccoby, & Levin, 1957; Sears, Whiting, Nowlis, & Sears, 1953). Studies of dependency can be grouped into four categories: child-rearing antecedents of dependency, effects of disturbances in dependency relationships, effects of situational factors on dependent behavior, and differences between high- and low-dependent children. The present study falls into the fourth category; its purpose is to determine whether dependency relates systematically to intentional learning and incidental learning in preschool children.

Intentional learning is learning which occurs as a result of specific training accompanied by instructions to learn; incidental learning can be distinguished from intentional learning by the absence of any specific training (McGeoch & Irion, 1950). Of particular interest to the developmental psychologist is the incidental learning of social cues. At the preschool level much of the incidental learning of social cues occurs as a result of *active imitation* by the child of the behaviors of prestigeful adults and peers (Bandura & Huston, 1961; Mussen & Conger, 1956).

There is theoretical support for a positive relationship between dependency and imitation. According to Freudian theory, a necessary condition for either aggressive or anaclitic identification is that the child be *dependent* upon the parent (Bronfenbrenner, 1960). In both types of identification the child is likely to become highly imitative.

There is also experimental support for the above relationship. Bandura and Huston (1961) reported that high-dependent children showed more imitative behavior than did low-dependent children. In the two studies of Bandura, Ross, and Ross (1961, 1963) high-dependent children showed more imitation of aggression than did low-dependent children. Ross' (1962) study of the imitation of deviant behaviors also provides evidence for a positive relationship between the two variables.

[1] This article is based on a dissertation submitted to Stanford University in partial fulfillment of the requirements for the PhD. The author wishes to express her appreciation to Jerry Wiggins, Albert Bandura, Quinn McNemar, and Pauline Sears, who served as members of her doctoral research committee.

Reprinted from the *Journal of Personality and Social Psychology*, 1966, **4**, 374–381, by permission of the author and The American Psychological Association.

Three other studies provide indirect support for a positive relationship between dependency and imitation. Cairns (1959) and Endsley and Hartup (1960) showed that high-dependent children tended to be more oriented towards obtaining social reinforcers than were low-dependent children. Jackubczak and Walters (1959) found that high-dependent children tended not to respond independently and consequently were more likely to depend on the cues produced by the behavior of adult and peer models than were low-dependent children.

What implications does this dependency-imitation relationship have for the socialization process? Is the high dependent-high imitator at an advantage in a learning situation? The high-dependent child should have a substantial advantage over the low-dependent child in a learning situation in which the model shows no irrelevant behaviors; that is, the high imitator should perform better than the low imitator if the task is to do *everything* the model does. But most learning situations provide the child with opportunities to observe the model performing many verbal and motor behaviors that are irrelevant to the learning task. Under these circumstances, we would predict that the low-dependent child should perform better because he tends to respond more independently and more selectively and as a consequence is trying to learn less material than is the high-dependent child in the same time period.

The present experiment was designed to determine whether the inclusion of relevant and irrelevant behaviors in a learning task would result in intentional and incidental learning scores which would differentiate high-dependent from low-dependent children. In the experimental situation (intentional learning), an adult female model (AM) taught high-dependent and low-dependent preschool children how to run a post office (PO). During the teaching session (incidental learning), the model exhibited behaviors which were either partially relevant or completely irrelevant to the successful performance of the learning task. The child's initial role in this situation was that of a learner; following the training session the child performed in the role of controller and instructor. Each child interacted first with the AM and then with a child trained to act as a customer (CC) and as a learner. The following hypotheses were tested:

1. The low-dependent children would obtain higher intentional learning scores than would the high-dependent children.

2. The high-dependent children would show more evidence of incidental learning than would the low-dependent children particularly in regard to the behaviors completely irrelevant to the learning task.

3. The low-dependent children would exhibit more general independence behavior in the experimental situation than would the high-dependent children.

METHOD

Subjects

Fifty-two white preschool children (26 boys, 26 girls) ranging in age from 3 years, 9 months, to 5 years, 5 months, with a mean age of 4 years, 7 months, served in this study. These subjects were all enrolled in the Stanford Village Nursery School, Stanford University, and had all participated in previous experiments conducted at this school. Stanford-Binet intelligence scores were available on all subjects. Since the subjects came primarily from professional, business, and graduate-student homes, the sample was skewed upwards in socioeconomic status and intelligence. None of the subjects had either a physical handicap or a severe health problem.

Selection Variable

The 52 subjects were selected on the basis of ratings of their dependent behavior from the 101 children in the school who were 3 years, 9 months, or older. Five members of the teaching staff of the Nursery School independently rated all children of this age range on five scales of dependent behavior. These scales measured the extent to which the child showed instrumental dependency, sought reassurance, sought physical proximity, displayed negative attention-getting behavior, and exhibited positive attention-getting behavior. A series of interrater reliabilities of the subjects' total dependency scores was estimated by means of the Pearson product-moment correlation. The degree of interrater agreement was fairly high: the reliabilities ranged from .68 to .83 with an average coefficient of .77. Each child's final dependency score was obtained by summing his total dependency scores and then computing the mean of these scores.

As a check on the validity of the dependency ratings, the dependency behavior of each subject in the experimental situation was recorded, and the experimenter made two kinds of longitudinal observations of the subjects in the Nursery School. The first observation concerned the presence or absence of help seeking while dressing: the experimenter noted whether or not the child sought help in putting on or taking off his clothes. Each child was observed for 8 consecutive weeks during the first session that he attended each week. The observation was made when the child arrived at the Nursery School and when he dressed to go home. A second observation was made by the experimenter of those children who lived within walking distance of the Nursery School. The purpose of this observation was to determine how many children came and went home by themselves rather than with an adult or an older child. These data were also collected during the first session the child attended each week for 8 consecutive weeks. High-dependent children differed significantly from the low-dependent children on all three comparisons: They showed more dependency behavior in the experimental situation (boys, $t = 3.91$, $p < .001$; girls, $t = 3.62$, $p < .001$, one-tailed); they more often sought help with dressing (boys, $x^2 = 4.12$, $df = 1$, $p < .025$; girls, $x^2 = 3.03$, $df = 1$, $p < .05$, one-tailed); and they walked to school with others more often than did the low-dependent children ($x^2 = 3.72$, $df = 1$, $p < .05$, one-tailed).

The 13 boys and 13 girls with the highest final dependency scores were selected as high-dependent subjects, and the 13 boys and 13 girls with the lowest final dependency scores were selected as low-dependent subjects. These 52 subjects were each assigned either to 1 of the 4 experimental groups of 10 subjects each (high-dependent boys, low-dependent boys, high-dependent girls, low-dependent girls) or to 1 of the 2 control groups of 6 subjects each (high- and low-dependent boys, high- and low-dependent girls).

A statistical check using the Kruskal-Wallis one-way analysis of variance by ranks technique (Siegel, 1956) established that the groups did not differ in age, intelligence scores, or ordinal position.

Experimenters

The author acted both as the AM for the 40 subjects in the four experimental groups and as the adult customer (AC) for all subjects in the study. Six preschool girls were trained to serve as CCs: the CC first mailed letters and then was taught the postman role by the subject. Both the AC and the CC were well known to the subject in all cases. Each of the six preschool girls was trained individually for the CC role by the experimenter and participated in the experiment seven or eight times. Although the CCs were willing to serve more often, the experimenter felt that it was increasingly difficult for them to resist telling the subject what to do in the experimental situation.

Equipment

The experimental materials included a small wooden structure resembling a store with a cash register, stamps, a rubber postmark stamp and pad, scales, pencils, paper, play money, two chairs, and an area under the counter for parcels. To the left of the PO there was a chair and a table with a telephone and a telephone pad and pencils, and above the table a balloon with a wastepaper basket beneath it. A mailbox and a small artificial garden stood off to one side. A hat bar with three hats was directly behind the PO. The telephone was connected to a telephone in the observation room.

Procedure for Experimental Groups

Each subject was contacted individually in the Nursery School by the AM and was invited to come to the experimental room to play in the AM's PO. The AM brought the subject to the doorway of the room, paused, and said,

Look [subject's name], this is a post office. See, there is the mailbox, and the cash register, and the telephone and the stamps. Would you like me to show you what a postman (post lady) does and then as soon as you know how to be a postman, I'll come and mail letters at your post office and I'll ask one of your other friends to come and mail letters, too.

As soon as the subject had indicated that he would like to learn to be the postman, the AM took him into the experimental room and began teaching him how to be a postman. During this session the AM had to teach the subject seven sets of behaviors needed to run a PO (intentional learning). These sets of behaviors were postman behavior; collecting money and giving change; cash-register procedures; letter regulations—kind of stamp, post-mark, where to mail; telephone dialing; and telephone answering. As the AM taught the subject, she emphasized each set of intentional learning behaviors by verbal repetition, repeated demonstrations, requiring the subject to practice some of the behaviors, verbally rewarding him when it was appropriate to do so, and brief explanations about the reason for certain of the behaviors. As the AM demonstrated each set of intentional learning behaviors, she also exhibited certain partially relevant and completely irrelevant behaviors (incidental learning). The partially relevant incidental learning behaviors consisted of verbal and nonverbal behaviors that had some connection to the sets of intentional learning, for example, "I'll call you later," or taking an indirect route to the mailbox. The completely irrelevant incidental learning behaviors consisted of verbal and nonverbal behaviors that were functionless in the situation, for example, "Doodle, doodle, doodle," or putting one foot on the chair when telephoning.

The following excerpt from the script shows the exact procedure used to teach the subject one set of intentional learning behavior, telephone answering. In this excerpt, intentional learning responses are italicized and followed by (INT), and incidental learning responses are italicized and followed by (INC).

The telephone rings. Every time the telephone rings during the training session the AM goes through the following telephone routine:

The AM picks up a pencil from the counter and *sticks it behind her right ear* (INC), looks at the subject and says, "Oh, there's the telephone, I'll answer it." The AM goes to the telephone, *puts her left foot on the telephone chair* (INC), puts her hand on the receiver, turns to the subject and says, *"When you answer the telephone say 'post office'* (INT), don't say 'Hello,' *say 'post office'* (INT). The AM now picks up the receiver and says *"post office"* (INT), then she picks up a pencil from the telephone table and *taps a balloon that is hanging near the table* (INC). She *continues to tap the balloon* (INC) as she says, "Well, I'm pretty busy, I'm teaching [subject's name] to be a postman. *I'll call you later"* (INC). The AM pauses, still *tapping the balloon* (INC), then says, "Goodbye." She puts the receiver down, *doodles on the telephone pad* (INC), saying *"Doodle, doodle, doodle"* (INC) as she does so, tears off the sheet of paper and *crumples it up* (INC), says, *"Ready, aim, fire"* (INC) and *throws it into the basket* (INC). Then the AM returns to the PO, sits down, turns to the subject and says, *"Now, remember* (INC), [subject's name], when the telephone rings don't say 'Hello,' *say 'post office'* " (INT).

When the AM had taught the subject the seven sets of intentional learning behaviors, she told the subject that he was the postman now and that she would come and mail a letter at the PO. The AM then left the experimental room, and the scoring period began.

Learning Scores

Each of the 40 subjects in the experimental groups was scored for performance of intentional behaviors and incidental behaviors. During the scoring period, the subject first acted as postman for the AM, and the CC and then taught the CC the postman's tasks. The scoring period ended when the subject indicated that he had finished showing the CC how to be a postman.

Dependent and Independent Behavior Scores

The observers recorded all dependent and independent responses made by the subject during the entire experimental session. The categories used were the same as those used by Beller (1955).

Procedure for Learning Scoring

The telephone rings. The observer says she is calling from the other PO and asks the subject what special clothes a postman has to wear. Now the AM, acting as the AC, comes in with a letter, squats at the counter, and says to the subject, "I'd like to mail a birthday letter, please." The AC gives information only if the subject asks for it. When the subject indicates that he is finished with the letter, the AC says warmly, "You're a good postman. I like mailing letters at your post office. I think I'll go and get some more letters to mail." The AC goes out. The telephone rings. The observer asks when to give money back to someone who buys stamps. The AC returns with an ordinary letter and follows exactly the same procedure as above. The telephone rings. The observer asks the subject how to dial the telephone. The AC comes back in with a parcel and follows exactly the same procedure as above. The telephone rings, and the observer asks which stamps go on the different kinds of letter.

Now the AM comes to the door with the CC. The AM says, "Here another friend of yours who wants to mail letters and parcels at your post office." The AM remains in the anteroom while the CC mails an ordinary letter with silver for stamps, a birthday letter with a bill, and a parcel with a bill. As the CC goes in and out the telephone only if the subject shows signs of leaving. When the CC has finished her mailing, the AM comes to the door of the experimental room with her and says to the subject, "You're a good postman, would you show [CC's name] how to be a postman? You show her all the things a postman does." The AC now remains in the anteroom until the subject and CC come out. The telephone rings during the teaching session only if the subject requests it—for example, "I wish the telephone would ring"—or if the subject tells the CC to answer the telephone if it rings.

Now the CC and the subject come out. The AC asks the subject who he would like to be if he played again, the postman or the customer. The AC takes the subject back to the Nursery School and notes whether the child returned willingly or whether he was reluctant, that is, pleaded, argued, resisted physically, bargained, etc., with regard to leaving the experimental room.

Procedure for Control Groups

Groups 3 and 6 were used to provide evidence that the intentional and incidental behaviors learned by the subjects in the four experimental groups occurred as a result of this experimental session rather than as a result of some earlier experience of the subjects. The scorers recorded each subject's behavior in the control sessions in considerable detail in order to determine whether any of the behaviors that the AM exhibited for the experimental groups were shown by the subjects in the control groups.

In the control-group sessions the AM brought the subject in "to play post office," and allowed the subject to play as he wished. The AM gave help and information only if the subject requested it, with two exceptions: The AM offered to act as an AC and also to bring in a CC; and later, the AM encouraged the subject to teach the CC how to be a postman. The session ended whenever the subject decided that he had finished showing the CC how to be a postman. The control sessions lasted an average of 25 minutes.

Observers

Experienced psychology students naive as to the purpose of the experiment and the dependency status of the subjects recorded both the learning responses and also the dependent-independent responses made by the subject. Percentage agreement was used as a measure of interobserver agreement in the scoring of the experimental and control sessions. Percentage agreement was obtained by dividing the number of agreements between the two observers by the number of agreements plus the number of disagreements. An agreement was counted whenever the two observers recorded a given behavioral act in the same category on the score sheet. Zero entries by both observers were not counted as agreements. An omission by one observer when the other observer made a tally was considered a single disagreement. Interscorer agreement was 94%.

Relevance of Incidental Learning

One hypothesis was concerned with the extent to which the high- and low-dependent children differed in the learning of adult behaviors that were completely irrelevant to the central learning task. For this analysis two judges independently assigned each of the behaviors of the AM to one of three categories: centrally relevant, peripherally relevant, and completely irrelevant. A comparison of the two sortings showed that the judges disagreed in one instance, and this behavior was omitted from the analysis.

In addition to the experimental protocols and the longitudinal observations of the subjects' dependency behavior in the Nursery School, information was collected in interviews with the mothers of the subjects, and postexperimental observations were made of the subjects.

Mother Interviews

The mother of each subject was interviewed to determine what report, if any, the child had made about his experience in the experiment. The experimenter then described the experimental procedure to the mother, arranged for her to observe an experimental session if she wished to, discussed the subject's performance in the experiment if the mother asked about it, and answered any other questions of a more general nature about the subject.

Two judges (the experimenter and a graduate [student]) read the mother interviews to determine whether the subject had reported *facts* about the PO or had described the *equipment* to his parents. This decision was relatively easy to make since the majority of the subjects had talked mainly about either the facts or the equipment, but not both. The judges agreed on all but two of the interviews; these two interviews contained reports of both facts and equipment and could not be assigned to one category to the exclusion of the other.

The judges then reread the mother interviews to determine whether mothers were primarily interested in their children's *achievement* or in their *social skill*. Once again the judgement was not a difficult one because mothers who wanted to discuss achievement-type topics generally did not mention social skills and vice versa. The judges agreed on all but three of the interviews which could not be placed definitely in either category.

Postexperimental Observations

A simple frequency count was made of the number of subjects who requested a second turn in the experiment after they had returned to the Nursery School. Some children requested a second turn later the same day, while others asked several days or a week later.

RESULTS

It was hypothesized that the low-dependent children would obtain higher intentional learning scores than would the high-dependent children. As the findings in Table 1 indicate, this hypothesis was confirmed for both sexes.

The second hypothesis was that the high-dependent children would show more evidence of incidental learning in the experimental situation than

TABLE 1. COMPARISONS OF INTENTIONAL LEARNING SCORES OF LOW-DEPENDENT AND HIGH-DEPENDENT BOYS AND GIRLS

Group	N	M	SD	t
Low-dependent boys	10	37.6	9.04	1.79 *
High-dependent boys	10	31.0	6.26	
Low-dependent girls	10	41.8	6.76	2.31 **
High-dependent girls	10	34.4	6.68	
All low-dependent Ss	20	39.7	8.39	2.57 ***
All high-dependent Ss	20	32.7	6.80	

* $p < .05$, 1-tailed.
** $p < .025$, 1-tailed.
*** $p < .01$, 1-tailed.

would the low-dependent children. Analysis of the incidental learning scores yielded significant differences for both sexes. These results are contained in Table 2.

It was also hypothesized that when the responses performed by the AM were categorized in terms of their relevance to the intentional learning task, that is, learning to run the PO, the high-dependent children would learn more of the completely irrelevant responses than would the low-dependent children. The two groups did differ as predicted (boys, $t = 3.77$, $p < .001$; girls, $t = 2.07$, $p < .03$, one-tailed test).

The *total learning scores* (intentional and incidental) of the high-dependent and low-dependent groups were compared. The expectation that the high-dependent children would be less selective and, as a result, would reproduce the adult model's behaviors more often than did the low-depend-

TABLE 2. COMPARISONS OF INCIDENTAL LEARNING SCORES OF HIGH-DEPENDENT AND LOW-DEPENDENT BOYS AND GIRLS

Group	N	M	SD	t
High-dependent boys	10	29.5	12.92	3.52 ***
Low-dependent boys	10	12.7	6.12	
High-dependent girls	10	23.5	14.61	2.11 **
Low-dependent girls	10	12.1	5.95	
All high-dependent Ss	20	26.5	14.11	4.00 ****
All low-dependent Ss	20	12.4	6.06	

** $p < .025$, 1-tailed.
*** $p < .005$, 1-tailed.
**** $p < .0005$, 1-tailed.

ent children was confirmed for boys ($t = 2.49$, $p < .025$, one-tailed), but not for girls.

The hypothesis that the low-dependent children would exhibit more general independence behavior in the experimental situation than did the high-dependent children was also supported for boys only ($t = 2.97$, $p < .005$, one-tailed).

Although no hypotheses were advanced concerning differences in expressed preference for the role of either the controller, that is, postman, or the consumer, that is, customer, analysis of the interview data indicated that low-dependent children of both sexes preferred the controller role, while the high-dependent children preferred the consumer role (boys, $\chi^2 = 5.21$, $df = 1$, $p < .05$; girls, $\chi^2 = 4.12$, $df = 1$, $p < .05$, two-tailed).

In the mother-interview data, there were two interesting differences between the low-dependent and high-dependent groups. First, the low-dependent children reported the *facts* that they learned in the experimental situation to their parents, while the high-dependent children described the *equipment*, particularly the two-way telephone. These differences were significant for boys ($\chi^2 = 3.91$, $df = 1$, $p < .05$, two-tailed) and girls ($\chi^2 = 4.12$, $df = 1$, $p < .05$, two-tailed). Second, the mothers of the low-dependent children seemed to be very interested in the *achievement behavior* of their children, while the mothers of the high-dependent children appeared to be mainly concerned with their children's *social skills*. These differences were significant for both boys' mothers ($\chi^2 = 4.14$, $df = 1$, $p < .05$, two-tailed) and girls' mothers ($\chi^2 = 5.63$, $df = 1$, $p < .02$, two-tailed).

The results from the sessions for the control-group subjects provide convincing evidence that the intentional and incidental behaviors exhibited by the experimental group's subjects occurred as a result of this experimental session rather than as a result of some previous exposure or experience. The behaviors that the adult model exhibited for the experimental group rarely occurred in the control-group sessions.

DISCUSSION

The results of this study clearly supported the two major hypotheses. Low-dependent children learned more of the intentional behaviors and less of the incidental behaviors than did the high-dependent children.

It will be recalled that the experimenter predicted that the low-dependent children would *select* from the adult model's behaviors and as a result would have less material to learn than did the high-dependent children in the same amount of time. Two different score comparisons provided support for this belief. First, the intentional-incidental learning ratio was greater for the low-dependent group (3.4:1) than it was for the high-dependent group (1.2:1), which suggests that the low-dependent children were more selective, while the high-dependent children tended to pay equal attention to all of the AM's behaviors. Second, the total learning scores, that is, intentional plus incidental learning, of the high-dependent boys were greater than those of the low-dependent boys.

These differences in learning scores may reflect differences in what Klein (1958) has called *cognitive controls.* Klein and his associates have used the cognitive variable *leveling-sharpening* to describe the loss or preservation of distinctions among a series of stimuli. It is possible that the less selective attention of the high-dependent children was *leveling,* and the more selective attention shown by the low-dependent children was *sharpening.*

There is some evidence that the motivational value of the situation differed for the two groups. The experimental situation was more attractive to the low-dependent children (they were more reluctant to leave and were more eager for a second turn); the low-dependent children like the controller role, whereas the high-dependent children preferred the consumer role.

Bahrick (1954) and Bahrick, Fitts, and Rankin (1952), in a study of the effects of different incentives on the perceptual selectivity of adults in a psychomotor task situation, reported that increasing the attractiveness of a central task (the intentional learning) facilitated the subject's performance on that task, but in general interfered with his performance on three peripheral tasks (incidental learning). Our findings support Bahrick's: Learning to be a postman was more attractive to the low-dependent children; hence, the low-dependent children learned more of the intentional behaviors and less of the incidental behaviors than did the high-dependent children.

On the basis of all the available information on the children and their parents, it was apparent that the low-dependent children set a high value on achievement behavior, were rewarded at home for achievement behavior, and saw the experimental situation as an achievement situation. In contrast, the high-dependent children set a lower value on achievement behavior, were rewarded at home for exhibiting social skills such as interacting well with other children, and were unconcerned about the achievement aspects of the experimental situation. Achievement situations apparently represented a potential source of reinforcement to the low-dependent children as a result of parental interest in, and reward of, achievement in the home.

The hypothesis that low-dependent children would show more evidence of independence in the experimental situation than did high-dependent children was confirmed for boys but not for girls. The following explanation is offered for the failure to confirm this hypothesis in the case of the girls. Independence is a result of socialization processes. In training a child to be independent, the mother teaches him two kinds of behavior, *general independence behaviors,* for example, taking the initiative, wanting to do things by himself, etc., and a set of *specific independence behaviors,* for example, drinking from a cup, dressing himself, etc. General independence is usually thought of as a masculine trait in our culture; as a result, even in the preschool years, the two sexes experience different training in general independence behavior. Boys are likely to be given direct teaching, praise, and encouragement from their parents for this kind of behavior; girls are likely to be discouraged or nonrewarded if they exhibit very much general independence (Mussen & Conger, 1956). In contrast, the specific independence behaviors are common to both sexes, and although there are marked variations in the age at which training in specific independence behavior begins and the severity with which it is accomplished, the two sexes seem to be subjected to approximately the same kind of training and demands in the preschool years.

In studying the *general independence behavior* of preschool boys and girls we would expect, according to the above reasoning, to find that boys exhibit more general independence behavior than girls do and that the range in boys' scores would be greater than that in girls' scores due to the restrictions usually imposed on the amount of general independence that girls may exhibit. For *specific independence behavior,* however, we would not expect to find between-sex differences in either amount or range of this behavior. The results of our study support this reasoning. Boys showed more general independence behavior and also more variation in this behavior; within-sex comparisons showed that only in the case of boys did the low-dependent children differ from the high-dependent. In the specific independence behaviors there were no differences between the sexes, but within both sexes low-dependent children showed these behaviors more often than did high-dependent children.

SUMMARY

An adult model taught 26 high-dependent and 26 low-dependent preschool children how to run a post office (intentional learning) and at the same time displayed various partially relevant and completely irrelevant behaviors (incidental learning). Each child first served as postman and then taught another child the role. The hypotheses that low-dependent children would show more intentional and less incidental learning than did the high-dependent children were confirmed at the .01 and .0005 levels, respectively. However, there was evidence that the experimental situation was more attractive to the low-dependent children because these children and their parents placed a higher value on achievement behavior than did the high-dependent children and their parents.

REFERENCES

Bahrick, H. P. Incidental learning under two incentive conditions. *Journal of Experimental Psychology,* 1954, 47, 170–172.

Bahrick, H. P., Fitts, P. M., & Rankin, R. E.   Effect of incentives upon reactions to peripheral stimuli. *Journal of Experimental Psychology*, 1952, **44**, 400–406.

Bandura, A., & Huston, A. C.   Identification as a process of incidental learning. *Journal of Abnormal and Social Psychology*, 1961, **63**, 311–318.

Bandura, A., Ross, D., & Ross, S. A.   Transmission of aggression through imitation of aggressive models. *Journal of Abnormal and Social Psychology*, 1961, **63**, 575–582.

Bandura, A., Ross, D., & Ross, S. A.   Imitation of film-mediated aggressive models. *Journal of Abnormal and Social Psychology*, 1963, **66**, 3–11.

Beller, E. K.   Dependency and independency in young children. *Journal of Genetic Psychology*, 1955, **87**, 25–35.

Bronfenbrenner, U.   Freudian theories of identification and their derivatives. *Child Development*, 1960, **31**, 15–40.

Cairns, R. B.   The influence of dependency anxiety on responsivity to social reinforcers. Unpublished doctoral dissertation, Stanford University, 1959.

Endsley, R. S., & Hartup, W. W.   Dependency and performance by preschool children on a socially reinforced task. *American Psychologist*, 1960, **15**, 399. (Abstract)

Jackubczak, L. F., & Walters, R. H.   Suggestibility as dependency behavior. *Journal of Abnormal and Social Psychology*, 1959, **59**, 102–107.

Klein, G. S.   Cognitive control and motivation. In G. Lindzey (Ed.), *Assessment of human motives*. New York: Rinehart, 1958. Pp. 87–118.

McGeoch, J. A., & Irion, A. L.   *The psychology of human learning*. New York: Longmans, Green, 1950.

Mussen, P. H., & Conger, J. J.   *Child development and personality*. New York: Harper, 1956.

Ross, S. A.   The effect of deviant and non-deviant models on the behavior of preschool children in a temptation situation. Unpublished doctoral dissertation, Stanford University, 1962.

Sears, R. R., Maccoby, E. E., & Levin, H.   *Patterns of child rearing*. Evanston, Ill.: Roe, Peterson, 1957.

Sears, R. R., Whiting, J. W. M., Nowlis, V., & Sears, P. S.   Some child-rearing antecedents of aggression and dependency in young children. *Genetic Psychology Monographs*, 1953, **47**, 135–235.

Siegel, S.   *Nonparametric statistics for the behavioral sciences*. New York: McGraw-Hill, 1956.

chapter five

Independence
and Achievement

5.1 Introduction

One of the aims of socialization, in addition to making the maturing child responsive to adults and peers, is to teach him to reach some of his goals unaided, to act independently. Some writers have viewed independence as the absence of dependence and have placed independence and dependence at opposite poles of a single continuum. However, independence often suggests that certain positive features characterize a child's social behavior, such as initiative, self-assertion, unaided and effortful striving, in addition to infrequent attempts to gain nurturance from others. Independence, then, is more than merely a lack of dependence.

As in the case of dependence, there is evidence that independent action changes with age; as the child grows older the frequency of independent behavior increases (Joel, 1936; Heathers, 1955). Probably this shift is due to the decreased reinforcement dependency behaviors elicit, combined with direct reward and encouragement for independent action. For example, many years ago Fales (1944) provided nursery school children with both training in taking off their wraps and praise for successful displays of this independent behavior. The increase in independence shown by the experimental subjects as opposed to a group of nontreated controls illustrates very clearly the importance of reinforcement in acquiring independence.

Just as independence is more than the mere absence of dependence, the concept of achievement usually refers to more than independent action. By achievement, one generally means that the subject is not merely executing a task without assistance, but is trying to perform well with the aim of eliciting positive reinforcement for his demonstrated competence in the task. An emphasis on evaluation of performance against some standard of excellence is the distinguishing characteristic of achievement behavior. Achievement behavior may be defined as "behavior directed toward the attainment of approval or the avoidance of disapproval for competence of performance in situations where standards of excellence are applicable" (Crandall, Katkovsky, & Preston, 1960). Instead of approaching this topic by examining achievement behavior, a number of investigators have focused on the study of achievement motivation or need for achievement. Originally developed by McClelland (See McClelland, Atkinson, Clark, & Lowell, 1953) need for achievement (n Ach) refers to a relatively stable acquired disposition to strive for success whenever behavior can be evaluated against a standard of excellence. Individual differences in the strength of the achievement motive are usually measured through scoring of fantasy productions produced by TAT or TAT-like stimuli. Despite its wide acceptance as a measure of achievement motivation, this index is plagued by a number of problems, such as low reliability of n Ach scores. In addition there has been some difficulty in replicating studies, particularly those using the TAT test as a measure.

Unlike most topics in social and personality development, achievement owes a relatively minor debt to classical Freudian theory. Instead the forerunners of modern research efforts can be traced to neo-Freudians such as Alfred Adler and Gestaltists such as Kurt Lewin. In fact, Lewin's early systematic investigations of levels of aspiration led to a recognition of the role of cognitive variables such as anticipations, expectations, and standards on achievement behavior (Crandall, 1963).

While independence and achievement are clearly not identical phenomena, a number of studies have found that independence of adults characterizes achievement-oriented children (Sontag, Baker, & Nelson, 1958; Crandall, Preston, & Rabson, 1960). In addition, McClelland, Atkinson, Clark, and Lowell (1953) found college students who were high in need for achievement conformed less to the opinions of other students in social influence situations.

Winterbottom (1958), in her pioneering investigation of the child-rearing correlates of achievement motivation, suggests that the critical factor separating high- and low-achievement boys is their independence training. In her study of 9-year-old boys, she found that the mothers of the boys rated high in achievement motivation expected self-reliant behavior relatively early and placed fewer restrictions on their sons' spontaneous independent strivings. In addition, these mothers provided larger and more frequent reinforcements whenever their sons successfully performed independently. The powerful influence of this independence training is indicated by Feld's (1959) follow-up study, in which he found that the early training was still predictive of the boys' achievement motivations in adolescence. In fact, the mother's encouragement of independence in the adolescent period was negatively correlated with the boys' achievement motivation; early training in independence appears more effective than later independence training (Hartup, 1965).

Further support of Winterbottom's (1958) findings comes from a longitudinal investigation of the stability of achievement behavior from childhood to adulthood (Moss & Kagan, 1961). The effect of maternal acceleration of developmental skills on a variety of childhood achievement behaviors, including intellectual, athletic, mechanical, and artistic, were examined. Adult achievement behavior was indexed by recognition-seeking activities (for example, striving for vocational recognition) and concern with intellectual competence. These investigators report that maternal acceleration from ages 6 to 10 was a moderately successful predictor of high concern for intellectual competence in adulthood for both males and females. Moreover, striving for achievement and recognition was markedly stable between ages 6 to 10 and adulthood.

In a later study of parental influences on achievement, Rosen and D'Andrade (1959) examined the influence of both mothers and fathers on the achievement behaviors of their sons. Instead of employing a questionnaire approach, these investigators used a quasi-experimental technique involving observations of the parent's behavior while the son worked on a series of achievement tasks. Their use of a structured parent-child interaction situation is an important methodological innovation that avoids many of the problems that plague questionnaire-based studies. Their observations revealed that the parents of boys with high achievement motivation typically set higher standards of excellence for their sons and generally anticipated better task performance than parents of boys with low achievement motivation. In addition, the former parents, especially the mothers, more readily reinforced their son's task success and punished their failure to reach performance goals. Other studies have found support for the role of positive reinforcement in the development of achievement. Crandall, Preston, and Rabson (1960) reported that mothers who rewarded their children's achievement efforts had children who displayed a high degree of achievement striving in nursery school. In addition, the fathers of high n Ach boys in the Rosen and D'Andrade study tended to be less dominant and interfered les with their sons' decision making than fathers of boys with low achievement motivation. Moreover, it appears to be mainly the dominant father that interferes with the development of achievement motivation, for a dominant mother does not have this detrimental effect.

As the Rosen and D'Andrade study indicated, parental standard-setting behavior is an important aspect of achievement. In their article in this section, Mischel and Liebert (1966) have experimentally investigated some of the conditions that facilitate the adoption and maintenance of achievement standards. Children may acquire these standards not only by direct instruction by parents (Rosen & D'Andrade) and other socializing agents but also by observing the standards other people employ (Bandura & Kupers, 1964). In real-life situations children are often exposed to both sets of influences; parents display or exhibit their own standards and at the same time directly impose different criteria on their offspring. The Mischel and Liebert findings indicate that standards are more likely to be adopted and maintained when there is consistency between the standards parents directly impose on their children and the criteria they apply to their own behavior.

The impact of parental attitudes and practices on children's achievement behavior may depend on a variety of factors, including the sex of the parent and child and the type of achievement behavior. Crandall, Dewey, Katkovsky, and Preston (1964), in the next article in this section, report that parental behaviors, particularly maternal behaviors, are more often predictive of girls' intellectual achievement performance than of boys'. Mothers of high-achieving girls tend to set high standards for their daughters but tend to be low in affection and nurturance. Fathers, on the other hand, who praise and reward their daughters' intellectual accomplishments and avoid criticizing their achievement efforts have high-achieving daughters. Possibly the girls with cold mothers but rewarding fathers are identifying with the masculine achievement role.

The finding that achievement behaviors of males and females differ in susceptibility to parental influence implies that different motivations may underlie the achievement efforts of boys and girls. Association between girls' achievement behavior and affiliative and approval-seeking behavior have been reported by a number of investigators (Sears, 1962; Tyler, Rafferty, & Tyler, 1962); no such relationships have emerged for boys. These results suggest that girls may employ achievement behavior as a means of attracting adult attention and approval, while boys may strive to achieve for the sake of achieving.

A number of other characteristics distinguish high- and low-achieving children. One of the best predictors of intellectual success appears to be the child's expectancy of how well he will perform. Children who expect to do well in a task are found to persist longer, try harder, and succeed more than children who do not expect to perform well (Crandall & McGhee, 1967). Another important discriminating feature is the extent to which children believe that they, rather than other people, are responsible for their intellectual or academic successes and failures. Crandall, Katkovsky, and Crandall (1965) have recently designed a scale to tap this belief and report positive relationships between belief in self-responsibility for academic performance and achievement test scores, on one hand, and report card grades, on the other, among elementary school children.

In addition, high achievers are better able to work under delayed reinforcement conditions and are able to delay immediate reinforcement for the sake of a larger, but delayed, reward. This ability is particularly important in achievement; successful task completion often requires persistence under conditions of minimal immediate feedback. Academic success, particularly, requires the capacity to work toward a long-range goal with little immediate reinforcement. Mischel (1961), using as subjects Trinidadian boys, found support for this hypothesized relationship between achievement motivation and the capacity to delay gratification. Children with high and low achievement motivation are also distinguished by the kinds of tasks they prefer and their strategies in achievement situations. High achievement-motivated people often prefer moderately difficult tasks which involve a challenge rather than tasks with complete certainty of success, but they are not necessarily gamblers and, in fact, prefer tasks of moderate difficulty when skill or ability is involved. When faced with a task, these people take moderate risks rather than no risks or extreme risks. In the final article in this section, McClelland (1958) presents research with children that illustrates this preference for moderate risk-taking. He notes that the risk-taking pattern of the children with high need for achievement is very similar to the usual behavior of the businessman who operates neither in a traditional manner nor like a gambler, but chooses to behave in a manner whereby his skill is most likely to pay off in subjective feelings of success. In his book *The Achieving Society*, McClelland (1961) has presented evidence supporting this hypothesized link between need for achievement and preference for entrepreneurial occupations. Drawing on data from the U.S.A., Poland, and Italy, he demonstrated that subjects with high n Ach scores preferred business occupations. In a recently completed longitudinal study, McClelland (1965) found that significantly more college students scoring high in n Ach than students low in achievement motivation were engaged in entrepreneurial occupations 14 years after graduation.

REFERENCES

Bandura, A., & Kupers, C. J. The transmission of patterns of self-reinforcement through modeling. *Journal of Abnormal and Social Psychology*, 1964, **69**, 1–9.

Crandall, V. J. Achievement. In H. W. Stevenson (Ed.), *Child Psychology: The sixty-second yearbook of the National Society for the Study of Education*, Part 1. Chicago: The National Society for the Study of Education, 1963. Pp. 416–459.

Crandall, V. J., Katkovsky, W., & Preston, A. A conceptual formulation of some research on children's achievement. *Child Development*, 1960, **31**, 784–797.

Crandall, V. J., Dewey, R., Katkovsky, W., & Preston, A. Parents' attitudes and behaviors and grade-school children's academic achievement. *Journal of Genetic Psychology*, 1964, **104**, 53–66.

Crandall, V. C., Katkovsky, W., & Crandall, V. J. Children's beliefs in their own control of reinforcements in intellectual-academic achievement situations. *Child Development*, 1965, **36**, 91–109.

Crandall, V. C., & McGhee, P. E. Expectancy of reinforcement as a determinant of academic competence. Unpublished manuscript, Fels Research Institute, 1967.

Crandall, V. J., Preston, A., & Rabson, A. Maternal reactions and the development of independence and achievement behavior in young children. *Child Development*, 1960, **31**, 243–251.

Fales, E. Genesis of level of aspiration in children from one and one-half to three years of age. Reported in Lewin, K., *et al.*, Level of aspiration, in J. Mc. V. Hunt (Ed.), *Personality and the behavior disorders*, Vol. 1. New York: Ronald Press, 1944. Pp. 333–378.

Field, S. C. Studies in the origins of achievement strivings. Unpublished doctoral dissertation, University of Michigan, 1959.

Hartup, W. W. Early pressures in child development. *Young Children*, 1965, **21**, 271–283.

Heathers, G. Emotional dependence and independence in nursery-school play. *Journal of Genetic Psychology*, 1955, **87**, 37–57.

Joel, W. Behavior maturity of children of nursery school age. *Child Development*, 1936, **7**, 189–199.

McClelland, D. C. Risk-taking in children with high and low need for achievement. In J. W. Atkinson (Ed.), *Motives in fantasy, action, and society*. Princeton, N.J.: Van Nostrand, 1958.

McClelland, D. C. *The achieving society*. Princeton, N. J.: Van Nostrand, 1961.

McClelland, D. C.   N achievement and entrepreneurship: A longitudinal study. *Journal of Personality and Social Psychology*, 1965. Pp. 389–392.

McClelland, D. C., Atkinson, J. W., Clark, R. A., & Lowell, E. L.   *The achievement motive*. New York: Appleton-Century-Crofts, 1953.

Mischel, W.   Preference for delayed reinforcement and social responsibility. *Journal of Abnormal and Social Psychology*, 1961, **62**, 1–7.

Mischel, W., & Liebert, R. M.   Effects of discrepancies between observed and imposed reward criteria on their acquisition and transmission. *Journal of Personality and Social Psychology*, 1966, **3**, 45–53.

Moss, H. A., & Kagan, J.   Stability of achievement and recognition seeking behaviors from early childhood through adulthood. *Journal of Abnormal and Social Psychology*, 1961, **62**, 504–513.

Rosen, B., & D'Andrade, R.   The psychosocial origins of achievement motivation. *Sociometry*, 1959, **22**, 185–252.

Sears, P. S.   Correlates of need achievement and need affiliation and classroom management, self-concept and creativity. Unpublished manuscript, Laboratory of Human Development, Stanford University, 1962.

Sontag, L. W., Baker, C. T., & Nelson, V. L.   Mental growth and personality development: A longitudinal study. *Monograph of the Society for Research in Child Development*, 1958, 23 (2).

Tyler, Y. B., Rafferty, J., & Tyler, B.   Relationships among motivations of parents and their children. *Journal of Genetic Psychology*, 1962, **101**, 69–81.

Winterbottom, M.   The relation of need for achievement in learning experiences in independence and mastery. In J. Atkinson (Ed.), *Motives in fantasy, action and society*. Princeton, N. J.: Van Nostrand, 1958. Pp. 453–478.

SUPPLEMENTARY READING

Crandall, F. J.   Achievement. In H. W. Stevenson (Ed.), *Child psychology: The sixty-second yearbook of the national society for the study of education*, Part I. Chicago: University of Chicago Press, 1963. Pp. 416–459.

Crandall, V. C.   Achievement behavior in young children. *Young Children*, 1964, **20**, 76–90.

McLelland, D. C.   *The achieving society*. New York: Van Nostrand, 1961. Pp. 336–390.

5.2 The Relation of Need for Achievement
to Learning Experiences in Independence and Mastery[1]

Marian R. Winterbottom

Research regarding the origins of the need for achievement has focused on the social conditions in which the growing person learns to be motivated for achievement. For example, McClelland and Friedman (1952) have found significant correlations between *n* Achievement scores obtained from the folk tales of eight American Indian tribes and the age and severity of independence training in those cultures. McClelland (1951a, 1951b) has derived from a theory of motivation a list of variables to be related to achievement motivation. His discussion directs attention to the number of experiences in independent mastery, the age at which the training is given, and the emotional accompaniments of the training as important conditions for the development of an achievement motive in the child.

In order to investigate further these hypotheses within an American community, the author studied a group of twenty-nine eight-year-old boys and their mothers, living in a small, middle-class, midwestern community in 1952. The group was relatively homogeneous economically and socially. The children all attended the same school and were in the same grade and same range of intelligence. The strength of *n* Achievement in the boys was related to dimensions of independence and mastery training as reported by their mothers in interviews conducted by the experimenter. Mothers were chosen as the initial group for study because of their close contact with children during the early formative years and because of the strong emotional ties of children to their mothers. Later in the paper we will discuss the importance of father and siblings in this learning, but the evidence presented will primarily be concerned with mothers and sons.

THE HYPOTHESES AND PROCEDURE

Mother's standards of training in independence and mastery (demands). The hypotheses relevant to this aspect of training state that mothers of boys

---

[1] This article is based on a dissertation submitted in partial fulfillment of the requirements for the degree of Doctor of Philosophy in the University of Michigan, 1953. The writer wishes to express her appreciation to Dr. J. W. Atkinson for his valuable guidance through the research.

Reprinted with abridgement from J. Atkinson (Ed.) *Motives in Fantasy, Action, and Society,* Princeton, N. J., Van Nostrand, 1958, pp. 453–478, by permission of the author and Van Nostrand Co., Inc.

who are high in n Achievement (a) will make a greater number of demands for independence and mastery, (b) that they will reward the child more frequently and more intensely, and (c) that they will give this training at an earlier age than mothers of boys who are low in n Achievement. These hypotheses are in accordance with McClelland's (1951a, 1951b) argument that as achievement cues are followed frequently by emotional changes, the cues take on the characteristic of arousing these emotional changes in an anticipatory way. McClelland has further specified that experiences early in life will be more decisive in this respect because there will be greater generalization of the learning and because emotional responses to parents are more intense at earlier ages.

Information regarding this aspect of training was obtained through interviews with each mother. The data presented comes from a questionnaire which each mother filled out and which included a list of twenty kinds of independence and mastery behaviors that she might consider as goals of her training. A mother was asked to put a check beside each item she considered to be a goal of her training and to indicate the age by which she expected her child to have learned the behavior. The demands were:

To stand up for his own rights with other children.

To know his way around his part of the city so that he can play where he wants without getting lost.

To go outside to play when he wants to be noisy or boisterous.

To be willing to try new things on his own without depending on his mother for help.

To be active and energetic in climbing, jumping, and sports.

To show pride in his own ability to do things well.

To take part in his parents' interests and conversations.

To try hard things for himself without asking for help.

To be able to eat alone without help in cutting and handling food.

To be able to lead other children and assert himself in children's groups.

To make his own friends among children his own age.

To hang up his own clothes and look after his own possessions.

To do well in school on his own.

To be able to undress and go to bed by himself.

To have interests and hobbies of his own. To be able to entertain himself.

To earn his own spending money.

To do some regular tasks around the house.

To be able to stay alone at home during the day.

To make decisions like choosing his clothes or deciding how to spend his money by himself.

To do well in competition with other children. To try hard to come out on top in games and sports.

The emotional consequences of the training were also assessed in the questionnaire. The hypotheses were that children who are more intensely and frequently rewarded for accomplishment are more highly motivated and that children who are more frequently and intensely punished for failure are more highly motivated. . . .

Following the demands scale, there were two lists of alternative parental reactions to the child's behavior. One list is concerned with what the mother does when the child fulfills her expectations. The other list is concerned with what she does when he does not fulfill her demands. The list of alternative reactions to "good" performance in the child is made up of three rewarding reactions:

1. Kiss or hug him to show how pleased you are.
2. Tell him what a good boy he is. Praise him for being good.
3. Give him a special treat or privilege.

and three relatively neutral reactions:

4. Do nothing at all to make it seem special.
5. Show him you expected it of him.
6. Show him how he could have done better.

The list of alternative reactions to the "bad" performance in the child is made up of three punishment items:

1. Scold or spank him for not doing it.
2. Show him you are disappointed in him.
3. Deprive him of something he likes or expects, like a special treat or privilege.

and three relatively neutral items:

4. Don't show any feeling about it.
5. Point out how he should have behaved.
6. Just wait until he does what you want.

The items in each scale were randomized, and mothers were asked to make three choices among the six possibilities.

Two measures can be obtained from each scale. First, the number of rewards or punishments chosen from the six items. . . . Second, the rewards and punishments are assumed to vary in intensity. It is assumed that direct physical rewards or punishments are affectively more intense than less personal reactions on the part of the mother. Verbal praise or punishment is assumed to be second in affective intensity; rewards or punishments which involve objects or privileges, least intense. The rewards and punishments have been listed above in their assumed order of intensity.

The final part of the mothers' questionnaire listed the twenty independence or achievement activities again and asked the mothers to indicate the independence and success which their children had achieved relative to other children. Mothers were asked to rate their children as showing a particular behavior more, less, or to the same degree as other children the same age. This measure was included in order to obtain the mother's picture of the child's achievements. It was expected that the mothers of boys who are high in n Achievement would rate their sons higher than the mothers of boys who are low in n Achievement. . . .

In addition to failure to achieve mastery, there are certain aspects of independence and mastery that a mother may prohibit, and these prohibitions are likely to effect the achievement motivation of her child. To test the hypothesis that restrictions will have an effect opposite to that of demands, a list of twenty behaviors that a mother might want to discourage was added to the questionnaire. Each of these restrictions corresponded in content to one of the demand items. For example, the demand "standing up for his rights with other children" was converted to the restriction "not to fight with other children." As with the demands, the mother was asked to check a restriction if she considered it a goal of her training and to indicate the age by which she expected it to be learned. . . .

The restrictions were followed by a list of rewarding and punitive reactions identical to those following the demands. The specific hypotheses to be tested were that boys who are high in n Achievement experience fewer restrictions, later in training, and with less intense rewards and punishments.

The imaginative measure of n *achievement.* Some young children showed that they often find it difficult to give imaginatively rich stories in four minutes (the standard time) when pictures are used to elicit thematic apperception. Lowell (1953a) has used verbal cues with this age group with much more success and without the distracting description-provoking effects of pictures. Hence, two sets of verbal cues, similar but not identical to Lowell's, were used in this study. One set of four was given under what has been called Relaxed Orientation, where every effort is made to put the subject at ease and instructions are given to reduce as much as possible any "test atmosphere." The experimenter said: "What I have for you today is a sort of game. I'm interested in storytelling and I'd like you to tell some stories. It would be hard to make up stories about just anything, so I'm going to tell you what to make up a story about. I'll give you an idea, and you tell me a story about it. Make up a real story with a beginning and an end just like the ones you read. Tell me as much about your story as you can, and I'll write down what you say. Let's try one for practice. Tell me a story about a little boy who is in school."

During the practice story the experimenter asked leading questions similar to those usually printed on the story form when stories are written, i.e.,

What is happening in this story? What happened before? How did the story begin? What is the boy thinking about—how does he feel? What will happen—how will the story end?

At the end of the practice story, the experimenter said: "Now you have the idea. You can tell me the rest of your stories in the same way. I'll ask you what is happening, what happened before, how the people think and feel, and how the story ends. You can tell the story by answering my questions."

The verbal cues about which the child was to tell the story were (1) A mother and her son. They look worried. (2) Two men standing by a machine. One is older. (3) A boy who has just left his house. (4) A young man sitting at a desk.

At the end of the "relaxed" stories, another condition was introduced: Achievement Orientation. The child was told that he would be given a puzzle test [2] which would tell how smart he was and on which he should try his best because he was to be compared to others in his class. After three minutes of work on the test and during a "rest period," a second set of stories was collected in response to the following verbal cues: (1) A father and son talking about something important. (2) Brothers and sisters playing. One is a little ahead. (3) A young man alone at night. (4) A young man with his head resting on his hands.

The stories were scored according to the criteria for achievement-related imagery developed by McClelland *et al.* (1953a). Scoring reliability was checked on twenty stories. . . . The product-moment correlation between the two scorings was .92. The over-all percentage agreement in scoring particular categories was 73 per cent.

The median n Achievement score of 5.0 for the 29 boys under Achievement Orientation was greater ($p < .06$ in the expected direction) than the median score of 3.8 under Relaxed Orientation. But since there is no evidence that the two forms of the measure were equivalent, little can be made of this difference except to note that it is in the expected direction.

Treatment of the data. For the analysis of results presented in this paper, the distributions of both Relaxed and Achievement-oriented n Achievement scores are divided at the medians forming high and low n Achievement groups on each measure. Results are reported in terms of each of these measures and also in terms of another division of subjects into a group ($N = 10$) who were high (i.e., above the median scores) on both Relaxed and Achievement-oriented scores versus a group ($N = 10$) who were low (i.e., below the median scores) in both conditions. This particular breakdown isolates a group who, as Martire has argued elsewhere . . . , show strong generalized motivation to achieve irrespective of the situation cues

---

[2] A form of the Carl Hollow Square test was used which was difficult enough so that no child completed it in three minutes.

and a group who are relatively low in motivation to achieve irrespective of situation cues.

RESULTS

n *Achievement and demands for independence and mastery.* The hypothesis that mothers of the high n Achievement group would report more demands was not confirmed. The median number of demands made by mothers of both high and low n Achievement groups was 19–20 in each of the comparisons, a result indicating that almost all of the mothers chose all of the items as goals of training by age ten.

However, the hypothesis that mothers of boys who are high in n Achievement would make these demands *earlier* is supported. By the age of eight, approximately half the demands of the total group were made. If we consider the demands made before the age of eight as *early* demands, we can compare mothers of high and low n Achievement groups on the number of early demands they make. Table 1 shows the median number of early de-

TABLE 1. MEDIAN NUMBER OF EARLY DEMANDS (THROUGH AGE SEVEN) REPORTED BY MOTHERS OF BOYS WHO WERE HIGH AND LOW IN n ACHIEVEMENT

	Measure of n Achievement					
n Achievement	Relaxed Orientation		Achievement Orientation		Both	
	N	Md.	N	Md.	N	Md.
High	15	10	14	11	10 (HH)	15.5
Low	14	7	15	6	10 (LL)	5.5
p *		.01		.004		.002

* Probability of the difference in predicted direction by Mann-Whitney U Test (303).

mands made by mothers of high and low n Achievement groups. It is clear in each of the three comparisons that the mothers of boys who had high n Achievement scores reported significantly more demands through the age of seven than the mothers of boys who were low in n Achievement.

Figure 1 shows the cumulative curves for demands over all ages by the mothers of the boys who were above and below the median n Achievement scores on both measures. This particular figure dramatizes an effect that is also apparent but slightly less pronounced in cumulative curves drawn in terms of either Relaxed or Achievement-oriented n Achievement scores taken separately (1953b).

When the number of demands made from age eight to ten are considered, the relationship is reversed. Mothers of boys who are high in n Achievement

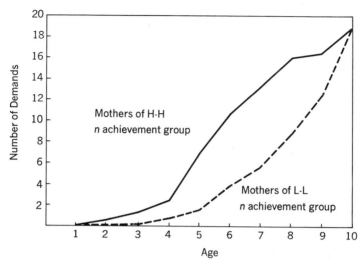

FIGURE 1. Cumulative average number of demands for independence and mastery at each age (1 to 10 years) by mothers of boys who were high (N = 10) and low (N = 10) on both relaxed and achievement orientation measures of n Achievement. (Courtesy of D. Van Nostrand Company, Inc.)

choose fewer items beyond the age of eight than mothers of boys who are low in n Achievement. This relationship is undoubtedly a function of the limited number of items to be chosen. The mothers of boys who are high in n Achievement have already used up significantly more of the items in the list by age eight and hence there are fewer remaining to be chosen.

Rewards for fulfilled demands and n achievement. . . . The hypotheses are that mothers of boys who are high in n Achievement will be more frequently and intensely rewarding when demands for independence and mastery are fulfilled and will be more frequently and intensely punishing when these demands are not fulfilled.

More mothers of boys who are high in n Achievement report using **all** three types of rewards—verbal, object, and physical—than mothers of boys who are low in n Achievement ($p = .05$–$.10$). It is assumed that some form of physical affection like hugging or kissing is more intensely rewarding than either verbal praise or object rewards. There are no differences between mothers of high and low n Achievement boys in frequency of verbal or object rewards. However, mothers of high n Achievement boys report more physical affection as reward for fulfilled demands than mothers of low n Achievement boys ($p < .05$).

Punishments for unfulfilled demands and n achievement. None of the comparisons between mothers of high and low n Achievement boys in use of punishment for unfilled demands reveals a significant difference. Apparently mothers of high and low n Achievement children are much the same in their reactions to the child's failure to fulfill demands, at least as we have measured these reactions.

Mother's evaluation of son's accomplishments. We may turn now to the mother's evaluation of her son's accomplishments in relation to those of other children. The hypothesis that mothers of boys who are high in n Achievement will be more likely to rate their children as more skillful is confirmed. An index of the favorableness of each mother's judgments of her son was obtained by subtracting the number of times the son was rated worse than average from the number of times he was rated better than average on the list of twenty demands. A plus score indicates a predominance of positive judgments; a minus score indicates a preponderance of negative judgments. . . . In each of the comparisons, the mothers of high n Achievement boys are more positive in their evaluations than mothers of low n Achievement boys ($p = .025–.05$). . . .

It is difficult to say whether the difference in judgments corresponds to a real difference in achievement levels in the two groups, or whether the mother's own evaluation of her son's achievement has influenced the ratings. Several behavioral ratings made by the boys' teachers in another phase of this study . . . provides some independent evidence of observable differences in the behavior of the two groups. According to the ratings of teachers, the boys who were high in n Achievement appeared significantly more motivated for success in school work, more independent, more successful in social groups (i.e., popular), and more pleased when they did succeed than the boys who were low in n Achievement. But ratings of success in school work, sports and games, and in leadership did not discriminate significantly between the two motivation groups, although the trend always favored the high n Achievement group. However, there still may be some justification for considering the ratings of a mother as more indicative of her general evaluation of the child's performance. In this light, the data provide additional suggestive evidence that the mothers of boys who are high in n Achievement tend to be more rewarding, i.e., they take a more positive view of the child's behavior.

n *Achievement and restrictions upon independent activity.* The first hypothesis to be tested is that mothers of high n Achievement children are less restrictive than mothers of low n Achievement children. Table 2 shows that this hypothesis is confirmed. By the age of ten, mothers of the high n Achievement group have selected only 12 to 13 of the restrictions; mothers of the low n Achievement group have selected 16 to 17, significantly more in each of the three comparisons.

It was further hypothesized that the restrictions imposed by the mothers of the high n Achievement group would come later than the demands for

TABLE 2. MEDIAN NUMBER OF TOTAL RESTRICTIONS (THROUGH AGE TEN) AND
EARLY RESTRICTIONS (THROUGH AGE SEVEN) REPORTED BY MOTHERS
OF BOYS WHO WERE HIGH AND LOW IN n ACHIEVEMENT

	Measure of n Achievement					
	Relaxed Orientation		Achievement Orientation		Both	
n Achievement	High	Low	High	Low	High-High	Low-Low
N	15	14	14	15	10	10
Total restrictions	12.17	16.5 *	13	16 *	12.25	17.25 *
Early restrictions	9.0	6.4 *	9.0	6.5 *	10.25	6.25 *

* p of difference $< .05$ in predicted direction by Mann-Whitney U Test (303).

independent accomplishment. A comparison between mothers of high and
low n Achievement groups in making early restrictions, i.e., through the
age of seven, shows that mothers of the high n Achievement boys actually
impose more early restrictions than mothers of the low n Achievement group
(Table 2 and Figure 2). But the question is, Do the mothers of the high n
Achievement group make more demands or restrictions at any early age?

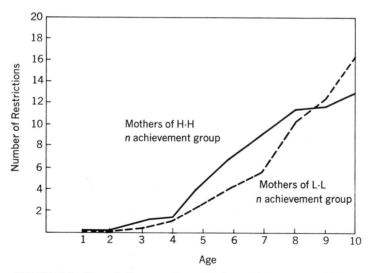

FIGURE 2. Cumulative average number of restrictions upon
independence and mastery at each age (1 to 10
years) by mothers of boys who were high (N = 10)
and low (N = 10) on both relaxed and achievement orientation measures of n Achievement.
(Courtesy of D. Van Nostrand Company, Inc.)

The number of demands and restrictions made by each mother through age seven was compared. . . . Mothers of boys who are high in n Achievement make more demands than restrictions during the early years ($p = .05$). But mothers of boys who are low in n Achievement do not. In other words, mothers of the high n Achievement boys report fewer restrictions through age ten but more early restrictions (through age seven) than mothers of boys who are low in n Achievement. However, the restriction training of the high n Achievement group does not precede their demand training; through age seven their training is characterized by a preponderance of positive demands.

Rewards and punishments administered in restrictive training. . . . The pattern of rewards and punishments in connection with restrictions tends to be similar to the pattern for demands but is less consistent in the three comparisons. There is no evidence to support the hypothesis that the boys who are high in n Achievement experience less frequent and less intense reward and punishment in connection with restrictions. On the contrary, . . . the mothers of boys who are high in n Achievement report administering all three types of rewards and using some form of physical affection to reward restrictive training more frequently than mothers of boys who are low in n Achievement. These differences are not significant, however, when the Achievement-Orientation score is the index of strength of n Achievement. . . .

DISCUSSION

The data presented provide a basis for description of the differences in the learning experiences of boys who have relatively high or low n Achievement scores on the fantasy measure used. The high n Achievement group have earlier training in our list of independence and mastery behaviors. They have fewer experiences in being restricted in these areas, and though restriction training comes earlier for them, it has been preceded by a good deal of training in independence. Their mothers take a more positive view of their accomplishments and are more often and more affectively rewarding. There is no evidence that the high n Achievement group is more frequently punished. All of these conclusions are limited by the measures used. Interviews and questionnaires from mothers may not give an accurate representation of what actually went on during training. The sample of fantasy we used may often miss important kinds of fantasies which may relate to achievement behavior but which are not easily verbalized, or which are not elicited in this situation.

Though it is difficult to evaluate the meaning of our questionnaire data and how it relates to the actual behavior of the mother, there is some possibility of examining the stories of the two groups of children in order to understand the context of fantasy in which the achievement imagery occurs and what clues it may give to other determinants which we have not considered. In order to do this fairly systematically, though without any check on reliability, twenty-five stories that were scored for achievement imagery were selected from the lowest and highest scorers. These stories were analyzed for differences in the stories other than in achievement imagery itself.

Most of the stories were centered around competitiveness. Both the high and low groups had nine stories each, involving competition with children though the resolutions of the stories were different. The high group resolved all the stories with someone winning. Four stories mentioned instances of aggression and cheating in the process of winning, though never leading to success. The low group had instances of resolution by the winner giving up the prize, or the loser refusing to play, or someone getting hurt or changing the theme of the story.

Competition between a young man and an older man occurred seven times in the stories of high n Achievers but not at all in the low group. The stories of the high group contained four references to aggression between the two, two references to someone being hurt, two references to helping each other, and no resolutions where the younger lost out. The low group, when they used the younger-older man theme, structured the stories twice as the older man helping the younger, once as the younger man admiring the older man's accomplishment, and three times as the young man being fired or worried about the possibility. There were no instances of aggression, bragging, or open competition.

These stories suggest that the context of the achievement imagery is limited more for the low group than the high group. Competitiveness is restricted to their own age group and does not get expressed with older men. Also cheating and aggression are not themes which accompany the achievement fantasy of the low group. It may be that the occurrence of such possibilities and subsequent avoidance of their expression may reduce the expression of ambitions involving them. These stories lead one to believe that a son's relationship with his father may be as important an area to investigate as his relationship with his mother, especially in an attempt to understand the restriction of fantasies that may be present and unexpressed or avoided. The emotional meaning of achievement fantasies is not well understood and is likely far more complex than our data suggest. Investigation of the determinants of achievement motives that have their sources in the psychosexual nature of the child may be helpful.[3] The competitiveness with older men certainly suggests this as a direction for research. The age of independence and mastery training of the child would then be seen in relation to his developmental level. The results which indicate the im-

---

[3] The lack of correspondence between the research on n Achievement in young men and women suggests this direction as well as an investigation of different methods of training.

portance of training before the age of eight do not justify the assertion that the earlier the training the more it contributes to the development of achievement motivation and fantasy. There may be particular age ranges during which an environment which encourages independence and achievement fits particularly well the needs of the growing child.

Another area for investigation is the parent's response to the child's fantasies, especially if the child expresses them in play or conversation. The parental response may be directly encouraging or inhibiting of certain types of fantasy. There is some suggestive evidence in a few cases that the n Achievement of parents (measured by using pictures) is related to the n Achievement of their children.[4] The available evidence, while not conclusive, reinforces the notion that certain kinds of fantasies are expressed in families and that these may vary and affect the child's expression of similar ideas.

The discussion of these other leads which require investigation indicates the author's belief that the determinants of n Achievement are undoubtedly very complex. Within the framework of all the possible determinants, this study has shown the importance of the nature of the child's experience in gaining independence and mastery as his learning is guided by his mother. The kinds of goals she chooses to train the child for, the age at which she wants them learned, and her general evaluation of her child's performance have been shown to be of some importance in contributing to the development of his motivation to achieve.

SUMMARY AND CONCLUSIONS

The results indicate that mothers of children with strong achievement motivation differ from mothers of children with weak achievement motivation in the following respects:

a. They make more demands before the age of eight.

b. They evaluate their children's accomplishments higher and are more rewarding.

c. The total number of restrictions made through age ten is less but the total number of restrictions made through age seven is greater.

d. Even though they make more restrictions through age seven the number of demands they make at this early age exceeds the number of restrictions.

No difference between the two groups was found in the total number of demands made, the number and intensity of punishments for demands and restrictions. It is concluded that early training in independence and mastery contributes to the development of strong achievement motivation.

[4] From the initial analysis of data collected by Miss Joanne Steger at Connecticut College, New London, Connecticut.

REFERENCES

1. McClelland, D. C. *Personality.* New York: Wm. Sloane Associates, 1951.
2. McClelland, D. C. Measuring motivation in phantasy: the achievement motive. In H. Guetzkow (Ed.), *Groups, leadership and men.* New York: Carnegie Press, 1951.
3. McClelland, D. C., Atkinson, J. W., Clark, R. A., & Lowell, E. L. *The achievement motive.* New York: Appleton-Century-Crofts, 1953.
4. McClelland, D. C., & Friedman, G. A. A cross-cultural study of the relationship between child-training practices and achievement motivation appearing in folk tales. In G. E. Swanson, T. M. Newcomb, & E. L. Hartley (Eds.), *Readings in social psychology.* New York: Holt, 1952.
5. Winterbottom, Marian R. The relation of childhood training in independence to achievement motivation. Unpublished doctoral dissertation, University of Michigan, 1953.

5.3 The Psychosocial Origins of Achievement Motivation [1]

Bernard C. Rosen and Roy D'Andrade

The purpose of this study is to examine the origins of achievement motivation (*n* Achievement) within the context of the individual's membership in two important groups: family and social class. Specifically, this paper explores, through the observation of family interaction, the relationship be-

[1] This paper is a condensed report of an investigation supported by a research grant (M–1495) to the senior writer from the National Institute of Mental Health, Public Health Service. The generous support, advice, and encouragement of David C. McClelland is gratefully acknowledged. The contributions of James Sakoda for his help on statistical procedures, Shirley Rosen for her work in administering the Thematic Apperception Test and in the preparation of the manuscript, and Marion Winterbottom for her work in scoring the TAT protocols are deeply appreciated. Roland Bonato, Diane D'Andrade, and June Schmelzer assisted in the collection of the data. David Bakum and Thomas Shipley made many helpful suggestions.

A special expression of thanks is due Superintendent Richard C. Briggs, Mansfield School system; Arthur H. Illing, Manchester School system; and Charles Northrup, Windham School system; Principals Stephen J. Ardel, Buchanan School; Harriet Atwood, Highland Park School; David J. DiSessa, Annie Vinton School; Esther Granstrom, Bowers School; Robert L. Perry, Natchaug School; Catherine Shea, Verplanck School; Lawrence Smith, Windham Center School.

tween achievement motivation and certain child-training practices, and the relationship between these practices and the parent's social class membership.

Since many socialization practices are known to be dissimilar between social groups (3, 4), it might be expected that independence training practices would also differ. A study by McClelland et al. (8), later replicated by Rosen (10), demonstrated this to be the case: middle-class parents place greater stress upon independence training than lower-class parents. The deduction from this finding that classes differ in their level of n Achievement was shown to be correct by Rosen (9) who found that, on the average, n Achievement scores for middle-class adolescents were significantly higher than those for their lower-class counterparts.

Significantly, although these studies flow logically from one another, in none of them were all three variables—group membership, child training practices, and n Achievement—studied simultaneously. Furthermore, there were certain gaps in these studies which called for theoretical and methodological modifications and additions. The nature of these gaps, and the contributions which it was the research objective of this study to make, are as follows:

Theoretical. The keystone around which studies of the origins of achievement motivation have been built is the notion that training in independent mastery is an antecedent condition of n Achievement (6, 15). This approach grew out of McClelland's and his associates' theory of the nature and origins of motivation. They argue that all motives are learned, that "they develop out of repeated affective experiences connected with certain types of situations and types of behavior. In the case of achievement motivation, the situation should involve 'standards of excellence,' presumably imposed on the child by the culture, or more particularly by the parents as representatives of the culture, and the behavior should involve either 'competition' with those standards of excellence or attempts to meet them which, if successful, produce positive effects or, if unsuccessful, negative effect. It follows that those cultures or families which stress competition with standards of excellence or which insist *that the child be able to perform certain tasks well by himself* . . . should produce children with high achievement motivation" (7).

Two distinctly different kinds of child-training practices are implicit in this theory. The first is the idea that the child is trained to do things "well"; the second, the notion that he is trained to perform tasks "by himself." The former has been called *achievement training* (2) in that it stresses competition in situations involving standards of excellence; the latter has been called *independence training* in that it involves putting the child on his own. The failure to disentangle these two concepts has resulted in a focus of attention upon independence training largely to the exclusion of achievement training, although the former is primarily concerned with developing self-reliance, often in areas involving self-care-taking (e.g., cleaning, dressing, amusing, or defending oneself). Although both kinds of training practices frequently occur together, they are different in content and consequences and needed to be examined separately.

Methodological. This study departed from two practices common in studies of the origins of *n* Achievement. The first practice is to derive data exclusively from ethnographic materials; the second to obtain information through questionnaire-type interviews with mothers. Interviews and ethnographies can be valuable sources of information, but they are often contaminated by interviewer and respondent biases, particularly those of perceptual distortion, inadequate recall, and deliberate inaccuracies. There was a need for data derived from systematic observation of parent-child relations. . . . In this study, experiments were employed which enabled a team of investigators to observe parent-child interaction in problem-solving situations that were standardized for all groups and required no special competence associated with age or sex.

Hypotheses

This study was designed to provide data that would permit testing two basic hypotheses.

1. Achievement motivation is a result of the following socialization practices: (a) *achievement training,* in which the parents set high goals for their son to attain, indicate that they have a high evaluation of his competence to do a task well, and impose standards of excellence upon tasks against which he is to compete, even in situations where such standards are not explicit; (b) *independence training,* in which the parents indicate to the child that they expect him to be *self-reliant,* while at the same time permit him relative *autonomy* in situations involving decision making where he is given both freedom of action and responsibility for success or failure; (c) *sanctions,* rewards and punishments employed by parents to ensure that their expectations are met and proper behavior is reinforced. Although each contributes to the development of achievement motivation, achievement training is more important than independence training. Neither [is] effective without supporting sanctions.

2. Differences in the mean level of achievement motivation between social classes is in part a function of the differential class emphases upon independence and achievement training: middle-class parents are more likely than lower-class parents to stress self-reliance, autonomy, and achievement in problem-solving situations, particularly those involving standards of excellence. They are more likely to recognize and reward evidences of achievement, as well as to be more sensitive of and punitive toward indications of failure.

The subjects were 120 persons who made up 40 family groups composed of a father, mother, and their son, aged 9, 10, or 11. A Thematic Appperception Test was administered individually and privately to 140 boys aged 9, 10, or 11. The subject was presented with a set of four ambiguous pictures and asked to tell a story about each. His imaginative responses were then scored according to a method developed by McClelland and his associates which involves identifying and counting the frequency with which imagery about evaluated performance in competition with a standard of excellence appears in the thoughts of a person when he tells a brief story under time pressure. This test assumes that the more the individual shows indications of evaluated performance connected with affect in his fantasy, the greater the degree to which achievement motivation is part of his personality (7). The Pearsonian coefficient of correlation between the two scorers was 87. Subjects with scores in the bottom quartile were leveled as having low n Achievement, those with scores in the top quartile as having high n Achievement.

Forty boys, matched by age, race, IQ, and social class were chosen for further study. All were white, native born, and between 9 and 11 years of age; the average was 10 years. Half of the boys had high n Achievement scores, half had low scores. In each achievement motivation category, half of the boys were middle class, half were lower class.

Experimental Tasks

The observers wanted to create an experimental situation from which could be derived objective measures of the parents' response to their son as he engaged in achievement behavior. Tasks were devised which the boy could do and which would involve the parents in their son's task performance. . . . The observation of the parents' behavior as their son engaged in these experimental tasks provided information about the demands and the amount of independence the child had developed in relations with his parents.

In creating the experimental tasks an effort was made to stimulate two conditions normally present when boys are solving problems in the presence of their parents: (1) tasks were constructed to make the boys relatively dependent upon their parents for aid, and (2) the situation was arranged so that the parents either knew the solution to the problem or were in a position to do the task better than their son. . . .

Five tasks were constructed, each designed to attack the problem from a somewhat different angle and yet provide certain classes of data that could be scored across tasks. The five tasks in this study are as follows:

1. *Block Stacking.* The boys were asked to build towers out of very irregularly shaped blocks. They were blindfolded and told to use only one hand in order to create a situation in which the boy was relatively depend-

nt upon his parents for help. His parents were told that this was a test of heir son's ability to build things, and that they could *say* anything to their on but could not touch the blocks. A performance norm was set for the xperiment by telling the parents that the average boy could build a tower f eight blocks; they were asked to write down privately their estimate of ow high they thought their son could build his tower. The purposes of his experiment were (a) to see how high were the parents' aspirations for nd evaluations of their son, e.g., if they set their estimates at above or below he norm; (b) to see how self-reliant they expected or permitted their son o be, e.g., how much help they would give him.

There were three trials for this task. The first provided measures of arental evaluations and aspirations not affected by the boy's performance; he second and third estimates provided measures affected by the boy's erformance. In addition to securing objective measures of parental aspiraion-evaluation levels, the observers scored the interaction between subjects, hus obtaining data as to the kind and amount of instructions the parents ave their son, the amount of help the son asked for or rejected, and the mount and kind of affect generated during the experiment.

2. *Anagrams.* In this task the boys were asked to make words of three etters or more out of six prescribed letters: G, H, K, N, O, R. The letters, vhich could be reused after each word was made, were printed on wooden locks so that they could be manipulated The parents were given three dditional letter blocks, T, U, and B, and a list of words that could be uilt with each new letter. They were informed that they could give the boy new letter (in the sequence T, U, B) whenever they wished and could ay anything to him, short of telling him what word to build. There was a 0-minute time limit for this experiment. [Since this is a familiar game, no fforts were made to explain the functions of the task.]

3. *Patterns.* In this experiment the parents were shown eight patterns, raduated in difficulty, that could be made with Kohs blocks. The subjects vere informed that pattern 1 was easier to make than pattern 2, pattern 3 vas more difficult than 2, but easier than 4, and so forth. The subjects were old this was a test of the boy's ability to remember and reproduce patterns uickly and accurately. Each parent and boy was asked to select privately hree patterns which the boy would be asked to make from memory after aving seen the pattern for 5 seconds. All three patterns were chosen *before* he boy began the problem solving so that his performance in this task vould not affect the choice of the patterns. Where there were differences of hoice, [the subjects were asked to make a group decision. The observers cored] (a) the number of acts each subject contributed to the decision-aaking process, (b) the number of times each individual imitated a decision, nd (c) the number of times each subject was successful in having the group ccept his decision or in seeing to it that a decision was made.

4. *Ring Toss.* In this experiment each member of the group was asked to choose privately ten positions, from each of which the boy was to throw three rings at a peg. The distance from the peg was delineated by a tape with 1-foot graduations laid on the floor. The subjects were told that this was a test of discrimination and judgment and that after each set of three tosses they would be asked to make a judgment as to the best distance from which to make the next set of tosses. Group decisions were made as to where the boys should stand.

5. *Hatrack.* The Maier Hatrack Problem was used in this experiment. The boy was given two sticks and a C-clamp and instructed to build a rack strong enough to hold a coat and hat. His parents were told that this was a test of the boy's ability to build things. In this task no one was given the solution at the beginning of the experiment. For the first time the parents had no advantage over the boy—a most uncomfortable position for many parents, particularly the fathers. This stress situation was created deliberately to maximize the possibility of the problem generating effect, as was often the case, with some hostility being directed at the observers. After seven minutes the parents were given the solution to the problem.

EXPERIMENTAL FINDINGS

Achievement Training and Achievement Motivation

Measures of achievement training were obtained from the estimates and choices made by the parents in three tasks: Block Stacking, Patterns, and Ring Toss. Each task provided measures of achievement training which though positively related to one another, were sufficiently independent to require their being treated as separate scores. . . .

Parental Aspirations and Evaluations

The parents' estimates of how well their son would do in the Block Stacking task are considered measures of their aspirations for and evaluations of him. In this case the estimates were made against a stated norm. The parents' first estimate, unaffected by any previous performance in this task, is conceived to be primarily a measure of parental aspirations for the boy. . . The fathers and mothers of boys with high n Achievement scores on the average give higher estimates, but the differences are not statistically significant. However, when father's and mother's scores are summed together the differences between parental group is significant ($F = 4.09$, $p < .05$).

The score for the second and third trials was considered as a measure of the parents' aspiration evaluation of the boy as affected by his performance against a given standard of excellence. . . . The data show that the mothers of boys with high n Achievement scores give considerably higher estimates for the second and third trials of this task than do the mothers of boys with low scores ($F = 10.28$, $p < .005$). The differences between the fathers, although in the predicted direction in that the fathers of boys with high n

Achievement scores tend to give higher estimates, are not statistically significant.

The Patterns task was designed to provide additional and supplemental measures of parental aspiration-evaluation levels. . . .

We had expected that the parents of boys with high achievement motivation scores would choose the more difficult patterns for their sons. The data indicate a difference in this direction, but the differences are small and not significant for either parent.

Parental Standards of Excellence

In the last two experiments, parents had been asked to make their estimates or choices in situations where standards were explicit (as in the Block Stacking task where a group performance norm had been given, or in the Patterns task where the complexity of the patterns had been clearly graded by the experimenters) and therefore it could not be clearly seen whether parents differed in their tendencies to impose standards upon the problems their children were expected to solve. The Ring Toss experiment was devised for this purpose. In this experiment no norm or group standard of excellence was set by the investigators. Each parent was asked to make ten choices of "the best place for your son to stand." After each choice the boy threw three rings at the peg. A measure of the height of the standard of excellence each parent sets for the boy was derived by summing the choices (number of feet the boy is asked to stand from the peg) of each parent. . . . The fathers and mothers of high n Achievement boys, on the average, chose positions further from the peg than the parents of children with low achievement motivation. The differences, however, are significant only in the case of the mothers ($F = 5.47$, $p < .25$). Combining the scores for fathers and mothers increases the differences between parental groups ($F = 6.99$, $p < .01$).

The Anagrams experiment involved another task for which the investigators had set no explicit standard of excellence [and] . . . had been designed primarily to provide measures of independence training. The sum of the times at which new letters (the parents shared three letters) were given by both (or either) parents was treated originally as a measure of self-reliance training, i.e., the longer the parents delayed in giving the boy new letters the more indication that they expected him to work longer and harder at a problem on his own. This experiment revealed a clear difference between parental groups but not in the direction we predicted: the parents of high n Achievement boys gave new letters *sooner* than the parents of boys with low Achievement ($F = 6.28$, $p < .025$).

This finding . . . prompted a reevaluation of the task and a further (albeit a post facto) interpretation of the data. . . . We were mistaken in assuming that this task would only measure self-reliance training. . . . The parents (especially the mothers) of boys with strong achievement motivation . . . tended to perceive the task not so much as one which their son should do on his own, *but as a challenge to do well.* The boy with strong motivation tended to receive letters sooner, we believe, because his parents were eager to see him make more words and because of their reluctance to frustrate him to a point where his motive to excel in this important area would be destroyed.

Achievement Training and Performance Levels

The behavior of people with high achievement motivation is characterized by persistent striving and general competitiveness. It would follow from this, other things being equal, that boys with high achievement motivation would perform better than those with low motivation. Boys with high *n* Achievement tend to build higher towers of blocks, construct patterns faster, and make more words in the Anagrams task. The differences are significant in the case of the Block Stacking task ($F = 8.16$, $p < .005$), but not for the Patterns and Anagrams experiments. In the latter two tasks the individual's performance is very greatly affected by his intelligence. Since IQ score was one of the variables controlled in this study, . . . the superior performance of high *n* Achievement boys appears to be more a function of greater self-reliance and zest in competitive activity than of intelligence. Thus, boys with high achievement motivation tend to ask for less aid . . . are more likely to reject offers of help from ther parents . . ., and appear to get more pleasure out of participating in the experiments—they show less evidence of negative affect . . . and more of positive feelings . . . . Although for only one of these variables—ask aid ($F = 5.76$, $p < .05$)—is there significant difference between groups, the direction of the differences in all four cases consistently points to greater self-reliance and self-assurance on the part of boys with high need for achievement.

In the Ring Toss experiment there was no question of whether superior performance by high *n* Achievement boys had influenced their parents to make significantly higher choices, because in this task high *n* Achievement boys were less successful in placing rings around the peg than their low Achievement peers. The reason for this is simple: the parents of high *n* Achievement boys tended to place their sons farther away from the peg and consequently the number of their successes were smaller; the tetrachoric correlation between the number of successes and the distance away from the peg is —.31.

INDEPENDENCE TRAINING, SANCTIONS, AND
ACHIEVEMENT MOTIVATION

Earlier we distinguished between achievement training and independence training; the latter was broken down into two components: self-reliance training and the granting of relative autonomy in decision making. Associated with *both* independence and achievement training are sanctions—rewards and punishments—administered by the parents to reinforce ap propriate behavior in the child. The data to index these variables were obtained by examining the interaction between parents and child as they engaged in the experimental tasks, and by observing the decision-making process in those instances where the subjects were asked to make a group estimate or choice of what the boy should do.

Sanctions

Typically, positive and negative reinforcements are associated with any learning situation—rewards for success and punishment for failure. We had predicted that the parents of boys with high achievement motivation would score higher on Warmth (positive affect) and lower on Rejection (negative affect) than the parents of low n Achievement boys. The data show that the mothers of high n Achievement boys score significantly higher on Warmth than the mothers of low n Achievement boys ($F = 8.87$, $p <$ .01). The differences between fathers, although in the predicted direction, are not significant ($F = 4.13$, $p < 1.0$).

Parental Profiles and Motivation

In the analysis of data so far the relationship of each variable to achievement motivation was examined separately. The Split Plot type of analysis of variance was next employed to permit the examination of all variables simultaneously for each parent. . . . A mean score for each variable for fathers and mothers was computed and the distance from the mean in standard deviations was plotted; the profiles for fathers are shown in Chart 1, for mothers in Chart 2.

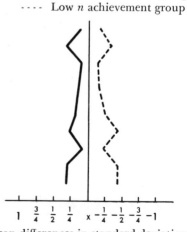

—— High n achievement group
- - - - Low n achievement group

Fewer specific directions
More nonspecific directions
Fewer pushing statements
More autonomy
Less rejection
More warmth
Total choice, Ring Toss
Total estimates, Patterns
2nd and 3rd estimates, Block Stacking
1st estimate, Block Stacking

$$1 \quad \tfrac{3}{4} \quad \tfrac{1}{2} \quad \tfrac{1}{4} \quad x \quad -\tfrac{1}{4} \quad -\tfrac{1}{2} \quad -\tfrac{3}{4} \quad -1$$

Mean differences in standard deviations

CHART 1. Profiles for fathers: High n Achievement group and low n Achievement group.

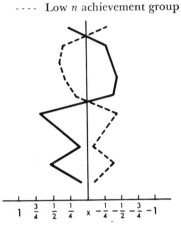

Fewer specific directions
More nonspecific directions
Fewer pushing statements
More autonomy
Less rejection
More warmth
Total choice, Ring Toss
Total estimates, Patterns
2nd and 3rd estimates, Block Stacking
1st estimate, Block Stacking

Mean differences in standard deviations

CHART 2. Profiles for mothers: High *n* Achievement group and low *n* Achievement group.

A Split Plot analysis of variance reveals that there are significant differences *in levels* between the profiles of the parents of boys with high achievement motivation and the parents of boys with low *n* Achievement. The difference in levels for fathers is greater ($F = 10.09$, $p < .005$) than for mothers ($F = 4.77$, $p < .05$). By difference in level we mean that when the scores for each variable are summed for each parent, the parents of high *n* Achievement boys have a significantly higher *total* score than the parents of low *n* Achievement boys. Thus, although some variables are not significant when tested separately, and others only barely significant, when the scores of all the variables are pooled together each contributes something to the total variance and the result is a significant difference between groups. This is most apparent in Chart 1 where the fathers' profiles are compared. It can be seen that the mean scores for the fathers of boys with high achievement motivation are higher for every variable, where "highness" was predicted as being positively related to high *n* Achievement. It should be remembered that the scores for S, P, Rejection, and Autonomy were reversed so that what appears as a "high" score in the chart is in fact, a low score. In the case of these four variables, low parental scores were predicted as tending to produce high *n* Achievement. The difference between the two groups of fathers is not great, it is the *consistency* of the direction of these differences which when summed together make for a significant difference between the two groups. . . .

The profiles for mothers are not parallel so that, even when level differences are taken out, the profiles for the mothers of high *n* Achievement boys remains significantly different from that of the mothers of low n Achievement boys ($F = 2.30$, $p < .025$). . . . There are . . . some reversals in that mothers of high n Achievement boys give fewer nonspecific directions, more pushing statements, and are more dominant than the mothers of low n Achievement boys.

Social Class and Child-Training Practices

The data reveal class differences, but with one exception they are not significant; nor is it always the middle-class group whose scores are in the direction hypothesized as generating high n Achievement. . . . The one clear difference between middle- and lower-class parents for a measure of achievement training is Total Choices, Ring Toss. In this case it is the lower-class parent who tends to place the boy farthest away from the peg ($F = 6.99$, $p < .01$), quite in variance with what we had anticipated, and for which no satisfactory explanation can be offered. . . .

In the case of our two measures of sanctions, Warmth and Rejection, we found, as was expected, that the middle-class father and mother are warmer and less rejecting than lower-class parents. The greatest difference is among fathers ($F = 4.13$, $p < .06$).

These data, though sometimes in the direction predicted, indicate that the training practices of middle-class parents are not on the whole markedly different from those of lower-class parents. However, it may be that by controlling n Achievement we, in effect, cancelled out for this sample any differences in training which might normally differentiate the social classes.

DISCUSSION AND SUMMARY

The question of how achievement training, independence training, and sanctions are related to achievement motivation may be rephrased by asking, How does the behavior of parents of boys with high n Achievement differ from the behavior of parents whose sons have low n Achievement?

. . . The observers' subjective impressions are that the parents of high n Achievement boys tend to be more competitive, show more involvement, seem to take more pleasure in the problem-solving experiments, [appear to be] more interested and concerned with their son's performance; they tend to give him more things to manipulate rather than fewer; on the average they put out more affective acts. More objective data show that the parents of a boy with high n Achievement tend to have higher aspirations for him to do well at any given task, and they seem to have a higher regard for his competence at problem solving. They set up standards of excellence for the boy even when none is given, or if a standard is given will expect him to do "better than average." As he progresses they tend to react to his performance with warmth and approval, or, in the case of the mothers especially, with disapproval if he performs poorly.

Fathers and mothers both provide achievement training and independence training, but the fathers seem to contribute much more to the latter than do the mothers. Fathers tend to let their sons develop self-reliance by giving hints . . . rather than always telling "how to do it" . . . They are less likely to push . . . and more likely to give the boy a greater degree of autonomy in making his own decisions. Father of high n Achievement boys often appear to be competent men who are willing to take a back seat while their sons are performing. They tend to beckon from ahead rather than push from behind.

The mothers of boys with high achievement motivation tend to stress achievement training rather than independence training. In fact, they are likely to be more dominant and to expect less self-reliance than the mothers of boys with low n Achievement. But their aspirations for their sons are higher and their concern over success greater. Thus, they expect the boys to build higher towers and place them farther away from the peg in the Ring Toss experiment. As a boy works his mother tends to become emotionally involved. Not only is she more likely to reward him with approval (Warmth) but also to punish him with hostility (Rejection). *In a way, it is this factor of involvement that most clearly sets the mothers of high* n *Achievement boys apart from the mothers of low* n *Achievement boys:* the former score higher on every variable, except specific direction. And although these mothers are likely to give them less option about doing something and doing it well, observers report that the mothers of high n Achievement boys tend to be striving, competent persons. Apparently they expect their sons to be the same.

The different emphasis which the fathers and mothers of high n Achievement boys place upon achievement and independence training suggests that the training practices of father and mother affect the boy in different ways. Apparently, the boy can take and perhaps needs achievement training from both parents, but the effects of independence training and sanctions, in particular Autonomy and Rejection, are different depending upon whether they come from the father or mother. In order for high n Achievement to develop, the boy appears to need more autonomy from his father than from his mother. The father who gives the boy a relatively high degree of autonomy provides him with an opportunity to compete on his own ground, to test his skill, and to gain a sense of confidence in his own competence. The dominating father may crush his son (and in so doing destroys the boy's achievement motive), perhaps because he views the boy as a competitor and is viewed as such by his son. On the other hand, the mother who dominates the decision-making process does not seem to have the same affect on the boy, possibly because she is perceived as *imposing her standards* on the boy, while a dominating father is perceived as *imposing himself* on the son. It may be that the mother-son relations are typically more secure than those between father and son, so that the boy is better able to accept higher levels of dominance and rejection from his mother than his father without adverse affect on his need to achieve. Relatively rejecting, dominating fathers, particularly those with less than average warmth—as tended to be the case with the fathers of low *n* Achievement boys—seem to be a threat to the boy[s] and a deterrent to the development of *n* Achievement. On the other hand, above-average dominance and rejection, coupled with above-average warmth, as tends to be the case with mothers of high *n* Achievement boys, appear to be a spur to achievement motivation. It will be remembered that the fathers of high *n* Achievement boys are on the average less Rejecting, less Pushing, and less Dominant—all of which points to their general hands-off policy.

REFERENCES

1. Bales, R. F. *Interaction process analysis*. Cambridge, Mass.: Addison-Wesley, 1951.
2. Child, I. L., Storm, T., & Veroff, J. Achievement themes in folk tales related to socialization practice. In J. W. Atkinson (Ed.), *Motives in fantasy, action and society*. Princeton, N.J.: Van Nostrand, 1958.
3. Erickson, M. C. Social status and child-rearing practices. In T. Newcomb and E. Hartley (Eds.), *Readings in social psychology*, New York: Holt, 1947.
4. Havighurst, R. J., & Davis, A. Social class differences in child-rearing. *Amer. sociol. Rev.*, 1955, **20,** 438–442.
5. Hollingshead, A., & Redlich, F. Social stratification and psychiatric disorders. *Amer. sociol. Rev.*, 1953, **18,** 163–169.
6. McClelland, D. C., & Friedman, G. A. A cross-cultural study of the relationship between child-training practices and achievement motivation, appearing in folk tales. In G. E. Swanson, Newcomb, T. M., & Hartley, E. L. (Eds.), *Readings in social psychology,* New York: Holt, 1952.
7. McClelland, D. C., Atkinson, J. W., Clark, R., & Lowell, E. *The achievement motive*. New York: Appleton-Century-Crofts, 1953.
8. McClelland, D. C., Rindlisbacher, A., & deCharms, R. Religious and other sources of parental attitudes toward independence training. In D. C. McClelland (Ed.), Studies in motivation. New York: Appleton-Century-Crofts, 1955.
9. Rosen, B. C. The achievement syndrome: a psychocultural dimension of social stratification. *Amer. sociol. Rev.*, 1956, **21,** 203–211.
10. Rosen, B. C., ethnicity, and the achievement syndrome. *Amer. sociol. Rev.*, 1959, **24,** 47–60.
11. Sakoda, J. M. Directions for a multiple-group method of factor analysis. Mimeographed paper, University of Connecticut, June, 1955.
12. Sears, R. R., Maccoby, Eleanor E., & Levin, H. *Patterns of child rearing*. Evanston, Ill.: Row, Peterson, 1957.
13. Strodtbeck, F. L. Family interaction, values, and achievement. In D. C. McClelland, A. L. Baldwin, U. Bronfenbrenner, & F. L. Strodtbeck (Eds.), *Talent and society*. Princeton, N.J.: Van Nostrand, 1958.

14. Tryon, R. C. *Cluster analysis*. Ann Arbor, Mich.: Edwards Brothers, 1939.
15. Winterbottom, M. R. The relation of need for achievement to learning experiences in independence and mastery. In J. W. Atkinson. *Motives in fantasy, action, and society*. Princeton, N.J.: Van Nostrand, 1958.

5.4 Effects of Discrepancies between Observed and Imposed Reward Criteria on their Acquisition and Transmission [1]

Walter Mischel and Robert M. Liebert

A critical aspect of self-control is the individual's own self-administration and regulation of the rewards and punishments which are available to him without external contraints. Humans evaluate their own performance and frequently set standards which determine, in part, the conditions under which they self-administer or withhold numerous readily available gratifications and a multitude of self-punishments. Failure to meet widely varying self-imposed performance standards often results in self-denial or even harsher self-punishments whereas attainment of difficult criteria more typically leads to liberal self-reward and a variety of self-congratulatory responses. Although research concentrating on infrahumans may find it easy to neglect this phenomenon, it is apparent that for humans self-administered reinforcers constitute powerful incentives for learning and potent reinforcers for the maintenance of behavior patterns. In spite of the importance of self-reward as a human process there have been relatively few experimental investigations of its antecedents.

Kanfer and Marston (1936b) provide some support for the direct conditioning of "self-reinforcing responses" and found that adults who were encouraged for judging their responses as accurate on an ambiguous noncontingent task increased their rate of self-reinforcement and rewarded themselves more frequently on a new learning task than those who were discouraged from judging their responses as accurate. The same authors also found that the frequency of self-reinforcement is partly dependent on such

[1] This study was supported by Research Grant M-06830 from the National Institutes of Health, United States Public Health Service. Grateful acknowledgment is due to the administrators and teachers of the Whisman School District who generously cooperated in this research. The help of Karen Nesbitt and Laura Gellman who served as the "models" is also acknowledged.

Reprinted from the *Journal of Personality and Social Psychology* 1966, **3**, 45–53, by permission of the authors and the American Psychological Association.

variables as the correctness of the individual's responses and the degree of similarity between the training and generalization tasks (Kanfer, Bradley, & Marston, 1962; Kanfer & Marston, 1963a).

An effective means of influencing children to adopt particular self-reward criteria consists of exposing them to the criteria exhibited by models. It has been demonstrated that mere observation of a model's self-reward patterns, without direct reinforcement to the observer, can result in their adoption by the observer even in the model's absence (Bandura & Kupers, 1964).

In life situations reward standards usually are transmitted by individuals who exhibit their own self-reward criteria and also reinforce the observer's adherence to particular criteria. The modeled and directly reinforced behaviors may not be congruent and the criteria used by social agents for administering rewards to themselves often are discrepant with the standards which they directly impose on others. Consider, for example, the father who tries to influence his child towards self-denial and work while he simultaneously and persistently indulges himself. Although frequent reference is made to the importance of "consistency" in child-rearing practices, usually this refers to consistency in the use of direct training techniques across different situations and the effects of consistency or discrepancy between direct training and modeling procedures remain unexplored. The present study therefore investigated the effects of discrepancies in the stringency of the self-reward criteria used by an adult and the standards he imposed on a child.

Children participated with a female adult model in a task which seemingly required skill but on which scores were experimentally controlled. A plentiful supply of tokens which could be exchanged for rewards was available to both the model and the subject. In one experimental group the model rewarded herself only for high performances but guided the subject to reward himself for lower achievements; in a second condition the model rewarded herself for low performances but led the subject to reward himself only for higher achievements; in the third group the model rewarded herself only for high performances and guided the child to reward himself only for equally high achievements. After exposure to these experimental procedures measures were obtained of the children's self-reward patterns displayed in the model's absence.

The following hypotheses were advanced concerning children's reward criteria in the absence of the model as a function of the initial standards imposed on them and displayed by the model.

It was reasoned that the reward criteria adopted by subjects will be a function of both the criteria they observed a model use for herself and those she imposed on them directly. When the observed and imposed criteria are consistent they should be adopted most readily. Therefore, greatest stringency will be shown by children who were held to a stringent standard and also observed a model who was stringent with herself. These children should be more likely to use higher standards for reward than either children who received the same stringent direct training but observed a lenient model or those who were permitted leniency themselves. Moreover, when the observed and imposed criteria are discrepant, the less stringent alternative will be adopted. When the criterion leading to more reward is the one that subjects were directly trained to adopt they should have little conflict about rewarding themselves generously in the model's absence and should maintain the lenient criterion on which they were trained. In contrast, those who were trained to be stringent but observed a more lenient model should be tempted to reward themselves more liberally when there are no external constraints. In the model's absence their behavior should reflect conflict about adopting the lower criteria yielding more frequent reward used by their own model and the more stringent standards which had been imposed on them. Therefore it was anticipated that subjects would adopt lenient criteria more frequently when they had been permitted greater leniency themselves than when they observed it in another.

The design also investigated the effects of the children's role on their self-administered reward schedules and on the criteria they imposed upon others. When there is a discrepancy between the reward criteria imposed on the child and the standards he observed used by the model the criteria that the child adopts in the model's absence and in the absence of other external constraints may be affected by his role. First, the subject may more readily adopt his model's criteria, as opposed to those on which he received direct training, when he himself becomes the model or demonstrator for another person than when he remains in the role of only a performer. Second, given that each subject is placed in both roles, and becomes both a demonstrator and a performer, the sequence in which these roles occur may affect the extent to which he adopts the criteria displayed by his model or those to which he was directly trained. Specifically, if following the initial interactions with the model the situation is structured so that the child immediately becomes the model or demonstrator for another person (say a younger child) he may be more likely to adopt the pattern displayed by his own model than if he is given this role after he has already practiced extensively as a performer. If such effects occur they would indicate that role factors may be important determinants of the acquisition and transmission of self-reward patterns. In contrast, if the criteria adopted by the child, both for his self-reward and for rewarding others, are primarily a function of his prior experience with observed and imposed reward standards as discussed above, the effect of such role variables would be minimal.

The following manipulations were used to test the effect of placing the child into the role of model or demonstrator as opposed to the role of performer and of varying the sequence of these roles. After the child's interaction with the adult model, half the children became "demonstrators" of the game for another younger child, alternating with him for a series of trials, and thereafter performed alone on additional trials. Half the subjects participated in the reverse sequence, first performing alone and then alternating trials with a younger child to whom they demonstrated the game. Both sequences took place in the absence of the experimenter as well as the model.

It is apparent from the above that the design permitted investigation of the effects of the independent variables not only on the acquisition of self-reward criteria but also on the transmission of these standards by subjects to others (the younger child) when the subject controls the available reinforcers. No differences in the criteria used by the subject for himself and those he imposes on the other child were anticipated. That is, the same between-treatment differences predicted for self-reward criteria were expected for the transmission of these standards to another person.

METHOD

Subjects and Experimenters

Subjects were 54 fourth-grade children (30 boys and 24 girls) from two elementary schools in the Stanford area. One adult male was the experimenter for all subjects. Two adult females served as models, with one model used for each subject. Each model was employed with an equal number of children from each treatment condition. In the phases of the experiment dealing with the transmission of reward criteria, each experimental subject was confronted with a younger child. The younger child was always drawn from the second grade of the subject's school and was of the same sex as the subject. A different second-grade child was used with each experimental subject.

Summary of Design

Each subject was randomly assigned to one of three model-subject interactions. One third of the children observed stringent reward criteria modeled but were led to use lenient criteria; one third observed lenient reward criteria modeled but were led to use stringent criteria; the remainder observed a model who used stringent criteria for herself and applied the same criteria to the child. Thereafter, in the absence of the model, half the subjects in each group demonstrated the game to another younger child and then performed alone, whereas the other half went through the reverse sequence, first performing alone and then demonstrating.

Apparatus

The apparatus was a modification of a bowling game used by Bandura and Whalen (1966) and consisted of a miniature bowling alley with a 3 foot runway at the end of which there were seven signal lights. Each light was labeled with a score, the score of 5 occurring once whereas scores of 10, 15, and 20 each appeared twice. The lights and scores were displayed on an upright partition facing the bowler. Whereas the Bandura and Whalen apparatus was controlled manually by the experimenter, the present version contained a series of concealed electronic relay switches which were preset for each subject in order to control in a standardized manner the entire sequence of scores for all trials. This apparatus permitted all trials to occur in the absence of the experimenter and the latter recorded all data from behind a one-way observation window. The target area was screened from the subject's view by shields which covered the terminal area of the runway and encircled the ostensible targets so that the child had no knowledge of whether or not the bowling balls were striking the target area and was dependent on the electric score signals for feedback. Pretesting indicated that the procedure appealed to the subjects and no doubts were raised about its credibility.

Procedure

Each subject was taken individually by the experimenter from his classroom to a three-room research trailer located on the school premises. The experimenter said he was from a toy company and that a new toy, something like a bowling game, was being tried out on children of this age group to see how they liked it. Upon reaching the trailer, the subject was introduced to the female experimental confederate who served as the model and was told that she would show him the game. The experimenter then left and observed and recorded the procedure from the trailer's observation room.

The model showed and explained the game to the child and demonstrated by rolling one trial, also indicating that both players would write down their scores on special score sheets at the end of each roll. She then called attention to a bowl of white chips, used as tokens, and explained that "the chips are worth valuable prizes at the end, and the more chips, the better the prize." Wrapped packages of toys were visible in the trailer. No other statements describing the reward tokens were made and each player was given a container for collecting his tokens. Tokens, rather than candy or other rewards, were used to avoid satiation effects during the experiment. The model and child alternated turns for a total of 10 trials each, the model taking the first turn. The scores for both model and child were always in a fixed 10-trial sequence and the same sequence was used in each series of subsequent test trials described below. The model's program was 5, 20, 10, 15, 15, 20, 20, 10, 20, 15, whereas the subject's program was always 20, 10, 15, 20, 20, 5, 15, 5, 10, 5.

Discrepancies between Modeled and Imposed Reward Criteria

The model-subject discrepancy treatments involved the following variations in the discrepancy of the scores for which the model rewarded herself and those for which she guided the subject to reward himself.

In the *stringent criterion modeled lenient criterion imposed* treatment (M_{20}, $S_{15/20}$) the model rewarded herself only for scores of 20 but led the subject to reward himself for scores of 15 or 20. Whenever the model's score was 20 she took a token and made approving comments such as, "That's a good score. That deserves a chip." or "I can be proud of that score. I should treat myself for that." In contrast, whenever her score was below the criterion of 20 she refrained from taking a token and commented with obvious self-disapproval, "That's not a very good score. That doesn't deserve a chip." or "Well, I can't be very proud of that. I can't treat myself for that low score." Using a fixed memorized script she addressed similar approving comments to the child whenever his score was either 15 or 20 and made parallel critical comments whenever his score was below 15.

In the *lenient criterion modeled, stringent criterion imposed* condition ($M_{15/20}$, S_{20}) the model used the same pattern of self-reward and self-disapproval and applied the same positive and negative commentary to the child's performance, but adopted a lower performance level for rewarding her own performance, while using a higher performance level for positively evaluating the child's performance. When the model's score was either 15 or 20 she expressed approval and helped herself to a token and when her scores were below 15 she expressed disapproval at her own performance and refrained from rewarding herself. However, she showed approval of the child's performance and commented that a chip was deserved only on trials when the child's score was 20, making her negative comments for all lower scores.

In the *stringent criterion modeled, stringent criterion imposed* condition (M_{20}, S_{20}) the model displayed her self-reward pattern only for scores of 20 and likewise commented positively on the child's performance only when he obtained scores of 20, indicating for all other performances that they did not deserve a chip and showing dissatisfaction.

Previous research (Bandura & Kupers, 1964) has already demonstrated that children exposed to a model's self-reward criteria in a similar experimental situation adopt the model's criteria whereas children in a no-model control group adopt essentially randomly distributed self-reward patterns that are unrelated to performance level. A no-model group therefore was not employed in the present study.

After both model and subject completed 10 trials the model said she had to leave and did so, collecting her own chips with enthusiasm and noting they would be exchanged now for valuable prizes. The experimenter returned and spent 5 minutes with the child on a simple unrelated guessing game which was used to reduce any immediate emotional arousal resulting from the treatments before the next phase of the experiment commenced.

Role Treatments

After the model-subject interactions described above, the following variations were used to investigate role effects. Namely, half the children in each model-subject discrepancy treatment were left alone for 10 trials to be performers (P) by themselves. The experimenter instructed them to bowl and help themselves to rewards as they pleased and then exited. Following these 10 trials the experimenter reentered with a younger child (O). He introduced the two children, asking the subject to demonstrate (D) the game to O, and left the two alone with each other until they had alternated turns for 10 trials each. This was the performer-demonstrator or P-D sequence. With the other half of the subjects in each treatment group the above sequence was reversed. These subjects immediately demonstrated the game to the younger child, the two children taking turns for 10 trials each, and thereafter the subject was left alone to perform by himself for another 10 trials (demonstrator-performer or D-P sequence). Thus, by comparing behavior when the subject is a performer and when he is a demonstrator basic role differences can be tested, and by comparing the P-D and D-P orders role sequence effects may be examined.

Measures of Reward Patterns

The dependent measures collected from subjects in both sequences were the scores for which self-reward occurred when performing alone (self-reward when performer), when demonstrating the game to the other child (self-reward when demonstrator), as well as the scores for which the subject rewarded the other child (rewards other). All dependent measures were collected in the absence of both the model and experimenter and were recorded by the latter through an observation window.

RESULTS

Inspection of the data in each treatment for males and females separately indicated no trends for sex differences and male and female data were therefore combined for all analyses. More than 92% of all subjects used either scores of 20-only or scores of 15 or 20 as the reward criteria. The data therefore required a nonparametric test and chi-square comparisons of reward for scores of 20-only as opposed to scores below 20 were used in all contingency tables with N greater than 20.[2] Fisher exact tests were used when N was below 20.

The experimental procedures used to guide the subject to reward himself only for particular contingencies in the model's presence, by means of the model's verbal approval and disapproval, were completely effective. In all treatment conditions subjects without exception rewarded themselves in the model's presence whenever she indicated that the score was deserving and never when she commented negatively on the performance. The effectiveness of this guidance procedure made it possible to use all subjects for investigating the effects of the experimental variables on behavior in the model's absence.

[2] All chi-squares were corrected for continuity.

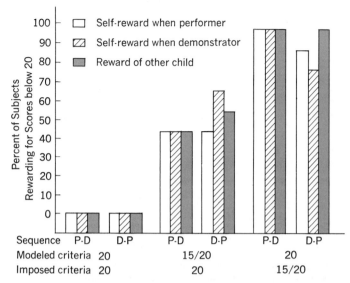

FIGURE 1. Self-reward when the subject is a performer or a demonstrator and reward of the other child, as a function of the performer-demonstrator (P-D) or demonstrator-performer (D-P) sequence and the initial criteria exhibited by the model and imposed on the subject.

Figure 1 shows the percentage of subjects who administered rewards for scores below 20 in each treatment group in all model-absent phases of the experiment. Note that whether the child was a performer first or a demonstrator first did not appear to affect appreciably his reward criteria within each model-subject discrepancy treatment. Fisher exact test comparisons of subjects who rewarded for scores below 20 as opposed to scores of 20-only in the P-D as opposed to the D-P sequence within each discrepancy treatment yielded no p values approaching significance. Therefore, subsequent comparisons between discrepancy treatments combined subjects from both the D-P and P-D sequences.

Comparisons of the discrepancy treatments for each phase of the experiment separately, are summarized in Table 1. The findings clearly support the hypotheses. The greatest stringency was shown by subjects who observed a stringent model and were themselves held to the same stringent criterion (M_{20}, S_{20}). These children made reward contingent on a higher performance level more often than those who obtained identical direct training but from a model who used a more lenient criterion for her own self-reward ($M_{15/20}$, S_{20}). Likewise, comparisons between discrepancy groups showed, as expected, that children who were trained on a stringent criterion but observed a more lenient model ($M_{15/20}$, S_{20}) were more frequently stringent than those who

TABLE 1. Treatment Comparisons of Subjects Rewarding for Scores of 20-Only or Scores Below 20 in Each Phase

Treatment comparisons	Phases		
	Self-reward (performer) χ^2	Self-reward (demonstrator) χ^2	Rewards other child χ^2
M_{20}, S_{20} versus $M_{15/20}$, S_{20} [a]	7.8 **	11.2 ***	9.48 **
$M_{15/20}$, S_{20} versus M_{20}, $S_{15/20}$ [a]	8.1 **	3.46 *	9.48 **
M_{20}, $S_{15/20}$ [a] versus M_{20}, S_{20}	28.53 ***	25.3 ***	32.1 ***

Note.—All chi-squares corrected for continuity, $df = 1$.

[a] Indicates the treatment in each comparison in which more subjects rewarded for scores below 20; M = modeled criterion, S = criterion, imposed on subject.

 * $p < .10$, two-tailed.
 ** $p < .01$, two-tailed.
 *** $p < .001$, two-tailed.

were permitted more lenient self-reward but observed a model who was stringent in her own self-reward (M_{20}, $S_{15/20}$).

Moreover, these differences hold at each phase of the experiment: the treatments affected the subject's self-reward both as a performer and as a demonstrator as well as the reward criteria he imposed on the younger child when demonstrating the game to him. It is of interest that the effects resulted in p values less than .01 in all but one instance. The one exception was the chi-square comparison of self-reward in the two discrepancy treatments when the subject served as a demonstrator and this yielded the least impressive p value ($< .10$, two-tailed). Closer examination of these data with Fisher exact tests revealed that for this phase the discrepancy treatments resulted in the expected differences when the subject served as a performer first ($p < .025$) but not when he served as a demonstrator first ($p < .30$). Thus, although the D-P as opposed to the P-D role sequences resulted in no significant differences within each discrepancy treatment, apparently they did, in this instance, act as mediating variables affecting differences between the discrepancy treatments. The lack of difference between the two discrepancy treatments on the self-reward schedule used when the subject was initially in the role of a demonstrator seems due to the more frequent adoption by these children of the model's own reward criteria rather than the criteria that the model imposed on them. These trends are reflected graphically in Figure 1 which shows a tendency for subjects in the D-P sequence in each discrepancy condition to adopt the model's standards rather than those imposed on them.

The children tended to use the same criteria for administering rewards in each phase of the experiment (Figure 1). When the modeled and imposed reward standards were the same (M_{20}, S_{20}) all subjects rewarded themselves for the same criteria when performing alone and when demonstrating, and applied the same standards to the younger child. Likewise, when the modeled and imposed reward criteria were discrepant, subjects in the P-D sequence showed perfect consistency in the reward criteria they employed across all phases of the experiment. In contrast, however, among the 18 children in the two discrepancy treatments who were in the D-P sequence, 5 used different criteria for themselves when serving as demonstrators and when performing alone. When they served as demonstrators, 4 of these subjects rewarded themselves for the same criteria that their model had used for herself rather than in accord with the standards she had imposed on them. This occurred with equal frequency in both discrepancy treatments. In the treatment in which the model had been stringent but had permitted leniency, 2 children rewarded themselves more stringently when demonstrating than when performing. Likewise, in the treatment in which the model had been lenient but had guided the child to be stringent, 2 children rewarded themselves more leniently when they served as demonstrators than when they performed alone. These trends, while not significant, suggest that emulation of the model occurs more readily when the child is immediately placed in the role of a model himself than when he is placed initially in the role of a performer. Comparisons of the number of subjects in the D-P as opposed to the P-D sequence who used the same criteria for themselves when they served as demonstrators and when they performed alone revealed that children who began as demonstrators tended to use different criteria more often than those who began as performers ($\chi^2 = 3.71$, $df = 1$, $p < .06$).

DISCUSSION

The results of this experiment show that patterns of self-reinforcement may be affected jointly by the criteria displayed by social models and the standards directly imposed on the observer, with the resultant behavior determined by a predictable interaction of both factors. The hypothesized effects of discrepancies and consistency between observed and imposed reward criteria received strong support. As predicted, when modeled and imposed reinforcement criteria were of different stringency, subjects adopted the more lenient alternative for themselves and this occurred more frequently when they were permitted self-reward for a relatively low standard but observed a model rewarding herself for higher achievements than when they were held to stringent criteria while observing a model displaying a more lenient self-reward pattern. Subjects in both these conditions adopted more lenient self-reward patterns than those who were held to a stringent self-reward criterion and observed the model using an equally stringent reward schedule for herself. Most interesting is the fact that children who were trained on a stringent criterion by a model who was similarly stringent with herself adopted and transmitted more stringent reward criteria than those who received the identical direct training but from a model who exhibited greater leniency in her own self-reward.

When the modeled and imposed standards were consistent they were adopted in the model's absence without a single deviation in spite of the relative stringency of the criterion and the desirability of the rewards which were freely available for self-administration without external constraints. Extremely precise, but not perfect, adoption of reinforcement patterns was also obtained in the Bandura and Kupers (1964) study in which children observed a model's self-reward patterns without themselves being administered any direct differential reinforcement. As Bandura and Kupers noted, it is likely that precise matching is enhanced when relevant normative data for performance quality are lacking or ambiguous. The fact that in the present study children who witnessed a model rewarding herself for a high standard and who were led to use the same high criterion for themselves adopted it in her absence without any deviations reflects the potency of combining modeling procedures with direct behavior guidance and reinforcement. It should also be noted that in the present study, in contrast to previous investigations on the modeling of self-reinforcement patterns, the apparatus permitted the subject to perform and to regulate his own reward schedules in the absence of both the model and the experimenter on all test trials. The maintenance of the predicted reward patterns in the absence of all external restraints further indicates that the variables studied in this experiment are determinants of behaviors frequently used as indices of self-control or "internalization."

Placing the subject in the role of a demonstrator for another person, as opposed to leaving him alone in the role of performer, had only minimal effects and the reward patterns of children in these two role conditions were not significantly different within each main model-subject discrepancy treatment. Notice (Figure 1) that there were no role effects whatsoever when the modeled and imposed reward schedules were identical. It is of interest, however, that role variables apparently did have indirect effects on the subject's self-reward schedule in the two model-subject discrepancy conditions when the subject was in the role of demonstrator with another younger child (self-reward when demonstrator in Figure 1). In this role, subjects who began as demonstrators (D-P sequence) tended to use the reward criteria displayed by their own model rather than the criteria that were imposed on them to a somewhat, although not significantly, greater degree than did subjects who were first placed in the role of a performer. Thus, in the D-P sequence, but not in the P-D sequence, subjects who had observed a stringent model became slightly more stringent and those who had observed a more lenient model became somewhat more lenient in their self-reward when they themselves served in the role of models. Apparently immediate practice of the demonstrator's role, prior to extensive practice in the performer's role, facilitates adoption of the modeled as opposed to directly trained behaviors.

Subjects tended to transmit to others the same reward patterns which they adopted for themselves as a function of the criteria which they had observed modeled and which had been imposed on them. On the whole, the children were extremely consistent in the criteria they used for their own self-reinforcement, both in their roles as performers and demonstrators, and in those they transmitted to another person when they served as his model. However, when subjects were immediately placed in the role of performers they showed perfect consistency in the reward criteria they used for themselves and those they imposed on another child, whereas when they served as demonstrators first there was some inconsistency. The differences in extent of inconsistency as a function of role treatments are suggestive of what might be considered "role discrimination." That is, the inconsistency shown by some subjects who served first as demonstrators reflected their use of the model's standards rather than those imposed on them by the model but only when they became models themselves.

The design of the present study appears to have utility for investigating the transmission as well as the acquisition of patterns of self-reward and further investigation of role variations and other variables affecting the "cultural transmission" of self-control patterns seems open to meaningful investigation through this paradigm.

The predicted effects of the model-subject discrepancy treatments were so strong both when the modeled and imposed behaviors were identical, and when the child was permitted lenient self-reward but observed the model rewarding herself stringently, that there was virtually no variance in the children's subsequent behavior. However, when the child was held to a stringent criterion but observed a model who was lenient with herself, approximately half the children adopted and transmitted the stringent standards imposed on them and half used the more liberal criteria which they had observed. The prediction and manipulation of behavior in this kind of discrepancy condition appears intriguing for future research and an investigation is planned to isolate some of the determinants affecting whether the individual adheres to the more self-denying schedule which was imposed on him or adopts the more generous patterns which he observed exhibited by a social agent. In addition to individual differences in previous social learning histories such factors as the attributes of the model, including his similarity to the subject, and the subject's role seem to be relevant variables.

In the present experiment, data on the children's willingness to delay immediate but less valued gratification for the sake of more valued but delayed rewards, elicited in simple real choice situations, were collected in the manner described previously (e.g., Mischel & Gilligan, 1964). No relationships approaching significance were found between this aspect of self-control and the children's behavior following the discrepancy treatments. Although certainly not definitive, this finding is in accord with numerous other recent investigations on self-control in pointing to the specificity of different aspects of self-control behavior and suggesting that such behaviors as delay of gratication and the regulation of self-reward schedules for particular performance contingencies may be relatively independent and governed by different antecedents without any underlying unitary moral agency (Aronfreed, 1964; Bandura & Walters, 1963).

The overall findings of this experiment appear to have clear implications for socialization practices and therapy. The study demonstrated that consistency in the standards which an individual is trained to use for himself and those he observes used by social agents facilitates the adoption and transmission of these standards and pointed to some of the variables that can determine the performance levels which the person adopts for his own self-reward and for reinforcing others. Many cultural and individual differences reflect differences in the kinds and liberalness of criteria used for the administration of rewards and punishments. There is abundant clinical evidence that for troubled individuals the inappropriate regulation of self-administered rewards and punishments often is a central problem. A host of deviant behavior patterns, such as psychopathy, masochism, depression, sadism, etc., may be construed as reflecting the inappropriate regulation of self-administered rewards and punishments and the imposition of excessively harsh or generous standards on other people. The isolation of antecedents of this aspect of self-control therefore seems to have particular importance.

SUMMARY

An adult (M) alternated turns with child Ss in a bowling game with experimentally controlled scores and abundantly available rewards. The treatments involved discrepancies between the performance criteria used by M to reward himself and those he imposed on S. Thereafter, Ss continued the game in M's absence, with free access to rewards. To examine "role-taking" effects, $\frac{1}{2}$ the Ss in each treatment performed alone 1st and then demonstrated the game to another younger child (O), with the sequence reversed for the remainder. As anticipated, reward schedules in the adult's absence were most stringent when both M and S had initially adhered to a high criterion and least when S had been permitted to reward himself for low achievements. Ss who were trained to reward themselves only on a stringent criterion and observed M reward himself similarly, maintained more stringent schedules than those who had been given the same stringent direct training for self-reward but by an M who rewarded himself leniently. The criteria Ss imposed on O tended to be identical with those they imposed on themselves and role taking had only indirect effects.

REFERENCES

Aronfreed, J. The origin of self-criticism. *Psychological Review*, 1964, **71**, 193–218.
Bandura, A., & Kupers, Carol J. The transmission of self-reinforcement through modeling. *Journal of Abnormal and Social Psychology*, 1964, **69**, 1–9.
Bandura, A., & Walters, R. *Social learning and personality development.* New York: Holt, Rinehart, & Winston, 1963.
Bandura, A., & Whalen, Carol K. The influence of antecedent reinforcement and divergent modeling cues on patterns of self-reward. *Journal of Personality and Social Psychology*, 1966, in press.
Kanfer, F. H., Bradley, Marcia A., & Marston, A. R. Self-reinforcement as a function of degree of learning. *Psychological Reports*, 1962, **10**, 885–886.
Kanfer, F. H., & Marston, A. R. Conditioning of self-reinforcing responses: An analogue to self-confidence training. *Psychological Reports*, 1963, **13**, 63–70. (a)
Kanfer, F. H., & Marston, A. R. Determinants of self-reinforcement in human learning. *Journal of Experimental Psychology*, 1963, **66**, 245–254. (b)
Mischel, W., & Gilligan, Carol. Delay of gratification, motivation for the prohibited gratification, and responses to temptation. *Journal of Abnormal and Social Psychology*, 1964, **69**, 411–417.

5.5 Parents' Attitudes and Behaviors and Grade-School Children's Academic Achievements

Vaughn Crandall, Rachel Dewey, Walter Katkovsky, and Anne Preston

PROBLEM

Since the time of Binet's pioneering attempts to predict children's academic achievements from their performances on intelligence tests, psychologists and educators have been concerned with factors producing individual differences in young children's scholastic attainments. Early research addressed to this question was primarily devoted to the role which general intellectual abilities played in academic performances. More recently, educational and child-development researchers have concerned themselves with factors other than ability which might also contribute to performance differences. Personality variables such as achievement motivation and anxiety have been brought into the picture. The achievement need has been the center of re-

Reprinted from *The Journal of Genetic Psychology*, 1964, **104**, 53–66, by permission of the authors and the Journal Press.

cent concerted research efforts by a number of investigators: e.g., McClelland and his colleagues (1, 6). So, too, has anxiety been used as a predictor variable for intellectual and academic performances: e.g., McCandless and Castaneda (5); Sarason, Davidson, Lighthall, Waite, and Ruebush (7).

Research on determinants of such achievement performances has indicated that both ability and motivational variables are useful and necessary predictors. Another broad, and basic, question still remains: What are the *antecedents* of differences in children's intellectual achievement motivations and performances? In other words, what environmental factors in children's everyday experiences facilitate or impede the development of intellectual and academic competence? Many persons and situations influence a child's personality development. Parents, teachers, siblings, and peers all interact with a child in the course of his daily experiences, and each of these individuals can be an important social reinforcer of the child's behaviors. This is true whether the area of personality under consideration is the development of aggressive, dependent, affiliative, or achievement behaviors.

Concerning the development of achievement motivations and behaviors, it is apparent to the careful observer that most children have developed, by the time they enter grade school, fairly consistent differences in the values they attach to intellectual and academic achievements, in their expectations of success in these activities, in the standards they use to judge their efforts, and in the methods and strategies they employ in their attempts to attain achievement goals. What factors produce these differences? This is the general question to which this research is directed. The present article describes one study of a larger research project concerned with parents as identification models and reinforcers of young children's achievement behaviors.[1] The investigation explored relationships between parents' attitudes and behaviors and their early-grade-school-age children's academic performances.

METHODS

Sample

The sample was comprised of 120 Ss: 40 early-grade-school-age children, and their fathers and mothers. The child sample contained 20 boys and 20 girls equally distributed in the second, third and fourth grades at the time the children were administered academic-achievement tests. The socioeconomic status of the families was assessed by Hollingshead's Two Factor Index of Social Position (4). The proportions of families in Hollingshead's social classifications I through V were 10, 30, 29, 31 and zero respectively,

[1] This study was a part of the project "Parents as identification models and reinforcers of children's achievement development," partially supported by USPH Grant M-2238, awarded the first-listed author.

TABLE 1. Intelligence and Academic-Achievement-Test
Performances of the Children

	Number of children
Stanford-Binet *IQ*	
Below 100	2
100–114	9
115–129	13
130–144	14
145 and over	2
Reading age *vs.* chronological age	
RA less than CA	2
RA 1–9 months beyond CA	7
RA 10–19 months beyond CA	19
RA 20–29 months beyond CA	5
RA 30–39 months beyond CA	4
RA 40–49 months beyond CA	2
Arithmetic age *vs.* chronological age	
AA less than CA	5
AA 1–9 months beyond CA	12
AA 10–19 months beyond CA	13
AA 20–29 months beyond CA	7
AA 30–39 months beyond CA	3

indicating that all but the lowest social classification was reasonably represented. Slightly more than one-half of the fathers and one-fourth of the mothers were college graduates. Table 1 presents information regarding the intellectual levels and academic-achievement test performances of the children. The children's intellectual abilities were assessed with the Stanford-Binet Intelligence Test; their academic performances, with the California Achievement Test.[2] As indicated in Table 1, the children of the study were intellectually superior to national norms; all but two had *IQs* above 100, and approximately three-fourths of the children obtained scores more than one standard deviation above the national average. The mean *IQ* of the group was 124. Intellectual abilities within the sample, however, varied appreciably. The children's *IQs* ranged from 79 to 164, with a *SD* of 16. As might be expected from their intelligence-test scores, the children's performances on the standard academic-achievement tests were generally above grade level. Only two of the children were reading below grade level, and only five were not performing at or above their grade level in arithmetic.

[2] The second author of this report administered the academic-achievement tests. Appreciation is expressed to Dr. Virginia Nelson, who gave the Stanford-Binet Intelligence Tests to the children.

Assessment of Parent Attitudes and Behaviors

The parents were interviewed individually at the Fels Research Institute for the Study of Human Development. To prevent communication between parents, each set of parents was interviewed concurrently but separately.[3] The interview sessions averaged from two-and-one-half to three hours, and were electronically recorded for subsequent interview analyses. Two interviews were given each parent during the interview session. The first was concerned with the parent's attitudes and reported behaviors toward his child's everyday achievement efforts. This interview covered four achievement areas, only one of which—the intellectual achievement area—is relevant to the present study. The second interview covered several general (nonspecific to achievement) behaviors of the parents. These included parental affection, rejection and nurturance.[4] Copies of the parent interview schedules and rating scales may be obtained.[5]

First Interview

Interview I obtained information regarding the following parental attitudinal and behavioral variables:

a. The parent's attainment value for his child's intellectual performances. This referred to the degree of importance or value the parent attached to his child's intellectual achievements. This rating assessed the intensity of the parent's desire that his child show interest and participate in intellectual activities; and the value the parent placed on his child's effort, persistence, and competence in these situations.

b. The parent's evaluation of his child's intellectual competence. This variable was concerned with the level of competence the parent felt his child characteristically demonstrated in intellectual activities.

c. The parent's satisfaction-dissatisfaction with his child's intellectual-achievement performances. Ratings of this variable focused on the amount of satisfaction *vs.* dissatisfaction the parent expressed regarding his child's intellectual-achievement performances. This rating was exclusively concerned with relevant parental feelings as these were expressed to the interviewer; the parent's reported overt reactions (praise, criticism, etc.) to his child's efforts were *not* a part of the rating.

d. The parent's minimal standards for his child's intellectual achievement performances. Here the "personal yardstick" the parent used to judge his

---

[3] The fathers were interviewed by the third-listed author; the mothers, by the fourth author.

[4] A fourth general parental-behavior variable—dominance—was also assessed in Interview II for a study other than the present one, and is not discussed in this report.

[5] Virginia Crandall, Fels Research Institute.

child's intellectual performances was considered. The major judgment for this rating entailed the determination of the minimal level of intellectual competence below which the child's performance produced parental dissatisfaction and above which the parent felt more satisfied than dissatisfied with his child's efforts.

e. Parental instigation of intellectual activities. This (like the remaining variables of Interview I) was concerned with reported parental behaviors rather than parental attitudes. Parental instigation referred to the frequency and intensity of the parent's attempts to increase his child's participation and competence in intellectual activities. The parent's reactions to his child's efforts *after* he had performed were not included here. To be a relevant behavioral referent for this variable, the parent's behavior must have preceded some activity on the part of his child. Examples of instigation included such events as the parent arranging for his child to receive special lessons or experiences in some intellectual pursuit, the parent making a special effort to convey to his child the importance of intellectual experiences, and the parent encouraging and/or demanding that his child participate in intellectual-achievement activities.

f. The parent's participation with his child in intellectual-achievement activities. This variable pertained to the extent that the parent actively engaged in intellectual-achievement pursuits with his child. Both the frequency of parental participation and the amount of personal involvement while so engaged constituted rating referents for this variable.

g. Positive parental reactions. Here the frequency and intensity of the parent's positive reactions to his child's intellectual-achievement behaviors were assessed. These included the degree to which the parent responded favorably to his child's interest and participation in intellectual-achievement activities, as well as the parent's positive reactions to the effort and the competence his child exhibited in these pursuits. Positive parental reactions might take the form of direct verbal approval or other less-direct symbols of approbation, such as granting special privileges or giving rewards (e.g., money, gifts, etc.) for intellectual achievements.

h. Negative parental reactions. This variable was concerned with the frequency and intensity of disapproval and criticism which the parent expressed to his child for any lack of interest, participation, effort and/or competence in intellectual-achievement activities.

Second Interview

Interview II sampled the parents' reported behaviors with their children which were nonspecific to the children's intellectual-achievement performances, but were aspects of parent-child interaction which might possibly influence (either directly or indirectly) children's intellectual-achievement efforts. The variables rated were:

a. *Parental affection.* This variable pertained to the amount of overt affection and acceptance which the parent reported expressing toward his child.

b. *Parental rejection.* Here the raters focused on the degree that the parent directly expressed dissatisfaction with, was critical of, or punitive about, his child's general personality attributes or characteristic behaviors.

c. *Parental nurturance.* The behavioral referents for this rating were those relevant to the frequency and quality of emotional support and instrumental help given the child by the parent.

Rating Procedures and Methods of Data Analysis

The criterion rater for Parent Interview I rated all interviews of the 80 parents from typescripts of the interviews. Reliability raters rated 40 randomly picked father and mother interviews. All identifying information (e.g., parent, child, and sibling names, etc.) was removed before the interview protocols were rated. Interview II was rated after the rater listened to the interview recordings.[6] It was felt that, while the data in Interview I was concerned with specific parental attitudes and behaviors which could be assessed from typescripts, Interview II data included important parental feelings and expressions which were less likely to be represented accurately in typed protocols. For example, in Interview II, two fathers (or mothers) might say that their children were "little hellions" in certain situations; yet one parent might mean (and convey) that he thoroughly disapproved of this behavior, while a second parent might make the same statement, but indicate (through his intonation) that he actually approved of these behaviors on the part of his child.

The children's academic-achievement-test scores used in the study were achievement-ratio scores; the reading-achievement score for each child was his reading age divided by his chronological age, and his arithmetic score was obtained by dividing his arithmetic age by his chronological age.

Statistical analyses employed in the study were exclusively nonparametric tests. The rank-difference correlation was used for all measures of associa-

---

[6] The criterion rater for Parent Interview I was the senior author. The reliability raters for this interview were the third author, for the mother interviews; and the fourth author, for the father interviews. The criterion rater of Parent Interview II was Virginia Crandall. The reliability ratings (made from 40 randomly selected father and mother interviews) were done by the fourth author and the third author respectively.

tion, and Wilcoxon's Unpaired Replicates Test was employed for all assessments of differences (8).

Interrater Reliabilities

The interrater reliability coefficients for Parent Interview I are presented in Table 2. The magnitude of rater concordance for these variables, with one noticeable exception (the mothers' reported negative reactions), ranged from moderately acceptable to highly acceptable agreement. Interrater reliabilities of the mother interviews of Parent Interview II were, for the variables of affection, rejection, and nurturance respectively, .87, .61 and .68. Correlations of interrater agreement for the same variables in the father interviews were .76, .85 and .78.

TABLE 2. INTERRATER RELIABILITIES FOR PARENT INTERVIEW I
(PARENT ATTITUDES AND REPORTED BEHAVIORS TOWARD
THE CHILDREN'S INTELLECTUAL-ACHIEVEMENT EFFORTS)

Parent variable	Re. mothers	Re. fathers
Attainment value	.50	.80
Evaluation of competence	.78	.94
Satisfaction-dissatisfaction	.85	.96
Achievement standards	.63	.57
Instigation	.63	.76
Participation	.70	.84
Positive reactions	.86	.80
Negative reactions	.22	.79

The Child Variables

Relations between the children's *IQ*s and their scholastic-achievement-test performances were assessed. Intelligence-test scores correlated .57 and .59 with reading and arithmetic-achievement-test scores respectively for the girls, and .66 and .50 for the boys. These correlations are similar in magnitude to associations found in previous studies of children's intelligence and their performances on standard academic-achievement tests. These data indicate, as have the results of previous investigations, that general intelligence is one major factor in children's academic achievements. However, the fact that less than one-third of the variance was held in common by these sets of variables (i.e., intelligence- and achievement-test performance) suggests that other factors may also be influential. Parents' attitudes and behaviors influencing children's intellectual-achievement motivations and behaviors may account for some of this variance.

Relations between General Parental Behaviors and Children's Academic-Achievement-Test Performances

Associations between general parental behaviors (i.e., affection, rejection, and nurturance) and the children's reading- and arithmetic-test performances were evaluated separately by sex of parent and sex of child. Of the 24 correlations run, only three were significant beyond the .05 level of confidence according to Old's Tables (8). This is only slightly better than might be anticipated by chance. That the significant correlations obtained were probably not chance occurrences, however, is suggested by the fact that all significant associations pertained *only* to the mothers and their daughters. Girls who were competent readers had both less affectionate and less nurturant mothers than did the girls who demonstrated less proficiency in that academic area; correlations between the girls' reading-achievement-test scores and their mothers' affection and nurturance were —.38 and —.43 respectively. In addition, girls who performed better on the arithmetic-achievement test had mothers who were also relatively low on nurturance; the Rho obtained was —.45.

Why should low maternal nurturance and affection seem to foster academic competence in the girls? Several possibilities are likely. First, the affectionate and nurturant mothers, by rewarding their daughters' affection-seeking and dependent behaviors, may have "taught" these girls to expect such overtures to be more effective means of attaining personal security than behaviors requiring independent initiative and achievement striving. In contrast, girls who did not receive as much maternal affection and support, might have turned to other potential sources of satisfaction and security, such as achievement *per se*. Second, previous research has demonstrated that maternal nurturance fosters children's dependence and impedes the development of independence and achievement behaviors (3, 9). Restrictions of learning experiences in independence and achievement in the more highly nurtured girls of the present study may have produced (a) fewer possibilities for developing independent problem-solving techniques to handle achievement situations, and (b) less confidence (and more anxiety) regarding abilities to do so. One final explanation for the negative relations obtained between maternal nurturance and affection and the girls' academic achievements pertains to young girls' attempted identification with, and emulation of, their mothers. All parents act as learning models for, as well as direct reinforcers of, their children's behaviors. The mother who readily proffers love and help to her child may derive personal satisfaction from such maternal behaviors, and may serve as a model to her daughter to this effect. On the other hand, the mother who withholds affection or rejects her child's help-seeking and emotional support-seeking may be less involved with the maternal role and be more achievement-oriented. Consequently, her daughter is, to the degree she uses her mother as an identification model, more likely to emulate her mother's achievement behaviors, values and motivations, and to attempt to become competent in academic achievement situations.

Relations between Parents' Specific Attitudes and Behaviors toward Children's Intellectual Achievement Efforts and Children's Performances on Standard Achievement Tests

Data relevant to this portion of the study are summarized in Tables 3 and 4. The first four parent variables listed in these tables are attitudinal variables; the last four are behavioral variables. Each will be discussed in turn.

a. Attitudinal variables. The *attainment values* the parents placed on their children's intellectual competence were essentially unrelated to their children's academic-achievement-test performances. In fact, the only significant correlation of the eight pertaining to this variable was an unanticipated negative one: fathers who expressed strong desires that their daughters be intellectually competent had daughters who performed less adequately on the reading-achievement test than did daughters of fathers who were less concerned with their daughters' intellectual activities and abilities.

The mothers' *evaluations* of their children's general intellectual competence were associated with their children's academic performances, but the evaluations of the fathers were not. Both the boys' and girls' reading-test performances were positively and significantly related to their mothers' assessments of their general intellectual competence. The children's arith-

TABLE 3. PARENTS' ATTITUDES AND ACTIONS AND
CHILDREN'S READING ACHIEVEMENT *

	Mothers re.		Fathers re.	
Parent variable	Girls	Boys	Girls	Boys
Attainment value	−.14	.35	−.38	.03
Evaluations	.44	.48	.28	.21
Satisfaction-dissatisfaction	.51	.48	.38	.23
Standards	.48	.18	.15	.26
Instigation	−.52	.18	−.43	−.07
Participation	−.10	.06	−.28	−.25
Positive reactions	−.11	.09	.42	−.17
Negative reactions	−.27	−.18	−.45	.06

* Italicized correlations are significant at or beyond the .05 level of confidence (one-tailed test).

TABLE 4. Parents' Attitudes and Actions and
          Children's Arithmetic Achievement *

Parent variable	Mothers re.		Fathers re.	
	Girls	Boys	Girls	Boys
Attainment value	.17	.23	−.26	−.05
Evaluations	.23	.35	.20	.04
Satisfaction-dissatisfaction	.76	.28	.19	.07
Standards	.50	.00	−.12	.34
Instigation	−.42	.05	−.38	−.31
Participation	.13	.05	−.09	−.55
Positive reactions	.14	.01	.41	−.19
Negative reactions	−.33	−.24	−.44	−.14

* Italicized correlations are significant at or beyond the .05 level of confidence (one-tailed test).

metic-test performances were positively correlated with the mothers' evaluations, though falling just short of statistical significance. In contrast, none of the fathers' evaluations of their children was related to these children's scholastic-achievement, test-taking behaviors. This finding—that the mothers' evaluation of their children's general intellectual performances were similar to their children's academic performances, while the fathers' evaluations were not—may have been due to the fact that mothers are usually home to receive the after-school reports from their children regarding their academic successes and failures, while most fathers are not. In addition, it is a common observation that mothers far outnumber fathers in school situations where concrete information is provided regarding their children's academic performances, (e.g., PTA meetings and parent-teacher conferences). Finally, it may be that fathers more frequently based their judgments of their children's general intellectual competence on their intellectual performances observed in the home (e.g., efforts on puzzles, quiz games, etc.) than did the mothers.

Consistent with the findings on evaluations was the fact that the mothers' *satisfactions and dissatisfactions* with their children's general intellectual-achievement efforts were also more often positively associated with the children's achievement-test performances than were those of the fathers: three of the four significant correlations obtained pertained to the mothers' expressed satisfaction with the adequacy of their children's intellectual-achievement performances.

Parental *standards* for the children's general intellectual performances were unrelated to the children's demonstrated competence on the academic-achievement tests with two exceptions. Both of these pertained to the standards the mothers held for their daughters. Mothers who set high standards for their daughters' intellectual-achievement efforts, in contrast with mothers whose standards were less demanding, had daughters who were more proficient on both the reading- and arithmetic-achievement tests. These correlations, as well as a number of those found in the tables which follow, illustrate an inevitable problem inherent in most parent-child research. When significant correlations are obtained between parent and child behaviors, when might it be legitimate to assume the former caused the latter, and when might the opposite be true? The positive association of the mothers' achievement standards for their daughters and these girls' academic-test performances may have been a function of the following: (*a*) high maternal achievement standards induced the girls to strive for, and become proficient in, the academic areas under consideration, while low maternal standards produced the opposite effect; or (*b*) the mothers adjusted their intellectual-achievement standards for their daughters according to the girls' demonstrated academic proficiencies; or (*c*) the correlations obtained may be a function of both (*a*) and (*b*).

b. Behavioral variables. The remaining correlations listed in Tables 3 and 4 focus on reported parental behaviors rather than parental attitudes. The degree of the parents' *instigation* of their children toward intellectual-achievement pursuits was predictive of the children's achievement-test performances only for the girls. Girls who performed especially well on the tests had mothers and fathers who were *less* prone to encourage and push them toward intellectual activities than were parents of the less academically proficient girls. Regarding the parents' *participation* with the children in intellectual activities, these parental behaviors bore little relation to the competence the children demonstrated on the academic-achievement tests. In only one instance—i.e., the fathers' participation and their sons' performances on the arithmetic-achievement test—was the correlation significant; fathers of boys who were especially competent in this area spent less time with their sons in intellectual activities than did the fathers of the less competent boys. There was, thus, no evidence in the present study that the amount of parental participation with children in intellectual activities *per se* had any positive impact on the children's academic achievements. The negative correlations obtained between parental instigation and participation and the children's achievement-test performances suggest, though cannot prove, that these parental behaviors might be reactions to the children's efforts rather than antecedent and causal factors in these performances. It is possible, for example, that many parents of grade-school-age children—when the child's academic efforts are competent ones—feel little need to encourage such endeavors or to spend additional time with the children in these pursuits. Conversely, parents of a child who performs relatively poorly in academic situations may become concerned with his ineptitude, and increase their instigational efforts and participation with him in intellectual-achievement activities.

The two final antecedent variables of this study pertained to *parental*

reactions to the children's intellectual-achievement behaviors as these predicted the children's academic-achievement-test performances. These variables, historically, have been the major focus of attention of researchers concerned with parent behaviors as determinants of children's personality development. In the current investigation, an attempt was made to assess the
reactions of the parents to their children's intellectual-achievement efforts,
and to relate these reactions to the levels of performance which the children
evidenced on standard academic-achievement tests. The only finding indicating an influence of these parental behaviors on the children's performance—if a causal relationship is assumed—was a cross-sex one; both positive
and negative reactions of the fathers to their daughters' intellectual efforts
predicted their daughters' academic proficiency. The mothers' reactions, in
contrast, were essentially unrelated to their daughters' performances, while
neither the fathers' nor the mothers' reported praise or criticism was predictive of their sons' achievement-test scores. In short, the only evidence that
the parents' direct rewards and punishments may have influenced their
children's academic performances occurred exclusively between fathers and
their daughters. Girls who performed especially well on the reading-achievement test had fathers who more often praised and rewarded, and less often
criticized and punished, their general intellectual-achievement behaviors. A
similar relation obtained for the girls' arithmetic performances.

SIGNIFICANT FINDINGS

When the total pattern of significant correlations found in the current
study is evaluated, the most striking finding is that the parents' attitudes and
behaviors (both general and specific) were associated with their daughters'
performances on the scholastic-achievement tests much more frequently
than with those of their sons. Of the 18 significant correlations obtained
between the Parent Interviews I and II data and the children's demonstrated
academic competence, only three pertained to the boys. Why should these
differences obtain? One possibility for this finding is that grade-school-age
boys may differ from girls in their susceptibility to adult influence. Two
unpublished sets of data by the authors of this report support this idea.
First, ratings of free-play behavior of another sample of children in the same
age range as the current child sample revealed that the amount of the
children's achievement efforts and the amount of their approval-seeking
from adults were positively and significantly related for the girls (Rho $=$
.46), but unrelated (Rho $=$ .03) for the boys. In other words, the girls'
achievement strivings were directly related to their apparent desire for
approval from adults, while the boys' achievement behaviors were more
autonomously determined. It appeared that the boys had less need to use
adults' reactions to define the competence of their efforts than did the girls,
possibly because the boys may have developed more-internalized achievement standards. Additional evidence suggesting that young boys' achieve-

ment performances may be less contingent on the reactions of others than are those of girls' was obtained on the sample of Ss employed in the current study. As a part of a different (as yet unpublished) investigation, the children were administered a specially constructed Children's Intellectual Achievement Responsibility Questionnaire. This questionnaire was designed to measure the extent a child attributes his intellectual-achievement successes and failures to his own instrumental behaviors rather than as a product of the behaviors and reactions of other persons. The boys' belief in self-responsibility correlated positively with their performances on the academic-achievement tests used in the current study, while these variables were not significantly related for the girls. The specific correlations between the boys' belief in self-responsibility and their reading- and arithmetic-achievement-test performances were .49 and .36 respectively. For the girls, these correlations were —.16 and —.23. In summary, to the degree that boys' achievement striving has been found to be unrelated to their approval-seeking from adults, and, to the degree that their academic proficiencies were associated with their belief in self-responsibility, their achievement behaviors appeared to be more independent and autonomous of adult reactions than those of the girls. Because of this, parental attitudes and behaviors may have less impact on, and therefore be less predictive of, the academic performances of boys of this age than of girls. The findings of the current study are congruent with this possibility. It should be strongly emphasized, however, that this reasoning rests on several assumptions, as well as limited research data, and must await more definitive tests in future investigations.

SUMMARY

This study investigated relations between parents' attitudes and behaviors toward their children's general intellectual-achievement efforts, and their children's performances on standard academic-achievement tests. The sample was comprised of 40 early-grade-school-age children and their fathers and mothers. The children were administered standard intelligence and scholastic-achievement tests. The parents were individually interviewed regarding their general parental behaviors (affection, rejection, nurturance), as well as their specific attitudes and reactions to their children's everyday intellectual-achievement efforts.

The following results were obtained:

1. Correlations between the children's IQ scores and their performances on the scholastic-achievement tests were of the same general magnitude found in most past research on children's intelligence and academic performances.

2. General parental behaviors which significantly predicted the children's

academic-test performances pertained solely to mothers and their daughters; mothers of academically competent girls were less affectionate and less nurturant toward their daughters than were the mothers of the girls who were less proficient.

3. Certain specific attitudes and behaviors of the parents toward their children's intellectual-achievement behaviors were predictive of the children's academic-test performances; others were not. First, neither the mothers' nor fathers' expressed values for the children's intellectual experiences were positively associated with the children's observed performances. Second, both the mothers' evaluations of, and satisfactions with, their children's general intellectual competence were positively related to these children's actual academic performances, while those of the fathers were not. Third, parental instigation and participation, when correlations were significant, were negatively associated with the children's academic performances. Fourth, the positive and negative reactions of the parents to the children's intellectual-achievement efforts were predictive of the children's academic-achievement-test performances for father-daughter combinations only; the more proficient girls had fathers who more often praised, and less often criticized, their everyday intellectual-achievement attempts than did the less academically competent girls.

4. Many more significant relations obtained between the parents' attitudes and behaviors and their daughters' academic proficiency than occurred between these parental attitudes and behaviors and the boys' performances.

REFERENCES

1. Atkinson, J., *Ed.* Motives in Fantasy, Action and Society. New York: Van Nostrand, 1958.
2. Crandall, V. J., Katkovsky, W., & Preston, A. Motivational and ability determinants of children's intellectual achievement behaviors. *Child Devel.*, 1962, 33, 643–661.
3. Crandall, V. J., Preston, A., & Rabson, A. Maternal reactions and the development of independence and achievement behavior in young children. *Child Devel.*, 1960, 31, 243–251.
4. Hollingshead, A., & Redlick, F. Social stratification and psychiatric disorders. *Amer. Soc. Rev.*, 1953, 18, 163–169.
5. McCandless, B., & Castaneda, A. Anxiety in children, school achievement and intelligence. *Child Devel.*, 1956, 27, 379–382.
6. McClelland, D., Atkinson, J., Clark, R., & Lowell, E. The Achievement Motive. New York: Appleton-Century-Crofts, 1953.
7. Sarason, S., Davidson, K., Lighthall, F., Waite, R., & Ruebush, B. Anxiety in Elementary School Children. New York: Wiley, 1960.
8. Siegel, S. Nonparametric Statistics for the Behavioral Sciences. New York: McGraw-Hill, 1956.
9. Winterbottom, M. The relation of need for achievement in learning experi-

ences in independence and mastery. In J. W. Atkinson (Ed.), *Motives in Fantasy, Action and Society.* New York: Van Nostrand, 1958. Pp. 453–478.

5.6   Delay of Gratification, Need for Achievement, and Acquiescence in Another Culture [1]

Walter Mischel

Relationships between overt behavior on important psychological dimensions and relevant motives are much sought foundations in personality research. This paper explores the relationship between a person's choice preferences for immediate, smaller (ImR) as opposed to delayed, larger (DelR) reinforcement and his motive system. It thus seeks to extend our knowledge of preference for delayed gratification, some antecedents and correlates of which have already been investigated (Mischel, 1958, 1959, 1961). Here choice behavior with respect to preference for ImR or DelR is related to the need for achievement (n Achievement) as scored from fantasy material in the manner described by McClelland and his associates (McClelland, Atkinson, Clark, & Lowell, 1953).

The central aim is not primarily to elaborate the network of correlates of n Achievement, but rather, to clarify some of the variables relevant to preferences for ImR or DelR by relating such choices to a motive that is logically relevant and whose measurement and empirical correlates appear relatively firm. If this can be done, research on delay of gratification with human subjects and in choice situations, in which smaller, immediate gratifications are pitted against more long term, larger gratifications, should be somewhat more solidly anchored, albeit only on a correlational basis, to the data of other more elaborated domains of personality research.

The ability to delay immediate gratification for the sake of later, more gratifying outcomes has long been recognized as crucial in a multitude of

[1] Thanks are due to David C. McClelland and to Ralph Metzner for informative pre- and post-experimental discussions on some of the central problems dealt with in this paper, to John W. Whiting for important suggestions concerning the measures used and for his "magic man" procedure, and to Claire Gerschuni and Judith Vollmar for statistical computations. Grateful acknowledgment is also made to the Education Office of the Government of Trinidad and Tobago, and its officials for cooperation in testing within their schools. This study was carried out under the partial support of a grant from the Laboratory of Social Relations, Harvard University, and Grant M-2557(A) from the National Institute of Mental Health.

Reprinted from *Journal of Abnormal and Social Psychology* 1961, **62**, 543–552, by permission of the author and the American Psychological Association.

complex human situations; it figures importantly in a variety of theoretical formulations (e.g., Freud, 1922; Rapaport, 1951; Singer, 1955). In spite of this recognition, there is a relative paucity of relevant experimental research. Recently, however, a number of investigations (e.g., Levine, Glass, & Meltzoff, 1957; Levine, Spivack, & Wright, 1959; Singer, Wilensky, & Mc-Craven, 1956; Spivack, Levine, & Sprigle, 1959) have inquired into the correlates of "delaying capacity," primarily as inferred from the frequency of human movement (M) Rorschach responses. In contrast to this line of research, the present study is part of a larger research program that approaches the problem of delay of gratification by using direct measures of preference for ImR or DelR in particular choice situations. Thus far, with children from other cultures as subjects, preference for DelR as opposed to ImR has been found to relate positively to social responsibility and to accuracy of time statements, negatively to delinquency (Mischel, 1961), positively to intelligence (Melikian, 1959), and positively to the presence (as opposed to the absence) of the father within the home under some conditions (Mischel, 1958, 1959). The method also has been used to test cross-cultural hypotheses experimentally with respect to differences in delay of gratification (Mischel, 1959).

Research on the need for achievement requires no new summary (e.g., Atkinson, 1958). It is consistent with past theorizing and research on n Achievement that high n Achievement should be related to preference for DelR as opposed to ImR. The essence of the definition of n Achievement is "competition with a standard of excellence" (McClelland et al., 1953). Implied in such striving is the ability to delay and postpone the relatively trivial but immediately available for the sake of later but more important outcomes. Achievement fantasies may be thought of in part as reflecting as well as sustaining and mediating the individual's strivings for future rewards and attainments of excellence. Indeed, imbedded in the operations for scoring n Achievement is the criterion of "long-term involvement." [2] Clearly there can be little realization (and thus little maintenance) of the motive to compete with a standard of excellence unless the person is able to delay immediate but smaller gratifications and to choose instead larger future rewards and goals.

A direct and positive relationship between preference for DelR and n Achievement, then, is to be expected for the following reasons. It has been argued (Metzner, 1960) that one of the crucial conditions that facilitates the development of the ability to delay gratification is the acquired reward

---

[2] Since "long-term involvement" is a criterion used in scoring for the presence of Achievement Imagery, and may have direct overlap with the ability to delay reinforcement, it is important to note that on only seven of the protocols did this criterion serve as the basis for Achievement Imagery scoring, and three of these protocols were given by subjects not consistently preferring delayed, larger reinforcement on the choice measures.

value of working itself. Learning to delay starts when behaviors based only on the pleasure principle are either frustrated or punished. Then, fantasy becomes an acquired primary process substitute and work a secondary process detour, both of which are rewarded by eventual (larger) gratifications, thus ultimately becoming rewarding activities in their own right. Liking to work for its own sake is generally assumed to be a basic ingredient of the high n Achievement pattern. Presumably, persons high in n Achievement have learned to like work, and they have learned this in part as a response to demands to forego immediate gratification in favor of more long-term goals. That is, they have learned to tolerate waiting periods and in the course of such socialization have built up a general readiness to delay when it is demanded by conditions of people. Consequently, when persons high in n Achievement are given choices between immediate, smaller rewards and delayed, larger ones, the balance between the negative valence of waiting and the positive valence of the delayed, larger reward is weighted in favor of the latter because the former is relatively minor for them. This is in contrast to the state of affairs with persons who have not learned work as a response to the delay situation, or who have not acquired intrinsic interest in achievement (i.e., persons low in n Achievement). The anticipated positive relationship between preference for DelR and n Achievement does not depend on an absolute preference by individuals high in n Achievement for the delayed alternative, but, rather, applies equally to relatively less nonavoidance of the delayed alternative on their part.

In addition to the central aim of testing the relationship between the need for achievement and patterns of preference for reinforcement with respect to delay of gratification, the paper also presents data relevant to the measurement and correlates of n Achievement itself, and to further correlates of preference for ImR or DelR. Especially for use in cross-cultural research, in which verbalizations in response to Thematic Apperception Test (TAT) pictures appropriate for the usual scoring of n Achievement often are difficult or impossible to obtain, alternative n Achievement measures are much needed. Graphic materials ("doodles") scored for n Achievement (Aronson, 1958) have been used with young children. The present study offers another alternative to measuring n Achievement via the TAT, far simpler than the Test of Insight (French, 1958), and possibly appropriate for use in many cultures.

Further, an attempt was made to use a measure—suitable for research in another culture—of simple acquiescence or "agreeing tendency." Much recent research with United States samples (e.g., Bass, 1956; Messick & Jackson, 1957) has focused on the response set to agree, and an intensive investigation of the problem (Couch & Keniston, 1960) has related "yeasaying" as opposed to "naysaying" to two personality syndromes. These syndromes are conceptually germane to the present distinction concerning preference for ImR-DelR. "Yeasayers were shown to be individuals with weak ego controls, who accept impulses without reservation, and . . . easily respond to stimuli exerted on them. The naysayer inhibits and suppresses his impulses . . ." (p. 173). The former "can freely indulge in impulse gratification" whereas "the egos of naysayers take over the controlling functions of the parents, and the suppression of impulses is subsequently self-maintained and self-rewarded" (p. 173). A cluster of scales including impulsivity and dependency characterized the positive end of the agreeing tendency; the disagreeing tendency was defined by scales including ego strength, responsibility, and trust. Further, in interviews, yeasayers (in contrast to naysayers) described themselves as ". . . unreflective, quick to act, easily influenced, and unable to tolerate delays in gratification" (p. 170).

Clearly, these two personality syndromes are directly relevant to preference for ImR-DelR. Indeed, I have reasoned previously (Mischel, 1958), with some direct experimental support (Mahrer, 1956), that "trust," or the expectancy that the promised delayed reward is forthcoming, is a basic factor in preference for DelR, and empirically have related preference for DelR to social responsibility (Mischel, 1961). It is to be expected that DelR preference should be related to naysaying and ImR preference to yeasaying and to the personality syndromes associated with each. Similarly, in the realm of n Achievement research, numerous attempts, mostly with mixed or dubious success (e.g., Samelson, 1958) have been made to relate n Achievement inversely to conforming behavior. Acquiescence may be thought of as a special case of conforming in an ambiguous situation, and again in the present research the often expected but rarely attained relationship between n Achievement and nonacquiescence was anticipated.

Lastly, data were also collected on social responsibility, as measured by an independently validated scale (Harris, 1957), substantially correlated with other measures of adjustment and maturity. Replication was thus sought for a previously established positive relationship between measures of preference for DelR (as opposed to ImR) and social responsibility (Mischel, 1961) and to determine the extent of interrelationship between social responsibility and the other variables measured in this study.

The over-all methodological aim is to aid the development of relatively simple but quantifiable techniques for testing psychological hypotheses in cultures much different from our own in which measures developed in the United States are inappropriate or excessively cumbersome. Such techniques are needed if the generality of psychological principles established on United States samples is to be extended to grossly different populations.

METHOD

Subjects

A total of 112 Trinidadian Negro children (68 boys and 44 girls), all in the age group 11–14, with a modal age of 13, were tested in a government school located near the capital city. The school contained children from the urban environs, primarily from the lower middle and lower socioeconomic strata of the society.

Measures of Preference for ImR or DelR

Three preference measures (a behavioral choice and two questionnaire items) were used to elicit preference for ImR or DelR. These were selected on the basis of earlier research with comparable Trinidadian samples. The general procedures used in the pretesting and selection have been described in detail (Mischel, 1959, 1961). Briefly, the behavioral measure consisted of a choice between ImR or DelR in the form of a small candy bar (costing approximately 10 cents) available immediately *or* a much larger candy bar (costing approximately 25 cents) for which the subject must wait one week.[3] The reward choice was administered as the last item in the total procedure and was structured as a way of "thanking" the subjects for their cooperation. The two verbal items, one inserted near the beginning, the other near the middle of the procedure, were:

1. I would rather get ten dollars right now than have to wait a whole month and get thirty dollars then.
2. I would rather wait to get a much larger gift much later than get a smaller one now.

Previous research (Mischel, 1961) has shown that the subject's responses over three such measures are significantly interrelated and that the three measures in combination tend to provide a more useful classification of subjects with respect to ImR or DelR preferences than does a single measure. Consequently, following the 1961 procedures, subjects were divided for purposes of data analysis into "Consistent ImR" (ImR preference over the three measures), "Consistent DelR" (consistent DelR preferences over the three measures), and "Inconsistent R" (one ImR and two DelR responses, or the reverse). Although the predictions center on differences between the Consistent ImR and Consistent DelR groups, results are also presented in terms of the number of DelR choices out of the total three possible made by the subject, i.e., 3 DelR, 2 DelR, 1 DelR, or 0 DelR.

Measures of n Achievement

Two measures of n Achievement were used. The first was the standard group-administered procedure developed by McClelland and his associates

---

[3] The size of the immediately available reinforcement used here was deliberately greater than that used in past work (Mischel, 1961) in order to increase the probability of a more equal dichotomy in the immediate, smaller versus delayed, larger choice distribution.

(1953), using five TAT-type cards.[4] The second measure was an innovation, in the form of an open-ended aspiration question. The latter was introduced in the context of "let's pretend there is a magic man": "Now let's pretend that the magic man who came along could change you into anything that you wanted to be, what would you want to be?" Subjects were instructed to answer in one word.

Measure of Acquiescence

A simple measure of acquiescence or conformity suitable for large scale research in other cultures—simple to answer, simple and rapid in administration, and meaningful in other cultural contexts—was sought. The measure adopted consisted of the following instructions, administered orally by the experimenter:

I have something in mind. I am closing my eyes and concentrating and thinking of it . . . it is something that you might agree with or that you might disagree with . . . you might disagree with what I'm thinking of or you might agree with it . . . if you agree put down a Y for Yes; if you disagree put down a N for No. (This was repeated twice, reversing the position of Y and N in the sequence of instructions.) Now I'm concentrating on it (closing eyes); go ahead.

Measure of Social Responsibility

Social responsibility was determined by response to a quite carefully constructed and independently validated Social Responsibility Scale (Harris, 1957). The Social Responsibility Scale (SRS) used has been found to correlate substantially with other measures of personal and social adjustment and was designed to "discriminate children who have, with their peers, a reputation for responsibility as contrasted with children who have little reputation for responsibility" (p. 326). All items from the 50-item SRS (Harris, 1957, called "Social Attitudes Scale," p. 324, Table 1), with the exception of Item 50, were administered in the modified form described earlier (Mischel, 1961).

Procedure

The experimenter was introduced as an American from a college in the United States interested in gathering information on the children in the various schools of the island. To help with this the subjects were asked to answer a number of questions. The details of the instructions are similar to those previously reported (Mischel, 1961). Subjects were seated sufficiently

[4] The five TAT-type pictures used were two men ("inventors") in a shop working at a machine; a boy in a checked shirt at a desk, an open book in front of him; a man at his desk in a dark office; a man looking at photos; a family at dinner. They were administered in printed booklets with the standard four questions printed for each picture on a separate page. The only modification made in the reproduction of the cards was a darkening of the pigmentation of the people in the pictures.

far apart from each other to give reasonable assurance that their choices were made independently. All testing was done in group settings in large classrooms, with two sessions. All measures except the TAT and the candy choice were given in the first session.

RESULTS AND DISCUSSION

Examination of both sex and age in relation to preference for DelR or ImR revealed no differences approaching statistical significance and consequently the male and female data and all age groups were treated collectively in subsequently analyses.

n Achievement and Preference for Delayed Reinforcement

Inspection of the responses to the five TAT-type cards indicated that the protocols were, on the whole, impoverished and short, with relatively little elaboration, a finding not unexpected for this culture. Simplified scoring for n Achievement was therefore decided upon. Protocols were scored only for presence or absence of achievement imagery (AI or UI, scored $+1$ or -1), or doubtful achievement imagery (TI, scored 0), in the manner described by McClelland et al. (1953), without continuing additional scoring of AI cards. This simplified procedure avoided the necessity for making subtler and potentially less reliable scoring decisions on relatively fragmentary responses that would be especially difficult to interpret, as normative scoring samples are not available for the culture. Since the range of scores obtained with the shortened scoring method for five cards extended from $+5$ to -5, and since any lack of discrimination through simplified scoring is likely to result in inability to reject the null hypothesis, the procedure seemed justifiable.

Comparison of subjects with respect to delay of reinforcement patterns as they related to n Achievement was done as follows. Subjects were first divided into Consistent ImR, Consistent DelR, and Inconsistent R, to categorize their choices with respect to the three measures of preference for ImR or DelR, the choice preferences with respect to DelR also being shown in terms of the number of DelR choices made by the subject out of the three total possibilities. Thus the Consistent ImR group contains all subjects with 0 DelR choices, the Inconsistent group is further subdivided into subjects with one as opposed to subjects with 2 DelR choices, and the Consistent DelR group contains all subjects with 3 DelR choices.

Table 1 presents the means and standard deviations of n Achievement scores for subjects in each of these categories with respect to reinforcement preference. As anticipated, the mean n Achievement score of Consistent DelR subjects as compared to Consistent ImR subjects is significantly higher ($t = 2.61$; $p < .01$). (One-tailed tests of significance are used throughout this paper.) The hypothesized relationship between preference for ImR as opposed to DelR and n Achievement is thus strongly supported. Similarly,

TABLE 1. Reinforcement Preference with Respect to Delay in Relation to n Achievement Scores, Aspirations, and Acquiescence

Reinforce-ment Preference N DelR [a]	n Achievement			n Achievement Distribution of Scores [b]					Aspirations [c]			Acquies-cence	
	N	M *	SD	−5 to −3	−2 to −1	0	+1 to +2	+3 to +5	Oc-cupa-tional	Achieve-ment Trait	Per-sonal Trait	Yes	No
Consistently delayed 3	37	.92	2.35	1	12	6	7	11	18	4	14	25	12
Inconsistent 2	18	1.11	} 2.32	0	4	4	6	4	8	2	7	12	6
1	27	−.74		8	4	6	8	1	4	5	17	21	6
Consistently immediate 0	30	−.70	2.62	11	6	3	5	5	9	0	17	27	3
Totals	112			20	26	19	26	21	39	11	55	85	27

[a] N of delayed reward choices made by subject.

[b] Subject's total score for the five TAT cards: N of subjects in each category of distribution.

[c] N of subjects giving Occupational aspirations, Achievement Trait aspirations, and Personal Trait aspirations; seven subjects failed to state any aspirations.

* t of 3 DelR versus 0 DelR on mean n Achievement $= 2.61$, $p < .01$; t of 3 DelR $+ 2$ DelR versus 1 DelR $+ 0$ DelR on mean n Achievement $= 3.78$, $p < .001$.

if subjects are dichotomized into "High DelR" (2 or 3 DelR responses, $M = .98$; $SD = 2.22$), and compared on mean n Achievement with "Low DelR" (0 or 1 DelR response, $M = −.41$; $SD = 2.46$), the resulting t is 3.78 ($df = 110$; $p < .001$). Clearly, subjects showing greater preference for DelR have significantly higher n Achievement scores than subjects with lesser preference for DelR. Of secondary interest is the fact that the mean n Achievement scores of subjects in the Inconsistent R category are between those of the Consistent DelR and Consistent ImR groups. The difference in means between the Consistent DelR group and the Inconsistent R group reaches significance ($p < .05$), but the difference in means between the latter and the Consistent Imr group does not reach an acceptable level. If the data are analyzed in correlational terms, a point biserial correlation of .31 ($p < .01$) is obtained from the correlation of n Achievement scores with Consistent DelR or Consistent ImR choice. A Pearson correlation between the number of DelR choices (0–3) and n Achievement scores yields an r of .27 ($p < .005$).

Responses to the open-ended aspiration question used to measure n Achievement were classified into three categories that emerged from inspection of the data: "Occupational" responses and "Trait" responses, the latter being further subdivided into "Achievement Traits" and "Personal Traits." The first category contained all responses mentioning an occupation or profession (e.g., policeman, pilot, doctor, priest); the second contained all responses mentioning personal traits that appeared to be directly achievement-related (e.g., important, big shot, bright, successful); the third contained all other responses, and consisted of traits that were not explicitly achievement-related (e.g., nice, same, a baby, small, adult, brother, honest, kind, brown). Judgments of whether a response belonged in the second or third category were made by two raters with knowledge of the culture; ratings showed more than 90% agreement. The Occupational category was of course extended to include all possible occupational aspirations within the culture. Thus, for example, king, prince, queen were included in the first category since Trinidad is within the British Commonwealth and such aspirations are analogous to "president" in a United States sample. The major conceptual distinction between the aspirations in the first as opposed to the second and third categories is that the former are clearly long-term aspirations of a career type, whereas the latter are not necessarily long-term goals, and are not explicitly career goals, but rather personal qualities.[5]

Numerous other distinctions can of course be made in scoring such responses. The major reason for using the present categorization is that when Occupational and Achievement Trait categories were combined it classified responses into a dichotomy which is as close to a 50-50 division as it was possible to obtain and which also appears to draw, albeit grossly, the desired conceptual distinction. The alternative possible distinction between occupational responses and all others is firmer since it is not dependent on nearly as subtle a judgment as that entailed in discriminating between kinds of traits. Statistical comparisons were made in which the first category was opposed to the other two combined, as well as in which the first two categories were combined and opposed to the third.

To determine the usefulness of this open-ended aspiration question for measuring n Achievement, responses in each category were related to the mean of n Achievement scores as measured in response to the more standard TAT-type procedure. Table 2 presents the mean and standard deviations of n achievement scores for subjects giving aspiration responses in each of the three categories and in combined categories, as well as the number of subjects in various categorizations of the n Achievement distribution giving each kind of aspiration. The difference between the n Achievement means

[5] The crudeness of the present scheme should be clear. For example, "policeman," although an occupational aspiration, may be less related to striving for achievement than is the aspiration to be "honest."

TABLE 2. n Achievement in Relation to Aspirations and Acquiescence

n Achievement scores [a]	N of subjects giving each kind of aspiration			Acquiescence	
	Occupational	Achievement Traits	Personal Traits	Yes	No
Positive					
+3 to +5	13	2	6	15	6
+1 to +2	12	5	10	17	9
0	6	1	9	14	5
Negative					
−1 to −2	7	3	14	21	5
−3 to −5	1	0	16	18	2
Totals	39	11	55	85	27
n Achievement M	1.44	1.09	−.73	.04	.79
		1.36	−.42		
n Achievement SD	1.89	2.15	2.56	2.53	2.25
		1.96	2.59		

Note.—t of Occupational aspirations versus all other aspirations on mean n Achievement $= 3.88$; $p < .001$. t of Occupational aspirations + Achievement Trait aspirations versus Personal Trait aspirations on mean n Achievement $= 4.54$; $p < .001$.

[a] Total score for the five TAT cards.

of subjects giving Occupational responses as compared to all others is significant ($t = 3.88$; $p < .001$), the mean of n Achievement scores of subjects in the group giving occupational aspirations being significantly higher. Similarly, comparison of the mean n Achievement of subjects giving occupational responses or Achievement Traits versus all other responses results in a t of 4.54 ($p < .001$), the former having significantly higher n Achievement scores than the latter. A Pearson correlation between Occupational responses, Achievement Trait responses, and Personal Trait responses (assigned values from 2 to 0) and n Achievement scores yields an r of .41 ($p < .001$).

This short-cut method may serve as a useful alternative to the usual much longer procedure of scoring fantasy material for n Achievement, especially when the latter is difficult to obtain, as it is in many kinds of field work. Some very recent and independently formulated attempts to relate n Achievement to realism in vocational aspirations (Mahone, 1960) should be noted, and provide further encouragement for exploring relationships between motive variables and aspirations.

The data for the relationship between aspirations and reinforcement preference patterns with respect to delay are presented in Table 1. A chi square comparison of subjects giving 3, 2, 1, and 0 DelR choices with the number of responses given by these groups in each of the three aspiration categories cannot be made meaningfully since this results in an excess of expected frequencies that are less than 5. Combining categories, subjects giving 2 or 3 DelR choices ("High DelR") were compared with subjects giving 0 or 1 DelR choices ("Low DelR") in regard to the number of responses in each of the three categories of aspirations. This comparison results in a chi square of 7.49 ($df = 2$; $p < .05$). Subjects with "High" DelR preference tend to give more Occupational and fewer Personal Trait responses than subjects with "Low" DelR preference. Chi square analyses of High-Low DelR in relation to number of Occupational aspiration responses versus number of all other aspiration responses, or in relation to a combination of the Occupational category and the Achievement Trait category as opposed to the Personal Trait category, both show a significant relationship of the same nature ($p < .02$, chi squares corrected for continuity).

Acquiescence, Reinforcement Preference, and n Achievement

The acquiescence data for yeasaying or naysaying in an ambiguous situation are related to the reinforcement preference patterns in Table 1. Consistent DelR subjects gave 25 yes and 12 no responses; consistent ImR subjects gave 27 yes and 3 no responses. Application of the chi square test to these data results in an uncorrected chi square of 4.80 ($df = 1$; $p < .05$). Similarly, a dichotomization into "High DelR" as opposed to "Low DelR" to compare number of yes or no responses, results in an uncorrected chi square of 4.38 ($df = 1$; $p < .05$).[6] As anticipated, subjects high in preference for DelR gave relatively more no and fewer yes responses than did subjects low in preference for DelR.

In spite of its relative weakness, this association is striking since only one item was used to measure acquiescent yeasaying tendencies. The relationship between yeasaying and naysaying tendencies and reinforcement preference patterns would seem well worth further study with more reliable multiple measures to obtain yeasaying data. The present measure of acquiescence may have advantages in studying various aspects of acquiescent behavior by permitting easy manipulation of the reference group, e.g., merely changing the public identification of the examiner. The method may also be

---

[6] If extreme caution is used and the decision is made to apply the Yates correction for continuity on all 2×2 contingency tables, although all expected frequencies in each cell do exceed 5, the comparison of Consistent DelR with Consistent ImR subjects on acquiescence results in a chi square of 3.59; the comparison of the "High" versus "Low" preference for DelR dichotomy with acquiescence results in a chi square of 3.51. A chi square of 3.84 is required for $p < .05$ and of 2.71 for $p < .10$.

used readily to study conforming tendencies cross-culturally. The preponderance of yes responses in the present results may be taken as a caution against excessive generalizations about strong conforming tendencies in our own culture without reference to comparative data. The primary relevance of these data, however, is that they serve as an empirical link between the patterns isolated by Couch and Keniston (1960) to distinguish yeasayers and naysayers and the present distinction between subjects consistently preferring DelR or ImR. Clearly the patterns have strong conceptual overlap: the present findings provide support for their empirical overlap.

The n Achievement scores obtained both from the standard n Achievement measure and the aspiration measure were related to yeasaying as opposed to naysaying. Theoretical considerations about the personality correlates of high n Achievement lead to the anticipation that persons high in n Achievement should show less acquiescence or yeasaying. However, although the mean n Achievement scores (on the standard measure) of non-acquiescent subjects is higher ($N = 85$; $M = .04$; $SD = 2.53$) the difference clearly falls short of acceptable significance levels and can only be interpreted as a trend ($t = 1.35$; $.10 > p > .05$, one-tailed test). Table 2 shows the number of yes and no responses given to the acquiescence measure by subjects in various categorizations of the total distribution of n Achievement scores for the five TAT stories. Comparison of subjects with positive scores as opposed to subjects with negative scores on the number of yes versus no responses results in an uncorrected chi square of 3.59 which approaches but does not reach an acceptable significance level ($p < .10$; chi square corrected for continuity $= 2.72$, $p < .10$). If subjects with zero and negative n Achievement scores are combined and compared with subjects having positive n Achievement scores, this represents the closest median split possible, using all subjects on the yes-no dichotomy. An uncorrected chi square of 2.73 with $p < .10$ results. In sum, a trend of such dubious statistical significance appears to characterize the relationship between our measure of acquiescence and the TAT n Achievement measure that we cannot safely reject the null hypothesis. As such, the present findings share the uncertain conclusions about the relationship between acquiescence and n Achievement obtained by other investigators (e.g., Samelson, 1958).

The data also permit a test of the relationship between the aspiration measure of n Achievement and acquiescence (Table 3). If subjects giving Occupational aspirations are combined with those giving Achievement Trait aspirations and compared to those giving Personal Trait aspirations with respect to the frequency of the yes or no responses, the resulting chi square does not approach statistical significance. However, comparison of subjects giving Occupational aspirations with those giving all other aspirations on acquiescence results in a chi square of 4.27 (corrected for continuity), $p < .05$. Subjects giving Occupational aspirations, when compared to those giving all other aspirations, significantly show relatively less yeasaying and

TABLE 3. ACQUIESCENCE IN RELATION TO EACH CATEGORY
OF ASPIRATIONS

	Aspirations		
Acquiescence	Occupational	Achievement Traits	Personal Traits
Yes	24	10	44
No	15	1	11

Note.—Chi square comparison of Occupational aspiration; with all others on Yes versus No: $x^2 = 4.27$ (corrected for continuity); $p < .05$.

more naysaying. It is of interest that the aspiration measure of n Achievement is thus significantly related to acquiescence whereas results from the more standard fantasy measure of n Achievement fall short of statistical significance. Even more clear-cut relationships may perhaps be expected when data that lend themselves to more detailed and subtle scoring are employed and when multiple acquiescence measures are used.

Social Responsibility in Relation to the Other Measures

As regards the SRS, the relationship between preference for DelR and social responsibility reported earlier (Mischel, 1961) is replicated. A Pearson correlation of .28 ($p < .005$) is obtained between number of DelR choices (0–3) and SRS scores. Using t tests, significant differences between means ($p < .01$) are obtained when "High DelR" subjects (3 and 2 DelR choices) are compared with "Low DelR" subjects (1 and 0 DelR choices). The means and SDs of the former are 31.25 and 4.28, and of the latter 29.05 and 3.70. A secondary finding of considerable interest (Table 4) is a strong relationship between SRS and n Achievement ($r = .40$, $p < .001$ with TAT measure; $r = .33$, $p < .001$ with aspiration measure). This appears to be one of the very few instances in which a significant positive correlation is obtained between n Achievement and a *questionnaire* measure. Theoretically, although not specifically predicted, it seems extremely plausible that social responsibility and achievement motivation should be interrelated. Operationally, it is encouraging that at least in this cultural setting, questionnaire data do appear correlated with scores based on fantasy material.

An Overview

Summarizing the results, Table 4 presents the intercorrelations of preference for DelR, the two n Achievement measures, and SRS. Preference for DelR, n Achievement measured by two different but intercorrelated methods (TAT and open-ended aspirations), and SRS scores are all significantly and positively interrelated. The acquiescence measure is not significantly

TABLE 4. Intercorrelations of Preference for Delayed, Larger
Reinforcement (DelR), n Achievement, and
Social Responsibility (SRS) ($N = 112$)

	n Achievement		SRS
	TAT	Aspirations [a]	
Preference for DelR	$r = .27$ **	$C = .26$ *	$r = .28$ **
n Achievement			
TAT		$r = .41$ ***	$r = .40$ ***
Aspirations [a]			$r = .33$ ***

[a] $N = 105$.
* $p < .05$ ($x^2 = 7.49$, $df = 2$).
** $p < .005$.
*** $p < .001$.

associated with social responsibility scores ($r = .06$, $p < .20$), although, as
discussed above, low significant relationships do seem to hold between naysaying and preference for DelR and between naysaying and Occupational
(as opposed to all other) aspirations. Finally, partial correlations were computed between preference for DelR and n Achievement, holding SRS constant, and between preference for DelR and SRS, holding n Achievement
constant. In both cases, low but positive and still significant correlations
result ($r = .18$ and $.19$, respectively, $p < .05$). This finding suggests that the
major measures used to delineate the cluster of correlates associated with
preference for DelR as opposed to ImR, while themselves significantly intercorrelated, still appear to tap different aspects of the constellation.

The main import of the over-all findings is that they relate reinforcement
preference to other more thoroughly explored variables. When the present
findings are taken collectively with those obtained on other previously reported samples, a network of meaningful correlates becomes apparent. These
are interpreted as providing considerable evidence that an obviously crucial
but relatively unstudied dimension of behavior, the ability to delay the
relatively trivial but immediately available for the sake of larger but later
outcomes, can be explored usefully with relatively simple direct measures
of choice preference. The correlates of these choice preferences are becoming increasingly clear, although controlled studies of antecedents are still
lacking.

The simple preference patterns with respect to delay elicited thus far
provide only an early model and a prelude to more complex and subtler
batteries. In such batteries, delay preference patterns systematically sampling
a variety of value and need areas could be tapped, and the valences of particular intervening work and fantasy activities (in addition to the simple
waiting period over a time interval used at present) could be elicited. The

ultimate aim would be the construction of predictive individual topographies for complex choices on the dimension of delay, and the measurement of individual time lines.

The findings also support the fruitfulness of devising simple quantifiable measures for eliciting data on potentially complex dimensions in field research situations in other cultures. Although such field research is often thought to present serious methodological problems when quantifiable data on psychological dimensions are sought, the present results indicated, on the contrary, that exceedingly simple measures may serve to yield useful data that might only be elicited from more sophisticated subjects by much more complex methods. In the present situation, the subjects' lack of psychological sophistication appears to have been a strong asset in circumventing sources of error that so often bedevil comparable researches.

SUMMARY

This study, using 112 Trinidadian subjects aged 11–14, tested the relationship between preference for immediate, smaller (ImR) or delayed, larger (DelR) reinforcement in choice situations and (a) n Achievement, (b) acquiescence (yeasaying or naysaying in an ambiguous situation). The expected significant positive relationships between preference for DelR and n Achievement were found. The inverse relationship between preference for DelR and acquiescence was, as predicted, also obtained. n Achievement was inversely related to acquiescence but only as a statistically nonsignificant trend. Responses to a simple open-ended aspiration measure, appropriate for use in other cultures, were found to significantly differentiate high and low n Achievement subjects as measured by the standard procedure, more occupational aspirations being given by high n Achievement subjects. The possible usefulness of this aspiration measure as an alternative index of n Achievement in field work was suggested. Data on the interrelationships between a measure of social responsibility and the other variables were also presented. The over-all findings support the usefulness of relatively simple choice situations for eliciting preference for ImR as opposed to DelR in the attempt to elaborate the variables relevant to the ability to delay immediate gratification for the sake of later, larger outcomes, within the context of another culture. The present findings serve to elaborate the network of correlates of choice preferences for delayed, larger gratifications when these are opposed to smaller but immediately available rewards.

REFERENCES

Aronson, E.   The need for achievement as measured by graphic expression. In J. W. Atkinson (Ed.), *Motives in fantasy, action, and society*. Princeton: Van Nostrand, 1958. Pp. 249–265.

Atkinson, J. W. *Motives in fantasy, action, and society.* Princeton: Van Nostrand, 1958.

Bass, B. M. Development and evaluation of a scale for measuring social acquiescence. *J. abnorm. soc. Psychol.,* 1956, **53,** 296–299.

Couch, A., & Keniston, K. Yesayers and naysayers: Agreeing response set as a personality variable. *J. abnorm. soc. Psychol.,* 1960, **60,** 151–174.

French, Elizabeth G. Development of a measure of complex motivation. In J. W. Atkinson (Ed.), *Motives in fantasy, action, and society.* Princeton: Van Nostrand, 1958. Pp. 242–248.

Freud, S. *Beyond the pleasure principle.* New York Boni & Livewright, 1922.

Harris, D. B. A scale for measuring attitudes of social responsibility in children. *J. abnorm. soc. Psychol.,* 1957, **55,** 322–326.

Levine, M., Glass, H., & Meltzoff, J. The inhibition process, Rorschach human movement responses and intelligence. *J. consult. Psychol.,* 1957, **21,** 41–45.

Levine, M., Spivack, G., & Wright, B. The inhibition process, Rorschach human movement responses and intelligence: Some further data. *J. consult. Psychol.,* 1959, **23,** 306–312.

McClelland, D. C., Atkinson, J. W., Clark, R. A., & Lowell, E. L. *The achievement motive.* New York: Appleton-Century-Crofts, 1953.

Mahone, C. H. Fear of failure and unrealistic vocational aspirations. *J. abnorm. soc. Psychol.,* 1960, **60,** 253–261.

Mahrer, A. R. The role of expectancy in delayed reinforcement. *J. exp. Psychol.,* 1956, **52,** 101–105.

Melikian, L. Preference for delayed reinforcement: An experimental study among Palestinian Arab refugee children. *J. soc. Psychol.,* 1959, **50,** 81–86.

Messick, S., & Jackson, D. N. Authoritarianism or acquiescence in Bass' data. *J. abnorm. soc. Psychol.,* 1957, **54,** 424–426.

Metzner, R. Preference for delayed reinforcement: Some complications. Harvard Psychological Clinic, 1960. (Mimeo)

Mischel, W. Preference for delayed reinforcement: An experimental study of a cultural observation. *J. abnorm. soc. Psychol.,* 1958, **56,** 57–61.

Mischel, W. Preference for delayed reinforcement: Further cross-cultural applications. Harvard Psychological Clinic, 1959. (Mimeo)

Mischel, W. Preference for delayed reinforcement and social responsibility. *J. abnorm. soc. Psychol.,* 1961, **62,** 1–7.

Rapaport, D. *Organization and pathology of thought.* New York: Columbia Univer. Press, 1951.

Samelson, F. The relation of achievement and affiliation motives to conforming behavior in two conditions of conflict with a majority. In J. W. Atkinson (Ed.), *Motives in fantasy, action, and society.* Princeton: Van Nostrand, 1958. Pp. 421–433.

Singer, J. L. Delayed gratification and ego-development: Implications for clinical and experimental research. *J. consult. Psychol.,* 1955, **19,** 259–266.

Singer, J. L., Wilensky, H., & McCraven, Vivian G. Delaying capacity, fantasy and planning ability: A factorial study of some basic ego functions. *J. consult. Psychol.,* 1956, **20,** 375–383.

Spivack, G., Levine, M., & Sprigle, H. Intelligence test performance and the delay function of the ego. *J. consult. Psychol.,* 1959, **23,** 428–431.

5.7 Risk Taking in Children with High and Low Need for Achievement

David C. McClelland [1]

Previous research in this series has argued that *n* Achievement is a key factor in accounting for the behavior of entrepreneurs, particularly business entrepreneurs who play a large part in determining the extent of economic development of a country (260, 263). One of the striking characteristics of such entrepreneurs is their willingness to take calculated risks, to innovate in ways that have reasonable chances of success. If *n* Achievement is in fact related to such entrepreneurial behavior, it ought to predispose people in favor of taking moderate risks as opposed to either the extremely speculative or the extremely safe ones. The rationale for predicting such a linkage runs something like this: in an extremely safe undertaking at which anyone can succeed, the person with high *n* Achievement can get little achievement satisfaction out of accomplishing his objective. In an extremely speculative one, on the other hand, he not only is almost certain to frustrate his achievement aspirations, he also may feel that if he should by some outside chance succeed, his success could not be attributed to his own personal efforts but to luck or circumstances beyond his control.

A previous experiment has shown that subjects with high *n* Achievement do in fact tend, more than subjects with low *n* Achievement, to like those occupations which involve some risk or which are part of the entrepreneurial role (263). This preference exists apparently in male subjects over an age range of roughly 18 to 45, and both in Germany and America. Furthermore, Atkinson has shown in a preliminary experiment that female subjects with high *n* Achievement tend to perform somewhat better at longer odds where the chances of winning are 1 out of 3 than do subjects with low *n* Achievement whose peak performance comes when the chances of winning are 1 out of 2 (Ch. 20). The experiments to be reported here extend the range of risk phenomena to be investigated from occupational preferences and from performance under odds to the choice of the degree of risk under which a person prefers to operate. These are probably all coordinate phenomena, but free choice of the risk to be taken is an essential part of the behavior

[1] I am deeply indebted to the Office of Naval Research for funds necessary to carry out this project, to Roberta Cohen, Leon Gross, and Elliot Aronson for running the subjects and for helping score the protocols.

Reprinted from J. W. Atkinson (Ed.), *Motives in Fantasy, Action and Society*. Princeton, N.J.: Van Nostrand, 1958, pp. 306–321.

of entrepreneurs, who must actually seek out certain types of risk situations as well as perform well in them.

The research was performed on young children because the theory of achievement motivation presented elsewhere (272) argues that the motive is formed roughly between the ages of 5 and 9, and if so, its effect on risk-taking behavior should already be apparent at these ages and perhaps in purer form than later when the subjects may have learned all sorts of things about what risks one *ought* to take. Measuring *n* Achievement at such early ages has only recently become potentially feasible through the development by Aronson (Ch. 17) of a method for scoring for it from expressive "doodles" or scribbles. The words "potentially feasible" need underlining. Aronson found that certain doodle characteristics were fairly consistently correlated with *n* Achievement scores obtained in the usual way from written stories (272) across a number of samples of subjects, but he worked with male college students, and it is a very large jump indeed from them to five-year-old boys and girls on whom the main experiment to be reported here was performed. The measurement is feasible because five-year-olds can scribble while they cannot be easily got to tell stories yet; there is no certainty that their scribbles will reflect *n* Achievement at this age the way college student scribbles do at age 18. In fact, there are so many uncertainties or risky assumptions in the design of this experiment that it may be worth summarizing them in advance. It must be assumed 1) that stable individual differences in *n* Achievement have been formed by age five, 2) that these differences will be reflected in the scribbles children produce, 3) that fairly stable preferences for certain types of risk-taking have also been developed by age five, and 4) that the hypothesized connection between *n* Achievement and risk-taking exists and has already been developed by this time. Only if all of these assumptions hold can positive results be obtained to support the hypothesis that children with high *n* Achievement will prefer moderate risks as contrasted with children with low *n* Achievement who should show more variability in risk-taking behavior with greater choice of extremely safe or speculative risks.

PROCEDURE

Two groups of subjects were employed. The group on which the main experiment was performed consisted of 26 five-year-old children in kindergarten, 13 boys and 13 girls, who were tested individually by a female graduate student. While their background was essentially middle class, it varied widely, some of the children coming from homes of college professors and others from the Italian and Polish lower middle class or lower class homes typical of a city school district in New England. The second group of subjects consisted of 32 eight- and nine-year-olds from a third grade class in a Connecticut manufacturing city. They were tested in a group by a male college undergraduate.

The tests given the children consisted of the following: *the "doodle" measure of n Achievement.* The children were shown very briefly (for about three seconds) a large white piece of cardboard on which the first set of doodles used by Aronson (Design 1) had been drawn in black ink. They were supplied with a standard piece of blank typewriting paper, a box of colored crayons, and instructed to, "Let me see if you can make scribbles like these. If you can't remember all of them, you can make up your own." They were given as much time as they needed to produce some scribbles, and if necessary, were reminded not to draw pictures of things. The same procedure was followed a second time with a different set of doodles (Design 2), also used by Aronson. In the group experiment with the third graders, the only difference was that the doodles had been drawn on slides which were projected briefly on a screen in front of the class. The scribbles produced by the children were scored for the characteristics developed and described elsewhere by Aronson (Ch. 17). These characteristics may be described briefly as follows without going into the details of scoring definitions: *Line*—the number of scribbles (or scorable units) composed of "discrete" lines (characteristic of high *n* Achievement) minus the number of units composed of "fuzzy" or repetitious lines (characteristic of low *n* Achievement). *Space*—amount of unused space (characteristic of low *n* Achievement), computed as the maximum distance from any margin to the nearest mark on the paper. Aronson used the unused space at the bottom of the paper only, and this procedure was followed with the third graders, but with the five-year-olds it could not be used because it was not always clear what was the bottom of the paper since the children frequently changed their orientation with respect to the page. *Form*—the number of diagonals and S-shapes (characteristic of high *n* Achievement), and the number of multiple waves (characteristic of low *n* Achievement). The general principle underlying the differences in the scribbling characteristics of high and low *n* Achievement seems to be an avoidance by the "highs" of repetition, a tendency to use up space, to avoid going over the same line twice, etc., although it should be emphasized that the scoring system was established entirely empirically simply by correlating various characteristics with the standard *n* Achievement score obtained from content analysis of stories written to pictures. Additionally, since colored crayons were used with the five-year-olds (instead of pencils as in the Aronson experiment and as in the third grade experiment here), there was an opportunity to check a finding reported by Knapp (Ch. 26) that subjects with high *n* Achievement prefer blues and greens over reds and yellows. So a new measure was obtained, consisting simply of the number of blue or green units minus the number of red or yellow units, with those colors being omitted which were not easily classifiable as belonging either in one category or in the other.

Risk-taking tasks. (1) Ring toss. In the kindergarten study, one of the original Lewin "level of aspiration" tasks was used in which the subject is simply given a rope ring and asked to try and throw it over a peg placed on the floor. The subject is allowed to stand wherever he wants to and can, of course, stand right next to the peg or as far away as six or seven feet. He was given ten trials and the distance at which he stood for each trial was recorded. Obviously the risk of failure increases the further he stands from the peg. (2) The tilting maze board. In this commercial children's toy, a ball is placed at the start of a maze, and the child is supposed to roll it through the maze by manipulating two wheels which control separately the right-left or up-down tilt of the board. The difficulty is that holes are punched at various points throughout the maze path, and the objective is to see how far one can roll the ball before it drops through a hole. The holes are numbered in sequence and the child was asked to trace with his finger through the path to the point he was going to try to reach on the next trial. Each child in the kindergarten group was given ten trials. Again, the further along the path he set his level of aspiration, the greater he risked failure. (3) Dot connection. In the group experiment with the third graders it was not possible to use ring toss, but a group task as much like it as possible was developed. Subjects were instructed to put down as many or as few dots as they wanted to on a piece of paper and then to try and connect them with a line that does not cross itself. The procedure was repeated twice and the score was simply the number of dots that the person put down each time. It appeared obvious to the subjects that the fewer dots he puts down, the easier the task will be just as in the case of ring toss the closer he stands to the peg, the easier it will be to succeed. The fact is, however, that it is impossible to fail at the dot connection task. Any number of dots can be connected by a line that does not cross itself, but it was hoped that subjects would not discover this in the two trials they were given. (4) Word memory. The third graders were asked to write down a list of words which they were to be asked to recall at some later date in the testing. Again, they could put down as many or as few words as they liked. The procedure was repeated twice, and the score was simply the number of words they put down, and also the number which they correctly remembered. This task was more like ring toss in that the subjects could clearly fail, but it had the marked disadvantage that subjects could defeat the purpose of the test by putting down connected phrases or sentences. Other performance tasks were given to both groups of subjects as part of another study.

RESULTS

The first question to settle is whether there is any evidence that the scribbles are reflecting *n* Achievement among the five-year-olds. The most important evidence on this point will be supplied by the relationship between the doodle measure of *n* Achievement and risk taking, but there are also two other questions which should be answered in the affirmative, if the doodle score is valid. Is it internally consistent or reliable? And does the mean score increase with age as it should according to the general theory

TABLE 1. Mean Number of Determinants of n Achievement Score in "Doodles" Produced by Subjects of Different Age Levels

	Male College Students, aged around 18 ($N = 75$). After Aronson (Ch. 17)			Boys and Girls in Third Grade, aged around 9 ($N = 32$)			Boys and Girls in Kindergarten, aged around 5 ($N = 26$)		
	Doodle Design			Doodle Design			Doodle Design		
	1	2	Total	1	2	Total	1	2	Total
Total units scored	12.25	10.00	22.25	11.58	11.45	23.03	8.54	9.00	17.54
S D			7.64			7.51			8.23
No. "discrete" minus No. "fuzzy" lines (+) *	3.16	5.65	8.81	2.67	4.55	7.22	.23	3.00	3.23
S D			9.94			9.32			7.72
Space from bottom in cm. (−)	8.68	8.80	17.48	12.09	10.55	22.64	not comparable		
S D			10.45			13.40			
Total "forms"	6.81	4.49	11.30	3.55	2.34	5.89	2.49	2.80	5.29
S D			5.09			3.41			4.90
Diagonals (+)	2.88	2.51	5.39	1.03	.64	1.67	.42	1.19	1.61
S-shapes (+)	.77	.54	1.31	.79	.55	1.34	.15	.23	.38
Multiple waves (−)	3.16	1.44	4.60	1.73	1.15	2.88	1.92	1.38	3.30

* + = scored positively, − = scored negatively for n Achievement.
Courtesy of D. Van Nostrand Company, Inc.

of how the achievement motive develops (272)? The answer to the second question is contained in Table 1, which presents the mean number of scorable units and of the determinants of n Achievement score for each of the two doodle Designs for groups of subjects with modal ages of 5, 9, and 18 years. The total number of scorable units does not differ between ages 9 and 18, but the five-year-olds are significantly ($p < .02$) less productive on the average. The *line* score based on the number of "discrete" minus the number of "fuzzy" lines is the best single index of n Achievement developed by Aronson because it correlates highest by itself with n Achievement, probably because it is based on every scorable unit in the subject's protocol. Also, it should not be influenced by sheer quantity of output nor by the capacity of the subjects to produce various shapes. So in the present instance it permits the most unambiguous comparison of changes in mean n Achievement at different age levels. The mean increase it shows from age 5 to 9, though large, is of borderline significance ($t = 1.76$, $p < .10$) because of some extreme scores which make the variability large, but if a simple measure is taken of the proportion of individuals in each group who score above the mean for all 134 cases combined, it turns out that only 18.2% of the five-year-olds are above the mean as compared with 51.5% of the nine-year-olds ($X^2 = 8.28$, $p < .01$) and 54.7% of the 18-year-olds. Obviously this score shows its big increase between age 5 and age 9, which it should if it is really reflecting n Achievement, since this is supposedly the crucial period for the development of the achievement motive. Furthermore, the much smaller and insignificant increase between the ages of 9 and 18 is entirely consistent with the theory that the motive should be largely complete in its development in most people by the age of 9. Actually, of course, the comparison between the 9-year-olds and the 18-year-olds is not really very meaningful because the 18-year-olds are all males and they are from higher socioeconomic status on the average. Either one or both of these factors might be responsible for the slightly larger mean score in the 18-year-old group over and beyond age as such. Since use of space was measured differently for the 5-year-olds, it can be used only to compare the 9- and 18-year-olds. Here the difference is in the same direction as for the line index, showing more use of space (indicating higher n Achievement) at a near significant level ($t = 1.94$, $p \sim .05$) for the older group. The *form* determinants show age trends like those of the other two determinants, although some recomputations are necessary because the younger age groups show many fewer identifiable forms ($p < .001$). This difference in form output can be equated for by converting each of the form subtype means into the proportion they represent of the total form mean. If this is done, the following clearcut results are obtained. At age 18, 59% of the total form mean is accounted for by high n Achievement forms (diagonals and S-shapes) and 41% by low n Achievement forms (multiwave); at age 9 the proportions are 51% to 49%, and at age 5 they are 38% to 62%, respectively, yielding differences in favor of high n Achievement forms of 18%, 2% and −24% at ages 18, 9, and 5, respectively. Again, as in the case of the line score, the increase in high n Achievement indicators between ages 5 and 9 (26%) is larger than the increase between ages 9 and 18 (16%). So far as the figures in Table 1 go then, they support the hypothesis that the doodle measure is reflecting n Achievement since it increases with age just as it should if it were measuring n Achievement.

The other fact of importance to emerge from Table 1 is that the mean number of identifiable forms in both of the children's groups is much smaller and very significantly so ($t < .001$ in each case) than the mean number of identifiable forms for the college students. This finding has a direct bearing on the computation of the total n Achievement score from doodles and, also, on its reliability. Aronson had obtained his total score by simply quartiling the distribution of scores for a given scoring variable in response to the combined doodle Designs 1 and 2 and summing across the quartile scores (reversed in value, of course, for the negative indicators— i.e., use of space, and multiwaves). In the present instance the use of a separate quartile score for each of the three form determinants when they were so much less frequent would possibly weight random variations much more heavily than desirable, particularly as compared with the "discrete-minus-fuzzy line" score which is based on large numbers of instances. Therefore, a new composite "form" score was devised which consisted of the number of diagonals plus the number of S-shapes minus the number of multi-waves. If this score is quartiled and added to the quartile scores for the other two determinants—line and space—the much less frequent forms contribute only $\frac{1}{3}$ to the total score instead of a less justifiable $\frac{3}{5}$ of the total score for children who have difficulty making identifiable forms. A check of the new composite form score against n Achievement with the 75 subjects in the college student group used by Aronson (see the first column in Table 1) yielded a correlation of $+.23$ ($p < .05$), a value which is higher than the correlation of two of its components with n Achievement in this sample and slightly lower than the other. While the use of the composite form score thus seemed justified on both theoretical and empirical grounds, it had the disadvantage of curtailing somewhat the range of total doodle n Achievement scores by reducing the number of determinants from five to three. This was corrected by quartiling the distributions of scores for each of the three determinants *on each doodle Design separately* and then adding the resulting six quartile scores to obtain the final total score for an individual. This new method of obtaining the total n Achievement score from doodles was also checked against the regular n Achievement score in the same sample of 75 college students and the resulting correlation was .36, which is exactly the same value obtained by Aronson using his method of combining determinants to get a total score.

The internal consistency of the quartile scores can be obtained by correlating those obtained for doodle Design 1 with those for doodle Design 2. For the kindergarten group the correlation proved to be 13, for the 9-year-olds it was .38, which is more nearly comparable to that obtained by Aronson ($r = .44$). The value for the kindergarten group is discouragingly low and insignificant, but it probably is a serious underestimate of the true correlation caused by the coarse grouping of results into quartiles and also by two deviant cases in a very small sample. Several lines of evidence support this conclusion. First, the correlations of the determinant scores between doodle Design 1 and doodle Design 2 before being quartiled are .58 for discrete minus fuzzy lines, .53 for space, and .46 for the combined form score, each of these correlations being significant well beyond the .05 level. Secondly, if the split is made not between doodle Design 1 and doodle Design 2 but between a score made up of a combination of odd vs. even determinants, regardless of which doodle Design they come from, the resultant split-half correlation is +.30 (or +.43 if one extremely deviant case is discarded). Thirdly, the scores obtained separately from each doodle correlate about the same with a measure of risk-taking behavior explained below. In short, the evidence tends to support the belief that the true reliability of the doodle measure of n Achievement is somewhere around .40 as a conservative estimate, which, corrected for halving the test, comes to between .55 and .60 for the total score. Such a value is not high enough to give one much faith in the test score for a given individual, but it is high enough to demonstrate that there is significant internal consistency in this measure even in young children and to permit using the measure for studies of group differences.

The most important results on risk-taking among subjects with high and low n Achievement are summarized in Figure 1, which shows where the 5-year-olds stood in relation to the peg in the ring-toss task and what the probability of success was at various distances from the peg. The distributions of choice points for throwing are plotted separately for the 12 subjects

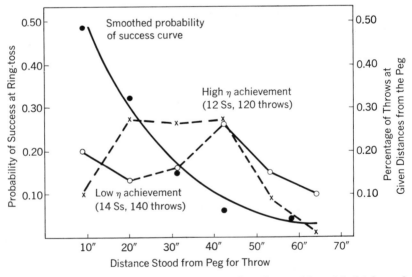

FIGURE 1. Percentage of throws made by 5-year-olds with high and low "doodle" n Achievement at different distances from the peg and smoothed curve of probability of success at those distances. 26 Ss, 10 throws each. Plotted at midpoints of intervals of 11 inches beginning with closest distance stood (4"–14", 5"–15", etc.). (Courtesy of D. Van Nostrand Company, Inc.)

above and the 14 subjects below the mean doodle n Achievement score. Obviously the variance of the throwing distances for the "lows" is considerably larger than the variance for the "highs" ($F = 1.83$, $p < .01$). Also, it is clear that, as predicted, the "highs" tend to concentrate their throws in the middle distance ranges (from 20 to 40 inches) where there is moderate probability of success (varying from around $p = .11$ to $p = .30$ to judge by the smoothed curve) whereas the "lows" show a disproportionate tendency to concentrate their shots either very close to the peg or very far away. Actually the grouping necessary to get large enough numbers to plot this graph obscures somewhat how different the "highs" and "lows" are at the extremes. For example, out of the 11 throws made standing as close to the peg as one could get (about 4 inches), 10 of them were made by "lows," whereas at the other extreme, of the 11 throws made at a distance of five feet or more (actually up to seven feet in one case), 10 of 11 of these throws were again made by "lows." While chi-square tests of significance are not strictly legitimate because of the unknown amount of correlation among the observations, they are of some interest as a rough test of significance. For example, if the frequencies in the two extremes of the distribution (farthest and nearest to the peg) are combined, it appears that 30% of the throws made by the "lows" are in these categories, whereas only 11% of the throws made by the "highs" are (chi-square $= 12.8$, $p < .01$). Or if the second farthest category is also added in, nearly $\frac{1}{2}$ of the throws (45%) of the "lows" are from extreme positions, whereas only $\frac{1}{5}$ of the "highs" are. Differences at each extreme taken separately are also significant. If the frequencies in the nearest or safest category are compared with those in the moderately safe middle distances from 15 to 36 inches, the "lows" show significantly more throws from the safest distance and the "highs" more from the moderately safe distances (chi-square $= 10.74$, $p < .01$). At the other extreme, if the throws from a moderately far distance (37 to 47 inches) are compared with the throws in the "very far" distances (48 inches and up), again the "highs" show significantly more "moderation" and the "lows" more "wild speculation" (chi-square $= 4.70$, $p < .05$).

The results for the tilting maze task are similar except that the distribution of estimates as to how far they could roll the ball is more nearly J-shaped rather than normal as in the case of ring-toss, which means that there is little or no opportunity for a difference between the "highs" and "lows" to show up at the "safe" end of the distribution of risks. That is, the task was so difficult that on 75% of 260 trials the subjects never got beyond the first hole and therefore there was a tendency to pile up levels of aspiration at the low end of the distribution. Nevertheless the difference between the "highs" and the "lows" at the "speculative" end of the distribution could and did show up. A split at the median of the distribution of estimates of how far they would roll the ball on the next trial show that 64% of the estimates of the "lows" were for hole 5 or beyond whereas only

43% of the estimates of the "highs" were this far out (chi-square $=$ 10.7, $p < .01$).

To return for a moment to the ring-toss task, one might expect that the subjects with high n Achievement might be more influenced by the actual success that they were having and might tend to gravitate toward a central tendency of the successful throws. Below such a midpoint, success would be easier but less satisfying, while above it, success would be more satisfying but too rare. The mean distance for the successful throws was 23 inches. The average distance at which a child stood on his ten throws was then computed and subtracted from 23 inches to get his deviation from this central tendency of the successful tries. The resulting distribution of devia-

TABLE 2. Frequencies and Percentages of Different Numbers of Dots Put Down to Be Connected by Ss with High and Low n Achievement

No. of Dots	High (16 Ss, two trials each)		Low (16 Ss, two trials each)	
3–8	2	6%	5	15%
9–14	12	38%	7	22%
15–20	11	34%	6	19%
21–26	3	9%	5	15%
27 & up	4	13%	9	28%

Courtesy of D. Van Nostrand Company, Inc.

tion scores was badly skewed as inspection of Figure 1 would demonstrate and had to be normalized by a square root transformation. The transformed deviation scores correlated with n Achievement score $-.40$, $p < .05$, indicating that the higher the subject's n Achievement score, the closer he tended to approximate in his risk-taking the central tendency of the successful throws. The n Achievement score based on each doodle Design is contributing about equally to this correlation, the correlations being $-.32$ for Design 1 alone and $-.28$ for Design 2 alone. Consequently, despite the low correlation between n Achievement scores based on Design 1 and Design 2, there is evidence they are both measuring the same characteristic because each correlates about the same with a third variable—e.g., tendency to take moderate risks.

Very similar results were obtained with the third graders, although they are somewhat less dramatic because the tasks used were not as adequate for testing the hypothesis as ring toss was. Table 2 summarizes the distribution of the numbers of dots the subjects with high and low n Achievement put down for themselves to connect. The frequencies are much smaller, but again 43% of the tasks set for themselves by the "lows" fall either in the easiest or the hardest category whereas only 19% of the tasks set for themselves by the "highs" fell in these extreme positions (chi-square $=$ 4.7, p $<$ .05). There is unfortunately no central tendency of success with this task, and so it was necessary to compute a deviation score simply from the mean number of dots put down for the two trials combined after this distribution of scores had been normalized by a square root transformation. The correlation of n Achievement score with the size of the individual's deviation from the means of these transformed scores was —.35, p $<$ .05, indicating again that the higher the n Achievement, the closer the subject tended to approximate "moderation" in setting a task for himself to accomplish. It may be noted in passing that in following the principle of transforming scores only when necessary because of an extreme skew in the distribution, *deviations* were transformed in the ring-toss experiment, whereas *raw scores* were transformed in the dot task *before* deviations were computed. However, if the transformations are made the other way in each case, the two resulting correlations of deviation scores with n Achievement do not differ from those reported by more than .01, (—.41 for ring toss and —.34 for the dot connection task).

Finally, the correlation between n Achievement and the deviation score from the central tendency of the average number of words listed for recall on the two trials in the word memory task was in the predicted direction ($r =$ —.20), but insignificant. The reason why it is not larger appears to lie partly in the fact that the distribution of words put down does not show much variability and partly because some of the children put down phrases (e.g., "I love you") which really defeated the purpose of the task as a method of estimating the degree of risk a subject would take in setting an easy or a difficult task for himself.

Could the results obtained be due simply to intelligence? Perhaps the way in which the doodles are scored for n Achievement simply reflects the intelligence of the child, and the more intelligent he is, the more likely he is to take moderate or sensible risks in setting tasks for himself. Unfortunately intelligence test scores were not available on the 5-year-olds, but Otis I.Q.'s were obtainable on 24 of the 32 subjects in the third-grade group. The correlation of these I.Q.'s with the doodle n Achievement score was .08 and with the deviation score estimate of moderate risk taking in the dot connection task was —.28. Both fall short of the .40 correlation needed for significance at the 5% level with this number of cases, although the latter correlation suggests that intelligence may also be a factor in influencing children to take calculated or moderate risks.

A final point of interest is the relationship between the doodle n Achievement score and the preference for blues and greens over reds and yellows discovered by Knapp (see Ch. 26). With the 5-year-olds who used colored crayons in making their doodles the correlation was a substantial .45, p $<$ .05, suggesting that this color preference may appear quite early in life and perhaps should be added as a determinant of the total n Achievement score obtained from doodles along with line, space, and form. It was added in the present experiment, and the correlation with the deviation score from the mean of the successful throws was recomputed. It dropped from —.40 to —.30, which is below the level of significance with this number of subjects. Unfortunately the sample is so small that it is hard to evaluate the significance of this drop, but the safest conclusion would appear to be that color preference in the doodle task ought to be correlated with the standard n Achievement score in several cross-validating groups as Aronson did with the other determinants before it is added to them.

DISCUSSION

This study itself represents a rather risky enterprise in that it involved a chain of at least four rather dubious assumptions, any one of which might not have been correct. The fact that positive results were obtained tends to strengthen confidence in all four of the assumptions, namely that individual differences in n Achievement have appeared by age 5, that doodles will sufficiently reflect those differences, that individual differences in risk taking have also appeared by age 5, and that n Achievement tends to predispose children even at this age toward taking moderate risks. Of particular importance is the evidence that n Achievement may be measured in children from their scribbles because the standard method of measuring n Achievement is not readily applicable during the crucial time period when the motive is supposed to be developed. To summarize, this evidence consists of a number of facts. First, there is significant internal consistency in the individual characteristics that make up the total doodle n Achievement score by age 5, indicating that children have developed characteristic ways of scribbling by the age of 5 which are stable from doodle to doodle. Secondly, the shift in mean scores for the determinants with age corresponds to the way n Achievement should increase with age, even to the point of there being a larger shift from age 5 to 9 than from age 9 to 18 (although this last comparison is not really legitimate because the groups are not matched). Third, the n Achievement score based on children's doodles will correctly predict which ones will tend to take moderate risks and which ones will swing between extremely safe and extremely speculative undertakings. It is of further interest to note that in the ring-toss experiment the distance at which the "highs" and "lows" differed most—namely, a median distance of 20 inches—showed a probability of success ($p = .32$) that was practically identical with the odds in Atkinson's experiment ($p = .33$) at which his subjects with high n Achievement (measured in the standard way) showed the greatest superiority in performance over subjects with low n Achievement (Ch. 20).

As an additional piece of evidence for this point it is worth noting in passing that the five-year-olds were also given the task of sorting 20 ESP cards into their respective suits in 30 seconds as part of another study and that subjects who were above the median in their performance on this task were also significantly more often above the median in n Achievement score based on doodles (chi-square $= 3.89$, $p < .05$). In other words, the subjects with presumed higher n Achievement based on their doodles actually performed better at a card-sorting task, and since faster performance was one of the basic validating criteria initially for the verbal n Achievement score, this may be taken as a fourth fact in support of the belief that what is being measured in the doodles is really n Achievement. As a fifth bit of supporting evidence for this belief, one could also cite the fact that the relationship between doodle n Achievement score and risk-taking was found not only once with five-year-olds but a second time with an older group of third graders. A sixth reason for accepting the doodle score as a measure of n Achievement lies in the fact that a possible alternative explanation of the results as being due to intelligence has apparently been ruled out by the zero order correlation of the score with intelligence. A seventh reason is the confirmation of the preference for blues and greens over yellows and reds among subjects with high n Achievement, a finding originally obtained by Knapp with the standard n Achievement score (Ch. 26). Finally, of course, one might reasonably expect that since Aronson found that the doodle score was significantly correlated with the verbal n Achievement score around age 18, the two measures should also correlate at earlier ages.

If we may accept the fact for the moment that we are really dealing with n Achievement in the doodle score, then the obtained relationship to risk-taking behavior has very important social and economic implications. What it suggests is that countries characterized by a low general level of n Achievement will contain a very high percentage of individuals who would be attracted simultaneously to very safe undertakings (as in traditionalist agriculture) and to fairly wild speculations in which the gain is very great but the probability of winning very small (as in lotteries). On the other hand, they will contain a very small percentage of individuals with high n Achievement who will be attracted to moderate risks with smaller gains but with greater probability of success. Yet it is this very class of entrepreneurs taking moderate risks who play a key role in successful social innovation and economic development. Furthermore, that both n Achievement and risk-taking propensities seem to be developed so early in life, too early for them to be part of the conscious ideational system of the child in all probability, is a fact which suggests the difficulty that later learning may have in modifying these early and partly unconscious tendencies. Consequently, even thorough knowledge of the value of moderate risk-taking, if acquired by subjects with low n Achievement later in life, may have little or no effect on the risks that they actually choose to take. In short, the data suggest that if one wants to modify n Achievement and risk-taking behavior at the time they are most easily influenced—e.g., at the time they are being formed—one will have to begin early, probably with the kind of independence and mastery training found by Winterbottom (Ch. 33) to be correlated with high n Achievement if it occurred roughly before the age of 8. The development of socially and economically backward areas by an indigenous class of entrepreneurs may then ultimately depend on changes in the home and in the preschool and early school years, rather than on adult education of the sort usually supported in foreign aid programs.

Finally, one may ask why it is that subjects with high n Achievement should prefer moderate risks, although the data do not admit of a really definitive answer. At the safe end of the continuum one may speculate that they take somewhat longer risks than the "lows" either because their confidence in their own ability is such that the subjective probability of success is increased over what it actually is or because their higher achievement drive would not be sufficiently rewarded by such a "safe" success, or both (cf. Ch. 20). At the speculative end of the continuum, they may reject some of the more extreme risks taken by the "lows" either because failure is more painful to them with their higher achievement drive or because they may be able to take very little personal credit for success if it comes in such a lucky enterprise, or both.

REFERENCES

McClelland, D.C.   Note on cyclical effects in successive administration of the TAT to the same persons. Unpublished manuscript, Wesleyan Univer., 1955.

McClelland, D. C.   Interest in risky occupations among subjects with high achievement motivation. Unpublished manuscript, Harvard Univer., 1956.

McClelland, D.C., Atkinson, J. W., Clark, R. A., and Lowell, E.L.   *The achievement motive*. New York: Appleton-Century-Crofts, 1953.

chapter six

Aggression

6.1 Introduction

Few topics in social development have received as much attention from the research investigator or stimulated as much concern and controversy among laymen as aggression. Because of the disruptive nature of this social behavior there is a need to understand its antecedents and thus to be able to effectively control and modify aggressive patterns.

Although social and developmental psychologists have spent much effort in attempting to define the concept of aggression in an unambiguous and objective fashion, the considerable debate that still prevails suggests that this issue is by no means settled. In the first paper in this section, Walters and Brown (1964) propose a social judgment approach to the problem of defining social behaviors such as aggression. According to this viewpoint (Bandura & Walters, 1963), behavior that is defined as aggressive in one situation may not be judged aggressive in another context. In determining whether a response is aggressive, an observer takes into account a variety of factors, including the antecedents of the response, the form of the response, and the characteristics of the agent and re-

cipient of the response. In the Walters-Brown paper the intensity
of the response was selected for study, and the results indicate that
this variable may be an important determinant of whether a response will be labeled aggressive. Responses of high intensity are
more likely to be labeled aggressive than are topographically identical responses of low intensity. The social judgment analysis suggests
that "a child does not learn aggressive habits nor does he acquire an
aggressive drive; what he learns are potentially harm-producing
responses which, if used in interpersonal transactions, are generally
labeled (and usually censured) as aggression" (Cowan & Walters,
1963, pp. 550–551).

The Walters-Brown study is the sole attempt to provide an experimental demonstration of the role played by social judgments in
categorizing social responses. It clearly indicates that the contribution of social judgments to the definition and labeling of social
behaviors can be studied in a rigorous and controlled manner.
Studies employing the Walters-Brown paradigm may provide further information concerning the criteria used by members of our
culture to discriminate among and label social phenomena.

The most influential statement offered to account for the development of aggression is the frustration-aggression hypothesis (Dollard,
Doob, Miller, Mowrer, & Sears, 1939). According to this position,
"the occurrence of aggressive behavior always presupposes the existence of frustration and, contrariwise, the existence of frustration
always leads to some form of aggression" (Dollard et al., 1939, p. 1).
In a revision of the hypothesis, Miller (1941) recognizes that other
responses, in addition to aggression, may occur when frustration is
present but continues to maintain that whenever an aggressive response occurs, it is instigated by frustration. This revision results
from research reports demonstrating that aggression is, by no means,
an inevitable response to frustration. Barker, Dembo, and Lewin
(1941), in a classic study, found that some children regressed when
frustrated rather than showing the increase in aggression that the
original frustration-aggression hypothesis predicted. Later studies
have indicated that personality differences are important in determining the nature of the reaction to frustration (Block & Martin,
1955; Otis & McCandless, 1955). In their study, Otis and McCandless
demonstrated that children with a "need for power" were more
aggressive under frustration than children who had a dominant
"need for affection."

Davitz (1952) has demonstrated that the response to frustration
can be experimentally modified by training. In his paper, he argues
that one of the determinants of the subject's reaction to frustration
is the nature of the response pattern that is dominant in his re-

sponse hierarchy at the time of frustration. By viewing personality characteristics as habitual ways of responding to certain classes of stimuli, the results of the Otis and McCandless study can be handled by Davitz's hypothesis. In his own study, Davitz trained subjects to be either aggressive or constructive and found that the kind of training significantly determined the nature of the reaction to frustration. Aggression was the prominent response to frustration only for the subjects rewarded for aggression in the previous training session, while subjects trained to give constructive responses responded constructively under frustration.

The study is important not only for demonstrating the modifiability of frustration reactions, but also for indicating an alternative way in which aggressive responses may be acquired, namely by direct training.

Buss (1961) summarized the current status of the hypothesis as follows: "the frustration-aggression hypothesis may have been a useful working hypothesis twenty years ago, but it has limited usefulness today. . . . Frustration is only one antecedent of aggression and it is not the most potent one" (1961, p. 28).

If frustration is not the sole antecedent of aggression, what are other determinants of this form of social behavior? Much attention has been directed at the role played by aggressive models in the learning and modifying of aggressive responses. Evidence that imitation may be important comes from field studies of the effects of different child-rearing practices on the development of aggression and secondly from laboratory experimental studies of the effects of direct exposure to real-life or film-mediated aggressive models. A number of interview studies (Bandura & Walters, 1959; Glueck & Glueck, 1950; Sears, Maccoby, & Levin, 1957) report a positive relationship between parental use of physical punishment and the incidence of aggressive behavior in children. As Bandura and Walters (1963a) suggest: "A parent who is severely punitive, especially if the punishment is physical, provides an aggressive model, the influence of which may more than counteract the inhibitory effects of punishment on the punished behavior" (p. 371). However, this correlational evidence is ambiguous and could be interpreted in a variety of ways. In addition to viewing the punitive parent as an aggressive model, it could be argued that these parents had to resort to physical punishment as a way of controlling children who already were highly aggressive. Finally, the punishment may be frustrating and result in an increase in aggression.

More definitive evidence of the relationship between aggressive models and the development of aggression comes from laboratory studies. Representative of this approach is a series of studies by

Bandura and his associates in which nursery-school children were exposed to real-life or film-mediated models (Bandura, Ross & Ross, 1963—see section on imitation). The experiments indicate that exposure to aggressive models does not lead to a reduction in the amount of aggression, as predicted by the catharsis hypothesis, but increases the degree of aggression displayed by observers. Moreover, Bandura's research suggests that observing aggressive models can have two effects. First, the fact that subjects reproduced many of the highly unusual and novel responses displayed by the model in a precise and exact way, illustrates that new ways of aggressive expression can be acquired through observation. Secondly, watching aggressive models may cause the subject to perform a variety of nonimitative aggressive responses that already exist in his repetoire. A variety of other investigators have provided similar evidence using children (Lovaäs, 1961; Mussen & Rutherford, 1961), adolescents (Walters & Llewellyn-Thomas, 1963), and adults (Berkowitz & Geen, 1966) as subjects.

A number of factors control the effect that exposure to violent displays will have on observers. The Bandura et al. study indicates that individual differences are important; boys are more susceptible to the influence of aggressive models than girls. The strength of the observer's aggressive habits may be important. In a recent study using college students, Geen (1967) found that subjects whose aggressive habit strength was experimentally increased showed more aggression following frustration and exposure to an aggressive film than subjects with weaker aggressive habits. Characteristics of the model may be important as well as subject factors. Male models, for example, appear to be more effective than female models in the transmission of aggression. The age and social status of the model (that is, peer or adult) must be taken into consideration also (see Hicks' study in section on imitation). A particularly important determinant of the effects of exposure on the observing child's aggressive responses may be the consequences the person anticipates for behaving aggressively. As the Bandura study (see section on imitation) indicated, seeing a model rewarded for aggression increased the probability of the child observer's behaving aggressively, while viewing the model punished tended to decrease or inhibit the aggressive behavior of the observer.

To what extent can we conclude from these studies that displays of violence in the mass media have similar effects? The Bandura et al. (1963) study indicates that the laboratory results may have relevance, particularly in light of their finding that film-mediated models are as effective as live models for eliciting and shaping aggressive behavior. However, as the Eron study (1963) indicates, caution is necessary in extrapolating conclusions about television aggression from the lab results. Although Eron's finding of a positive correlation between the extent of violence in favorite TV programs and peer-rated aggression in boys is consistent with the laboratory findings, his finding of a negative relationship between total length of TV viewing and aggression suggests that no simple statement can be made about the effects of violence in the mass media and aggression.

Berkowitz (1962) has pointed out that a variety of variables must be considered before any meaningful statement can be made concerning the probability that media violence will evoke aggression in later real-life contexts. First, the degree of association between the fantasy situation and (a) the situations in which the aggressive responses are originally learned and (b) the postfantasy setting must be taken into account. Secondly, the strength of the observer's aggressiveness habits may be important. Another determinant may be the intensity of the hostile tendencies elicited within the observer by the fantasy violence. A final factor noted by Berkowitz is the intensity of the guilt or aggression anxiety aroused by the aggressive display. When aggression anxiety is high, inhibition of aggressive behavior may result.

Aggressive responses are acquired not only through exposure to aggressive models, but also by direct reinforcement. In the interview studies (Bandura & Walters, 1959), it was found that parents of aggressive boys more actively encourage aggression than parents of nonaggressive children. Similarly laboratory experiments have demonstrated that aggression can be systematically increased through the provision of positive reinforcers. This finding is illustrated in the Walters and Brown study in this section and by a number of other reports (Cowan & Walters, 1963; Patterson, Ludwig & Sonoda, 1961; Walters & Brown, 1963). The Walters and Brown paper indicated that not only can the aggressive behaviors be increased by direct training, but aggressive responses acquired through reinforcement in a noninterpersonal situation may generalize to new situations involving interpersonal interaction.

The Lovaäs article examines another important aspect of aggression—hostile verbalizations—and demonstrates that the rate of occurrence of both verbal and nonverbal aggression can be increased by reinforcement procedures. More importantly, however, the Lovaäs research demonstrates that reinforcement effects generalize from one class of aggressive responses to another class—in this case from verbal to motor aggression. When aggressive verbal responses are reinforced, subjects show greater increases in nonverbal aggression than control subjects who are reinforced for nonaggressive verbalizations.

A similar result was reported recently by Loew (1967) using college students as subjects. These studies are significant for a variety of reasons. First, they emphasize the often neglected relationships between verbal and nonverbal behavior systems and suggest that the manipulation of verbal behavior is a potentially powerful means of regulating motor behavior. Second, these data serve as a reminder that attitudes may play an important role in shaping overt social actions.

Studies of reinforcement of aggression have generally employed adults as reinforcing agents or used some nonsocial reinforcer like candy or marbles to control aggressive behavior. However, a great deal of aggression is probably learned in interactions with peers. Patterson, Littman, and Bricker (1967) have recently provided data pertaining to this issue. In their research they made detailed observations of the aggressive exchanges between children in a nursery school setting. They found that the reaction of the victim of aggression was an important determinant of aggressive behavior. Specifically when the target child responded by withdrawing, by acquiescing to the aggressor's demands, or by crying, the aggressor was positively reinforced, and the probability that he would repeat the aggressive response and direct it toward the same victim was increased. Similarly, attempts at recovery of property (for example, a toy) or retaliation (hitting back) on the part of the victim led to a decrease in the aggressive behavior or a change in the choice of target. The study suggests that peers as well as adults are important reinforcing agents and that the reactions or feedback provided by the victim constitute an important class of reinforcing events for controlling aggressive behavior.

Not only is aggression maintained by positive reinforcement, but it may occur because of the permissive nature of the situation. The concept of permissiveness has been defined as "the willingness of a socialization agent to allow a given form of behavior to occur or to continue once it has commenced" (Bandura & Walters, 1963b, p. 130). Sears, Maccoby, and Levin (1957) have reported a positive correlation between the degree of aggression in the home and maternal permissiveness for aggression. These results held for 5-year-old children only; when the children were 12 years of age, no relationship remained between aggression and permissiveness. Other support for the relationship is provided by Bandura and Walters' finding of greater permissiveness on the part of the mothers of aggressive boys as compared to the mothers of nonaggressive boys.

The main context for laboratory studies of the effects of permissiveness is the doll play situation. In this situation, the child is typically confronted by a house filled with doll furniture and a set of dolls representing members of the family unit. While the child plays with the equipment, the kind, the direction, and often the intensity of the child's doll play aggression is recorded. (For a critical discussion of the research uses of doll play, see Levin and Wardell, 1962.) On the assumption that the situation has similarities to a real-life home situation, it has been used to explore the effects of parental child-rearing variables on the expression of aggression (Sears, Whiting, Nowlis, & Sears, 1953). The studies have reported that aggression increases both within sessions and across sessions when a permissive adult is present (Bach, 1945; Hartup & Himeno, 1959; Hollenberg & Sperry, 1951). It was generally assumed that a permissive adult lessened the child's fear of being punished for aggression and that this anxiety reduction process accounted for the increase in aggression. If this explanation is correct, session to session increases in aggression would be expected in the absence of an adult as well as in an adult's presence. However, in a later study, Siegel and Kohn (1959) found that aggression decreased when an adult was not present and increased only when a permissive adult was present. These results suggest that permissiveness represents more than mere neutralization of adult control; rather the nonreaction of the permissive adult in a situation where the child anticipates punishment may serve as a cue indicating tacit approval for aggressive play behavior.

Although a great deal of information is available concerning the conditions promoting increases in aggression, there is relatively little knowledge of ways to inhibit aggression. In fact, only one laboratory study of the effects of punishment on aggression has been reported. In their now classic experiment, Hollenberg and Sperry found that verbally punishing a child for doll play aggression was effective in decreasing, although only temporarily, the frequency and intensity of aggression in the doll play situation. A similar result has been reported by field investigators like Bandura and Walters (1959), who have found that punishment of aggression directed to parents effectively inhibited parentally aimed aggression. However, punishment of aggression may increase the frequency of aggression in situations distinctly dissimilar to that in which the punishment occurred. In support of this hypothesis, Hollenberg and Sperry found that children who were highly punished for aggression at home showed more doll play aggressiveness than children receiving less severe punishment for aggression in the home. Sears and his colleagues (Sears, Whiting, Nowlis, & Sears, 1953; Sears, Maccoby, & Levin, 1957) found positive relationships between children's nursery school aggression and maternal punitiveness for aggression. Similarly, Bandura and Walters (1959) and Eron, Walder, Torgo, and

Lefkowitz (1963) reported that punitive parents had children who were characterized as highly aggressive in their extrafamilial interactions with peers and in school.

A more effective way of inhibiting aggressive behavior may be to reinforce incompatible prosocial behaviors. In the final paper in this section, Brown and Elliott (1965) report the results of a recent study in which they used this approach to control aggression in a nursery school setting. By instructing teachers to ignore aggressive acts and to encourage cooperative, nonaggressive actions, these investigators effectively decreased the frequency of aggression. This technique is a potentially important one because it avoids some of the undesirable consequences usually associated with the use of punishment for suppressing aggression. For instance, it is unlikely that this approach would lead to increases in aggressive behavior in situations different from the disciplinary context.

REFERENCES

Bach, G. R.   Young children's play fantasies. *Psychological Monographs,* 1945, **59,** No. 2.

Bandura, A., & Walters, R. H.   *Adolescent aggression.* New York: Ronald Press, 1959.

Bandura, A., & Walters, R. H.   Aggression. In H. W. Stevenson (Ed.), *Child Psychology: The sixty-second yearbook of the National Society for the Study of Education,* Part 1. Chicago: The National Society for the Study of Education, 1963. Pp. 364–415.

Bandura, A., Ross, D., & Ross, S. A.   Imitation of film-mediated aggressive models. *Journal of Abnormal and Social Psychology,* 1963, **66,** 3–11(a).

Bandura, A., & Walters, R. H.   *Social learning and personality development.* New York: Holt, Rinehart, and Winston, Inc., 1963.

Bandura, A., & Walters, R. H.   Aggression. In *Child Psychology: The sixty-second yearbook of the National Society for the Study of Education,* Part I. Chicago: The National Society for the Study of Education, 1963. Pp. 364–415.

Barker, R. G., Dembo, T., & Lewin, K.   Frustration and regression: An experiment with young children. *University of Iowa Studies in Child Welfare,* 1941, **18,** No. 1.

Berkowitz, L.   *Aggression: A social psychological analysis.* New York: McGraw-Hill, 1962.

Berkowitz, L., & Geen, R. G.   Film violence and the cue properties of available targets. *Journal of Personality and Social Psychology,* 1966, **3,** 525–530.

Block, J., & Martin, B.   Predicting the behavior of children under frustration. *Journal of Abnormal and Social Psychology,* 1955, **51,** 281–285.

Buss, A. H.   *The psychology of aggression.* New York: Wiley, 1961.

Brown, P., & Elliott, R.   Control of aggression in a nursery school class. *Journal of Experimental Child Psychology*, 1965, **2**, 103–107.

Cowan, P. A., & Walters, R. H.   Studies of reinforcement of aggression: 1. Effects of scheduling. *Child Development*, 1963, **34**, 543–552.

Davitz, J. R.   The effects of previous training on postfrustration behavior. *Journal of Abnormal and Social Psychology*, 1952, **47**, 309–315.

Dollard, J., Doob, L. W., Miller, N. E., Mowrer, O. H., & Sears, R. R. *Frustration and aggression.* New Haven: Yale University Press, 1939.

Eron, L. D.   Relationship of TV viewing habits and aggressive behavior in children. *Journal of Abnormal and Social Psychology*, 1963, **67**, 193–196.

Eron, L., Walder, L. O., Torgo, R., & Lefkowitz, M. M.   The relationship between social class and parental punishment for aggression and of both to an independent measure of child aggression. *Child Development*, 1963, **34**, 849–867.

Geen, R.   Frustration, attack, and prior training in aggressiveness as antecedents of aggressive behavior. Unpublished doctoral dissertation. University of Wisconsin, 1967.

Hartup, W. W., & Himeno, Y.   Social isolation versus interaction with adults in relation to aggression in preschool children. *Journal of Abnormal and Social Psychology*, 1959, **59**, 17–22.

Hollenberg, E., & Sperry, M.   Some antecedents of aggression and effects of frustration in doll play. *Personality*, 1951, **1**, 32–43.

Levin, H., & Wardell, E.   The research uses of doll play. *Psychological Bulletin*, 1962, **59**, 27–56.

Loew, C. A.   Acquisition of a hostile attitude and its relationship to aggressive behavior. *Journal of Personality and Social Psychology*, 1967, **5**, 335–341.

Loväas, O. I.   Effect of exposure to symbolic aggression on aggressive behavior. *Child Development*, 1961, **32**, 37–44(a).

Miller, N. E.   The frustration-aggression hypothesis. *Psychological Review*, 1941, **48**, 337–342.

Mussen, P. H., & Rutherford, E.   Effects of aggressive cartoons on children's aggressive play. *Journal of Abnormal and Social Psychology*, 1961, **62**, 461–464.

Otis, N. B., & McCandless, B.   Responses to repeated frustrations of young children differentiated according to need area. *Journal of Abnormal and Social Psychology*, 1955, **50**, 349–353.

Patterson, G. R., Littmon, R. A., & Bricker, W.   Assertive behavior in children: A step toward a theory of aggression. *Monographs of the Society for Research in Child Development*, 1967, **32**, No. 5 (Serial No. 113).

Patterson, G. R., Ludwig, M., & Sonoda, B.   Reinforcement of aggression in children. Unpublished manuscript, University of Oregon, 1961.

Sears, R. R., Maccoby, E., & Levin, H.   *Patterns of child rearing.* New York: Harper, 1957.

Sears, R. R., Whiting, J. W. M., Nowlis, V., & Sears, P. S.   Some child-rearing antecedents of aggression and dependency in young children. *Genetic Psychology Monograph*, 1963, **47**, 135–234.

Walters, R. H., & Brown, M.   Studies of reinforcement of aggression: III. Transfer of responses to an interpersonal situation. *Child Development*, 1963, **34**, 563–572.

Walters, R. H., & Brown, M.   A test of the high magnitude theory of aggression. *Journal of Experimental Child Psychology*, 1964, **1**, 376–387.

Walters, R. H., & Llewellyn-Thomas, E.   Enhancement of punitiveness by visual and audiovisual displays. *Canadian Journal of Psychology*, 1963, **16**, 244–255.

SUPPLEMENTARY READING

Bandura, A., & Walters, R. H.   Aggression. In H. W. Stevenson (Ed.), *Child Psychology: The sixty-second yearbook of the national society for the study of education,* Part I. Chicago: University of Chicago Press, 1963. Pp. 364–415.

Berkowitz, L.   *Aggression: A social-psychological analysis.* New York: McGraw-Hill, 1962.

Buss, A. H.   *The psychology of aggression.* New York: Wiley, 1961. Pp. 266–298.

6.2   A Test of the High-Magnitude Theory of Aggression[1]

Richard H. Walters and Murray Brown

Acts tend to be labeled as aggressive if the agent's behavior is capable of producing pain, damage, or loss to others under circumstances that are not thought to justify this outcome. The labeling of an act as aggressive thus involves both a value judgment and the identification of a response sequence as possessing characteristics that are likely to inflict pain, damage, or loss on others. According to the high-magnitude theory of aggression, proposed by Bandura and Walters (1963a,b; Walters, 1964), the possession of high intensity is one such characteristic.

There are several aspects of the high-magnitude theory that perhaps need

---

[1] The authors wish to express their appreciation to the Kitchener School Board and to the Principal and Staff of Smithson School for their cooperation in this study. Thanks are due to Roland Hersen for acting as the experimenter's assistant, and to Knil De, Eunice Desmond, and Ruth Franks for serving as observers. The research was supported by the Ontario Mental Health Foundation, Grant No. 42.

Reprinted from *Journal of Experimental Child Psychology* 1946, **1**, 376–387, by permission of the authors and Academic Press.

to be distinguished. In the first place, whereas a mild response may be regarded as nonaggressive, a topologically similar, but more intense, response may be judged to be aggressive. For example, a child who gently tugs at its mother's skirts is likely to be regarded as displaying dependent behavior, whereas violent pulling may be categorized as aggression. In either case, the goal of the response may be to attract the mother's attention; nevertheless, the social judgments elicited by the two responses differ considerably.

A second, related aspect of the theory deals with the widely accepted frustration-aggression hypothesis. Frustration, defined as delay of reward (Bandura and Walters, 1963a), may increase the intensity of the responses for which reward is delayed; on account of this increase in intensity, the agent's behavior may be regarded as aggressive. Thus, although, according to the theory, frustration is neither a necessary nor a sufficient condition for the eliciting of aggressive responses, frustrating circumstances often elicit acts that are judged to be aggressive.

A third aspect of the theory, which the present study was designed to test, concerns the learning of responses that are likely to be labeled as aggressive. High-magnitude responses may be acquired in a wide variety of situations that would not ordinarily be classified as frustrative (for example, play) and generalize to other situations. Under the conditions of acquisition, the high-magnitude responses may not be judged to be aggressive; however, these responses may generalize to other situations in which they are regarded as instances of aggression. Bandura and Walters (1963a) give the example of a child who is taught by his father, through a discrimination-training process, to strike hard on a punch-ball. Once the intense hitting response has been established, it may be elicited in interpersonal situations in which it could inflict pain on others. Generalization of this kind may occur not only in respect to a specific kind of response, for example, hitting, but also in respect to the characteristic of intensity itself. As Bandura and Walters (1963b) have suggested, mothers who ignore mild overtures from their children and attend only when the behavior is frequent and intense may be unwittingly reinforcing socially undesirable high-magnitude responses that may generalize widely; these mothers are thus likely to have children who are judged to be "troublesome" and "aggressive."

In one of a series of investigations into the effects of positive reinforcement on aggressive behavior, Walters and Brown (1963) demonstrated that children who had been intermittently reinforced for hitting a Bobo doll showed more "physically aggressive" responses in an interpersonal competitive-game situation than did children who had been continuously reinforced for hitting responses. Although it was not possible, at the time, to measure the intensity of the reinforced hitting responses, one may suspect that the intermittently reinforced children made more intense responses when reward was withheld and had, in fact, been reinforced for intense, effortful behavior. When these children were made to compete with others in interpersonal situations demanding physical contact, the generalization of the characteristic of intensity may have resulted in their displaying more responses that the observers considered to be classifiable as physically aggressive.

The purpose of the present study was to compare, in physical-contact games, the behavior of children who had been trained to give high-magnitude responses and that of children who had been trained to give low-magnitude responses. During the games, the occurrence of responses falling into selected physical-aggression categories was noted by one or two "naive" observers. It was predicted that children trained to give high-magnitude responses would show more physically aggressive behavior than children who had been trained to give low-magnitude responses. One assumption underlying this prediction was that training in high-magnitude, effortful behavior would be reflected in an increased number of responses of sufficient intensity to be judged by the observers as falling into one or other of the physical-aggression categories. Unfortunately, there is no practicable means of securing objective measures of the intensity of children's responses in competitive-game situations like those employed in this study, and consequently this underlying assumption cannot be directly verified.

The study was conducted in two parts. In Part 1 the response utilized in training was hitting; if used in interpersonal situations, such a response would ordinarily be regarded as aggressive. In Part 2 of the study, a lever-pressing response was used in training; the specific response was similar to that used by Lövaas (1961) as an instance of non-aggressive behavior.

METHOD: PART 1

Subjects

Sixteen grade 2 boys served as Ss. Their ages ranged from 7 years, 3 months to 9 years, 8 months; the mean age was 7 years, 10 months. The Ss were randomly selected from the available pool of boys in the two grades. Since each boy was to be tested under both a high-intensity and a low-intensity training condition, eight boys were randomly assigned to each of the two possible orders of training.

Competitors

An additional 16 boys were selected from the grade 2 classes to compete with Ss in the testing situation. The Ss and competitors (Cs) were randomly paired.

Apparatus

The apparatus was an automated Bobo doll, described in previous publications (Bandura and Walters, 1963b; Cowan and Walters, 1963). Each time a child struck the doll's stomach, the occurrence of the response and its intensity were recorded on an Esterline-Angus recorder. Intensity was recorded by means of a Clark CS-5-50 pressure cell (0–50 pounds). Since the force of the hits versus the recorder pen deflection was a nonlinear uncalibrated function, only the relative force of hits could be determined.

When the toy was struck by the child, the clown's eyes and a flower in his buttonhole lit up. In addition to the minimal reinforcement that the lights presumably supplied, reinforcements in the form of glass marbles were provided for selected responses. The marbles were contained in a Gerbrand's Universal Dispenser located beside the Bobo doll and were released from the dispenser by means of a remote-control button. When released, the marbles fell into a tin can placed immediately underneath the dispenser. The location of the can, together with the noise of the dropping marbles, ensured that S was aware that some of his responses were being reinforced.

The Angus-Esterline recorder and the remote control for the dispenser were both located behind a transportable one-way vision booth that had been set in one corner of the experimental room.

Training procedure

Each boy received two training sessions on the Bobo doll, each session being followed later in the same day by a testing session. An assistant of E, who was stationed behind the observation booth during the training session, noted the recorded incidence and intensity of S's responses and operated the dispenser.

First training session. On the morning of one day, S was brought to the experimental room by E and instructed as follows: "Do you see this toy? You may play with it if you like. You play with it by hitting it right here (E points to the clown's stomach) and you may keep anything you win." At this instant the operations recorder was turned on by E's assistant, and E removed himself to a table where he appeared to be occupied with books and papers.

In order to establish the intensity of responses for which S was to be reinforced, he was given an initial 2-minute period of play, during which marbles were dispensed on a fixed-interval schedule of one marble every 30 seconds. This period also served to familiarize S with the equipment and the reinforcement procedure.

Following this 2-minute period, E said, "O.K. Now let's rest for a minute." During this rest period, E's assistant calculated the intensity level at which S was to be reinforced during the training period.

After the 1-minute rest period, E said, "Now you can play with the toy again, if you like." During the training period, eight Ss were reinforced for responses that were more intense than the ten most intense responses that they gave during the initial 2 minutes of responding; the remaining Ss were reinforced for responses that were less intense than the ten least intense responses that were registered during the initial play period.

All Ss were allowed to play with the toy until they had made 15 reinforced responses. The E then said to S, "That's enough. You may keep all you won. You may go back to your room now."

Second training session. The second training session, which occurred exactly 2 weeks later, was identical with the first, except that the assignment of Ss to the two experimental conditions was reversed. The Ss previously trained to respond with high-intensity responses were now trained to respond with low-intensity responses, and vice versa.

Testing procedure

In the afternoon of each day on which he received training, S was brought back to the experimental room and was told that he was going to play some games. He was instructed to be seated while E fetched someone with whom he might play.

Two observers, who had no knowledge of the purpose of the experiment and who were unaware of the condition under which S had been trained, were located behind the one-way vision booth.

As soon as E returned with C, he said, "Come over here, fellows. We are going to play some games." The S and C followed E to a rectangular game area, approximately 10×12 feet, which had been marked out on the floor. On reaching the game area, E said, "We're going to play some games. Will you go over there (motioning S to one corner of the rectangle), and will you go over there (motioning C to another corner)."

During the session, S and C interacted during two competitive games, "Cover the Cross" and "Scalp" [previously used by Davitz (1953) and Walters and Brown (1963)], and during an intervening free-play period.

"Cover the Cross." In the center of the game area was an "X" consisting of two strips of black mystic tape. The E instructed the competitors as follows: "Do you see this X-mark? Now, the winner of this game is the one who is on the X-mark when I call 'Stop.' You can do anything you like to get on the X-mark or to get the other fellow off. Now, when I say 'Go,' you start; and remember, the one who has some part of his body completely covering the X-mark when I call 'Stop' is the winner. And if you play the games real well, I'll give you each some marbles." The game was continued for 3 minutes, after which E cried "Stop" and said "——— is the winner" or "There's no winner in this game," depending on the outcome.

Free play. E now said, "Now, you can do anything you like for the next little while, but do something together. Go ahead; do something together." If at the end of each 30-second interval of the free-play period, S and C were not playing together, E told them, "Go ahead; play together some more." At the end of 2 minutes, E said, "Let's play one more game."

"Scalp." E bound self-adhesive elastic bandages around the arms of both S and C. He then said, "You see these things around your arms. They are

your 'scalps.' This is your 'scalp' (pointing to S's bandage), and this is your 'scalp' (pointing to C's bandage). Now, in this game the winner is the one who takes the 'scalp' from the other fellow but keeps his own on. Now, just like in the 'X-game,' you can do anything you like to take the other fellow's scalp from his arm and to protect your own. When I say 'Go,' you start; and remember, it is just as important to keep your own 'scalp' on as to take off the other fellow's 'scalp.' And if you really play the game well, I'll give you each some marbles when we are all finished."

The game was played for 2 minutes. If there was a winner before this time, E simply said, "Let's have another game." The bandages were then once more wrapped around the boy's arm. Time lost in re-starting the game was not included in the 2-minute period.

At the end of 2 minutes, whether the game was completed or not, E said, "O.K., fellows. That's enough." To avoid Ss' telling about their experiences to their schoolmates, E continued, "Since you both played the games so well, I am going to give each of you some marbles, but I do not want you to tell anyone about it or about anything that happened down here." The S and C were then returned to their classrooms.

The first and second testing sessions were carried out in an identical manner. Moreover, each S interacted with the same C in each testing session.

Measures

Ratings during testing were made only on the boy in the pair who served as S. The observers were supplied with specially prepared sheets, listing a number of conventional physical-aggression categories, similar to those previously used by Walters and Brown (1963). These categories were butting, kneeing, elbowing, kicking, punching, pulling, pushing, twisting hand, and sitting on back.

The total testing time was divided into 20-second intervals. If an observer judged that a response falling into one of the physical-aggression categories occurred during any 20-second interval, he placed a line in the appropriate box on the rating sheet. A response of a particular kind was scored only once within a single 20-second interval. This procedure was employed to eliminate the problem of determining what constituted a single response. The average of the total numbers of responses assigned by the two raters was regarded as S's aggression index for the testing session.

METHODS: PART 2

Subjects and competitors

The Ss were 16 kindergarten and grade 1 boys from the same school as the grade 2 boys used in Part 1 of the study. Their ages ranged from 5 years, 0 months to 7 years, 0 months; the mean age was 6 years, 3 months. The Cs were kindergarten and grade 1 boys who were randomly paired with Ss from their own grade.

The design and the testing procedure of Part 2 of the study were precisely the same as those employed in Part 1. Consequently, only the apparatus and the training procedure require describing.

Apparatus

The training apparatus consisted of a lever-pressing device which was secured to a wooden platform 36 inches long and 24 inches wide. The lever enabled a ball to be propelled toward the top of a 29-inch column. The front and sides of the column were made of clear plastic, while the rear consisted of a board marked out in 14 equal intervals. The intervals were signified by red lines on a white background and were boldly numbered.

The lever protruded 5 inches from a box at the base of the column. The end of the lever inside the column formed a cup, designed to hold a ping-pong ball. When the lever was depressed, the ball was propelled upwards; the height to which the ball was propelled was indicated in terms of the interval divisions on the back of the column.

The difficulty with which a ball could be propelled upwards was determined by a weighted wooden panel that was connected with springs to the part of the lever inside the column and also to the lower-front inside wall of the column. If the springs were disconnected from the lever, a gentle press easily sent the ball to the top of the column; when the weights and springs were attached to the lever, the ball could be propelled to the top of the column only if considerable force was employed. Whenever the ball hit the ceiling of the column, which was made of tin, a clanging noise was produced.

The marble dispenser, used in conjunction with the Bobo doll, was employed to dispense reinforcements for responses in the lever-pressing task. The arrangements were similar to those employed with the Bobo doll, except that the remote control for the marble dispenser was left outside the one-way vision booth and was manipulated by E.

Training procedure

Instructions to S were as follows: "Do you see this toy? You may play with it, if you like. You play with it by holding it like this and pressing down. (E demonstrates by gripping the lever, with his thumb placed on a piece of scotch tape that was affixed to the lever at a point about half way along its length.) Make sure the ball has settled before you depress the lever."

In order to establish the intensity level at which S was to be reinforced, he was allowed an initial "practice" period, consisting of 20 presses on the lever. The E recorded the level the ball reached after each press. At the end of this "base-line" period, E said, "O.K. Now, let's rest a minute." The E then calculated the level at which S was to be reinforced. After a 1-minute break, E told S, "Now, you can play with the toy again, and this time you may keep anything you win."

Each S was tested twice, as in Part 1 of the study. Under the high-intensity training condition, the weights and springs were attached to the lever, and S was reinforced only for responses that projected the ball as high as, or higher than, the point that it reached in the fifth highest trial of the initial 25-trial period. Under the low-intensity condition, the springs and weights were disconnected, and S was reinforced only for responses that projected the ball to a lower level than that which it reached on the fifth lowest trial of the initial 25-trial period. If, under the low-intensity condition, S had reached the maximum level possible on sixteen or more of the 20 initial trials, he was reinforced for any responses that did not propel the ball to the top of the column.

The Ss were, under each training condition, allowed to play with the toy until they had made fifteen reinforced responses. The E sat behind S during the reinforcement procedure; the remote control of the dispenser was hidden behind a curtain so that S was not aware of E's role in dispensing the marbles. Thus, the reward procedure was not dissimilar to that employed in Part 1 of the experiment in spite of the fact that E himself controlled the reinforcers. After S had received 15 reinforcements, E said, "That's enough. You may keep all you won. Now we are going to play some games, so why don't you sit here (E points to a chair) while I get someone to play with you."

As in Part 1, all Ss were tested twice, once following training under the high-intensity condition and once following training under the low-intensity condition, with order effects controlled. During testing, S's responses were recorded by two observers. One of these was a housewife who had no knowledge of the purpose of the experiment or of the experimental conditions; the other was E's assistant. The judgments made by the "naive" observer were used in statistical analyses.

RESULTS

Inter-rater reliabilities for the aggression indices were 0.89 and 0.94 for Parts 1 and 2 of the study, respectively.

Table 1 gives the group means and SD's for these indices. Type II analyses of variances (Lindquist, 1953) showed that children tested under the high-intensity conditions, both on the Bobo doll and on the lever-pressing task, had significantly higher mean physical-aggression indices than those trained under the corresponding low-intensity conditions ($F = 5.43$; $p < 0.05$ for Bobo-doll training; $F = 10.14$; $p < 0.01$ for lever-pressing training). The effects of differential training in high-magnitude and low-magnitude responses were thus similar for two groups of subjects varying in age and trained on very different types of tasks. Neither analysis yielded a significant main effect for order of treatment or a significant interaction effect.

TABLE 1. Group Means and Standard Deviation of
Aggression Indices [a]

| | Type of training | | | |
| | High intensity | | Low intensity | |
Task	Mean	SD	Mean	SD
Hitting				
High first	26.7	7.35	22.0	7.29
High second	27.9	5.17	23.4	4.07
Lever pressing				
High first	21.2	7.79	16.2	6.85
High second	19.5	5.87	14.5	5.89

[a] $n = 8$ in each group; repeated measures design

Since the dependent measures in Part 1 and Part 2 were precisely the same, a supplementary Type III analysis of variance (Lindquist, 1953) was carried out by using the data from both parts of the study. The analysis yielded a highly significant main effect attributable to the differential reinforcement of high-intensity and low-intensity responses ($F = 14.08$; $p < 0.001$), and also a significant difference between Ss used in Part 1 and those used in Part 2 of the study ($F = 11.87$; $p < 0.005$). This latter effect cannot, however, be attributed to the single factor of type of training (hitting versus lever-pressing), since the two sets of Ss differed in age and were rated by different observers.

DISCUSSION

Observation of the raters indicated that they did not score every competitive physical-contact response of the subjects as an instance of aggression. After ratings had been completed, the "naive" raters were questioned concerning the criteria that had been employed in deciding whether a particular physical-contact response, for example, pushing, should be scored in one of the physical-aggression categories. Their replies indicated that they had utilized to a large extent an intensity criterion ("force") in making their judgments. It is therefore probably safe to conclude that habits of responding with high or low intensity set up during training generalized to the competitive game situation, and that, as a result, children trained under the high-intensity condition exhibited more responses classifiable as aggressive than did children trained under the low-intensity condition.

The study does not provide an ideal test of the high-magnitude theory. Such a test would entail securing an objective measure of the intensity of the responses made in the testing situation, together with judgments of observers concerning both the incidence and the strength of responses that they would categorize as aggressive. Technical difficulties obviously preclude objective measures of intensity of responses made during social-interaction sequences of the kind used in this study. The use of the competitive-game and free-play situations nevertheless had the advantage that it rendered the data comparable to those previously secured by Walters and Brown (1963). It is now reasonable to suppose that the relatively high aggression of children trained by Walters and Brown on an FR 1:6 schedule was due to the differential reinforcement of the intense hitting responses of these children during the training period.

In Part 1 of the study it was more difficult for children under the high-intensity condition training, than for children under the low-intensity condition, to reach criterion during training. On the average, children under the former condition were reinforced only once every twelve responses; in contrast, children under the latter condition were reinforced, on the average, once every eight responses. It could therefore be argued that the difference between the two groups of subjects represented a motivational (frustration) effect and was not the outcome of differential reinforcement.

The motivational interpretation is rendered less convincing by the outcome of Part 2 of the study. The lever-pressing equipment was designed in such a way that the production of low-intensity responses was difficult for the children. While E did not actually count the number of responses made by each S during training, it was quite evident that children under the low-intensity condition took considerably more trials to reach criterion than did children under the high-intensity condition. The obtained difference between the intensity groups must therefore be attributed to the transfer of previously reinforced habits of response.[2]

In spite of some methodological shortcomings, the findings from Parts 1 and 2, taken together, demonstrate the need for re-evaluation of customary approaches to the problem of aggression. Walters and Parke (1964) have argued that the traditional motivational categories of social-psychological research, for example, dependency and aggression, are "quasi-evaluative" in nature. "It is suggested that motives of this kind are not characteristics of human agents, but constructs by means of which human beings order social phenomena and evaluate behavior in terms of its acceptability or non-acceptability within a given cultural context" (pp. 271–272). It follows, from this point of view, that children do not, strictly speaking, acquire social habits or social drives; on the other hand, they may learn characteristic response-components, or modes of response, common to all or most acts that are customarily placed in a specific motivational category, so that their

---

[2] The difficulty of the tasks was assessed by testing ten children not included in the study, five under the high-intensity condition and five under the low-intensity condition. Each child was required to press the lever until he had obtained 15 reinforcements. The ratio of reinforced to total responses was 1:1.6 for children under the high-intensity condition and 1:4.9 for children under the low-intensity condition; the distributions of responses to criterion for the two groups did not overlap.

behavior is in many contexts judged to be, for example, aggressive or dependent. This theoretical approach further implies that the response components or modes of response in question may be acquired in contexts in which they would not be subsumed under a social-motivation label. The data from Part 2 of the study support this implication. The generalization of high-magnitude responses from the lever-pressing situation, in which such responses could hardly be classified as aggressive, to the play situation, in which they were classified as aggressive, is an example of the kinds of transfer of learning that would be predicted by the theory.

Although the observers primarily employed the criterion of "force" in determining whether they should classify a response as aggressive, they also mentioned the use of a second criterion, "expression," which has not yet been considered in expositions of the social-judgment approach to the problem of aggression. While facial expression, gestures, and body posture can provide indications of the intensity or effortfulness of behavior, they may influence judgments concerning social motives in other ways than this. Any thorough investigation into the learning of social judgments will undoubtedly have to evaluate the role of cues that are provided by the facial and bodily expression of agents.

SUMMARY

The high-magnitude theory of aggression predicts that training in high-intensity responses will lead a child to behave in interpersonal situations in ways that will be labeled as aggressive. In Part 1 of the study, grade 2 children were twice trained on an automated Bobo doll; in one training session they were reinforced for high-intensity hitting responses, while in the other training session they were reinforced for low-intensity hitting responses. Following each training session, each child competed in physical-contact games with a grade 2 child who did not otherwise participate in the study. The Ss' physically aggressive responses were recorded by observers. In Part 2 of the study, kindergarten and grade 1 children were twice trained in a nonaggressive lever-pressing task; the children were reinforced in one training session for high-intensity responses and in the other session for low-intensity responses. The testing procedure was the same as in Part 1. In both parts of the study, children were judged to be more aggressive following high-intensity training than following low-intensity training.

REFERENCES

Bandura, A., & Walters, R. H. Aggression. In *Child psychology: The sixty-second yearbook of the National Society for the Study of Education*. 1963, pp. 364–415. (a)

Bandura, A., & Walters, R. H. *Social learning and personality development.* New York: Holt, Rinehart, and Winston, 1963. (b)

Cowan, P. A., & Walters, R. H. Studies of reinforcement of aggression. I. Effects of scheduling. *Child Develpm.,* 1963, **34,** 543–552.

Davitz, J. R. The effects of previous training on postfrustrative behavior. *J. abnorm. soc. Psychol.,* 1952, **47,** 309–315.

Lindquist, E. F. *Design and analysis of experiments in psychology and education.* Boston: Houghton Mifflin, 1953.

Lövaas, O. I. Interaction between verbal and nonverbal behavior. *Child Develpm.,* 1961, **32,** 329–336.

Walters, R. H. On the high-magnitude theory of aggression. *Child Develpm.,* 1964, **35,** 303–304.

Walters, R. H., & Brown, M. Studies of reinforcement of aggression: III. Transfer of responses to an interpersonal situation. *Child Devlpm.,* 1963, **34,** 563–572.

Walters, R. H., & Parke, R. D. Social motivation, dependency, and susceptibility to social influence. In L. Berkowitz (Ed.), *Advances in experimental social psychology.* Vol. 1. New York: Academic Press, 1964. Pp. 231–276.

6.3   The Effects of Previous Training on Postfrustration Behavior [1]

Joel R. Davitz

In recent years the concept of frustration has been central in both mental hygiene and social psychology. Psychologists and other social scientists have shown their interest in frustration and its effects by developing several theories, by performing a number of experiments and by using the concept of frustration to account for the deviant behavior of persons and of social groups. In spite of this extensive interest, many issues relating to the effects of frustration remain unresolved and the current theories remain incompletely tested.

The research reported here deals with the influence of one variable upon reactions to frustration. The principal hypothesis is that a person's response to frustration will be affected by his previous experience in situations similar to that in which frustration is encountered. Specifically, the experiment studies the differential effects of *aggressive training* and of *constructive*

[1] The writer wishes to express his appreciation to Professors Irving Lorge, Laurance F. Shaffer, Edward J. Shoben, Jr., and Lincoln Moses of Teachers College, Columbia University, for their invaluable assistance in the present study.

Reprinted from the *Journal of Abnormal and Social Psychology,* 1952, **47,** 309–315, by permission of the author and The American Psychological Association.

training on the responses to frustration made by children seven to nine years of age.

In order to develop the theoretical rationale for the present study, three major theories of frustration presented in the recent literature will be critically reviewed. The frustration-aggression hypothesis, which assumes a high degree of correlation between frustration and an "instigation to aggression," interprets postfrustration behavior in terms of direct aggression, displaced aggression, or substitute activity (*3, 4*). That direct or indirect aggression is not a universal response to frustration has been widely discussed in the literature of frustration-aggression criticism. Thus, the category of "substitute activity" necessarily covers an extremely wide range of behavior. The interpretation of this wide range of nonaggressive behavior as substitute activity, "substitute" only from the perspective of a theoretician anticipating aggression, requires the manipulation of unverified inferred variables, and does not provide an adequate general theoretical framework within which to analyze, predict, and understand this behavior.

The frustration-regression theory suggests that the change of behavior which occurs after frustration is predominantly in the direction of regression (*1*). While there is little question that regression may occur as a result of frustration, a change of behavior in this direction is certainly not the only possible change in direction. There are instances in the classroom every day in which the change of behavior after frustration is in the direction of growth rather than regression. There would seem to be no general factor in frustration per se which determines the direction of behavioral change, and the a priori assumption that the change is always in one direction is not consistent with everyday observations. Therefore, because it predicts a change of behavior after frustration in only one direction, viz. regression, the frustration-regression theory does not provide a general theory of frustration.

Maier has suggested that postfrustration behavior is nonmotivated behavior without a goal (*6*). This challenge of the postulate that all behavior is motivated rests on Maier's experiments with animals forced to respond in insoluble problem situations. Maier observed that these animals developed consistent patterns of behavior, yet there was no apparent goal, and he concludes that postfrustration behavior is qualitatively different from motivated behavior because it is behavior without a goal. Maier's theoretical position restricts the definition of motivation to goal-seeking, neglecting the widely recognized definition of motivation in terms of antecedent conditions. The chief criticism of Maier's position is that his basic experimental data, upon which he bases his fundamental postulate of motivated and nonmotivated behavior, can be adequately interpreted and predicted in terms of avoidance behavior, utilizing the concepts of learning theory and without invoking a new theoretical sphere of nonmotivated behavior.

Having briefly examined these theories of frustration, it is suggested that a general theory of frustration cannot be restricted to the prediction of a particular mode of response or to a particular directional change of behavior after frustration. This critical examination also suggests that frustration theory may be most fruitfully treated in terms of a more general theory of adjustment, rather than in terms specific to frustration alone.

It is suggested that postfrustration behavior tends toward adjustment, and that the process of adjustment may be analyzed in terms of learning theory as suggested by Shaffer (10) and Miller and Dollard (7). For purposes of this study, frustration is defined as the blocking of drive-evoked behavior. When this behavior is blocked and the drive continues, the cumulative intensification of the drive evokes an emotional response. The particular pattern of behavior evidenced by the organism is a function of the organism's hierarchy of responses related to the emotional stimulation and the particular situation in which frustration is encountered. While it is suggested that this hierarchy of responses is a significant determinant of the organism's postfrustration behavior, it is recognized that this is not the only determining factor. The intensity of the original frustrated drive and the resultant emotional response, the degree to which the original drive-evoking situation continues to impinge upon the organism, and the degree of active punishment involved in the frustrating circumstances may be several other factors involved in this complex process.

Frustration theory is treated as merely one case of a general adjustment theory employing the concepts of learning theory. No specific behavioral responses are predicted as general results of frustration nor is the direction of behavioral change, either in terms of regression or growth, suggested as a general rule. As in all cases of behavior, the analysis of postfrustration behavior involves the interaction of a particular organism and a particular situation, and the theoretical framework suggests general relationships among the various factors involved in this interaction.

The principal focus of the present research was the development of differential response tendencies, prior to subjecting the subjects (Ss) to frustration. One group of Ss was trained aggressively before frustration, and another group was trained to act constructively. All Ss were trained in the same physical setting as that in which the effects of the frustration were observed. It was assumed that the training received would develop in the individuals of each group a specific behavioral tendency related to that physical situation, and it was hypothesized that their learned behavioral tendencies would differentially affect the behavior of each of the groups following frustration.

The two major hypotheses of the study were:

1. Subjects trained aggressively will behave more aggressively after frustration than will subjects trained constructively.

2. Subjects trained constructively will behave more constructively after frustration than will subjects trained aggressively.

Procedure

The experimental procedure may be divided into four major sections: (a) free play; (b) training; (c) frustration; and (d) free play. In the first experimental session each of the ten groups was allowed free play with any of the materials in the experimental playroom. This was followed by a series of training sessions in which five groups were trained aggressively and five groups were trained constructively. The final sequence of the experiment consisted of a frustrating situation followed by a second period of free play.

The experimental population consisted of 40 subjects, 24 girls and 16 boys between the ages of seven and nine, selected from a group of children in residence at a summer camp. The mean age of the subjects was 100 months and the standard deviation of age was nine months. The total population was divided into five pairs of experimental groups (10 groups), each pair matched on the basis of age and sex. There were four Ss in each group, and the particular type of training, aggressive or constructive, assigned to each group was determined in a random manner.

The playroom was twelve feet long and nine feet wide, and it was bounded on one end by a black wire screen which permitted cameras, placed at a small opening in a wall fourteen feet from the screen, to record the behavior during the pre- and postfrustration play sessions. The play materials, which were arranged in an identical fashion before each free play session, consisted of clay, three dolls, building logs, dump truck, large plastic punching doll, hammer, saw, nails, and wood. Each group received seven thirty-minute training sessions.

Aggressive training is defined as that which encourages and rewards behavior the goal of which is injury to some object or person. The aggressive training was a series of games designated as: Cover the Spot, Scalp, and Break the Ball. These games are briefly outlined below.

Cover the spot. At the center of a mat placed on the floor was a small x marked in black chalk. Each S was instructed to cover the spot with some part of his body, and that person covering the spot at the end of the game was the winner. Only one person could cover the spot at one time, and it was emphasized to the Ss that there were no rules limiting their aggressive behavior during the game.

Scalp. A piece of cloth was tied around the arm of each subject and he was informed that this was his scalp. The object of the game was to tear the scalps from the other S's arm while protecting one's own scalp.

Break the ball. Each S was provided with a ping pong ball which was placed on the floor and could not be touched by hand. The object of the game was to break everyone else's ping pong ball while protecting one's own ball.

The several games described above were played for a period of ten minutes and repeated during the seven training sessions. During these training sessions a chart for each group was kept on the wall, and the winner of each game was awarded a star on this chart. Throughout these sessions aggressive behavior was praised and encouraged by the experimenter (*E*), and, in general, there was a high degree of aggressive behavior evidenced.

TABLE 1. EXPERIMENTAL PROCEDURE

Section	Session	Procedure	Time
I.	1.	Prefrustration free play	18'
II.	2.	Training *	30'
	3.	Training	30'
	4.	Training	30'
	5.	Training	30'
	6.	Training	30'
	7.	Training	30'
	8.	Training	30'
III.	9.	Frustration	15'
IV.	10.	Profrustration free play	18'

* During the training sessions (2–8), five groups of *S*s were trained aggressively and five groups of *S*s were trained constructively.

Constructive training is defined as that which encourages and rewards behavior involving the use of materials for the construction of designated objects. The constructive training consisted of drawing murals and completing jigsaw puzzles. During four sessions a long sheet of paper was placed on the wall and a box of crayons was placed on the floor. Instructions were given to draw a single picture on the entire sheet of paper, and *E* emphasized the constructiveness of each *S* as well as the cooperation of the group. During the remaining sessions, each group was presented with a jigsaw puzzle containing thirty pieces. The *S*s were told that if the pieces were put together correctly, they would form a picture of American Indians or a familiar fictional character. When the group completed the first puzzle, a second puzzle was provided, and this was continued until the end of each training period. Throughout the training periods all aggressive behavior was discouraged by *E*, while constructiveness, on the other hand, was praised and encouraged.

The final phase of the experiment consisted of the frustration and a second free play session. The *S*s were seated on the floor next to a projector outside of the playroom and told that they were to see movies. Five reels of film, arranged next to the projector, were contained in boxes which displayed the titles of the film and a picture of the leading character. The first reel was shown completely. At the start of the second reel, each S was given a bar of candy, and at the climactic point of the film, E stepped in front of the seated Ss, removed the candy from their hands, and ushered them into the playroom. As E locked the screen door of the playroom, he made the following statement, "You cannot have any more candy or see any more films, but you can play with anything in the room." Although the Ss could see the projector, which continued to run, through the screen door, the movie screen was not visible. E did not answer any questions and made no comment on behavior. In no case was there any contact between groups during the final phase of the experiment.

The behavior evidenced in the pre- and postfrustration free play sessions was recorded on moving picture film for a period of eighteen minutes, starting in each case with the moment the Ss entered the playroom. Two eight-mm. cameras with automatic self-winding devices and wide angle lenses were used for this purpose. In order to analyze the data, the pre- and postfrustration behavior recorded on film was observed and written protocols of the behavior of each S were made. Pre- and postfrustration periods were not identified and the observations were made independently by two observers. During each viewing of the film the observers made a continuous record of a single S. These protocols were compared, differences between observers noted, and the procedure was repeated until agreement between observers was reached concerning the behavior of each S.

RESULTS

The data were analyzed in terms of the two major hypotheses, and the statistical analysis pertaining to each hypothesis will be presented separately.

Aggressiveness

It is hypothesized that Ss trained aggressively will evidence more aggressive behavior after frustration than will Ss trained constructively. The eighty protocols of behavior, including the records of pre- and postfrustration behavior of all forty Ss, were presented to four judges, who were asked to rank the protocols in order of aggressiveness. The playroom and materials were described to the judges; however, the pre- and postfrustration sessions and the individual Ss were not identified. The eighty protocols were presented in random order, and the protocols were ranked independently by each judge. The judges were doctoral students in psychology who had previous experience in ranking procedures.

The agreement among judges was determined by the coefficient of concordance as presented by Kendall (5, p. 61). All four judges agreed that twenty protocols evidenced no aggression and could not be ranked along the aggression continuum. Including these protocols in the evaluation of agreement among judges would result in a spuriously high coefficient of concordance, since the concordance of judges on protocols not on the continuum is $+1$. Therefore, in computing the coefficient of concordance these protocols were omitted. The value of the coefficient of concordance, corrected for ties, for the four rankings of sixty protocols was found to be .903,[2] indicating an extremely high degree of agreement among judges.

In the following analysis of the data, the pre- and postfrustration ranks of each S were determined by summing the ranks assigned to each protocol by the four judges and arranging these summed ranks in order from the lowest to the highest sum. It should be noted that the form of the population of ranks cannot be specified; therefore, the analysis of the data is in terms of non-parametric inference.

In order to test the major hypothesis concerning aggressiveness, the pre- and postfrustration ranks of each S were compared, and a gain of rank was indicated by a $+$; a loss in rank, by a $-$. The null hypothesis which was tested may be stated as follows: The probability of gains after frustration of the aggressively trained group is less than, or equal to, the probability of gains of the constructively trained group. The null hypothesis would be rejected for a high number of gains in the aggressive group.

Only pairs of ranks (the pre- and postfrustration ranks of each individual) were considered. Therefore, these observations may be treated as independent, and the significance of the difference of gains and losses between the two groups may be tested by the ordinary method of chi-square. In computing chi-square, the ties for each group were split, half added to the number of gains and half to the number of losses in each group. This procedure increased the numerator of chi-square, thus providing the most conservative estimate of probability. The obtained chi-square corrected for continuity is 3.63. However, the hypothesis under consideration is a one-sided hypothesis and the chi-square values is in terms of a two-sided hypothesis. For moderate samples, if chi-square has one degree of freedom, the square root of chi-square has a distribution which is the right hand half of a normal distribution. Therefore, in order to test the present one-sided hypothesis, the chi-square value must be converted into the equivalent value in terms of a unit normal deviate. This value is 1.90; therefore, the null hypothesis is rejected

---

[2] Since there were a number of ties within the rank order of each rater, the computation of W must correct for these ties.

$$W = \frac{S}{\frac{1}{12}(m)^2\left[(m^3-n)-m\sum_{T^1}T^1\right]}$$

where W is the coefficient of concordance; m is the number of raters; n is the number of ranked protocols; S is the sum of the squares of deviations from the mean rank;

$$\sum_{T^1}T^1 = \frac{1}{12}\sum_t(t^3-t)$$

where t is the number of ties in the rank order of each rater.

at the .05 level of significance. It is concluded that aggresively trained Ss behaved more aggressively after frustration than constructively trained Ss.

The equivalence of the location of prefrustration ranks of the two groups is evaluated by the *median test* as presented by Mood (*8*, p. 394). The hypothesis that the two population medians are equal is tested. The resulting value of chi-square is 1.6 and the hypothesis cannot be rejected even at the .10 level of significance. Therefore, we may conclude that in terms of the location in the rank order of aggressiveness before frustration, the aggressive and constructive groups were equivalent.

TABLE 2. RANK ORDER OF AGGRESSIVENESS, PRE- AND POSTFRUSTRATION

	Constructive				Aggressive		
Subject	Pre	Post	Difference *	Subject	Pre	Post	Difference *
1	40	48	−	21	70	55	+
2	38	70	−	22	70	50	+
3	59	70	−	23	70	52	+
4	70	70	0	24	42	70	−
5	8	7	+	25	5.5	10.5	−
6	31	35	−	26	4	1	+
7	9	5.5	+	27	15.5	10.5	+
8	34	47	−	28	12	2	+
9	19	70	−	29	58	54	+
10	20.5	39	−	30	56	70	−
11	23.5	70	−	31	70	70	0
12	22	51	−	32	45.5	57	−
13	26	15.5	+	33	49	53	−
14	20.5	43	−	34	60	23.5	+
15	29.5	13	+	35	27.5	18	+
16	32	25	+	36	70	44	+
17	70	70	0	37	33	17	+
18	70	70	0	38	45.5	14	+
19	70	29.5	+	39	36	3	+
20	41	70	−	40	37	27.5	+
	Gains	6			Gains	14	
	Losses	11			Losses	5	
	Ties	3			Ties	1	

* + indicates gain in rank; − indicates loss in rank; 0 indicates no change in rank.

Constructiveness

It is hypothesized that the constructively trained Ss will behave more constructively after frustration than the aggressively trained subjects. The analysis of the data in terms of this hypothesis is essentially the same as the procedure discussed above in terms of aggressiveness. The eighty protocols were ranked from most to least constructive by five judges, and the agreement among judges was determined by the coefficient of concordance. The value of the coefficient of concordance was found to be .904,[3] indicating an extremely high degree of agreement among judges.

The pre- and postfrustration protocols were arranged in rank order of constructiveness by taking the sum of ranks assigned to each protocol by the five judges. Correcting for continuity, the resulting value of chi-square was 5.10. This value was converted to the corresponding value in terms of a unit normal deviate and the value 2.25 was obtained. Therefore, the null hypothesis, that the probability of gains of the constructively trained group is less than, or equal to, the probability of gains of the aggressively trained group, was rejected at the .02 level of significance. It may be concluded that the constructively trained Ss behaved more constructively after frustration than the aggressively trained Ss.

The equivalence of the location of prefrustration ranks of the two groups is evaluated by the *median test*. The hypothesis that the population medians are equal is tested. The resulting value of chi-square is 0.4, and the hypothesis cannot be rejected even at the .10 level of significance. Therefore, it may be concluded that in terms of location in the rank order of constructiveness before frustration, the constructive and aggressive groups were equivalent.

CONCLUSIONS

Both of the experimental hypotheses were supported by the experimental results. Therefore, it may be concluded that under the conditions specified in the present experiment previous training in situations similar to that in which frustration is encountered is a significant determinant of the organism's postfrustration behavior. These results are in contrast with past studies of frustration which have interpreted postfrustration behavior primarily in terms of the frustrating situation itself.

The experimental results do not seem to be consistent with the frustration-aggression hypothesis as a general theory of frustration. While fourteen of the Ss of the aggressively trained group behaved more aggressively after frustration, the postfrustration behavior of five subjects was ranked as less aggressive than their prefrustration behavior. The evidence countering the frustration-aggression hypothesis is even more striking when the constructively trained group is considered; 11 of the 20 Ss in this group behaved less aggressively after frustration, while only six behaved more aggressively. Fur-

---

[3] The coefficient of concordance, W, is obtained by the following formula: $W = 12S/[m^2 (n^3-n)]$, where W is the coefficient of concordance; m is the number of raters; n is the number of protocols ranked; S is the sum of the squares of deviations from the mean rank.

thermore, it does not seem reasonable to interpret the general decrease of aggressiveness evidenced by the constructive group and the increase of constructiveness evidenced by 12 members of this group as "substitute activity." It would seem to be more consistent with objective psychological theory to interpret these results in terms of a general theory of adjustment rather than in terms of a specific mode of response such as aggression.

TABLE 3. RANK ORDER OF CONSTRUCTIVENESS, PRE- AND POSTFRUSTRATION

Constructively Trained				Aggressively Trained			
	Rank		Direction of		Rank		Direction of
Subject	Pre	Post	difference *	Subject	Pre	Post	difference *
1	24	21	+	21	37	41	−
2	17	8	+	22	22	47	−
3	12	9.5	+	23	14	30.5	−
4	15	11	+	24	13	29	−
5	68.5	76	−	25	67.5	80	−
6	45	3	+	26	77	75	+
7	74	78	−	27	61	73	−
8	38	36	+	28	66.5	79	−
9	62	7	+	29	33	48.5	−
10	51	6	+	30	56.5	46	+
11	48.5	1	+	31	23	25	−
12	50	68.5	−	32	44	40	+
13	52	71	−	33	53	34	+
14	56.5	28	+	34	27	60	−
15	39	55	−	35	35	64.5	−
16	32	70	−	36	5	42	−
17	16	20	−	37	30.5	63	−
18	26	2	+	38	4	64.5	−
19	18	58.5	−	39	43	72	−
20	19	9.5	+	40	54	58.5	−
	Gains	12			Gains	4	
	Losses	8			Losses	16	

* + indicates gain in rank; − indicates loss in rank.

The frustration-regression theory suggested by Barker, Dembo and Lewin (*1*), and Maier's (*6*) interpretation of postfrustration behavior as behavior without a goal, are not supported by the data. While growth and constructiveness as defined in this study are not synonymous, there is a close relationship between these two concepts. Therefore, to interpret the increase of constructiveness as evidenced by 16 of the 40 subjects in this experiment in terms of regression or behavior without a goal does not seem to be a valid theoretical procedure. While 22 Ss did evidence less constructiveness after frustration, it is obvious that the change of behavior is not necessarily in the direction of regression. Previous training is at least one factor which determines this change of direction.

It should be noted that in the experiment presented her the two major hypotheses are interdependent. The data used for testing the two hypotheses were obtained from the same population and the behavior of each S was treated in terms of aggressiveness and constructiveness. All other things being equal, a high degree of constructiveness was associated with a low degree of aggressiveness, and vice versa, as indicated by a rank order correlation of —.83 between aggressive and constructive ranks of the 40 subjects.

The effects of prefrustration training in this experiment were not invariant. Six individuals within the constructively trained group behaved more aggressively after frustration and four Ss in the aggressively trained group behaved more constructively after frustration. This indicates that while the experimental training was a significant factor in terms of the behavior of the group, the total past history of the individual must be considered in predicting and understanding his behavior after frustration.

It has been demonstrated that postfrustration behavior cannot be treated only in terms of the stimulus conditions associated with the frustration. The external stimulus conditions of the frustrating situation were identical for the aggressive and constructive groups, while the previous training of the groups differed. Therefore, in this case the previous training was the significant factor which determined the differences of the change of behavior in the two groups after frustration. It is suggested that previous experience in situations similar to that in which frustration occurs is one factor which must be considered in the understanding of postfrustration behavior.

The results of this single experiment are presented neither as conclusive evidence of the inadequacy of present frustration theories nor as final evidence of the effects of previous experience on postfrustration behavior. For the writer, the most significant result is a realization of the need for further experimental study in this area.

REFERENCES

1. Barker, R., Dembo, T., & Lewin, K. *Frustration and regression: an experiment with young children.* Univ. of Iowa Studies, Studies in Child Welfare, **18**, No. 1.
2. Dixon, W. J., & Massey, F. J. *Introduction to statistical analysis.* Eugene, Oregon: Univ. of Oregon Press, 1950.
3. Dollard, J., Doob, L. W., *et al. Frustration and aggression.* New Haven: Yale Univ. Press, 1939.

4. Dollard, J., Doob, L. W., *et al.* The frustration-aggression hypothesis. *Psychol. Rev.,* 1941, **48,** 337–342.

5. Kendall, M. G. *Rank correlation methods.* London: Griffin, 1948.

6. Maier, N. *Frustration: the study of behavior without a goal.* New York: McGraw-Hill, 1949.

7. Miller, N. E., & Dollard, J. *Social learning and imitation.* New Haven: Yale Univ. Press, 1941.

8. Mood, A. G. *Introduction to theory of statistics.* New York: McGraw-Hill, 1950.

9. Sears, R. R. Non-aggressive reactions to frustration. *Psychol. Rev.,* 1941, **48,** 343–346.

10. Shaffer, L. F. *The psychology of adjustment.* Boston: Houghton Mifflin, 1936.

6.4 Relationship of TV Viewing Habits and Aggressive Behavior in Children [1]

Leonard D. Eron

Since the advent of television, popular writers and journalists have linked increased rates of crime and delinquency to the increased production of TV sets, much as, in the past, the same effects have been ascribed to radio, movies, dime novels, and comic books. Television executives have stoutly maintained at the same time that, "there is no direct relationship between action or the physical contact that occurs in television and activity of children who are viewing—except in deviant cases, of course" (Aubrey, 1962). However, little convincing research evidence has been amassed either to substantiate or refute the assertion that TV is the cause of an increase in delinquency or is in any way related to overt behavior in real life. An extensive, well designed survey study carried out in England (Himmelweit, Oppenheim, & Vance, 1958) provided no conclusive answer. This study found no more aggressive or delinquent behaviors among children who viewed TV than among their control group who did not watch TV at all. However, these authors, on the basis of their study of the television habits of over

[1] The data on which this article is based derive from a larger study, "The Psychosocial Development of Aggressive Behavior," which has been generously supported by Grant M1726 from the National Institute of Mental Health, United States Public Health Service, and the Columbia County Tuberculosis and Health Association, Incorporated, New York. Thanks are due also to the IBM Watson Scientific Computing Laboratory at Columbia University for making computer time available without charge and to the elementary schools in Columbia County for their continued cooperation in this study.

Reprinted from the *Journal of Abnormal and Social Psychology,* 1963, **67,** 193–196 by permission of the author and The American Psychological Association.

5,000 youngsters in England, did state that they felt the important question was not how long a child watches television but rather what he sees. Schramm, Lyle, and Parker (1961) in a study of American children came to a like conclusion and Newton Minnow, Chairman of the Federal Communications Commission, has made similar statements about the quality of TV programming, especially for children.[2] Although in the laboratory it has been possible to demonstrate that exposure of children to aggressive behavior portrayed in a film increases the probability of aggressive responses to an immediately subsequent frustration (Bandura, Ross, & Ross, 1963); evidence as to the long-term effect of TV programming on real-life behavior has not been forthcoming.

It has been possible, in a larger investigation of the psychological antecedents of aggressive behavior in children (Eron, Laulicht, Walder, Farber, & Spiegel, 1961), to accumulate data which indicate that there is a relationship between such TV habits and aggressive behavior in real life.

METHOD

Subjects and Procedure

Two groups of subjects were included. The first consisted of 367 boys and 322 girls who were in the third grade in a semirural county of New York's Hudson Valley in the spring of 1960. They comprised all children whose mothers had been interviewed in a study of aggressive behavior of all third graders in the county (875). Also included were 277 boys and 245 girls whose fathers had been interviewed in this same study. There is a large degree of overlap between the two samples and thus separate analyses were done for mother and father.

The measures of aggressive behavior and TV viewing were obtained independently of each other. The former was a peer rating measure (Guess Who?) in which each child rated every other child in his classroom on 10 items having to do with specific aggressive behaviors. A description of the scale and a detailed account of its derivation, scoring, reliability, and validity are contained in a monograph by Walder, Abelson, Eron, Banta, and Laulicht (1961) and in an article by Banta and Walder (1961). Information about TV habits was taken from three questions in a 286-item interview administered individually in the respondent's home. This interview is an extension and refinement of the one described in an article by Eron, Banta, Walder, and Laulicht (1961). The specific questions were:

How often does [Name] watch TV during the week?
How often does [Name] watch TV during the weekend?
What are [Name's] three favorite TV programs?

[2] Address to the Radio and Television Executives Society, New York, September 22, 1961.

Two scores were obtained: total number of hours spent in viewing TV; and amount of violence in programs watched. Independent estimates by fathers and mothers of hours watched correlated .54 with each other. While information from father thus cannot be substituted for information from mother and vice versa, this is a sufficiently high relationship to indicate that there is some degree of validity in the reports of viewing hours noted by these independent observers and they were not answering randomly. To obtain the violence score, all TV programs mentioned by the respondents were categorized as to whether or not they emphasized antisocial aggression. No classification was permitted on the basis of the title alone. The raters had to be familiar with the content of the programs mentioned before assigning a rating. This was not difficult since the majority of inhabitants of this area can receive only one channel, and at most three, and the raters were familiar with the programs mentioned. Indication that the raters were not influenced by the program titles, but responded only to the content, is seen in the classification of some westerns as violent and some as nonviolent, of some mysteries as violent and some as nonviolent. For example, the *Lone Ranger* and *Perry Mason* were classified as nonviolent while *Have Gun–Will Travel* and *77 Sunset Strip* were classified as violent.

As one check on the validity of the information itself, i.e., whether the parents were actually giving us the children's three favorite programs or just making it up, we compared the programs mentioned independently by the fathers and mothers for those 509 children both of whose parents were interviewed. Average percentage agreement in naming the child's three favorite programs was 63 which, although again not permitting substitution of father information for mother information, is surprisingly high, considering the number of choices possible. Further evidence of the validity of the violence rating (as well as of the number of hours watched) is seen in the similarity of results whether the mother or father is the informant, which is discussed in the Results section below. Agreement between two independent raters in the categorization of all programs mentioned was 94%.[3] With the remaining 6%, discussion between the raters resolved the differences. On the basis of these ratings each subject was then assigned a score indicating extent of violence observed in TV viewing: 1, no violent programs mentioned; 2, one violent program mentioned; 3, two violent programs mentioned; 4, three violent programs mentioned. For the first measure a threefold classification of hours watched—0–4, 5–9, 10 and over—was used. Since these two variables, hours watched and extent of violence, are not completely independent, two simple randomized analyses of variance (Lindquist, 1953) were then done with aggression score as the dependent variable and, in one case, hours watched and, in the other case, violence ratings of programs as

[3] Thanks are due Irene Quinn and Anne Yaeger for their aid in making these ratings.

the independent variables. These analyses were done separately for boys and girls, mothers and fathers.

RESULTS AND DISCUSSION

The results of the analyses of variance are summarized in Table 1. There is a strong positive relationship between the violence rating of favorite pro-

TABLE 1. ANALYSIS OF VARIANCE RELATING TV HABITS OF BOYS AS REPORTED BY PARENTS TO AGGRESSION AS RATED BY PEERS

Informant	TV variable	Source	df	MS	F
Mothers	Violence rating	Treatments	3	980.07	
		within groups	363	233.54	4.196 **
Fathers	Violence rating	Treatments	3	550.59	
		within groups	273	198.22	2.925 *
Mothers	Hours watched	Treatments	2	731.57	
		within groups	364	236.96	3.087 *
Fathers	Hours watched	Treatments	2	19.95	
		within groups	274	203.38	$<$1.00

** $p < .01.$
* $p < .05.$

grams, whether reported by mothers or fathers, and aggression of boys as rated by their peers in the classroom. There is also a significant negative relationship between amount of time spent in viewing TV as reported by mothers and aggression of boys. Although the results for fathers of boys are in the same direction for number of hours watched, they are not significant. There was no significant relationships when TV habits of girls were reported either by mothers or fathers. The magnitude and direction of the differences for boys can be seen in Tables 2 and 3. As the amount of violence increases, the aggression rate of the boys also increases; however, as total amount of time watched increases, aggression scores decrease.

Aside from the fact that definite relationships are thus established between TV viewing habits and aggressive behavior in real life, these findings are interesting for a number of other reasons important in child rearing research.

TABLE 2. MEAN AGGRESSION SCORES ACCORDING TO VIOLENCE RATING OF TV PROGRAMS WATCHED

Informant	1	2	3	4
Mother	14.44	14.97	18.32	28.54
Father	12.44	14.23	18.92	20.67

TABLE 3. MEAN AGGRESSION SCORES ACCORDING TO
NUMBER OF HOURS WATCHED

| | Hours | | |
Informant	0–4	5–9	10+
Mother	24.26	16.48	15.25
Father	16.00	14.17	14.75

1. They substantiate the assertions of Himmelweit et al. (1958), Schramm et al. (1961), and Minnow (see Footnote 2) that the relationship of behavior to the quality of programing is of a different order than is relationship of behavior to the sheer amount of time spent in watching TV. In general, boys who watch TV more are not as aggressive as boys who watch it less. Is this because they are by temperament less active; is it because they discharge their aggressive impulses in this fantasylike way and thus do not have to act them out in real life; or is it because their time is taken up in watching TV and they have less opportunity to act out aggression? On the other hand, boys who watch more violence on TV are more likely to be aggressive than boys who watch less violence. Is this because aggressive boys prefer violent programs; or is aggressive drive increased by such viewing; or are the subjects modeling their behavior after that of the characters on the TV programs? This survey study of real-life behavior cannot furnish definitive answers as to cause and effect relationships by itself. It can only demonstrate that a relationship exists. However, buttressed by manipulative laboratory studies, such as that of Bandura et al. (1963), we can speculate with some confidence that TV viewing does affect real-life behavior, and that the modeling variable is a crucial one. The drainage hypothesis, as an explanation for the lowered aggression of children who watch TV for longer hours, is unlikely in light of the results of other manipulative studies which show a direct relationship between aggression expressed in fantasy and overt behavior (Buss, 1961).

2. This study contributes further evidence that mothers and fathers are not equally good observers in all areas of child behavior. A previous article demonstrated areas in which fathers gave us better information than mothers (Eron, Banta, Walder, & Laulicht, 1961). However, for the present purposes, it seems, fathers do not have as good information as mothers. They very likely do not know about the child's daytime TV behavior and thus cannot give accurate details of total time watched. However, they are usually home in the evening hours and perhaps watch TV along with their children and thus are familiar at least with programs viewed then. Also their children are likely to talk to them about what they see on TV but not give them accurate reports of just how much time is spent in front of the

TV. Mother, however, is on hand and can observe for herself; thus her estimates are more relevant. At any rate, when mother and father agree as to what they tell us about their children, we can be more certain we are approximating the truth, especially when the observations of each relate in the same way to an independent criterion.

3. A final observation is the difference in results obtained with boys and girls. This is another indication that it is impossible to generalize from boys to girls in research on socialization, especially as far as the variable of aggression is concerned. This was pointed out by Sears, Whiting, Nowlis, and Sears (1953) a decade ago and is not due merely to the fact that boys score higher on all kinds of measures of aggression than do girls which has been a monotonous finding for even more years (Levin & Wardwell, 1962).

SUMMARY

Information about TV habits, (a) length of time watched and (b) extent of violence in favorite programs, was obtained from 689 mothers and 522 fathers in individual interviews having to do with the psychosocial antecedents of aggressive behavior in their children. This information was related to ratings of aggressive behavior of 3rd-grade children made by their peers. It was found that there was a significant positive relationship between the violence ratings of favorite programs as reported by both mothers and fathers and aggressive behavior of boys as rated in school. Also there was a significant negative relation between total time watched by boys as reported by mothers and aggressive behavior. The results for fathers' reports in this latter case were in the same direction, although not significant. No consistent relationships were noted between girls' TV habits as reported by either mother or father and aggression as rated in school by the peers.

REFERENCES

Aubrey, J. T. Testimony before Federal Communications Commission. *N. Y. Times,* January 26, 1962.

Bandura, A., Ross, Dorothea, & Ross, Sheila A. Imitation of film-mediated aggressive models. *J. abnorm. soc. Psychol.,* 1963, **66,** 3–11.

Banta, T. J., & Walder, L. O. Discriminant validity of a peer-rating measure. *Psychol. Rep.,* 1961, 9, 573–582.

Buss, A. H. *The psychology of aggression.* New York: Wiley, 1961.

Eron, L. D., Banta, T. J., Walder, L. O., & Laulicht, J. H. Comparison of data obtained from mothers and fathers on childbearing practices and their relation to child aggression. *Child Develpm.,* 1961, **32,** 457–472.

Eron, L. D., Laulicht, J. H., Walder, L. O., Farber, I. E., & Spiegel, J. P. Application of role and learning theories to the study of the development of aggression in children. *Psychol. Rep.,* 1961, 9, 291–334. (Monogr. Suppl. No. 2-V9)

Himmelweit, Hilde T., Oppenheim, A. N., & Vance, Pamela. *Television and the child: An empirical study of the effect of television on the young.* New York: Oxford Univer. Press, 1958.

Levin, H., & Wardwell, Elinor. The research uses of doll play. *Psychol. Bull.*, 1962, **59**, 27–56.

Lindquist, E. F. *Design and analysis of experiments in psychology and education.* Boston: Houghton Mifflin, 1953.

Schramm, W. A., Lyle, J., & Parker, E. B. *Television in the lives of our children.* Stanford: Stanford Univer. Press, 1961.

Sears, R. R., Whiting, J. W. M., Nowlis, V., & Sears, Pauline S. Some child rearing antecedents of aggression and dependency in young children. *Genet. Psychol. Monogr.*, 1953, **47**, 135–234.

Walder, L. O., Abelson, R. P., Eron, L. D., Banta, T. J., & Laulicht, J. H. Development of a peer-rating measure of aggression. *Psychol. Rep.*, 1961, **9**, 497–556. (Monogr. Suppl. No. 4-V9)

6.5   Interaction between Verbal and Nonverbal Behavior [1]

O. Ivar Lovaas [2]

Experimental investigations on the relation between verbal and nonverbal behavior date back as far as Lehmann's study (5) on the effect of verbal labels upon discrimination. Since then, research has been oriented around discrimination learning, generalization, transfer, transposition, problem solving, etc. Thus, previous research on the relation between verbal and nonverbal behavior has been frequently tied in with traditional areas of psychological inquiry where most often the nonverbal behavior has been employed as an index of the effect of verbal behavior on a hypothesized basic process, such as discrimination. The conceptual formulations designed to cover the empirical findings have been primarily concerned with the cue properties (or discriminative stimulus properties) of the two kinds of behavior—the two behaviors have been thought to interact in so far as one provides discriminative stimuli for the other. Esper states this interaction in

[1] This study was supported by grant M-2208 from the National Institute of Health, United States Public Health Service.

[2] The author expresses his gratitude to Professors Donald M. Baer and Sidney W. Bijou for their assistance, particularly on the conceptual aspects in this study. He is also grateful for the cooperation of the staff of the Nursery School, Gatzert Institute of Child Development.

Reprinted from *Child Development* 1961, **32**, 329–336, by permission of the author and the Society for Research in Child Development.

a broad formulation: "the stimuli associated with each type of response are among the conditioned elicitors of the other . . ." (2, p. 446). A similar paradigm is employed by Kurtz and Hovland (4) to deal with the more specific problem of the effect of verbal behavior on discrimination; they apparently conceive of the effect as due to attending behavior elicited by the verbal response. Miller's (7) formulations on acquired equivalence and distinctiveness of cues similarly rely on the cue properties of the verbal behavior in effecting a change in nonverbal behavior. Indeed all mediational hypotheses assume that it is the cue properties of the (hypothetical) verbal response that provide the "connecting link" to other behaviors.

In so far as one is concerned with the effect of verbal behavior on specific problems such as discrimination learning and concept formation, one can perhaps adequately conceptualize the relations observed by considering only the stimulus properties of the verbal behavior. It is apparent that in so doing one limits oneself to only one of several possible interactions between the two behaviors. It is, for example, conceivable that the two classes of behavior could interact on the basis of having common reinforcing stimuli, common emotional states which influence either behavior, etc. An analysis in these terms becomes more appropriate when one deals with broader classes of verbal and nonverbal behavior, for example, if one deals with social behavior, as in the study to be reported.

The purpose of the present study was to determine the effect of strengthening one class of verbal responses on a class of nonverbal responses. A bar-pressing response reinforced by aggressive doll action was observed immediately after a verbal conditioning session during which one group of children was reinforced for emitting aggressive verbal responses and the other group was reinforced for emitting nonaggressive verbal responses.

METHOD

Apparatus and Subjects

The research was conducted in the laboratory of the Gatzert Institute of Child Development. One room, the observation room, was equipped with one-way mirrors and sound equipment. The E (experimenter) could present the various experimental treatments from this room without being observed by S (subject). The other room, the "playroom," contained the apparatus or toys with which S would play and a partition behind which A (an adult assistant) could sit.

There were three pieces of apparatus in the playroom. Two of these, the doll apparatus and the ball-toy, have been described earlier (6). Briefly, the doll apparatus, or "striking dolls," was arranged so that each depression of a lever in the box on which the dolls were placed would make one doll strike the other on the head with a stick. The ball-toy consisted of a ball within a cagelike structure; the ball could be flipped up and down inside the cage by depression of a lever at the base of the cage. Depression of these levers also activated electric counters. The two were placed on a table, enabling S to operate both simultaneously.

The third piece of apparatus was a "talk-box," a 15 by 12 by 12 inch wooden box, placed on a table at the opposite wall from the table containing the dolls and the ball-toy. A microphone, inside the talk-box, was wired into the observation room and enabled recordings of S's verbalizations on a Gray Audograph recorder. Two dolls were fastened in a sitting position on top of the box. These dolls originally were similar in appearance, but one, "the bad doll," had been made very dirty; the other doll, "the good doll," was neat and clean. Reinforcement, in the form of small trinkets, could be delivered automatically to S through a chute emptying into a small tray on the side of the talk-box.

The Ss were children from the Institute's Nursery School. They were above average in intelligence (1). Nineteen children, age 3–5 to 4–7, were randomly selected from this group (but Ss known to be uncooperative were not asked). Five Ss were eliminated during the experiment, two because they expressed definite desire to leave, two others because they failed to respond to the verbal conditioning procedure (one could not be differentially conditioned, the other did not respond verbally at all), the fifth one because he had an identical ball-toy at home. The remaining 14 Ss had experiences as Ss in other experiments, but had no previous contact with the apparatus employed in this study. The Ss were seen in the morning while they were engaged in free play.

Procedure

A, a female adult who had visited the nursery prior to the experimental run and acquainted herself with the children, invited S to the playroom to "play some games." S was first made briefly acquainted with the playroom and then introduced to the striking dolls and the ball-toy. A pressed the lever on the dolls once and said, "When you press this bar (demonstrates) this (pointing) will happen. Now you do it (S is induced to press the lever five times). Now look here (pointing to ball-toy), when you press this lever (demonstrates) this (pointing) will happen. Now you do it (S is induced to press the lever five times). Now you play with the toys while I sit in my chair." S received a three-minute period of play, timed from the S's initial depression of either lever. This period constituted the pre-experimental or operant level of behavior for the striking dolls and the ball-toy.

A returned on signal by E and placed the dolls and the ball-toy out of S's view. She then seated him in front of the talk-box and said, "This is a talk-box; when you talk to this box, it will give you toys right here (points to reinforcement tray). Now see here are two dolls. This (pointing) is the good doll; this (pointing) is the bad doll. Say 'good doll' (if necessary coaches S to say, 'good doll'; this response is reinforced). See what you got; this is your toy; you can keep it. Now say, 'bad doll' (coaching if necessary;

this response is also reinforced). See what the box gave you; this is your toy to keep. Now you sit here and tell the box all about the dolls; tell the box what is going to happen to the dolls." The dolls were included to give S discriminative stimuli for emitting aggressive or nonaggressive verbal responses. Additional instructions were needed for about one-fourth of the Ss equally distributed between the groups. If, after two minutes and again after four minutes, S had made no response that could be reinforced, A told him from behind her screen: "Say, 'good doll' (S is reinforced for saying this); now say, 'bad doll' (also reinforced); now talk about the dolls."

The Ss were divided into two groups of seven each. One group was reinforced for aggressive verbal behavior (AV-group), the other for verbal behavior other than aggressive (NAV-group). The criterion used for deciding whether a verbal response was aggressive or not was whether it was derogatory to the dolls or denoted a wish on the part of the child to damage or hurt the dolls. In fact, the only responses the AV-group emitted that fulfilled this criterion were: "bad doll," "dirty doll," and "doll should be spanked."

The Ss from the AV-group and the NAV-group were matched in pairs on sex, age, number of reinforcements, and length of the verbal conditioning period. The magnitudes of the last two variables were determined by the AV-member of each pair who invariably was run first.

The verbal conditioning procedure necessitated initially reinforcing both aggressive and nonaggressive verbal responses (e.g., "good doll" and "bad doll") for both the NAV- and AV-groups to produce a high rate of verbal responding. A high rate of responding was defined as at least 12 reinforceable verbal responses within any two-minute period. A reinforceable verbal response was any word, phrase, or sentence. The criterion of high rate was reached from two to eight minutes after initiation of the verbal conditioning period. Once the high rate was reached, the AV-group became selectively reinforced for aggressive verbal responses while the NAV-group was reinforced for verbal responses other than aggressive ones. In the NAV-group, affectionate responses were reinforced as little as possible. If "good doll" reached a high rate, reinforcement was withheld in order to extinguish this response and produce other verbal responses. This condition was introduced to insure that any difference in subsequent play behavior between the two groups would not be a function of a contrast between "aggressive" and "friendly" verbal responding, but rather between aggressive and nonaggressive responding ("friendly" verbal responses could be incompatible with subsequent aggressive behavior, hence the data would be less clear than otherwise).

The length of the conditioning period was determined by S in the AV-group. The period was terminated after six minutes once a high rate of aggressive verbal responses was established (not less than 20 reinforceable aggressive verbal responses in a three-minute period). Thus, the conditioning period lasted anywhere from six to 14 minutes.

When the conditioning period was terminated, A told S that the "talk-box" did not work any more, helped him put his trinkets in a paper bag, and told him: "I will keep these toys for you while you play some more with this (pointing to the striking dolls) and this (pointing to the ball-toy) for just a few minutes more." The child was then allowed to play with the striking dolls and ball-toy for a period of four minutes. At the end of the four-minute period, *A* came out, gave *S* a thank you and his trinkets, and accompanied him back to his nursery school group.

A interacted with *S* in a matter-of-fact manner. She remained behind her partition except when she introduced apparatus. She did not interact with him unless he came over to her chair, at which point she said: "I'll sit here and you be over there for a few minutes more."

RESULTS AND DISCUSSION

Changes in the verbal behavior as a function of the verbal conditioning are presented in Figure 1. Number of aggressive and nonaggressive verbal

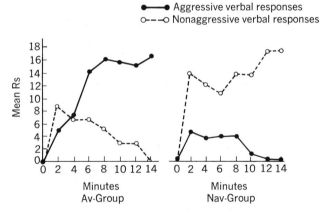

FIGURE 1. **Mean number of aggressive and nonaggressive verbal responses over successive two minute periods in the verbal conditioning period. Aggressive verbal conditioning group presented separately from the verbal conditioning group.**

responses was summed and averaged over successive two-minute periods for the various *S*s; the average aggressive and nonaggressive verbal responses for each group are presented in Figure 1. Since some *S*s reached the criterion of adequate verbal conditioning after six minutes, the last two-minute intervals give the verbal responding of decreasing numbers of *S*s. Thus, Figure 1 is only an approximate presentation of the changes in verbal behavior. The figure indicates that both objectives of the verbal conditioning were affected: first, there is an initial increase in the rate of responding, and secondly, there is subsequent differentiation of aggressive and nonaggressive verbal responses. It should be noted that these Ss emitted a very limited range of verbal responses. This was particularly true of the AV-group which in general was limited to "bad doll" or "dirty doll."

The effect of the verbal conditioning on the subsequent play behavior was calculated by taking the total number of responses for each S on the striking dolls and the ball-toy and converting this into the following score: $100 \times$ total responses on the dolls $\div$ total responses on dolls and ball. This percentage gives the relative amount of aggressive play behavior and was calculated for each S both before and after the verbal conditioning procedure. The group means are presented in Table 1. As can be observed, the

TABLE 1. Mean Proportion of Aggressive Responding before and after Verbal Conditioning

	Before Verbal Conditioning	After Verbal Conditioning
Aggressive conditioning	55.2	78.4
Nonaggressive conditioning	55.4	59.4

Note.—Proportion $= 100 \times$ total Rs on doll/total Rs on doll $+$ ball.

level of aggressive responding prior to the verbal conditioning is identical for the two groups. There is a significantly higher proportion of aggressive play behavior following the verbal conditioning period for the AV-group Ss who were conditioned to make aggressive verbal responses ($t = 2.326$, $df = 12$, $p < .05$, two-tailed test). In other words, some control of nonverbal aggressive behavior was achieved by manipulating the children's verbal aggressive behavior.

In evaluating these results, four possibilities should be considered. First of all, the aggressive verbal response, since it is reinforced and not punished, becomes a discriminative stimulus which marks the occasion when nonverbal aggressive behavior will be reinforced, or at least not punished. In popular terms, the aggressive verbal behavior provides a "green light" for subsequent aggressive nonverbal responding.

The second interpretation to be considered deals with the reinforcing stimuli held in common by the verbal aggressive and the nonverbal aggressive behavior. The common reinforcing stimuli may be primary (e.g., tension reduction) as well as secondary (e.g., other forms of self-stimulation). Frequently it appears that in everyday life verbal behavior achieves consequences similar to those of nonverbal behaviors (e.g., both may achieve the removal of some noxiously stimulating person); hence one would expect them also to have numerous secondary reinforcers in common. To the extent that the two response systems have reinforcing stimuli in common, it would be unlikely that an operation upon one system would not also change characteristics of responding in the other system. Both an increase and a decrease could be brought about in subsequent aggressive nonverbal behavior depending upon the operations on the verbal aggressive behavior. For example, one should be able to bring about a "sensitization" for aggressive reinforcers by presenting these briefly to the verbal mode of responding. This sensitization should bring about a subsequent increase in nonverbal responding for that reinforcer. This may well account for the effect observed in the present study. Insofar as the reinforcing stimuli are common between the two response systems, it also should be possible to "satiate" the organism on the reinforcer by presenting it amply for the one mode of responding, whereupon one would observe a subsequent decrease in responding for that reinforcer by the other mode of responding. The possibility of reducing nonverbal aggressive behavior by providing frequent and intensive verbal aggressive expression has been long recognized in clinical psychology, usually referred to by such terms as "cathartic expression." There is experimental evidence which supports this notion; for example, Feshbach (3) observed a decrease in aggressive behavior immediately following the writing of aggressive TAT stories.

The third manner in which verbal and nonverbal behavior may be seen to interact attributes to the verbal behavior a "directing" influence upon nonverbal behavior. This formulation presupposes that in the history of the person certain verbal and nonverbal behaviors have occurred together in such a manner that the verbal response becomes a discriminative stimulus for the nonverbal behavior.[3] This formulation may lead one to expect that one can vary the amount of generalization from verbal to nonverbal behavior by varying the degree to which the verbal behavior denotes the nonverbal behavior. For example, one would be led to expect more generalization than was observed in this study if the children in the AV-group had been reinforced for "doll should be spanked." This hypothesis is supported by observation of the behavior of some of the Ss in the NAV-group. For example, one of these Ss was reinforced for "what shall I say?" As this response increased in frequency with reinforcements, S got up from his chair and walked toward A to address his question to her.

Fourth and lastly, it is assumed that aggressive behavior has been associated with aversive stimuli in the past history of the child. It is conceivable that the occurrence of the verbal aggressive response allows for some extinction of the conditioned aversive stimuli associated with that response and that the effect of this extinction generalizes to the nonverbal response. If conditioned aversive stimuli suppress or inhibit aggressive responding, the effect to be expected would be an increase in subsequent nonverbal aggressive responding. In view of the resistance of aversive stimuli to extinction, this relationship is perhaps the least likely explanation of the present data.

---

[3] Informal observation on the Ss while they were being verbally conditioned further confirms that such behavior was being emitted; many Ss in the AV-group raised their voices and became quite loud, thrashed around, pounded the table, etc.

SUMMARY

The purpose of the present research was to determine the effect of strengthening one class of responses on another. A bar-pressing response reinforced by aggressive doll action was observed immediately after the children had undergone a verbal conditioning session during which one group of children was reinforced for emitting aggressive verbal responses; the other group was reinforced for nonaggressive verbal responses. The results of the study gave evidence for an increase in aggressive nonverbal behavior following reinforcement of aggressive verbal behavior. In other words, some control of nonverbal aggressive behavior was achieved by manipulating verbal aggressive behavior.

In evaluating these results, four possibilities should be considered: (a) the verbal aggressive behavior becomes a discriminative stimulus which marks the occasion when nonverbal aggressive behavior will be reinforced or at least not punished. (b) To the extent that the two response systems have reinforcing stimuli in common, operating upon one system might also change characteristics of responding for these stimuli by the other system (e.g., by sensitization of or satiation for the common reinforcer). (c) The verbal response has a "directing" influence on the nonverbal response since it functions as a discriminative stimulus for that response. (d) Occurrence of the verbal aggressive response allows for some extinction of the conditioned aversive stimuli associated with that response; the effect of this extinction generalizes to the nonverbal response and thereby reduces the amount of aversive stimuli inhibiting the nonverbal aggressive responding.

REFERENCES

1. Bijou, S. W. Patterns of reinforcement and resistance to extinction in young children. *Child Develpm.*, 1957, **28**, 47–54.
2. Esper, E. A. Language. In C. Murchison (Ed.), *A handbook of social psychology*. Clark Univer. Press, 1935. Pp. 417–460.
3. Feshbach, S. The drive-reducing function of fantasy behavior. *J. abnorm. soc. Psychol.*, 1955, **50**, 3–11.
4. Kurtz, K. H., & Hovland, C. I. The effect of verbalization during observation of stimulus objects upon accuracy of recognition and recall. *J. exp. Psychol.*, 1953, **45**, 157–164.
5. Lehmann, A. Über Wiedererkennen. *Phil. Stud.*, 5, 96–156.
6. Lovaas, O. I. Effect of exposure to symbolic aggression on aggressive behavior. *Child Develpm.*, 1961, **32**, 37–44.
7. Miller, N. E. Theory and experiment relating psychoanalytic displacement to stimulus-response generalization. *J. abnorm. soc. Psychol.*, 1948, **43**, 173–176.

6.6 Some Antecedents of Aggression and Effects of Frustration in Doll Play [1]

Eleanor Hollenberg and Margaret Sperry

The fantasies expressed in doll play by young children are presumably the products of the same motivations and life history experiences that determine interpersonal behavior in real life. The special character of the doll play situation provides for different weightings of the drives and other antecedents, to be sure, and therefore the actual content of the play is in some ways quite different from the content of real life activity. But it must be assumed that fantasy activity is a product of the same basic psychologic processes that govern all other behavior. In order to understand fantasy performances, then, one must discover the particular antecedent conditions or factors that are associated with particular forms of fantasy.

The present study was designed to test a set of theoretically coherent hypotheses which deal with the antecedents of the frequency and intensity of doll play aggression. These latter variables were measured in terms of behavior units occurring during four fifteen-minute doll play sessions. The antecedent variables investigated were frustration, punishment of aggression, and permissiveness toward aggression. The first section of this paper will examine the effects of frustration in the home, as rated on the basis of mother interviews. The second part will examine the effects of both home punishment and punishment experimentally induced during the doll play itself. In the third section, the cumulative influence of experimental permissiveness will be investigated.

THE EXPERIMENT

Fifty-three children, between the ages of three and six years, enrolled in the State University of Iowa preschool, were the subjects of this study. Each child participated in four fifteen-minute doll play sessions separated by two to five days. The doll play equipment consisted of a roofless, one story, six room house, realistically furnished (Phillips, 1945), and a standard family

[1] This study was conducted under the direction of Robert R. Sears at the Iowa Child Welfare Research Station as part of a larger project supported in part by a grant from the Rockefeller Foundation. Members of the research staff who participated in the design and analysis of mother interviews were Vincent Nowlis, John W. M. Whiting, Lois Jean Carl, Helen Faigin, John McKee, and the authors.

Reprinted from the *Journal of Personality* 1951, **1**, 32–43, by permission of the authors and Duke University Press.

of dolls—mother, father, boy, girl, and baby (Robinson, 1946). At the start
of each session the child and a female experimenter, with whom he was
acquainted, examined and identified the dolls and rooms. The child was
then asked to invent a story about the family of dolls who lived in the house
and was assured that he could make them do anything he wanted them to
do. An observer concealed behind a one-way screen kept a record of the
child's doll play activity with respect to the type, the agent, and the object
of each response which was made.

This study is a combination of two experiments, each conducted by a
different experimenter. The first was a comparison of the effects of experimentally induced punishment and permissiveness. Twenty-three children
were used, divided into two sub-groups; they will be referred to respectively
as the Experimentally Punished group (five girls, six boys) and the Control
group (five girls, seven boys). For the former group, the punishment, which
was introduced in the *second* session only, consisted of verbal disapproval
of each aggressive response. For example, if the child kicked the baby doll,
the experimenter said, "No, John, don't you know that nice boys shouldn't
do a thing like that?" The other three sessions for the group were characterized by high permissiveness, as described by Pintler (1945). For the Control
group, all four sessions were conducted under conditions of high permissiveness.

The second experiment utilized thirty children, in four sessions which,
like those of the Control group in the above experiment, were permissive.
For each of these children, two measures of home experiences were available. These were *frustration* and *punishment for aggression*. They were
obtained in the form of ratings made from intensive interviews of the
children's mothers with respect to their child training practices. Ratings of
degree of frustration were based on the number and kinds of restrictive
rules, the lack of responsiveness to the child's needs or requests, and the
degree to which the mother forced the child to comply with her own motivations without regard to the child's interests. Separate ratings, on ten-point
scales, were made on six areas of child training: feeding during infancy,
weaning, toileting, cleanliness, health and danger, and eating. These six
sets of ratings were then converted to standard scores, and combined addi-
tively to provide a single measure of home frustration.

Punishment for aggression is broadly defined as inducing pain or discomfort in the child when he acts in an aggressive or asocial manner. The
punishment ratings were based on interview reports of the frequency, intensity and duration of such responses as spanking, threatening, isolating,
denying privileges and derogating.

The reliability of these ratings of the interview records, as measured by
the product-moment correlation between two independent raters, ranged
from 0.57 to 0.70 on the six frustration scales. For the punishment scale, the
correlation between two raters was 0.71.

On the basis of the scores described above, these thirty children have been divided into sub-groups, during the course of data analysis, depending upon which antecedent home variable was being investigated. For example, when home frustration was the relevant factor, the fifteen children whose mothers were rated in the lower half of the frustration distribution, constituted the Low Frustration group; the fifteen children whose mothers were rated in the upper half of the distribution constituted the High Frustration group. The Low Punishment and High Punishment groups were similarly obtained. In the last section below, which deals with the effects of experimental permissiveness, the performances of all thirty children have been combined, and they are described as the Total group.

The measure of aggression was obtained from the records of the children's doll play behavior. Though these records also include all other types of response which occurred, such as dependency, nurturance and noninteractive behavior, aggression is singled out for study in this investigation. It was defined as any behavior resulting in injury, destruction, derogation or irritation of another. Two measures of aggression, frequency and intensity, were recorded. *Intense aggression* included physical punishment, physical injury and the destruction of equipment; in contrast, *attenuated aggression* included mischief, verbal aggression, and the inducing of discomfort. In order to eliminate the effects of the intensity measures of individual differences in frequency, intensity has been presented in percentage form— *Frequency of Intense Aggression/Total Frequency of Aggression*. In both experiments the reliability of observer agreement for intense and total aggression ranged from 0.72 to 0.85.

THE EFFECT OF FRUSTRATION ON AGGRESSION

The first hypothesis to be tested is that *frustration increases the strength of drive and thus results in an increase of aggressive responses.*

It is assumed that interference with the attainment of a goal produces a heightened drive state, frustration-produced drive, which can be reduced by any response that removes the source of frustration. Furthermore, it is assumed that the strength of this frustration drive increases both with the frequency and degree of interference and with the strength of the response suffering interference (Dollard et al., 1939). Depending upon the conditions of learning, aggressive, dependent, withdrawing, or other responses (Whiting, 1944) may be instrumental in reducing the strength of the frustration-produced drive. Whichever class of responses is repeatedly rewarded will tend to become dominant and thus will be evoked in other frustrating situations. It is assumed that since our competitive culture rewards aggression as a response to interference by other persons, aggression becomes a dominant response to frustration.

It should be pointed out that no assumption is made as to whether or not frustration itself produces an aggressive drive, but simply that frustration increases the general drive level, thereby increasing the probability of the occurrence of aggressive responses. Although the relationship between the motivational effect of frustration and a specific acquired drive of aggression is a problem of importance, the present study is not designed to throw light on this matter. In other words, the present hypothesis is concerned simply with the relationship between frustration as an antecedent condition and the occurrence of aggressive responses as a consequence. To particularize the general hypothesis for the present experimental data, children who are severely frustrated by their mothers at home will be more frequently and more intensely aggressive in doll play than children who are mildly frustrated.

The results obtained are shown in Table 1. The differences between the

TABLE 1. FRUSTRATION AND AGGRESSION (Mean frequency and intensity of aggressive acts in the first doll play session* for children whose mothers were rated in the *upper* and *lower* halves of the distribution on the frustration scale)

Mother Frustration	N	Mean Freq. Agg. Acts	Mean Percent Intense Agg.
High	7 girls 8 boys	12.3	57.0
Low	8 girls 7 boys	7.5	39.6

* Session I scores are used to test the relationship between home variables and doll play aggression, because it is felt that permissiveness during the course of doll play sessions, which will be discussed in Section IV, differentially affects the high and low frustration and punishment groups.

high and low frustration groups are in the predicted direction but are not statistically significant. Thus, the first hypothesis is not strongly confirmed. However, as will be shown in Section III, when the effects of punishment are controlled, the predicted differences are significant for the low punishment group.

THE EFFECTS OF PUNISHMENT ON AGGRESSION

The second hypothesis is that *punishment of aggression (a) decreases the frequency and intensity of aggression in the situation in which punishment occurs, and (b) increases the frequency and intensity in situations distinctly dissimilar to that in which the punishment occurred.*

Due to the conditions of social interaction and the process of socialization, children are punished as well as rewarded for aggression. Therefore, stimulus situations which tend to evoke aggression simultaneously elicit the anticipation of punishment, i.e., aggression anxiety. This results in a conflict between two incompatible tendencies—the tendency to express aggression, and the tendency to avoid expression of aggression.

Following Miller (1944), we assume that these tendencies summate algebraically. Thus, if the tendency to express aggression remains constant, the probability that aggression will occur decreases as aggression anxiety increases. If aggression anxiety becomes greater than the tendency to express aggression, it is probable that aggression will be inhibited.

The application of this principle to the present data requires that children who are experimentally punished for aggression in the doll play situation should (1) express less doll play aggression after being punished than before being punished, and (2) should express less aggression than a control group which has not been punished.

Figure 1 shows that for the Experimentally Punished group, the means

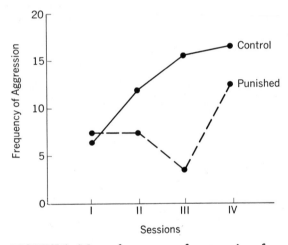

FIGURE 1. Mean frequency of aggression for experimentally punished group (N = 12) and control group (N = 11) in four doll play sessions. Experimentally induced punishment was introduced in the punishment group during session II only.

are in the predicted order. That is, the mean of session III, after punishment, is lower than the mean of session I, before punishment, though this difference is not statistically significant.

It is interesting to note that although there is no decrease in aggression between the first session and the second session, in which punishment occurred, aggression decreases markedly in the third session. The difference between the means of sessions II and III is significant at approximately the 5 per cent level of confidence (obtained t = 2.1). It appears that the first session permissiveness increases the probability of occurrence of aggression, and it may therefore be assumed that the Experimentally Punished group has, like the Control group, a higher tendency to aggression at the beginning of the second session. The introduction of punishment, however, increases aggression anxiety and thus holds the actual expression during that full session to the same average level as occurred in the first session. The second session punishment then has the effect of increasing aggression anxiety and reducing the expression of aggression in session III even further.

The Control group, however, which has been permitted to be aggressive throughout, is significantly more aggressive on session III than the Punished group. This difference is well beyond the 1 per cent level of confidence (obtained t = 4.2).

In the fourth session, the aggression of the punished group rises again. This is consistent with a session to session increase in aggression resulting from a decrease in aggression anxiety due to the reinstatement of permissiveness. This process will be discussed more fully in the section dealing with the third hypothesis.

Figure 2 shows that punishment affects the intensity of aggression in the same way as it affects the frequency of aggression. The only statistically reliable difference is found in session III, where the aggression of the punished group is significantly less intense than that of the Control group (obtained t = 2.1).

The above results support the first part of the second hypothesis, that punishment of aggression decreases the frequency and intensity of aggression in the situation in which punishment occurs.

The second part of the second hypothesis, namely, that punishment for

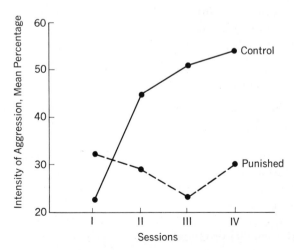

FIGURE 2. Mean percent of intense aggression in experimentally punished group and control group in four doll play sessions.

aggression *increases* aggression in situations distinctly dissimilar to that in which the punishment occurred, involves the postulates of (1) stimulus generalization of conflicting response tendencies, and (2) conflict-produced drive.

1. Stimulus Generalization of Conflicting Response Tendencies

Miller (1944) presents evidence that both approach and avoidance responses generalize with decreasing strength along a dimension of stimulus similarity from the point at which they are established. The generalization of avoidance responses, however, has a steeper slope than the generalization of approach responses, i.e., the former generalize to a narrower range of similar situations. We are assuming that the tendencies to express aggression and aggression anxiety follow the same principles as the approach and avoidance responses of Miller's study. Thus even though a child may be so severely punished that he will not express aggression in the punishing situation, it follows from this assumption of differential generalization of aggression and aggression anxiety that he will express aggression in a situation distinctly dissimilar from that in which he was punished.

In order to relate this paradigm to the conditions of this study, it should be made explicit that our dimension of similarity ranges from the real life home, which is considered as the original point of reinforcement for both aggression and aggression anxiety, to the doll family home. Because most of the socialization, and the punishment it incurs, is induced by the mother in the home, and because the conditions of permissive doll play have none of these punishing characteristics, it is assumed that these points on the similarity dimension are widely separated, and thus are sufficiently dissimilar to permit the dissipation of generalized aggression anxiety. It follows from Miller's formulation that children who are punished for aggression by their mothers will be most inhibited at home, but will be able to express their aggression in situations very dissimilar to home, as, for example, in permissive doll play.

2. Conflict-produced Drive

Whereas Miller specifies *where* on a stimulus dimension a response will occur, Whiting's (unpublished) hypothesis of conflict-produced drive further specifies *how strongly* it will occur at a given point. In his statement of this principle, he postulates that a state of conflict, i.e., the simultaneous evocation of two incompatible response tendencies, increases the drive level, thereby increasing the frequency and intensity of the occurring responses. The strength of this drive varies positively with the product of the two tendencies. Thus, if the tendency to express aggression is constant, the strength of the conflict-produced drive will increase with an increase in anxiety.

It should be pointed out that the above formulation is similar to the assumption, discussed earlier, that frustration produces drive. In a conflict situation, before the conflict is resolved, the tendency to perform either the approach or avoidance response is believed to be interfered with by the presence of the other. Since frustration was defined as *any* interference with goal-directed activity, and the interference of competing responses is a class of frustrating events, therefore it too should produce drive.

In summary, stimulus generalization specifies the situations in which a response is most likely to occur. Conflict-produced drive specifies that in those situations the occurring response will be stronger if a competing response is present. Thus, the specific hypothesis to be tested is that children who are highly punished for aggression at home will be more frequently and intensely aggressive in doll play than children who are mildly punished.

The relevant data are presented in Table 2, and support the hypothesis.

TABLE 2. PUNISHMENT AND AGGRESSION (Mean frequency and intensity of aggressive acts in the first doll play session for children whose mothers were rated in the upper and lower halves of the distribution on the punishment scale)

Mother Punishment	N	Mean Freq. Agg. Acts	Mean Percent Intense Agg.
High	7 girls 8 boys	13.5	55.4
Low	8 girls 7 boys	6.9	41.2

The difference between the frequency means approaches the 5 per cent level of confidence (obtained t = 1.9). The difference between the means of intensity, although it is in the predicted direction, is not statistically significant.

Tables 1 and 2 demonstrate that there is a tendency for both home punishment and home frustration to increase aggression. One might suspect that these measures are correlated; i.e., that highly punishing mothers are also highly frustrating. This is not the case. The product-moment correlation coefficient is .17 and not statistically significant.

THE COMBINED EFFECTS OF FRUSTRATION AND PUNISHMENT

Since punishment and frustration are relevant variables with respect to aggression, more revealing relationships can be shown if both these factors are taken into account simultaneously, rather than singly. The 30 children were divided, therefore, into four groups: (1) low frustration-low punishment (N = three boys, five girls); (2) low frustration-high punishment (N = four boys, three girls); (3) high frustration-low punishment (N = four boys, three girls); (4) high frustration-high punishment (N = four boys, four girls).

For example, the child whose mother was in the lower half of the frustration distribution and the lower half of the punishment distribution was placed in group 1; the child whose mother was in the upper half of the frustration distribution and lower half of the punishment distribution was placed in group 3; etc. From the first two hypotheses it follows that the high frustration-high punishment group should be the most aggressive in doll play, and that the low frustration-low punishment group should be the least aggressive, and the high-low and low-high groups should fall between these two extremes. The theory is not precise enough to predict the order of the two intermediate groups. It can be seen from Figures 3 and 4 that the low

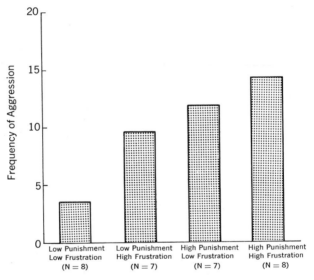

FIGURE 3. **Mean frequency of aggression during session 1 in four subgroups divided with reference to low and high experiences of frustration and punishment at home.**

frustration-low punishment group is the least aggressive, the high frustration-high punishment group the most aggressive, and the high-low groups fall in between. In Figure 3, the difference in frequency between the high frustration-high punishment group and the low frustration-low punishment group is the greatest, but due to the extreme variability within the former group, this difference is not statistically significant. However, for the low frustration groups, the obtained t for the difference between low and high punishment is 2.1. For the low punishment group, the obtained t for the difference between low and high frustration is 2.2. Both these differences are significant at the 5 per cent level of confidence. In Figure 4 none of the differences in

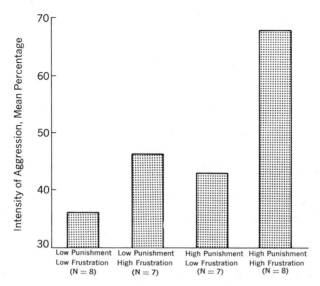

FIGURE 4. Mean percent of intense aggression during session 1 in four subgroups divided with reference to low and high experiences of frustration and punishment at home.

intensity between the groups are significant, although the trends are in the predicted order.

THE EFFECT OF PERMISSIVENESS ON AGGRESSION

We now come to the third hypothesis, that *permissiveness with respect to aggression reduces the anticipation of punishment and/or increases the anticipation of reward for aggression, and thus results in an increase of aggression.*

This hypothesis stems from previous discussions of reward and punishment. The only problem which arises here is whether permissiveness increases the anticipation of reward, decreases the anticipation of punishment, or both. If, for these subjects and conditions, a precise formulation of the slopes of generalization of reward and punishment were known, it might be possible, on the basis of the rate of increase of aggression, to choose among these possibilities. However, since the potential effects of these alternatives are in the same direction—that is, an increase in aggression—any choice among them is, for the purposes of this paper, simply a matter of preference. In any case, the expectation is that under conditions of permissive doll play there will be a progressive increase in the frequency and intensity of aggression from the first to the fourth session.

The results are presented in Table 3. These data clearly support the

TABLE 3. PERMISSIVENESS AND AGGRESSION (Mean frequency and intensity of aggression for four doll play sessions)

Group	I	II	III	IV	t bet. I and IV
Frequency					
Control (N = 11)	6.9	12.3	15.6	16.2	3.1
Total (N = 30)	10.2	17.3	21.3	21.9	2.8
Intensity					
Control (N = 11)	22.5	45.0	51.3	54.2	5.4
Total (N = 30)	48.3	49.5	63.5	74.3	3.7

hypothesis. All differences between the means of sessions I and IV are significant at or beyond the 1 per cent level of confidence.

SUMMARY AND CONCLUSIONS

This study, which is based on two experiments, deals with the effects of home frustration, home and experimental punishment, and experimental permissiveness on the frequency and intensity of aggressive doll play behavior of fifty-three nursery school children.

In one experiment, thirty children participated in four doll play sessions under permissive conditions. For these children, measures of frustration and punishment in the home, based on mother interviews, were available.

In the other experiment, twelve children were experimentally punished for aggressive behavior in the second of four doll play sessions. For the remaining eleven children, who served as a control for the punished group, all four sessions were conducted under permissive conditions.

The results can be summarized as follows:

1. Children who are severely frustrated by their mothers at home tend to be more aggressive in doll play than children who are mildly frustrated. When the effects of home punishment are taken into account, this relationship shows up more clearly.

2. Children who are highly punished for aggression at home tend to be *more* aggressive in doll play than children who are mildly punished.

3. Children who are experimentally punished for doll play aggression are significantly less aggressive in doll play than nonpunished children.

4. Under conditions of permissive doll play, there is a significant increase in aggression from the first to the last session.

The above findings have been discussed within a theoretic framework which utilizes the constructs and assumptions of frustration-produced drive, conflict-produced drive, stimulus generalization, and reduction of anxiety.

REFERENCES

Dollard, J., Doab, L. W., Miller, N. E., Mowrer, O. H., & Sears, R. R. *Frustration and Aggression.* New Haven: Yale University Press, 1939.

Miller, N. E. Experimental studies of conflict. In J. McV. Hunt (Ed.), *Personality and the behavior disorders.* New York: Ronald Press, 1944.

Phillips, Ruth. Doll play as a function of the realism of the materials and the length of the experimental session. *Child Development,* 1955, **16,** 123–143.

Pintler, Margaret H. Doll play as a function of experimenter-child interaction and initial organization of materials. *Child Development,* 1945, **16,** 145–166.

Robinson, Elizabeth F. Doll play as a function of the doll family constellation. *Child Development,* 1946, **17,** 99–120.

Whiting, J. M. W. The frustration complex in Kwoma society. *Man,* 1944, **44,** 140–144.

6.7   Control of Aggression in a Nursery School Class [1,2]

Paul Brown and Rogers Elliot

The aim of the present study was to add to the data of the field of social learning theory (Bandura and Walters, 1963), at several points. First, among the techniques of controlling operant social behavior, simple extinction (Williams, 1959), simple reinforcement (Azrin and Lindsley, 1956), or both of them in combination (Zimmerman and Zimmerman, 1962; Ayllon and Michael, 1960; Baer, Harris, and Wolf, 1963) have been employed frequently with children. Second, the use of explicit learning techniques has been shown effective in young nursery school subjects (Ss) in two recent papers (Baer *et. al.,* 1963; Homme, de Baca, Devine, Steinhorst, and Rickert, 1963). Finally, antisocial acts of the assertive-aggressive kind are known to have operant components which are extinguishable (Williams, 1959) and reinforcible (Cowan and Walters, 1963).

With the above as background, we took seriously the following:

[1] This is a report of work done by the first author, under the direction of the second, in partial fulfillment of the requirements of the senior courses in independent research at Dartmouth.

[2] The authors thank Edith Hazard, director, and the members of the staff of the Hanover Nursery School. Not only did they make this study possible, they made it very enjoyable.

Reprinted from *Journal of Experimental Child Psychology* 1965, **2,** 103–107, with permission of the authors and the Academic Press.

Theorizing and experimentation on the inhibition of aggression have focused exclusively on the inhibitory influence of anxiety or guilt, on the assumption that response inhibition is necessarily a consequence of pairing responses with some form of aversive stimulation. The development of aggression inhibition through the strengthening of incompatible positive responses, on the other hand, has been entirely ignored, despite the fact that the social control of aggression is probably achieved to a greater extent on this basis than by means of aversive stimulation (Bandura and Walters, 1963, p. 130).

We set out to control the aggressive behavior of all of the boys in an entire nursery school class, by using as techniques the removal of positive generalized reinforcement (attention) for aggressive acts, while giving attention to cooperative acts.

METHOD

Subjects

The subjects were the 27 males in the younger (3- to 4-year-old) of the two groups at the Hanover Nursery School. Observation and teachers' reports made it clear that the younger boys were more aggressive than any other age-sex subgroup.

Ratings

Aggressive responses were defined by enumeration of the categories of the scale devised by Walters, Pearce, and Dahms (1957). The scale has two major subcategories—physical aggression and verbal aggression. Each of these is subdivided into more concrete categories; e.g., under physical aggression are categories labeled "pushes, pulls, holds"; "hits, strikes"; "annoys, teases, interferes"; and there are similar specific descriptions (e.g., "disparages"; "threatens") under the verbal category.

The observations of the behavior were made by two raters, both undergraduates at Dartmouth.[3] They were trained in the use of the scale, and given practice in observing the class during the free-play hour from 9:20 to 10:20 in the morning. Such observation was possible because the rater could stand in a large opening connecting the two spacious play areas. The rating scale had the categories of aggressive behavior as its rows, and 12 five-minute intervals as its columns. The raters simply checked any occurrence of a defined behavior in the appropriate cell.

One rater observed on Monday, Wednesday, and Friday mornings; the other observed on Tuesday and Thursday. On two of the four observed Wednesday sessions, both raters observed, so that interrater reliability could be estimated. At the conclusion of the study, the raters were interviewed to determine what changes, if any, they had observed in the behavior

[3] We thank James Miller and James Markworth for their assistance.

of teachers and children, and whether they had surmised the research hypothesis.

Procedure

The pre-treatment period was simply a one-week set of observations of aggressive responses by the younger boys, to furnish a reference response rate. Two weeks later the first treatment period was initiated by the teachers and the first author (see below) and it lasted for two weeks. Ratings were taken during the second week of this period. The teachers were then told that the experiment was over, and that they were no longer constrained in their behavior toward aggressive acts. Three weeks after this another set of ratings was taken to assess the durability of the treatment effect. Finally, two weeks after this follow-up observation, the treatment was reinstituted for two weeks, and, again, observations were made in the second of these weeks.

The teachers were the agents of treatment (along with the first author) and they were instructed verbally, with reference to a typed handout, which read in part as follows:

There are many theories which try to explain aggression in young children. Probably most are partly true and perhaps the simplest is the best. One simple one is that many fights, etc. occur because they bring with them a great deal of fuss and attention from some adult. If we remember that just 3 or 4 short years ago these children would have literally died if they were not able to command (usually by crying) attentive responses from some adult, we can see how just attending to a child could be rewarding. On the other hand, when a child is playing quietly most parents are thankful for the peace and leave well enough alone. Unfortunately, if attention and praise is really rewarding, the child is not rewarded when he should be. Thus, many parents unwittingly encourage aggressive, attention-getting behavior since this is the only way the child gets some form of reward. Of course this is an extreme example but it would be interesting to see if this matter of attention is really the issue, and the important issue especially in a setting where punishment of behavior is not a real option.

At the school I have noticed that whenever it has been possible cooperative and non-aggressive acts are attended to and praised by teachers. During the intervening week we would like to exaggerate this behavior and play down the attention given to aggressive acts. I hope to concentrate on the boys, but if a boy and girl are concerned that is perfectly all right.

Briefly, we will try to ignore aggression and reward cooperative and peaceful behavior. Of course if someone is using a hammer on another's head we would step in, but just to separate the two and leave. It will be difficult at first because we tend to watch and be quiet when nothing bad is happening, and now our attention will *as much as possible* be directed toward cooperative, or non-aggressive behavior. It would be good to let the most aggressive boys see that the others are getting the attention if it is possible. A pat on the head, 'That's good Mike,' 'Hello Chris and Mark, how are you today?' 'Look what Eric made,' etc. may have more rewarding power than we think. On the other hand, it is just as important during this week to have no reprimands, no 'Say you're sorry,' 'Aren't you sorry?' Not that these aren't useful ways of teaching proper behavior, but they will only cloud the effects of our other manner of treatment. It would be best not even to look at a shove or small fight if we are sure no harm is being done; as I mentioned before, if it is necessary we should just separate the children and leave.

RESULTS AND DISCUSSION

The Raters

The correlation between the raters of total aggressive responses checked in each of 24 five-minute periods was 0.97. This is higher than the average interrater correlation of 0.85 reported by Walters, et al. (1957), but their raters were working with a one-minute, rather than a five-minute observation petriod.

When interviewed, one rater said that the only change he saw in the children was in the two "most troublesome" boys, who at the end (the fourth-rating period) seemed less troublesome. The other noticed no change in any of the children, even though his ratings described the changes shown in Table 1. One rater had noticed, again during the fourth-rating period, that

TABLE 1. AVERAGE NUMBER OF RESPONSES IN THE VARIOUS RATED CATEGORIES OF AGGRESSION

Times of observation	Categories of Aggression		
	Physical	Verbal	Total
Pretreatment	41.2	22.8	64.0
First treatment	26.0	17.4	43.4
Follow-up	37.8	13.8	51.6
Second treatment	21.0	4.6	25.6

the first author was being "especially complimentary" to one of the troublesome boys, and the other rater did not notice any change in the behavior of any adult.

Aggressive Responses

Table 1 presents the average daily number of physical, verbal, and overall aggressive responses in each of the four periods of observation. Analyses of variance of the daily scores as a function of treatments yielded F ratios ($df = 3, 16$) of 6.16 for physical aggression ($p < 0.01$), 5.71 for verbal aggression ($p < 0.01$), and 25.43 for overall aggression.

There seems little doubt that ignoring aggressive responses and attending cooperative ones had reliable and significant effects upon the behavior of the children.

Verbal aggression did not recover after the first treatment, while physical aggression did. Since we were rating children, not teachers, we offer the following speculation with only casual evidence. We believe the teachers find it harder to ignore fighting than to ignore verbal threats or insults. It is certainly true that the teachers (all females) found aggression in any form fairly difficult to ignore. During treatment periods, they would frequently look to the first author as if asking whether they should step in and stop a fight, and they often had the expression and behavior of conflict when aggressive, especially physically aggressive behavior occurred—i.e., they would often, almost automatically, move slightly toward the disturbance, then check themselves, then look at the first author. The more raucous scenes were tense, with the teachers waiting, alert and ready for the first bit of calm and cooperative behavior to appear and allow them to administer attention. The teachers, incidentally, were skeptical of the success of the method when it was first proposed, though they came ultimately to be convinced of it. What made its success dramatic to them was the effect upon two very aggressive boys, both of whom became friendly and cooperative to a degree not thought possible. The most aggressive boys tended to be reinforced for cooperative acts on a lower variable ratio than the others, because teachers were especially watchful of any sign of cooperation on their parts.

CONCLUSION

As Allen, Hart, Buell, Harris, and Wolf (1964) have pointed out recently, the principles involved in the present application of controlling techniques are simple. What makes this and other demonstrations of them successful in a real-life setting is systematic observation, systematic application, and systematic evaluation.

REFERENCES

Allen, Eileen K., Hart, Betty, Buell, Joan S., Harris, Florence R., & Wolf, M. M. Effects of social reinforcement on the isolate behavior of a nursery school child. *Child Develpm.*, 1964, **35,** 511–518.

Ayllon, T., & Michael, J. The psychiatric nurse as a behavioral engineer. *J. exp. anal. Behav.*, 1959, **2,** 323–334.

Azrin, N. H., & Lindsley, O. R. The reinforcement of cooperation between children. *J. abnorm. soc. Psychol.*, 1956, **52,** 100–102.

Baer, D. M., Harris, Florence R., and Wolf, M. M. Control of nursery school children's behavior by programming social reinforcement from their teachers. *Amer. Psychologist*, 1963, **18,** 343. (Abstract).

Bandura, A., & Walters, R. H. *Social learning and personality development.* New York: Holt, 1963.

Cowan, P. A., & Walters, R. H. Studies of reinforcement of aggression. I. Effects of scheduling. *Child Develpm.*, 1963, **34,** 543–551.

Homme, L. E., de Baca, P. C., Devine, J. V., Steinhorst, R., & Rickert, E. J.   Use of the Premack principle in controlling the behavior of nursery school children. *J. exp. anal. Behav.*, 1963, **6**, 544.

Walters, J. C., Pearce, Doris, and Dahms, Lucille.   Affectional and aggressive behavior of preschool children. *Child Develpm.*, 1957, **28**, 15–26.

Williams, C. D.   The elimination of tantrum behavior by extinction procedures. *J. abnorm. soc. Psychol.*, 1959, **59**, 269.

Zimmerman, Elaine H., and Zimmerman, J.   The alteration of behavior in a special classroom situation. *J. exp. anal. Behav.*, 1962, **5**, 59–60.

chapter seven

Sex-Role Development

7.1 Introduction

Sex typing is the process by which the child learns the behaviors and attitudes culturally appropriate to his sex. Attempts to account for the acquisition of sex-typed patterns have generally employed the Freudian concept of identification. Although there has been much debate over the meaning and usefulness of the construct (see Bronfrenbrenner, 1960, for a review), it is still the most popular starting point for discussions of sex-role development.

Within classical Freudian theory, two processes of identification are distinguished—anaclitic and aggressive identification. According to the anaclitic notion, the child is motivated to reproduce the behaviors of a parent because of a threatened withdrawal of parental affection. Learning theorists (for example, Mowrer, 1950; Sears, 1957) in extending this theory have focused on the role of parental warmth and nurturance in promoting parent-child identification. Both boys and girls initially form an anaclitic bond with their mothers; however, this form of identification is generally considered to be more important for girls than for boys since girls can maintain this identification pattern while boys are required to shift to the father as a sex-role model. Defensive identification or "identification with the aggressor," which involves adoption of parental behaviors through fear of punishment, facilitates the boy's shift to the father. Freud viewed this type of identification as the outcome of the resolution of the Oedipus complex, in which the boy adopts the characteristics of his father, his rival for his mother's affection, and thereby reduces the anxiety associated with anticipated paternal punishment.

According to a third viewpoint (Parsons, 1955), parental power, defined as the ability to control the dispensing of rewards and punishments, is the main basis for parent-child identification. Children are assumed to identify with the most powerful parent. In addition, Parsons suggests that children learn expressive behavior patterns mainly from the mother, while the role of the father is primarily instrumental. In an extension of the theory, Johnson (1963) argues that the father responds differentially to sons and daughters and the mother does not; therefore, the father should be more important than the mother in the development of sex typing of both boys and girls. Evidence relating to these theoretical positions is discussed below.

The underlying assumption of the identification theories is that the adoption of the parent of the same sex as an identificatory model facilitates the acquisition of appropriate sex-typed behaviors. As a result, research has focused on the conditions that promote this identification process.

According to the anaclitic theory of identification, the child identifies with and imitates the behavior of the parent who is warm and nurturant. There is a good deal of support for this claim that warmth in the same-sex parent facilitates sex typing by promoting an identification with the parent. In a study of high school boys, Payne and Mussen (1956) found that subjects who were highly identified with the father possessed more sex-typed masculine behavior and attitudes and perceived their fathers as more nurturant than minimally identified boys. Later studies have confirmed these findings (Mussen & Distler, 1959, 1960), and in their article in this section, Mussen and Rutherford (1963) report that warmth in the same-sex parent facilitates sex-typing in both girls and boys. Recent experimental studies also suggest that a nurturant model is imitated more than a nonnurturant adult (Bandura & Huston, 1961; Mussen & Parker, 1965).

The fact that the father plays an important role in the development of femininity in girls is of additional interest. Highly feminine girls had masculine fathers who encouraged their daughters to participate in feminine activities; however, neither the mother's femininity nor her reinforcement of her daughter's feminine behavior were related to the girl's sex typing. The lack of relationships between boys' masculinity and parental characteristics suggests that boys' sex typing is less affected by familial influences. Hetherington (1968) has also found that more parental and child-rearing variables relate to femininity in girls than to masculinity in boys. In part, this is due to the greater encouragement given girls to sustain their family orientation; boys, however, are encouraged to be independent and oriented toward extrafamilial influences (Hetherington, 1968). The fact that the female role is less clearly defined than the male role probably contributes to this relationship as well.

In spite of the importance of warmth for sex typing of both boys and girls, there is some evidence that parental warmth may be more important in promoting appropriate sex typing in girls than in boys. This conclusion is based on the Hetherington and Frankie study (1967) which examined the effects of parental warmth, dominance, and conflict on imitation in children. (Imitation was used as a behavioral measure of identification in this study.) This study found not only that warmth is more critical for girls, but also that parental dominance may be more critical for boys' sex typing. Additional evidence supporting the effects of parental power on sex typing and identification was provided in an earlier study by Hetherington (1965), in which sex typing was assessed by sex-role preferences and identification measured by parent-child similarity. Boys from father-dominant homes displayed more masculine sex-role preferences and were more highly identified with the father than boys from mother-dominant families. Similarly, Mussen and Distler (1959) found that highly masculine boys viewed their fathers as more powerful than more feminine boys did. Recent research employing college student populations have confirmed these relationships between paternal dominance and appropriate sex typing in boys (Heilbrun, 1965; Moulton, Burnstein, Liberty, & Altucher, 1966).

Although these findings indicate that paternal dominance is a critical antecedent of masculinity in boys, other research has shown that the dominant father does not disrupt sex typing in girls (Hetherington, 1965). In fact, there is some evidence that a dominant father may accentuate femininity in girls (Hetherington, 1968). This finding, in conjunction with the Mussen and Rutherford data, provides substantial support for the role theory approach to sex typing (Brim, 1958; Johnson, 1963; Parsons, 1955), which suggests that masculine and feminine behavior patterns are acquired, in part, through interaction with the opposite-sex parent.

Although a father-dominant family arrangement may be a more

favorable context for the acquisition of sex-typed patterns in children of both sexes, it is still probably more important for boys than for girls. Boys, unlike girls, are required to shift their identification model from their mother, the initial identification object, to the father in order to acquire appropriately masculine traits. A powerful father would facilitate the shift. Secondly, since a dominant father is acting in a culturally masculine fashion, he provides a more appropriate sex-role model than a nondominant, or passive, father (Hetherington, 1968).

Although there is considerable support for both the anaclitic and power theories of identification, evidence in support of the defensive theory of identification has not only been extremely scanty but somewhat equivocal. Hetherington and Frankie (1967) have provided support for the "identification with the aggressor" hypothesis. According to their findings, defensive identification is likely to occur in a home characterized by high parental conflict and low warmth in both parents.

Another way of exploring the role of the father in sex typing involves studying the consequences of paternal absence. If the father model is critical for the boy's acquisition of appropriate sex-typed behaviors, boys with no father present should clearly be less masculine. The effects of father absence have been explored in a variety of studies, but the results have not always clearly supported the predicted disruption of sex typing in boys. Bach (1946), for example, in comparing father-absent and father-present boys during World War II, found less aggressive fantasy in the doll-play themes of the father-absent boys. McCord, McCord, and Thurber (1962), however, found father-absent boys more aggressive than boys from intact homes. One of the critical variables that may, in part, account for the discrepancy is the age of the child at the time of the father-son separation. Theoretically, the loss of a father model is more disruptive of sex typing during the early years of a child's life, when father identification is incomplete, than at some later point when masculine behaviors have already been acquired. In order to test this proposition, Hetherington (1966) compared father-present boys with father-absent boys whose father had left either before or after the child was 5 years of age. Only when the father-son separation occurred during the first 4 years of the child's life were there indications of disrupted sex typing and lowered aggression. The sex typing and aggressive patterns of the late separated boys were similar to father-present subjects. In fact, the greater aggression shown by boys in the McCord et al. study is attributable mainly to the boys in the 6 to 12 age range. Younger boys from father-absent homes that were otherwise normal were clearly less aggressive.

An additional factor which may contribute to the lack of consistency in the father-absence studies may be the time at which sex-typed behaviors are measured. Boys with fathers absent may be slower in becoming sex typed since there is no adult model in the home, and when sex typing occurs, it may be less stable and thus result in erratic compensatory masculinity. In fact, studies which assess father-absent boys in nursery school usually find them more feminine and less aggressive than father-present boys. In elementary school, the father-absent boys show unstable masculinity and in adolescence they frequently show a delinquent behavior pattern which might be considered compensatory masculinity.

Although most research has concentrated on the impact of father absence on boys, recent evidence suggests that girls may also be affected. The sex-role typing of female preschoolers and preadolescents from father-absent homes is not disrupted, but the delayed impact of the family arrangement is reflected in the heterosexual relationships of these girls during adolescence. In a study of the effects of parental absence on girls, Hetherington (1967) found two extremes: either accelerated dating, combined with assertive, provocative behavior with boys or extremely retarded dating accompanied by anxiety and shyness in heterosexual situations. The finding that these girls were unable to adequately handle adolescent cross-sex relationships provides further support for the role-theory suggestion that the father contributes to the sex typing of both girls and boys.

In the final article in this section, some of the consequences of sex-role identification are explored. The selection is part of a larger work entitled *Birth to Maturity* (1962), in which Kagan and Moss explore in detail the differential stability of behaviors between childhood and adulthood. The subjects of this longitudinal investigation were observed and rated along a variety of social and intellectual dimensions from birth to adolescence. When the subjects were in their twenties, they were reinterviewed and rated again on each of the same dimensions. As the summary indicates, the degree to which a behavior is stable from childhood through adulthood is determined by the appropriateness of the behavior for the subject's particular sex. In our culture, certain behaviors, such as aggression and competitiveness, are more appropriate for males than for females; similarly, passive, dependent behavior is more appropriate for females. As a result, females tend to show greater stability for passive, dependent behaviors, and males for aggression.

Constitutional factors may also play a role in determining the stability of sex-typed behaviors. (See Hamburg & Lunde, 1966, for a recent review.) Evidence based on observations of neonates suggests that girls are more likely than boys to display motoric passivity (Bell, 1960; Knop, 1946). Boys, however, may be constitutionally predisposed to behave aggressively. Males have a higher proportion of muscle tissue than girls (Garn, 1958), and neonatal boys appear to be less sensitive to pain than infant girls (Lipsett & Levy, 1959). Moreover, infant male monkeys show a greater proclivity for aggressive play than infant female monkeys (Harlow, 1962; Harlow & Harlow, 1965). "It is possible that the differential stability of dependency and aggression for males and females is the product of a complex interaction in which constitutional variables find support in the behavioral rules promoted by the child's culture" (Kagan & Moss, 1962, p. 119).

REFERENCES

Bach, G. R.   Father-fantasies and father-typing in father-separated children. *Child Development*, 1946, **17,** 63–80.
Bandura, A. & Huston, A. C.   Identification as a process of incidental learning. *Journal of Abnormal and Social Psychology*, 1961, **63,** 311–318.
Bell, R. Q.   Relations between behavior manifestations in the human neonate. *Child Development*, 1960, **31,** 463–478.
Brim, O. G.   Family structure and sex role learning by children: A further analysis of Helen Koch's data. *Sociometry*, 1958, **21,** 1–16.
Bronfrenbrenner, U.   Freudian theories of identification and their derivatives. *Child Development*, 1960, **31,** 15–40.
Garn, S. M.   Fat, body size, and growth in the newborn. *Human Biology*, 1958, **30,** 265–280.
Hamburg, D. A., & Lunde, D. T.   Sex hormones in the development of sex differences in human behavior. In E. E. Maccoby (Ed.), *The development of sex differences.* Stanford: Stanford University Press, 1966. Pp. 1–24.
Harlow, H. F.   The heterosexual affectional response system in monkeys. *American Psychologist*, 1962, **17,** 1–7.
Harlow, H. F., & Harlow, M. K.   The affectional system. In A. M. Schrier, H. F. Harlow & F. Stollnitz (Eds.), *Behavior of nonhuman primates.* Vol. 2. New York: Academic Press, 1965. Pp. 287–334.
Heilbrun, A. B.   Sex differences in identification learning. *Journal of Genetic Psychology*, 1965, **106,** 185–193.
Hetherington, E. M.   A developmental study of the effects of sex of the dominant parent on sex-role preference, identification and imitation in children. *Journal of Personality and Social Psychology*, 1965, **2,** 188–194.
Hetherington, E. M.   Effects of paternal absence on sex-typed behaviors in Negro and white preadolescent males. *Journal of Personality and Social Psychology*, 1966, **4,** 87–91.
Hetherington, E. M.   Effects of paternal absence on sex-typed behavior in adolescent girls. Unpublished manuscript, University of Wisconsin, 1967.

Hetherington, E. M. The effects of familial variables on sex role typing, parent-child similarity and imitation in children. In J. P. Hill (Ed.), *Minnesota Symposia on Child Psychology*, Vol. I. Minneapolis: University of Minnesota Press, 1967. Pp. 82–107.

Hetherington, E. M. & Frankie, G. Effects of parental dominance, warmth, and conflict of imitation in children. *Journal of Personality and Social Psychology*, 1967, **6**, 119–125.

Johnson, M. M. Sex role learning in the nuclear family. *Child Development*, 1963, **34**, 319–333.

Kagan, J. & Moss, H. A. *Birth to Maturity*. New York: John Wiley, 1962.

Knop, C. The dynamics of newly born babies. *Journal of Pediatrics*, 1946, **29**, 721–728.

Lipsitt, L. P. & Levy, N. Electrotactual threshold in the neonate. *Child Development*, 1959, **30**, 547–554.

McCord, J., McCord, W., & Thurber, E. Some effects of paternal absence on male children. *Journal of Abnormal and Social Psychology*, 1962, **64**, 361–369.

Moulton, R. W., Burnstein, E., Liberty, P. G., & Altucher, N. Patterning of parental affection and disciplinary dominance as a determinant of guilt and sex-typing. *Journal of Personality and Social Psychology*, 1966, **4**, 356–363.

Mowrer, O. H. *Learning theory and personality dynamics*. New York: Ronald Press, 1950.

Mussen, P. H. & Distler, L. Masculinity, identification, and father-son relationships. *Journal of Abnormal and Social Psychology*, 1959, **62**, 461–464.

Mussen, P. H. & Distler, L. Child-rearing antecedents of masculine identification in kindergarten boys. *Child Development*, 1960, **31**, 89–100.

Mussen, P. & Parker, A. Mother nurturance and girls' incidental imitation learning. *Journal of Personality and Social Psychology*, 1965, **2**, 94–96.

Mussen, P. & Rutherford, E. Parent-child relations and parental personality in relation to young children's sex-role preferences. *Child Development*, 1963, **34**, 589–607.

Parsons, T. Family structure and the socialization of the child. In T. Parsons & R. F. Bales (Eds.), *Family socialization and interaction process*. New York: Free Press, 1955. Pp. 35–131.

Payne, D. E. & Mussen, P. H. Parent-child relations and father identification among adolescent boys. *Journal of Abnormal and Social Psychology*, 1956, **52**, 358–362.

Sears, R. R. Identification as a form of behavioral development. In D. B. Harris (Ed.), *The concept of development*. Minneapolis: University of Minnesota Press, 1957. Pp. 149–161.

SUPPLEMENTARY READING

Biller, H. B., & Borstelmann, L. J. Masculine development: An integrative review. *Merrill-Palmer Quarterly*, 1967, **13**, 253–294.

Hetherington, E. M. The effects of familiar variables on sex-role typing, parent child similarity and imitation in children. In J. P. Hill (Ed.), *Minnesota Symposium on child psychology*, Vol. 1, Minneapolis: University of Minnesota Press, 1968.

Kagan, J. Acquisition and significance of sex typing and sex-role identity. In Lois W. Hoffman & . L. Hoffman (Eds.), *Review of Child development research*, Vol. I. New York: Russell Sage, 1964. Pp. 137–167.

Maccoby, E. E. (Ed.), *The development of sex differences*. Stanford: Stanford University Press, 1966.

7.2 Parent-Child Relations and Parental Personality in Relation to Young Children's Sex-Role Preferences [1]

Paul Mussen and Eldred Rutherford

According to classical psychoanalytic theory, the identification process originates in the child's hostility toward his like-sexed parent and consequent fear of that parent's retaliation. In contrast, the more recently formulated developmental identification hypothesis considers the process to be motivated by warmth and affection toward that parent whose characteristics and responses are then taken on as a "total pattern" (*2, 13, 18, 22, 28, 29*).

Most of the available evidence supporting this latter hypothesis has been derived from studies of boys' identification with their fathers. If the hypothesis has general validity, however, it should apply equally well to the girl's identification with her mother. This hypothesis would not predict, as classical psychoanalysis theory does, that the process is more confused, complex, and slower for girls than for boys (*18, 22, 28*).[2]

[1] This study was supported by the National Institute of Mental Health, United States Public Health Service, under Research Grant M–3217.

The authors wish to express their appreciation to A. B. Campbell, Assistant Superintendent of Schools of Berkeley, Frank Wylde, Principal of the Jefferson School, and Mrs. Sue Callan, Mrs. Georgia Johnson, Mrs. Virginia Allison, Miss Marcia Morgen, and Mrs. Ruth Lockwood, first grade teachers for their cooperation in this study.

[2] In fact, Sears *et al.* have argued that the opposite is true, stating: ". . . We are inclined to believe that the boy's shift (from identification with mother to identification with the father) retards the smooth development of the (identification) process. His gradual adoption of a new model is doubtless somewhat frustrating to him, and puts him in a state of conflict as to whom he should act like. Thus we might expect not only that boys in their sixth year would be less fully identified

Reprinted from *Child Development* 1963, **34**, 225–246, by permission of the authors and the Society for Research in Child Development.

The primary purpose of the present investigation was to test the developmental identification hypothesis further to determine its general validity and its usefulness in understanding the process of the girl's identification with her mother. A major aspect of the basic design paralleled that of two earlier studies of the antecedents of father identification in kindergarten boys (20, 21) in which masculinity was found to be related to perceptions of the father as more rewarding and nurturant and also the more powerful source of punishment.

In addition to testing the developmental identification hypothesis, the study was designed to permit investigation of the association between certain parental variables not directly related to that hypothesis and one criterion of identification with the same-sexed parent, the development of appropriate sex-role preference. For the sake of simplicity of presentation, the hypotheses tested may be categorized in terms of the relation between sex-role preference and (a) parent-child relationships, (b) parental personality characteristics, and (c) parental encouragement of appropriate sex-typing. A series of hypotheses with parallel versions for boys and girls was formulated.

1. *Hypotheses concerning parent-child relationships.* This category includes the most central hypotheses of this study, those derived from the developmental identification hypothesis. More specifically it was hypothesized that femininity (female sex-role preference) in little girls—generally assumed to be a product or manifestation of identification with the mother —is related to rewarding, nurturant, and affectionate relationships with that parent (hypothesis Ia). Mother-daughter relationships were evaluated, first from the child's point of view, by means of projective doll play, and, secondly, from the mother's account of her interactions with her daughter, given in response to interview questions.

Since most of the research was conducted in a coeducational public grammar school, data on boys were also collected. It was therefore possible to achieve something that is rare in research in personality and development: a replication (but with more subjects) of an earlier study and thus additional independent checks on the developmental, defensive, and role-taking hypotheses of identification as applied to boys. All the hypotheses received some support in the earlier study (20). The developmental hypothesis states that masculinity in young boys is related to positive, affectionate father-son relationships (hypothesis Ib).

2. *Hypotheses concerning consequents of parental personality structure.* Both theory and empirical findings suggest that certain aspects of parental

---

with their fathers, than girls with their mothers, but that they would have a less complete identification with the adult role in general than girls would have. Also, this means they would show less indication of high conscience, as well as other signs of identification, than girls" (28, p. 384).

personality structure would have facilitative effects on the child's appropriate sex identification. Thus it was hypothesized that self-acceptance on the part of the like-sexed parent would promote femininity in girls (hypothesis IIa) and masculinity in boys (hypothesis IIb). The prediction is based on the assumption that the parent who accepts himself (or herself) is satisfied with his own sex role and is therefore more likely than the parent who is not self-accepting to reward responses replicating his (her) own. Helper found that children were more likely to emulate the characteristics of a mother who approved of herself (i.e., accepted herself) as model for her children (12). McCandless has pointed out that, if the girl's mother is successful and, hence, self-accepting, "she provides the best available model for the appropriate sex role" (16, p. 347). The same kind of reasoning probably applies to the boy, i.e., a self-accepting father provides the best model for the son.

In addition, self-acceptance on the part of the opposite-sexed parent may contribute to the development of appropriate sex-typing of his (her) child's behavior. Assuming that self-acceptance is related to approval of—and respect for—others, the self-accepting mother or father is more likely than the parent who lacks this characteristic to approve of his opposite-sexed child's sex-appropriate responses, rewarding and encouraging them. Thus, it is hypothesized that the mother's self-acceptance would be related to the boy's masculinity of interests (hypothesis IIIa), while the father's self-acceptance would be similarly related to the girl's femininity of interests (hypothesis IIIb).

On the basis of learning theory, it was hypothesized that, in general, more masculine fathers and more feminine mothers would foster their daughters' femininity (hypothesis IVa) and their sons' masculinity (hypothesis IVb). The rationale underlying these hypotheses was twofold. First, it was assumed that highly feminine women and masculine men are good models for their like-sexed children and provide more distinctive cues for their children's sex-appropriate responses and attitudes. Secondly, it seems plausible to assume such parents are more cognizant of those interests and responses that are sex-appropriate and those that are inappropriate. They might then be expected to reward sex-appropriate responses, thus increasing their frequency and intensity, and to discourage and punish sex-inappropriate behavior.

3. *Hypotheses concerning parental encouragement of sex-typed behavior.* Parents may directly encourage their child's participation in activities (games, hobbies, etc.) traditionally engaged in by members of the child's own sex and may even participate in such activities with the child. By doing this, they make it clear to the child that they approve and perhaps expect certain kinds of behavior while others are considered inappropriate. They delineate for the child the distinctive cues of sex-typed behavior and, simultaneously, differentially reward such behavior, thus increasing its habit

strength. By generalization, other sex-appropriate responses, not specifically rewarded, may also become more intense and frequent. It was therefore hypothesized that strong parental encouragement of participation in sex-appropriate activities would implement the feminization of girls (hypothesis Va) and the masculinization of boys (hypothesis Vb).

METHOD

Psychoanalytic theory holds that identification with the like-sexed parent follows resolution of the Oedipus complex which takes place around the age of 5 or 6 years. Moreover, it is generally agreed that the child becomes increasingly aware of his sex identification at this time, e.g., "at the kinder-garten-first grade level, the little girl is faced with the inevitability of her femininity" (16, p. 347). For these reasons, first grade children, between $5\frac{1}{2}$ and $6\frac{1}{2}$ years of age, would seem to be ideal subjects for the study of the familial antecedents of sex-typing of behavior and interests.

Femininity and masculinity of interests were assessed by means of the IT Scale, a projective test of sex-role preference (3) which was administered to 57 girls and 46 boys in the first grade of a middle class public school. In this test, the child is given a card with a figure drawing unstructured as to sex and referred to as IT. He is then presented with groups of pictures of toys, objects, and activities and asked to choose, from among these, the things that IT would like. The underlying assumption of the test is that "the child will project himself or herself into the IT figure on the basis of his own sex-role preference and will attribute to IT the child's own role preference." (3, p. 5). Scores ranged from 0 (exclusively feminine choices) to 84 (exclusively masculine choices).

To designate male and female subjects high and low in sex-typing, the distributions of the IT Scale scores for each sex separately, were dichotomized at the median. The 29 girls with scores ranging from 0 to 70 were considered high in femininity (i.e., low in masculinity), while the other 28 girls, whose scores were over 70, were considered low in femininity (relatively high in masculinity). Among the boys, the highly masculine group, 24 subjects, scored more than 81 on the IT scale, while the 22 considered low in masculinity had scores ranging between 19 and 80.

Doll Play

About a week after the IT test was administered, each subject was tested individually in a structured doll play situation involving a mother doll, a father doll, and a child doll of the subject's own sex. The subject was asked to use the dolls in playing out, and thus completing, nine incomplete stories designed to elicit the child's attitudes toward, and perceptions of, his (her) parents.[3] The following is illustrative:

[3] Dittoed copies of the full set of nine stories and the interview questions may be obtained by writing to the authors.

The child wants a certain toy. He can't reach it. He goes into the living room to get help. Both Mommy and Daddy are busy reading. What happens?

In telling the stories, which were completely recorded, the child could depict either father or mother as nurturant and/or punitive. The following scores were derived from the children's stories: Mother Nurturance (MN) and Father Nurturance (FN) scores were the total number of stories in which the mother or father, respectively, gave the child in the story help, care, comfort, or attention. Total Nurturance (TotN) score was the sum of the MN and FN scores. Mother Punishment (MP) and Father Punishment (FP) scores were the number of stories in which the mother and father disciplined, spanked, criticized, or in any way punished the child. Mother Power (MPow) and Father Power (FPow) scores were the number of stories involving either nurturant or punitive relationships with the mother or father, i.e., MN plus MP, and FN plus FP.[4]

Mother Interviews

The other, perhaps more objective, source of information on parent-child relationships consisted of interviews with the mothers, but for many reasons, it was possible to interview only 19 mothers of girl subjects—11 mothers of highs and eight mothers of lows. The interviews consisted of 32 open ended questions, some of them with suggested probes, adapted and somewhat modified from the interview schedules used by Sears, Maccoby, and Levin (28). These dealt with various aspects of mother-daughter relationships such as restrictions and demands on the child, types of discipline used, warmth and affection, punitiveness, the child's dependence, and conscience development. Interviews lasted between one and two hours and were conducted by trained interviewers who asked the questions in a prescribed order using the exact wording given in the schedule. All interviews were electrically recorded.

Following completion of the interviews, a trained rater listened to the recordings and then rated each of them on 19 scales taken from Appendix B of *Patterns of Child Rearing*, e.g., warmth of mother to child, acceptance-rejection, and child's conscience (28).[5] It should be noted that neither the interviewer nor the rater were informed of the real purpose of the research and knew nothing about the subjects beforehand. Consequently, neither

---

[4] Since the scoring categories were very explicitly defined, interrater agreement was high. Two scorers agreed in over 90 percent of their scores for 10 protocols (90 stories).

[5] The two interview raters were trained in scoring comparable interviews with other mothers, but based on the same questions, before they scored the interviews involved in this study. On these "practice" ratings, they achieved 91 percent agreement, based on five interview protocols.

the interviews nor the ratings could be biased by any knowledge of hypotheses or of the method of selecting the interviewees.

Assessment of Parental Personality

In order to test hypotheses IIa, IIb, IIIa, IIIb, IVa, and IVb as simply and directly as possible, two scales of the California Psychological Inventory, the Femininity and Self-Acceptance scales, were mailed to both parents of each of the subjects. The Femininity scale purports to measure femininity of interests and attitudes, while the Self-Acceptance assesses "factors such as sense of personal worth, self-acceptance, and capacity for independent thinking and action" (*11*, p. 12).

The inventories were completed and returned by 32 girls' mothers (14 mothers of highs, 18 mothers of lows) and by 30 girls' fathers (14 fathers of highs, 16 fathers of lows). Among the parents of the boys, 22 mothers (8 of highs, 14 of lows) and 18 fathers (7 of highs, 11 of lows) returned the tests.

Measurement of Parental Encouragement
of Appropriate Sex-Typed Activities

All the parents of the subjects were also sent a "play and games list," a list of 50 well known sex-typed children's games, play activities, and hobbies, taken from a list of activities that had been shown to differentiate significantly between the preferences of the two sexes (*25*). Parents were instructed to complete the questionnaires separately and independently, indicating, for each activity, whether they had "actually played the game with their child," "encouraged the child to play the game," or "discouraged the child from playing the game."

The responses to each item (game or activity) were scored in terms of the child's sex. If the parent indicated that he actually played a girls' game with his daughter, or a boys' game with his son, the item was scored $+2$. Each indication of simple encouragement of the child's playing a sex-appropriate game or participating in a sex-appropriate activity was scored $+1$, while "discouraging the child" from an activity or game appropriate to his sex was scored -2. The sum of the scores on the 50 items constituted the parent's "encouragement of appropriate sex-typed behavior" score. This score was used in testing hypotheses Va and Vb dealing with parental encouragement of the child's sex-typed activities and behavior.

RESULTS

Verification of the major hypotheses involved comparing the highs and lows in sex-typing of interests in relevant variables derived from doll play, maternal interviews (in the case of the girl subjects only), parental scores on the CPI, and parental responses to the "play and games" questionnaires. In the interests of simplicity of exposition, the results of the comparisons of the two groups of boys, including the replication of the Mussen and Distler study *(20)*, will be presented first. In general, the present findings on boys substantiate those of the earlier study and may therefore serve as a point of reference for the evaluation and interpretation of the data relevant to the process of identification in girls.

Analysis of Boy's Doll Play Responses

The mean scores of the variables evaluated from the doll play responses of the high and low masculinity groups of boys are given in Table 1. In general, these findings clearly substantiate those of the Mussen-Distler study *(20)*.

TABLE 1. MEAN SCORES OF BOYS HIGH AND LOW IN MASCULINITY ON FAMILY PERCEPTION (DOLL PLAY) VARIABLES

Variable	High Masculinity Group (N = 24)	Low Masculinity Group (N = 22)	t	p [a]
Father Nurturance (FN)	1.3	.8	1.66	.05
Mother Nurturance (MN)	.9	1.3	1.33	ns
They Nurturance (TN)	.3	.4	.18	ns
Total Punishment (TotP)	2.5	2.5	.24	ns
Father Punishment (FP)	2.3	1.7	1.33	$<.10$
Mother Punishment (MP)	1.4	1.6	.41	ns
They Punishment (TP)	.6	.6	.00	ns
Total Punishment (TotP)	4.3	3.9	.67	ns
Father Power (FPow)	3.6	2.5	2.19	$<.025$
Mother Power (MPow)	2.3	2.9	1.10	ns

[a] In evaluating the significance of differences in this and the following tables, *p* values were calculated in terms of a one-tail test when there was *specific* prediction (from hypothesis) about the direction of the difference between the groups. Otherwise, two-tail tests were used.

The present data, like those of the earlier study, demonstrate that boys with highly masculine interests told significantly more stories involving father nurturance, i.e., scored higher on the average in Father Nurturance (FN) than boys low in masculinity. These data, then, provide further evidence supportive of the developmental hypothesis, showing that "young boys are more likely to identify strongly with their fathers, and thus to acquire masculine interests, if they perceive their fathers as highly nurturant and rewarding" *(20, p. 353)*.

Table 1 also reveals that there was a tendency (reliable only at the 10 percent level) similar to that discovered in the other study (reliable at the 6 percent level, in that instance) for the highly masculine boys to have higher mean Father Punishment (FP) doll play scores than the less masculine boys. This is in accord with what was predicted on the basis of the defensive identification hypothesis which holds that identification with the father is based on perceptions of him as punitive, threatening, and hostile. However, in both studies, the evidence supportive of this hypothesis was much less impressive than that confirming the developmental identification hypothesis.

Since the Father Power (FPow) score was composed of the Father Nurturance (FN) and Father Punishment (FP) scores, the highly masculine boys, of course, received higher scores in this variable, i.e., perceived their fathers as more powerful than the other group. This may be regarded as support for the role-taking hypothesis of identification which maintains that sex-role learning depends upon the amount of the child's interaction with the identificand and the latter's power or control over the child.

In summary, the findings of the present investigation—involving a larger sample of subjects than the Mussen and Distler study (20) and a different definition of high and low masculinity status (above and below the median score for the entire group rather than extreme scores)—in essence replicated those of the earlier study. In both studies, the most salient variables appeared to be the father's nurturant and (to a less marked degree) punitive qualities, the substantially father-identified (i.e., those with strongly sex-typed interests) tending to view their fathers as possessing more of both.

The present results are also consistent with those of other studies in showing that, for boys, sex-typing of interests is more directly related to perceptions of their fathers than to feelings about their mothers. Thus, as Table 1 shows, none of the mother-child interaction variables, derived from the doll play, significantly differentiated the high and low masculinity groups.

Analysis of CPI and Play and Games List Data of Boys' Parents

The data collected from the parents failed to confirm any of the hypotheses concerning the relations between boys' sex-role preferences and parental personality characteristics (hypotheses IIb, IIIb, and IVb) or parental encouragement of sex-appropriate activities (hypothesis Vb). There was no evidence that sex-typing of parental interests and attitudes (high masculinity of fathers and high femininity of mothers) or parental self-acceptance, as measured by the CPI, fostered high degrees of masculinity in the sons. Moreover, neither the fathers or mothers of the highly masculine boys differed significantly from the other parents in their responses to the "play and games" list. Hence these hypotheses were rejected.

It may be concluded that the boy's perception of his father as a nurturant and powerful individual is of paramount importance in his development of masculinity, but there is no evidence that his parents' personality structures, particularly degree of sex-typing and self-confidence, have any significant influence. Moreover, parental encouragement of their son's participation in masculine activities does not seem to have a significant effect on the youngster's sex-role preferences. In other words, it appears that, if a father is warm and nurturant in his relationships with his son, the latter is likely to become highly masculine, even if the father does not have this characteristic or a high degree of self-acceptance and even if he does not encourage his son to participate in traditionally masculine activities. On the other hand, a ruggedly masculine, self-confident father who has poor relationships with his son is not likely to produce a highly masculine son, even if he actively attempts to stimulate his son's participation in typical male activities.

Analysis of Girls' Doll Play Responses

The means of the doll play scores of the girls low and high in femininity, used in testing hypothesis Ia, are presented in Table 2. As indicated in the

TABLE 2. Mean Scores of Girls High and Low in Femininity on Family Perception (Doll Play) Variables

Variable	High Femininity Group ($N = 29$)	Low Femininity Group ($N = 28$)	t	p[a]
Mother Nurturance (MN)	1.5	1.1	1.65	.05
Father Nurturance (FN)	.8	.5	1.34	ns
They Nurturance (TN)	.2	.3	.21	ns
Total Nurturance (TotN)	2.6	1.9	2.12	<.05
Mother Punishment (MP)	2.4	2.0	1.14	ns
Father Punishment (FP)	1.9	1.9	.07	ns
They Punishment (TP)	.6	.7	.11	ns
Total Punishment (TotP)	4.9	4.6	.30	ns
Mother Power (MPow)	3.9	3.0	1.93	<.05
Father Power (FPow)	2.7	2.5	.18	ns

[a] See footnote to Table 1.

table, the groups differed significantly in Mother Nurturance (MN) scores, the mean score of the highly feminine girls in this variable being significantly higher than that of the girls low in femininity. The finding is entirely consistent with, and supports, the developmental identification hypothesis which holds that girls will identify strongly with their mothers—and consequently become more feminine—if they perceive their mothers as warm, nurturant, affectionate, and rewarding.

As the data summarized in Table 2 show, highly feminine girls, compared with girls low in femininity, regarded their mothers as significantly more powerful (i.e., obtained higher scores in MPow). This finding seems analogous to the finding that highly masculine boys scored significantly higher in FPow than the other boys. There is a major difference between the findings for the two sexes, however. The highly masculine group's high FPow scores were due to the group's significantly, or nearly significantly, higher scores in *both* components of the FPow, i.e., in Father Nurturance (FN) and Father Punishment (FP). The highly feminine group's significantly higher Mother Power scores, on the other hand, are almost entirely attributable to the higher scores in only one of the components of that score, Mother Nurturance (MN). The two groups of girls did not differ significantly in the Mother Punishment (MP) variable. It may therefore be concluded that the development of a high degree of femininity is importantly influenced by the girl's perceptions of her mother as an important, warm, and gratifying person, but not by the extent to which she is perceived as punitive and threatening.

It may be tenably assumed that strong fear of loss of maternal love would be reflected in perceptions of the mother as harsh and punitive. If this is true, according to the defensive identification hypothesis, highly feminine girls would obtain relatively higher Mother Punishment (MP) scores than the other girls. This was not the case; the defensive identification hypothesis, as applied to girls, received no support from these data.

While the mean score of the highly feminine girls in Father Nurturance (FN) was greater than that of the other group, the difference was not statistically significant. Since the Total Nurturance (TotN) score is essentially a composite of the Mother Nurturance (MN) and Father Nurturance (FN) scores, the mean score of the highly feminine girls in this variable was, of course, also significantly higher, the difference being attributable primarily to the group difference in MN.

Analysis of Maternal Interviews

These interviews were designed to elicit information on mother-daughter relationships from the mother's point of view, similar to the information obtained on father-son relationships in the Mussen-Distler study (*21*). The interview protocols were rated on 19 variables, taken from the Sears, Maccoby, and Levin study (*28*). These included: warmth of mother to child; acceptance-rejection; mother's use of withdrawal of love, scolding, physical punishment, deprivation, and reasoning as disciplinary techniques; restrictions imposed upon the child and expectancy of good conduct; child's conscience, tendency to admit guilt.

Only one of the 19 rating variables significantly differentiated the two groups. While it is true that one significant difference might have been expected on the basis of chance alone, it is interesting to note that the differentiating variable, "warmth of mother to child," is of paramount theoretical importance. The mean rating for the highly feminine group in this variable was 4.1, while for the other group, it was 3.4 ($t = 1.75$, $p < .05$). As predicted on the basis of the developmental identification hypothesis, young girls were more likely to identify with their mothers, and thus to acquire appropriately sex-typed interests and responses, if their mothers were warm, rewarding, and affectionate. Thus this finding from the interview reinforces the doll play Mother Nurturance (MN) finding and further supports the developmental identification hypothesis.

The interview data, like those from doll play, failed to provide any confirmation for the defensive identification hypothesis and, in fact, contained some suggestive evidence contradictory to that hypothesis. While none of the interview punishment variables was significantly differentiating, there was a slight, statistically nonsignificant, tendency for the mothers of the girls low in femininity to be rated higher in "use of withdrawal of love as a disciplinary technique" (mean rating for mothers of the highs was 1.8, for mothers of the lows 2.4; $t = 1.51$, $p < .20$ for two tail test). If the defensive identification hypothesis is valid, and if it assumed that frequent use of this technique [6] is likely to evoke fear of loss of maternal love, it would be expected that extensive use of this technique would produce high mother-identification and, consequently, high femininity in the daughter. According to these results, however, a high degree of use of this technique by the mother, if it has any effect, tends to produce *less* femininity in the daughter.

There were some striking parallels between these interview findings and those derived from a study of child-rearing antecedents of masculine identification in kindergarten boys (21). Maternal interviews in that study showed that, compared with the other fathers, the fathers of highly masculine boys were warmer and more affectionate toward their sons, a finding analogous to the group differences in maternal warmth in the present study. Moreover, the mothers of the highly feminine girls did not differ significantly from the other mothers with respect to the punishment variables, and the fathers of the two groups of boys were not found to differ in degree of punitive or threatening treatment of their sons (although it will be recalled that in doll play there was a tendency for the highly masculine boys to portray their fathers as more punitive) (20, 21).

Analysis of CPI Results of Girls' Parents

It has been hypothesized that, compared with the other parents, the parents of highly feminine girls would be more self-accepting and self-assured individuals (hypotheses IIa and IIIb), with appropriately sex-typed interests, opinions, and orientations (hypothesis IVa). The hypotheses were tested by comparing the self-acceptance and femininity (in reverse, masculinity) scale scores of the CPI inventories completed by the two groups of parents. Parental scores in these scales are summarized in Table 3.

As that table shows, hypothesis IIa was clearly confirmed. As predicted, the mothers of the highly feminine girls scored significantly higher than the

---

[6] It has been suggested that withdrawal of love is regarded as extremely harsh punishment by girls (4).

TABLE 3. Mean Scores on Personality Measures (CPI) of Parents of Girls High and Low in Femininity

Variable	High Femininity Group (N = 15)	Low Femininity Group (N = 16)	t	p [a]
Self Acceptance				
Mother	22.1	18.5	2.82	<.005
Father	19.8	21.7	1.35	ns
Femininity				
Mother	24.2	24.1	.26	ns
Father	16.7	18.7	1.35	<.10

[a] See footnote to Table 1.

other mothers in the CPI self-acceptance scale, indicating that they possess greater self-confidence, self-assurance, and "capacity for independent thinking and action." The relation between the mothers' security and self-confidence and the daughters' level of femininity may be interpreted in several ways. Perhaps mothers with these characteristics are more able than less secure mothers to maintain warm, affectionate relationships with their daughters, thus fostering their daughter's femininity. Or, mere possession of these characteristics—which must be evident to the child—may make her a stable, successful, and consequently, desirable model for the daughter to emulate. These explanations are, of course, not mutually exclusive and both of them may be valid.

The data did not provide any evidence supportive of hypothesis IVa as it applied to mothers. The mothers of highly feminine girls were not found to be more feminine than the mothers of the other girls. It may be inferred that girls are likely to express a high degree of female sex-role preference if their mothers are warm, nurturant, and self-accepting (self-confident), though not necessarily highly feminine. The nature of the mother-child relationships and the mother's personal security are basic determinants of the girl's acquisition of feminine orientations, but the degree of the mother's femininity in itself does not appear to exert an important influence. In other words, so far as we are able to determine, the differences between the two groups of girls in the degree of feminine sex-role preference cannot be attributed to differences in the quantity or intensity of sex-appropriate characteristics or cues presented by their mothers, for the two groups of mothers are approximately equal in this respect. Rather it may be assumed that the more feminine little girls are more strongly motivated than the others to imitate their mothers' behavior as a consequence of their allegiance to that parent. This may have either or both of the following consequents. The feminine cues presented by the mother may have greater vividness or be more distinctive for the girl (i.e., she pays closer attention to them) and hence she is more likely to assimilate more of these characteristics into her own role behavior. Or, being strongly motivated to imitate her mother, she may also emulate the behavior of other women, some of whom present more highly feminine models than the mother does. In terms of this latter explanation, it may be suggested that the daughter who is securely identified as a female does not need to duplicate her mother's behavior in toto but finds other appropriate, sometimes more feminine, models among others in her environment.

While the two groups of fathers did not differ significantly from each other in either the CPI Femininity or Self-Acceptance scales (Table 3), there was a trend consistent with, and supportive of, that part of hypothesis IVa which concerns the girls' fathers. The fathers of the highly feminine group tended to be more masculine in interests and orientations (scored more masculine, or lower, on the Femininity scale) than the fathers of the other group. Perhaps more highly masculine fathers are more aware of the behaviors appropriate for both sexes and, consequently, are better able to discriminate and reward appropriately sex-typed responses in their daughters, thus encouraging and promoting their feminization.

Analysis of Parental Responses to Play and Games List

The parents' direct encouragement of their daughters' participation in sex-appropriate play and activities (hypothesis Va) was measured by the play and games list score. The data are summarized in Table 4.

TABLE 4. Mean Scores on Encouragement of Sex-Appropriate Behavior by Parents of Girls High and Low in Femininity

Variable: Play and Games List	High Femininity Group		Low Femininity Group			
Play and Games List	N	Mean	N	Mean	t	p [a]
Mother	14	31.9	17	32.2	.13	ns
Father	11	29.0	15	19.9	1.97	<.05

[a] See footnote to Table 1.

Contrary to what was predicted on the basis of hypothesis Va, the scores of the mothers of the highly feminine girls on this questionnaire did not differ significantly from those of the other mothers. Hypothesis Va, as it relates to the mothers of the girls, was therefore refuted. In brief, the two groups of mothers appeared to be alike in the extent to which they participated with their daughters—and encouraged participation—in feminine games and activities. Apparently the mothers of highly feminine girls provide good models and in subtle ways motivate their daughters to emulate them. According to these data, they accomplish this primarily by interacting warmly and affectionately with their daughters and by revealing their security and self-confidence, rather than by being highly feminine in interests and orientation or by directly stimulating the girl's participation in sex-appropriate female activities.

Hypothesis Va as it related to the fathers of the girls was supported, however. The fathers of the highly feminine group apparently provide much more encouragement and stimulation of their daughters' participation in sex-appropriate activities, scoring significantly higher, on the average, on the play and games list than the fathers of the other girls (Table 4). Clearly, these fathers play an important and direct role in steering their daughters into feminine role preferences.

DISCUSSION

The results on boys' father identifications—and consequent appropriate sex-typing of their behavior—are essentially in agreement with those of previous studies. An unexpected finding was that, for girls, the process of identification with the like-sexed parent—assessed in terms of degree of appropriate sex-role preference—appears to be much more complexly determined and contingent upon a greater number of antecedent conditions. This was somewhat surprising in view of the fact that much current psychological theorizing emphasizes that the establishment of appropriate sex identification is as difficult—or perhaps more difficult—for boys as for girls (2, 18, 22, 28).

According to the data of this study, the most crucial determinant of the development of masculinity in young boys is the nature of the father-son relationship. Appropriate sex-role preference in boys was found to be directly correlated with nurturant, affectionate relationships with the father, a finding fully consistent with the developmental identification hypothesis and the conclusions of other studies (19, 20, 21, 26). There was also a tendency for highly masculine boys to perceive their fathers as punitive and threatening, a finding supportive of the defensive identification hypothesis. In general, it may be concluded that the boy who sees his father as a highly salient and powerful person in his life—instrumental in both rewarding and punishing him—is likely to develop highly sex-appropriate responses. Except for those pertaining to father-son relationships, none of the hypotheses about the acquisition of masculine sex-role preference was supported in the present study. That is, according to these data, appropriate sex-typing of boys was not influenced by the boys' relationships with their mothers, the personality structures of their parents (self-acceptance and relative degrees of masculinity or femininity), or parental encouragement of specifically sex-typed activities.

The acquisition of femininity by young girls is not so simply determined, however. In a way that is analogous to the boys' development of masculine interests, a positive mother-daughter relationship is of paramount importance in the girl's establishment of appropriate sex-role preference. In addition to this factor, however, aspects of the parents' personality structure —e.g., high degree of maternal self-acceptance and self-confidence—appear to be conducive to the establishment of a high degree of femininity in the daughter. Furthermore, while the mother's personality and interrelationships with her son seem to have little influence on the boy's sex-role preference, the father's personality and behavior appear to be important factors in the daughter's development of femininity. The father's possession of a high degree of masculinity of interests and attitudes and his active encouragement of the girl's participation in appropriate sex-typed activities tend to foster the girl's development of appropriate sex-role preference.

From a synthesis of these data it may be inferred that the boy who loves his father (regards him as nurturant) and perceives him as a powerful person is highly motivated to incorporate some of that parent's behavior and personal qualities, including his sex-typed characteristics and interests. By generalization, he tends to view other men in the same way and emulates their behavior, thus reinforcing his masculine identification. This may occur even though the parents do not strongly encourage, or give direct tuition in, masculine activities and even though the father is not an outstanding model of masculinity or personal security.

It seems that the boy, being strongly motivated to become masculine—initially as a consequence of his positive feelings toward his father—maintains, and probably increases, this motivation. Under these conditions, there is little need for his parents to present clear-cut models of sex-typing or excellent personal adjustment or to exert strong pressure toward masculinizing him. In brief, given positive father-son relationships, no specific family socialization techniques are required for the boy's achievement of a high level of male typing.

The process of female typing in the little girl, while directly related to mother-daughter relationships, is also facilitated by the presence of a highly adequate mother as the feminine model and a father who tends to be aware of the behavior expected of a young girl, encouraging his daughter to act in feminine ways (i.e., to participate in girls' games).

It may be concluded that, in the development of the young child's appropriate sex-typing, the girl's family must play more forceful and direct roles as teachers and socializers than the boy's. The reasons for this are not clear, but we may speculate that the boy receives more assistance and support from the general social environment in the process of establishing appropriate sex-role behavior than the girl does. This may be true for several reasons. For one thing, in American culture—particularly in the middle class group from which most of these subjects come—maleness (being a male and acting like one) is relatively highly valued, while being a female and behaving in feminine ways are relatively less valued and rewarded (15). Evidence for this comes from the finding that, when asked, boys seldom, if ever, state that they wish they were girls, while girls frequently state that they wish they were boys (30). Moreover, masculine characteristics are rated as more desirable by children and adults of both sexes (17). Among nursery school children, boys identify significantly more strongly with their fathers than with their mothers, while girls often identify with both mother and father (5). Boys generally become firmly sex-typed in their behavior earlier than girls do (24). From these facts it may be inferred that society strongly motivates the boy to acquire his own sex-role characteristics and rewards him for acquiring them. The girl is not so strongly motivated in this way to become feminine and is less likely to be highly rewarded for it if she does.

Moreover, as common observation attests, behavior considered appropriate for boys is more clear-cut and well-defined, and boys' violations of approved behavior are more likely to elicit punishment and hence to be extinguished. For example, young boys can wear cowboy outfits and play ball but would be severely ridiculed if they wore dresses or played with dolls. Little girls, on the other hand, can wear either outfit and play either game without suffering such harsh social criticism. In short, boys can acquire masculine behavior and interests relatively more simply than girls can assimilate femininity partially because the cues for sex-appropriate masculine behavior are more distinct, easier to discriminate, and hence easier to learn.

From the point of view of learning theory, the role of the parents in masculinizing their sons is primarily that of providing initial motivation to acquire masculine characteristics and behavior. The general social-cultural milieu further implements the masculinization by presenting numerous, well articulated, and distinct cues for the male sex role and rewards the boy for learning these. If the boy is already highly motivated to learn this kind of behavior as a consequence of his relationships with his father, he will not have difficulty acquiring these behaviors.

For girls, the social-cultural milieu gives less support in the assimilation of her sex role. Due to the relatively lesser value of the feminine role in middle-class American culture and the relative paucity and nondistinctiveness of cues associated with the female sex role among young children, her parents must assist her in several ways if she is to achieve a high degree of femininity. More specifically, parents are forced to assume three feminizing functions with their daughters, only one of which is like the parents' role in masculinizing boys. They must evoke motivation to acquire femininity, and, in addition, they help the feminizing process by presenting some cues for discriminating the sex roles and by directly encouraging the girls to adopt at least certain kinds of behavior characteristic of the feminine role.

It is also possible that, for young boys, masculinization is facilitated by

their tendency to have higher activity levels and greater freedom of movement. These probably permit them to seek out and establish more numerous
and intense social relationships outside the home than girls do. Some of the
boy's peers and friends are likely to be excellent models of masculine behavior, and by imitating these people, the boy's own appropriate sex-typing
will be strengthened. Young girls, having more limited freedom to make
contacts outside the home, may find fewer good models of sex-appropriate
behavior to emulate. For this reason, the establishment of a high degree of
sex-typing in girls may be relatively less influenced by factors outside the
home than the masculinization of boys and more importantly affected by
parental personality structure and direct efforts at sex-typing.

The data of the present study are consistent with at least one aspect of
psychoanalytic theory, for they indicate that, as that theory maintains, the
achievement of sex-identification is more complicated for girls than for boys.
The greater difficulty involved in feminine than in masculine sex-typing
may, however, be plausibly—and probably more parsimoniously—attributed
to certain features of the social structure that promote the boys' acquisition
of appropriate sex-role behavior more than they do the girl's.

It is impossible to know, without empirical tests, the extent to which
findings such as these can be generalized. The results might have been different if other criteria of strength of identification were used. For example, it is
possible that the achievement of a high degree of same-sex parental modeling, another criterion of identification (as distinguished from sex identity,
the criterion used here), is in fact more complex for boys than for girls in
our society. It is at least possible that different manifestations of identification are related to different processes. Thus, as Mowrer has suggested (18),
sex typing may depend on developmental identification while conscience
development or parental modeling may depend on defensive identification.

SUMMARY

This study was designed to test several hypotheses dealing with boys'
father-identifications and girls' mother-identifications as these are reflected
in the degree of appropriate sex-role preference. The sex-role preference of
46 first grade boys and 57 first grade girls was determined by means of the
IT scale. Boys above the boys' median masculinity score and girls above the
median for femininity (i.e., below the median for masculinity) were considered to have developed high degrees of appropriate sex-role identification
while the others were considered low in this dimension.

The major hypotheses concerned the relations between parent-child interactions and identifications with the like-sexed parent. Doll play techniques
provided the basis for assessing the subjects' perceptions of their parents.
Analysis of these data substantially supported the developmental identifi-

cation hypothesis for both sexes. That is, compared with members of their own sex low in appropriate sex-role identification, highly masculine boys and highly feminine girls perceived their like-sexed parents as significantly warmer, more nurturant, and more affectionate. Maternal interviews with the girls' mothers buttressed the doll play findings, the mothers of the highly feminine girls being rated significantly higher than the other mothers in "warmth toward the child." Among the boys—but not among the girls— there was also evidence supportive of the defensive identification hypothesis, for the highly masculine group tended to perceive their fathers as more punitive as well as more rewarding.

The other hypotheses investigated were related to parental characteristics —specifically mothers' femininity, fathers' masculinity, and self-acceptance— and parental encouragement of the child's participation in sex-appropriate activities as antecedents of high degrees of sex-typing. These were evaluated from parental questionnaires which included the CPI Femininity and Self-Acceptance scales and a play and games list in which the parent indicated whether he (she) encouraged or discouraged his (her) child's participation in certain typically male and female activities.

There was no evidence that high masculinity of fathers, femininity of mothers, parental self-acceptance, or encouragement of their son's participation in masculine activities had any significant effect on the boy's masculinization. Apparently the boy's perceptions of his father as a nurturant and powerful individual are crucial in his development of masculinity, but his parents' personality structure and their pressures toward sex-typing him are not significantly influential.

The young girl's feminization, on the other hand, appears to be facilitated by several factors in addition to warm mother-daughter relationships. Thus, the mothers of highly feminine girls were found to be significantly more self-accepting, but more feminine or more encouraging of their daughters' participation in feminine activities, than the mothers of girls low in femininity.

Fathers of the highly feminine girls also appear to play a vastly important role in their daughters' feminization. Compared with the fathers of girls low in femininity, these fathers tended to be more masculine and gave their daughters significantly more encouragement to participate in feminine activities. It may be concluded that the feminization of young girls involves a greater number of, and more complex, determinants than does the masculinization of boys. In the development of the child's appropriate sex-typing, the girl's family appears to play more forceful and direct roles as teachers and socializers than the boy's. It is suggested that this is true because the male role is more highly valued in middle class American culture and because behavior considered appropriate for the boy is more clear-cut and well-defined. In short, it may be that the boy receives more assistance and support from the general social environment in the process of sex-typing than the girl does.

REFERENCES

1. Bronfenbrenner, U.   The study of identification through interpersonal perception. In R. Tagiuri & L. Petrullo (Eds.), *Person perception and interpersonal behavior.* Stanford Univer. Press, 1958. Pp. 110–130.
2. Bronfenbrenner, U.   Freudian theories of identification and their derivatives. *Child Develpm.,* 1960, **31,** 15–40.
3. Brown, D. G.   Sex role preference in young children. *Psychol. Monogr.,* 1956, **70,** No. 14 (Whole No. 421).
4. Burton, R. V., Maccoby, Eleanor E., & Allinsmith, W.   Antecedents of resistance to temptation in four-year-old children. *Child Develpm.,* 1961, **32,** 689–710.
5. Emmerich, W.   Parental identification in young children. *Genet. Psychol. Monogr.,* 1959, **60,** 257–308.
6. Freud, Anna.   *The ego and the mechanisms of defense.* New York: International Universities Press, 1946.
7. Freud, S.   The passing of the Oedipus-complex. In *Collected papers,* Vol. II. London: Hogarth, 1925. Pp. 269–282.
8. Freud, S.   On narcissism: an introduction. In *Collected papers,* Vol. IV. London: Hogarth, 1925. Pp. 30–59.
9. Freud, S.   *Group psychology and the analysis of the ego.* London: Hogarth Press, 1949.
10. Freud, S.   Some psychological consequences of the anatomical distinction between the sexes. In *Collected papers,* Vol. V. London: Hogarth, 1950. Pp. 186–197.
11. Gough, H. G.   *The California psychological inventory.* Palo Alto: Consulting Psychology Press, 1957.
12. Helper, M. M.   Learning theory and the self-concept. *J. abnorm. soc. Psychol.* 1955, **51,** 184–194
13. Kagan, J.   The concept of identification. *Psychol. Rev.,* 1958, **65,** 296–305.
14. Levin, H. & Sears, R. R.   Identification with parents as a determinant of doll play aggression. *Child Develpm.,* 1956, **27,** 135–153.
15. Lynn, D. B.   A note on sex differences in the development of masculine and feminine identification. *Psychol. Rev.,* 1959, **66,** 126–135.
16. McCandless, B. R.   *Children and adolescents.* Holt, Rinehart & Winston, 1961.
17. McKee, J. P., & Sherriffs, A. C.   The differential evaluation of males and females. *J. Pers.,* 1957, **25,** 356–371.
18. Mowrer, O. H.   Identification: a link between learning theory and psychotherapy. In *Learning theory and personality dynamics.* Ronald, 1950. Pp. 573–616.
19. Mussen, P.   Some antecedents and consequents of masculine sex-typing in adolescent boys. *Psychol. Monogr.,* 1961, **75,** No. 2 (Whole No. 506).
20. Mussen, P., & Distler, L.   Masculinity, identification, and father-son relationships. *J. abnorm. soc. Psychol.,* 1959, **59,** 350–356.
21. Mussen, P., & Distler, L.   Child rearing antecedents of masculine identification in kindergarten boys. *Child Develpm.,* 1960, **31,** 89–100.
22. Parsons, T.   Family structure and the socialization of the child. In T. Parsons

& R. F. Bales (Eds.), *Family, socialization, and interaction process.* Free Press, 1955. Pp. 35–131.

23. Payne, D. E., & Mussen, P. H. Parent-child relations and father identification among adolescent boys. *J. abnorm. soc. Psychol.,* 1956, **52,** 358–362.
24. Rabban, M. Sex-role identification in young children in two diverse social groups. *Genet. Psychol. Monogr.,* 1950, **42,** 81–158.
25. Rosenberg, B. G., & Sutton-Smith, B. The measurement of masculinity and femininity in children. *Child Develpm.,* 1959, **30,** 373–380.
26. Sears, P. S. Child-rearing factors related to playing of sex-typed roles. *Amer. Psychologist,* 1953, **8,** 431. (Abstract)
27. Sears, R. R. Identification as a form of behavior development. In D. B. Harris Harris (Ed.), *The concept of development.* Univer. of Minnesota Press, 1957. Pp. 149–161.
28. Sears, R. R., Maccoby, E. E., & Levin, H. *Patterns of child rearing.* Harper & Row, 1957.
29. Stokes, S. M. An inquiry into the concept of identification. In W. E. Martin & C. B. Stendler (Eds.), *Readings in child development.* Harcourt, Brace, 1954. Pp. 227–239.
30. West, J. *Plainville, U.S.A.* Columbia Univer. Press, 1945.

7.3 Effects of Parental Dominance, Warmth, and Conflict on Imitation in Children [1]

E. Mavis Hetherington and Gary Frankie

Most theories of identification agree that identification is based on a process or processes whereby the child, through imitation, modeling, or introjection acquires traits, characteristics, and values similar to the parents. Although there is agreement in the defining characteristics of identification, the various theories diverge in their emphases on the relative importance of different motivational and learning conditions leading to identification. Three variables have frequently been hypothesized by the different theories as affecting identification; namely, parental power, parental warmth, and parental aggression.

Parsons (1955) has emphasized the importance of total parental power in the development of identification. According to Parsons, the child identifies with the parent because he determines or mediates both the rewards and

[1] This study was supported by the Research Committee of the Graduate School of the University of Wisconsin with funds provided by the Wisconsin Alumni Research Foundation.

Reprinted from the *Journal of Personality and Social Psychology,* 1967, **6,** 119–125, by permission of the authors and the American Psychological Association.

punishments the child receives. Several studies (Hetherington, 1965a; Mussen & Distler, 1959, 1960) do indeed suggest that parental power or dominance influences sex typing in boys. The Hetherington (1965a) study also indicated that parental dominance had little effect on sex typing in girls, although paternal dominance increased father-daughter similarity on non-sex-typed traits without interfering with mother-daughter similarity.

Learning theorists focus on anaclitic identification and the effects of warmth and nurturance in the development of identification. Considerable evidence has been accumulated indicating that identification and appropriate sex-role typing are facilitated for both-sex children by warmth in the same-sex parent (Helper, 1955; Mussen & Distler, 1959, 1960; Mussen & Rutherford, 1963; Payne & Mussen, 1956; Sears, 1953).

Psychoanalytic theorists have emphasized the role of fear of punishment and defensive identification with a threatening model. Most of the support for this position has been in clinical case studies, anecdotal evidence, or naturalistic observations such as the German concentration camp studies (Bettelheim, 1943). The Mussen and Distler (1959, 1960) studies did offer some evidence that highly masculine boys perceived their fathers as more punitive as well as more nurturant than feminine boys. No relationship was found between punitiveness and sex typing in girls in a subsequent study by Mussen and Rutherford (1963).

Bandura (1962) has suggested that identification and imitation are synonymous since both encompass the tendency for a person to match the behavior, attitudes, or emotional reactions exhibited by models. If this is true, then the same variables thought to be significant in identification should be salient in the child's imitation of the parent. Experimental studies have found that children imitate a powerful model (Bandura, Ross, & Ross, 1963) or a nurturant model (Bandura & Huston, 1961). Two studies using parents as models have also found that both boys and girls imitate the dominant parent (Hetherington, 1965a), and that maternal nurturance increases imitation by daughters (Mussen & Parker, 1965). Although there is evidence that children imitate aggressive behavior in others, there is only limited evidence that they emulate the behavior of an aggressive model when the aggression is directed toward themselves. A recent study by Mischel and Grusec (1966) has found that children rehearsed aggressive behaviors directed at them more when the model was high in control, and transmitted the aversive behaviors more when the model was high in rewardingness.

Perhaps one reason why evidence for identification with the aggressor is at best suggestive is that it can only be found in certain restricted circumstances. Sarnoff (1951) has suggested that three conditions are essential in producing defensive identification: a hostile individual who directs his aggression toward another person, a victim who is dependent upon the aggressor, and a situation involving stresses and limitations which prevent the victim from escaping the hostile behavior of the aggressor. On the basis of clinical and sociological observations, and Sarnoff's criteria for identification with the aggressor, defensive identification with a hostile dominant parent seems most likely to occur in a stressful home in which both parents are lacking in warmth. Such a home situation would offer the child no escape by seeking a closer relationship with a warm nondominant parent. A stressful, conflictual family relationship should add to the child's feeling of helplessness and increase his tendency toward defensive identification. The present study attempted to test this hypothesis.

A second purpose of the present study was to investigate further the effects of the different variables postulated to affect identification. There seems to be ample evidence that warmth and power do affect identification; a necessary step would appear to be to investigate the interactions of these variables and to find if there are situations under which warmth or dominance are particularly influential. For example, there has been some suggestion in the literature that parental power is more important in the identification of boys than of girls and that warmth is more salient for girls (Hetherington, 1965b; Mussen & Rutherford, 1963).

To test these hypotheses the present study investigated the effects of parental warmth, dominance, and conflict on imitation of parents by boys and girls.

METHOD

Subjects

Subjects were 80 male and 80 female nursery-school and kindergarten children and their parents randomly selected from a large pool of 310 families in which the parents had already taken the Structured Family Interaction Task. These families lived in small Wisconsin towns and most would probably be classified as lower middle class. The ages of the children ranged from 4 years, 4 months to 6 years, 5 months. Half of the subjects were from high-conflict homes and half were from low-conflict homes. Within each conflict group half of the subjects were from mother-dominant homes and half from father-dominant homes. Groups were further subdivided on the basis of all possible mother-father warmth combinations. Thus within each conflict-dominance group there were four warmth combinations: mother high-father low, mother low-father high, mother high-father high, and mother low-father low.

The measures of dominance, conflict, and maternal and paternal warmth were not significantly correlated, although there was an insignificant trend for parental warmth to be associated with low conflict. The number of subjects within each cell in the total populations sampled was approximately equal. These ranged from $N = 13$ in the father-dominant, low-conflict, both-parents-warm, boys group to $N = 9$ in the father-dominant, high-conflict, both-parents-warm, girls group.

Experimental Design

The study utilized a 2 × 2 × 2 × 2 × 4 mixed factorial design involving parental dominance, conflict, sex of subject, parent imitated, and parental warmth combination. Each individual subject had two scores, one for imitation of his mother and one for imitation of his father.

Parental Measures

The parental measures of warmth, hostility, conflict, and dominance were obtained from a structured family-interaction task adapted from a procedure developed by Farina (1960). Each parent was seen individually in a quiet room in his own home. He was read 12 hypothetical problem situations involving child behavior and asked how he would handle them when he was by himself. The instructions were as follows:

> We are interested in knowing how a father/mother handles situations that come up when his wife/husband is not around. I'm going to read some situations that _____ might or might not really have been involved in. Imagine that this situation has arisen and that your wife/husband is not around and you must handle the problem yourself.

Both parents were then brought together and asked to arrive at a compatible solution on handling these children's problems.

The instructions for the joint interaction sessions were as follows:

> You have talked about how you would handle these various situations if you were alone; now I would like to go through these situations again, and have you discuss them and come to some agreement as to how you would handle the problem if you were both there. Imagine the situation arising, you are both at home and must deal with the situation. I want you to continue the discussion until you can come to some agreement on how you would handle the problem if you were together, then say "Agreed" and we will go on to the next situation.

The discussion of each problem continued until both parents said the terminating signal, "agreed." The experimenter participated only minimally in the discussion in order to clarify scoring responses. All interviews were tape-recorded and scored later.

In the previous studies, for which the interaction task was initially run (Hetherington, 1965a, 1965b), the results of all 12 situations were used; however, since many parents complained of fatigue and became restless during the last part of the joint interaction sessions only the responses on the first 7 situations were utilized in this study.

The seven situations were as follows:

1. Your son/daughter loses his/her temper while playing with a toy and intentionally breaks it.
2. You have friends over in the evening. Your son/daughter keeps getting out of bed to see what's going on.

3. Your son/daughter has a friend over to play. The friend wants to play with one of _____'s favorite toys but _____ won't let him.

4. A neighbor calls up and complains that your son/daughter has been throwing rocks at her child.

5. You have gone out of your way to buy something nice for your child and then he/she throws it aside and says he/she doesn't like it.

6. Your child has been asked several times to tidy up his/her room. You find his/her room still a mess and him/her watching TV.

7. You have taken your son/daughter out to dinner in a restaurant as a special treat. He/she is behaving in a generally noisy, ill-mannered way although you have warned him/her to quiet down.

Parental dominance measure. The index for parental dominance was comprised of five of the measures previously used by Farina (1960), which were: speaks first, speaks last, passive acceptance of spouse's solution, percent of total speaking time, and the amount of yielding from original individual solution to the joint solution. Total scores on each of these measures were used to classify the index as indicating mother or father dominance. If three or more indexes indicated paternal dominance, the family was classified as father dominant; if three or more indicated maternal dominance, the family was classified as mother dominant.

Parental conflict measure. The parental conflict measures were the same as those used by Farina (1960): total time spoken, disagreements and aggressions, interruptions, frequency of simultaneous speech, and failure to agree. Total time spoken was included as a measure of parental conflict, since it was assumed that the greater the conflict and disagreement the longer it would take to resolve differences and come to a mutually acceptable solution on handling problems. These scores were converted to z scores and combined into a single conflict index. Families which scored above the group mean in conflict were classified as high-conflict homes; those below the mean were classified as low-conflict homes.

Warmth-Hostility measure. The mother and father were separately rated on a 6-point warmth-hostility scale ranging from 1—extremely warm, nurturant, and affectionate; clearly proud of the child, concerned with and enjoys the child as a person; understanding and empathic—to 6—marked hostility, anger, and punitiveness toward the child; little sympathy or attempt to understand the child's behavior; always interprets the child's behavior in the worst light. Ratings of parental warmth were done on the basis of both the individual sessions and the joint interaction session. A parent scoring below the group mean for his sex was classified as high in warmth; those above the mean were classified as low in warmth.

All the measures on the Structured Family Interaction Task which had previously exhibited any unreliability were rated by two judges. These included the yielding measure of the dominance scale, the warmth-hostility scale, and the conflict measures. Interjudge reliability was .94 for the yielding measure, .81 for the warmth-hostility ratings, and mean interjudge reliability on the conflict measures was .86.

Imitation Task

Each child was run on an imitation task where he watched each parent alternately perform for four trials in a free-play situation. Each parent was preinstructed, given a practice session without the child present, and given a small inconspicuous card to carry summarizing his role in the imitation task. Following the second, fourth, sixth, and eighth trials the child was given a 5-minute session in the playroom. The parental behaviors involved postural, motor, and verbal responses associated with playing with a group of toys and games previously determined to be of equal interest to male and female children. An attempt was made to use activities and behaviors which were appropriate for adults rather than some of the bizarre behaviors used in previous studies. Thus the activities involved were some in which an adult might participate without appearing too ludicrous, such as golf putting, shooting rubber darts at a target, a game of ball throwing at a target which automatically ejected the ball, etc. The parental behaviors involved such things as making predetermined distinctive comments following success or failure, always selecting a toy of a given color and saying, "_____ is my lucky color," squatting and lining up golf shots, pulling up a chair, sitting sideways and shooting with two hands in the dart game, and so on.[2] The set of imitative responses assigned to a given parent and the parent performing first were randomly determined. Parents were always absent from the room during the child's test series.

A male and female observer checked the imitative responses on a response check list; perfect interrater agreement was found in the scoring of 95% of the specific imitative responses. The imitation scores were obtained by summing the frequency of responses the child made which were similar to those of a given parent.

RESULTS AND DISCUSSION

The basic analysis of variance for the imitation scores is presented in Table 1. The significant main effect of parent imitation and the significant Sex of Subject $\times$ Parent Imitation interaction indicate that although mothers were imitated more than fathers, boys imitated the father more than the mother ($M = 16.82$, 15.22, respectively, $p < .10$),[3] while girls imitated the mother more than the father ($M = 19.65$, 12.06, respectively, $p <$

---

[2] Complete details on the imitation procedures may be obtained by writing to the senior author.

[3] Probability values are based on two-tailed t tests, unless otherwise noted.

TABLE 1. ANALYSIS OF VARIANCE OF THE IMITATION SCORES

Source	df	MS	F
Conflict (C)	1	116.40	2.85 *
Dominance (D)	1	1.95	<1.00
Sex of S (S)	1	2.28	<1.00
Warmth (W)	3	600.03	14.71 ***
C × D	1	14.03	<1.00
C × S	1	3.00	<1.00
C × W	3	10.61	<1.00
D × S	1	114.00	2.80 *
D × W	3	32.19	<1.00
S × W	3	59.91	1.47
C × D × S	1	.03	<1.00
C × D × W	3	2.80	<1.00
C × S × W	3	3.55	<1.00
D × S× W	3	40.35	<1.00
C × D × S × W	3	13.83	<1.00
Error (a)	128	40.78	
Parent imitation (P)	1	717.00	19.77 ***
C × P	1	3.83	<1.00
D × P	1	4096.95	112.99 ***
S × P	1	1688.20	46.56 ***
W × P	3	1048.75	28.92 ***
C × D × P	1	141.79	3.91 *
C × S × P	1	8.78	<1.00
C × W × P	3	4.56	<1.00
D × S × P	1	1762.51	48.61 ***
D × W × P	3	11.79	<1.00
S × W × P	3	61.64	1.70
C × D × S × P	1	2.27	<1.00
C × S × W × P	3	7.56	<1.00
C × D × W × P	3	53.06	1.46
D × S × W × P	3	45.35	1.25
C × D × S × P × W	3	16.41	<1.00
Error (b)	128	36.26	

* $p < .10$.
*** $p < .01$.

.05). The significant Dominance × Parent Imitation and Warmth × Parent Imitation interactions support the previous findings that parental warmth and dominance are important factors in identification. The means for the Dominance × Parent Imitation interaction show that the dominant parent was imitated more; in a mother-dominant home the means for imitation of the mother and father were 20.94 and 10.78, respectively ($p < .05$), and in a father-dominant home means for imitation of the mother and father were 13.94 and 18.10, respectively ($p < .05$). In looking at the means for the Warmth $\times$ Parent Imitation interaction, it is obvious that a parent high in warmth is imitated more than a parent low in warmth. Mean imitation of the mother under the various warmth conditions was as follows: mother high–father high, 21.25; mother low–father high, 12.85; mother high–father low, 23.27; and mother low–father low, 12.40 (critical difference = 2.73, $p < .05$). It can be seen that a mother high in warmth was imitated more than one low in warmth, regardless of the level of paternal warmth. The same type of results were also obtained for mean imitation of the father under the various warmth conditions: father high–mother high, 16.72; father low–mother high, 10.92; father high–mother low, 17.35; and father low–mother low, 12.77 (critical difference = 2.73, $p < .05$). Also significant ($p < .05$) is the difference between imitation of a highly warm mother and a highly warm father (i.e., comparing imitation of the mother in the warmth conditions of mother high–father high, and mother high–father low versus imitation of the father in the conditions of father high–mother high and father high–mother low). This finding suggests that maternal warmth facilitates imitation of the mother more than paternal warmth facilitates imitation of the father.

However, these general findings must be qualified when we look at the means for the significant Dominance $\times$ Sex $\times$ Parent Imitated interaction presented in Table 2. Under mother dominance both boys and girls imitated the mothers more. Under father dominance, however, boys imitated the father more while girls continued to imitate the mother. This suggests that parental dominance has a more important effect on the identification of boys than of girls. The age range of the subjects in this study, 3–5, is considered a particularly important transition period in identification for boys where identification must shift from the mother to the father. Paternal dominance may play an extremely salient role in facilitating this shift for boys. It might also be suggested that a dominant father offers a more appropriate role model for boys than does a nondominant father.

TABLE 2. Means for the Dominance $\times$ Sex $\times$ Parent Imitated Interaction

Parent imitated	Mother dominant		Father dominant	
	Boys	Girls	Boys	Girls
Mother	20.47	21.40	9.98	17.90
Father	10.22	11.35	23.42	12.78

Note.—Critical difference (2-tailed t test, $p < .05$) = 2.67 or comparison of mother versus father imitation within a column, and 2.73 for comparison across columns.

For the girls, who do not need to shift their identification, maternal warmth seems to be the most salient variable in imitation. When the warmth-combinations variable is broken down into the orthogonal factors of mother and father warmth, the interaction of these factors with sex of subject (presented in Table 3) shows that maternal warmth interacts sig-

TABLE 3. ANALYSIS OF VARIANCE FOR SEX OF SUBJECT ×
WARMTH EFFECTS INTERACTIONS

Source	df	MS	F
S × Warmth	3		
S × MW	1	161.03	3.95 **
S × FW	1	1.13	<1.00
S × MW × FW	1	17.58	<1.00

Note.—S = sex, MW = mother warmth, FW = father warmth.
** $p < .05$.

nificantly with sex of subject while paternal warmth facilitates imitation to an equal degree in boys and girls. The means for the significant Maternal Warmth × Sex of Subject interaction are presented in Table 4 and show that maternal warmth affects the girl's imitation more than it does the boy's.

The means for the marginally significant ($p < .06$) Conflict × Dominance × Parent Imitated interaction are presented in Table 5. The pattern of differences in this table suggests that in a stressful home situation having high conflict there is more imitation of the dominant parent than is found in a home having low conflict. This appears to be particularly true if the mother is the dominant parent.

In order to permit clearer evaluation of the interaction of specific variables, and in order to assess the possibility of defensive identification occurring under the previously hypothesized conditions of Sarnoff's (1951) study, the means for all subgroups are presented in Table 6. The means essential for the defensive identification analysis are outlined.

TABLE 4. MEANS FOR THE SIGNIFICANT
SEX OF SUBJECT ×
MATERNAL WARMTH
INTERACTION

Sex	Maternal warmth	
	High	Low
Girls	18.66	13.05
Boys	17.41	14.64

TABLE 5. MEANS FOR THE CONFLICT × DOMINANCE ×
PARENT IMITATED INTERACTION

Conflict	Mother dominant: Parent imitated		Father dominant: Parent imitated	
	Mother	Father	Mother	Father
High	22.52	10.82	13.77	19.05
Low	19.35	10.75	14.10	17.15

Note.—Critical difference = 2.73, 2-tailed t test, $p < .05$.

It was assumed that the conditions most likely to lead to identification with the aggressor would be a home in which there is a high conflict and in which both parents were low in warmth. In such a situation there would be no warm supportive parent to whom to turn for succor so that the child might attempt to minimize his insecurity by identifying with a powerful, punitive model. Under the less stressful situation of a low-conflict home or a home in which there is some protection from a warm parent, there should be less tendency to imitate a hostile aggressive parent. Since these assump-

TABLE 6. MEAN IMITATION SCORES

Homes	Parent imitated	Warmth combinations							
		Mother low– Father low		Mother high– Father low		Mother low– Father high		Mother high Father high	
		Boys	Girls	Boys	Girls	Boys	Girls	Boys	Girls
Mother dominant High conflict	Mother	20.6	20.2	28.4	27.6	15.0	16.6	25.6	26.2
	Father	8.8	7.8	7.2	9.0	12.4	15.6	12.0	13.8
Low conflict	Mother	13.2	14.2	25.6	27.2	15.0	15.0	20.4	24.2
	Father	10.5	10.0	6.4	8.6	12.0	14.0	12.8	12.0
Father dominant High conflict	Mother	6.8	7.6	13.0	25.4	9.0	11.8	11.2	25.4
	Father	22.5	15.6	19.8	10.4	27.8	14.6	27.8	14.2
Low conflict	Mother	7.0	9.6	13.6	25.4	7.4	13.0	11.8	25.0
	Father	20.6	7.0	16.4	9.6	26.2	16.2	26.6	14.6

Note.—Means for evaluating defensive identification under Sarnoff's (1951) criteria are outlined. Critical difference = 6.3, 1-tailed t test, $p < .05$, for comparing mother imitation versus father imitation at a given level of all other variables. For other comparisons critical difference = 6.5, 1-tailed t, $p < .05$.

tions produce directional hypotheses, one-tailed t tests were used in testing the differences in Table 6.

It can be seen that under high conflict, with both parents low in warmth, there is indeed a significant tendency for both boys and girls to imitate the dominant parent regardless of sex of the parent. If either the nondominant parent is warm or conflict is reduced, there is a trend toward less imitation of the aggressive dominant parent, so that the dominant parent is not imitated significantly more than the nondominant one. This trend does not hold in the case of boys with dominant fathers, however. The boy's tendency to imitate a dominant father overrides the effects of variations in conflict and warmth. In contrast, maternal warmth appears to be particularly salient for girls. Even under conditions of high conflict and paternal dominance there is marked imitation of warm mothers by daughters.

In summary, the results seem to be congruent with those of past studies which have found that both parental warmth and power are important in the identification of girls, and paternal dominance is important in the identification of boys. This is in agreement with the earlier findings of Mussen and Rutherford (1963) and Mussen and Distler (1959, 1960). Some support was found for identification with the aggressor under very restricted conditions involving high stress and low warmth in both parents, which might be assumed to result in a sense of extreme helplessness on the part of the child.

SUMMARY

This study investigated the effects of parental dominance, warmth, and conflict on imitation of parents by boys and girls. Parental warmth and dominance were found to be salient variables in identification; however, parental dominance was more important for imitation by boys while maternal warmth was more effective with girls. Support was found for identification with the aggressor under the conditions of a high-conflict home where both parents were low in warmth.

REFERENCES

Bandura, A. Social learning through imitation. In M. R. Jones (Ed.), *Nebraska symposium on motivation: 1962.* Lincoln: University of Nebraska Press, 1962. Pp. 211–269.

Bandura, A., & Huston, A. C. Identification as a process of incidental learning. *Journal of Abnormal and Social Psychology,* 1961, **63,** 311–318.

Bandura, A., Ross, D., & Ross, S. A. A comparative test of the status envy, social power, and the secondary-reinforcement theories of identification learning. *Journal of Abnormal and Social Psychology,* 1963, **67,** 527–534.

Bettelheim, B.   Individual and mass behavior in extreme situations. *Journal of Abnormal and Social Psychology*, 1943, **38**, 417–452.

Farina, A.   Patterns of role dominance and conflict in parents of schizophrenic patients. *Journal of Abnormal and Social Psychology*, 1960, **61**, 31–38.

Helper, M. M.   Learning theory and the self-concept. *Journal of Abnormal and Social Psychology*, 1955, **51**, 184–194.

Hetherington, E. M.   A developmental study of the effects of sex of the dominant parent on sex-role preference, identification, and imitation in children. *Journal of Personality and Social Psychology*, 1965, **2**, 188–194. (a)

Hetherington, E. M.   The effects of parental dominance on imitation of sex typed behaviors. Unpublished manuscript, University of Wisconsin, 1965. (b)

Mischel, W., & Grusec, Joan.   Determinants of the rehearsal and transmission of neutral and aversive behaviors. *Journal of Personality and Social Psychology*, 1966, **3**, 197–205.

Mussen, P., & Distler, L.   Masculinity, identification and father-son relationships. *Journal of Abnormal and Social Psychology*, 1959, **59**, 350–356.

Mussen, P., & Distler, L.   Child rearing antecedents of masculine identification in kindergarten boys. *Child Development*, 1960, **31**, 89–100.

Mussen, P., & Rutherford, E.   Parent-child relations and parental personality in relation to young children's sex-role preferences. *Child Development*, 1963, **34**, 589–607.

Mussen, P. H., & Parker, A. L.   Mother nurturance and girls' incidental imitative learning. *Journal of Personality and Social Psychology*, 1965, **2**, 94–97.

Parsons, T.   Family structure and the socialization of the child. In T. Parsons & R. F. Bales (Eds.), *Family socialization and interaction process*. Glencoe, Ill.: Free Press, 1955. Pp. 35–131.

Payne, D. E., & Mussen, P. H.   Parent-child relations and father identification among adolescent boys. *Journal of Abnormal and Social Psychology*, 1956, **52**, 358–362.

Sarnoff, I.   Identification with the aggressor: Some personality correlates of anti-semitism among Jews. *Journal of Personality*, 1951, **20**, 199–218.

Sears, P. S.   Child-rearing factors related to playing of sex-typed roles. *American Psychologist*, 1953, **8**, 431. (Abstract)

7.4   Effects of Paternal Absence on Sex-typed Behaviors in Negro and White Preadolescent Males

E. Mavis Hetherington

This study investigated the effects of father absence on the development of sex-role preferences, dependency, aggression, and recreational activities of Negro and white preadolescent boys. All children had mothers but no father

Reprinted from the *Journal of Personality and Social Psychology* 1966, **4**, 87–91, by permission of the author and the American Psychological Association.

substitutes present in the home and no contact with the fathers subsequent to separation.

In previous studies of the effects of father absence on the development of children, total and final absence of the father usually had not occurred. The father was either temporarily away due to war (Bach, 1946; Sears, Pintler, & Sears, 1946) or to occupational demands (Lynn & Sawrey, 1959; Tiller, 1958). An exception to this is the McCord, McCord, and Thurber (1962) study of boys from broken homes. These studies frequently indicated disruption of masculine identification in boys whose fathers were absent. Boys with fathers absent from the home tended to be less aggressive in doll-play situations (Sears et al., 1946), had father fantasies more similar to those of girls (Bach, 1946), and were more dependent (Stolz et al., 1954; Tiller, 1958) than boys whose fathers were living in the home. In contrast to these findings McCord et al. found no differences in dependency between boys from homes in which the father was absent and those in which the father was present and found the former group was more aggressive. The Lynn and Sawrey study also indicated that boys deprived of regular contact with their fathers made stronger strivings toward masculine identification shown by preference for a father versus a mother doll in a Structured Doll Play Test, and manifested an unstable compensatory masculinity. They found no differences between boys whose fathers were absent and those whose fathers were present in ratings of dependency in the doll-play situation and attribute this to a "compensatory masculine reluctance to express dependency [p. 261]."

It might be expected that if boys with absent fathers in contrast to those with a father present manifest compensatory masculinity they would score high on behaviors associated with masculinity such as independence, aggression, masculine sex-role preferences, and participation in activities involving force and competition. Moss and Kagan (1961) suggested that for boys, participation and skill in sports is closely involved with maintenance of sex-role identification. However, if father absence results in a direct expression of a failure to establish masculine identification, boys without fathers would be rated low on the previous variables.

The age at which separation from the father occurs could differentially affect the form of disrupted identification in boys. Early separation may result in greater disruption of sex-typed behaviors than would later separation when identification is well under way or completed. Early separation might result directly in less masculine sex-role behaviors since identification with the father has never developed. In contrast later separation may have little effect on these behaviors or result in exaggerating masculine behavior in an attempt to sustain the already established masculine identification with the major role model, the father, absent.

It might also be expected that the effects of father absence would interact with the race of the family. It has frequently been suggested that the Negro family structure is basically matriarchal (Karon, 1958). Maternal dominance has been demonstrated to have a disruptive effect on sex typing in boys (Hetherington, 1965; Mussen & Distler, 1959). In such mother-dominated families, absence of the father might be expected to have a less disruptive effect on sex-typed behavior of boys than it would in a father-dominant family.

Kardiner and Ovesey (1951) suggest that Negroes have strong inhibited aggressive needs which are displaced and expressed in competitive sports. It would therefore be predicted that Negroes would be rated lower in overt social aggression than would white boys, but would show a marked preference for aggressive, competitive activities.

METHOD

Subjects were 32 Negro and 32 white first-born boys between the ages of 9 and 12, who were attending a recreation center in a lower-class urban area. Sixteen of the boys in each group were from homes in which both parents were present, and 16 from homes in which the father was absent. In half of the father-absent homes for Negro and white families, separation had occurred at age 4 or earlier, and in half, after age 6. Father separation was caused by desertion, divorce, death, and illegitimacy. No father substitutes lived in the home. There were no significant differences in causes of father separation between groups, although illegitimacy was a cause only in the early groups.

Forty-nine of the subjects were only children, seven subjects had a younger male sibling, and eight subjects had a younger female sibling. These subjects were distributed approximately evenly across groups, although there was a slightly larger proportion of only children in the group of children whose fathers left early than in the groups whose fathers were present or had left the home after age 6.

Procedure

Two male recreation directors who had known the subjects for at least 6 months rated them on 7-point scales measuring dependence on adults, dependence on peers, independence, aggression, and on an activities test. The scales ranged from 1, very rarely and without persistence, to 7, very often and very persistently. Interrater reliabilities ranged from .85 to .94. All subjects were also individually administered the It Scale for Children (ITSC; Brown, 1956).

Measures

Scales for dependence and independence were based upon those used by Beller (1957). The aggression scale was based on that of Sears, Whiting, Nowlis, and Sears (1953). Behaviors involved in each scale were more fully elaborated as in Beller (1957), but used behaviors appropriate to the age group of the present study. A total rating for each of these three scales was obtained.

Rating Scale for Dependence on Adults was comprised of ratings of:

1. How often does the boy seek physical contact with adults?
2. How often does the boy seek to be near adults?
3. How often does the boy seek recognition (any form of praise and punishment) from adults?
4. How often does the boy seek attention from adults?

Rating Scale for Dependence on Peers was composed of the same items as dependence on adults oriented toward children.

Rating Scale for Independence involved the following four of Beller's autonomous achievement-striving scales:

1. How often does the boy derive satisfaction from his work?
2. How often does the boy take the initiative in carrying out his own activity?
3. How often does the boy attempt to overcome obstacles in the environment?
4. How often does the boy complete an activity?

Rating Scale for Aggression involved in the following items:

1. How often does the boy act to necessitate correction, scolding, or reminding?
2. How often does the boy ask for special privileges?
3. How often does the boy attack other children on their property to show envy?
4. How often does the boy threaten adults?
5. How often does the boy threaten other children?
6. How often does the boy destroy the property of the Center or of other children?
7. How often does the boy derogate others?
8. How often does the boy quarrel with other children?
9. How often does the boy display undirected aggression?
10. How often does the boy attack other children physically?
11. How often does the child exhibit displaced aggressive attacks?

The Activities Test was comprised of ratings on a 7-point scale ranging from 1, very rarely participates in this activity, to 7, very often and persistently participates in the activity. Five activities in each of four categories were rated. In standardizing the Activities Test three recreation directors were asked to sort a group of 48 activities into the following four categories. Only those in which the three judges agreed were retained.

1. Physical skill involving contact—boxing, wrestling, football, basketball, battle ball.

2. Physical skill not involving contact—foot-racing, bowling, horseshoes, table tennis, darts.

3. Nonphysical competitive games—dominoes, checkers, scrabble, monopoly, cards.

4. Nonphysical, noncompetitive games—reading, watching television, building things, working on puzzles, collecting things.

Total ratings for each of the four types of activities were obtained.

TABLE 1. Means for Father Separation Early, Father Separation Late, and Father Present, Negro and White Boys

	Father present		Early		Late	
	White	Negro	White	Negro	White	Negro
Dependency on adults	15.69	15.19	14.25	14.00	12.75	13.00
Dependency on peers	15.31	15.50	17.62	18.25	18.25	19.12
Independence	15.75	15.69	18.25	15.37	15.25	18.25
Aggression	39.87	47.06	32.00	30.75	51.00	52.12
ITSC	67.56	70.69	53.50	55.00	65.12	73.25
Physical contact	20.62	23.62	14.87	18.87	21.50	21.87
Physical noncontact	21.06	18.75	15.37	17.50	21.12	17.00
Nonphysical, competitive	21.44	20.81	16.87	18.62	20.12	17.62
Nonphysical, noncompetitive	17.69	16.62	24.25	22.37	21.37	19.12

The ITSC (Brown, 1956) is a test of sex-role preference which presents the child with an ambiguous figure (It) and asks the child to select from a group of toys and objects those that "It" prefers. A high score indicates masculine preference.

RESULTS

Separate two-way analyses of variance involving race and father status (early absent, late absent, and present) were calculated for each scale. When significant F ratios were obtained, t tests between means were calculated. Table 1 presents the means for all groups on all variables.

The analysis of variance of total dependence on adults yielded no significant differences; however, the analysis of dependence on peers yielded a significant F ratio ($F = 10.18$, $p < .005$) for father status. Subsequent t tests indicated that both early-separated and late-separated boys were significantly more dependent on peers than were the boys with fathers living in the home ($t = 2.23$, $p < .05$; $t = 2.90$, $p < .005$).

No significant differences were found between groups on total independence scores.

The analysis of total aggression scores indicated a significant effect of father status ($F = 10.39$, $p < .005$) on aggressive behavior. Both boys who were deprived of their fathers after age 6 and boys whose fathers are present manifested more aggression than boys who were deprived of their fathers at an early age ($t = 3.20$, $p < .005$; $t = 2.21$, $p < .05$, respectively).

The results of the ITSC also yielded a significant effect for father status ($F = 4.966$, $p < .025$). Boys experiencing late separation from the father and boys from unbroken homes have more masculine sex-role preferences than early-separated boys ($t = 2.32$, $p < .05$; $t = 3.14$, $p < .005$).

The Activities Test indicates that early-separated boys play fewer physical games involving contact than do either late-separated boys or boys with fathers living in the home ($t = 2.06$, $p < .05$; $t = 2.60$, $p < .025$). Negro boys tend to play more games of this type than do white boys ($t = 2.22$, $p = .05$). It should be noted that this is the only significant racial difference found in the entire study. No significant effects were obtained in the analysis of physical activities involving no contact or in nonphysical competitive activities. However, a significant effect ($F = 8.236$, $p < .005$) for father status was found in nonphysical, noncompetitive activities. Early-separated boys spend more time in these activities than do boys living with both parents.

It seemed possible that the obtained differences between early- and late-separated boys were a result of the total time elapsed since the father left the home, rather than the developmental stage at which separation occurred.

TABLE 2. CORRELATIONS AMONG ALL VARIABLES FOR ALL SUBJECTS

	1	2	3	4	5	6	7	8	9
1. Dependence on adults	1.00	.02	−.25 **	.06	.04	.04	.06	.11	−.06
2. Dependence on peers		1.00	−.10	.06	.04	−.02	.03	−.26	.10
3. Independence			1.00	.05	.02	−.01	.11	.17	−.17
4. Aggression				1.00	.21 *	.40 ****	.22 *	−.01	−.33 ***
5. ITSC					1.00	.38 ***	.02	.09	−.29 ***
6. Physical contact						1.00	.13	.03	−.59 ****
7. Physical noncontact							1.00	.17	−.16
8. Nonphysical, competition								1.00	−.23
9. Nonphysical, noncompetition									1.00

* $p = .10$.
** $p = .05$.
*** $p = .01$.
**** $p = .001$.

The early-separated children may have had more time for a loss of cathexsis on masculine behaviors. In order to investigate this possibility, an attempt was made to compare subjects in the early- and late-separation groups who had been deprived of their fathers for 6 years. The resulting Ns in each group were too small to permit an adequate analysis of the scores ($N = 4$ in early separated, $N = 3$ in late separated); however, the results appeared to parallel those of the total early- and late-separated groups.

The small sample size and predominance of only children did not permit a satisfactory analysis of the effects of family size and sex of sibling on the behavior studied.

Table 2 presents the intercorrelations among all variables studied for all subjects.

Dependence on adults but not on peers is negatively related to independence. Masculine sex-role preferences, aggressive behavior, and participation in physical activities cluster together. Conversely, it appears that boys who enjoy nonphysical, noncompetitive activities are low in masculine sex-role preferences, aggression, and in participation in activities involving physical contact or nonphysical competition.

DISCUSSION

The results of the study indicate that absence of the father after age 5 has little effect on the sex-typed behaviors of boys. These boys in most respects do not differ from boys who have their fathers present. They are similar in their independence, dependence on adults, aggression, and sex-role preferences. In preferences for activities involving physical force or competition which might permit socially accepted expression of compensatory masculinity we again find no differences. An increased dependence on the adult all-male staff of the recreation center might have been expected if the boys lacking fathers were seeking attention from other adult males as father substitutes. This did not occur. It appears that any frustrated dependency needs which loss of a father might have produced do not generalize to other adult males. In fact there was a trend for boys with no fathers to be less dependent on adults ($F = 2.56, p < .10$). The greater dependence on peers of boys who had lost their fathers early or late is difficult to explain. It may be that loss or lack of a father results in a mistrust of adults with a consequent compensatory increase in dependence on peers. This general pattern of relations was reported by Freud and Burlingham (1944) in their studies of children separated from their parents by World War II. These children showed strong ties to their peers but few emotional ties to adult caretakers in institutions.

Boys who lost their fathers early, before identification can be assumed to have been completed, showed considerable deviation in sex-typed traits. They are less aggressive and show more feminine sex-role preferences than the other boys. They also participate less in physical games involving contact and more in nonphysical, noncompetitive activities. This preference for the latter type of activity could be considered an avoidance of activities involving the appropriate masculine behaviors of competition and aggressive play. An alternative explanation might be that it is a manifestation of social withdrawal since the activities in that category tend to be ones which involve a minimum of social interaction. It is difficult to accept this interpretation in view of the high dependency on peers ratings obtained by these boys. One could speculate that these boys make unsuccessful dependent overtures to peers, are rebuffed, and remain socially isolated.

The results suggest that adequate masculine identification has occurred by age 6 and that this identification can be maintained in the absence of the father. If the father leaves in the first 4 years before identification has been established, long-lasting disruption in sex-typed behaviors may result.

The predictions concerning racial differences were only partially confirmed. Differences between Negro and white boys in overt aggression which would be expected if Negroes inhibit direct expression of aggression were not obtained. However, the predicted high participation of Negroes in competitive activities involving contact was found. On the basis of this study it must be concluded that the behavior of Negro and white boys observed in the setting of a recreation center appears very similar.

SUMMARY

This study investigated the effects of race, father absence, and time of departure of the father on sex-typed behaviors of preadolescent males. If the father left after the age of 5, sex-typed behaviors are similar to those of boys from homes in which the father is present; however, if the father left in the first 4 yr. of life considerable disruption of these behaviors are found. Both groups of boys with fathers absent are significantly more dependent on their peers than father-present boys. The only racial difference obtained indicated that Negro boys participate more in competitive activities involving force than do white boys.

REFERENCES

Bach, G. R.   Father-fantasies and father typing in father-separated children. *Child Development,* 1946, **17,** 63–79.

Beller, E. K.   Dependency and autonomous achievement-striving related to orality and anality in early childhood. *Child Development,* 1957, **29,** 287–315.

Brown, D. G.   Sex-role preference in young children. *Psychological Monographs,* 1956, **70** (14, Whole No. 421).

Freud, A., & Burlingham, D. T.   *Infants without families.* New York: International Universities Press, 1944.

Hetherington, E. M. A developmental study of the effects of sex of the dominant parent on sex-role preference, identification, and imitation in children. *Journal of Personality and Social Psychology,* 1965, **2,** 188–194.

Kardiner, A., & Ovesey, L. *The mark of oppression.* New York: Norton, 1951.

Karon, B. P. *The Negro personality.* New York: Springer, 1958.

Lynn, D. B., & Sawrey, W. L. The effects of father-absence on Norwegian boys and girls. *Journal of Abnormal and Social Psychology,* 1959, **59,** 258–262.

McCord, J., McCord, W., & Thurber, E. Some effects of paternal absence on male children. *Journal of Abnormal and Social Psychology,* 1962, **64,** 361–369.

Moss, H. A., & Kagan, J. Stability of achievement and recognition seeking behaviors from early childhood through adulthood. *Journal of Abnormal and Social Psychology,* 1961, **62,** 504–513.

Mussen, P., & Distler, L. Masculinity, identification, and father-son relationships. *Journal of Abnormal and Social Psychology,* 1959, **59,** 350–356.

Sears, R. R., Pintler, M. H., & Sears, P. S. Effects of father-separation on preschool children's doll play aggression. *Child Development,* 1946, **17,** 219–243.

Sears, R. R., Whiting, J. W. M., Nowlis, H., & Sears, P. S. Some childrearing antecedents of dependency and aggression in young children. *Genetic Psychology Monographs,* 1953, **47,** 135–234.

Stoltz, L. M., et al. *Father relations of war-born children.* Stanford: Stanford University Press, 1954.

Tiller, P. O. Father-absence and personality development of children in sailor families: A preliminary research report. *Nordisk Psykologi,* 1958, Monogr. No. 9.

7.5 Differential Stability of Behavior as a Function of Sex Typing

Jerome Kagan and Howard A. Moss

The most dramatic and consistent finding of this study was that many of the behaviors exhibited by the child during the period 6 to 10 years of age, and a few during the age period 3 to 6, were moderately good predictors of theoretically related behaviors during early adulthood. Passive withdrawal from stressful situations, dependency on family, ease-of-anger arousal, involvement in intellectual mastery, social interaction anxiety, sex-role identification, and pattern of sexual behavior in adulthood were each related to reasonably analogous behavioral dispositions during the early school years. Figure 1 summarizes the differential stability of these seven classes of responses from childhood to adulthood. These results offer strong support

Reprinted from J. Kagan, and H. A. Moss, *Birth to Maturity, A Study in Psychological Development,* by permission of the authors and John Wiley & Sons, Inc., 1962. Pp. 266–276.

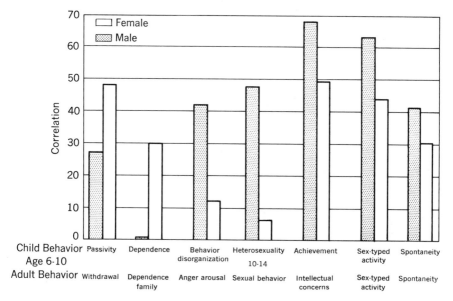

FIGURE 1. Summary of relations between selected child behaviors (6 to 10 years of age) and phenotypically similar adult behaviors.

to the popular notion that aspects of adult personality begin to take form during early childhood.

However, the degree of continuity of these response classes was intimately dependent upon its congruence with traditional standards for sex-role characteristics. The differential stability of passivity, dependency, aggression, and sexuality for males and females emphasizes the importance of cultural rules in determining both behavioral change and stability.

Passive and dependent behavior are subjected to consistent cultural disapproval for men but not for women. This disapproval is communicated to the child through the direct rewards and punishments issued by peers and adults as well as the behavior of role models, be they real or the product of the public media. It is not surprising, therefore, that childhood passivity and dependency were related to adult passive and dependent behavior for women, but not for men, and that the men had greater difficulty than the women in recognizing the tachistoscopically presented dependency scenes.

A low threshold for anger, direct aggressive retaliation, and frequent sexual behavior, on the other hand, are disproportionately punished in females, whereas males are given greater license in these areas. The data revealed that childhood rage reactions and frequent dating during pre-adolescence predicted adult aggressive and sexual predispositions, respectively, for men but not for women. As might be expected, the women had greater difficulty than the men in accurately describing the tachistoscopically presented aggressive pictures and described themselves as less aggressive than the men on the self-rating questionnaire.

Intellectual mastery and adoption of appropriate sex-typed interests are positively sanctioned for both sexes, and both of these behaviors showed a high degree of continuity for males and females from the early school years through adulthood. In selected instances even preschool behavior was related to a similar disposition in adulthood. For example, the preschool girl's involvement in achievement tasks predicted her concern with intellectual mastery in adulthood ($r = .44$; $p < .05$).

Even the children who were reared by families that did not consciously attempt to mold the child in strict concordance with traditional sex-role standards responded to the pressures of the extrafamilial environment. The aggressive girls learned to inhibit direct expression of overt aggressive and sexual behavior; the dependent boys gradually placed inhibition on urges toward dependent overtures to others.

Moreover, the occurrence of derivatives of child behavior was related to the sex-role appropriateness of the childhood response. Passivity among boys predicted noncompetitiveness, sexual anxiety, and social apprehension in adult men, but not direct dependent overtures to parents or love objects. A tendency toward rage reactions in young girls predicted intellectual competitiveness, masculine interests, and dependency conflict in adult women, but not direct expression of aggression. It appears that when a childhood behavior is congruent with traditional sex-role characteristics, it is likely to be predictive of phenotypically similar behaviors in adulthood. When it conflicts with sex-role standards, the relevant motive is more likely to find expression in theoretically consistent substitute behaviors that are socially more acceptable than the original response. In sum, the individual's desire to mold his overt behavior in concordance with the culture's definition of sex-appropriate responses is a major determinant of the patterns of continuity and discontinuity in his development.

Not all of the childhood reactions displayed long-term continuity. Compulsivity and irrational fears during childhood were not predictive of similar responses during adulthood. Moreover, task persistence and excessive irritability during the first three years of life showed no relation to phenotypically similar behaviors during later childhood.

However, when a response displayed long-term stability, it was likely to be congruent with sex-typed behavior standards. The relevance of sex-role identification in directing behavioral choices is supported by investigations indicating that the child begins to differentiate the culture's definition of masculine and feminine characteristics and activities very early in development. Hartup and Zook (1960) have reported that even 3-year-olds are aware of the interests and objects that comprise the exterior decor of males and females in this culture. Other investigators (Kagan, 1956b; Kagan and Lemkin, 1960c; Kagan, Hosken and Watson, 1961b; Gardner, 1947) have reported that children from 5 to 10 years of age view the male, in relation to the female, as more competent, more aggressive, and more fear arousing, but less nurturant. The belief that aggressive behavior is more appropriate for males than for females is apparently acquired early in development and no doubt contributes to the girls' suppression of overt aggressive responses.

Osgood's (1957) work with the semantic differential suggests that adults categorize most objects and qualities with respect to their position on three dimensions: good-bad, potent-impotent, and active-passive. The qualities that define the potency and activity demensions resemble, in large measure, the stereotyped conceptions of male and female sex-typed traits. For example, the adjectives *large, strong, loud, heavy, bass, rough,* and *rugged* have the highest factor loadings on the potency factor. The adjectives *agitated, sharp, ferocious, tense, hot, angular, active,* and *fast* have the highest loadings on the activity factor. The above sets of adjectives are more commonly applied to males, whereas their polar opposites are typically attributed to females. Aggressive behavior is closely related to the potent and activity dimensions, whereas passive-dependent behavior is allied with impotence and inactivity.

Comprehension of the world is much like the game of twenty questions, with the child attempting to understand new experiences through successive categorizations from broad to narrow labels. It would appear that the masculine or feminine quality of an activity or object is one of the first questions implicitly asked by the child. Having determined the answer to this question, his behavior toward it (i.e., approach or avoidance) will depend on his sex-role identification.

The universe of appropriate behaviors for males and females is delineated early in development, and it is difficult for the·child to cross these culturally given frontiers without considerable conflict and tension.

One of us recalls a conversation between a female college student (*S*) and his 3½-year-old daughter (*D*).

> *D:* "What are you studying?"
> *S:* "Psychology, for your daddy."
> *D:* "Are you going to be a psychologist?"
> *S:* "Yes."
> *D:* "Are you going to be a mother?"
> *S:* "Yes, I think so."
> *D:* (After a puzzled pause) "Well, you can't be a psychologist and a mother too."

Social-class membership is an additional variable of constraint with respect to the specific sex-role values adopted by the child. Certain behaviors (e.g., interest in art and music) would be more acceptable to middle-class than to lower-class males, and vocational aspirations are, of course, highly dependent on social-class position. Thus knowledge of the sex and social class of a child allows one to make an unusually large number of predictions about his future interests, goals, vocational choice, and dependent, aggressive, sexual, and mastery behaviors. The behavioral face that is typically exposed to the social environment derives much of its topography from the cultural rules for sex and social class appropriate behaviors.

SEX-ROLE IDENTIFICATION AS A GOVERNOR OF BEHAVIOR

The preceding discussion places the construct of sex-role identification in a central position in directing the selective adoption and maintenance of several behavior domains. The expression of aggression, competitiveness, passivity, dependency, or sexuality is determined, in part, by the individual's assessment of the congruence of the behavior with traditional sex-role standards. For many individuals are motivated to behave in a way that is congruent with a hypothetical ego ideal or idealized model that embodies the essential qualities of masculinity or femininity.

This motive—like Festinger's (1957) construct of cognitive dissonance vs. consonance—locates both the goal state as well as the incentive conditions in the cognitive system of the individual rather than in the outside world. The motive paradigm chosen by psychologists in the behavioral tradition is derived from the hunger, thirst, pain model used with animals. In this model, the conditions that create motives (or drives) as well as the reward stimuli that gratify motives are defined primarily in terms of external stimulus events (e.g., frustration, rejection, or loss of loved one as motive arousing conditions; perception of injury in another or receipt of love as goal states).

We do not reject the usefulness or validity of this orientation. It seems necessary, however, to acknowledge the relevance of a need—perhaps unique to humans—to act and to believe in ways that are congruent with previously established standards. The incentive and goal stimuli for this motive are not always external events but evaluations of the match between a belief or proposed response and an internalized standard. Each individual has a cognitive picture of the person he would like to be and the goal states he would like to command—an idealized model of himself. Any behavior or belief that increases the discrepancy between the individual's evaluation of himself and his idealized model provokes anxiety and is likely to be shunned; any behavior that decreases the discrepancy between the evaluation of self and model is rewarding and is likely to be practiced.

It would appear that the desire to be an *ideal male* or *ideal female*, as defined by the individual, comprises an essential component of everyman's model. Thus the position of a response on a cognitive dimension ranging from *highly masculine* to *highly feminine* is a primary determinant of its acceptability and, therefore, of its probability of occurrence.

THE EARLY SCHOOL YEARS AS A CRITICAL PERIOD

The continuity between child and adult behavior generally became manifest during the first four years of school. This relation was clearest for the behavior of withdrawal (for women), involvement in task mastery, social spontaneity, and degree of adoption of traditional sex-typed interests.

The poorer predictive power of behavior during the preschool years suggests that developments during the age period 6 to 10 induce important changes in the child's behavioral organization. The primary events of this period include (a) identification with parents and the concomitant attempt to adopt the values and overt responses of the parent, (b) the realization that mastery of intellective skills is both a cultural requirement as well as a source of satisfaction, and (c) the encounter with the peer group. The latter experience forces the child to accommodate, to some degree, to the values and evaluations made by peers. For some children, peer experiences strengthen patterns of dominance, social spontaneity, and positive self-evaluation. For others, peer rejection and a perception of marked deviation from peer-valued attributes lead to social anxiety, social submission, and a sense of ineffectiveness. Some children in the latter group develop compensatory domains of competence not involving peer interactions. Those who are unable to do so continue to anticipate failure when faced with task or social challenges.

It would appear that, for some children, the first four years of contact with the school and peer environments (i.e., during ages 6 to 10) crystallize behavioral tendencies that are maintained through young adulthood.

The present findings argue that those children who display intense strivings for mastery during the early years of school are likely to maintain this behavioral posture. The strategy of selecting bright, highly motivated fourth graders for special educational programs implicitly assumes that these children will not suddenly cease to exert efforts at task mastery. The results of this study support this assumption.

However, these data also suggest that withdrawal from anticipated task failure, among girls especially, grows rapidly during the early school years, and remedial or therapeutic intervention should be applied earlier in the curriculum than is now the case.

BEHAVIOR AND MOTIVES

These conclusions about developmental continuities refer primarily to *behaviors*, not to *motives*. It is not suggested, for example, that the lack of relation between child and adult dependent behavior for men implies no continuity of dependency motivation. The longitudinal material did not allow for the reliable assessment of purely motivational constructs, and we have tried to avoid stating conclusions about motive states. This is an unfortunate lacuna but an unavoidable one. The difficulty in assessing motivational variables from overt behavior is not merely a function of the inhibiting influence of motive-related conflict and anxiety upon expression of goal-related behavior. The evidence presented in Chapters Four and Six indicated that aggressive or sexual behavior in boys and men might occur in the service of strengthening the individual's sex-role identification rather than be directed toward goal states traditionally regarded as endpoints for an aggressively or sexually motivated act. Thus absence as well as presence of certain forms of aggressive or sexual behavior are ambiguous as indexes of motive intensity. The valid assessment of motive constructs is one of the most perplexing and exasperating problems facing contemporary psychology and one that may not be solved until we discover lawful relations between the child's history of social experiences and his behavior. It is hoped that the results from this project are a small step in that direction.

SEX DIFFERENCES IN PATTERNS OF RELATIONSHIPS

A frequent but not always welcome finding in psychological research involves sex differences in the pattern of correlations among similar or identical variables. We found many such differences in our material.

There were striking sex differences in ease of recognition of the tachistoscopically presented scenes and in scores on some of the self-rating scales. Moreover, delayed recognition of the dependency scenes was related to independent indexes of conflict for men but not for women. Delayed recognition of aggressive scenes showed the opposite pattern. Independent indexes of aggressive conflict predicted delayed recognition for women but not for men.

The intercorrelations among the interview variables yielded dramatic sex differences. For women, for example, dependency on love object and parents was positively associated, but each was independent of dependency on friends. For men, however, dependency on love object was unrelated to parental dependency but positively associated with dependency on friends. Competitiveness, retaliation, and anger arousal were all positively intercorrelated for the adult men. For the women, on the other hand, competitiveness was independent of both retaliation and anger arousal.

One of the clearest examples of the divergent meanings of phenotypically similar traits occurred with the correlations involving intellectual mastery (interview variable 35). Our intellectually oriented men, in contrast to the intellectual women, were less competitive, more likely to withdraw to stress. The differences between the correlations for the men and women for competitiveness and withdrawal were both significant (p < .01).

Dependency, aggression, sexuality, and achievement conflict differentially with the standards for sex-typed behaviors and, therefore, are in different hierarchical organizations for the sexes. Thus we should not expect the intercorrelations among these related behaviors to be similar for men and women. It is suggested, furthermore, that many phenotypically similar behaviors may be *of different psychological significance for males and females*. To illustrate, aggressive behavior in a group of school-age children (hitting, pushing, verbal taunts) is typically regarded as evidence of hostile motivation. However, these responses could be the product of different motives in boys and girls. Traditional sex-typed values regard some forms of aggression as a critical attribute of masculinity. Thus boys who are striving to identify with a masculine ideal will be prompted to push a peer, to grab a toy, to jeer at a teacher. These behaviors may not necessarily reflect hostile needs but may be the child's way of announcing to the social environment, "I am a boy, I am capable of executing those behaviors that help to define my role." Thus a boy may employ a shove or verbal taunt as a way of greeting a peer—a "hello" if you wish. *This use of aggression in a girl is unlikely.* For this reason, aggressive behavior with peers is probably a more accurate index of hostile motivation in girls than in boys.

Similarly, initiation of sexual behavior among adolescents and adult males is often used as a way of supporting a traditional masculine identification. The positive relation, for men, between traditional masculine interests in early childhood and frequency of sexual behavior in adolescence and adulthood supports this statement. Women are less likely to initiate sexual behavior as a means of strengthening their self-image as women.

This discussion suggests a more general statement. Overt aggressive, sexual, dependent, and mastery behaviors can serve different purposes (i.e., have different motivational bases for men and women). This is not an original conclusion, for psychology has long acknowledged that the same class of behavior in two individuals may have different causes. But we have occasionally ignored this axiom in interpreting empirical data.

It is more difficult to explain the sex differences in intercorrelation patterns obtained from test scores (e.g., perceptual performance, projective tests, etc.) that are not related directly to sex-typed behaviors. On the basis of what we know of sex-typed characteristics, it is possible that the hierarchy of motives in a psychological testing situation differs for the sexes. Let us assume, for example, that females are generally more concerned with gaining the examiner's acceptance, giving socially appropriate responses, and avoiding failure, in the broad sense of the term. Males are probably more concerned with the accuracy of their responses and with displaying their cognitive skills and efficiency at analyzing conceptual materials. These sex differences in orientation to examiner, approach to test material, and motive for accurate performance might lead to similar responses which were provoked by different motives and, consequently, were of different psychological significance.

For example, females who perform well on problems requiring analysis and complex reasoning tend to reject a traditional feminine identification. Males with high performance scores, on the other hand, do *not* reject a masculine identification. Thus men and women with masculine interests and values achieve high scores on complex intellective problems (Milton, 1957). Since degrees of identification with one's sex-role have implications for a variety of behavioral dispositions, we would not except the correlations between problem-solving ability and scores derived from personality tests to be similar for the sexes.

One tentative conclusion is suggested. It may be unwise to pool data for males and females without first examining the data for sex differences. This means more than merely computing means and standard deviations, for many of our variables showed no significant differences in these two parameters *but yielded different patterns of intercorrelations*. If the data had been pooled, many of the relationships between child and adult behavior would have been negligible. For the positive correlation for one sex would have been diluted by the zero order relationship for the other. It is likely that many studies in the literature or in a file drawer would have led the investigator to draw different conclusions if separate analyses had been made for males and females.

REFERENCES

Festinger, L. *A theory of Cognitive Dissonance.* Evanston: Row, Peterson, 1957.

Gardner, R. L. Analysis of Children's attitudes toward fathers. *Journal of Genetic Psychology,* 1947, 70, 3–28.

Hartup, W. W., & Zook, E. A. Sex-role preferences in three- and four-year-old children. *Journal of Consulting Psychology,* 1960, 24, 420–426.

Kagan, J. The child's perception of the parent. *Journal of Abnormal and Social Psychology,* 1956b, 53, 257–258.

Kagan, J., Hasken, B., & Watson, S. The child's symbolic conceptualization of the parents. *Child Development,* 1961b, 32, 625–636.

Kagan, J., & Lemkin, J. The child's differential perception of parental attributes. *Journal of Abnormal Psychology,* 1960c, 61, 440–447.

Milton, G. A. The effects of sex role identification upon problem solving skill. *Journal of Abnormal and Social Psychology,* 1957, 55, 208–212.

Osgood, C. E., Suci, G. J., & Tannenbaum, P. H. *The Measurement of Meaning,* Urbana: University of Illinois Press, 1957.

chapter eight

Moral Development

8.1 Introduction

The study of moral development in children involves tracing the processes by which the child internalizes a set of culturally defined norms of social conduct. Traditionally, the end product of this development was described as a conscience or superego. Discussions of moral development can be conveniently divided into three parts—behavioral, affective, and cognitive aspects of morality. The behavioral aspect has generally referred to the child's ability to resist temptation in the absence of external surveillance. The affective aspect focuses on the emotional reaction of the child to transgression. The existence of internalized norms is inferred from emotional reactions such as guilt which may follow violation of these standards. Much of the research in this area has been influenced by psychoanalytic theory. The third approach to moral development has been judgmental or cognitive; the stress has been on tracing developmentally children's use and interpretation of rules for judging the correctness of behavior in various situations involving moral conflict. Piaget's pioneering studies are the main inspiration for research into the judgmental aspects of morality. Each of these facets of moral development is represented in the papers of this section.

In support of the assumption that learning plays an important role in shaping moral conduct, Walters, Parke, and Cane (1965) report the results of a recent experimental examination of the effects of punishment and imitation on resistance to temptation in young children. The findings indicate that punishment can affect the degree to which children resist temptation, but the effectiveness of punishment is contingent on its timing; punishment delivered at the initiation of a deviant response sequence is more effective than punishment occurring after the deviation has been completed. However, timing is only one of a variety of parameters which may affect the operation of punishment.

A variable of considerable importance is the verbal rationale or explanation which accompanies the punishment. Aronfreed (1965), using an experimental paradigm somewhat similar to that of Walters, Parke, and Cane, provided subjects with a brief explanation for not handling the taboo toy at the same time that they were punished. The addition of the verbal rationale significantly increased response inhibition in the children he used as subjects. More important, however, was the impact that the explanation had on the effectiveness of early- and late-timed punishment. When the late-timed punishment was accompanied by a verbal rationale, the late punishment was as effective an inhibitor as an early-timed punishment. These results suggest that cognitive factors play an important role in children's resistance to temptation. The laboratory findings are supported by field studies which have yielded positive relationships between parental use of reasoning as a preferred technique of discipline and nonaggressive, conforming behavior among children. Sears, Maccoby, and Levin (1957) reported a positive correlation between maternal use of reasoning and the development of conscience in children. Similarly, Gleuck and Gleuck (1950) found that parents of delinquent boys made relatively little use of reasoning in comparison to parents of nondelinquent boys.

In another study of the effects of punishment on resistance to temptation, Parke and Walters (1967) found that the intensity of punishment is important; high intensity punishment produces greater resistance to deviation than low intensity punishment. In the same study, these investigators examined the effects of the relationship between the agent and recipient of punishment and found that subjects who were punished by an agent with whom they had experienced positive interaction showed greater resistance to deviation than subjects who had had only impersonal contact with the punishment agent. (Studies by Zigler and his colleagues have found the relationship factor to be important in studies of positive social reinforcement as well. See the section on social reinforcement.) The studies clearly indicate that punishment is an effective way of controlling children's resistance to deviation.

In addition to punishment, imitation may play an influential role in the development of self-control in children. A number of investigators have shown that exposure to a model breaking a prohibition increases the probability that the observer will deviate (Blake, 1958; Ross, 1962). As the Walters, Parke, and Cane (1965) study indicates, the consequences associated with the model's deviant behavior are important determinants of the extent to which the observer will likewise deviate. When no apparent consequence or a rewarding outcome ensues, the observer is likely to break the prohibition and touch the forbidden toys; but when the model is punished, the observer tends not to deviate. The combined findings of the Walters *et al.* study suggest that punishment, both direct and vicarious, is an important determinant of resistance to deviation in children.

Certain individual differences may be important in determining the child's resistance to temptation. Since most resistance to temptation situations offer the child an immediate gratification if he violates a prohibition, one of the personality factors that is relevant to high resistance to deviation is the capacity to defer gratification. In the next paper, Mischel and Gilligan (1964) report an experimental test of the proposed relationship between the willingness to delay gratification and resistance to temptation. The experiment is one of a series carried out by Mischel and concerned with the correlates of the capacity to defer an immediate reward in favor of a delayed, but more valued, gratification. On the basis of a series of realistic choices between small immediate (for example, a small candy bar) and larger delayed (a large candy bar delivered in one week) alternatives, subjects are classified into high and low delay groups. In this experiment, children of each type were placed in an experimentally controlled shooting gallery game in which they were required to cheat by falsifying their scores in order to accumulate sufficient points for a prize. Subjects who preferred delayed gratification cheated less than subjects preferring immediate rewards, a finding which confirms the Mischel and Gilligan hypothesis. This result is consistent with Mischel's (1961) earlier finding that Trinidadian delinquents exhibited a greater preference for immediate rewards than a nondelinquent and socially responsible group of control boys. As Block and Martin (1955) noted, tolerance for delay as indexed by "ego control" is also predictive of other social behaviors such as aggression. In their study, subjects high in ego control reacted less aggressively when frustrated than subjects weak in this characteristic.

Another determinant of the resistance to temptation examined by Mischel and Gilligan was the strength of the motivation to obtain the prohibited gratification. In their experiment, prizes in the form of badges signifying proficiency in the task were available for accumulating a large number of points in the shooting game. Since subjects with a high need for achievement would be more motivated to win such a prize than subjects with a low need for achievement, it was predicted that the former would cheat more in this situation. As expected, when cheating was instrumental to achievement, the achievement-oriented subjects resisted temptation much less than low achievement-oriented children.

This finding concerning the role of incentives in resisting temptation is reminiscent of the pioneering work of Hartshorne and May (1928), who were among the first investigators to give explicit recognition to the role of situational factors in studies of deviant behavior. Their pioneering work indicated that different situations elicit different proportions of individuals yielding to temptation. They argued that consistency in resistance to deviation from one context to another was due mainly to the similarity of external cues in the different situations. Confirmation of the importance of situational cues in eliciting deviant responses has recently been provided by Nelson, Grinder, and Mutterer (1967). Such factors as the risk of detection and the attractiveness of the incentive are clearly important. Moreover, an individual incentive was found to produce more cheating than a collective or group prize. However, their data clearly indicated that situational factors alone could not account for cheating patterns. Both individual differences and situational elicitors must be considered in studies of resistance to temptation.

Some additional observations by Mischel concerning the origins of the capacity for delay of reward suggest that parental models may be important in the acquisition of delay of gratification patterns. For example, Mischel (1958) found that children from the Trinidadian Negro subculture, in which immediate self-reward is the prevailing gratification pattern, displayed a greater preference for immediate rewards than children of Trinidadian Indians, who characteristically exhibited self-denying delayed-gratification behavior. More explicit evidence that social models contribute to the development of these patterns is provided by the experimental investigation by Bandura and Mischel (1965). Children were exposed to a model who exhibited delay behavior that was opposite to the child's preferred pattern. Exposure to a model produced substantial modifications in the preferences of the children as indexed by a test following the observation of the model. Moreover, when the children were retested one month later, evidence of the model-produced shifts was still present. Social models, then, are clearly effective in modifying not only resistance to temptation (Walters, Parke, & Cane) but gratification patterns as well. As in the case of resistance to deviation, social models, in conjunction with directly experienced rewards and punishments, are probably highly effective means of acquiring and maintaining delay of gratification behavior.

Instead of focusing on the prevention of deviant activity, many researchers have examined the reactions of the child following a transgression. Traditionally, resistance to deviation and the response to transgression have been viewed as indices of the same end product —a conscience or superego. A person with a well-developed conscience was expected to show high resistance to deviation and when he did submit to temptation, to exhibit relatively severe guilt. In psychoanalytic theory it was assumed that the expectation of guilt prevented deviant behavior. However, recent research has shown that these two indices have different parental antecedents and are not highly correlated. Knowledge of guilt reactions is of little aid in predicting resistance to temptation.

One of the primary purposes of the Hoffman and Saltzstein (1967) paper, included in this section, is to isolate those parental disciplinary practices that are associated with a highly developed guilt reaction following transgression. These investigators correlated the child's guilt response, as assessed from a story completion test, with three different types of discipline. Power-assertive discipline is characterized by the use of physical punishment and material deprivation. Nonassertive techniques were classified as love withdrawal, whereby the parent gives direct but nonphysical expression of disapproval, or as induction, a technique in which the parent focuses on the painful consequences of the child's act for the parents and others. The use of an inductive disciplinary approach was highly related to the presence of guilt following violation of a standard and also to other indices of moral development, such as confession, acceptance of responsibility, consideration for other children, and internalized moral judgments. Power assertion, however, tended to be negatively related to guilt and other indices of moral behavior, while love withdrawal produced few significant relationships. Interestingly, the mother's disciplinary practices were mainly responsible for the results, suggesting that the father may be less important than the mother for moral development.

In addition to tracing the child-rearing antecedents of guilt and other indices of moral development, some recent attempts have been made to experimentally analyze the reinforcement conditions controlling the operation of specific reactions to transgression. Underlying this approach is the assumption that there are important differences not only among various responses to deviation, but in their developmental antecedents as well. Support for this view is evidenced by Aronfreed's (1961) finding that children give a wide variety of different responses to a hypothetical transgression, including confession, apology, self-criticism, and reparation. Moreover, social class and sex-role differences are associated with different reaction patterns. Middle class children, for example, tend to use self-criticism more often than working class subjects, and girls use confession as a response to transgression more than boys.

In his experimental study in this section, Aronfreed (1963) demonstrated that the reinforcement conditions affecting children's use of two moral responses, self-criticism and reparation, were different. Self-critical responses are more likely to be made when the socialization agent provides the child with explicit standards of evaluation than when cognitive structure is minimized. Reparation, however, tends to occur when the child, rather than the agent, has active control over the corrective or punitive consequences of transgression.

In a later experiment concerning the origins of self-criticism, Aronfreed (1964) has shown that the timing of punishment plays an important role in the establishment of the tendency to criticize one's behavior following a transgression. According to Aronfreed's analysis, the critical determinant in the acquisition of a self-critical response is the presentation of a critical label at the point of punishment termination. The child tends to utilize the critical label following subsequent transgression because of the anxiety-reducing cue function that the label previously acquired through its association with punishment termination. Therefore the timing of punishment plays an important role not only in producing resistance to temptation, but in the acquisition of responses to transgression as well; the timing of punishment onset is more important for the induction of response inhibition, and punishment termination is more vital for the acquisition of self-critical responses.

The general implication of Aronfreed's research is that different reactions to transgression "should be treated as distinct moral phenomena and not as equivalent reflections of an underlying unitary phenomenon such as "conscience" (Aronfreed, 1961, p. 239).

The third approach to moral development has stressed the cognitive or judgmental aspects of morality. The aim of research in this area has been to delineate the changes occurring with age in the child's understanding and interpretation of moral rules. "In contrast to the 'superego strength' view of moral learning as a matter of increased strength of conscience responses, the developmental approach views moral learning in terms of age-related sequences of changes by which moral attitudes emerge from qualitatively different premoral attitudes and concepts" (Kohlberg, 1963, p. 313).

Piaget's *The Moral Judgment of the Child* (1948) has primarily been responsible for the recent research on the cognitive aspects of morality. According to Piaget, two clearcut stages of moral development—the heteronomous and autonomous stages—can be distinguished and 7 years is the approximate dividing age. In the first or heteronomous stage, two defects in cognitive functioning limit the young child's understanding of moral rules. Because of the first limitation—"realism"—the child is unable to distinguish subjective and objective phenomena and hence views adult rules as fixed external entities. The second defect—"egocentrism"—leads the child to confuse his own and other person's perspectives; the result is a failure to regard moral rules as relative to various individuals and purposes. Children at each of the two moral stages differ in their definitions of right and wrong and in their conception of justice. In the heteronomous stage, for example, children judge the severity of an act in terms of the amount of physical damage and disregard the intentionality of the action. Only in the autonomous stage does intent replace consequence as the basis for judgment. Similarly the younger child believes in immanent justice rather than in naturalistic causality and favors expiative over restitutive justice. Subsequent tests of Piaget's two-stage theory have shown at least that some aspects of his moral judgment categories form genuine developmental dimensions in that they "increase regularly with age, regardless of the child's nationality in Western cultures, his social class, his religion, or the particular stories or situations about which the child is questioned" (Kohlberg, 1964, p. 398). These data argue against a learning theory interpretation of moral judgments as products of direct cultural instruction. A learning theory approach may be more appropriate for explaining moral conduct data, which in contrast to moral judgments, vary greatly with situational and background differences.

The most extensive non-Piagetian account of moral judgment has been undertaken by Kohlberg (1963a, b; 1964). This theorist differs from Piaget in viewing moral development as an extended and complex process rather than a single step from heteronomous to autonomous morality. Instead of merely two stages of moral judgment, Kohlberg's investigations have revealed six distinct stages, which are assumed to form an invariant sequence.

Secondly, Kohlberg's analysis assumes that the passage from one stage to the next involves an integration and displacement of modes of thought associated with earlier stages. Support for these assumptions has been provided by the recent experimental work of Turiel

(1966), in which subjects of a known stage of moral development were exposed to examples of moral reasoning either one stage below, one stage above, or two stages above their present stage of moral development. The finding that subjects assimilated moral reasoning associated with one stage higher than their own more readily than two stages higher lends support to Kohlberg's fixed sequence notion. Moreover, subjects accepted moral judgments one stage higher more readily than moral judgments one stage lower than their own; this finding supports Kohlberg's second assumption concerning the integration of lower stages into higher stages of thought.

REFERENCES

Aronfreed, J. The nature, variety, and social patterning of moral responses to transgression. *Journal of Abnormal and Social Psychology,* 1961, **63,** 223–241.

Aronfreed, J. The effect of experimental socialization paradigms upon two moral responses to transgression. *Journal of Abnormal and Social Psychology,* 1963, **66,** 437–448.

Aronfreed, J. The origin of self-criticism. *Psychological Review,* 1964, **41,** 193–218.

Aronfreed, J. Punishment learning and internalization: Some parameters of reinforcement and cognition. Paper presented at the Biennial Meeting of the Society for Research in Child Development, Minneapolis, March, 1965.

Bandura, A., & Mischel, W. Modification of self-imposed delay of reward through exposure to live and symbolic models. *Journal of Personality and Social Psychology,* 1965, **2,** 698–705.

Blake, R. R. The other person in the situation. In R. Tagiuri & L. Petrullo (Eds.), *Person perception and interpersonal behavior.* Stanford: Stanford University Press, 1958. Pp. 229–242.

Block, J., & Martin, B. Predicting the behavior of children under frustration. *Journal of Abnormal and Social Psychology,* 1957, **51,** 281–285.

Gleuck, S., & Gleuck, E. *Unraveling juvenile delinquency.* Cambridge: Harvard University Press, 1950.

Hoffman, M. L., & Saltzstein, H. D. Parent discipline and the child's moral development. *Journal of Personality and Social Psychology,* 1967, **5,** 45–57.

Kohlberg, S. L. Moral development and identification. In H. Stevenson (Ed.), *Child Psychology: 72nd Yearbook of the National Society for the Study of Education.* Chicago: University of Chicago Press, 1963(a). Pp. 277–332.

Kohlberg, L. The development of children's orientations toward a moral order. I. Sequence in the development of moral thought. *Vita Humana,* 1963, **6,** 11–33 (b).

Kohlberg, L. The development of children's orientations toward a moral order. II: Social experience, social conduct, and the development of moral thought. *Vita Humana,* 1964, Vol. 7.

Mischel, W.   Preference for delayed reinforcement: An experimental study of a cultural observation. *Journal of Abnormal and Social Psychology,* 1958, **56,** 57–61.

Mischel, W.   Preference for delayed reinforcement and social responsibility. *Journal of Abnormal and Social Psychology,* 1961, **62,** 1–7.

Mischel, W., & Gilligan, C.   Delay of gratification, motivation for the prohibited gratification, and responses to temptation. *Journal of Abnormal and Social Psychology,* 1964, **69,** 411–417.

Nelsen, E. A., Grinder, R. E., & Mutterer, M. L.   Sources of variance in behavioral measures of honesty in temptation situations. Unpublished manuscript, University of Wisconsin, 1967.

Parke, R. D., & Walters, R. H.   Some factors influencing the efficacy of punishment training for inducing response inhibition. *Monograph of the Society for Research in Child Development,* 1967, **32,** No. 1 (Serial No. 109.)

Piaget, J.   *The moral judgment of a child.* Glencoe, Ill.: Free Press, 1948. (First published in French, 1932.)

Ross, S. A.   The effect of deviant and nondeviant models on the behavior of preschool children in a temptation situation. Unpublished doctoral dissertation, Stanford University, 1962.

Sears, R. R., Maccoby, E. E., & Levin, H.   *Patterns of child rearing.* Evanston: Row, Peterson and Co., 1957.

Turiel, E.   An experimental test of the sequentiality of developmental stages in the child's moral judgments. *Journal of Personality and Social Psychology,* 1966, **3,** 611–618.

Walters, R. H., Parke, R. D., & Cane, V. A.   Timing of punishment and the observation of consequences to others as determinants of response inhibition. *Journal of Experimental Child Psychology,* 1965, **2,** 10–30.

SUPPLEMENTARY READING

Aronfreed, J.   The concept of internalization. In D. A. Goslin & D. C. Glass (Eds.), *Handbook on socialization theory.* New York: Rand-McNally, 1968.

Bandura, A., & Walters, R. H.   *Social learning and personality development.* New York: Holt, Rinehart and Winston, 1963. Pp. 162–223.

Becker, W. C.   Consequences of different kinds of parental discipline. In L. W. Hoffman & M. L. Hoffman (Eds.), *Review of child development research,* Vol. I. New York: Russell Sage, 1964. Pp. 169–208.

Kohlberg, L.   Development of moral character and moral ideology. In L. W. Hoffman & M. L. Hoffman (Eds.), *Review of child development research,* Vol. I. New York: Russell Sage, 1964. Pp. 383–431.

Walters, R. H., & Parke, R. D.   The influence of punishment and related disciplinary techniques and social behavior of children: Theory and empirical findings. In B. A. Maher (Ed.), *Progress in experimental personality research,* Vol. IV. New York: Academic Press, 1968. Pp. 179–228.

8.2 Timing of Punishment and the Observation of Consequences to Others as Determinants of Response Inhibition [1]

Richard H. Walters, Ross D. Parke, and Valerie A. Cane

The role of punishment in the socialization of children has received considerable emphasis in theoretical discussions but has seldom been explored in laboratory studies. Perhaps partly for humanitarian reasons and perhaps partly because ethical and practical considerations limit the range of intensities of punishment that may be used in investigations with human subjects, psychologists have readily accepted the "legend" (Solomon, 1964) that punishment is an extremely ineffective means of controlling human behavior. In this respect most parents have probably been wiser than the "experts"; the renewed interest in punishment on the part of psychologists and the more cautious approach taken in recent theoretical discussions of this topic (e.g., Church, 1963; Solomon, 1964) are therefore welcome developments. The available research evidence strongly suggests that punishment may have very diverse (and sometimes very dramatic) effects, and that these effects are dependent on such parameters as the intensity and timing of punishment, the sequencing and scheduling of rewarding and punishing events, the strength and nature of the punished response, and the relative status of the agent and the recipient of punishment (Aronfreed, 1964; Bandura and Walters, 1963; Church, 1963; Martin, 1963; Mowrer, 1960a,b; Solomon and Brush, 1958 Solomon, 1964).

The purpose of this study was to investigate the effects of one of these parameters, the timing of punishment, on the resistance to deviation of children who, following direct punishment training, were exposed to a deviant model. Since the consequences of the responses to a social model have a considerable influence on the extent to which the model's behavior is imitated (Bandura, Ross, and Ross, 1963; Walters, Leat, and Mezei, 1963), consequences were varied in such a way as to permit an investigation, in a

[1] This study was supported by the Public Health research grant 605-5-293 of the (Canadian) National Health Grants Program, the Ontario Mental Health Foundation grant 42, and the Defense Research Board of Canada grant 9401-24. The authors are indebted to the Superintendent of Public Schools of Waterloo and to the Principals and Staff of Northdale and Brighton Schools. Thanks are due to Patsie Hutton and Keith Barnes for assisting as observers.

Reprinted with abridgement from *Journal of Experimental Child Psychology*, 1965, **2**, 10–30, by permission of the authors and Academic Press.

single experimental design, of some of the effects of both directly and vicariously experienced punishment.

TIMING OF PUNISHMENT

A theoretical basis for predicting the effects of timing of punishment has been offered by Mowrer (1960a,b). According to Mowrer, the execution of a prohibited act is accompanied by a sequence of response-produced cues, each providing sensory feedback. A punishment may be presented at any point during this sequence and result in a relatively direct association of a fear-motivated avoidance response with the response-produced cues occurring at the time that the punishment is administered. If the punishment occurs only when the deviant act has been completed, fear will be most strongly associated with the stimuli produced by the agent's preparatory responses. In contrast, punishment that occurs at or near the time that an act is initiated will result in a relatively strong association between the agent's preparatory responses and the emotion of fear; in this case, even the initiation of the deviant act will arouse fear that motivates incompatible prosocial or avoidance responses. Once an act has been initiated, secondary positive reinforcers associated with the instrumental behavior involved in the commission of the act may serve to maintain and facilitate the response sequence and thus to some extent counteract the inhibitory effect of punishment. Consequently, it may be argued, the earlier a punishment occurs in a deviant response sequence, the more effectively will it prevent the subsequent commission of the act.

Mowrer's account perhaps overemphasizes both the role of kinesthetic feedback and that of the emotion of fear, and underemphasizes the part played by perceptual-cognitive factors that are associated with the functioning of distance receptors. Visual and auditory cues accompanying the commission of a deviant act may be as closely associated with punishment experiences as kinesthetic feedback; since such cues are far more readily discriminable, they probably also play a more important role in the maintenance of behavioral control. This consideration does not, however, change the basic prediction generated by Mowrer's theory.

HYPOTHESIS 1. *Children who receive punishment as they begin to perform a class of responses will subsequently show greater resistance to deviation than children who receive punishment only on completion of responses of this class, provided that the deviant behavior falls in the same general category as the responses made during the punishment training session.*

CONSEQUENCES OF RESPONSES TO MODELS

Previous investigations (Bandura, 1965; Bandura *et al.*, 1963; Walters *et al.*, 1963; Walters and Parke, 1964) have demonstrated that the observation of a social model who receives punishment for a class of responses leads to response inhibition in the observer. The consequence of the model's response apparently serves as a cue signifying to the observer the nonpermissibility of the punished response within a given social context (Walters and Parke, 1964). Similarly, the observation of a reward to a model may signify the permissibility of a response class even if the rewarded response has previously been prohibited for the observer (Walters et al., 1963; Walters and Parke, 1964). Under some circumstances, the observation of a model's performing a prohibited or socially disapproved act (for example, aggression) with no adverse consequences to himself may suffice as a cue to the observer that the act may be performed (Walters and Llewellyn-Thomas, 1963); the inhibitions created in the observer may thus be overcome either by rewarding a model who performs the disapproved responses or simply by not punishing the model's behavior (Walters and Parke, 1964).

HYPOTHESIS 2. *Children who observe a model punished for acts that they have been prohibited from performing will show greater resistance to deviation than children who see a model rewarded or receive no punishment for these acts.*

METHOD

Subjects.   Eighty kindergarten and Grade 1 boys, with a mean age of 6 years, 5 months served as Ss. The boys were randomly assigned to one of eight conditions in a 2 × 4 factorial design involving two timing-of-punishment conditions (early vs. late punishment) and four film conditions. Under three of the four film conditions, the children were shown a colored film sequence depicting an interaction between a 6-year-old boy and a female adult who performed a mother role; the remainder of the children saw no film.

Equipment.   For the timing-of-punishment manipulations, the equipment and procedures were similar in some respects to those used by Aronfreed and Reber (1964). Nine pairs of toys (one attractive, one unattractive) were used in a series of training trials. One toy in each pair was large, well detailed, and well made, and of interest to boys (e.g., cars, guns, and trucks); the other toy in each pair was smaller, less detailed, and in some cases sex-inappropriate (e.g., toy dishes, a bracelet, and a plastic doll).

Three film-sequences, similar to those used by Walters and Parke (1964), were prepared for the film manipulations. The sequences were identical, except for the addition of "endings" to two of the films. Complete correspondence was ensured through the use of copies of an original edited sequence. The film showed an adult female, presumably a mother, indicate to a child through a single gesture that he should not play with toys that had been set on a nearby table; the adult then sat the child in a chair beside the table, gave him a book to read, and left the room. After her departure, the child put the book aside and proceeded to play with the prohibited toys.

Play continued for approximately 4 minutes. The play sequence displayed the child playing with a number of attractive toys similar to those used in the punishment-training sessions. . . .

Endings were added to two of the films. The reward-movie ending showed the adult return to the room, sit beside the child, hand him toys and play with him affectionately. For the punishment-movie ending, the adult, on returning, pulled the child up from the floor, where he was playing, snatched the toy from him, spanked him, and once again sat him on the chair with the book. In the no-consequences film, the mother did not re-enter. Because children are used to seeing sound-accompanied movies in school settings, a tape recording of background music was played during the showing of the films. The recording was identical for all children.

The children were tested in a mobile laboratory, divided into an experimental room and an observation room by a partition containing two one-way vision mirrors. A diagram of the experimental arrangements is provided in Fig. 1.

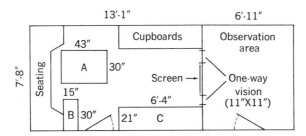

FIGURE 1. Experimental arrangements.

On Table A were displayed three rows of toys, three toys in each row. When S was seated at one end of the table, the first row of the toys was readily accessible to him, the toys in the second row were accessible if he stood up in front of the table, while the third row could be reached only if S walked around the table. A folding table (B) was used to display toys during the punishment-training session; when not in use, these toys were placed on Table C, which also held a Bolex 18-5 projector and a Uher 4000-S portable tape recorder.

Procedure

The E brought S from his classroom to the mobile laboratory. She interacted with him in a relaxed and friendly manner and informed him that he was about to play a game with her. If S had been assigned to a film condition, he was also told that he would be shown a movie.

Punishment training. The S was seated behind Table B and instructed as follows:

"I'm going to put some toys out here on the table. Each time I'm going to put down two toys, and here is what I want you to do. I want you to pick the toy that you would like to play with. I want you to pick it up, hold it, and think about it for a while. Be sure you pick it up, hold it, and think about it. Now, if I ask you, I want you to tell me what the toy is or what it is used for. Do you understand?"

After S indicated that he understood the nature of the task, E continued, "Now, some of these toys are for another boy, and you're not supposed to touch them. So if you touch a toy that is for the other boy, I'll tell you. O.K.?"

Following these instructions, E uncovered the toys on Table C and commenced the punishment training. On each of nine trials E placed a pair of toys before S. The order of presentation of pairs of toys was constant for all Ss, and the position of the attractive toy was consistently alternated over the nine training trials, so that it appeared at S's left on odd-numbered trials and on his right on even-numbered trials.

Each time S selected the attractive toy, E verbally punished him by saying, "No, that's for *the other boy*." For Ss in the early-punishment condition, E administered the punishment as S's hand neared the attractive toy, but before he touched it. As E spoke, she covered the forbidden toy and removed it from the table. The unattractive toy was left undisturbed for a few seconds to give S an opportunity to make the alternative choice. If he did so, he was asked to describe the toy. Almost all Ss immediately selected the unattractive toy when rebuked for choosing the attractive toy.

For Ss in the late-punishment condition, the punishment was presented only after S had picked up the attractive toy and held it for 2–3 seconds. The E took the toy from S's hand while administering the same rebuke as was used for early-punished Ss. Again S was given an opportunity to choose and describe the unattractive toy.

If, on any trial, S chose the unattractive toy first, E said, "What is it?" or "What is it used for?" Following S's description of the toy, E acknowledged the response by a simple "O.K." and removed both the toys from the table.

Resistance-to-deviation test. On completion of the punishment session the toys on Table C were covered. The S was then seated behind Table A, which contained three rows of toys, similar to, and in some cases identical with, those used in the punishment-training session. After removing the cloth covering these toys, E told all Ss, "These toys are *for the other boy* so you had better not touch them." If S was under a film condition, E added, "Now, I'm going to show you a movie." She then switched on the projector and the tape-recorded music. As soon as the movie had ended, E gave the next set of instructions. Ss under the no-film condition received these instructions immediately after being seated at Table A.

Then E said, "Before we play the game, I have to go and get something, so would you like to sit here and read this book while I am gone." (*E*, at this point, placed a dictionary on the table before *S*.) "I'm going to close the door when I go out so that nobody will come in and bother you. O.K.?"

Measures

An observer, who was seated behind the one-way vision screen, recorded *S*'s choices during the punishment-training session, thus providing a record of the number of punishments received by each *S*. In addition, during the test for resistance to deviation, the observer recorded on a specially prepared record sheet the times at which *S* touched and ceased to touch individual toys. The sheet was set up in such a way that, during the 15-minute period of *E*'s absence from the room, the observer's only task was to record times, read from a Heuer-Century Stopwatch, in the appropriate squares which designated specific toys.

From the observer's records, the following scores were calculated: the latency of *S*'s first deviant response, the number of times he deviated, and the total time for which he deviated. Weighted deviation scores were calculated in the following manner: a deviation involving one of the three most accessible toys was scored 1; a deviation involving one of the toys in the second row was scored 2; and *S*'s touching a toy in the third row was scored 3. A weighted-number-of-deviations and a weighted-time score were then obtained by multiplying the number of times *S* touched toys in each class, and the amount of time for which he handled them, by the appropriate weights. These scores had previously been employed by Walters *et al.* (1963) and Walters and Parke (1964). Since in both the earlier studies somewhat similar results were obtained with unweighted and weighted scores, only the weighted scores were utilized in this study. Weighted scores were preferred because they make use of more of the available information and reduce the number of ties in analyses based on ranking methods.

RESULTS

Reliability of measures

A second observer was present while 16 *S*s were tested. Rank-order correlation coefficients were used as indices of interrater reliability for the resistance-to-deviation measures. These correlations were 1.00, 1.00, and 0.94 for the latency, number of deviations, and duration of deviations, respectively. Reliability of scoring was above 0.94 for all three classes of responses made by *S* during the test for observational learning.

Punishment-training data

A 2 × 4 analysis of variance indicated that there were no significant differences among the eight groups of *S*s in respect to the number of punishments received ("incorrect" choices made) during the punishment-training

TABLE 1. Group Means and Medians on Three Indices of
Resistance to Deviation [a]

Punishment conditions	Model Rewarded		No Consequence		Model Punished		No Film	
	Mean	Median	Mean	Median	Mean	Median	Mean	Median
Early								
Latency (seconds)	590.1	750	333.2	144.5	697.0	900	624.5	900
Weighted deviations	5.2	1	3.7	4	2.5	0	2.9	0
Weighted duration	64.5 [b]	2.5	15.3	12.5	0.7	0	16.4	0
Late								
Latency (seconds)	269.0	71.5	345.6	270.5	543.1	576	299.3	141
Weighted deviations	7.4	4.5	6.8	5.5	2.7	1.5	6.2	4.5
Weighted duration	33.7	11	32.7	131	9.5	2	30.9	14

[a] $n = 10$ in each group.
[b] Mean $= 11.3$, excluding one extreme case.

session. Group differences in resistance to deviation cannot therefore be
attributed to this variable. The mean number of punishments received by
Ss under the early-punishment and late-punishment conditions were 4.1
and 3.8, respectively.

Over-all tests of predicted effects

The distributions of resistance-to-deviation data for some groups of Ss
were markedly skewed; consequently, Table 1 gives both group medians and

TABLE 2. Significance of Main and
Overall Effects [a]

A. Model effects (Kruskal-Wallis H-tests; $df = 3$)
   Latency: $H = 6.54$; $p < 0.10$
   Weighted deviations: $H = 8.86$; $p < 0.05$
   Weighted duration: $H = 8.93$; $p < 0.05$

B. Punishment effects (Mann-Whitney U-tests)
   Latency $z = 2.32$; $p < 0.02$
   Weighted deviations: $z = 2.67$; $p < 0.01$
   Weighted duration: $z = 2.27$; $p < 0.03$

C. Over-all effects (Kruskal-Wallis H-tests; $df = 7$)
   Latency: $H = 14.08$; $p < 0.05$
   Weighted deviations: $H = 16.74$; $p < 0.02$
   Weighted duration: $H = 14.69$; $p < 0.05$

[a] H and z corrected for ties.

group means for the latency, weighted-deviations, and weighted-duration indices.

Most differences were in predicted directions. Model-rewarded and no-consequence Ss deviated more quickly, more often, and for longer periods of time than did model-punished Ss. Differences between early-punishment and late-punishment Ss were remarkably consistent across all film conditions; under each condition, the early-punishment Ss showed greater resistance to deviation.

Table 2 reports the results of nonparametric tests of main effects; it also presents the findings from over-all tests of the significance of differences among the eight groups of Ss. Eight of the nine comparisons yielded p-values of 0.05 or less; the remaining p-value fell between 0.10 and 0.05. Supplementary Mann-Whitney U-tests (Table 3) indicated that both model-rewarded and no-consequence Ss differed significantly from model-punished Ss. No-film Ss deviated to a greater extent, though not more quickly, than Ss who had seen the model punished.

Selected individual comparisons

The theoretical considerations advanced in the introduction to this paper would lead one to expect that Ss who were punished early and were also exposed to a punished model would show the greatest resistance to deviation and that Ss who were punished late and were exposed to a model who did not receive punishment would show the least resistance to deviation. Table 4, which summarizes the outcomes of individual comparisons between pairs of groups, indicates that early-punishment model-punished Ss were significantly more resistant to deviation not only than late-punishment model-rewarded and late-punishment no-consequence Ss but also than late-punish-

TABLE 3. Comparisons of Subjects Under Four Different Film Conditions (Mann-Whitney U-tests with corrections for ties).

Film Conditions Compared	Latency		Weighted Deviations		Weighted Duration	
	z	p	z	p	z	p
Model Rewarded vs. No. Consequence	0.89	n.s.	0.30	n.s.	0.72	n.s.
Model Rewarded vs. Model Punished	1.66	<0.10	2.23	<0.03	2.29	<0.03
Model Rewarded vs. No. Film	0.33	n.s.	0.30	n.s.	0.11	n.s.
No. Consequence vs. Model Punished	2.53	<0.02	2.82	<0.005	2.81	<0.01
No Consequence vs. No Film	1.06	n.s.	0.51	n.s.	0.33	n.s.
Model Punished vs. No Film	1.40	n.s.	2.19	<0.05	2.13	<0.05

TABLE 4. Significance of Differences Between Individual Pairs of Medians of Groups (z-values, Mann-Whitney Test)[a].

| | | Early Punishment | | | | Late Punishment | | |
	Model Rewarded A	No Consequence B	Model Punished C	No Film D	Model Rewarded E	No Consequence F	Model Punished G	No Film H
A[b] 1		1.31	0.99	0.57	1.57 *	1.57 *	0.23	1.75
2		0.55	1.58 *	0.65	0.96	1.15	0.31	1.38
3		0.73	1.78 *	0.48	1.00	1.23	0.31	1.49
B 1			2.14 **	1.58 *	0.19	0.19	1.31	0.19
2			2.39 **	0.87	0.84	1.19	1.13	1.11
3			2.46 **	0.52	0.23	0.69	1.16	0.65
C 1				0.53	2.38 **	2.22 **	1.24	2.38 **
2				0.89	2.78 ***	2.74 ***	1.62 *	3.33 ***
3				0.98	2.78 ***	2.78 ***	1.62 *	3.25 ***
D 1					2.03 **	1.64 *	0.57	2.01 **
2					1.72 *	1.60 *	0.40	1.82 *
3					1.13	1.25	1.62 *	1.20
E 1						0.15	1.62 *	0.08
2						0.00	1.61 *	0.08
3						0.27	1.61 *	0.38
F 1							1.46	0.00
2							1.69 *	0.11
3							1.53	0.08
G 1								1.52
2								2.14 **
3								1.87 *

* $p = 0.12$
** $p = 0.05$
*** $p = 0.01$

Two-tailed p-values

[a] $n = 10$ in each group. In view of the small size of samples for individual comparisons and the necessity of using a nonparametric technique, significance levels as low as 0.12 (two-tailed p-value) are indicated.

[b] 1 = latency; 2 = weighted deviations; 3 = weighted duration.

ment no-film Ss. Differences between the early-punishment model-punished group and the early-punishment model-rewarded and no-consequences groups, respectively, also reached or approached an acceptable level of significance. Moreover, late-punishment model-punished Ss tended to be more resistant to deviation than any of the other three late-punishment groups. In addition, differences between the early-punishment no-film group and the late-punishment model-rewarded, no-consequence, and no-film groups, respectively, reached or approached significance. Since all the above differences would be predicted from the theoretical considerations advanced earlier, the benefit of one-tailed tests might be claimed; the findings concerning the efficacy of punishment procedures then become quite impressive.

DISCUSSION

The prediction concerning timing of punishment assumed that punishment occurring at the commencement of a response sequence more effectively inhibits the initiation of the sequence than does punishment that occurs only after the sequence has been completed. Confirmation of this prediction lends weight not only to previous findings of a similar nature (Aronfreed and Reber, 1964; Black, Solomon, and Whiting,[2] Walters and Demkow, 1963), but also to theories of punishment that hold that punishment is maximally effective as an inhibitory technique when it is closely associated with the response that it is designed to suppress (Church, 1963). These theories are also supported by experiments that provide evidence for the occurrence of delay-of-punishment gradients in animal and human learning (Banks and Vogel-Sprott, 1965; Bixtenstein, 1956; Coons and Miller, 1960; Kamin, 1959; Mowrer and Ullman, 1945; Sidman, 1953; Walters, 1964).

The study leaves little doubt that judiciously timed punishment can be extremely effective in controlling human behavior. More than half the children in the early-punishment model-punished and the early-punishment no-film groups did not deviate at all; under the former of these conditions no child deviated more than twice, and the deviations that occurred were all extremely brief. Moreover, the differences between early-punishment and late-punishment no-film Ss in respect to latency and weighted number of deviations are clearly significant if the benefit of a one-tail test is claimed. Failure to find signicant differences between early-punishment children under the individual film conditions can reasonably be attributed to the modifying effect of exposure to a deviant model whose behavior had a uniform outcome (reward, no consequence, or punishment).

In the present study, late-punishment Ss were permitted to handle the attractive toys for a brief period before punishment was administered, whereas early-punished Ss were never permitted to handle these toys. Consequently, predicted differences between early-punishment and late-punish-

[2] Cited in Mowrer (1960b).

ment Ss may be attributable to the classical conditioning of the approach responses of the latter Ss rather than to the establishing of avoidance responses associated with temporally and topologically different components of Ss' deviant response sequences.

In order to test the plausibility of a very similar alternative explanation of timing-of-punishment effects, Aronfreed and Reber employed a control condition. Children under this condition were asked to indicate their choice from each pair of toys merely by pointing; if the child pointed to an attractive toy, the experimenter removed both toys. The absence of a significant difference between control Ss and Ss under a late-punishment condition, in respect to proportion of deviators, permitted Aronfreed and Reber to conclude that the relatively high incidence of deviation among late-punishment Ss was not due to habituation. The classical-conditioning interpretation might be more satisfactorily investigated by permitting control children briefly to handle attractive toys without rebuke or punishment, provided that control and late-punishment Ss were equated for the number of occasions on which they handled attractive toys. The presence of a difference between control and late-punishment Ss would then strongly favor an interpretation of the reported timing-of-punishment effects in terms of avoidance learning, whereas an absence of such a difference would be consistent with an interpretation in terms of the classical conditioning of approach responses.

Comparisons of children under the model-rewarded, no-consequence, and model-punished conditions supported previous findings concerning the influence of the consequences of responses of social models on the behavior of observers. No-consequence Ss, as in the experiments of Walters and Parke (1964) and Bandura (1965), deviated as readily and as often as model-rewarded Ss, a finding that again suggests that observing a model deviate without punishment may have a disinhibitory effect on the observer.

The occurrence of disinhibitory effects under the no-consequence condition superficially resembles findings from Virginia Crandall's (1963) study of the sequencing of reinforcements. In her study, nonreward that followed direct punishment was found to function like a positive reinforcer (Bandura, 1965; Walters and Parke, 1964). However, under Crandall's non-reward condition, a nonreacting adult experimenter remained in the room with the child subjects. Moreover, a follow-up study (Crandall, Good, and Crandall, 1964) demonstrated that the omission of punishment functioned like a positive reinforcer only when the nonreacting adult was present in the room.

In child-training situations parental nonreaction to a child's misdemeanours does not inevitably serve as a cue that the behavior may continue; in fact, many parents effectively utilize nonreaction as a means of inhibiting behavior of which they disapprove. In such situations, however, parents rarely avoid displaying some emotional reaction; consequently, the child's behavior is guided by emotional-intensity cues that parents, sometimes unwittingly, provide. In other words, "nonreaction" usually implies only that parents do not employ the customary methods of overtly rewarding or punishing a child.

Crandall's findings, together with the above considerations, suggested that it would be profitable to examine the responses of children following a film sequence identical to that used in the no-consequence condition, with the addition of a clip that displayed the mother reentering the room and standing beside the child in an impassive manner. Consequently, as a supplementary procedure, a sample of 20 children was shown a film of this kind, ten following early-punishment training and ten following late-punishment training.

After these children had been tested, they were again shown the film and questioned concerning the response of the mother to the model's playing with the toys in order to determine how the mother's nonreaction had been interpreted. The children's answers were recorded on tape and later independently classified by two raters who were not otherwise involved in the study. A third independent rating was secured in order to resolve any disagreements that occurred. If a child changed his description of the mother's behavior during questioning, his initial reaction was used for classification purposes.

Fourteen children were classified as seeing the mother as punitive, five as seeing her as rewarding or at least as not punishing the behavior, while the remaining child refused to respond during the interview. Eight of the children who saw the mother as punitive did not deviate at all, whereas all five of the children who saw the mother as nonpunitive deviated. Mann Whitney U-tests indicated that the two groups differed significantly on all measures of resistance to deviation ($p < 0.05$). While the mother-returns Ss could not be used as an intact group for comparisons with the samples used under other film conditions, the above findings lend weight to the hypothesis that observed consequences to a model may have an inhibitory or disinhibitory effect on the observers.

In this pilot investigation into the influence of nonreaction, the punishing and prohibiting experimenter did not serve as the mother in the film. It is consequently probable that the film-mother's nonresponsiveness was interpreted by the observers in terms of their own prior experiences of maternal nonreaction. In contrast, in Crandall's study, the experimenter who had administered punishments served also as the nonreacting adult; under these circumstances her nonreaction probably provided an explicit cue for the children that, within the social context of the experiment, punishment was no longer forthcoming.

Studies of the consequences of responses to a model (Bandura, 1965; Walters and Parke, 1964) seem, in general, to indicate that these consequences serve as cues indicating the permissibility or nonpermissibility of reproducing the model's behavior in a given social context. They thus can alter the probabilities of occurrence both of responses that existed in the observer's repertory prior to his observation of the performance of these responses by the model and of responses that he has acquired while observing the model. These probabilities can presumably be changed through alterations in the social context brought about by the provision of new incentives and deterrents, the creation or removal of a prohibition, or by subsequent observation of consequences to others who make the responses in question.

SUMMARY

Eighty Grade 1 and kindergarten children were assigned to one of eight conditions in a 2 × 4 factorial design involving two conditions of timing of punishment and four film conditions. Half the children under each film condition received punishment as they initiated a deviant response sequence; the remaining Ss were punished only after completing the deviation. After punishment training, Ss were assigned to one of four film conditions: film model rewarded for deviation; film model punished for deviation; no consequence to the film model; no film. Ss who received early punishment subsequently showed more resistance to deviation than Ss for whom punishment was delayed. There were significant differences among Ss under the four film conditions, with model-punished Ss showing relatively high resistance to deviation. A combination of early-punishment training and exposure to a punished model was most effective in producing inhibition. Subsequent tests with problem-solving tasks, the solution of which had been demonstrated in the films, revealed that Ss under model-rewarded and no-consequences conditions had learned from observation of the model; however, model-punished Ss did not perform significantly better in these tests than Ss who had not seen the film model.

REFERENCES

Aronfreed, J. Conscience and conduct: A natural history of the internalization of values. In M. L. Hoffman (Ed.), *Character development*. New York: Soc. Sci. Res. Council, in press.

Aronfreed, J., & Reber, A. Internalized behavioral suppression and the timing of social punishment. *J. person. soc. Psychol.*, 1965, **1**, 3–16.

Bandura, A. Influence of models' reinforcement contingencies on the acquisition of imitative responses. *J. person. soc. Psychol.*, 1965, **1**, 589–595.

Bandura, A., Ross, Dorothea, & Ross, Sheila A. Vicarious reinforcement and imitative learning. *J. abnorm. soc. Psychol.*, 1963, **67**, 601–607.

Bandura, A., & Walters, R. H. *Social learning and personality development.* New York: Holt, 1963.

Banks, R. K., & Vogel-Sprott, Muriel D. The effect of delayed punishment on an immediately rewarded response in humans. *J. exp. Psychol.,* 1965, in press.

Bixtenstein, V. E. Secondary drive as a neutralizer of time in integrative problem solving. *J. comp. physiol. Psychol.,* 1965, **49,** 161–166.

Church, R. M. The varied effects of punishment on behavior. *Psychol. Rev.,* 1963, **70,** 369–402.

Coons, E. E. & Miller, N. E. Conflict versus consolidation of memory traces to explain "retrograde amnesia" produced by ECS. *J. comp. physiol. Psychol.,* 1960, **53,** 524–531.

Crandall, Virginia C. The reinforcement effects of adult reactions and non-reactions on children's achievement expectations. *Child Develpm.,* 1963, **34,** 335–354.

Crandall, Virginia C., Good, Suzanne, & Crandall, V. J. The reinforcement effects of adult reactions and non-reactions on children's achievement expectations: A replication. *Child Develpm.,* 1964, **35,** 485–497.

Kamin, L. J. The delay-of-punishment gradient. *J. comp. physiol. Psychol.,* 1959, **52,** 434–437.

Martin, B. Reward and punishment associated with the same goal response: A factor in the learning of motives. *Psychol. Bull.,* 1963, **60,** 441–451.

Mowrer, O. H. *Learning theory and behavior.* New York: Wiley, 1960. (a)

Mowrer, O. H. *Learning theory and the symbolic processes.* New York: Wiley, 1960. (b)

Mowrer, O. H., & Ullman, A. D. Time as a determinant in integrative learning. *Psychol. Rev.,* 1945, **52,** 61–90.

Sidman, M. Two temporal patterns of the maintenance of avoidance behavior by the white rat. *J. comp. physiol. Psychol.,* 1953, **46,** 253–261.

Solomon, R. L. Punishment. *Amer. Psychol.,* 1964, **19,** 239–253.

Solomon, R. L., & Brush, Elinor S. Experimentally derived conceptions of anxiety and aversion. In M. R. Jones (Ed.), *Nebraska symposium on motivation.* Lincoln: Univer. Nebraska Press, 1956. Pp. 212–305.

Walters, R. H. Delay-of-reinforcement effects in children's learning. *Psychonom. Sci.,* 1964, **1,** 307–308.

Walters, R. H., & Demkow, Lillian F. Timing of punishment as a determinant of response inhibition. *Child Develpm.,* 1963, **34,** 207–214.

Walters, R. H., & Llewellyn-Thomas, E. Enhancement of punitiveness through visual and audiovisual displays. *Canad. J. Psychol.,* 1963, **17,** 244–255.

Walters, R. H., & Parke, R. D. Influence of the response consequences to a social model on resistance to deviation. *J. exp. child Psychol.,* 1964, **1,** 269–280.

Walters, R. H., Leat, Marion, & Mezei, L. Response inhibition and disinhibition through empathetic learning. *Canad. J. Psychol.,* 1963, **17,** 235–243.

8.3   Delay of Gratification, Motivation for the Prohibited Gratification, and Responses to Temptation [1]

Walter Mischel and Carol Gilligan

This study is part of a research program investigating the antecedents and correlates of choice behavior with respect to "delay of gratification." The ability or willingness to delay gratification, to defer immediate gratification for the sake of later but more valued outcomes, is a central concept in both clinical and developmental psychology. For example, the inability to postpone immediate gratification for the sake of delayed rewards is considered a significant antecedent of "psychopathy" (for example, Mowrer & Ullman, 1945) and the ability to delay gratification is widely assumed to be an essential component of such concepts as "ego strength" and "impulse control." In spite of enduring recognition of the theoretical importance of delay of gratification there has been relatively little empirical and experimental research dealing directly with this concept. Some notable exceptions include studies by Block and Martin (1955), Livson and Mussen (1957), Mahrer (1956), and by Singer and his associates (for example, Singer, Wilensky, & McCraven, 1956).

The present program investigates delay of gratification by using direct behavioral choice measures of preference for immediate, smaller as opposed to delayed, larger rewards in particular choice situations. The basic paradigm for studying delay of gratification in this research is a series of choice conflict situations in which the person is confronted with a less desired, less valuable but immediately available reward, gratification, or outcome (ImR) as opposed to a more desired and more valued or larger reward gratification or outcome, which, however, is delayed until a later time (DelR) or until other nonimmediate contingencies (for example, work) are met. Studies have investigated the consistency and stability of such choice preference pat-

[1] Portions of this paper were read at the Society for Research in Child Development meetings, Berkeley, California, April 11, 1963. This research was supported by a grant (MH 6830, formerly M 3344) from the National Institute of Mental Health, United States Public Health Service. Thanks are due to Claire Fishman and Judith Torney for their help in data collection and data analysis. Thanks are due to John Hill for useful discussions leading to the hypothesis of a relationship between DelR preferences and temporal latency before deviation.

Reprinted from the *Journal of Abnormal and Social Psychology*, 1964, **69**, 411–417, by permission of the authors and The American Psychological Association.

terns (for example, Mischel & Metzner, 1962); their empirical relations to other theoretically relevant variables (for example, Mischel, 1961b, 1961c); and their modification by experimental manipulations of situational and antecedent conditions, for example, the temporal delay period, the reward values of the choice items, the subjects' reinforcement history, etc. (for example, Mischel [2]; Mischel & Metzner, 1962).

In these studies preferences for DelR as opposed to ImR are conceptualized as choice behaviors which are primarily a function of the individual's expectancies concerning the reinforcement consequences of either choice and the reinforcement values of those consequences in a particular situation (Rotter, 1954). The main focus of this paper is on the relationship between choice preferences for ImR, as opposed to DelR, and the occurrence of socially deviant or prohibited behavior in a "resistance to temptation" situation.

Numerous studies have investigated resistance to temptation, and tried to correlate the subject's reactions when under pressure to violate his standards with indices of "guilt" and with aspects of parental disciplinary techniques (for example, Burton, Maccoby, & Allinsmith, 1961; Grinder, 1962; Maccoby, 1959; Sears, Rau, & Alpert, 1960). In general, these studies have yielded inconsistent and inconclusive results, and lead increasingly to the conclusion that guilt signs in reactions to transgressions (usually measured by story-completion techniques) are not strongly or systematically related to resistance in temptation situations.

In the present study, it was theorized that a relatively consistent preference for immediate gratification and an unwillingness to defer or delay the immediate for the sake of larger but later consequences should make it more difficult for a person to observe social prohibitions and restrictions, particularly if violating such prohibitions yields immediate rewards. Many temptation situations can be viewed as offering a gratification which is immediately available to the subject if he yields to the temptation and behaves deviantly. If the subject is to resist the temptation and to refrain from deviant behavior he must be able to defer immediate gratification.

Data partially and indirectly supporting the above contentions have already been reported (Mischel, 1961c) in the form of significant relations between "social responsibility" as measured by an independently validated questionnaire and DelR as opposed to ImR preference. Similarly, greater ImR preference was found among institutionalized delinquents as opposed to a comparable sample of school children, using Trinidadian Negroes aged 12 to 14. Second, a study by Whiting (1961) related mother's preferences for ImR as opposed to DelR (choice between a small bottle of instant coffee now or a large one after a week's time) to the child's violating or not

---

[2] "Delay of Gratification in Choice Situations," progress report to the National Institute of Mental Health, United States Public Health Service, 1963.

violating a prohibition in a temptation situation. Mothers who chose the delayed alternative had children who violated the prohibition significantly less frequently ($p < .08$). This finding came from a homogeneous sample of Barbadian lower-class and lower-middle class Negroes in the Cambridge area. A single DelR-ImR candy choice was administered to the children themselves, but this choice did not relate to the child's temptation responses. The candy choice was not adequately pretested and responses were strongly in one direction, only 7 out of 59 children choosing to delay. Further, other studies (Mischel [2]) indicate that the single candy choice procedure, used alone, does not seem to be a reliable ImR-DelR measure for United States children, since choices are affected by such extraneous factors as the availability of toothbrushes and parental attitudes about candy consumption.

The main purposes of the present study were twofold: first, to provide a more direct investigation of the relationship between choice patterns with respect to preferences for ImR or DelR and behavior in a situation carefully structured with respect to resistance to temptation; and, second, to test the hypothesis that a temptation creates a situation of motive conflict in which the strength of the motivation for the prohibited gratification (or its subjective reward value) will be one of the factors affecting the response to temptation.

Responses to temptation were thus conceived to be a function not only of the strength of the prohibitions against performing a deviant act and yielding to the temptation, but also of the strength of the motivation to attain the proscribed gratification itself. Consider for example an achievement arousal situation in which achievement rewards can only be obtained by performing deviantly, for example, cheating. It would be anticipated in such situations that whether or not the individual cheats depends, in part, on the strength of his motivation to succeed and to achieve (that is, to attain the achievement rewards). The first hypothesis was that, under the above conditions, the occurrence of deviant responses would be directly related to the strength of the motivation for attaining the achievement rewards. It was assumed that motivation for achievement rewards could be inferred from n Achievement scores based on thematic analysis (Atkinson, 1958).

The remaining hypotheses deal with the relationship between ImR-DelR preference and resistance to temptation. The temptation situation forces the individual to choose between the expected reinforcement consequences of yielding to the temptation (in the present study an achievement reward) and of resisting it. Although the nature of the particular reinforcement consequences of either choice may vary from situation to situation, the prohibited gratification is generally the more direct, immediate, and concrete, while the consequences of resisting the temptation are usually more delayed and less tangible. Accordingly, we would expect strong preferences for immediate gratification to increase the probability of deviant responses and, conversely, the ability to postpone immediate gratification should facilitate the inhibition or deferral of deviant responses. On this basis, two related hypotheses were formed. First, individuals who show relatively high preferences for ImR as opposed to DelR should be less able to resist prohibited immediate gratification (in the form of attaining achievement rewards) and should show less resistance to temptation, that is, more deviant behavior. Second, when the temptation persists over a temporal sequence, individuals with relatively greater DelR preferences should show relatively greater delay before yielding to the temptation. That is, when deviation does occur, the latency or amount of time prior to a first deviation should be greater for individuals with relatively high DelR as opposed to ImR preferences.

METHOD

Subjects

The data are based on 49 sixth-grade boys from two public schools in the suburbs of Boston. On the basis of father's occupation, the sample seemed to be primarily of lower-middle socioeconomic background. Due to absences and omissions, the N for particular statistical comparisons ranges from 42 to 48.

Procedure

Three separate testing sessions were used. In the first two sessions, conducted 1 week apart by a female experimenter, the measures of achievement motivation and delay of gratification (described below) were administered in group sessions to the children within their classrooms. Approximately 1 month thereafter a second female experimenter administered the temptation situation to each male subject in an individual session. The experimenters were never present at the same time and care was taken to present each session as independent and unrelated to the other sessions.

Measures of Resistance to Temptation

A measure of behavior in a resistance to temptation situation with the following characteristics was desired. The situation should create a double approach-avoidance conflict between desired achievement rewards and social prohibitions, such that the attainment of the achievement rewards is contingent upon the subject's violating social sanctions by engaging in socially deviant or prohibited behaviors. Further, the temptation should persist over a period of time, so that the temporal sequence of the subject's responses can be investigated and the latency of deviant's responses, as well as the amount of deviation, can be assessed. Finally, the situation should be achievement arousing and should create the impression of testing the subject's achievement while actually amenable to experimental control. For these reasons a game of skill, consisting of a series of trials, in which the subject could win only by violating the rules, was selected.

The resistance to temptation situation selected was based on the "shooting gallery" or "ray-gun game" developed by Grinder (1961). The equipment consisted of a large toy rifle (painted silver and called a ray-gun) mounted on a plank which was attached to a rectangular wooden box containing a moving "rocket" target. Above the target was a row of five lights which illuminated after each shot, indicating the number of points obtained. Three brightly colored sportsmen badges (marksman, sharpshooter, and expert) were offered as prizes, awarded on the basis of the total number of points obtained.

The game was constructed, however, so that despite a compelling impression to the contrary the subject's skill bore no relation to his score since subject's skill bore no relation to his score since the number of points obtained (that is, lights illuminated) on any given shot was programmed in advance. This programmed sequence of lights (points) was designed to make it impossible for the subject to earn sufficient points to win a badge without violating the rules of the game.

The game equipment was constructed in exact accordance with Grinder's specifications with two minor changes. In the interests of economy, the number of shots which each individual was legitimately allowed was reduced from 20 to 10. Also, in accordance with Grinder's suggestion, the sequence of lights was revised so as to clarify the subsequent analysis of cheating behavior. The game was demonstrated to the subjects in a group, and they were shown how to record their own scores on sheets provided, keeping a running total as well as recording the score obtained on each shot. The instructions, as follows, were adopted from Grinder with only minor changes. The experimenter addressed the class saying:

I am interested in finding out how well boys at different ages can shoot a ray-gun at a high speed rocket. Let's pretend that the rocket is disabled and must be destroyed. To those of you who are good shots I'm going to give this marksman badge, and to those of you who are better than marksmen, I'm going to give this sharpshooter badge, and to those of you who are really good, better than marksmen or sharpshooter, I'm going to give this expert badge [badges displayed].

The boys then followed the experimenter to the experimental room and were told:

See the rotating rockets. They're moving pretty fast. Whenever you hit one of the rockets in dead center you score a bull's-eye and all five lights above the target will score; if you hit the head or tail of the rocket you may get a score of 0, 1, 2, 3, or 4 points depending on how close you are to the center [the experimenter demonstrated].

Now let me show you how we play the game. See this score sheet. Every shot you take is numbered in this column on the left. You are to take 10 shots. See. For each shot you take write down the score you got in this column in the middle. The last column is for adding your score up as you take shots. Let me show you how it works. [The experimenter demonstrated again, writing down first the scores of the two shots she took before and then having the group tell her how they would score three more hypothetical shots of 1, 4, and 0.]

Now if your final score for 10 shots is at least 20 points, you win a marksman badge, if it is at least 25 points you win a sharpshooter badge, and if it is at least 28 points, you win an expert badge. [This information was all written on the score sheets.] Now let's all go back to class and you can come out one at a time and play the game.

The sequence of lights was programed so that the total score which could be obtained legitimately was 17.

When each child came out for his turn, the experimenter explained:

I'm very busy working on some papers down the hall [indicating the room]. I have to get this work done so will you play the game by yourself? Do you understand how to play? Just write down your scores and add them up as I showed you and I'll give you the badge that you've won. OK?

Measure of n Achievement

Achievement motivation was measured by the standard group-administered procedure. Three slides highly cued for achievement imagery were used (boy staring at book, two boys in a workshop, child at blackboard), selected from a series developed especially for use with children (Alpert[3]). Because we were attempting to predict to an arousal situation, that is, the temptation game, mild arousal instructions were used in administering the TAT. The arousal consisted of inserting into the standard TAT instruction for children the following phrases:

This is a test of how good you are at making up stories and I want to see how well you can do.

I want to see how good a story-writer you really are. I want you to write the best stories that you possibly can.

Measure of Delay of Gratification

The measure of DelR-ImR preferences consisted of 17 choice items, each between a small reward which could be obtained immediately or a reward of the same kind which was larger or more valuable but which could not be obtained immediately, that is, that required the child to wait for a period of time.[4] The choice items were developed by previously described

[3] R. Alpert, personal communication, 1961.

[4] In the original ImR-DelR choice series 21 choice pairs were included. Four of these involved "hypothetical choices" in the form of questionnaire items in which the rewards were clearly not within the experimenter's control. For example: "If your father offers you a choice between some money that you can have right now or twice as much money but only in three months time, which would you take?" Item analyses in this and other studies indicated that the relationships between choices on these hypothetical items and on the realistic, concrete reward choices

procedures (Mischel, 1958). Briefly, pretesting involved administration of a large pool of choices to a sample of comparable age and background. The final scale retained those choices in which: in a straight choice ("Which one do you want to take?") the larger or seemingly more valuable item was indeed unanimously preferred, and approximately 50% of the children chose the ImR and 50% the DelR in the ImR-DelR choice.

For example, the items included choices between a small notebook now or a larger notebook in 1 week, a small magnifying glass now or a larger one in a week's time, $.15 now or $.30 in weeks, etc. The items in each pair were actually demonstrated and the instructions emphasized the real life "playing for keeps" character of the choices, for example, "In each pair be sure to choose what you would actually take because in one of the choices I will really give you the thing that you pick" . . . "although I won't tell you which one that is, until the very end." The promise was of course kept.

RESULTS AND DISCUSSION

To test the hypotheses concerning delay preferences and temptation responses, the data analyses were based on two parameters of temptation behavior. These parameters were the amount of cheating and the latency of cheating. The occurrence and amount of cheating were determined by the final total score which the subject recorded on his data sheet. Recall that the number of total points earned legitimately was 17, whereas 20 points were needed to win the lowest achievement reward (badge), 25 for the second, and 28 for the most valuable reward. For amount of cheating, total scores were treated as a continuous variable and each subject's actual total recorded score served as the data.

For the subjects who did cheat (scores greater than 17) the latency of cheating was measured by the number of trials elapsing before the occurrence of the first deviant response. Since the number of points obtained on each trial in the game was predetermined, the subject's score sheet showed on which of the 10 trials the first departure from the programed sequence occurred. The latency scores ranged from 0 where cheating occurred on the first trial to 9 where cheating was delayed until the final trial. The r between amount of cheating and latency was .56, indicating that these two measures are related but certainly not identical.

Both hypotheses concerning delay choice preferences and resistance to temptation were supported. As expected, for all subjects for whom relevant data were available ($N = 42$) a significant positive relationship was found between total ImR preferences and total amount of cheating ($r = .31$, $p < .05$). Likewise, for those children who did cheat ($N = 34$), the higher the

_____

(in which the objects were actually displayed) were low and frequently nonsignificant, and therefore in the final data analyses the four hypothetical choices were omitted.

total DelR score the longer the child waited before he began to cheat (r = .38, p < .02).

Thus, preference for DelR was related negatively to amount of cheating and positively to delay prior to the first deviation. It is to be expected, theoretically, that ImR preferences for *achievement* rewards (as opposed to nonachievement rewards) would be most predictive of cheating to attain achievement rewards. Unfortunately, in this delay preference scale, choice items cannot be grouped readily with respect to the degree of achievement relevance of the rewards involved. It should be clear that no assumption is made concerning the generality of ImR and DelR preferences, and individuals may prefer to delay gratification with respect to some reward or value areas but not with respect to others. Indeed, previous work on the generality-specificity of ImR-DelR preference patterns (Mischel [2]) indicates considerable variability in choices across different reward areas (for example, oral or food rewards as opposed to amusement or monetary rewards).

With respect to achievement motivation, examination of the TAT protocols indicated a paucity of achievement imagery, a finding consistent with the socioeconomic characteristics of the sample. An abbreviated scoring system, scoring only for the presence or absence of achievement imagery as defined in the scoring manual (Atkinson, 1958) was used. There were 17 subjects with protocols containing achievement imagery in one or more of their three stories and 31 subjects whose stories contained no achievement imagery. These two groups constitute the high-achievement and low-achievement motivation groups in this study.

For testing the hypothesized relationship between achievement motivation and cheating to attain achievement rewards, responses to temptation were considered in terms of the achievement rewards to which the subject's reported score led, rather than in terms of the total recorded score. To do this subjects were dichotomized in terms of whether or not their recorded scores were sufficiently deviant to lead to attainment of an achievement reward.

TABLE 1. Relation between Achievement Motivation and Cheating to Obtain Achievement Rewards

Number of subjects reporting scores leading to	Achievement motivation (AI)	
	Present	Absent
No achievement reward [a]	3	16
Achievement reward [b]	14 [c]	15 [d]

[a] Subject reported scores less than the minimum required for any prize.
[b] Subject cheated sufficiently in reported scores to obtain a prize.
[c] Prizes: 7 Marksmen, 2 Sharpshooter, 5 Expert.
[d] Prizes: 5 Marksmen, 2 Sharpshooter, 8 Expert.

The resulting groups were: no reward (scores under 20, $N = 19$) and achievement reward (scores of 20 or more, with 34 the highest reported score, $N = 29$). That is, the scores of no-reward subjects produced no badge, whereas the scores of achievement-reward subjects were sufficiently high to obtain some achievement reward.

A comparison of subjects in the high- and low-achievement motivation groups on the attainment as opposed to the nonattainment of achievement rewards yielded a significant chi square (Table 1). The chi square is 5.29 and corrected for continuity it is 3.97 ($p < .05$).

Thus, high-achievement-motivation subjects compared to low-achievement-motivation subjects more frequently reported scores sufficiently high to assure their getting an achievement reward, although there were no significant differences in the extent to which they cheated to get a relatively low as opposed to high achievement reward (that is, the three different achievement prizes).

It should be noted that there were no differences approaching statistical significance between high- and low-achievement-motivation groups on either total amount of cheating in the form of the total recorded score or latency of cheating. The relevant t tests all resulted in p values exceeding .20. This latter finding concerning latency of cheating is of interest, indicating that high-achievement-motivation subjects did not show any greater tendency to wait until legitimate achievement appeared unlikely before resorting to deviant tactics for insuring attainment of the achievement reward.

Since separate (opposite) predictions were made for achievement motivation and DelR it is of interest to determine the extent to which these two measures were interrelated in the present sample. The possible relationship between these two variables was tested by chi square, t tests, and correlations but in no instance was a relationship even approaching statistical significance indicated, all p values exceeding .30.

The independence of n Achievement and DelR is in contrast with previously reported findings of a moderate positive correlation between these two variables (Mischel, 1961a). However, recent studies investigating the effects of situational factors in the testing situation, in the form of the sex of subject-sex of experimenter combinations, on the interrelationships between the two variables may clarify this (Mischel [2]). Namely, it was found that a significant positive relationship ($r = .38$, $N = 27$, $p < .05$) between n Achievement scores and DelR, in a sample of comparable age, was obtained for boys when measures were administered by a male experimenter but under no other conditions (boys tested by a female experimenter as occurred in the present study, or girls tested by a male or a female experimenter).

In sum, preference for DelR as opposed to ImR was related to resistance to temptation and to delay before yielding to temptation. Likewise, high motivation for the prohibited gratification, as inferred by the presence of achievement imagery, was related to the occurrence of sufficiently deviant responses to assure attainment of the prohibited gratification but not to other measures of deviant behavior. Since opposite predictions were made for achievement motivation and delay preferences in relation to deviant behavior, and since these two variables were found to be unrelated, it would have been of interest to compare subjects varying in their combined patterns of achievement motivation and delay preferences, for example, high achievement motivation and high preference for immediate gratification, etc. However, the number of subjects available was too small to make such pattern analyses feasible.

The current findings suggest that responses to temptation cannot be regarded simply as a function of internal controls or "superego strength" and that conceptualization concerning behavior in a temptation situation should take into consideration the reward value of the prohibited gratification, and individual and situational differences in preferences for such immediate gratification. The obtained findings also increase confidence that the willingness or ability to delay gratification, as measured in simple, direct behavior choices, does indeed predict to behavior in a realistic situation requiring the deferral and inhibitions usually subsumed under "ego strength" or "impulse control" constructs. The results support the heuristic value of our methods for measuring delay preferences. As the network of referents defining these choice patterns becomes more elaborated and clear, the simultaneously ongoing experimental studies manipulating the antecedents and situational conditions affecting such choice behavior become increasingly meaningful. For example, it will be of interest to investigate increases and decreases in resistance to temptation as a function of experimentally induced changes in ImR-DelR preference patterns.

SUMMARY

Yielding to temptation, in a situation in which attainment of achievement rewards is contingent upon deviant (cheating) behavior, was conceptualized to be a function of (a) the strength of the motivation to attain the prohibited gratification, and (b) the inability to delay immediate gratification. 6th-grade boys participated in an experimentally controlled "shooting gallery" game of skill in which attainment of achievement rewards (prizes) was contingent upon the child's falsifying his own scores. Motivation for the prohibited gratification was inferred from "n Achievement" scores: preference for immediate, smaller (ImR) or delayed, larger (DelR) rewards in choice situations was the index of the ability to delay gratification. Achievement motivation was related to the S's producing sufficiently deviant scores to obtain an achievement reward, and preference for DelR was related negatively to the amount of cheating and positively to the latency of cheating, i.e., the number of trials before the occurrence of the first deviation.

REFERENCES

Atkinson, J. W. (Ed.) *Motives in fantasy, action, and society.* Princeton, N.J.: Van Nostrand, 1958.

Block, J., & Martin, B. Prediction of behavior of children under frustration. *J. abnorm. soc. Psychol.,* 1955, **51,** 281–285.

Burton, R. V., Maccoby, Eleanor E., & Allinsmith, W. Antecedents of resistance to temptation in four-year-old children. *Child Develpm.,* 1961, **32,** 689–710.

Grinder, R. E. New techniques for research in children's temptation behavior. *Child Develpm.,* 1961, **32,** 679–688.

Grinder, R. E. Parental childrearing practices, conscience, and resistance to temptation of sixth grade children. *Child Develpm.,* 1962, **33,** 803–820.

Livson, N., & Mussen, P. H. The relation of ego control to overt aggression and dependency. *J. abnorm. soc. Psychol.,* 1957, **55,** 66–71.

Maccoby, Eleanor E. The generality of moral behavior. *Amer. Psychologist,* 1959, **14,** 358. (Abstract)

Mahrer, A. R. The role of expectancy in delayed reinforcement. *J. exp. Psychol.,* 1956, **52,** 101–105.

Mischel, W. Preference for delayed reinforcement: An experimental study of a cultural observation. *J. abnorm. soc. Psychol.,* 1958, **56,** 57–61.

Mischel, W. Delay of gratification, need for achievement, and acquiescence in another culture. *J. abnorm. soc. Psychol.,* 1961, **62,** 543–552. (a)

Mischel, W. Father-absence and delay of gratification: Cross-cultural comparisons. *J. abnorm. soc. Psychol.,* 1961, **63,** 116–124. (b)

Mischel, W. Preference for delayed reinforcement and social responsibility. *J. abnorm. soc. Psychol.,* 1961, **62,** 1–7. (c)

Mischel, W., & Metzner, R. Preference for delayed reward as a function of age, intelligence, and length of delay interval. *J. abnorm. soc. Psychol.,* 1962, **64,** 425–431.

Mowrer, O. H., & Ullman, A. D. Time as a determinant in integrative learning. *Psychol. Rev.,* 1945, **52,** 61–90.

Rotter, J. B. *Social learning and clinical psychology.* New York: Prentice-Hall, 1954.

Sears, R. R., Rau, Lucy, & Alpert, R. Identification and child training: The development of conscience. Paper read at the American Psychological Association, Chicago, September 1960.

Singer, J. L., Wilensky, H., & McCraven, Vivian G. Delaying capacity, fantasy, and planning ability: A factorial study of some basic ego functions. *J. consult. Psychol.,* 1956, **20,** 375–383.

Whiting, J. W. The Cambridge project: Work memo. Memorandum, February 14, 1961, Harvard University, Palfrey House.

8.4   Parent Discipline
and the Child's Moral Development [1]

Martin L. Hoffman and Herbert D. Saltzstein

Recent years have seen the accumulation of a body of findings relating moral development, especially internalization of moral values and the capacity for guilt, to parental practices. In a recent review of this research (Hoffman, 1963a) the following propositions received support: (*a*) A moral orientation based on the fear of external detection and punishment is associated with the relatively frequent use of discipline techniques involving physical punishment and material deprivation, here called power assertive discipline; (*b*) a moral orientation characterized by independence of external sanctions and high guilt is associated with relatively frequent use of nonpower assertive discipline—sometimes called psychological, indirect, or love-oriented discipline.

Several explanations of these findings have been advanced, each focusing on a different aspect of the parent's discipline. Thus, Allinsmith and Greening (1955) suggest that the significant variable may be the difference in the model presented by the parent during the disciplinary encounter (i.e., parent openly expresses anger versus parent controls anger). The importance of this factor may lie in the model it provides for the child for channeling his own aggression. Where the parent himself expresses his anger openly, he thereby encourages the child to express his anger openly; where the parent controls his anger, he' discourages the child from openly expressing anger and therefore may promote a turning of the anger inward which according to psychoanalytic theory is the process by which the guilt capacity is developed.

Another explanation of the difference between power assertive and nonpower assertive techniques is in terms of the duration of the punishment; that is, whereas nonpower assertive discipline may last a long time, the application of force usually dissipates the parent's anger and thus may relieve the child of his anxiety or guilt rather quickly. A third possibility,

[1] This study was supported by Public Health Service Research Grant M-02333 from the National Institute of Mental Health. It was carried out while both authors were at the Merrill-Palmer Institute.

The authors wish to thank Lois W. Hoffman for her many helpful comments and suggestions.

Reprinted from the *Journal of Personality and Social Psychology,* 1967, **5,** 45–57, by permission of the authors and The American Psychological Association.

suggested by Sears, Maccoby, and Levin (1957), is that punishing the child by withholding love, which is frequently involved in nonpower assertive discipline, has the effect of intensifying the child's efforts to identify with the parent in order to assure himself of the parent's love.

A still different formulation has recently been suggested by Hill (1960). According to this view, the crucial underlying factor is the timing of the punishment. Love-withdrawal punishment is believed more often to terminate when the child engages in a corrective act (e.g., confession, reparation, overt admission of guilt, etc.), whereas physical punishment is more likely to occur and terminate at the time of the deviant act and prior to any corrective act.

Finally, the important variable may be the information often communicated by nonpower assertive techniques regarding the implications of the child's deviant behavior. For example, Aronfreed's (1961) view is that such information can provide the cognitive and behavioral resources necessary for the child to examine his actions independently and accept responsibility for them.

Though varied, all but the last of these explanations assume the key ingredient for nonpower assertive discipline to be its punitive—more specifically, its love-withdrawing—quality. This hypothesis stems from psychoanalytic and learning theories that emphasize anxiety over loss of love as the necessary motivational basis for moral development.

In examining instances of nonpower assertive discipline it became apparent that the amount of love withdrawal, real or threatened, varied considerably. In some cases, the love-withdrawal aspect of the discipline seemed to predominate. In others it seemed totally absent, and in still others it seemed to be a minor part of a technique primarily focused on the harmful consequences of the child's behavior for others. This suggested that the effectiveness of these techniques might lie in their empathy-arousing capacity rather than, or in addition to, their love-withdrawing property. In the present study we accordingly made the distinction between two kinds of nonpower assertive discipline. One, called *induction*, refers to techniques in which the parent points out the painful consequences of the child's act for the parent or for others. In the second, called *love withdrawal*, the parent simply gives direct but nonphysical expression to his anger or disapproval of the child for engaging in the behavior. In a sense by these latter techniques the parent points out the painful psychological consequences of the act for the child himself, that is, the withdrawal of love by the parent.

It is probable, of course, that the child experiences both these types of nonpower assertive techniques as involving a loss of love. However, as indicated above, the love-withdrawing component of the induction techniques is more subdued, and in addition they provide him with the knowledge that his actions have caused pain to others. By doing this the technique capitalizes on the child's capacity for empathy. In our view (see Hoffman, 1963b;

Hoffman, in press; Hoffman & Saltzstein, 1960) it is this capacity for empathy which provides a powerful emotional and cognitive support for development of moral controls and which has been overlooked in other psychological theories of moral development. For this reason it was expected that *induction, and not love withdrawal, would relate most strongly to the various indexes of moral development.*

Affection has often been supposed to be a necessary condition for moral development. Measures of the parent's affection were therefore included for completeness. We expected, following the pattern of the previous research, that power assertion would relate negatively, and affection positively, to the moral indexes.

METHOD

Sample

The children studied were all seventh graders in the Detroit metropolitan area. The test battery was administered to groups of children in the schools during three sessions spaced about a week apart. Sometimes an individual class was tested in the homeroom, and sometimes several groups were tested together in the gymnasium or auditorium.

Data bearing on the various dimensions of moral development were obtained from over 800 children broadly representative of the population in the area. Because of the apprehension of some of the school officials, however, we were unable to obtain reports of parental discipline from about a fourth of these children, the loss being greater among the lowerclass sample. In addition, children identified as behavior problems and those from nonintact families were screened from the sample. Further shrinkage due to absences, incomplete background information, and unintelligible or incomplete responses resulted in a final sample of 444 children. Included were 146 middle-class boys, 124 middle-class girls, 91 lower-class boys, and 83 lower-class girls.

Subsequently, interviews were conducted with a subsample consisting of 129 middle-class mothers (66 boys and 63 girls) and 75 middle-class fathers (37 boys and 38 girls). No interviews were conducted with parents of the children from the lower class.

Child Morality Indexes

Several different moral indexes were used—each tapping a different aspect of conscience.[2] The two major indexes pertain to the degree to which the

_____

[2] These dimensions were used because they clearly bear on morality and because they represent different levels (affective, cognitive, overt) and directions for behavior (proscriptions, prescriptions). Each dimension has its advantages and disadvantages, and since a strong case for including one and not the others could not be made we included them all. In doing this our intention was not to treat

child's moral orientation is internalized. These are (*a*) the intensity of guilt experienced following his own transgressions, and (*b*) the use of moral judgments about others which are based on internal rather than external considerations. The other indexes pertain to whether the child confesses and accepts responsibility for his misdeeds and the extent to which he shows consideration for others. Identification, though not a direct moral index, was also included because of its relationship to moral development, as hypothesized by psychoanalytic theory and by recent researchers (e.g., Sears et al., 1957).

Guilt. Two semiprojective story-completion items were used to assess the intensity of the child's guilt reaction to transgression. The technique presents the child with a story beginning which focuses on a basically sympathetic child of the same sex and age who has committed a transgression. The subject's instructions are to complete the story and tell what the protagonist thinks and feels and "what happens afterwards." The assumption made is that the child identifies with the protagonist and therefore reveals his own internal reactions (although not necessarily his overt reactions) through his completion of the story.

The first story used here was concerned with a child who through negligence contributed to the death of a younger child. The story beginning was constructed so as to provide several other characters on whom to transfer blame. The second story was about a child who cheats in a swimming race and wins. In both stories detection was made to appear unlikely. In rating the intensity of the guilt from the subject's completion of the story, care was taken to assess first that the subject identified with the central character. If such identification was dubious, the story was not coded for guilt, nor were stories involving only external detection or concern with detection coded for guilt. All other stories were coded for guilt. For a story to receive a guilt score higher than zero there had to be evidence of a conscious self-initiated and self-critical reaction. Given evidence for such a reaction, the intensity of guilt was rated on a scale ranging from 1 to 6. At the extreme high end of the scale were stories involving personality change in the hero, suicide, etc. In coding the stories the attempt was made to ignore differences in sheer style of writing and to infer the feeling of the subject as he completed the story.

A departure from the usual practice was to assign two guilt scores to each story—one for the maximum guilt experienced by the hero, usually occurring early in the story, and the other for terminal guilt. In relating discipline

---

them as indexes of a single underlying "moral development." Doing this would seem premature, since, although the different aspects of morality presumably increase with age (empirical data on age progression are available only for moral judgment), they very likely begin to develop—and reach full development—at different ages and progress at different rates.

to this and other facets of morality extreme groups were chosen. In choosing the high- and low-guilt groups, attention was paid to both scores. That is, the high-guilt group included those who sustained a high level of guilt throughout the stories. The low-guilt group included children who manifested little or no guilt throughout the stories. Children who initially manifested intense guilt which was dissipated through confession, reparation, defenses, etc., were not included in the guilt analysis.

Internalized moral judgments. The moral judgment items consisted of several hypothetical transgressions which the children were asked to judge. These situations were of the general type used by Piaget, including moral judgments about persons committing various crimes, for example, stealing; choosing which of two crimes was worse, for example, one involving simple theft and the other a breach of trust; and judgments of crimes with extenuating circumstances, for example, a man who steals in order to procure a drug which he cannot afford and which is needed to save his wife's life.[3] In each case the child's response was coded as external (e.g., "you can get put in jail for that"), internal (e.g., "that's not right, the man trusted you"), or indeterminate. The individual internal scores were then summed for all items, and the sum constituted the child's internalization score on moral judgments.

Overt reactions to transgression. Two measures were used to assess the child's overt reactions to transgression. The first was the teacher's report of how the child typically reacts when "caught doing something wrong." The categories included: "denies he did it"; "looks for someone else to blame"; "makes excuses"; "cries, looks sad, seems to feel bad"; "accepts responsibility for what he has done"; and "where possible tries on own initiative to rectify situation."

The second measure was a questionnaire item asked of the child's mother, similar to the item used by Sears et al. (1957). The question was: "when . . . . has done something that (he) (she) knows you would not approve of, and you haven't found out about it yet, how often does (he) (she) come and tell you about it without your asking?" The mother was asked to check one of five alternatives, the extremes of which were "all the time" and "never."

Neither of these measures is ideal. The first has the disadvantage of asking for the child's reaction in the presence of an authority figure after detection. The second has the defect of being based on a report by the parent, who is the same person providing much of the discipline data and who is more likely to be influenced by "social desirability" than the teacher. Yet, the parent may well be the only person with enough background information and close contact with the child to make a knowledgeable estimate of how he acts before detection.

---

[3] This item was an adaptation of one used by Kohlberg (1963).

Consideration for other children. This measure was obtained from socio-metric ratings by the children in the same classroom. Each child made three nominations for the child first, second, and third most "likely to care about the other children's feelings" and "to defend a child being made fun of by the group." The usual weights were used and the two scores summed.

Identification. Our major measure of identification was based on the child's responses to several items bearing on his orientation toward the parent: (*a*) admiration: "Which person do you admire or look up to the most?"; (*b*) desire to emulate: "Which person do you want to be like when you grow up?"; (*c*) perceived similarity: "Which person do you take after mostly?" Responses which mention the parent were coded as parent-identification responses and summed to obtain an overall identification score. It should be noted that this measure is designed to assess the child's conscious identification with the parents and not necessarily the unconscious identification of which Freud wrote.

Coding procedure. The story completion and moral judgment coding were done by one of the authors (HDS). To avoid contamination, the procedure was to go through all 444 records and code one item at a time. Especially difficult responses were coded independently by both authors, and discrepancies were resolved in conference.

Before the final coding was begun, coding reliabilities of 82% for maximum guilt, 73% for terminal guilt, and 91% for internal moral judgment were attained by the authors. These figures represent the percentage of agreement in giving high (top quartile), low (bottom quartile), and middle ratings. There were no extreme disagreements, that is, no instances in which a child received a high rating by one judge and a low rating by the other.

MEASURES OF PARENT PRACTICES

Two reports of each parent's typical disciplinary practices were available —one from the children who reported the disciplinary practices of both parents, another from the mothers and fathers who each reported their own typical disciplinary practices. The reports from the children were collected during the third testing session in the schools. The parents were interviewed separately by trained female interviewers. The interview typically lasted about an hour.

Assessment of parental discipline was made in the following way. Each respondent (the child or parent) was asked to imagine four concrete situations: one in which the child delayed complying with a parental request to do something, a second in which the child was careless and destroyed something of value, a third in which he talked back to the parent, a fourth situation in which he had not done well in school. Following each situation was a list of from 10 to 14 practices. The respondent was asked to look over the list, then rate the absolute frequency of each and finally to indicate the first, second, and third practice most frequently used.[4] These three choices were weighted, and the scores summed across the four situations. The practices listed represented our three main categories. The first category, *power assertion,* included physical punishment, deprivation of material objects or privileges, the direct application of force, or threat of any of these. The term "power assertion" is used to highlight the fact that in using these techniques the parent seeks to control the child by capitalizing on his physical power or control over material resources (Hoffman, 1960). The second category, *love withdrawal,* included techniques whereby the parent more or less openly withdraws love by ignoring the child, turning his back on the child, refusing to speak to him, explicitly stating that he dislikes the child, or isolating him. The third category, *induction regarding parents,* includes appeals to the child's guilt potential by referring to the consequences of the child's action for the parent. Included are such specifics as telling the child that his action has hurt the parent, that an object he damaged was valued by the parent, that the parent is disappointed, etc.

These lists were administered to each parent twice, once with instructions to select the techniques which he used at present, and next to select those he remembers using when the child was about 5 years old. Reports of past discipline were not asked of the children because it was unlikely that they could remember parent practices used several years before.

The above measure of induction is a limited one in that it only included instances where the parent made references to the consequences of a transgression for the parent himself. To supplement this, an additional measure of induction was constructed. This dealt with the parent's reaction to two situations in which the child's transgression had harmful consequences for another child. In the first situation the child, aged 5, aggresses against another child and destroys something the other child has built, causing the other child to cry. In the second situation the parent sees his child aged 6–10 making fun of another child. The parent was asked what he would have done or said in such a situation, and his reaction was coded along a 3-point scale for the degree to which he (the parent) makes reference to and shows concern for the *other* child's feelings. The scores were summed to arrive at a measure of the parent's use of *induction regarding peers.*

Assessment of the parent's affection for the child was also obtained from the child and from the parent. The child was given a list of 19 behaviors indicating affection, approval, criticism, advice giving, and participation in child-centered activities and asked to indicate along a 4-point scale how often the parent engaged in such behaviors. The affection score was a simple weighted sum for the affection and approval items.

A slightly different measure was used to obtain affection data from the parents. They were given a list of eight behaviors indicating affection, ap-

---

[4] Ratings of the absolute frequency were included primarily to make sure the respondent thought about all the items in the list before ranking them.

proval, qualified approval, and material reward and asked to indicate along a 4-point scale how often they engaged in such behaviors when the child "did something good." The affection score was a weighted sum for the affection items.

Background information. The family's social class was determined from the child's responses to questions about the father's occupation and education. The distinction was basically between white collar and blue collar. In a few cases, families initially classified as middle class were later recategorized as lower class as a result of more accurate and specific information from the parent about the father's actual occupation and education.

Data analysis. The data were analyzed separately for middle-class boys, middle-class girls, lower-class boys, and lower-class girls. The procedure for each of these subsamples was to form two groups—one scoring high and one scoring low on each moral development index—and then to compare these groups on the child-rearing-practice scores obtained in the child reports and (in the case of the middle class only) the parent interviews. In forming the comparison groups, the cutoff points were made as close as possible to the upper and lower quartile points within each subsample.

The test of significance used throughout was the median test.

Control on IQ. An important feature of this study, which was not true in the previous moral development research, was the control on intellectual ability which was instituted. Scores on either the California Test of Mental Maturity or the Iowa Tests of Basic Skills were found—with social class controlled—to relate positively to internalized moral judgments and consideration for others, negatively to confession, and negatively to parent identification. This suggested that some of the findings previously reported in the literature might be the artifactual results of a lack of IQ control. In forming the high and low quartile groups for these variables we therefore controlled IQ—to the point of making the high-low differences in IQ negligible. Since IQ did not relate to guilt, there was no need to control IQ in the guilt analysis.

RESULTS AND DISCUSSION

To facilitate presentation of the results, the significant findings relating moral development indexes and parental discipline are summarized in Tables 1 and 2 for the middle-class sample and Tables 4 and 5 for the lower-class sample.[5] Included in each table are relationships between each

---

[5] Seven pages of tables giving medians for each of the high and low quartile groups have been deposited with the American Documentation Institute. Order Document No. 9079 from the ADI Auxiliary Publications Project, Library of Congress, Washington, D.C. 20540. Remit in advance $1.25 for microfilm or $1.25 for photocopies and make checks payable to: Chief, Photoduplication Service, Library of Congress.

TABLE 1. STATISTICALLY SIGNIFICANT RELATIONS BETWEEN CHILD'S MORALITY INDEXES AND MOTHER'S DISCIPLINE TECHNIQUES: MIDDLE CLASS

Morality index	Power assertion			Love withdrawal			Induction re parent			Induction re peers [a]		
	Boys	Girls	Sum	Boys	Girls	Sum	Boys	Girls	Sum	Boys	Girls	Sum
Guilt (child's response)		-p*	-c*, -n*, -p*				+c*	+p*	+c*, +n*, +p*	+p*		+p**
Internal moral judgment (child's response)		-n*	-c*		-c*	-c*		+c*	+c*			
Confession (mother's report)	-p**		-p**				+n*		+c*			
Accepts responsibility (teacher's report)	-c*	-c*, -n*	-c**, -n**		+n*		+c*, +n*, +p*		+c**			
Consideration for other children (peers' ratings)	+n*	-p*		-p*				+n*, +p*	+c*		+p**	+p**
Identification (child's response)	-c*	-c*	-c**		-n*		+p*	+c*	+c*			

Note.—The data sources of the significant findings summarized in Tables 1, 2, and 4–6 are indicated as follows: c (child report), n (parent report of current practices), p (parent report of past practices).

[a] Data on induction regarding peers are incomplete since these data were obtained only from the parent reports of past practices.

** $p < .01$.

* $p < .05$.

549

TABLE 2. STATISTICALLY SIGNIFICANT RELATIONS BETWEEN CHILD'S MORALITY INDEXES AND FATHER'S DISCIPLINE TECHNIQUES: MIDDLE CLASS

Morality index	Power assertion			Love withdrawal			Induction re parent			Induction re peers		
	Boys	Girls	Sum	Boys	Girls	Sum	Boys	Girls	Sum	Boys	Girls	Sum
Guilt (child's response)												
Internal moral judgment (child's response)		−c*						+c*				
Confession (mother's report)	+p*		+p*		+c*		−p*		−p*			
Accepts responsibility (teacher's report)	−c**		−c*			+c*		+c***	+c**			
Consideration for other children (peers' ratings)	+n*		+p*		−c*							
Identification (child's response)												

* $p < .05$.
** $p < .01$.

550

TABLE 3. STATISTICALLY SIGNIFICANT RELATIONS BETWEEN CHILD'S MORALITY INDEXES AND PARENT'S COMPOSITE INDUCTION SCORE: MIDDLE CLASS

Morality index	Mother's induction			Father's induction		
	Boys	Girls	Sum	Boys	Girls	Sum
Guilt (child's response)	+*	+*	+*			
Internal moral judgment (child's response)	+*	+*	+**			
Confession (mother's report)	+**			+***		
Accepts responsibility (teacher's report)	+*			+*		
Consideration for other children (peers' ratings)		+**	+*			
Identification (child's response)	+*					

* $p < .05$.
** $p < .01$.
*** $p < .005$.

of the six indexes of moral development and each of the four measures of parental discipline: power assertion, love withdrawal, induction regarding parents, and induction regarding peers. Tables 1 and 2 are based on present discipline as reported by the child and present and past discipline as reported by the parent. Since the parent's report was not available for the

TABLE 4. STATISTICALLY SIGNIFICANT RELATIONS BETWEEN CHILD'S MORALITY INDEXES AND MOTHER'S DISCIPLINE: LOWER CLASS

Morality index	Power assertion			Love withdrawal			Induction re parents		
	Boys	Girls	Sum	Boys	Girls	Sum	Boys	Girls	Sum
Guilt (child's response)				+c*					
Internal moral judgment (child's response)							+c*		
Accepts responsibility (teacher's report)									
Consideration for other children (peers' ratings)	+c*						+c*		
Identification (child's response)				−c*	−c*				

Note.—Interview data were not obtained from the lower-class parents. Thus all entries in Tables 3 and 4 are based on child reports. For the same reason lower-class data on confession and on induction regarding peers were unavailable.

* $p < .05$.

TABLE 5. STATISTICALLY SIGNIFICANT RELATIONS BETWEEN CHILD'S MORALITY
INDEXES AND FATHER'S DISCIPLINE: LOWER CLASS

Morality index	Power assertion			Love withdrawal			Induction re parent		
	Boys	Girls	Sum	Boys	Girls	Sum	Boys	Girls	Sum
Guilt (child's response)	$-c$*				$+c$*				
Internal moral judgment (child's response)									
Accepts responsibility (teacher's report)									
Consideration for other children (peers' ratings)									
Identification (child's response)	$-c$*			$-c$*			$+c$*		$+c$*

* $p < .05$.

lower-class sample, Tables 4 and 5 are based solely on the child's report of
present parental discipline.

Middle-class discipline. The overall pattern of the findings in the middle
class provides considerable support for our expectations, at least with respect
to the mother's practices. Thus the frequent use of power assertion by the
mother is consistently associated with weak moral development. The use
of induction, on the other hand, is consistently associated with advanced
moral development. This is true for both induction regarding parents and
induction regarding peers. In all, there are a large number of significant
findings especially for the major moral indexes—guilt and internalized
moral judgments.

In contrast to the mothers, few significant findings were obtained for
fathers—for boys as well as girls—and those that were obtained did not fit
any apparent pattern.

A further step in the analysis of induction was to combine all indexes of
this category into a composite index. The results, presented in Table 3,
were quite striking in the case of mothers for all the moral indexes. Significant findings, all in the expected direction, were obtained for boys on guilt,
internal moral judgments, confession, and acceptance of responsibility; and
for girls on guilt, internal moral judgments, and consideration for others.
When both sexes are combined, the findings are significant for all the moral
indexes. The findings on identification are significant only for boys, however.

In contrast to induction, love withdrawal relates infrequently to the
moral indexes (see Table 1). Further, in most cases in which significant
relations between love withdrawal and moral development do occur, they

prove to be negative. Taken as a whole, the importance of the distinction between love withdrawal and induction has been clearly demonstrated by these findings.

In sum it is a pattern of infrequent use of power assertion and frequent use of induction by middle-class mothers which generally appears to facilitate the facets of morality included in this study.[6]

There is, however, one major exception to this pattern. The peers' reports of the boys' consideration for other children is positively related to the mother's report of their present use of power assertion (Table 1). A possible explanation of this finding is that our measure of consideration is a poor one especially for the boys. In particular, there is no built-in provision to assure that the behavior is based on internal motivation. The motive behind such behavior in the case of boys might instead often be a need for approval by peers. Why this should be the case for boys and not for girls remains unclear. It should be noted, however, that consideration is a more deviant value for boys than girls. Evidence for this is provided from a measure of values administered to the children. The largest sex difference found was on the consideration item ("goes out of his way to help others"). The girls valued this trait more than the boys ($p < .001$). Thus consideration does appear to have a different meaning for the two sexes.

Lower-class discipline. In discussing the lower-class findings the lack of parent interview data must be kept in mind. Nevertheless, there are several very apparent contrasts with the middle-class sample. Foremost among these is the general paucity of significant relationships between the child's moral development and his report of parental discipline. This is especially striking in the case of the mother's discipline. Furthermore, of those significant relationships that emerge, two are inconsistent with our expectations. First, as with the middle-class sample, the boy's consideration is related positively to the mother's use of power assertion. Second, in contrast with the findings for the middle-class boys, guilt is positively associated with the mother's use of power assertion or induction. In summary, our expectations were not confirmed for the lower-class sample, and no general conclusion may be drawn.

[6] The question might be raised here as to the extent to which these findings should be interpreted as independent. Do induction and power assertion exert independent influence on morality, or are they but two aspects of the same influence; for example, do the measures used require that someone high on induction is necessarily low on power assertion? The findings in Table 1 suggest the influences are largely independent. That is, there are only a few instances in which negative power assertion findings and positive induction findings for the same subsample were obtained with the same measure. In most cases the findings for the two types of discipline were obtained with different measures, and in some instances a finding was obtained for one but not the other (e.g., guilt in boys relates to induction, but not to power assertion).

The infrequent relationships between the child's moral development and the mother's discipline, compared to the middle-class sample, suggest that the lower-class mother's discipline may be less crucial and singular a variable. This in turn may be due to several factors. First, the mothers more often work full time in the lower than in the middle class. Second, the combination of large families and less space may result in the parent and child interacting with many other people besides each other. Third, according to the more traditional family structure usually found in the lower class (e.g., Bronfenbrenner, 1958), the father is more often the ultimate disciplining agent. In our sample, for example, boys more often reported that their mothers had the fathers do the disciplining ("says she'll tell your father") in the lower class than in the middle class ($p < .01$). Fourth, lower-class children are encouraged to spend more time outside the home than middle-class children. For all these reasons the socializing process may be more diffuse in the lower class; that is, it may be more equally shared by the mother with the father, with siblings, members of the extended family, the child's peers, and others.[7]

Further research comparing the two classes needs to be performed. One might conjecture that because of the more diffuse socialization process in the lower class the basis of internalization may be quite different for children in the two classes, with consequent differences in the kind of morality that develops.

Affection. The relations between affection and the six moral indexes are presented in Table 6. The most notable features of this table are first, as expected, the relationships are positive; second, most of the findings, as with the discipline data, were obtained for middle-class mothers. It should also be noted that most of the findings are based on the child's report.

Role of the father. Several studies of delinquency (e.g., Glueck & Glueck, 1950; McCord & McCord, 1958; Miller, 1958) suggest that the father is important in the development of internal controls. Our findings, especially in the middle class, seem to suggest that this is not so. Relatively few significant relationships were obtained between paternal discipline and the child's morality, and several were in a direction opposite to that expected.

Of course, it is possible that the role of the father is more important than indicated in this study. For example, the father might provide the cognitive

[7] Another possible explanation for the paucity of findings in the lower class is that the lower-class children are very low on morality. Thus if the upper quartile of the lower class on morality were like the lower quartile of the middle class, there would be no reason to expect similar associations for the two classes. This possibility can be discounted since there was no overlap between the lower-class upper quartile and the middle-class lower quartile. And although there was a general tendency for the lower class to be lower on morality than the middle class, the difference was significant only for internal moral judgment and consideration for others, and only for girls.

TABLE 6. STATISTICALLY SIGNIFICANT RELATIONS BETWEEN CHILD'S MORALITY INDEXES AND PARENT'S AFFECTION

Morality index	Middle Class						Lower class					
	Mothers			Fathers			Mothers			Fathers		
	Boys	Girls	Sum	Boys	Girls	Sum	Boys	Girls	Sum	Boys	Girls	Sum
Guilt (child's response)	+c*		+c*									
Internal moral judgment (child's response)		+c*	+n*			+n*						
Confession (mother's report)	+c*		+c*			+p*						
Accepts responsibility (teacher's report)		+n*			+n*							
Consideration for other children (peers' ratings)	+p*	+c*	+c*				+c*			+c*		
Identification (child's response)	+c***	+c***	+c**				+c*					

* $p < .05$.
** $p < .01$.

content of the standards by direct instruction rather than by his discipline techniques. Lacking data on direct instruction, we could not test this possibility. Another possibility is that the role of the father is a less direct one. That is, he may affect the moral development of the child by his relationship to the mother and his influence on the discipline techniques chosen by the mother. This is indicated in a study of preschool children where evidence was found suggesting that women who are treated power assertively by their husbands tend to react by using power assertive discipline on their children (Hoffman, 1963c). It may also be that the father's role is ordinarily latent in its effects and only becomes manifest under exceptional circumstances such as those often associated with delinquency. That is, under normal conditions with the father away working most of the time and the mother handling most of the disciplining, as in our middle-class sample, the father's importance may lie mainly in providing an adequate role model that operates in the background as a necessary supporting factor. Under these conditions, the specific lines along which the child's moral development proceeds may be determined primarily by the mother's discipline. An adequate role model is lacking, however, in extreme cases as when there is no father, when the father is a criminal, or when the father is at home but unemployed, and this may account for the findings obtained in the delinquency research.

Methodological issues. Any study of child rearing and moral development that relies on indexes of discipline and morality from the same source is open to the criticism that the relationships that emerge are due to the lack of independence of the sources. If that source is the child himself, the suspicion might be held that the child's report of parental discipline is simply another projective measure of the child's personality. It should be noted that in the present study the relationships between the child's morality and the parent's report of discipline were generally in the same direction as those involving the child's report of discipline. (We refer here to the middle-class-mother findings.) In addition, over half the significant findings for each sex involve relations between measures obtained from different respondents.

Further support for our findings comes from a recent review in which our threefold discipline classification was applied to the previous research (Hoffman, in press). Since most studies used a power assertive-nonpower assertive dichotomy, as indicated earlier, the raw data were examined (and recoded where necessary) to determine whether love withdrawal, induction, or some other form of nonpower assertion was responsible for the findings. The results were clearly consistent with ours. Since a wide range of theoretical and methodological approaches were involved in the studies reviewed, our confidence in the findings reported here is considerably strengthened.

A common problem also relevant to the present design is that no definitive conclusion may be drawn about causal direction of the relationships obtained. Any solution to this will have to wait upon application of the experimental method or longitudinal studies. Nevertheless, some support for the proposition that discipline affects moral development, rather than the reverse, may be derived from the fact that several findings bear on the use of discipline in the past. If these reports are assumed to be reasonably valid, to argue that the child's moral development elicits different discipline patterns (rather than the reverse) necessitates the further assumption that the child's morality has not changed basically from early childhood. This is an unlikely assumption in view of common observations (e.g., about the child's changing acceptance of responsibility for transgression) and the findings about the developmental course of moral judgments obtained by Piaget (1948), Kohlberg (1963), and others.

Theoretical discussion. In this section we will analyze the disciplinary encounter into what we believe to be some of its most basic cognitive and emotional factors.

First, any disciplinary encounter generates a certain amount of anger in the child by preventing him from completing or repeating a motivated act. Power assertion is probably most likely to arouse intense anger in the child because it frustrates not only the act but also the child's need for autonomy. It dramatically underscores the extent to which the child's freedom is circumscribed by the superior power and resources of the adult world. This is no doubt exacerbated by the fact that power assertion is likely to be applied abruptly with few explanations or compensations offered to the child. (The empirical evidence for a positive relation between power assertion and anger has been summarized by Becker, 1964.)

Second, a disciplinary technique also provides the child with (a) a model for discharging that anger, and may provide him with (b) an object against which to discharge his anger. The disciplinary act itself constitutes the model for discharging the anger which the child may imitate.

Third, as much animal and human learning research has now shown, what is learned will depend on the stimuli to which the organism is compelled to attend. Disciplinary techniques explicitly or implicitly provide such a focus. Both love withdrawal and power assertion direct the child to the consequences of his behavior for the actor, that is, for the child himself, and to the external agent producing these consequences. Induction, on the other hand, is more apt to focus the child's attention on the consequences of his actions for others, the parent, or some third party. This factor should be especially important in determining the content of the child's standards. That is, if transgressions are followed by induction, the child will learn that the important part of transgressions consists of the harm done to others.

Fourth, to be effective the technique must enlist already existing emotional and motivational tendencies within the child. One such resource is the child's need for love. This factor depends on the general affective state of the parent-child relationship, the importance of which may be seen in the consistent relationship obtained between affection and the moral indexes (Table 6). Given this affective relationship, some arousal of the need for love may be both necessary for and capable of motivating the child to give up his needs of the moment and attend to (and thus be influenced by) the parent's discipline technique. Too much arousal, however, may produce intense feelings of anxiety over loss of love which may disrupt the child's response especially to the cognitive elements of the technique. All three types of discipline communicate some parental disapproval and are thus capable of arousing the child's need for love. But it is possible that only inductions can arouse this need to an optimal degree because the threat of love withdrawal implicit in inductions is relatively mild. Also, it is embedded in the context of a technique which *explicitly or implicitly* suggests a means of reparation. Inductions are thus less likely to disrupt the child's response —as well as his general affective relationship with the parent—than either love withdrawal which may arouse undue anxiety, or power assertion which arouses anger and other disruptive affects.

The second emotional resource, empathy, has long been overlooked by psychologists as a possibly important factor in socialization. Empathy has been observed in children to occur much before the child's moral controls are firmly established (e.g., Murphy, 1937). We believe that it is a potentially important emotional resource because it adds to the aroused need for love the pain which the child vicariously experiences from having harmed another, thus intensifying his motivation to learn moral rules and control his impulses. Of the three types of discipline under consideration, induction seems most capable of enlisting the child's natural proclivities for empathy in the struggle to control his impulses. As indicated in greater detail elsewhere (Hoffman, 1963b; Hoffman, in press; Hoffman & Saltzstein, 1960), we view induction as both directing the child's attention to the other person's pain, which should elicit an empathic response, and communicating to the child that he caused that pain. Without the latter, the child might respond empathically but dissociate himself from the causal act. The coalescence of empathy and the awareness of being the causal agent should produce a response having the necessary cognitive (self-critical) and affective properties of guilt.

It follows from this analysis that power assertion is least effective in promoting development of moral standards and internalization of controls because it elicits intense hostility in the child and simultaneously provides him with a model for expressing that hostility outwardly and a relatively legitimate object against which to express it. It furthermore makes the child's need for love less salient and functions as an obstacle to the arousal of empathy. Finally, it sensitizes the child to the punitive responses of adult authorities, thus contributing to an externally focused moral orientation.

Induction not only avoids these deleterious effects of power assertion, but also is the technique most likely to optimally motivate the child to focus his attention on the harm done others as the salient aspect of his transgressions, and thus to help integrate his capacity for empathy with the knowledge of the human consequences of his own behavior. Repeated experiences of this kind should help sensitize the child to the human consequences of his behavior which may then come to stand out among the welter of emotional and other stimuli in the situation. The child is thus gradually enabled to pick out on his own, without help from others, the effects of his behavior, and to react with an internally based sense of guilt. Induction in sum should be the most facilitative form of discipline for building long-term controls which are independent of external sanctions, and the findings would seem to support this view.

Love withdrawal stands midway between the other two techniques in promoting internalization. It provides a more controlled form of aggression by the parent than power assertion, but less than induction. It employs the affectionate relationship between child and parent perhaps to a greater degree than the other two techniques, but in a way more likely than they to produce a disruptive anxiety response in the child. However, it falls short of induction in effectiveness by not including the cognitive material needed to heighten the child's awareness of wrongdoing and facilitate his learning to generalize accurately to other relevant situations, and by failing to capitalize on his capacity for empathy.

The weak and inconsistent findings for love withdrawal suggest that anxiety over loss of love may be a less important factor in the child's internalization than formerly thought to be the case. Before drawing this conclusion, however, the possibility that love withdrawal is only effective when the parent also freely expresses affection, as suggested by Sears et al. (1957), should be considered. We were able to test this hypothesis by examining the relation between love withdrawal and the moral indexes within the group of subjects who were above and below the median on affection, and also within the upper and lower quartile groups. The results do not corroborate the hypothesis: the relations between love withdrawal and the moral indexes do not differ for the high- and low-affection groups.

In an earlier study with preschool children, however, love withdrawal was found to relate negatively to the expression of overt hostility in the nursery school (Hoffman, 1963b). It was possible to make a similar test in the present study since teacher ratings of overt hostility were available. Here, too, love withdrawal related negatively to hostility outside the home ($p < .05$).[8] We

[8] Power assertion related positively to hostility ($p < .05$), and induction showed a slight nonsignificant negative relation.

Some relevant experimental evidence is also available. Gordon and Cohn (1963) found that doll-play aggression expressed by children in response to frustration decreased after exposure to a story in which the central figure, a dog, searches unsuccessfully for friends with whom to play. Assuming the story arouses feelings of loneliness and anxiety over separation in the child—feelings akin to the emo-

also found that love withdrawal is used more when the child expresses hostility toward the parent than in other types of discipline situations. These findings suggest that the contribution of love withdrawal to moral development may be to attach anxiety directly to the child's hostile impulses, thus motivating him to keep them under control. Psychoanalytic theory may thus be correct after all in the importance assigned love withdrawal in the socialization of the child's impulses. Our data, however, do not support the psychoanalytic view that identification is a necessary mediating process. That is, we found no relation between love withdrawal and identification (Tables 1–4). It remains possible, of course, that a form of unconscious identification which may not be tapped by our more consciously focused measure serves to mediate between the parent's love withdrawal and the child's inhibition of hostile impulses—as suggested in psychoanalytic theory.

In any case, our data do tend to show that love withdrawal alone is an insufficient basis for the development of those capacities—especially for guilt and moral judgment—which are critical characteristics of a fully developed conscience.[9]

SUMMARY

7th-grade children were assessed on several dimensions of moral development by means of paper-and-pencil tests and ratings by parents, teachers, and peers. Extreme groups were formed along each of these dimensions, and they were compared on measures of parental discipline based on reports by the children themselves and by each of the parents. Discipline techniques were coded into 3 categories: power assertion, in which the parent capitalizes on his power and authority over the child; love withdrawal, i.e., direct but nonphysical expressions of anger, disapproval, etc.; and induction, consisting of the parent's focusing on the consequences of the child's action for others. Data from middle- and lower-class boys and girls were analyzed separately. IQ was controlled for each analysis. With considerable—but not complete—consistency, advanced development along the various moral dimensions was associated with infrequent use of power assertion and frequent use of induction among the middle-class sample. Love withdrawal, on the other hand, related infrequently to moral development.

---

tional response to love-withdrawal techniques—these findings may be taken as further support for the notion that love withdrawal may contribute to the inhibition of hostility.

[9] It should be noted that love withdrawal might relate positively to guilt as defined in psychoanalytic terms, that is, as an irrational response to one's own impulses. Clearly our concept of guilt is quite different from the psychoanalytic, pertaining as it does to the real human consequences of one's actions.

REFERENCES

Allinsmith, W., & Greening, T. C. Guilt over anger as predicted from parental discipline: A study of superego development. *American Psychologist,* 1955, **10**, 320. (Abstract)

Aronfreed, J. The nature, variety, and social patterning of moral responses to transgression. *Journal of Abnormal and Social Psychology,* 1961, **63**, 223–241.

Becker, W. Consequences of different kinds of parent discipline. In M. L. & L. W. Hoffman (Eds.), *Review of child development research,* Vol. 1. New York: Russell Sage Foundation, 1964. Pp. 169–208.

Bronfenbrenner, U. Socialization and social class through time and space. In E. E. Maccoby, T. M. Newcomb, & E. L. Hartley (Eds.), *Readings in social psychology.* New York: Holt, 1958. Pp. 400–425.

Glueck, S., & Glueck, E. *Unraveling juvenile delinquency.* New York: Commonwealth Fund, 1950.

Gordon, J. E., & Cohn, F. Effect of fantasy arousal of affiliation drive on doll play aggression. *Journal of Abnormal and Social Psychology,* 1963, **66**, 301–307.

Hill, W. F. Learning theory and the acquisition of values. *Psychological Review,* 1960, **67**, 317–331.

Hoffman, M. L. Power assertion by the parent and its impact on the child. *Child Development,* 1960, **31**, 129–143.

Hoffman, M. L. Childrearing practices and moral development: Generalizations from empirical research. *Child Development,* 1963, **34**, 295–318. (a)

Hoffman, M. L. Parent discipline and the child's consideration for others. *Child Development,* 1963, **34**, 573–588. (b)

Hoffman, M. L. Personality, family structure, and social class as antecedents of parental power assertion. *Child Development,* 1963, **34**, 869–884. (c)

Hoffman, M. L. Socialization practices and the development of moral character. In M. L. Hoffman (Ed.), *Character development in the child.* Chicago: Aldine, in press.

Hoffman, M. L., & Saltzstein, H. D. Parent practices and the development of children's moral orientations. In W. E. Martin (Chm.), Parent behavior and children's personality development. Current project research. Symposium presented at American Psychological Association, Chicago, September 1, 1960.

Kohlberg, L. The development of children's orientations toward a moral order. *Vita Humana,* 1960, **6**, 11–33.

McCord, J., & McCord, W. The effect of parental role model on criminality. *Journal of Social Issues,* 1958, **14**, 66–75.

Miller, W. Lower class culture as a generating milieu of gang delinquency. *Journal of Social Issues,* 1958, **14**, 5–19.

Murphy, L. B. *Social behavior and child personality.* New York: Columbia University Press, 1937.

Piaget, J. *The moral judgment of the child.* Glencoe, Ill.: Free Press, 1948.

Sears, R. R., Maccoby, E. E., & Levin, H. *Patterns of child rearing.* Evanston, Ill.: Row, Peterson, 1957.

8.5   The Effects of Experimental Socialization Paradigms upon Two Moral Responses to Transgression

Justin Aronfreed

The development of moral behavior has proved to be remarkably refractory to psychological analysis and empirical study, despite the increasing attention that has been given to it. The difficulties in a psychological treatment of the origins of moral responses are undoubtedly related to the virtual absence of experimentation in which the conditions presumed to effect their establishment and maintenance have been systematically varied. There have been some informative assessments (1; 14; and 30, Ch. 10; and 33, Ch. 11) of moral responses in the context of variations in parental child rearing practices. But despite the theoretical ingenuity exercised in interpreting the results of these surveys, the very limited extent and magnitude of the relationships uncovered make it apparent that we have as yet only a restricted understanding of how such responses are acquired.

Contemporary conceptions of moral development tend to attribute a wide array of relevant phenomena to a unitary psychological structure established through a single process of acquisition. Thus, in the psychoanalytic formulation (9, Ch. 6; 12, Ch. 8), various aspects of internalized morality are subsumed under the concept of the superego and are viewed as collectively acquired through the mechanism of identification. Even more detailed and behavioral accounts of moral development are inclined to treat different forms of response as more or less equivalent criteria of the "extent of development of conscience" (30, Ch. 10), of the "severity of standards" (1), or of the "strength of superego formation" (14).

This assumption of an underlying unity in the forms and sources of moral behavior may obscure some important differences between specific responses and their distinct antecedents. For example, most of the psychological research on moral behavior has focused on its prohibitive and punitive components. Yet people are obviously moral in a broader sense than that of merely avoiding or reacting to transgressions. They also come to find many of their actions intrinsically rewarding, quite aside from any consequent external approval. Even the relatively monolithic psychoanalytic conception distinguishes between the punitive superego and the rewarding ego ideal. And if we think of moral responses as being acquired through social sanctions and becoming, in varying degrees, independent of these sanctions, then it seems clear that the reinforcements which originally define

Reprinted from *Journal of Abnormal and Social Psychology,* 1963, **66,** No. 5, 437–448.

transgressions and their consequences may be very different from those which define actions to be experienced as rewarding or praiseworthy.

Significant distinctions can also be made even among responses which reflect the punitive and prohibitive functions of morality. Many years ago, Hartshorne and May (13) concluded from their studies of deceit and self-control that moral behavior was highly dependent on the external situation and often did not accord with verbalized moral judgment. More recently, Mowrer (26, Ch. 10), in applying learning concepts to socialization, has reproduced a letter from R. L. Solomon that describes work in progress, on internalization in dogs, in terms which suggest that resistance to temptation and reactions to transgression may derive from two patterns of reinforcement which are, to some extent, independent of one another. Hill (15) has proposed that different types of internalized response to transgression may follow from different learning processes which vary in the temporal relations and reinforcement contingencies between the child's responses and the onset or termination of punishment. And Whiting (31) has used cross-cultural observations to infer that effective moral control in the absence of direct external supervision need not rest on the experience of guilt and that a degree of internalization is possible merely through the fear of real or imagined external sources of punishment.

The findings of a survey previously reported by the writer (3) indicated that children's internalized responses to transgression assume a great variety of forms and often reveal little evidence of cognitive resources of moral judgment usually associated with the phenomenon of guilt. The response of self-criticism, for example, was very circumscribed in its frequency of occurrence. Confession, apology, reparation, and commitments to modify future behavior were common, but the greater proportion of such responses appeared without the explicit application of a standard of judgment to the transgression. Furthermore, numerous responses were characterized by the perception of externally defined consequences of transgression. Although all of the responses found in the survey were internalized, in the sense that they occurred without external observation of the transgression and in the absence of any explicit or threatened punishment, there was no basis for assuming that the responses were alternate manifestations of a single, more fundamental reaction. There was, on the contrary, striking confirmation that the different responses were attributable to different patterns of social reinforcement in that they were predictably related to the socio-economic status and sex role of the child, and, to a lesser degree, to maternal disciplinary practices.

The two experiments reported in the present paper are attempts to examine the specific conditions of reinforcement affecting children's use of two moral responses, self-criticism and reparation, in controlled socialization paradigms. The second experiment, in replicating the first, introduced certain conceptual and methodological refinements.

EXPERIMENT I

One of the implications of the survey described above is that transgressions may apparently be socially defined for a child in a minimally cognitive context. The internalized behavioral consequences of a transgression would certainly require discrimination, since there must be distinct response cues to which they are attached, but it would seem that such consequences encompass a much broader class of behavior than that for which self-evaluation or judgment is a prerequisite. There is considerable recent evidence (17, 21, 27) that a normative framework of standards for evaluating actions, in contrast to what are merely expectations about their consequences, is not simply a natural feature of cognitive development and social exposure, as has been suggested by Piaget (28). It appears instead to be a variable function of particular social roles and cultural settings which the child has experienced.

Self-criticism, viewed in its bare essentials as a consequence of transgression, is the use of a verbal-symbolic referent to one's own behavior, thoughts, or feelings. As such, it represents a response in which the individual takes action, through the internal mediation of his own cognitive resources, with respect to himself as the object of action. The active quality of the self-critical response was recognized by earlier social-psychological theorists such as J. M. Baldwin (4) and G. H. Mead (22), who, while they were primarily concerned with morality as a phenomenon of valuation and consciousness, nevertheless viewed a moral response as being one in which the individual was capable of taking the role of another with respect to himself. The same property of action can be seen to apply to reparation, which uses the individual's own behavioral resources to correct or ameliorate the effects of a transgression. Although reparative responses may simply reduce unpleasant feeling without necessarily implying self-evaluation, they are always constructive or restitutive, and therefore require some kind of manipulation of one's own behavior as well as of the external environment.

The active, self-corrective character of moral responses such as self-criticism and reparation suggests that their establishment might depend on the extent to which a child has been previously socially reinforced for evaluating and acting upon its own behavior. A child who has been encouraged to make corrective or punitive responses to its socially unacceptable behavior would be expected to more frequently resolve subsequent transgressions through its own critical and reparative actions, even in the absence of external sanctions, than a child who has experienced the consequences of transgression in events outside of its own control. One might also expect that a child's self-mediated resources for responding to transgression would be enhanced by the incorporation of explicitly verbalized standards into its socialization. A cognitive context for punishment would provide evaluative labeling responses for the child to act upon its own behavior with self-criticism. It would also provide, therefore, additional cues for appropriate reparative responses of a kind quite different from those provided by the stimulus of the transgression itself. A number of studies (1; 3; 20; 30, Ch. 10), in which reasoning and the reinforcement of self-punitive reactions were subsumed under the category of "psychological," "love oriented," or "induction" techniques of discipline, have reported a positive relationship between the use of such techniques and the child's self-corrective activity and independence of external events in responding to transgression.

The basic procedure of the experiments reported in this paper was to use mild disapproval and deprivation to punish the child repeatedly for an act of aggression carried out on 10 successive training trials. In the first experiment, two distinct treatments were employed. One treatment maximized cognitive structure through the verbalization of an explicit standard in reference to the aggressive acts, and also gave the child control over the evaluation and punishment of the transgression. In the second treatment, cognitive structuring was minimal, and evaluation and punishment of the child's behavior were entirely in the experimenter's control. A common test trial at the end of both treatments, where a more destructive transgression occurred in the contrived breaking of a doll, was designed to elicit self-critical and reparative responses when the experimenter's punitive socializing role was terminated. The specific moral responses to be observed during the test trial were not made by the child in the course of the experimental treatment, in order that their appearance might be taken to reflect generalized response tendencies and not merely isolated pieces of behavior repeatedly attached to a stimulus situation. The nature of the aggressive acts was purposely made unusual and somewhat removed from ordinary experience, so as to minimize the effects of the child's predispositions and maximize the effects of the procedure.

Method

Subjects. The subjects for the first experiment were 57 fifth-grade girls drawn from two public schools in a large urban school system.[1] Both of the schools served fairly homogeneous socioeconomic areas of a working-class character. The children were randomly assigned to the two experimental conditions in roughly equal numbers.

Procedure. Each subject was individually taken by the experimenter, who was a male, from her classroom to the experimental room, where she was asked to sit in front of one end of a rectangular piece of composition board resting upon a small table. The board was roughly 2 × 3.5 feet in size. Twenty-four toy soldiers of the small plastic variety were thickly clus-

---

[1] The author is indebted to a number of administrators and teachers in the Philadelphia public school system, whose cooperation made the experiments possible.

tered in a triangular formation at the other end of the board. Behind the base of the formation, at the very edge of the board, stood a wooden doll about 6 inches in height, with clearly feminine features and a black uniform not unlike a skiing outfit. A large cloth-padded cardboard box rested on a chair just beyond the far edge of the board and behind the doll. The box was below the height of the board's surface, so that the interior was not visible to the subject when she was seated. The experimenter sat to one side of the board toward the far end. On a table adjacent to the experimenter's right hand were some recording sheets, a box of small Tootsie Rolls, and an instrument to be introduced as the "pusher" (actually a miniature hoe, roughly 2 feet long).

After the experimenter and the subject were seated, the experimenter used one of two procedures which were identical in all aspects not relevant to the experimental treatment, including the specification of the behavior to be punished and the nature of the punishment. The procedures differed only in their degree of cognitive structuring and in the direction of control over evaluation and punishment. In the High Cognitive Structure-High Control condition, the subject's activity was repeatedly put into the context of standards verbalized along the dimensions of careful-careless and gentle-rough, and the subject was also asked to evaluate and punish her own actions. In the Low Cognitive Structure-Low Control condition, only the minimal cognitive framework necessary to clarify the task was used, and evaluation and punishment were under the experimenter's control. The task in which the child was required to engage was arranged so that some degree of aggression was inevitable, since the children might otherwise have made punishment inappropriate by simply inhibiting any action construed as a transgression.

HIGH COGNITIVE STRUCTURE–HIGH CONTROL. The verbal instructions given by the experimenter were as follows (italicized words and statements were used only in this condition):

I have something here for you to do. The Army uses it to pick people for a special kind of work. *To do this work, you have to be very careful and gentle. Being careful and gentle is the most important thing.*

Here's the way we do it. Back here there is a nurse in a special uniform [experimenter points to doll]. She is important in case anyone gets sick, and all of the soldiers love her because she is so good to everyone. Whenever there's any danger, she has to leave the field by going back into this box [experimenter indicates box by lifting it from chair]. Here's how she goes into the box. You push her off the board with this pusher. You can't lift the pusher; you must keep it down on the board when you push [experimenter demonstrates, then hands pusher to the subject].

Now the soldiers guard the nurse very carefully. They stand all around her like this [experimenter points to soldiers]. Of course, to push her off, you will have to push through the soldiers, and so you will knock some of them over, *even though you're trying to be careful and gentle* [this is, in fact, obviously true, as the spacing between the soldiers is much too narrow to permit the pusher's blade to pass without toppling some of them]. The idea is to see how many of the soldiers you will knock down. If you knock down just a few, that's good. If you knock down a lot of them, that's not so good. *When you use the pusher, try to be as careful and gentle as you can.*

Here is a pile of thirty Tootsie Rolls for you [experimenter places pile and small empty box in front of the subject]. When we're all through, you may keep however many you have left. Each time, after you push off the nurse, *you* look at the number of soldiers you knocked down, *and you decide how careless and rough you've been.* Then *you decide* how many Tootsie Rolls *you* should take from your pile. *You* take the number of Tootsie Rolls *you* think is right and put them in the box here. Those are the Tootsie Rolls you lose. *You* might take one Tootsie Roll, or two, or three, but not more than three. *The amount you take depends on how careless and rough you think you've been.*

The subject then went through a series of 10 training trials. The experimenter began the first trial by saying:

Remember to keep the pusher down on the board. Push off the nurse and knock down as few soldiers as you can. *And be as careful and gentle as you can.* All right, go ahead.

The experimenter began all subsequent trials by simply saying:

Okay, go ahead.

On each trial, after the nurse had been pushed over, the experimenter said:

All right. You knocked down some soldiers, *so you decide how careless and rough you've been.* Take *as many Tootsie Rolls as you think is right and put them into the box.*

While the subject was making the Tootsie Roll payment, the experimenter reset the nurse and fallen soldiers. Just as the subject put the Tootsie Rolls into the box, the experimenter casually said:

Good!

This verbal reinforcement was intended to make it somewhat easier for the child to continue the self-depriving behavior.

LOW COGNITIVE STRUCTURE–LOW CONTROL. The procedure in this condition was initially the same as that indicated in the first three paragraphs of instructions under the first condition described above, except that the italicized portions for maximizing cognitive structure were eliminated here. The experimenter then continued as follows (italicized words and statements were used only in this condition):

Here is a pile of thirty Tootsie Rolls for you [experimenter places pile and small empty box in front of the subject]. When we're all through, you may keep however many you have left. Each time after you push off the nurse, *I* look at the number of soldiers you knocked down. Then *I* decide how many Tootsie Rolls you should take from your pile. *I* take the number of Tootsie Rolls *I* think is right and put them in the box here. Those are the Tootsie Rolls you lose. *I* might take one Tootsie Roll, or two, or three, but not more than three.

The subject then went through the series of 10 training trials. The experimenter began each trial in the same way as indicated above under the first condition, except that the italicized statement (for the first trial) was eliminated. On each trial, after the nurse had been pushed over, the experimenter said:

All right. You knocked down some soldiers, *so I'll have to take—let's see—[one, two, three] Tootsie Rolls.*

The experimenter then removed the Tootsie Rolls and reset the nurse and soldiers. Since there was always considerable disarray, the experimenter had freedom to vary the number of Tootsie Rolls he took on different trials. This flexibility was used to equate the total loss of Tootsie Rolls for children under this condition with the total loss for children under the first condition, where they controlled their own losses.

TEST TRIAL. The eleventh trial of both of the experimental treatments was planned as an apparently unexpected disruption due to the breaking of the nurse doll. The bottom half of one leg of the doll was detachable, having been prepared so that it was attached only by a tiny screw and could be unobtrusively removed by the experimenter with only a few gentle turns. Since the experimenter had to be present during the test trial to observe the child's responses, some change in the situation had to occur to indicate to the child that the previous punitive consequences of transgression were no longer forthcoming. Accordingly, the experimenter terminated his role as a socializing agent on this trial and used nondirective, apparently casual verbal stimuli to make the situation more appropriate for the child to show her own overt reactions to transgression.

When the subject pushed off the nurse on this trial, the experimenter looked into the box with a surprised expression and said:

Oh, my—it's broken.

While making this statement, the experimenter reached into the box with both hands, as though slowly picking up the doll, and quickly removed the leg. This procedure took only 2 or 3 seconds, and the child could not see the interior of the box. The experimenter held up the doll in one hand and the detached leg in the other, and, looking at them (but not directly at the child), added:

And we don't have another nurse here to use for this—[1] I wonder why it broke.

This last query, spoken reflectively as though the experimenter were thinking to himself, was an indirect verbal stimulus to elicit a self-critical response in those subjects in whom it might be prepotent.

If the subject gave any response to Stimulus 1 that was relevant to the cause of the doll's breaking, whether or not it was self-critical, the experimenter went on to the third stimulus (given below). If the response was not clearly relevant to the doll's breaking, or if the subject gave no response, the experimenter presented Stimulus 2:

Why do you think it broke?

This second question was meant to provide a stronger eliciting stimulus for self-criticism. Then, regardless of the responses to the first two stimuli, Stimulus 3 was:

Well, now that it's broken, I wonder what we should do.

This third comment was spoken reflectively and was the first indirect stimulus intended to elicit reparative responses. If the subject offered any response that was relevant to the implied question, whether or not it was reparative, the experimenter terminated the test trial procedure. If the subject gave no response, or one that was not relevant to the question, the experimenter then presented the final, stronger eliciting Stimulus 4:

What do you think we should do now?

Then, regardless of the subject's response to this last question, the test trial procedure was always terminated. The subject's responses to all of the experimenters verbal stimuli were written down verbatim as they occurred.

Closing procedure. A closing procedure was used to put the subject at ease about her performance and to invoke her cooperation in not discussing the experiment with other children. Informal checks, as well as the children's behavior during the experiment, indicated that excellent security was maintained.

Results and Discussion

It was apparent that all of the children took the experimental situation seriously and that, without respect to treatment, they uniformly paid close attention to the loss of Tootsie Rolls and exercised care in pushing over the nurse. Almost all of the children were visibly concerned about the breaking of the doll, though their responses were quite variable. Some self-critical responses were given to the experimenter's first, rhetorical verbal stimulus (1), but the majority appeared only when the second, more direct stimulus (2) was presented. Likewise, most of the reparative responses occurred to the direct question (4) rather than to the indirect stimulus (3). Frequency counts were taken of the number of children who showed any instance (one or more) of each of the two types of response, to either the direct or indirect stimuli, and of the number of children who showed no evidence of the response.

Self-critical and reparative responses were independently identified .by highly specified criteria which required virtually no judgment or interpretation. A response was classified as self-critical if the child, in accounting for the doll's breaking, referred to her behavior in pushing it—for example, any response indicating that she had not pushed the nurse "the right way," had pushed it too hard, had pushed it so that it did not hit the box properly, etc. The fact that only four of the children actually used the words "careless" or "rough" suggests that self-critical responses did not represent merely what the child regarded as appropriate verbalizations of the experimenter's words and that they followed from a more general self-evaluative orientation induced by the procedure. Responses were classified as reparative when they indicated the child's perception that the effects of transgression could be corrected or ameliorated through her own resources for constructive action. These responses invariably took the form of suggestions for repairing the doll or continuing the procedure, even without the doll, in some alternative way.

Table 1 shows the frequency of self-critical and reparative responses under each of the experimental conditions. Both types of responses were significantly more likely to occur when cognitive structure and the child's control over punishment had been maximized than they were when there had been minimal cognitive structure and control. It is interesting to note that children who gave no self-critical responses, particularly those in the Low Cognitive Structure-Low Control condition, often attributed the breaking

TABLE 1. FREQUENCY OF SELF-CRITICAL AND REPARATIVE
RESPONSES UNDER CONDITIONS OF HIGH
COGNITIVE STRUCTURE-HIGH CONTROL AND
LOW COGNITIVE STRUCTURE-LOW CONTROL

Type of response	High cognitive structure-high control ($N = 29$)	Low cognitive structure-low control ($N = 28$)
Self-criticism		
Present	18	7
Absent	11	21
Reparation		
Present	16	8
Absent	13	20

Note.—Frequencies represent number of subjects who show any instance (one or more) of a given response and number of subjects who show no evidence of the response. Chi square values for 2 × 2 contingency tables (employing correction for continuity) are as follows: Self-criticism, $x^2 = 6.52$, $p < .01$, one-tailed test; Reparation, $x^2 = 3.15$, $p < .05$, one-tailed test.

of the nurse to factors external to their own actions. Thus, they might indicate that the nurse was poorly constructed, that it was broken by the physical impact with the cloth-padded box, or that it had been given too much use. Analogously, children who did not make reparative responses sometimes simply indicated their inability to make any constructive suggestion. Some made comments to the effect that the experimenter should decide what ought to be done.

While the experimental effects confirmed expectations, they were limited to indicating that, in response to a transgression in the absence of external punishment, the children's use of cognitive and behavioral resources to act upon either their own actions or the external environment was a function of the extent to which they had previously been provided with such resources and encouraged to use them. The design of the experiment reflected a conceptualization of the antecedents of self-criticism and reparation that obscured certain more detailed and explicit interpretations of the findings. The socialization paradigms were constructed in a manner that made it impossible to separate the effects of cognitive structuring from those of control over punishment. Since the two moral responses bore a parallel relationship to the experimental treatments, it could not be ascertained whether contingencies existed between them or whether they had independent antecedents which had been subsumed together in the treatments. For example, the two responses might be viewed as interchangeable variants of a single generalized response tendency or, alternatively, as separate response tendencies induced by common features of treatment. It was even possible that one of the responses was induced only secondarily through the mediation of the other.

In order to examine the antecedents of the two moral responses more closely, a second experiment was designed to permit cognitive structure and control over punishment to vary independently of one another and to go beyond merely drawing a parallel between the properties of the responses and the resources provided by the socialization paradigms. Conceptual changes were introduced which emphasized the functional significance of the responses and outlined the specific mechanisms through which the two antecedent variables might have different behavioral consequences. Self-criticism and reparation, while they might both be instances of the child's active use of its own resources, were clearly distinct responses, and it was difficult to imagine that they did not have distinct determinants. One obvious possibility that suggested itself was that self-criticism, a cognitive and evaluative response, might be more affected by the articulateness of standards provided for the child than by the degree of control over punishment. Conversely, a reparative response, oriented toward actively correcting the effects of transgression, would seem more closely related to whether a child was given responsibility for its own deprivation than to the amount of cognitive structuring present.

The second experiment also utilized a different kind of sample in order to expand the generality of the expected findings. Previous evidence (2, 3; 30, Ch. 10) of the relationship of moral responses to socioeconomic status and sex role suggested the desirability of using middle-class boys as subjects, in contrast to the working-class girls used in the first experiment. Replication of the findings, under such a sampling variation, would indicate that the experimental effects could not be attributed to an interaction of the procedures with predispositions already attached to particular social roles.

EXPERIMENT II

The conceptual framework of the second experiment proceeded from the view that a behavior may be defined as a transgression to the extent that it has been exposed to negative (punitive) sanctions. The social punishment results in the behavior itself becoming a cue for an effective response that may be given the general designation of anxiety, though it might well have various qualities dependent on the nature of the punishment. When the anxiety is no longer contingent on the actual presence of punishment, it may be regarded as the first and invariant component of any internalized moral response to transgression. The anxiety is reducible by a number of different responses which acquire instrumental value because they reproduce certain significant cues which are often associated, in the original socializing situation, either with the avoidance or termination of punishment or with the attenuation of the anticipatory anxiety that precedes punishment. The child may then make the relevant cue producing responses to reduce the anxiety aroused by subsequent transgressions, even in the absence of external punishment. The use of the term guilt, in this framework, would be appropriate only when the moral responses have a self-evaluative, cognitive component.[2]

The cues associated with anxiety reduction may, in certain instances, be stimulus aspects of the child's own responses which were originally effective in arresting or terminating punishment. Children frequently learn that their reparative responses (as well as other responses, such as confession) are followed by this kind of direct external reinforcement. In the self-deprivation condition of the first experiment, the child made a reparative response, on each training trial that terminated a punitive situation and the anxiety aroused by it. Presumably, such training might well have induced a corrective or ameliorative disposition on the test trial, when there was no punishment, even if explicit standards of evaluation had not been provided. In naturalistic socialization, of course, reparation may also be followed by

[2] What is being described here, of course, is nothing more than a learning process having two aspects which correspond to varieties of classical and instrumental conditioning. Mowrer (25) has described the reinforcement value of cues associated with the termination of punishment (and anxiety) as being crucial to a complete account of secondary reinforcement. A number of animal studies relevant to this phenomenon have recently been summarized by Beck (5).

positive reinforcement, and the experimenter's saying the word "Good!" when the child removed her own Tootsie Rolls might be taken as analogous to such a reinforcement.

Direct external reinforcement of a moral response does not provide, however, a very satisfactory account of the origins of self-criticism. The self-critical response is not easily open to observation by others (it is not ordinarily verbalized). Its initial appearance in very young children, among whom it is more often overt, is frequently quite vigorous and sudden. Furthermore, it actually reproduces an aspect of the socializing agent's punitive behavior, and the manner in which its external reinforcement could be controlled by the agent is not readily apparent. For example, in the experimental socialization paradigm with high cognitive structure, only the experimenter had used evaluative labels during training to refer to the children's behavior. The appearance of a self-critical response on the test trial may be viewed, then, as an adoption of the experimenter's role, a phenomenon with many of the properties commonly referred to as imitation or identification.

Freud (11, Ch. 3; 12, Ch. 8) at various times attributed the child's adoption of a model's behavior both to the desire to reproduce the characteristics of a loved object and to the desire to defend against the anxiety aroused by the threatening or aggressive aspects of the model. These two motive sources have been elaborated and modified by others (6; 10, Ch. 9; 24, Ch. 21; 29), but without a description of the specific reinforcement mechanisms through which the modeling takes place. Direct external reinforcement has been suggested to explain certain forms of imitation (7, 23), and Hill (15) has recently attempted to use it to derive the origins of self-criticism. Other theorists (26, Ch. 3; 30, Ch. 10; 33, Ch. 11) have taken the view that the child reproduces stimulus properties of a model's behavior which are already secondary reinforcers because of their association with the model's affection and nurturance. A form of observational learning has also been proposed (8, 19), in which reinforcements or their affective consequences are somehow vicariously generalized from model to subject. Finally, a number of recent theoretical treatments specify that, because of the resources or goal states controlled by the model but desired by the subjects, it becomes self-reinforcing for the subject to maximize the perceived similarity between self and model (16) or to covertly practice (toward the self and others) role actions of the model which occur in close contiguity to the subject's own responses (18) or which maintain drive reducing effects through their translation into control over the resources in fantasy (32).

The reinforcement mechanisms outlined above are awkward in their application to the experimental paradigm in question here (and to the ordinary socialization situation), where the child makes a response that is previously made only by the socializing agent and that is clearly associated with punishment. It is difficult to see how the self-critical response could have been directly reinforced during the training trials, why the child would reproduce aspects of a nonnurturant experimenter's role which obviously do not result in pleasurable experience, or why the child would receive vicarious satisfaction in perceiving the experimenter's criticism of its actions. Likewise, the motivation for reproducing the experimenter's control of punitive resources is not apparent. The child may, of course, have been making implicit self-critical responses during training, but we are still left with the problem of why the responses are made at all and of how they are reinforced.

A solution to the problem is made possible by considering that moral responses may acquire instrumental value for reducing the anxiety aroused by a transgression through more than one pattern of reinforcement. Not only may they reproduce cue aspects of those behaviors of the child which were originally associated with avoidance or termination of punishment, as in the case of reparation, but they may also reproduce cue aspects of the previous punitive behavior of a socializing agent. After a child has had some experience with a transgression, punishment itself may come to serve as a cue signifying the attenuation of the anxiety that accompanies its anticipation. When a child's punishment incorporates the verbalization of evaluative labels in reference to its actions, the labels, like any other component of punishment, may become cues for the termination of the anxiety that comes to be directly attached to the transgression. The child can then subsequently itself make the evaluative response, even in the absence of external punishment, and thus reproduce the anxiety reducing cues in its own behavior.[3]

We may assume that, as a result of the training procedures, the child begins to experience anxiety each time the soldiers are knocked down. Under high cognitive structuring, the experimenters critical evaluation ("careless" and "rough") becomes part of the anticipated punishment associated with the termination of the anxiety. The place of the verbal criticism in the punishment, and its timing with respect to onset and termination of anxiety, would therefore be expected to motivate the child to reproduce the critical responses during the test trial, regardless of the degree of direct control that the child has exercised over the loss of Tootsie Rolls.

Method

Subjects. The subjects for the second experiment were 68 fifth-grade boys from another public school in the same urban school system from which the girls for the first experiment had been drawn. The school was in a residential area having an entirely middle-class population. Seventeen children were randomly assigned to each of four experimental conditions.

---

[3] An appreciation of this cue value of punishment is useful in understanding why some children's predominant response to transgression might lie in the perception of punishment in the actions of other people or in impersonal fortuitous events.

Procedure. The second experiment used the same experimenter used in the first one. The procedures were also, in most essential respects, the same as those of the first experiment. They differed from the original procedures primarily in using four rather than two distinct conditions, and in introducing minor changes of instruction and treatment into two of the four conditions, in order to permit cognitive structuring and control over punishment to vary independently of one another. There were now two conditions in which explicit standards of evaluation were presented. The initial portion of the instructions for both of these conditions was identical to that described under the first three paragraphs of general instructions for the first experiment, including the italicized sections for maximizing cognitive structure. There were, likewise, two conditions of low cognitive structure using the same initial instructions, but with the italicized sections removed. The procedure within each of the two sets of conditions then bifurcated so as to introduce variation in the degree of control over punishment.

HIGH COGNITIVE STRUCTURE–HIGH CONTROL. The instructions continued here as shown in the fourth paragraph of instructions under the original High Cognitive Structure–High Control condition.

HIGH COGNITIVE STRUCTURE–LOW CONTROL. Here the experimenter continued the procedure as follows (italicized words and statements were used only under the condition with low control):

Here is a pile of Tootsie Rolls for you [experimenter places pile and empty box next to the subject's right hand]. When we're all through, you may keep however many you have left. Each time, after you push off the nurse, *I* look at the number of soldiers you knocked down, and *I* decide how careless and rough you've been. Then *I* decide how many Tootsie Rolls *I* should take from your pile. *I* take the number of Tootsie Rolls *I* think is right and put them in the box here. Those are the Tootsie Rolls you lose. *I* might take one Tootsie Roll, or two, or three, but not more than three. The amount *I* take depends on how careless and rough *I* think you've been.

The experimenter's statements in initiating trials were again the same as those described for the original High Cognitive Structure–High Control condition (initiation of trials did not carry any manipulation of the Control variable). The experimenter's procedure in terminating each trial was to say:

All right. You knocked down some soldiers, so *I* decide how careless and rough you've been. *I'll have to take—let's see—[one, two, three] Tootsie Rolls.*

LOW COGNITIVE STRUCTURE–HIGH CONTROL. After the common initial portions of the instructions, the procedure here continued as follows (italicized words and statements were used only under the condition with high control):

Here is a pile of thirty Tootsie Rolls for you [experimenter places pile and empty box next to the subject's right hand]. When we're all through, you may keep however many you have left. Each time, after you push off the nurse, *you* look at the number of soldiers you knocked down. Then *you* decide how many Tootsie Rolls *you* should take from your pile. *You* take the number of Tootsie Rolls *you* think is right and put them in the box here. Those are the Tootsie Rolls you lose. *You* might take one Tootsie Roll, or two, or three, but not more than three.

The experimenter initiated trials in the way described under the original Low Cognitive Structure–Low Control condition (initiation of trials did not carry any manipulation of the control variable). In terminating each trial, the experimenter said:

All right. You knocked down some soldiers. *Take as many Tootsie Rolls as you think is right and put them into the box.*

LOW COGNITIVE STRUCTURE–LOW CONTROL. The remainder of the instructions and procedure in this condition was the same as that described for the original Low Cognitive Structure–Low Control condition in the first experiment.

For all four of the experimental treatments summarized above, the test trial and closing procedures were identical to those used in the first experiment.

Results and Discussion

The criteria for establishing the presence of self-critical and reparative responses were the same as those described in the report of the first experiment. Table 2 shows the frequencies of occurrence and nonoccurrence of the

TABLE 2. FREQUENCY OF SELF-CRITICAL AND REPARATIVE
RESPONSES UNDER FOUR CONDITIONS OF COGNITIVE
STRUCTURE AND CONTROL OF REINFORCEMENT
AT PUNISHMENT TERMINATION

Type of response	High cognitive structure		Low cognitive structure	
	High control	Low control	High control	Low control
Self-criticism				
Present	11	10	5	4
Absent	6	7	12	13
Reparation				
Present	14	4	10	6
Absent	3	13	7	11

Note.—$N = 17$ in each of the experimental groups. Frequencies represent number of subjects who show any instance (one or more) of a given response and number of subjects who show no evidence of the response.

two types of response under each of the four experimental conditions. Chi square values for the comparisons evaluating the effect of each independent variable upon each of the two responses are presented in Table 3. The two tables indicate a series of significant differences which are almost entirely those expected. Self-critical responses are more likely to appear when the socialization paradigm provides explicit standards of evaluation than when cognitive structure is minimal. It is also clear that the effect of cognitive structuring on self-criticism is in no way contingent on the degree of control over punishment given the child, since the effect is equally apparent under conditions of both high and low control. Control over punishment alone, when separated from any variation in cognitive structure, obviously has no effect whatsoever on self-criticism. It seems reasonable to conclude, therefore, that a socialization situation in which the child actively uses its own resources in responding to transgression, as happens under conditions of self-deprivation, does not in itself evoke a generalized response tendency of action with respect to one's own behavior, of which self-criticism is one form. It would appear that the reinforcement of a self-critical response requires that punishment be associated with the verbalization of specific cognitive labels.

The effects of the experimental treatments on reparative responses, while generally in the anticipated direction, are not quite as definitive as the effects on self-criticism. Control over punishment, rather than cognitive structuring, is the major source of variation. But its effect is clearly apparent only

TABLE 3. CHI SQUARE VALUES FOR FREQUENCY COMPARISONS OF SELF-CRITICAL AND REPARATIVE RESPONSES UNDER FOUR CONDITIONS OF COGNITIVE STRUCTURE AND CONTROL OF REINFORCEMENT AT PUNISHMENT TERMINATION

	Chi square value	
Comparison	Self-criticism	Reparation
High Cognitive Structure versus Low Cognitive Structure		
High Control	2.95 *	1.28
Low control	3.04 *	0.14
Both groups	7.22 **	0.06
High Control versus Low Control		
High Cognitive Structure	0.00	9.56 **
Low Cognitive Structure	0.00	1.06
Both groups	0.06	9.94 **

Note.—Chi square values for 2×2 contingency tables (employing correction for continuity) based on frequencies in Table 2.

* $p < .05$, one-tailed test.

** $p < .01$, one-tailed test.

under the condition of high cognitive structure. There is some tendency for control over punishment to affect reparative responses even when cognitive structure is minimal, but the tendency does not attain statistical significance. Since cognitive structure per se does not significantly affect reparative responses, its effect on these responses might be interpreted as a secondary or modifying one. Reparation seems to be reinforced primarily by giving the child active control over the corrective or punitive consequences of transgression. It is quite possible, however, that explicit cognitive labeling adds another dimension to this control, and facilitates reparation through the additional cue values which it provides. Such an interpretation might find some tentative support in the fact that, given the condition of high control over punishment, there is a tendency for reparative responses to be more frequent when cognitive structure is maximized. It is obvious, in any case, that self-criticism and reparation cannot be thought of as alternative or equivalent responses to transgression deriving from a single pattern of socialization. Nor can either one of the responses be viewed as a fundamental reaction to transgression through which the other is only secondarily mediated. The two responses must be regarded as outcomes of distinct patterns of social reinforcement, even though these patterns may happen to be intimately interwoven in the ordinary course of child rearing relationships.

Certain restraints need to be recognized in interpreting the results of these experiments. While there was no punishment on the test trial, so that the moral responses observed showed internalization in the sense of being independent of the original negative reinforcements on which they were based, some ambiguity remains as to the degree of internalization, since the experimenter had to be present in order to observe the children's responses. Further, the effect of the punishment itself, being compounded of disapproval and deprivation, is difficult to evaluate precisely. The use of terms like "careless" and "rough" might have created a greater perceived intensity of punishment, a possibility conceivably reflected in the fact that minimal cognitive structuring seemed to depress even the impact of high control over punishment on reparative responses. Finally, the treatments are not entirely divorced from the child's previous socialization, and generalization or transfer may have entered into their inducement of moral responses. An unequivocal demonstration of the conditions necessary to establish a new moral response tendency would require the use of symbolic referents with no previous evaluative connotation and a more exact control over the timing of punishment with respect to the behavior of both the child and the socializing agent.

SUMMARY

In an initial experiment on the antecedents of self-criticism and reparation, 57 fifth-grade girls were equally assigned to two treatments: High

Cognitive Structure–High Control and Low Cognitive Structure–Low Control. Each S was repeatedly punished for an aggressive act on 10 training trials. On the test trial, a more destructive act was contrived to elicit internalized moral responses. In a second experiment, using the same techniques but designed to distinguish independent antecedents, 68 fifth-grade boys were equally assigned to each of four treatments: High Cognitive Structure–High Control. High Cognitive Structure–Low Control, Low Cognitive Structure–High Control, and Low Cognitive Structure–Low Control. Induction of self-criticism was significantly related to E's cognitive structuring during training. Reparative responses were a function of whether S or E controlled punishment. The two moral responses were concluded to be the consequences of distinct patterns of social reinforcement and not attributable to a unitary entity such as "conscience" or "superego."

REFERENCES

1. Allinsmith, W.   The learning of moral standards. In D. R. Miller and G. E. Swanson (eds.), *Inner conflict and defense*. New York: Holt, 1960, pp. 141–76.
2. Aronfreed, J.   Moral behavior and sex identity. In D. R. Miller and G. E. Swanson (eds.), *Inner conflict and defense*. New York: Holt, 1960, pp. 177–93.
3. Aronfreed, J.   The nature, variety, and social patterning of moral responses to transgression. *J. abnorm. soc. Psychol.*, 1961, **63**, 223–40.
4. Baldwin, J. M.   *Social and ethical interpretations in mental development*. New York: Macmillan, 1906.
5. Beck, R. C.   On secondary reinforcement and shock termination. *Psychol. Bull.*, 1961, **58**, 28–45.
6. Bronfenbrenner, U.   Freudian theories of identification and their derivatives. *Child Develpm.*, 1960, **31**, 15–40.
7. Church, R. M.   Transmission of learned behavior between rats. *J. abnorm. soc. Psychol.*, 1957, **54**, 163–65.
8. Darby, C. L., & Riopelle, A. J.   Observational learning in the rhesus monkey. *J. comp. physiol. Psychol.*, 1959, **52**, 94–98.
9. Fenichel, O.   *The psychoanalytic theory of neurosis*. New York: Norton, 1945.
10. Freud, Anna.   *The ego and the mechanisms of defense*. New York: International Univer. Press, 1946.
11. Freud, S.   *New introductory lectures on psychoanalysis*. New York: Norton, 1933.
12. Freud, S.   *The problem of anxiety*. New York: Norton, 1936.
13. Hartshorne, H., & May, M. A.   *Studies in the nature of character*. Vol. 1. *Studies in deceit*. New York: Macmillan, 1928.
14. Heinecke, C. M.   Some antecedents and correlates of guilt and fear in young boys. Unpublished doctoral dissertation, Harvard University, 1953.
15. Hill, W. F.   Learning theory and the acquisition of values. *Psychol. Rev.*, 1960, **67**, 317–31.

16. Kagan, J. The concept of identification. *Psychol. Rev.*, 1958, **65**, 296–305.
17. Kohlberg, L. Moral development and identification. *Yearb. Nat. Soc. Stud. Educ.*, 1963.
18. Maccoby, Eleanor E. Role-taking in childhood and its consequences for social learning. *Child Develpm.*, 1959, **30**, 239–52.
19. Maccoby, Eleanor E., & Wilson, W. C. Identification and observational learning from films. *J. abnorm. soc. Psychol.*, 1957, **55**, 76–87.
20. MacKinnon, D. W. Violation of prohibitions. In H. A. Murray (ed.), *Explorations in personality: A clinical and experimental study of fifty men of college age.* New York: Oxford Univer. Press, 1938, pp. 491–501.
21. MacRae, D., Jr. A test of Piaget's theories of moral development. *J. abnorm. soc. Psychol.*, 1954, **49**, 14–18.
22. Mead, G. H. *Mind, self, and society.* Chicago: Univer. Chicago Press, 1934.
23. Miller, N. E., & Dollard, J. *Social learning and imitation.* New Haven: Yale Univer. Press, 1941.
24. Mowrer, O. H. *Learning theory and personality dynamics.* New York: Ronald, 1950.
25. Mowrer, O. H. *Learning theory and behavior.* New York: Wiley, 1960. (a)
26. Mowrer, O. H. *Learning theory and the symbolic processes.* New York: Wiley, 1960. (b)
27. Peel, E. A. Experimental examination of some of Piaget's schemata concerning children's perception and thinking, and a discussion of their educational significance. *Brit. J. educ. Psychol.*, 1959, **29**, 89–103.
28. Piaget, J. *The moral judgment of the child.* Glencoe, Ill.: Free Press, 1948.
29. Sanford, N. The dynamics of identification. *Psychol. Rev.*, 1955, **62**, 106–18.
30. Sears, R. R., Maccoby, Eleanor E., & Levin, H. *Patterns of child rearing.* Evanston, Ill.: Row, Peterson, 1957.
31. Whiting, J. W. M. Sorcery, sin, and the superego: A cross-cultural study of some mechanisms of social control. In M. R. Jones (ed.), *Nebraska symposium on motivation: 1959.* Lincoln: Univer. Nebraska Press, 1959, pp. 174–95.
32. Whiting, J. W. M. Resource mediation and learning by identification. In I. Iscoe and H. W. Stevenson (eds.), *Personality development in children.* Austin: Univer. Texas Press, 1960, pp. 112–26.
33. Whiting, J. W. M., & Child, I. L. *Child training and personality: A cross-cultural study.* New Haven: Yale Univer. Press, 1953.

8.6   An Experimental Test
of the Sequentiality of Developmental Stages
in the Child's Moral Judgments [1]

Elliot Turiel

Moral development has been approached from different viewpoints. Developmental theories such as Piaget's (1948) focus on the cognitive processes underlying moral responses and assume that the organization of these processes is different at different stages of development. The greater part of developmental research on morality has stemmed from Piaget's theory of moral stages, stages supported only to a limited extent by subsequent investigations (see Kohlberg, 1963b). Kohlberg (1958, 1963a) has postulated the following set of moral stages, which are based on children's reasoning in response to hypothetical moral conflicts (Kohlberg, 1963a):

Stage 1: Punishment and obedience orientation.

Stage 2: Naive instrumental hedonism.

Stage 3: Good-boy morality of maintaining good relations, approval of others.

Stage 4: Authority-maintaining morality.

Stage 5: Morality of contract and democratically accepted law.

Stage 6: Morality of individual principles of conscience [pp. 13–14].

While space does not permit a detailed definition of Kohlberg's stages nor of his methods for the elicitation and stage classification of responses, the Method section should clarify the nature of his data.

Kohlberg postulated that his stages define a sequence normally followed by each individual. The sequence of the stages is hypothesized to be invariant, with the attainment of a mode of thought dependent upon the attainment of the preceding mode, requiring a reorganization of the preceding

[1] This study is based on a dissertation presented to Yale University in candidacy for the degree of Doctor of Philosophy. It was conducted while the author held a United States Public Health Service predoctoral fellowship. The author wishes to express his gratitude to the members of the dissertation committee: Edward Zigler, Irvin Child, Merrill Carlsmith, and Robert Abelson. The author is also indebted to Lawrence Kohlberg for his invaluable advice and aid. Thanks are due to Rita Senf for her critical reading of the manuscript.

Reprinted from the *Journal of Personality and Social Psychology* 1966, **3**, 611–618, by permission of the author and The American Psychological Association.

modes of thought. Evidence for this hypothesis (Kohlberg, 1963a, pp. 15–17) consists, first, of findings of age differences, in various cultures, consistent with the notion of sequence and, second, of findings of a "Guttman quasi-simplex" pattern in the correlations between the various types of thought, a pattern expected if they form a developmental order.

While this evidence supports the validity of the stages as forming a fixed sequence, there has been no experimental evidence. The aim of the present research was to subject Kohlberg's hypotheses to an experimental test. In particular, the concept of developmental sequence suggests some hypotheses regarding developmental change and learning of new moral concepts. The plan of the study was to select subjects at varying developmental stages, expose them to moral reasoning that differed from their dominant stage, and then test the amount of learning and generalization of the new concepts. First, part of the Kohlberg moral judgment interview was administered to determine the subject's dominant stage. With the remaining part of the Kohlberg interview, the subject was then exposed to concepts corresponding to a stage differing from his own. Some subjects were exposed to the stage that was one below their own, some to the stage one above, and some to the stage two above. Finally the subject was retested on the entire interview. If Kohlberg's stages do form a fixed developmental sequence, so that the attainment of a mode of thought is dependent on the attainment of the preceding mode, then it is expected that subjects exposed to the stage directly above their dominant stage would show more usage of that stage on the retest than would subjects exposed to stages two above or one below.

Thus this study was designed to test the following two hypotheses:

1. That Kohlberg's stages form an invariant sequence so that an individual's existing mode of thought determines which new concepts he can learn. It was expected that subjects exposed to reasoning corresponding to a stage directly above their dominant stage would be influenced more than those exposed to reasoning corresponding to a stage further above.

2. That each stage represents a reorganization of the preceding stages, and in effect is a displacement of those stages. If each stage is a reorganization of the preceding stages, rather than an addition to them, then a tendency to reject lower stages would be expected, so that subjects exposed to a stage one above would be influenced more than those exposed to a stage one below their own.

METHOD

Subjects

This experiment used 44 seventh-grade boys from the New Haven public schools, between the ages of 12–0 and 13–7. These boys, chosen at random from the school files, were from the middle socioeconomic class, as determined by their parents' occupation and educational level.

Scoring Methods

An individual's developmental stage is determined by using Kohlberg's (1958) moral judgment interview, which contains nine hypothetical conflict stories and corresponding sets of probing questions. The following story is an example:

In Europe, a woman was near death from a special kind of cancer. There was one drug that the doctors thought might save her. It was a form of radium that a druggist in the same town had recently discovered. The drug was expensive to make, but the druggist was charging ten times what the drug cost him to make. He paid $200 for the radium and charged $2,000 for a small dose of the drug. The sick woman's husband, Heinz, went to everyone he knew to borrow the money, but he could only get together about $1,000, which is half of what it cost. He told the druggist that his wife was dying and asked him to sell cheaper or let him pay later. But the druggist said: "No, I discovered the drug and I'm going to make money from it." So Heinz got desperate and broke into the man's store to steal the drug for his wife. Should the husband have done that?

Two scoring procedures are available for determining a subject's scores on each of the six stages. (The stage with the highest score represents his dominant stage.) The first, a more global method, involves the use of rating forms devised by Kohlberg (1958). A second scoring procedure uses detailed coding forms (Kohlberg, 1958) for each of the nine situations of the interview. These coding forms were constructed and standardized on the basis of responses given by a large number of subjects. Each response listed in the coding forms has a stage assigned to it. A subject's responses to a given situation are divided into "thought-content" units, and each unit is assigned to a stage, as determined by the stage classification of that unit in the coding form. In this way the total number of units assigned to each stage is determined.

Design and Procedure

There were three steps in the experimental procedure. The subject's dominant stage was determined by a pretest interview. In the experimental session subjects were exposed, through role playing, to concepts that were either one below, one above, or two above their initial dominant stages. These experimental treatments will be referred to as -1, $+1$, and $+2$ treatments, respectively. The treatment groups were equated on IQ via the Ammons Full-Scale Picture Vocabulary Test. In a posttest interview the subjects' stage scores were reassessed to determine the influence of the treatment.

Pretest selection interview. During the first meeting each subject was individually administered six of the nine situations of the Kohlberg interview in order to determine his initial stage scores. A tentative assessment of each subject's scores was made using Kohlberg's global rating forms. Only those subjects whose scores on the dominant stage were twice as large as their scores on the next most dominant stage were retained. In all, 21 subjects were discarded, while the 48 retained were equally distributed among Kohlberg's Stages 2, 3, and 4.

Since the global rating system did not provide the sensitivity desired for the experiment, the protocols of subjects retained were rescored using Kohlberg's detailed coding forms. Only those subjects who then scored higher on their dominant stage, as determined by the global ratings, than on any other stage were retained. Four subjects were thus discarded, leaving a total of 44.

Experimental treatment conditions. All subjects of a given dominant stage were randomly assigned to the control group or to three experimental groups ($N = 11$ per group). In the experimental treatments, administered 2 weeks after the pretest, subjects were exposed to moral reasoning in individual role-playing situations with an adult experimenter. In one treatment the reasoning presented was one stage below the initial dominant stage (-1 treatment); the second treatment group was exposed to reasoning that was one stage above ($+1$ treatment); and in a third treatment the reasoning presented was two stages above ($+2$ treatment). Members of the control group were not seen by the experimenter for any kind of treatment.

Through role playing of the three remaining stories of the Kohlberg interview, experimental subjects were exposed to the new moral concepts. After each story was read the subject played the role of the main character in the story, and as the main character he was to seek advice about the problem from two friends. The experimenter played the parts of the two friends. The subject first asked one "friend" for "advice," with that friend's advice favoring one side of the conflict, and then asked the second friend, who favored the other side of the conflict. The reasoning was always at the stage appropriate to the subject's treatment condition. All the arguments used in the role playing were constructed by closely following the coding forms and thus are based on specific coded responses.

Illustrative examples of the treatment-condition arguments are based on the Kohlberg situation in which the husband's conflict is between stealing a drug or letting his wife die. The following two arguments, containing Stage 3 reasoning, represent what a Stage 2 subject in the $+1$ treatment was exposed to in this situation:

(*a*) You really shouldn't steal the drug. There must be some better way of getting it. You could get help from someone. Or else you could talk the druggist into letting you pay later. The druggist is trying to support his family; so he should get some profit from his business. Maybe the druggist should sell it for less, but still you shouldn't just steal it.

(*b*) You should steal the drug in this case. Stealing isn't good, but you can't be blamed for doing it. You love your wife and are trying to save her life. Nobody would blame you for doing it. The person who should really be blamed is the druggist who was just being mean and greedy.

The experimenter, while administering the treatment, did not know the subject's stage, since he had not scored the pretest, and did not know the experimental group of the subject; hence administration of the treatments was blind. The only exceptions were subjects exposed to "Stage 1" concepts who must have been in Stage 2, and those exposed to "Stage 6," who must have been Stage 4 subjects. The possibility of the experimenter recalling the subjects' stages since he previously interviewed them is unlikely because there were many lengthy interviews, and because a subject's stage is determined using the scoring guides.

Posttest interview. The posttest consisted of the six pretest situations plus the three situations of the experimental treatments; it was administered to the experimental subjects 1 week after the treatment, and to the control subjects 3 weeks after the pretest. Subjects were called to the experimental room individually, where they were told they would be asked questions regarding stories similar to the ones they had previously heard. (The repetition of some of the stories and questions did not seem to affect the subjects' willingness to respond. They generally responded with the same interest and concentration as in the pretest.)

Reliability and Scoring of Protocols

The results reported in this paper are based on the scores obtained through the detailed coding. The interviews were coded by the experimenter more than a year after their administration. The scorer had no knowledge of the identity of the protocol he was coding, nor of its experimental condition. All the pretests were scored separately from the posttests. The coding was carried out on a situation-by-situation basis rather than on a subject-by-subject basis; after all subjects' responses to the first situation were coded, all subjects' responses to the next situation were coded, and so on.

One estimate of the reliability of Kohlberg's detailed coding system is based on the independent coding by two judges of responses obtained from 17 subjects not used in this experiment. Scores for each subject consisting of the percentage of the statements falling into each of the six stages were calculated. A weighted score per subject was then obtained by multiplying the number of points at each stage by the number of the stage, summing these products, and dividing the sum by the total number of points. The product-moment correlation between the scores of the two judges was .94.

A measure of interjudge agreement on the scoring of the subjects in this experiment was obtained from the correlation between the scores of the author, who used the detailed coding system, and those of another scorer who used the global rating system. Under both scoring systems a subject receives a number of points on each stage, which can be converted into a single score by the procedure described above. A product-moment correlation of .78 was found for the original 48 subjects. Since the two scoring systems differ slightly, this correlation is a conservative estimate of the inter-judge reliability of the detailed coding system.

RESULTS

The analysis of the posttest interview, which included all nine moral judgment situations, was divided into the following two parts:

1. Stage scores were obtained from the posttest responses to the three situations used in the treatments and not in the pretest. Since the experimental subjects were directly influenced on those three situations, these scores, which will be referred to as "direct scores," represent the amount of direct influence of the treatment.

2. Posttest stage scores for the six situations used in the pretest represent the amount of indirect influence, or the tendency to generalize the treatment influence to situations differing from those on which subjects were directly influenced. The measure reflecting indirect influence is the difference between a subject's pretest and posttest scores on each stage. These change scores will be referred to as "indirect scores."

Direct Scores

The analysis of the direct scores involved the percentage of usage for each subject of the stage that is: one below the initial dominant stage (-1 scores), at the same stage as the initial dominant stage (0 scores), one above the initial dominant stage ($+1$ scores), and two above the initial dominant stage ($+2$ scores).[2]

The hypothesis was that an individual accepts concepts one stage above his own dominant position more readily than he accepts those two stages above, or those one stage below. Two specific hypotheses result from this general hypothesis that the $+1$ treatment would be the most effective; (*a*) that the $+1$ treatment causes more movement to $+1$ than the $+2$ treatment causes movement to $+2$ or the -1 treatment to -1, and (*b*) that the $+1$ treatment causes more $+1$ movement than does any other treatment.

Test of Hypothesis a.   Table 1 presents (in boldface type), for each experimental group, the mean amount of usage of concepts at the same stage as that of the treatment condition. Table 1 also presents the control group mean scores on the stages that are one below (-1 scores), one above ($+1$ scores), and two above ($+2$ scores) their dominant stage.

The experimental groups' scores may not reflect solely the influence of the experimental manipulations. To determine how much of these scores reflects factors other than the treatments, it is necessary to correct for the change that would have occurred independently of the experimental manipulations.

---

[2] The other scores, such as those of the stage two below or three above the dominant stage, are not reported because they did not show significant differences between the groups and do not add to the understanding of the problem.

TABLE 1. Mean Direct Posttest Stage Scores (In Proportions) on the Stages One Below (−1), the Same as (0), One Above (+1), and Two Above (+2) the Pretest Dominant Stage

Stage level relative to pretest dominant stage [a]	Condition groups [b]			
	−1 treatment	+1 treatment	+2 treatment	Control
−1	.336₁₁	.183₁₂	.209₁₃	.240₁₄
0	.283	.346	.374	.395
+1	.131₂₁	.266₂₂	.145₂₃	.122₂₄
+2	.057	.102	.099	.085

Note.—Dunnett t tests were computed for each boldface figure against each of the other three figures in the same row. Tests significant at the .05 level, Group 11 > 13; at the .025 level, 11 > 12; at the .005 level, 22 > 21, 22 > 23, 22 > 24.

[a] Each subject had received pretest scores at each developmental stage, the highest of these indicating his dominant stage. On the posttest, for each individual the proposition of his total score was calculated for each level listed in the left column.

[b] $N = 11$ in each group.

The best estimate of this change is provided by the control group, which had no treatment. It may be assumed that the scores of the control group are due to statistical regression and other artifactual sources.[3]

The experimental groups' scores were corrected by subtracting from those scores the corresponding control group scores. This subtraction was done in the following manner: The −1 mean of the control group was subtracted from the −1 mean of the −1 treatment group; the +1 mean of the control group was subtracted from the +1 mean of the +1 treatment group; the +2 mean of the control group was subtracted from the +2 mean of the +2 treatment group. The three corrected means (−1 = .096, +1 = .144, +2 =

[3] It may be a function of skewness that the −1 score of the control group was considerably larger than the +1 or +2 scores. Of the subject's series of scores one stage has the largest score while its adjacent stages have the next largest scores, with the more distant stages to the dominant stage having smaller scores. The subjects of this experiment tended to use the stages below the dominant stage more than those above, resulting in a positively skewed distribution on the six situations of the pretest. When the other three situations are included, more usage of the stage directly below the dominant stage, resulting in less skewness, would be expected. The control group and the experimental groups were originally very similar. There were no significant differences between the combined scores of the experimental groups and the scores of the control group, with the t values ranging from .10 to .65. We also compared each experimental group with the control group and found no significant differences.

.014) obtained in this way are presumably free of artifacts and thus represent the amount of influence of the experimental treatments.

The corrected means show that, as hypothesized, the direct influence of the $+1$ treatment was greater than that of the other two treatments. The corrected mean of the $+1$ treatment group was shown to be significantly greater than the corrected mean of the $+2$ treatment group by a one-tailed t test ($t = 3.55$, $p < .005$).[4] The one-tailed t test of the difference between the corrected means of the $+1$ treatment group and the -1 treatment group reached a borderline level of significance ($t = 1.43$, $p < .10$).

The corrected mean of the -1 treatment group was significantly greater than the corrected mean of the $+2$ treatment group ($t = 2.03$, $p < .05$).

Test of Hypothesis b.   We have demonstrated that the amount of usage of the treatment condition stage was greater in the $+1$ treatment group than in the other two experimental groups. While this result is necessary to demonstrate the greater influence of the $+1$ treatment, the $+1$ scores of the $+1$ treatment group must also be compared with the $+1$ scores of the other groups.

Table 1 contains the $+1$ scores of each of the four groups. The differences between the $+1$ score of the $+1$ treatment group and the $+1$ scores of the other groups were tested using Dunnett's t statistic, which is appropriate in simultaneously testing one group mean against each of several others (Winer, 1962). These t tests indicated that the $+1$ treatment was the most effective condition in moving subjects up one stage, since the $+1$ score of the $+1$ treatment group was significantly larger than the $+1$ scores of any other group (Table 1).

Other findings.   Table 1 also presents the -1, 0, and $+2$ scores for the four groups. The -1 score of the -1 treatment group was larger than the -1 scores of the other groups. However, the Dunnett t test indicates that the difference between the -1 score of the -1 treatment group and the -1 score of the control group did not reach significance ($t = 1.66$). The differ-

---

[4] Having subtracted the appropriate control score from the experimental condition score we then computed a t test for the difference between the corrected means. The standard error for this t test is complicated by the fact that we subtracted correlated groups from independent groups. However, the appropriate standard error may be shown to be:

$$\sqrt{s_1{}^2 + s_2{}^2 - r_{c_1c_2}s_1s_2}$$

where:

$s_1{}^2 = $ the MS_w for the $+1$ scores multiplied by $2/n$

$s_2{}^2 = $ the MS_w for the $+2$ scores multiplied by $2/n$

$n = $ the number of subjects in each group

$r_{c_1c_2} = $ the correlation between the $+1$ and $+2$ scores of the control group.

(We are indebted to Robert Abelson and Merrill Carlsmith for the derivation of this expression.)

ences between the -1 score of the -1 treatment group and the -1 scores of the $+1$ and the $+2$ treatment groups were both significant (Table 1).

Using Dunnett t tests, comparisons of the $+2$ score of the $+2$ treatment group with the $+2$ scores of the control group ($t < 1$), of the -1 treatment group ($t = 1.16$), and the $+1$ treatment group ($t < 1$), indicated that the $+2$ treatment did not show a significant effect.

Congruent with the hypothesis, the control group and the $+2$ treatment group showed the greatest usage of the dominant stage (0 scores). An analysis of variance comparing the control and the $+2$ treatment groups on the one hand, with the -1 and $+1$ treatment groups on the other hand, showed a significant difference ($F = 4.72$, $df = 1/32$, $p < .05$).

Conclusions regarding the direct scores. (*a*) The $+1$ treatment had a direct effect, an effect greater than that of either the -1 or $+2$ treatment. (*b*) Although not reaching an acceptable significance level, there was some suggestion that the -1 treatment had an effect in moving subjects down one stage. (*c*) The $+2$ treatment did not show a significantly greater effect than the control condition or the other experimental treatments in moving subjects up two stages.

Indirect Scores

The analysis of the indirect scores was similar to that of the direct scores. The indirect score is not a rating of responses on the posttest, but rather a measure of change from pretest to posttest. For each subject's stage scores we subtracted the pretest from the posttest scores and obtained change scores.

As indicated by Table 2, the pattern of results of the indirect scores was consistent with the hypotheses and with the results on the direct scores. The evidence is only suggestive since significant findings were minimal. A one-tailed t test ($t = 2.70$, $p < .025$) showed that the corrected mean of the $+1$

TABLE 2. MEAN INDIRECT POSTTEST STAGE SCORES (IN PROPORTIONS) ON THE STAGES ONE BELOW (-1), THE SAME AS (0), ONE ABOVE ($+1$), AND TWO ABOVE ($+2$) THE PRETEST DOMINANT STAGE

Stage level relative to pretest dominant stage	Condition groups [a]			
	-1 treatment	$+1$ treatment	$+2$ treatment	Control
-1	$+.057$	$+.001$	$+.009$	$+.045$
0	$-.045$	$-.043$	$-.022$	$-.061$
$+1$	$-.004$	$+.045$	$+.016$	$-.007$
$+2$	$-.016$	$-.002$	$+.008$	$+.010$

[a] $N = 11$ in each group.

treatment group (.052) was significantly larger than that of the +2 treatment group (—.002). The one-tailed t test of the difference between the corrected means of the +1 treatment group (.052) and the —1 treatment group (.012) reached a borderline level of significance ($t = 1.46$, $p < .10$). Although the +1 score of the +1 treatment group was larger than the +1 scores of the other groups, none of these differences was significant. No other relevant differences were significant.

DISCUSSION

The analysis of the direct scores showed that the +1 treatment was the most effective of the three treatments, with the +2 treatment being the least effective. The similarity between the patterns of the indirect and the direct scores suggests that the differential effect of the treatments represented something more than memorization of the specific verbalizations used in the treatments and that some change occurred in generalized moral concepts. This conclusion remains tentative since the results on the indirect scores were minimally significant and since the same interview form was used in the test-retest procedure.

The findings support Kohlberg's schema of stages as representing a developmental continuum, in which each individual passes through the stages in the prescribed sequence. If the stages do form a developmental sequence, then it should be easier for subjects to understand and utilize concepts that are directly above their dominant stage than concepts that are two stages above.

The developmental interpretation is also strengthened by the finding that subjects assimilated the next higher stage more readily than the lower stage, even though they could understand the concepts of the lower stage as well as, if not better than, those of the higher stage. Hence, we have an indication that the attainment of a stage of thought involves a reorganization of the preceding modes of thought, with an integration of each previous stage with, rather than an addition to, new elements of the later stages.

Causal Factors of Changes in Stage

The subjects exposed to the stage one above their dominant stage did learn to use some new modes of thought. A factor causing the use of new modes of thought may be *cognitive conflict*. Indeed, Smedslund's work with the concept of conservation (Smedslund, 1961a, 1961c, 1961d) indicates that cognitive conflict may lead to reorganization of structure. The concept of cognitive conflict is similar to the concept of disequilibrium, which Piaget and Inhelder have presented rather obscurely (Inhelder & Piaget, 1958; Piaget, 1950). They seem to be saying that movement from one structure to the next occurs when the system, by being challenged, is put into a state of disequilibrium. Thus change in structure would involve the establishment of a new equilibrium after the occurrence of disequilibrium.

Such a viewpoint is relevant to our study. Since subjects were exposed to new modes of thought through arguments justifying both sides of a moral conflict, they did not really receive solutions to the problems. Such a situation, which exposed subjects to cogent reasons justifying two contradictory positions, could have resulted in cognitive conflict arising from an active concern with both sides of the issue. When the arguments were too "simple," as in the −1 treatment, the subjects may not have become actively involved. When the arguments were too "complicated," as in the +2 treatment, the subjects may have not understood them. However, exposure to concepts one stage above, concepts within a subject's grasp, allowed him contact with new contradictory ideas requiring thought. Perhaps coping with concepts that had some meaning to the subjects led to new modes of thinking, or to a greater use of the stage that was one above the initial stage.

Related Studies

A study having a direct relation to the present research, by Bandura and McDonald (1963), attempts to demonstrate that Piaget's (1948) sequence of moral development changes is a function of reinforcement contingencies and imitative learning. The study assumed that Piaget's stages of moral development could be defined as a stage of "objective responsibility" (moral judgment in terms of the material damage or consequences), followed by a stage of "subjective responsibility" (judgment in terms of intention). Following one of Piaget's procedures, Bandura and McDonald assigned children to stages in terms of responses to paired storied acts, one being a well-intentioned act resulting in considerable material damage, and the other a maliciously motivated act resulting in very little material damage.

Their experimental treatments attempted to influence the subjects by reinforcing adult models who expressed judgments in opposition to the child's orientation, and by reinforcing any of the child's own responses that run counter to his dominant mode. Two measures of learning of the opposite orientation were obtained: the amount of learning during experimental treatment, and a posttest response to new stories immediately following the treatment. They showed that children could be influenced to judge on the orientation opposite to their initial one. Bandura and McDonald viewed this evidence as "throwing considerable doubt on the validity of a developmental stage theory of morality."

An adequate test of a stage theory of morality must deal with stages that are truly representative of mental structure rather than with specific verbal responses. Empirical tests of Piaget's moral judgment theory indicate that the stages do not meet the necessary criteria (Kohlberg, 1963b). However, the Bandura and McDonald study does not provide an adequate test of Piaget's theory because his two stages are not those of objective and subjective responsibility, but rather are those of heteronomous and autonomous orientations. The heteronomous and autonomous stages are each represented by 11 observable aspects (Kohlberg, 1963b) of children's definitions of right and wrong, of which the dimension of objective-subjective responsibility is only one. By studying only one dimension as manifested in children's choices between two alternatives Bandura and McDonald dealt with isolated surface responses, and not with the concept of stage or mental structure. In their experimental treatment one of two possible answers was reinforced. Therefore, the induced changes did not represent underlying structures, but instead represented switches to what the subjects thought were the correct answers.[5]

Another important deficiency in their procedure was the administration of the posttest immediately after the experimental treatment. As Smedslund (1961b) has demonstrated, the test of duration over time is a main criterion for distinguishing between cognitive structure and superficially learned responses. There was a small decrease in subjective responses given by objective children from the experimental treatment to the posttest, while there was no such decrease in the objective responses of subjective children. This finding, that downward movement was more stable than upward movement, is in contrast to our findings, in which upward movement was more stable. It is not surprising that the learning of surface verbal responses related to a lower stage can be retained for a short time. It is interesting that the learning of responses related to a higher stage was not entirely retained, even for such a short period of time.

In the present research we have worked with responses assumed to reflect mental structure and have found that the concept of developmental stage or mental structure has much relevance to the understanding of children's moral thinking. We suggest that the effectiveness of environmental influences depends on the relation between the type of concept encountered and developmental level.

SUMMARY

2 developmental propositions of Kohlberg's theory of moral judgments were tested: (a) that the stages form an invariant sequence, and, thus, more learning results from exposure to the stage directly above one's level than to stages further above; (b) that passage from 1 stage to the next involves integration of the previous stages, and, thus, more learning results from

---

[5] It must be pointed out that in the contrasting pairs of stories a well-intentioned act always resulted in much material damage, while the maliciously motivated act always resulted in little material damage. A child in the objective stage could easily have learned to more frequently designate, as being worse, that story which contained less material damage, thinking that it was the expected answer. Thus he could have given the "higher stage" answer without having learned the concept of intention.

exposure to the stage directly above than to the stage 1 below. First, Ss' stages were determined in a pretest. 44 Ss of Kohlberg's Stages 2, 3, and 4 were equally distributed among 3 experimental groups and 1 control group. In the treatment conditions, Ss were exposed to either the stage 1 below, 1 above, or 2 above the initial dominant stage. The control group was not administered a treatment condition. In a posttest the influence of the treatment conditions was assessed. The results confirmed the hypotheses since exposure to the stage directly above was the most effective treatment.

REFERENCES

Bandura, A., & McDonald, F. J. Influence of social reinforcement and the behavior of models in shaping children's moral judgments. *Journal of Abnormal and Social Psychology,* 1963, **67,** 274–281.

Inhelder, B., & Piaget, J. *The growth of logical thinking from childhood to adolescence.* New York: Basic Books, 1958.

Kohlberg, L. The development of modes of moral thinking in the years ten to sixteen. Unpublished doctoral dissertation, University of Chicago, 1958.

Kohlberg, L. The development of children's orientations toward a moral order: I. Sequence in the development of moral thought. *Vita Humana,* 1963, **6,** 11–33. (a)

Kohlberg, L. Moral development and identification. In W. H. Stevenson (Ed.), *Yearbook of the National Society for the Study of Education:* Pt. I. *Child psychology.* Chicago: University of Chicago Press, 1963. Pp. 277–332. (b)

Piaget, J. *The moral judgment of the child.* (Orig. publ. 1932) Glencoe, Ill.: Free Press, 1948.

Piaget, J. *The psychology of intelligence.* (Orig. publ. 1947) New York: Harcourt, Brace, 1950.

Smedslund, J. The acquisition of conservation of substance and weight in children: II. External reinforcement of conservation of weight and of the operations of addition and subtraction. *Scandinavian Journal of Psychology,* 1961, **2,** 71–84. (a)

Smedslund, J. The acquisition of conservation of substance and weight in children: III. Extinction of conservation of weight acquired "normally" and by means of empirical controls on a balance. *Scandinavian Journal of Psychology,* 1961, **2,** 85–87. (b)

Smedslund, J. The acquisition of conservation of substance and weight in children: V. Practice in conflict situations without external reinforcement. *Scandinavian Journal of Psychology,* 1961, **2,** 156–160. (c)

Smedslund, J. The acquisition of conservation of substance and weight in children: VI. Practice on continuous vs. discontinuous material in problem situations without external reinforcement. *Scandinavian Journal of Psychology,* 1961, **2,** 203–210. (d)

Winer, B. J. *Statistical principles in experimental design.* New York: McGraw-Hill, 1962.

Name Index

595

Subject Index

603